European Civil Procedure

De Gruyter Handbook

European Civil Procedure

Edited by
Xandra Kramer, Stefaan Voet and Adriani Dori

DE GRUYTER

ISBN 978-3-11-077526-6
e-ISBN (PDF) 978-3-11-078163-2
e-ISBN (EPUB) 978-3-11-078172-4

Library of Congress Control Number: 2025945801

Bibliographic information published by the Deutsche Nationalbibliothek
The Deutsche Nationalbibliothek lists this publication in the Deutsche Nationalbibliografie; detailed bibliographic data are available on the internet at http://dnb.dnb.de.

Cover image: Just_Super/iStock/Getty Images
Typesetting: Integra Software Services Pvt. Ltd.
Printing and binding: CPI books GmbH, Leck

www.degruyterbrill.com
Questions about General Product Safety Regulation:
productsafety@degruyterbrill.com

MIX
Papier | Fördert gute Waldnutzung
FSC® C083411

Foreword

European civil procedure has developed as an independent field of research and education over the past two decades. Influenced by human rights law on fair trial, European Union directives on among others consumer law, and boosted by the expanded competence of the European Union regarding judicial cooperation resulting from the Treaty of Amsterdam, national civil procedure has Europeanised.

In particular cross-border litigation in the European Union has been harmonised to a great extent through a series of regulations that cover, in particular, matters of international jurisdiction, recognition and enforcement of judgments, the service of documents and the taking of evidence, and a number of residual topics of judicial cooperation and legal aid. Moreover, full-fledged European procedures have been developed supporting cross-border enforcement of claims, in particular the European Order for Payment and Small Claims Procedure, and the Account Preservation Order. But also in many other areas, including collective redress, specialised courts, ADR and ODR, and legal aid, costs and funding EU law and, more general, European developments have influenced national civil procedure and cross-border litigation. Harmonisation in Europe has also been furthered through soft law, most notably the ELI-Unidroit Model European Rules of Civil Procedure. All these topics are covered in the present book, and expanded through reflections on the EU enlargement process, non-European perspectives from four jurisdictions and a broader outlook on the wider challenges of civil procedure in today's society.

The book is divided into three parts. Part I deals with the general themes regarding the development of European civil procedure, including the EU competence, historical perspectives, the principles of mutual trust and access to justice as foundational principles, the interaction between European and national civil procedure and innovation and the role of digitalisation in civil procedure. Part II deals with key topics of litigation and other means of dispute resolution. It starts with the service of documents as this is usually the first step in initiating litigation, and following the sequence of the procedure discusses the international jurisdiction, taking of evidence and the recognition and enforcement based on the general EU instruments. Two chapters address international jurisdiction and enforcement in family matters, maintenance, matrimonial property and succession. Uniform debt collection procedures, asset preservation, insolvency proceedings and specialised courts are discussed in separate chapters. The last three chapters focus on ADR and ODR as alternative pathways, collective redress and legal aid, costs and funding of civil litigation. Part III is dedicated to general and future outlooks on European civil procedure, including harmonisation through soft law, the EU enlargement process (Albania, Serbia and Ukraine) and perspectives from non-European jurisdictions (China, South Africa, the United States and Brazil) and wider challenges of European civil procedure.

https://doi.org/10.1515/9783110781632-202

We are grateful to all contributors to this book and hope this book will prove useful to advance the further development, study and application of European civil procedure.

The research and editing work for this book has benefitted from co-funding of the VICI project 'Affordable Access to Justice: towards sustainable cost and funding mechanisms for civil litigation in Europe' (project no VI.C.191.082), financed by the Dutch Research Council (NWO), and is supported by the European Civil Justice Centre. See www.euciviljustice.eu.

Xandra Kramer, Stefaan Voet and Adriani Dori
Rotterdam, Leuven, Genova, August 2025

Contents

Part II: Litigating and Other Means of Dispute Resolution in Europe

Part I: **Introduction and General Perspectives on European Civil Procedure**

Xandra Kramer*, Stefaan Voet, and Adriani Dori

Chapter 1
Introduction to European Civil Procedure

A The Scope and Dimensions of European Civil Procedure

#1 European civil procedure is a field that sits at the crossroads of national procedural autonomy and supranational legal integration. It traditionally governs the resolution of civil and commercial disputes that cross national borders, ensuring legal certainty and effective judicial cooperation among multiple jurisdictions.

#2 However, the term '**European civil procedure**' can be understood in both a narrow and a broad sense, depending on the perspective adopted. From a purely territorial or geographical perspective, in its narrower sense, it is often synonymous with **EU civil procedure**, referring to the legal framework and instruments established within the European Union (EU) to ensure effective cross-border dispute resolution. However, the scope of this book extends beyond the limits of the EU. It incorporates a broader European perspective, acknowledging the importance of legal developments in non-EU jurisdictions, like the UK, and exploring the role of comparative law and soft law in shaping civil procedure across Europe. This broader approach is crucial for understanding the full scope of civil procedural law, particularly in areas such as collective redress, legal aid, litigation funding, and soft law, where cross-jurisdictional comparisons provide valuable insights and influence EU civil procedure. While EU civil procedure forms the core of this discussion, this volume also recognises significant legal developments and procedural trends beyond the EU.

#3 At its most fundamental level, **European civil procedure in the narrower, EU-specific sense** consists of the rules, principles, and mechanisms facilitating cross-border dispute resolution within the EU. These rules primarily stem from EU regulations and instruments that coordinate national judicial systems within the EU to prevent legal fragmentation, conflicting jurisdictions, and conflicting judg-

Note: The research for this chapter was made possible by the co-funding of the VICI project 'Affordable Access to Justice: towards sustainable cost and funding mechanisms for civil litigation in Europe' (project no VI.C.191.082), financed by the Dutch Research Council (NWO). See www.euciviljustice.eu.

***Corresponding author: Xandra Kramer**, Erasmus University Rotterdam and at Utrecht University, e-mail: kramer@law.eur.nl
Stefaan Voet, KU Leuven, e-mail: stefaan.voet@kuleuven.be
Adriani Dori, Erasmus University Rotterdam, e-mail: dori@law.eur.nl

https://doi.org/10.1515/9783110781632-001

ments. Key examples include the Brussels I-bis Regulation, which sets the framework for jurisdiction and the recognition and enforcement of judgments; or the European Enforcement Order, European Payment Order, and Small Claims Procedures, which streamline litigation in specific contexts. Within this structured legal framework, other (more relaxed) judicial cooperation mechanisms—such as judicial networks or the assessment of national justice systems through numerical data and indicators—play a crucial role in enhancing efficiency and mutual trust among EU Member States. All these formal and informal instruments aim to strengthen access to justice, uphold the rule of law, and promote the smooth functioning of the internal market. Their importance is undisputable, all the more in our connected world where cross-border activities and commerce, digital transactions, and mobility have made procedural coordination more of a necessity than a mere political aspiration.

#4 However, **European civil procedure in a broader sense** is not merely a set of technical legal rules. It is part of a larger ecosystem of European-wide and national justice policies, regulatory trends, and socio-legal developments that shape how procedural laws function in practice, both locally and transnationally. Several broader dimensions warrant attention here. Beyond its role in structuring cross-border litigation, civil procedure intersects with overarching themes that have influenced—and continue to influence—its creation, evolution, and effectiveness. These include the protection of fundamental rights, the impact of technological advancements, and the economic dynamics and pressures on access to justice. In particular, the growing demand for efficient, cost-effective dispute resolution has driven the development of innovative financial models of litigation, such as third-party funding (TPLF). These trends have reignited debates about the tension between the affordability of justice and the need for a robust and fair procedural system across Europe. At the same time, they also reflect the ongoing relevance of Cappelletti and Garth's insights on overcoming barriers to access, which continue to shape current discussions on legal reforms across Europe.

#5 Perhaps the most significant dimension of this broader perspective of European civil procedure is the **relationship between procedural law and fundamental rights**. The Charter of Fundamental Rights of the EU (CFR), the European Convention on Human Rights (ECHR), and the case law of the Court of Justice of the European Union (CJEU) and the European Court of Human Rights (ECtHR) have shaped key procedural guarantees, reinforcing principles such as the right to a fair trial, access to justice, and effective judicial protection. Such legal fundaments ensure that the more 'technical' procedural legal rules are not applied per se in isolation but rather function within a broader system of fundamental rights protection. In this context, the **Europeanisation** of civil justice systems has led national procedural laws to increasingly align with EU standards, fostering consistency across jurisdictions and reinforcing the protection of fundamental rights within a unified, broader European legal framework.

#6 Another key development influencing European civil procedure is the rapid transformation of justice policies through **digitalisation** and **legal technology**, particularly in the times during and after the COVID-19 pandemic. AI-driven dispute resolution, online courts, and automated legal processes are redefining procedural efficiency and access to justice. At the same time, changes in legal funding models—such as the growing role of **third-party litigation funding**—are altering the dynamics of litigation, raising questions about fairness, transparency, and regulatory oversight. These **technological and financial developments** are reshaping procedural law in ways that cannot be fully captured by classical legal doctrine alone.

#7 Equally important is the role of **empirical legal research** and the **sociology** of civil procedure in understanding how procedural rules operate in practice. Legal norms do not exist in a vacuum. They affect individuals, businesses, and institutions in multiple ways, sometimes creating barriers rather than facilitating justice. Examining real-life litigation, who benefits from existing procedural mechanisms, where and why inefficiencies arise, and how access to justice can be improved offers valuable insights that go beyond the traditional doctrinal analysis that had for decades dominated the legal discipline of procedural law and delineated its traditional understanding but also limitations.

#8 In addition, the **rule of law** plays a pivotal role in the functioning of European civil procedure. The EU's emphasis on the rule of law is a fundament for its creation and underpins its commitment to ensuring justice, fairness, and consistency in legal processes across Member States. At the same time, a well-functioning civil procedure system contributes to **economic integration** by providing clear, predictable, and efficient mechanisms for resolving disputes, which is essential for maintaining trust in the internal market. A strong rule of law ensures that legal protections are upheld and citizens and businesses can rely on fair processes, contributing to stability and fostering **economic growth** within the EU.

#9 As a handbook, this volume focuses on the core aspects of EU civil procedure, offering a structured and accessible exploration of key concepts, legislative instruments, case law, and judicial cooperation mechanisms that guide the course of a litigation process within EU Member States. The **scope of the book**, however, extends beyond these core elements, as the broader perspectives and themes mentioned above are essential for anyone seeking a comprehensive understanding of European civil procedure. While this handbook cannot explore these interdisciplinary and empirical dimensions in full depth, conscious efforts have been made to complement the traditional doctrinal approach by integrating these broader perspectives, ensuring a more inclusive and dynamic view of the field.

B From Foundations to Impact: The Evolution and Reach of EU Civil Procedure

I The Evolution of European Civil Procedure

#10 European civil procedure has been developed gradually over the past decades, emerging from different sources. Important influences have been the fundamental rights of fair trial under Article 6 ECHR and, later, Article 47 EU Charter on Fundamental Rights (CFR). But particularly in the past 25 years, after the Treaty of Amsterdam became applicable, European civil procedure has developed rapidly in the EU. This section provides a brief overview of the foundations and framework, shortcomings of the present legislative framework and attempts at increasing coherence in EU civil procedure.

1 Foundations and Framework

#11 Before EU competence was extended to cover judicial cooperation in civil matters having cross-border implications pursuant to the Treaty of Amsterdam, entering into force in 1999, harmonisation of civil procedure in the EU was limited. The (then) European Court of Justice adopted the principle of **procedural autonomy** in its *Rewe* ruling in 1976, meaning that the Member States possess autonomy in enforcing substantive EU law relying on their domestic institutional and procedural rules.[1] In exercising these rights, the Member States procedural rules should not be less for the enforcement of EU law than for the enforcement of national law (**principle of equality**) and these procedural rules should not make it impossible in practice to exercise the rights which the national courts are obliged to protect (**principle of equivalence**).

#12 Gradually, the procedural laws of the Member States and other EU countries have been influenced by the requirements of **fair trial** under Article 6 ECHR and other fundamental rights. The extensive case law of the European Court of Human Rights has had an important influence on civil procedure and has resulted in **procedural harmonisation** across Europe.[2] This role was also taken up by the Court of Justice of the EU (CJEU), which, in particular, after the adoption of the EU Charter on Fundamental Rights (CFR), has progressively interpreted the fundamental

1 Case C-33/76 *Rewe-Zentralfinanz eG and Rewe-Zentral AG v Lanswirtschaftskammer für das Saarland* (16 December 1976) ECLI:EU:C:1976:188.

2 S Law and JT Nowak, 'Procedural Harmonisation by the European Court of Justice: Procedural Autonomy and the Member States' Perspective' in F Gascón Inchausti and B Hess (eds), *The Future of the European Law of Civil Procedure* (Intersentia 2020) 17.

rights to an effective remedy and a fair trial under the equivalent Article 47. But also before that, the CJEU has played a role in the development of European civil procedure in cross-border cases, in particular in its **autonomous interpretation** of the 1968 Brussels Convention on jurisdiction and the recognition and enforcement of judgments, currently the Brussels I-bis Regulation.[3]

#13 From 1999 onwards, European civil procedure has developed rapidly, resulting from the constitution of an **area of freedom, security and justice** (AFSJ) as regulated in Part Three, Title IV on the Area of Freedom, Security and Justice (AFSJ). In accordance with Article 67(1) of the Treaty on the Functioning of the European Union (TFEU), the Union shall constitute an area of freedom, security and justice, with respect for fundamental rights and the different legal systems and traditions of the Member States. Pursuant to Article 67(4) TFEU the Union shall facilitate access to justice, in particular through the **principle of mutual recognition**. Most civil procedure instruments have been established under this title and, and more specifically Article 81 TFEU which provides the legislative basis for **judicial cooperation** in civil matters having cross-border implications. However, also Article 114 TFEU regarding harmonisation measures relating to the **internal market** in specific policy areas have played an important role, in particular in the area of **consumer law**. Unlike Article 81 TFEU, the latter provision does not require 'cross-border implications' and can also concern domestic matters.[4]

#14 Along with access to justice and the fair trial principles emulating from fundamental rights law, the principle of **mutual trust** has become a pillar of EU civil justice.[5] It requires that Member States should have confidence in each other's legal system and courts and forms the basis of EU integration and judicial cooperation. It has been put to the test both in case law and in the literature, and has

3 Regulation (EU) 1215/2012 of 12 December 2012 on jurisdiction and the recognition and enforcement of judgements in civil and commercial matters (recast) [2012] OJ L351/1. See also J Meeusen, 'The Contribution of 'Brussels I' to the Process of EU Integration: A True Trailblazer for the Europeanisation and Constitutionalisation of Private International Law' in B Hess and K Lenaerts (eds), *The 50th Anniversary of the European Law of Civil Procedure* (Nomos 2020) 121.

4 See in greater detail on the legislative competence, Storskrubb, Chapter 2. Extensively on the EU competence in civil procedure and its limits: B Hess, *Europäisches Zivilprozessrecht* (2nd edn, De Gruyter 2021) 38–96.

5 X Kramer, *Procedure Matters: Construction and Deconstructivism in European Civil Procedure* (Eleven International Publishing 2013) 18; E Storskrubb, 'Mutual Trust in Civil Justice Cooperation in the EU' in A Bakardjieva Engelbrekt and others (eds), *Trust in the European Union in Challenging Times* (Springer 2019) 159; M Weller, '"Mutual Trust": A Suitable Foundation for Private International Law in Regional Integration Communities and Beyond?' in Collected Courses of the Hague Academy of International Law – Recueil des cours, vol 423 (Brill 2022).

been under pressure in recent years in particular due to political developments,[6] but should still be considered the cornerstone of judicial cooperation.[7]

#15 Over the past 25 years, a vast body of legal instruments has been established in the area of European civil procedure. Many of these deal with international civil procedure, others also apply in purely national cases, and some incidental rules of civil procedure are included in directives that primarily contain substantive law. Roughly, three strands of **harmonisation** of EU civil procedure can be distinguished, though EU civil procedure is largely diversified and is spread over different types of instruments with different scopes and aims.

#16 The first strand of harmonisation of civil procedure involves aspects of cross-border litigation that are in the realm of **private international law**. These are the EU regulations dealing with, in particular, international jurisdiction, the recognition and enforcement of judgments and **extrajudicial documents** (Brussels I-bis Regulation), the cross-border **service of documents**,[8] and the **taking of evidence**[9]. These rules are not intended to harmonise civil procedure as such, but aim to coordinate and bridge the legal systems involved in cross-border cases. However, they are essential in EU litigation and through the autonomous interpretation and in light of the principle of mutual trust endorsed by the CJEU, they are at the core of EU civil procedure.

#17 The second strand of harmonisation of EU civil procedure consists of a series of instruments that have introduced pan-EU civil procedures – the so-called second-generation instruments[10] – or that aim at harmonising specific topics of civil procedure. These include the Regulations on a European Order for Payment Procedure, a Small Claims Procedure, and an Account Preservation Order.[11] These provide uniform European procedures aimed at improving **cross-border enforcement**. Two Directives that do not introduce uniform procedures but rather provide minimum

6 See also the introduction to a special issue on the topic: M Glavina, 'Trust in and Between Courts in the Changing World of the 21st Century' [2024-1] Erasmus Law Review 15.

7 See also M Weller, Chapter 4.

8 Regulation (EU) 2020/1784 of 25 November 2020 on the service in the Member States of judicial and extrajudicial documents in civil or commercial matters [2020] OJ L405/40.

9 Regulation (EU) 2020/1783 of 25 November 2020 on cooperation between the courts of the Member States in the taking of evidence in civil or commercial matters [2020] OJ L405/1.

10 B Hess, 'The State of the Civil Justice Union' in B Hess, M Bergström and E Storskrubb (eds), *EU Civil Justice: Current Issues and Future Outlook* (Hart Publishing/Bloomsbury 2016) 1, 4.

11 Regulation (EU) 2015/2421 of 16 December 2015 amending Regulation (EC) No. 861/2007 establishing a European Small Claims Procedure and Regulation (EC) No. 1896/2006 creating a European order for payment procedure [2015] OJ L341/1; Regulation (EU) 655/2014 of 15 May 2014 establishing a European Account Preservation Order to facilitate cross-border debt recovery in civil and commercial matters [2014] OJ L189/59.

standards, but do have a **horizontal nature**, are the Mediation Directive[12] and of a more recent date, the Directive on Strategic lawsuits against public participation (**SLAPPs** Directive).[13] As the regulations on international civil procedure mentioned above, these second strand instruments are also based on Article 81 TFEU and are limited to cross-border cases.

#18 A third category of EU civil procedure rules consists of what are termed **sectorial or vertical instruments** that contain sector-specific rules introducing harmonised rules for a specific substantive area, mostly consumer law. These include notably the Consumer ADR directive[14] and the Representative Actions Directive for consumer **collective redress**.[15] A number of other **sectorial instruments** that regulate largely substantive issues also contain procedural rules on *inter alia* **provisional measures, evidence**, and **seizure**. These include the Directive on the Enforcement of **Intellectual Property Rights**[16] and the Directive on Damages for **Competition Law** Claims.[17] Unlike the other civil procedure instruments mentioned above, these are not based on Article 81 but on Article 114 TFEU, and they apply both in cross-border and domestic cases.

#19 Another noteworthy instrument that cannot be gathered under these categories is the Agreement on a **Unified Patent Court** (UPCA).[18] The UPCA has been signed by 24 Member States, but so far, has been ratified by only 18 and has been applicable since 1 June 2023. Along with the establishment of the Unified Patent Court (UPC), dealing with unitary and European patents, extensive Rules of Procedure of the Unified Patent Court were adopted.

#20 Apart from these legislative instruments, the development of EU civil procedure has been supported by policy initiatives and practical tools focusing on digitalisa-

---

12 Council Directive 2008/52/EC of 21 May 2008 on certain aspects of mediation in civil and commercial matters [2008] OJ L136/3.

13 Directive (EU) 2024/1069 of the European Parliament and of the Council of 11 April 2024 on protecting persons who engage in public participation from manifestly unfounded claims or abusive court proceedings ('Strategic lawsuits against public participation') [2024] OJ L2024/1069.

14 Directive 2013/11/EU of the European Parliament and of the Council of 21 May 2013 on alternative dispute resolution for consumer disputes and amending Regulation (EC) No 2006/2004 and Directive 2009/22/EC (Directive on consumer ADR) [2013] OJ L165/63. This Directive is currently under revision.

15 Directive (EU) 2020/1828 of the European Parliament and of the Council of 25 November 2020 on representative actions for the protection of the collective interests of consumers and repealing Directive 2009/22/EC [2020] OJ L409/27.

16 Council Directive 2004/48/EC of 29 April 2004 on the enforcement of intellectual property rights [2004] OJ 2004 L195/16.

17 Directive 2014/104/EU of 26 November 2014 on certain rules governing actions for damages under national law for infringements of the competition law provisions of the Member States and of the European Union [2014] OJ L349/1.

18 Agreement on a Unified Patent Court [2013] OJ C175/01. See G Antonopoulou, Chapter 19.

tion and the evaluation of civil justice systems. In 2010, the **e-Justice Portal** was launched as an 'electronic one-stop shop' in the area of justice.[19] It not only provides information on European and national justice systems, but also included dynamic forms as well as translation tools for the purpose of bringing claims in other Member States. **Digitalisation** of justice has been high on the agenda for many years, and after implementing digital communication in several separate instruments, in 2023, a Regulation on the digitalisation of judicial cooperation and access to justice was adopted.[20] This is an overarching regulation providing a framework for electronic communications, **videoconferencing**, **electronic signatures**, the legal effects of electronic documents and the electronic payment of **court fees**. The Regulation became applicable on 1 May 2025 and applies to thirteen instruments on civil justice cooperation. Another important policy tool is the **European Justice Scoreboard**, which, on an annual basis, measures and compares the performance of national courts in terms of the **efficiency**, **quality**, and **independence** of justice.[21]

2 Shortcomings: The EU Civil Justice Patchwork and Need for Coherence

#21 While the development of the EU civil procedure framework over the past 25 years is impressive in terms of the number of instruments and the coverage of key issues, the harmonisation of civil procedure in the EU also has its shortcomings. Inherent to the EU as a supranational order and the limited competence of the EU legislator, including the principles of **proportionality** and **subsidiarity** as laid down in Article 5 TFEU, EU civil procedure is based on piecemeal legislation and an ever-increasing body of separate instruments. An overarching architecture and systemic framing are lacking. While all of these instruments aim at improving access to justice and judicial cooperation between the Member States, both legislative techniques and scope differ significantly per instrument.

#22 As regards legislative technique, many instruments take the form of direct binding regulations. This, in particular, holds true for the private international instruments and those dealing with cross-border enforcement. These are based on Article 81 TFEU and aim specifically at regulating aspects of cross-border litigation, for instance, international jurisdiction, the enforcement of judgments, and the

19 See <https://e-justice.europa.eu/> accessed 21 April 2025.

20 Regulation (EU) 2023/2844 of the European Parliament and of the Council of 13 December 2023 on the digitalisation of judicial cooperation and access to justice in cross-border civil, commercial and criminal matters, and amending certain acts in the field of judicial cooperation [2023] OJ L2023/2844.

21 A Dori, *The Governance of EU Justice Reforms: The Role of the EU Justice Scoreboard and Country Specific Recommendations in Shaping National Judicial Systems* (Nomos 2025).

cross-border service and taking of evidence. These only require minimal, mostly practical implementation, for instance, designating competent authorities. However, a number of instruments, notably the Mediation and the SLAPPs Directive, are directives that include minimum harmonisation rules that need to be implemented by the Member States.

#23 Most other instruments, mentioned under the third strand above (see #18), are sector-specific directives based on Article 114 TFEU. The choice for either a directive or regulation is not always obvious, and some directives provide rather detailed rules, but sometimes this can be traced back to the political feasibility of proposed instruments. For instance, for the SLAPPs Directive, including procedural rules that have a direct impact on domestic civil procedure rules, view to the **proportionality principle**. It would have been unlikely that Member States would have agreed to expanding it to purely national cases.

#24 In part inherent to the different **legislative basis**, some instruments apply to most or all civil and commercial matters, for instance, the Brussels I-bis and the Service and Evidence Regulations, while others are limited to specific types of cases. Most of these focus on consumer law and aim to improve consumer redress, among other through collective actions (Representative Action Directive) or ADR (Consumer ADR Directive). A species in its own are those regulations that have introduced uniform civil procedures for cross-border cases: the European Order for Payment Procedure, the Small Claims Procedure and the Account Preservation Order. These procedures are not compulsory but optional, meaning that a creditor can choose the European procedure or available national procedures.

#25 Lastly, not all EU instruments, including rules on civil procedure, are applicable in all Member States. Denmark has a general **opt-out** of judicial cooperation instruments based on Article 81 TFEU, and only applies the Brussels I-bis and Service Regulation on the basis of a parallel agreement with the other Member States. Ireland has an **opt-in** possibility, and has so far made use of this and is thus bound by the instruments based on Article 81(2) TFEU. In addition, a number of regulations in the area of **private international law**, including rules on cross-border litigation, have been adopted on the basis of **enhanced cooperation** on the basis of Article 328 TFEU, as they lacked the required unanimity for **family law** matters pursuant to Article 81(3) TFEU.[22]

22 Regulation (EU) 2016/1103 implementing enhanced cooperation in the area of jurisdiction, applicable law and the recognition and enforcement of decisions in matters of matrimonial property regimes [2016] OJ L183/1 and Regulation (EU) 2016/1104 implementing enhanced cooperation in the area of jurisdiction, applicable law and the recognition and enforcement of decisions in matters of the property consequences of registered partnerships [2016] OJ L183/30.

#26 This fragmentation of EU civil procedure has been criticised in the literature, and has been called architectural deconstructivism[23] and constitutional incoherence[24]. While most instruments are helpful, the plurality and fragmentation of civil procedure rules in the EU undermine **coherence** and complicates the application of these instruments, while it may also affect effective access to justice. This has resulted in calls for more coherence, but not in concrete legislative action so far. The lack of coherence is in part inherent to the layered structure of the EU legal order and the reluctance of Member States to adopt horizontal instruments that are not limited to cross-border cases in the sense of Article 81 TFEU, or to adopt more horizontal instruments that would also apply in domestic cases on the basis of Article 114 TFEU.[25] The next subsection will address some EU and soft law initiatives that may contribute to a more coherent outlook on European civil procedure.

3 Towards a More Coherent Legal Framework: Minimum Standards and Model Rules

#27 The European Parliament has been active in the area of private international law and civil procedure, including on increasing coherence.[26] In 2015, the Research Service of the European Parliament issued a report on the Europeanisation of civil procedure[27], followed by a number of other studies.[28] In 2017, the European Parliament adopted a resolution with recommendations to the European Commis-

23 Kramer (n 5) 9.

24 E Storskrubb, 'EU Civil Justice at the Harmonisation Crossroads' in A Nylund and M Strandberg (eds), *Civil Procedure and Harmonisation of Law: The Dynamics of EU and International Treaties* (Intersentia 2019) 11, 18.

25 B Hess and X Kramer, 'From Common Rules to Best Practices in European Civil Procedure: An Introduction' in B Hess and Xandra Kramer (eds), *From Common Rules to Best Practices in European Civil Procedure* (Hart Publishing/Nomos 2017) 9, 25–27.

26 As to private international law, it commissioned a number of studies between 2012 and 2015: European Parliament: X Kramer and others, *A European Framework for Private International Law: Current Gaps and Future Perspectives* (Study European Parliament 2012); X Kramer, *Current Gaps and Future Perspectives in European Private International Law: Towards a Code on Private International Law?* (Briefing Note, European Parliament 2012); X Kramer, 'European Private International Law: The Way Forward' in *Workshop on Upcoming Issues of EU Law: Compilation of In-Depth Analyses* (European Parliament 2014) 77; J von Hein and G Rühl, 'Towards a European Code on Private International Law?' in *Cross-border Activities in the EU: Making Life Easier for Citizens* (Workshop for the JURI Committee, European Parliament 2015) 8.

27 European Parliamentary Research Service (Rafał Mańko), *Europeanisation of Civil Procedure: Towards common minimum standards?* (In-depth Analysis, European Parliament 2015).

28 See, in particular European Parliamentary Research Service (Magdalena Tulibacka, Margarita Sanz and Roland Blomeyer), *Common Minimum Standards of Civil Procedure* (European Parliament

sion on **Common Minimum Standards** of Civil Procedure in the European Union.[29] The draft Directive consists of 28 provisions containing rules on, among others, the commencement, conduct, and conclusion of civil proceedings, and aims to ensure the right of a fair trial as laid down in Article 47 EU Charter and Article 6 ECHR.[30] This ambitious initiative to provide a **horizontal framework** for European civil procedure, however, was not followed up by the European Commission.

#28 An important contribution to European civil procedure are the ELI-Unidroit Model European Rules of Civil Procedure, adopted in 2020.[31] Taking as point of departure the 2004 ALI-Unidroit Principles of Transnational Civil Procedure, and taking into account, in particular, the 1994 Storme report, the EU acquis, and the common traditions of European countries, this joint project of the European Law Institute and Unidroit to establish **model rules** on civil procedure officially started in 2014. Over a period of seven years, eight working groups worked on different areas of civil procedure, complemented by an overarching structure group that compiled and completed the different parts. This has resulted in an extensive set of 245 model rules divided into twelve parts. These include general provisions and more detailed rules on parties, case management, commencement of proceedings, proceedings preparatory to a final hearing, service, evidence, judgments, means of review, provisional and protective measures, collective proceedings, and costs.

#29 While the binding EU civil procedure rules are scattered over different instruments and do not rely on a uniform technique, scope or approach, the European Commission has invested in unifying and simplifying the use of civil procedure rules. It has done so, in particular, by setting up the above-mentioned e-Justice Portal (see #20) including the **European Judicial Atlas in Civil Matters**, developing **standard forms** attached to the instruments for various steps of the procedure, as well as invested in **judicial training** (*eg* through the European Judicial Training Network, EJTN). Also, the European Judicial Network (EJN), having national contact points facilitating judicial cooperation as well as other European networks, including the European Network of Councils for the Judiciary (ENCJ), have contributed to a more uniform application of, and perhaps coherent approach to European civil procedure.

2016); B Hess, *Harmonized Rules and Minimum Standards in the European Law of Civil Procedure* (In-depth Analysis, European Parliament 2016).

29 European Parliament Recommendation 2015/2084(INL) of 10 February 2017 on common minimum standards of civil procedure in the EU (4 July 2017).

30 X Kramer, 'Strengthening Civil Justice Cooperation: The Quest for Model Rules and Common Minimum Standards of Civil Procedure in Europe' in MA Rodrigues and H Zaneti Jr (eds), *Coleção Grandes Temas do Novo CPC – v.13 – Cooperação Internacional* (Juspodivm 2019) 591.

31 European Law Institute and Unidroit, *ELI-Unidroit Model European Rules of Civil Procedure. From Transnational Principles to European* Rules of Civil Procedure (OUP 2021). See also E Jeuland, Chapter 23.

II Impact of EU Civil Procedure on National Systems

#30 The impact of European civil procedure reaches further than the regulations and directives that explicitly deal with cross-border litigation or aspects of civil procedure, as the Europeanisation of civil procedure has also taken place more indirectly through human rights case law.[32] A certain degree of **harmonisation** has been achieved through the **human rights** case law of the European Court of Human Rights and the CJEU on the basis of Article 6 ECHR and Article 47 ECHR. The extensive case law of the CJEU on the various instruments of private international law and civil procedure, most prominently on the Brussels I-bis Regulation and its predecessors, and autonomously interpreting key concepts, also has an influence on civil procedure in the Member States that may reach beyond the application of those specific regulations and directives.

#31 Also, the application and interpretation of directives that mostly contain substantive law have led to the Europeanisation of civil procedure. This is most prominent in the area of consumer law through the various consumer directives. Most influential on the operation of civil justice systems has been the obligation to apply EU consumer law *ex officio*. But also in other areas, including data protection through the GDPR, **competition law**, intellectual property law, and **environmental law** harmonisation trends are visible.

#32 Lastly, more indirectly, through the EU Justice Scoreboard mentioned above (#20), European civil justice policy has an influence on civil procedure in the Member States. Since 2013, the Scoreboard has presented an annual overview of how Member States perform, focusing on essential criteria of an effective justice system, efficiency, quality, and independence. It has an impact on civil procedure through comparing Member States' performance, using mostly data of the European Commission for the Efficiency of Justice (**CEPEJ**) of the **Council of Europe** and by giving country-specific recommendations.

C Themes and Goals of the Book

I Objective and Structure

#33 As the previous section has shown, European civil procedure has undergone significant transformation in recent decades. Despite challenges and setbacks, it has evolved from a patchwork of national systems into an increasingly harmonised, coherent, and sophisticated legal framework, built on steadily expanding foundations and continuing to drive change across national procedural and justice sys-

32 See also A Ancery and B Krans, Chapter 6.

tems. The **objective** of this handbook is to offer an in-depth and thematically rich analysis of those developments, shedding light on the principles, mechanisms, and trends that define civil justice in today's European context.

#34 The **structure** of the volume reflects both its objective and the complexity and scope of the legal field. To this end, the book is organised in three parts, with each of them offering a distinct perspective on the subject. Part I addresses the background, core themes, and foundational questions that underpin the broader context of European civil procedure. Part II focuses on procedural stages, special mechanisms, and dispute resolution tools shaped by EU legal instruments. Part III broadens the scope to explore different approaches to harmonisation, the interplay with global developments and influences, and prospects for the future. Each of these parts is briefly outlined below.

II Content

1 Part I 'Introduction and General Themes'

#35 The first part of the book (Part I) sets the stage and addresses the key concepts, principles, and developments that underpin the European approach to civil procedure. Next to the legal infrastructure, it explores the historical, philosophical, political, and technological rationales that have driven the process of integration of procedural law across European jurisdictions. The themes selected are essential for understanding the evolution of European civil procedure, its ongoing transformation, and its connections to broader European legal and policy frameworks.

#36 Part I opens with Eva Storskrubb's 'Civil Justice and EU Competence' (Chapter 2), which traces how Articles 81 and 114 TFEU have progressively empowered the EU to shape civil procedural law. Remco van Rhee's 'The History of Civil Procedure in Europe' (Chapter 3) offers a historical overview, providing crucial context and highlighting the comparative traditions that have influenced European civil procedure. Matthias Weller examines 'Mutual Trust' (Chapter 4), the cornerstone of judicial cooperation, unpacking its legal significance, current tensions, and relevant supranational case law that form the backbone of European judicial cooperation.

#37 Burkhard Hess's contribution, 'Access to Justice' (Chapter 5), explores this fundamental procedural principle and its evolving significance within EU law. He highlights the constitutionalisation of civil procedure under Article 47 of the Charter of Fundamental Rights and assesses how efficiency, enforcement priorities, and the rise of ADR mechanisms are reshaping the role of access to justice principle. Alain Ancery and Bart Krans discuss 'EU Law and National Procedural Law' (Chapter 6), which focuses on the Europeanisation of civil procedure through the convergence of national rules and EU law. They emphasise the impact of EU general principles and directives, which significantly shape national procedures—often in unexpected ways, as illustrated by concrete examples. Finally, Anna Nylund's 'Innovation and Digitalisation' (Chapter 7) investigates how technological advancements and innovation, from e-filing systems to AI tools, are transforming civil justice and considers potential directions for future development.

2 Part II 'Litigating in Europe'

#38 Building on the conceptual, legal, historical, political, foundational, and technological groundwork laid in Part I, the second Part II of the handbook shifts focus to the practical realities of civil litigation within the EU framework. It guides the readers through the entire typical lifecycle of a cross-border civil case—from initiation to enforcement—while also addressing various specialised procedures and mechanisms that have shaped specific legal domains within the European AFSJ. The chapters in this part offer practical insights and doctrinal perspectives on how EU procedural rules operate in real-world disputes, highlighting both the synergies and tensions between national systems and EU law. Moreover, they also illustrate the growing interdependence between those systems and their rules and the key areas of reforms and innovation in European civil justice.

#39 It opens with Wendy Kennett's 'Service of Documents' (Chapter 8), which analyses the procedural steps and challenges involved in cross-border service under EU instruments. Geert van Calster follows with 'International Jurisdiction: Fundamental Principles' (Chapter 9), unpacking the core jurisdictional rules governing civil and commercial litigation within the EU. Pietro Franzina's 'International Jurisdiction in Civil and Commercial Matters' (Chapter 10) provides an in-depth discussion of the Brussels I-bis Regulation, highlighting recent jurisprudential developments. Jachin van Doninck and Wannes Vandenbussche address the cross-border 'Taking of Evidence' (Chapter 11), offering insights into procedural cooperation and the interplay between national authorities. Fernando Gascón Inchausti's 'Recognition and Enforcement: Fundamental Issues' (Chapter 12) provides an analysis of key principles and mechanisms that facilitate the circulation of judgments within the European AFSJ. Wolfgang Hau continues this thread with 'Recognition and Enforcement of Civil and Commercial Judgments' (Chapter 13), examining the Brussels I-bis Regulation's practical implications for national systems.

#40 The handbook then turns to specialised areas. Apostolos Anthimos's 'Family Matters' (Chapter 14) discusses the rules governing cross-border family cases. Anna Wysocka-Bar explores issues of jurisdiction, applicable law, and recognition in matters related to 'Property Regimes and Succession' (Chapter 15). Elena D'Alessandro focuses on 'Debt Collection and Special Procedures' (Chapter 16), examining legal tools such as the European Payment Order and Small Claims Procedure.

Carlos Santaló Goris's chapter on 'Asset Preservation and Provisional Measures' (Chapter 17) addresses procedural tools available to secure claims before final judgment. Vesna Lazić explores 'Insolvency Proceedings' (Chapter 18), tracing the evolution of EU rules and their harmonising impact.

#41 The final section of Part II looks ahead to emerging trends and institutional developments. Georgia Antonopoulou's 'Specialised Courts' (Chapter 19) assesses the rise of international commercial courts and the Unified Patent Court, analysing their role in transforming procedural landscapes and procedural venues of dispute resolution. Emma Van Gelder contributes 'Alternative Pathways: ADR/ODR' (Chapter 20), which evaluates non-judicial mechanisms as vital alternatives to litigation. Eva Lein's 'Collective Redress' (Chapter 21) examines the implications of the Representative Actions Directive and the evolving European approach to group litigation. John Sorabji closes this part with 'Legal Aid, Costs and Funding' (Chapter 22), discussing access to justice in light of legal expenses, litigation funding, and broader constitutional concerns.

3 Part III 'Future Outlook'

#42 The third part of the book (Part III) broadens the focus to explore future developments and the broader global context of European civil procedure. This Part looks forward but also outward, positioning European civil justice within an increasingly globalised legal environment.

#43 Emmanuel Jeuland opens this part with 'Soft Law and Best Practices' (Chapter 23), examining how non-binding instruments—particularly the ELI-Unidroit Rules—are contributing to the establishment of procedural standards across jurisdictions. He further analyses how soft law, collaborative networks, judicial evaluations and metrics, and judicial training initiatives foster convergence through shared principles of efficiency, fairness, and innovation.

#44 Of particular interest is the contribution of Monika Canco, Ana Harvey and Iryna Izarova who turn to 'European Civil Procedure and the EU Enlargement Process' (Chapter 24), focusing on the influence of EU procedural norms on candidate countries. Using Albania, Serbia, and Ukraine as examples, they show how civil justice reforms are increasingly driven by the accession process, aligning national systems with EU standards well before membership. This chapter underscores the depth of EU influence and the broader role of Europeanisation in shaping national legal frameworks.

#45 A global perspective is provided in 'European Civil Procedure from a Non-European Perspective' (Chapter 25), authored by Magdalena Tulibacka, Peter Chan, Mohamed Paleker, and Eduardo Silva de Freitas. This collaborative chapter explores both the EU's normative impact beyond its borders and the reciprocal insights offered by developments in North America, Latin America, and Asia.

#46 The handbook concludes with Alan Uzelac's 'Wider Challenges' (Chapter 26), a reflective analysis of the systemic pressures currently shaping European civil justice. Addressing issues from Brexit to global harmonisation and internal fragmentation, this chapter underscores the ongoing tension between procedural unification and diversity—a central challenge for the future of the EU's justice agenda.

D The Future of European Civil Procedure

#47 Finally, the question arises about the **future** of EU civil procedure. As previously discussed, and as demonstrated throughout the various chapters, EU civil procedure is dynamic, not static. It evolves in response to both legal and non-legal developments within the broader societal context in which it operates. It is crucial to consider what lies ahead. What future changes will shape EU civil procedure in the coming years and decades? What direction are EU justice policies heading? Three key questions emerge: Where is the focus shifting? What challenges still remain? And how should we prepare future generations for these changes

I Emerging Priorities Shifting Focuses in EU Civil Justice

1 Consumer Protection and Collective Redress

#48 As mentioned earlier (#18), a third category of EU civil procedure rules comprises sector-specific or vertical instruments. One of the most prominent examples today is **consumer protection**, particularly the resolution of consumer disputes. The **2013 Consumer ADR Directive** is currently undergoing revision.[33] A key priority moving forward is to clarify the role that Alternative Dispute Resolution (ADR) for consumers can and should play alongside traditional judicial processes in both national and cross-border disputes. In certain EU Member States, such as the Netherlands and Belgium, there is a proposal to grant consumer ADR bodies the right to refer questions to the courts for preliminary rulings.

#49 On the other hand, there is the already discussed **Representative Actions Directive**, which has been implemented in nearly all Member States. Its impact on national civil procedure, particularly regarding judicial case management and evidence gathering, which has traditionally focused on individual litigation, should not be underestimated. This is an area that warrants close attention. A remaining issue is the application of the Brussels I-bis Regulation in cross-border mass harm

33 See <https://commission.europa.eu/publications/revision-adr-directive-all-documents_en> accessed 21 April 2025.

cases and representative actions. The Representative Actions Directive states that the existing EU rules apply, but this has led to uncertainty and has sparked some (albeit limited) case law from the CJEU.[34] These developments could eventually prompt legislative action at the EU level.

#50 The trend towards collectivising civil procedure extends beyond the realm of consumer protection. It has also influenced areas such as **competition damages**[35] and **general data protection**[36]. However, this has resulted in **fragmented legislation** and a disjointed landscape for collective **private enforcement**. What is lacking is a comprehensive, uniform, and horizontal collective redress framework. In this regard, European policymakers have been criticised for adopting a 'silo mentality'.[37]

#51 Finally, there is the growing emphasis on **private litigation funding**, which is a relatively new development. In September 2022, the European Parliament adopted a resolution on responsible private funding of litigation, urging the European Commission to propose legislation to regulate Third Party Litigation Funding (TPLF) in the EU.[38] In March 2025, the Commission published its 'Study on Mapping Third Party Litigation Funding in the European Union',[39] while in October 2024 the European Law Institute (ELI) adopted its 'Principles Governing the Third Party Funding of Litigation'.[40] It remains to be seen whether these efforts will lead to EU-wide legislation. Regardless, private litigation funding – both within and outside the context of representative actions – will undoubtedly remain a significant feature of the litigation landscape and is important in securing access to justice.

---

34 See P Leupold, *Private International Law and Cross-Border Collective Redress. A Legal Analysis of Jurisdiction, Applicable Law, Pendency, Recognition and Enforcement under the Representative Actions Directive 1828/2020* (BEUC 2022) <https://www.beuc.eu/sites/default/files/publications/BEUC-X-2022-085_Private_International_Law_and_Cross-Border_Collective_Redress.pdf> accessed 21 April 2025.

35 Directive (EU) 2014/104 of 26 November 2014 on certain rules governing actions for damages under national law for infringements of the competition law provisions of the Member States and of the European Union Text with EEA relevance [2014] OJ L349/1.

36 Regulation (EU) 2016/679 of 27 April 2016 on the protection of natural persons with regard to the processing of personal data and on the free movement of such data [2016] OJ L119/1.

37 S Voet, 'Europe's Collective Redress Conundrum' (2018) 61 Japanese Yearbook of International Law 205.

38 European Parliament, 'Responsible private funding of litigation. European Parliament resolution of 13 September 2022 with recommendations to the Commission on Responsible private funding of litigation' 2020/2130(INL).

39 <https://commission.europa.eu/strategy-and-policy/policies/justice-and-fundamental-rights/civil-justice/civil-and-commercial-law/third-party-litigation-funding-tplf_en> accessed 21 April 2025.

40 <https://www.europeanlawinstitute.eu/news-events/news-contd/news/eli-publishes-principles-governing-the-third-party-funding-of-litigation-tpfl/> accessed 21 April 2025.

2 Digitalisation and AI in Civil Justice

#52 **Digitalisation** and AI will play an increasingly significant role in both national and EU civil justice systems. While their impact is still manageable at present, rapid **technological advancements** will soon require national and European policymakers to act swiftly and establish appropriate regulations. Existing frameworks will need to be updated, and new ones developed. On one hand, this involves addressing the effect of digitalisation on the conduct of civil proceedings (*eg* electronic service of documents). On the other hand, the impact extends beyond this traditional scope. We are witnessing the rise of AI-driven adjudication, which includes automated case management, predictive justice, and AI-assisted legal reasoning. Alongside the 2013 Consumer ADR Directive, the EU has introduced the Consumer ODR Regulation.[41] ODR, or Online Dispute Resolution, uses technology, primarily the internet, to resolve disputes through negotiation, mediation, or arbitration.[42] While the European Commission announced in 2023 that the ODR Regulation will be repealed, and the ODR platform has been discontinued, this form of dispute resolution will remain vital (*eg* through private platforms or future EU legislation or activities), particularly for resolving small consumer disputes, which in turn will help foster confidence in the internal market.

#53 In light of these developments, it is crucial to remain mindful of the **fundamental rights** that underpin EU civil procedure (see #5 and #12). While digitalisation and AI offer significant advances in efficiency and speed, it is essential that **procedural safeguards** – such as due process – continue to be upheld. These safeguards are enshrined in well-established legal frameworks and case law, and while they may be shaped differently in the digital age, they cannot be compromised. The challenge will be to strike a pragmatic yet robust balance between these principles.

3 Expanding the Role of (EU) Civil Procedure in Economic Governance

#54 Finally, it is essential to continually highlight the growing importance of EU civil procedure within the broader framework of EU **economic governance**. This framework – central to the Economic and Monetary Union – is designed to identify and address economic imbalances that could undermine national economies. In this context, European civil procedure plays a vital role in supporting **eco-**

---

41 Regulation (EU) 524/2013 of 21 May 2013 on online dispute resolution for consumer disputes [2013] OJ L165/1.

42 E van Gelder, *Consumer Online Dispute Resolution Pathways in Europe. Analysing the Standards for Access and Procedural Justice in Online Dispute Resolution Procedures* (Eleven International Publishing 2022).

nomic integration and ensuring the stability of the internal market (see #3, #8, and #13). Strengthening procedural safeguards in key areas such as competition law, financial disputes, and cross-border insolvency should remain a core priority moving forward. In this regard, the ELI-Unidroit Model Rules of European Civil Procedure (see #28) offer a valuable blueprint for achieving procedural harmonisation beyond sector-specific instruments.

II Key Challenges for the Future of European Procedural Law

#55 Three key challenges can be identified. First, there is a gradual but increasingly evident **erosion of mutual trust** within EU judicial cooperation. This decline is driven, in part, by growing concerns over the rule of law, particularly regarding judicial independence in certain Eastern European Member States. One possible, albeit controversial, response could be to reinforce the existing conditionality regime.[43]

#56 Second, the rise of **Euroscepticism** and national resistance to harmonisation presents a significant challenge. This tension, rooted in the broader subsidiarity versus uniformity debate, which always has been present, manifests as opposition to deeper procedural integration and a renewed emphasis on national constitutional identity. These dynamics became particularly visible in the context of cross-border enforcement following Brexit, re-emerged in the context of the implementation of the Representative Actions Directive, and might come up again in the implementation process of the SLAPPs Directive.

#57 Third and finally, longstanding **barriers to access to justice** persist, both financial and structural. **Litigation costs** continue to rise, partly due to the increasing specialisation of legal practice. As noted earlier (see #51), third-party litigation funding (TPLF) could provide an alternative financing mechanism, especially – but not exclusively – in collective proceedings. Additionally, there is a notable disparity in access to digital justice tools among EU Member States.[44] Addressing **digital vulnerability** is essential, not only within traditional judicial processes but also in alternative and online dispute resolution mechanisms, particularly in the consumer context.

---

43 Regulation (EU, Euratom) 2020/2092 of 16 December 2020 on a general regime of conditionality for the protection of the Union budget [2020] OJ L433/1. This is to be distinguished from the Annual Rule of Law Cycle, which is mere preventive tool, aiming to promote the rule of law and prevent challenges from emerging or deteriorating (see <https://commission.europa.eu/strategy-and-policy/policies/justice-and-fundamental-rights/upholding-rule-law/rule-law/annual-rule-law-cycle_en> accessed 21 April 2025).

44 See for example C Crea and A De Franceschi (eds), *The New Shapes of Digital Vulnerability in European Private Law* (Nomos 2024).

III The Future of European Civil Procedure Education and Training: How to Prepare the Future Generation?

#58 In a handbook on European civil procedure it is essential to look ahead to the future of **education** and **training** in this area. Earlier (see #29), the importance of **judicial training**, such as that provided by the European Judicial Training Network (EJTN) and the European Law Academy (ERA), was emphasised. For professional development, the Erasmus+ Programme plays a key role.[45] It offers valuable opportunities for lawyers and law students to participate in mobility and exchange initiatives, particularly through the 'Euro Lawyers Exchange Program', which supports internships in law firms and institutions across Europe. Expanding such **judicial networks** and cross-border legal education programs is crucial to promoting a harmonised interpretation and consistent application of EU procedural instruments.

#59 It is equally essential to adapt legal education to the evolving landscape of European civil procedure.[46] National civil procedure remains a fundamental component of legal education. At many universities, European civil procedure is either integrated into the national procedure course, combined with teaching or private international law, or taught as a separate subject. However, what is needed is the inclusion of EU civil procedure in a harmonised curriculum across Member States to prepare the future generation of EU policy makers, judges, lawyers and other legal professionals. Such a curriculum is also important to prepare for a possible **enlargement** of the EU in the years to come.[47] This would equip law students with a shared transnational perspective on litigation. Promoting a comparative and harmonised approach to European civil procedure in legal education is imperative. In this context, the ELI-Unidroit Model European Rules of Civil Procedure (see #28) could serve as an excellent teaching tool for transnational procedural law.

References

Crea C and De Franceschi A (eds), *The New Shapes of Digital Vulnerability in European Private Law* (Nomos 2024).

Dori A, *The Governance of EU Justice Reforms: The Role of the EU Justice Scoreboard and Country Specific Recommendations in Shaping National Judicial Systems* (Nomos 2025).

45 <https://erasmus-plus.ec.europa.eu/programme-guide/part-a/priorities-of-the-erasmus-programme/participate> accessed 21 April 2025.

46 See X Kramer and L Carballo Piñeiro (eds), *Research Methods in Private International Law. A Handbook on Regulation, Research and Teaching* (Edward Elgar 2024). Part III focuses on Shaping the Future Through Private International Law Methodology.

47 See M Canco, A Harvey and I Izarova, Chapter 24.

European Law Institute and Unidroit, *ELI-Unidroit Model European Rules of Civil Procedure. From Transnational Principles to European Rules of Civil Procedure* (OUP 2021).
European Parliament (Xandra Kramer and others), 'A European Framework for Private International Law: Current Gaps and Future Perspectives' (Study European Parliament 2012).
European Parliament, 'Responsible Private Funding of Litigation' European Parliament Resolution of 13 September 2022 with Recommendations to the Commission on Responsible Private Funding of Litigation, 2020/2130(INL).
European Parliamentary Research Service (Magdalena Tulibacka, Margarita Sanz and Roland Blomeyer), 'Common Minimum Standards of Civil Procedure' (European Parliament 2016).
European Parliamentary Research Service (Rafał Mańko), 'Europeanisation of Civil Procedure, Towards Common Minimum Standards?' (In-depth Analysis, European Parliament 2015).
Gelder van E, *Consumer Online Dispute Resolution Pathways in Europe. Analysing the Standards for Access and Procedural Justice in Online Dispute Resolution Procedures* (Eleven International Publishing 2022).
Glavina M, 'Trust in and Between Courts in the Changing World of the 21st Century' [2024-1] Erasmus Law Review 1.
Hess B, 'Harmonized Rules and Minimum Standards in the European Law of Civil Procedure' (In-depth Analysis, European Parliament 2016).
—— 'The State of the Civil Justice Union' in B Hess, M Bergström and E Storskrubb (eds), *EU Civil Justice: Current Issues and Future Outlook* (Hart Publishing/Bloomsbury 2016) 1.
—— *Europäisches Zivilprocessrecht* (2nd edn, De Gruyter 2021).
Hess B and Kramer X, 'From Common Rules to Best Practices in European Civil Procedure: An Introduction' in B Hess and X Kramer (eds), *From Common Rules to Best Practices in European Civil Procedure* (Hart Publishing/Nomos 2017) 9.
Kramer X, 'Current Gaps and Future Perspectives in European Private International Law: Towards a Code on Private International Law?' (Briefing Note, European Parliament 2012).
—— *Procedure Matters: Construction and Deconstructivism in European Civil Procedure* (Eleven International Publishing 2013).
—— 'European Private International Law: The Way Forward' in: *Workshop on Upcoming Issues of EU Law: Compilation of In-Depth* Analyses (European Parliament 2014) 77.
—— 'Strengthening Civil Justice Cooperation: The Quest for Model Rules and Common Minimum Standards of Civil Procedure in Europe' in MA Rodrigues and H, Zaneti Jr (eds), *Coleção Grandes Temas do Novo CPC – v.13 – Cooperação Internacional* (Juspodivm 2019) 591.
Kramer X and Carballo Piñeiro L, *Research Methods in Private International Law* (Edward Elgar 2024).
Law S and Nowak JT, 'Procedural Harmonisation by the European Court of Justice: Procedural Autonomy and the Member States' Perspective' in F Gascón Inchausti and B Hess (eds), *The Future of the European Law of Civil Procedure* (Intersentia 2020) 17.
Leupold P, *Private International Law and Cross-Border Collective Redress. A Legal Analysis of Jurisdiction, Applicable Law, Pendency, Recognition and Enforcement under the Representative Actions Directive 1828/2020* (BEUC 2022).
Meeusen J, 'The Contribution of 'Brussels I' to the Process of EU Integration: A True Trailblazer for the Europeanisation and Constitutionalisation of Private International Law' in B Hess and K Lenaerts (eds), *The 50th Anniversary of the European Law of Civil Procedure* (Nomos 2020) 121.
Storskrubb E, 'EU Civil Justice at the Harmonisation Crossroads' in A Nylund and M Strandberg (eds), *Civil Procedure and Harmonisation of Law: The Dynamics of EU and International Treaties* (Intersentia 2019) 11.
—— 'Mutual Trust in Civil Justice Cooperation in the EU' in A Bakardjieva Engelbrekt and others (eds), *Trust in the European Union in Challenging Times* (Springer 2019) 159.
Voet S, 'Europe's Collective Redress Conundrum' (2018) 61 Japanese Yearbook of International Law 205.

von Hein J and Rühl G, 'Towards a European Code on Private International Law?' in: *Cross-border Activities in the EU: Making Life Easier for Citizens* (Workshop for the JURI Committee, European Parliament 2015) 8.

Weller M, '"Mutual Trust": A Suitable Foundation for Private International Law in Regional Integration Communities and Beyond?' in Collected Courses of the Hague Academy of International Law – Recueil des cours, vol 423 (Brill 2022).

Eva Storskrubb*

Chapter 2
Civil Justice and EU Competence

A Introduction

#1 One of the central principles of EU law is the **principle of conferral** (alternatively the principle of attributed powers), today enshrined in Article 1 of the Treaty on the European Union (TEU). The principle entails that the Member States confer competence on the EU to attain the objectives outlined in the EU Treaties. Competence is in this context used to denote both legal authority and power.[1] The principle of conferral is also a means to delimit the competence of the EU. It is clarified in Article 5(2) TEU that the EU shall only act within the limits of the competence conferred upon it by the Member States. In addition, Article 4(1) TEU stipulates that the competences not conferred upon the EU remain with the Member States.

#2 In the EU Treaties the Member States grant **legislative competence** to the EU in a number of discrete and specific policy areas. The Treaty provisions providing specific legal foundations for the competence, called legal bases, include material restrictions as well as formal requirements on the process to enact EU legislation in the relevant area. Thus, the delimitation of power between the Member States and the EU in a specific area of EU law is regulated in detail. However, the legal bases can also be perceived as a means to protect the competence remaining with the Member States.[2] Should a legislative act of the EU breach the principle of conferral, ie should the EU exceed its competence, the act may be annulled by the Court of Justice of EU (CJEU), Articles 263–264 of the Treaty on the Functioning of the European Union (TFEU).

#3 Together with the principle of primacy, and the principle of sincere cooperation, Article 4(2), the principle of conferral entails a significant transfer of sovereignty from the Member States to the EU.[3] How the power conferred to the EU is exercised is governed by the principles of **subsidiarity** and **proportionality**, Article 5(3) and 5(4) TEU, which will not be analysed further here. This chapter aims at providing a comprehensive overview of the competence of the EU in the area of civil justice. First, a history of Treaty evolution will show the development of com-

---

1 K Bradley, 'Legislating in the European Union' in Catherine Barnard and Steve Peers (eds), *European Union Law* (4th edn, OUP 2023) 108.

2 ibid 110.

3 For the principle of primacy see declaration 17 to the Treaty of Lisbon.

***Corresponding author: Eva Storskrubb**, Uppsala University, e-mail: eva.storskrubb@jur.uu.se

https://doi.org/10.1515/9783110781632-002

petence in the area (section B). Second, it is pertinent to analyse the so-called competence catalogue as well as potential relevant legal bases in the EU Treaties (section C). Finally, the chapter will provide a brief future outlook (section D). The issues discussed in this chapter are fundamental to and relevant for all other chapters that deal with specific legislative instruments of EU civil justice. However, the broader debate on EU competence that is raised in this chapter is particularly connected to the discussion in Chapter 6 and in Chapter 7 of this book.

B The Evolution of Competence

I The Intergovernmental Period

#4 Historically, at the very start of the EU, then called the European Economic Community (EEC), there was no competence to legislate in the area of civil justice. However, Article 220 of the founding **Treaty of Rome** (in force 1958) included an impetus for intergovernmental action in certain aspects of private international law. Thus, at the very start, when the EEC commenced with its initial project of removing market barriers and creating a common market, it was already foreseen that cooperation in certain limited aspects of civil justice might become necessary.[4] However, the cooperation that was envisaged was solely private international law and solely intergovernmental treaties, not any competence to legislate. Two well-known treaties that were subsequently enacted in the field of private international law were the **Brussels Convention** in 1968 (on jurisdiction and the recognition and enforcement of judgments in civil and commercial matters) and the **Rome Convention** in 1980 (on choice of law for contractual disputes).[5]

#5 The potential for deeper market integration was furthered in a Treaty amendment called the **Single European Act** (in force in 1987). One of main changes was to ensure move from negative integration (removing market barriers) to positive integration (harmonising rules) that would support the establishment of an internal market. The new legal basis, Article 100a conferred on the European Community (EC) power to adopt measures to approximate the laws of the Member States by qualified majority to create the internal market. Article 100a is the precursor to current Article 114 TFEU.[6] The aim for deeper substantive market integration

4 E Storskrubb, *Civil Procedure and EU Law* (OUP 2008) 34–35. For the historic development of the EU see eg P Craig, 'The Development of the EU' in C Barnard and S Peers (eds), *European Union Law* (4th edn, OUP 2023) 10, 15.

5 G Barrett, 'Introduction' in G Barrett (ed), *Creating a European Judicial Space, Prospects for Improving Judicial Cooperation in Civil Matters in the European Union*, vol 30 (Academy of European Law Trier 2001) 8.

6 Craig (n 4) 20.

also led to the first significant academic debate on the necessity and desirability for a broader harmonisation of civil procedure. The starting point for this debate was the report of a group of academics that prepared detailed proposals for harmonised rules, the so-called **Storme Report**, published in 1994.[7] It was argued in the Report that the legal bases in the Treaties for the internal market provided competence for the EU to act also in the procedural field.[8] The Report also provided arguments on the necessity of procedural **harmonisation**. For example, it was argued that diverging procedural rules created procedural obstacles and that transparent and functioning rules for litigation for cross-border commercial actors were needed.[9]

#6 The findings of the report were both supported and criticised in the doctrine.[10] Critics raised arguments against both the issue of EU competence as well as the specific proposals and the exclusions from the project. In addition, the benefits and feasibility of harmonisation was questioned.[11] Regardless of this academic debate, it is notable that no general legislative action was taken in the procedural field under the legal basis of Article 100a during this period. Instead, there were unsuccessful attempts to create additional cross-border conventions via the **intergovernmental** route outside the formal EC framework.[12]

#7 During this early period, the lack of harmonised procedural rules came before the CJEU in the context of domestic court proceedings in which substantive EC law rights were raised. In such a case, there could arise situations in which the domestic procedural rule was considered to potentially hinder to the realisation of the substantive rights. Thus, from 1976 onwards, the CJEU has stipulated that the procedural rules must not be less favourable than those governing similar domestic actions (**principle of equivalence**); and must not make it virtually impossible or excessively difficult to exercise the rights conferred by Community law (**principle of efficiency**).[13]

---

7 M Storme (ed), *Rapprochement du Droit Judiciare de l'Union européenne - Approximation of Judiciary Law in the European Union* (Kluwer Law International 1994).

8 ibid 24–25.

9 ibid 9–18.

10 ibid 21–24, 36–37.

11 See eg PH Lindblom, 'Harmony of the Legal Spheres. A Swedish View on the Construction of a Unified European Procedural Law' (1997) 5 European Review of Private Law 11. See further, Storskubb (n 4) 21–24.

12 A-M Rouchaud, 'Le renforcement de la coopération judiciaire' in Université Jean Moulin, Faculté de Droit (eds), *Les effets des jugements nationaux dans les autres États membres de l'Union européenne* (Bruylant 2001) 19, 20–21.

13 The seminal cases are Case C-33/76 *Rewe-Zentralfinanz eG and Rewe-Zentral AG v Lanswirtschaftskammer für das Saarland* (16 December 1976) ECLI:EU:C:1976:188, and C-45/76 *Comet BV v Produktschap voor Siergewassen* (16 December 1976) ECLI:EU:C:1976:191. The case law has dealt with a multitude of domestic procedural and remedial rules and continues to grow (see Stor-

#8 This case law highlighted the fact that enforcement of substantive EU law rights is **decentralised**, entailing that the realisation of those rights relies on proceedings in national courts and hence on the national procedural rules. The case law of the CJEU in this respect also created the concept of national **procedural autonomy**, because the starting point for the CJEU in shaping the principles of equivalence and effectiveness was the fact that there was no procedural competence or harmonised procedural legislation in the EU at the time (only limited international conventions as mentioned above). However, the concept of national procedural autonomy only holds true until there is legislation in place at the EU level. As will be evident from the following sections of this Chapter, the progressive increase in the competence of the EU in the field of civil justice has led to a progressive increase in EU legislation in the field. Therefore, the procedural autonomy of the Member States is today significantly curtailed.

II Justice and Home Affairs

#9 The next treaty amendment came with the **Treaty of Maastricht**, which entered into force in 1993. The Treaty created the so-called Third Pillar in the structure of the Treaties for the new policy concept of **Justice and Home Affairs** (JHA).[14] Thus, separate from the traditional internal market framework, which remained in the First Pillar, a competence for the EC to act specifically in the field of justice was included in a separate part, the Third Pillar. The terms **judicial cooperation** in civil matters, as well as judicial cooperation in criminal matters, were used to denote these new fields of procedural 'common interest'.[15] However, there were no further specifications of what these terms meant or were intended to encompass. Further, it is notable that the Third Pillar was created because all Member States were not willing to relinquish sovereignty in the field of justice.

#10 Thus, the institutional structure and legislative process under the Third Pillar remained mainly **intergovernmental**. For example, the main instrument was conventions (rather than directives or regulations), the Commission did not have the right of initiative, there was a requirement of unanimity in the Council (rather

skrubb (n 4) 16–17. See also A Nylund (Chapter 7) in this volume and *inter alia* S Law and JT Nowak, 'Procedural Harmonisation by the European Court of Justice – Procedural Autonomy and the Member States' Perspective' in F Gascón Inchausti and B Hess (eds), *The Future of the European Law of Civil Procedure* (Intersentia 2020) 17, 27.

14 The Maastricht Treaty introduced the concept of citizenship of the EU. Some commentators have also considered the provisions on citizenship could form a legal basis for civil justice. See *inter alia* P-E Partsch, Le Droit International Privé Européen. De Rome à Nice (Larcier 2003) 269–275. See further, Storskrubb (n 4) 82–86.

15 Formally also in a separate Treaty, the EU Treaty, Article K.1.

than qualified majority voting), the European Parliament (EP) was excluded from the decision making only having a potential consultative role, and recourse to the CJEU was excluded. These features were perceived as disadvantages and were the basis for significant critique.[16] In the field civil justice only two conventions were adopted during this period, and due to slow transposition neither ever entered into force due to matters being overtaken by the following Treaty amendment in 1999.[17]

III The Area of Freedom, Security and Justice

#11 For civil justice, the hitherto most significant Treaty amendment was made arguably in the **Treaty of Amsterdam**, which entered into force in 1999. Juridical cooperation in civil matters was taken from the Third Pillar and placed in the First Pillar, ie in the community sphere of the Treaties. This can be seen as a response to the above-mentioned deficiencies encountered in the JHA era of civil justice. However, even though the move to the First Pillar was significant, there were still temporal limitations that entailed that many of the old features of the legislative process remained until 2003 an amendment in the Treaty of Nice.[18] In addition, the CJEU was given a special and more limited remit in the Treaty of Amsterdam, which crucially meant that the possibility to request a preliminary reference was limited to courts of last instance.[19] These structural and institutional limitations can be seen as a testament to a continued reluctance of the Member States to relinquish **sovereignty** in the area. An additional testament to such reluctance is that fact that three Member States, the UK, Ireland and Denmark formally opted out of judicial cooperation in civil matters. This added **fragmentation** and complexity to the policy area and resulted in these Member States not being bound by any enacted legislative acts in the area unless they were able to opt in based on specific terms.[20] In addition, judicial cooperation in the special field of family law remained under the old intergovernmental model, requiring unanimity in the Council.[21]

---

16 G Barrett, 'Cooperation in Justice and Home Affairs in the European Union – An Overview and a Critique' in G Barrett (ed), *Justice Cooperation in the EU, The Creation of a European Legal Space* (Institute of European Affairs 1997) 17.

17 Rouchaud (n 12) 22–23.

18 W Kennett, *Enforcement of Judgments in Europe* (OUP 2000) 15–19.

19 Storskrubb (n 4) 49–55.

20 J Monar, 'Justice and Home Affairs in the Treaty of Amsterdam: Reform at the Price of Fragmentation' (1998) 23 European Law Review 320, 321–324. See further Protocols 4 and 5 to the Treaty of Amsterdam.

21 Article 65(3) EC Treaty. See E Storskrubb, 'Civil Justice: The Contested Nature of the Scope of EU Legislation' in F Trauner and A Ripoll Servant (eds), *Policy Change in the Area of Freedom, Security and Justice* (Routledge 2015) 197, 204.

#12 Despite the above-mentioned limitations and the fragmentation, there were important developments in the Treaty of Amsterdam. Firstly, the specific legal basis for judicial cooperation in civil matters in Article 65 included a list of enumerated fields and measures that could be adopted under the policy area. In addition, the policy concept of the **Area of Freedom, Security and Justice** (AFSJ) was included in the Treaties and a five-year deadline was set for the creation of the AFSJ in Article 60. The deadline in the Treaties led to a political and institutional impetus to act and enact new EU legislation in the field of judicial cooperation in civil matters. In practice, a stream of policy documents including Action Plans of the Council and the Commission, as well as European Council Programmes steered this development, with regular updates by the Commission in so-called Scoreboards, that supported and monitored legislative action.[22] After the five-year deadline lapsed, this political impetus continued. In a ten-year period, between the Treaty of Amsterdam and the **Treaty of Lisbon** entering into force, ie 1999 to 2009, fifteen specific legislative acts had been enacted under the legal basis of judicial cooperation in civil matters as well as several overarching measures.[23]

#13 However, an issue of interpretation of the legal basis in Article 65, in other words, the interpretation of the competence of the EU, has arisen in the context of the legislative process concerning several of the above-mentioned fifteen measures. The issue of interpretation has concerned the limitation in Article 65, which entails that the EU can adopt measures in civil matters having cross-border implications. The present author has called the competence debate 'the cross-border struggle'. In practice, a debate between the EU institutions concerning whether the competence should be interpreted in a restrictive or expansive way.[24] The Commission has argued for a broad interpretation, and the Member States in the Council have acted as gatekeepers and consistently proposed a narrower interpretation. The EP during this period ultimately supported the Council in its strive to limit the understanding of cross-border matters.[25] This debate can be seen to reflect the sovereignty-sensitive nature of civil justice and the concomitant desire of the Member States to retain some level of **autonomy** in the field.

---

22 Storskrubb (n 4) 66–70, see further E Storskrubb, 'Civil Justice Extending its Tentacles' in P Craig and G de Búrca (eds), *The Evolution of EU Law* (3rd edn, OUP 2021) 770, 784–785.

23 See Storskrubb (n 21) 198 for a table of the acts and measures.

24 E Storskrubb, 'Civil Justice: Constitutional and Regulatory Issues Revisited' in M Fletcher, E Herlin-Karnell and C Matera (eds), *The EU as an Area of Freedom, Security and Justice* (Routledge 2017) 303, 307.

25 ibid 307–310; Storskrubb (n 21) 207–209.

IV The Lisbon Treaty

#14 The current Treaty, called the Treaty of Lisbon, entered into force in 2009. The new Treaty included changes to the legal basis for judicial cooperation in civil matters, now in Article 81 TFEU (hereinafter 'Article 81'). The legal basis will be analysed further below (Section C.II) but it can be noted that the cross-border wording has been retained. Furthermore, the list of measures has been increased and broadened. In addition, the **principle of mutual recognition** has been added to its wording. One significant structural reform for judicial cooperation in civil matters subsequent to the Treaty of Lisbon, is that **preliminary references** are now possible for all Member State courts and there are no derogations under Article 267 TFEU.[26]

#15 Further, it can be noted that for **family matters,** there are still special limitations in the legal basis, Article 81(3). As a main rule the old intergovernmental rule of unanimity in the council still applies. However, the provision now includes a so-called **passerelle clause**, which entails that the Council may, by unanimity, decide that certain aspects of family law can be dealt with in the ordinary legislative procedure.[27] This shows that family law is of particular sensitivity for the Member States that want to retain sovereignty in the field.[28] After the Treaty of Lisbon entered into force, there has been no use of the passerelle clause. Rather, the unanimity requirement for family matters has led to difficult negotiations for certain legislative instruments. For example, the so-called Rome III Regulation on the law applicable to divorce and legal separation. This has resulted in the regulation being enacted under EU rules of enhanced cooperation, which means that not all Member States participate in the specific legal act.[29]

#16 Finally, as regards structural matters, it can further be noted that the fragmentation was retained and the UK, Ireland and Denmark still remained formally outside the policy area, but with the option to opt-in. However, the Danish protocol was amended to make it easier for Denmark to opt in to legislative acts.[30] Notably, the position of the UK has changed after the Treaty of Lisbon due to **Brexit**; the UK naturally no longer has an option to participate in judicial cooperation in civil matters.[31]

---

26 G-R de Groot and J-J Kuipers, 'The New Provisions on Private International Law in the Treaty of Lisbon' (2008) 15 Maastricht Journal 109, 114.

27 ibid (n 26) 112–113.

28 J von Hein, 'EU Competence to Legislate in the Area of Private International Law and Law Reforms at the EU Level' in P Beaumont and others (eds), *Cross-Border Litigation in Europe* (Bloomsbury 2017) 21, 24.

29 ibid 30–31.

30 De Groot and Kuipers (n 26) 111.

31 For the situation post Brexit see *inter alia* P Beaumont, 'Some Reflections on the Way Ahead for UK Private International Law after Brexit' (2021) 17 Journal of Private International Law 1.

#17 Since the entry into force of the Lisbon Treaty in 2009, fewer instruments have been enacted under the legal basis Article 81 than during the above-mentioned 10-year period and the strong political impetus to create an AFSJ. However, many of the instruments have been reviewed and amended during this period. In addition, the focus has partly moved to more overarching and steering measures to support the functioning of the existing measures, such as the current push to **digitalise EU justice**, including civil justice.[32]

#18 During this period there has also partly been a shift in the institutional dynamic with respect to legislating in the field of civil justice. The EP does not have the power to initiate a legislative proposal, rather that power lies with the Commission.[33] Nonetheless, the EP has twice adopted so-called own initiative resolutions[34] calling upon the Commission to initiate legislation in the field of civil justice.[35] So far, none of these proposals has led to legislative action at the EU level and the impetus for them may have been different underlying interests. Nevertheless, these resolutions demonstrate surges of activism on the part of the Parliament, when it appears to want the EU to go further and deeper in the integration and harmonisation of civil justice than the Commission and, in particular, the Member States in the Council. It appears that the main actor that will have a gatekeeping role in the future will be the Council.[36]

#19 Further, it is interesting to note that one of the proposals of the EP was for a broader procedural act, called 'Common minimum standards of civil procedure'.[37] This proposal was partly inspired by the **soft-law project** of the European Law Institute and UNIDROIT called Model European Rules of Civil Procedure.[38] However, it can also been seen following in the footsteps of the Storme Report

32 Storskrubb (n 22) 781–783. See also A Nylund, Chapter 7, in this volume.

33 Article 294 TFEU regarding the ordinary legislative procedure.

34 Article 225 TFEU.

35 P8_TA(2017)0282 Common minimum standards of civil procedure, 4 July 2017 (2015/2084(INL)), [2018] OJ C334/39; and P9_TA(2022)0308 Responsible private funding of litigation, 14 September 2022 (2020/2130(INL)) [2023] OJ C125/2.

36 See further, E Storskrubb, 'EU Civil Justice at the Harmonisation Crossroads?' in A Nylund and M Strandberg (eds), *Civil Procedure and Harmonisation of Law: The Dynamics of EU and International Treaties* (Intersentia 2019) 11, 31.

37 P8_TA(2017)0282 (n 35). For an analysis of the proposal, see F Gascón Inchausti, 'The 2017 Directive Proposal on Common Minimum Standards of Civil Procedure in the European Union' in F Gascón Inchausti and B Hess (eds), *The Future of the European Law of Civil Procedure* (Intersentia 2020) 224.

38 <https://www.europeanlawinstitute.eu/fileadmin/user_upload/p_eli/Publications/ELI_UNIDROIT_Model_European_Rules.pdf> accessed on 30 March 2025. See further E Jeuland, Chapter 23, in this volume.

mentioned above, in the respect of attempting to promote further of harmonisation of procedural law in the EU. In addition, the Parliament resolution specifically argued that the **'cross-border' limitation** in Article 81 should be interpreted in a broad manner. Thus, trying to argue for a broader interpretation of the competence of the EU.[39]

V The Rise of Sector-Specific Regulation

#20 Separately from the above-mentioned evolution of a specific legislative competence in the Treaties (Article 81), a parallel development of **sector-specific procedural rules** has emerged in the EU. It is not a new phenomenon that substantive legislative instruments limited to a particular field of substantive EU law include private international rules. Originally, such rules were limited in scope and impact from a procedural point of view.[40] However, more recent developments, have entailed substantive EU legislative acts in sector-specific policy fields of EU law with a broader panoply of procedural rules. Thus, demonstrating a heightened procedural focus connected to enforcement of substantive EU law. Such developments have taken place in the areas of **intellectual property** rights, **competition law**, **consumer rights** and **employment law**.[41]

#21 The development of these more focussed sector-specific procedural measures commenced roughly at the same time as the Treaty of Amsterdam provided for a specific legal basis, now Article 81. However, these sector-specific measures have been enacted under different legal basis than Article 81. Most of the measures have been enacted based on the general **internal market** legal basis, ie Article 114 TFEU (hereinafter 'Article 114'). This means that legislative acts are not necessarily limited to cross-border matters. This development has been called a 'new

39 P8_TA(2017)0282 (n 35) para 9–11.

40 H Duintjer Tebbens, 'Les règles de conflit contenues dans les instruments de droit dérivé' in A Fuchs, H Muir Watt and E Pataut (eds), *Les conflits de lois et le système juridique communautaire* (Dalloz 2004) 102; T Andersson, 'Approximation of Procedural Law in Europe' in M Storme (ed), *Procedural Laws in Europe. Towards Harmonisation* (Maklu 2003) 56, 56–58.

41 See as examples: Directive 2004/48/EC on the enforcement of intellectual property rights [2004] OJ L157/45; Directive 2014/104/EU on certain rules governing actions for damage under national law for infringements of the competition law provisions of the Member States of the European Union [2014] OJ L349/1; Directive 2020/1828/EU on representative actions for the protection of the collective interests of consumers [2020] OJ L409/1; and Directive 2023/970/EU to strengthen the application of the principle of equal pay for equal work or work of equal value between men and women through pay transparency and enforcement mechanisms [2023] OJ L132/21. See further Storskrubb (n 24) 312–323, and A Ancery and B Krans, Chapter 6, in this volume.

approach' to procedural harmonisation,[42] 'vertical harmonisation',[43] as well as the 'invisible pillar' of EU civil justice.[44]

#22 The present author has called this development a **constitutional incoherence**. As noted above, the Member States in the Council have kept procedural development limited to cross-border matters and have never agreed to an expansive interpretation of the general procedural legal basis in Article 81. However, by using the legal basis of Article 114 for sector-specific legislative acts, it is possible harmonise procedural rules also for domestic matters. The Member States, thus, in certain instances accept a broader procedural competence, albeit only for specific sectors. This incoherence has become more pronounced due to the increase in sector-specific developments. Linked to the strict constitutional question on competence is an underlying tension between a restrictive and an expansive vision of EU civil justice as a whole, including all types of measures regardless of legal basis. The opposing visions relate to how far procedural harmonisation in the EU is considered practically feasible and politically desirable.

C Potential Legal Bases

I Introduction

#23 The presentation above on the evolution of the competence of the EU with respect to procedural law already demonstrated on a general level that there are diverging legal bases that can have different consequences with respect to the competence and its interpretation. This section seeks to analyse the potential **legal bases** as well as address the choice of legal basis in more detail. First, though, it should be noted that there are different types of competence in the Treaties, that are now also explicitly listed in the so-called **competence** catalogue, Articles 2–6 TFEU.

#24 Based on these general provisions, there are three categories of competence in the EU; exclusive, shared and ancillary (or complimentary) competence.[45] **Exclusive competence** means that in certain specific and limited areas only the EU

42 B Hess, 'Procedural Harmonisation in a European Context' in X Kramer and CH van Rhee (eds), *Civil Litigation in a Globalising World* (TMC Asser Press 2012) 164.

43 G Wagner, 'Harmonisation of Civil Procedure: Policy Perspectives' in X Kramer and CH van Rhee (eds), *Civil Litigation in a Globalising World* (TMC Asser Press 2012) 93, 101.

44 B Krans, 'EU Law and National Civil Procedure Law: An Invisible Pillar' (2015) 23 European Review of Private Law 568, and A Ancery and B Krans, Chapter 6, in this volume.

45 In addition, there are two special areas not falling under any of these categories, ie economic policy (Article 5 TFEU) and common foreign and security policy (see TEU, eg Article 24(1)). See Bradley (n 1) 112–115.

may adopt legislative acts, Article 3 TFEU. **Ancillary competence** means that EU may only carry out actions to support, coordinate or supplement the actions of the Member States, Article 6 TFEU. It is the least invasive of the categories of competences with respect to domestic law, since the exercise of competence may not in itself lead to harmonisation of national laws.[46] The most common category of competence is the **shared competence**, Article 4 TFEU. Shared competence entails that both the EU and the Member States may enact legislation in the field. Notably, when the EU has enacted legislation in a matter that falls under shared competence, the **pre-emption effect** means that the Member States are precluded from enacting legislation unilaterally on that specific matter. Thus, concurrent competence has been considered a better term for the category of shared competence, because the competence is *de facto* no longer shared after the EU has adopted rules, Article 4(3) TEU.[47]

#25 In Article 4 TFEU a number of policy areas of the EU are listed as falling within the category shared competence. Included in the list, are both the internal market and the AFSJ. Thus, both policy areas that are of importance for civil justice are included in the category of shared competence. According to Article 26(1) TFEU the EU shall establish and ensure the functioning of the internal market, and according to Article 67(1) the EU shall constitute an AFSJ. However, none of these general provisions constitutes a legal basis, ie a legal foundation in the Treaties indicating who may adopt legislative acts, what these acts may contain and what procedure must be followed.[48]

#26 As noted already in the introduction of this chapter, legal bases are often carefully worded and include material restrictions as well as formal requirements on the process to enact EU legislation in the relevant area. Such restrictions and requirements are a means to regulate in detail the delimitation of power between the EU and the Member States. However, to determine the correct legal basis in the Treaties may also be important for the **institutional balance** between the EU institutions. Depending on the type of procedure that must be followed under a specific legal basis, the institutions can have varied levels of power in the legislative process. The choice of the correct legal basis has thus been held by the CJEU to have constitutional importance.[49] It follows that EU legislator is obliged to identify a legal basis in each and every legal act.[50]

#27 It should be noted that there are two types of articles in the Treaties that serves as legal basis, sectoral and functional. The sectoral type of legal basis are articles

46 Bradley (n 1) 114.

47 ibid.

48 ibid 110.

49 K Bradley, 'Powers and Procedures in the EU Constitution: Legal Bases and the Court' in Paul Craig and Gráinne de Búrca (eds), *The Evolution of EU Law* (2nd edn, OUP 2011) 85–86, 94.

50 ibid 94.

that enable legislation in a specific policy field, whereas the functional type of legal basis is one that can be used for different policy fields to pursue a specified objective.[51] The legal basis in Article 81 appears to be a typical sectoral legal basis, that enables legislation for the specific policy field, ie civil justice. In addition, the legal basis in Article 114 appears to be a typical functional legal basis, under which it is possible to enact legislation in many policy areas such as consumer law and intellectual property law, including sector-specific procedural rules, as long as the specific functional objective of achieving the internal market is upheld.

#28 As noted by one commentor disputes regarding the correct legal basis often concern the choice between a sectoral and a functional legal basis.[52] In relation to EU civil justice, there have been no annulment cases brought before the CJEU for incorrect legal basis. However, as we have seen already above there have certainly been divergences in the interpretation of the legal bases by the central institutional actors. In addition, there are constitutional consequences in the choice of legal basis, related to the 'cross-border' limitation as well as to the fact that certain Member States have an opt-out under Article 81 but not under Article 114.

#29 Before analysing the two legal bases more closely, it should be noted that the CJEU has provided guidance on the correct choice of legal basis. The main rule is that the choice of legal basis must be based on objective factors, such as the aim and content of the relevant act, ie factors that can form the basis for judicial review.[53] Furthermore, a main purpose of the relevant legal act should be identified for the choice of legal basis, should there be several aims of the legal act. As a main rule, only one legal basis should be chosen based on the main aim. However, if there are multiple aims of the legal act and no main purpose can be identified, all relevant legal bases should be invoked as an exception.[54]

II Article 81

#30 For the purpose of the analysis here the first two paragraphs of the Article 81 are relevant. The third paragraph relates to the more stringent requirements for enacting measures in the special field of **family law** mentioned above. One way of limiting the scope these special rules for family law measures in the legal basis is to narrowly interpret the term 'family law'. An example of such a development is

51 ibid 86.
52 ibid 86.
53 ibid 91; see further R Manko, *Europeanisation of Civil Procedure – Towards Common Standards?* (European Parliament Research Service 2015) 13.
54 ibid 13.

the enactment of the Succession Regulation, that the institutions agreed was not a specific family law measure but rather a general civil law measure.[55]

#31 **Article 81(1)** stipulates that:

> The Union shall develop judicial cooperation in civil matters having cross-border implications, based on the principle of mutual recognition of judgments and of decisions in extrajudicial cases. Such cooperation may include the adoption of measures for the approximation of the laws and regulations of the Member States. (underlining added)

The cross-border limitation is thus included in the first part of the legal basis, giving the EU competence to develop legislation with respect to civil litigation with a cross-border element. In addition, the first part of the legal basis states that the EU may enact harmonising legislation, this means all kind of harmonisation not merely minimum rules.

#32 Article 81(2) stipulates that:

> For the purposes of paragraph 1, the European Parliament and the Council, acting in accordance with the ordinary legislative procedure, shall adopt measures, particularly when necessary for the proper functioning of the internal market, [. . .] (underlining added)

The second part of the legal basis tells us that the ordinary **legislative procedure**, under Article 294 TFEU, shall be used when enacting legislation. Furthermore, the EU should act in the field of civil justice cooperation particularly when necessary to support the functioning the internal market. This wording, that clearly connects legislation under Article 81 to the aims and the purpose of the internal market, was in the Treaty of Amsterdam worded more as a limiting condition, ie that the EU could only act when necessary for the internal market. In the current Treaty wording the connection with the internal market is rather worded as an open impetus for enacting legislation, not as a strict requirement.

#33 Article 81(2) continues with providing a functional list of the measures that may be enacted, namely measures:

> [. . .] aimed at ensuring:
> (a) the mutual recognition and enforcement between Member States of judgments and of decisions in extrajudicial cases;
> (b) the cross-border service of judicial and extrajudicial documents;
> (c) the compatibility of the rules applicable in the Member States concerning conflict of laws and of jurisdiction;
> (d) cooperation in the taking of evidence;
> (e) effective access to justice;

55 Von Hein (n 28) 24. Regulation (EU) No 650/2012 on jurisdiction, applicable law, recognition and enforcement of decisions and acceptance and enforcement of authentic instruments in matters of succession and on the creation of a European Certificate of Succession [2012] OJ L201/107.

(f) the elimination of obstacles to the proper functioning of civil proceedings, if necessary by promoting the compatibility of the rules on civil procedure applicable in the Member States;
(g) the development of alternative methods of dispute settlement;
(h) support for the training of the judiciary and judicial staff. (underling added)

In the Amsterdam Treaty (a)-(d) and (f) were included in the list. Thus, (e) and (g)-(h) were added in the current Lisbon Treaty. The first points in the list (a)-(d) include very specific procedural issues that are traditionally included in private international law or international procedural law. The actual measures enacted under the legal basis did indeed first deal with such typical cross-border issues, eg the **Service Regulation**, the **Evidence Regulation**, and the flagship regulation of the policy area the **Brussels I-bis Regulation** for international jurisdiction and recognition and enforcement of judgments.[56]

#34 Subsequent measures under Article 81 have gone further in breadth or in depth, some dealing with specific matters that have not been dealt with before in the international procedural law context.[57] Others creating discrete new EU procedures, ie **uniform** and optional cross-border procedures for civil and commercial matters.[58] Commentators have identified different generations in measures enacted within the policy area and the **second generation** is held to encompass the uniform EU procedures that go the furthest in harmonisation.[59] These more innovative or second generation measures have often been based on the legal basis in point (f) above, eg the **Legal Aid Directive** or the **European Account Preservation Order** (EAPO).[60] In other words the legal basis giving the EU competence to eliminate obstacles to the **proper functioning of civil proceedings** and promoted the compatibility of the rules on civil procedure. This is a quite a broad, even functional style, legal basis albeit limited to cases having cross-border implications.

56 Regulation (EC) 1393/2007 on the service of judicial and extrajudicial documents in civil or commercial matters [2007] OJ L324/79; Regulation (EC) 1206/2001 on cooperation between the courts in the taking of evidence in civil and commercial matters [2001] OJ L174/1; and Regulation (EC) 44/2001 [2001] repealed by Regulation (EU) 1215/2012 on jurisdiction and the recognition and enforcement of judgments in civil and commercial matters (recast) [2012] OJ L351/1.

57 Storskrubb (n 22) 776–778. See, for example, Regulation (EC) 805/2004 creating a European Enforcement Order for uncontested claims [2004] OJ L143/15 and Directive (EC) 2003/8 to improve access to justice in cross-border disputes by establishing minimum common rules relating to legal aid [2003] OJ L26/41.

58 Regulation (EC) 1896/2006 creating a European payment procedure [2006] OJ L399/1 and Regulation (EC) 861/2007 establishing a European Small Claims Procedure [2007] OJ L199/1, both amended by Regulation (EU) 2015/2421 [2015] OJ L341/1. Regulation (EU) 655/2014 creating a European Account Preservation Order to facilitate cross-border debt recovery [2014] OJ L189/59.

59 B Hess, 'The State of the Civil Justice Union' in B Hess, M Bergström and E Storskrubb (eds), *EU Civil Justice: Current Issues and Future Outlook* (Hart 2016) 1, 3–5.

60 Directive (n 57) and Regulation (n 58) see for both the first sentence of the Preamble.

#35 Interestingly, the EAPO is also based on point (e) in the legal basis, ie effective **access to justice**. By adding this point to the legal basis in the latest Treaty reform, the competence has arguably been extended, because it has to mean something different to point (f) that was already in the legal basis before, ie more than facilitating the proper functioning of civil proceedings. In addition, the word 'effective' seems to imply a proactive stance on potential procedural harmonisation, not only 'access to justice' as basic standard, but 'effective access to justice'.[61] However, the present author agrees with Hess, that there has been limited focus and discussion on what 'effective access to justice' actually means in the EU cross-border context.[62] In addition, this addition has not so far occasioned any significant new approach specifically on 'access to justice' with respect to legislation in the civil procedural field.

#36 The legal basis also includes (g) **alternative dispute resolution (ADR)** and (h) support for the **training** of the judiciary, which were added to the list in the latest Treaty reform. Such measures had *de facto* already at the time been enacted under the legal basis (under current point (f)).[63] However, the explicit mention of them in the legal basis reflects in a more transparent manner the scope of action possible. In addition, one can also consider that the competence has increased, to the extent that certain action with respect to ADR or judicial training can be argued not to fall within point (f), ie the proper functioning of civil proceedings.[64] For judicial training, one can also see that there has been an increased focus on judicial training programmes subsequent to the explicit addition to the legal basis.[65] Finally, aside from judicial training, the EU has, as already noted above, recently focussed more on further overarching measures, such as the current push to digitalise EU justice. Such measures are in contrast to judicial training not explicitly mentioned in the list in Article 81(2) but have based on both point (f) and (e) in the legal basis, ie the proper functioning of civil proceedings and access to justice.[66]

61 Storskrubb (n 4) 45.

62 B Hess, Chapter 5, section 3.3 in this volume.

63 Directive 2008/52/EC on certain aspects of mediation in civil and commercial matters [2008] OJ L136/3, and Decision (EC) 470/01 establishing a European Judicial Network [2001] OJ L 174/25 amended by Decision (EC) 568/09 [2009] OJ L168/35.

64 Storskrubb (n 4) 45.

65 COM(2011) 551 final Communication Building Trust in EU-wide Justice – A New Dimension to European Judicial Training, and the subsequent Council Conclusions [2011] OJ C361/7. See further < https://e-justice.europa.eu/topics/trainings-judicial-networks-and-agencies/training-justice-professionals/eu-judicial-training-policy_en≥ (accessed 30 March 2025), including the annual reports published since 2011 by the Commission.

66 See *inter alia* Regulation (EU) 2023/2844 on the digitalisation of judicial cooperation and access to justice in cross-border civil, commercial and criminal matters, and amending certain acts in the field of judicial cooperation [2023] OJ L2844/1.

III Article 114

#37 **Article 114** constitutes the well-known general legal basis for the internal market, Article 114(1)[67] stipulates that:

> Save where otherwise provided in the Treaties, the following provisions shall apply for the achievement of the objectives set out in Article 26. The European Parliament and the Council shall, acting in accordance with the ordinary legislative procedure and after consulting the Economic and Social Committee, adopt the measures for the approximation of the provisions laid down by law, regulation or administrative action in Member States which have as their object the establishment and functioning of the internal market.

The wording of the legal basis thus tells us that the ordinary legislative procedure shall be followed to achieve the aim of establishing a functioning internal market (Article 26 TFEU) and the EU is entitled to enact harmonising legal acts. However, the interesting question is the scope of the permitted measures under this seemingly broad functional legal basis.

#38 In its famous *Tobacco Advertising I* ruling the CJEU has set some limits on the competence under Article 114.[68] A mere abstract risk of disparities between national rules creating obstacles to trade is not sufficient to justify the use of Article 114, it must be likely that such national divergencies create obstacles to free movement and the harmonising legislation proposed must be specifically directed to preventing such obstacles.[69]

#39 One example of such justifications is included in the Commission's legislative proposal for creating procedural **collective redress** mechanisms for consumer cases.[70] For example, the Commission argued that European consumers face the same obstacles when seeking redress now as they did ten years ago, including, amongst other, excessive length of proceedings and lack of information. In addition, injunctions were not often used for cross-border infringements, and relevant actors from different Member States did not cooperate enough.[71] The enacted Directive includes, amongst other provisions on procedural expediency, bringing cross-border representative actions, and information for consumers and databases.[72]

---

67 There are additional sections to Article 114 relating to exclusions and Member States derogations, which are of limited application for civil procedural measures. However, the exclusion in Article 114(2) is relevant for employment law and notably Directive 2023/970/EU (n 41) has a separate legal basis.

68 Case C-376/98 *Germany v Parliament and Council* (5 October 2000) ECLI:EU:C:2000:54.

69 Bradley (n 49) 98.

70 Proposal for a Directive on representative actions for the protection of the collective interests of consumers, COM (2018) 184 final

71 ibid 8.

72 Directive (n 41) Articles 6, 13, 14 and 17.

D Future Outlook

#40 In the foreseeable future it is likely that the constitutional incoherence between generic cross-border procedural legislation and sector-specific procedural legislation based on the different legal bases will remain even though it has been identified as a matter of tension.[73] This creates diverging types of EU procedural law applicable in the Member State courts and also potentially different levels of impact on domestic procedural law. However, it can also be understood as a strategic choice of the Member States that still perceive the procedural field as a sovereignty sensitive one. From this perspective it is not necessarily negative to proceed in a piece-meal and multi-layered manner with incremental harmonisation. Since the Council has the power to act as gatekeeper in the legislative process, the Member States can as far as they agree (with qualified majority) control how far procedural harmonisation is taken under both the legal bases.

#41 What will be interesting to see in the future is how far the EU is prepared to continue to deepen civil procedural harmonisation under both legal bases. For example, with respect to generic civil justice measures, the application of the overarching measures of digitalisation are only in their inception and may potentially have significant impact on procedural development. With respect to sector-specific procedural measures, the implementation and actual practice with respect to the most recent measures in the field of consumer and employment law will be instructive.

References

Andersson T, 'Approximation of Procedural Law in Europe' in M Storme (ed), *Procedural Laws in Europe. Towards Harmonisation* (Maklu 2003) 56.

Barrett G, 'Cooperation in Justice and Home Affairs in the European Union – An Overview and a Critique' in G Barrett (ed), *Justice Cooperation in the EU, The Creation of a European Legal Space* (Institute of European Affairs 1997) 17.

—— 'Introduction' in Gavin Barrett (ed), *Creating a European Judicial Space, Prospects for Improving Judicial Cooperation in Civil Matters in the European Union*, vol. 30, (Academy of European Law Trier 2001) 8.

Beaumont P, 'Some Reflections on the Way Ahead for UK Private International Law after Brexit' (2021) 17 Journal of Private International Law 1.

Bradley K, 'Powers and Procedures in the EU Constitution: Legal Bases and the Court' in P Craig and G de Búrca (eds), *The Evolution of EU Law* (2nd edn, OUP 2011) 85.

—— 'Legislating in the European Union' in C Barnard and S Peers (eds), *European Union Law* (4th edn, OUP 2023) 108.

73 See also Magdalena Tulibacka 'Europeanisation of Civil Procedures: In Search of a Coherent Approach' (2009) 46 CMLR 1527, 1548.

Craig P, 'The Development of the EU' in C Barnard and S Peers (eds), *European Union Law* Duintjer Tebbens H, 'Les règles de conflit contenues dans les instruments de droit dérivé' in A Fuchs, H Muir Watt and E Pataut (eds), *Les conflits de lois et le système juridique communautaire* (Dalloz 2004) 102.
(4th edn, OUP 2023) 10.
Groot de G-R and Kuipers J-J, 'The New Provisions on Private International Law in the Treaty of Lisbon' (2008) 15 Maastricht Journal 109, 114.
Gascón Inchausti F, 'The 2017 Directive Proposal on Common Minimum Standards of Civil Procedure in the European Union' in F Gascón Inchausti and B Hess (eds), *The Future of the European Law of Civil Procedure* (Intersentia 2020) 224.
Hess B, 'Procedural Harmonisation in a European Context' in X Kramer and CH van Rhee (eds), *Civil Litigation in a Globalising World* (TMC Asser Press 2012) 164.
—— 'The State of the Civil Justice Union' in B Hess, M Bergström and E Storskrubb (eds), *EU Civil Justice: Current Issues and Future Outlook* (Hart Publishing/Bloomsbury 2016) 1.
Kennett W, *Enforcement of Judgments in Europe* (OUP 2000) 15–19.
Krans B, 'EU Law and National Civil Procedure Law: An Invisible Pillar' (2015) 23 European Review of Private Law 568.
Law S and Nowak JT, 'Procedural Harmonisation by the European Court of Justice – Procedural Autonomy and the Member States' Perspective' in F Gascón Inchausti and B Hess (eds), *The Future of the European Law of Civil Procedure* (Intersentia 2020) 17.
Lindblom PH, 'Harmony of the Legal Spheres, A Swedish View on the Construction of a Unified European Procedural Law' (1997) 5 European Review of Private Law 11.
Manko R, *Europeanisation of Civil Procedure – Towards Common Standards?* (European Parliament Research Service 2015).
Monar J, 'Justice and Home Affairs in the Treaty of Amsterdam: Reform at the Price of Fragmentation' (1998) 23 European Law Review 320.
Partsch P-E, *Le Droit International Privé Européen. De Rome à Nice* (Larcier 2003).
Rouchaud A-M, 'Le renforcement de la coopération judiciaire' in Université Jean Moulin, Faculté de Droit (eds), *Les effets des jugements nationaux dans les autres États membres de l'Union européenne* (Bruylant 2001) 19.
Storme M (ed), *Rapprochement du Droit Judiciare de l'Union européenne – Approximation of Judiciary Law in the European Union* (Kluwer Law International 1994).
Storskrubb E, *Civil Procedure and EU Law* (OUP 2008).
—— 'Civil Justice: The Contested Nature of the Scope of EU Legislation' in F Trauner and A Ripoll Servant (eds), *Policy Change in the Area of Freedom, Security and Justice* (Routledge 2015) 197.
—— 'Civil Justice: Constitutional and Regulatory Issues Revisited' in M Fletcher, E Herlin-Karnell and C Matera (eds), *The EU as an Area of Freedom, Security and Justice* (Routledge 2017) 303.
—— 'EU Civil Justice at the Harmonisation Crossroads' in A Nylund and M Strandberg (eds), *Civil Procedure and Harmonisation of Law: The Dynamics of EU and International Treaties* (Intersentia 2019) 11.
—— 'Civil Justice Extending its Tentacles' in P Craig and G de Búrca (eds), *The Evolution of EU Law* (3rd edn, OUP 2021) 770.
Tulibacka M, 'Europeanisation of Civil Procedures: In Search of a Coherent Approach' (2009) 46 CMLR 1527.
von Hein J, 'EU Competence to Legislate in the Area of Private International Law and Law Reforms at the EU Level' in P Beaumont and others (eds), *Cross-Border Litigation in Europe* (Bloomsbury 2017) 21.
Wagner G, 'Harmonisation of Civil Procedure: Policy Perspectives' in X Kramer and CH van Rhee (eds), *Civil Litigation in a Globalising World* (TMC Asser Press 2012) 93.

Cornelis Hendrik van Rhee*

Chapter 3
The History of Civil Procedure in Europe

A Introduction

#1 Within the European Union, the former Article 65 of the **Treaty establishing the European Community** (the ancestor of current Article 81 of the **Treaty on the Functioning of the European Union)** represents a milestone in the development of a harmonised European civil procedural law.[1] It empowered the European Union to adopt rules of civil procedural law in cross-border cases when necessary for the proper functioning of the internal market. Article 65 aimed at improving and simplifying the system of cross-border service of judicial and extrajudicial documents, improving and simplifying cooperation in the taking of evidence, improving and simplifying the recognition and enforcement of judgments in civil and commercial matters including decisions in extrajudicial cases, promoting the compatibility of the rules applicable in the Member States concerning conflict of laws and of jurisdiction and eliminating obstacles to the proper functioning of civil proceedings, if necessary by promoting the compatibility of the rules on civil procedure applicable in the Member States.

#2 It was not entirely clear how the boundaries were drawn by Article 65, in other words, how far the EU's competences under this article extended. Indeed, Article 65 left a margin of appreciation, although this margin was kept narrow since Member States were concerned about the EU gaining too much influence in the area of procedural law and judicial organisation. Nevertheless, the need for some **harmonisation** or **approximation** was felt by many, even where purely national cases were concerned. After all, differences in the procedural treatment of purely national cases can also have a disruptive effect on the functioning of the internal market and, in that sense, have cross-border implications. This is due to the fact that the availability of efficient procedures for handling cases and enforcing court decisions has a direct effect on the level of costs of the administration of justice. These costs are taken into account by providers of goods and services when making a decision on the availability of these goods and services in the different member states of the European Union. Large differences in litigation costs

1 See on Art. 65 for example T Drappatz, *Die Überführung des internationalen Zivilverfahrensrechts in eine Gemeinschaftskompetenz nach Art. 65 EGV* (Mohr Siebeck 2002).

***Corresponding author: Cornelis Hendrik van Rhee,** Maastricht University,
e-mail: chvanrhee@outlook.com.

https://doi.org/10.1515/9783110781632-003

can have an unjustifiable distorting effect on the functioning of the internal market.[2] This problem is still relevant today, since parties can exert little influence on the applicable procedural rules in their court cases due to the ***lex fori*** principle, meaning that courts will apply their own procedural rules without options for the litigants. Unlike, for example, in the area of contract law, where parties may opt for the substantive rules governing their contract, parties cannot choose the procedural law applicable to their case once it is brought before a particular court. Although a choice of forum by the parties is possible under certain circumstances, eg a choice of the Dutch court if parties want their case to be handled according to Dutch procedural rules, this does not offer solace under all circumstances as a choice of forum cannot always be easily realised, for example in light of later enforcement.

#3 The push for harmonised European rules of civil procedural law even where purely national cases are involved has its origins in a private initiative. Reference should be made to the 1994 report produced by a working group under the chairmanship of the late Professor **Marcel Storme (1930–2018)** from Ghent in Belgium.[3] As is well known, this report contains proposals to achieve uniform, harmonised regulation in certain areas of civil procedural law. Among other things, the **Storme Working Group** drafted rules on conciliation, the commencement of proceedings, the subject matter of the dispute, discovery and witness statements. The Project was seen as the driving force behind initiatives at the harmonisation of procedural law in Europe and beyond. It was taken into consideration within the context of the 2004 ***Principles and Rules of Transnational Civil Procedure*** by the American Law Institute (ALI) and UNIDROIT which provided rules on a global scale.[4] Within the European context, both the Storme Project and the Principles and Rules of Transnational Civil Procedure were considered when drafting the 2021 ***Model European Rules of Civil Procedure*** *of the European Law Institute* (ELI) and ALI.[5]

#4 These projects introduced lawyers to the problems that need to be overcome before any kind of harmonisation of civil procedural law can be achieved. These problems may partly have to be solved pragmatically, but it is my strong conviction that studying the **history of procedural law** may also be beneficial. After all, civil procedural law in the various European jurisdictions is even more

2 Cf M Storme (ed), *Rapprochement du droit judiciaire de l'Union européenne/Approximation of Judiciary Law in the European Union* (Wolters Kluwer 1994), 10ff.

3 Storme (n 2).

4 <https://www.unidroit.org/english/principles/civilprocedure/ali-unidroitprinciples-e.pdf> accessed 1 August 2024.

5 <https://www.europeanlawinstitute.eu/fileadmin/user_upload/p_eli/Publications/200925-eli-unidroit-rules-e.pdf> accessed 1 August 2024.

strongly marked by its history than the substantive civil law prevailing in these territories.

#5 In this contribution, I would like to consider to what extent the study of the history of procedural law can be used to promote harmonisation. Here, I will discuss two possibilities:[6]

1. Uncovering the historical relationship between the different systems of procedural law in Europe in order to bridge apparent differences.
2. Studying past attempts to create an **efficient procedure** by uncovering the reasons for past success or failure of procedural reform.

B The Relationship Between Different Procedural Systems in Europe

#6 It has been claimed that the differences between civil procedural law systems in Europe are so great that a harmonised or approximated procedural law, acceptable to all countries of the European Union, must be considered a utopia. The history of civil procedural law in Europe makes it clear, however, that the differences between the systems may not be as insurmountable as they appear at first sight. Knowledge of the history of civil procedural law can help to break down the often seemingly impenetrable walls between the procedural legal traditions in Europe. After all, legal history shows that these legal traditions are highly interrelated.

#7 Within Europe, at least three and possibly even four **traditions of procedural law** can be distinguished. These are the **Common Law tradition**, the **Romanic tradition** and the **Germanic tradition**. The Scandinavian countries belong to a fourth tradition, but it should be borne in mind that these countries have traditionally undergone much German influence.[7]

#8 The aforementioned legal traditions on the continent of Europe are rooted in **Romano-canonical procedural law** (ie, originally ecclesiastical law). This procedural law is an original creation of medieval jurists, in which elements of Roman law were combined with other material of mainly canon law origin and customary law from northern Italy. The result was a learned procedure, which gradually spread from the ecclesiastical courts to the various secular jurisdictions.[8]

---

6 Cf CH van Rhee, 'Civil Procedure: A European "Ius Commune"?' [2000] ERPL 589.

7 On legal traditions in procedural law, see CH van Rhee, *European Traditions in Civil Procedure* (Intersentia 2005).

8 See RC Van Caenegem in *International Encyclopedia of Comparative Law* (Volume 16: Civil Procedure, Chapter 2: History of European Civil Procedure) (Brill 1973).

#9 The current traditions of procedural law on the European continent are ultimately the result of the different fate of Romano-canonical procedural law in the French kingdom on the one hand and in the German countries on the other. Indeed, the **French Code of Civil Procedure of 1806** largely incorporated the procedural law as it had developed in the higher courts in France from the Middle Ages onwards. This procedural law had a clear Romano-canonical character, but also contained elements of originally French origin. It was laid down comprehensively for the first time in the important ***Ordonnance civile sur la réformation de la justice*** or ***Code Louis*** of 1667,[9] which did not apply to one particular court only, as was customary at the time, but to the entire French kingdom. The Napoleonic codifiers of 1806 largely incorporated this ordinance, which had been extensively commented on by, among others, **Robert-Joseph Pothier (1699–1772)**,[10] in their new ***Code de procédure civile***.[11] It was subsequently the procedural law of this code that was introduced in many of the territories subjugated by Napoleon in the early 19th century, including those of the present-day Netherlands and Belgium.

#10 In the German territories, developments were different. The ***Zivilprozessordnung* of 1877**, the first procedural code valid for the entire German Empire,[12] must be situated in the context of earlier codifications in the German territories. Although the *Zivilprozessordnung* cannot be viewed separately from the French *Code de procédure civile* (indeed, this French code had been in full force in the territories on the left bank of the Rhine until the introduction of the 1877 German code), it nevertheless has to a large extent its own, German character.[13] This is partly a consequence of the fact that earlier codifications for the individual territories that made up Germany at the time were a reaction against the learned, Romano-canonical procedural law, which was introduced at the German ***Reichskammergericht*** (the highest court of the Holy Roman Empire) at the end of the 15th century and which became known as the 'common procedural law' (***gemeines Prozessrecht***). However, this reaction did not mean that elements of learned procedural law completely disappeared from German proceedings. As a result, German procedural law still belongs to the Romano-canonical procedural group of civil procedural systems.

#11 The procedural law of the 1877 *Zivilprozessordnung* was of great importance for the development of procedural law in the traditionally German-oriented **Nordic countries**. In addition, the procedural law of **Austria** can be linked to German

9 F Isambert and others (eds), *Recueil général des anciennes lois françaises, depuis l'an 420 jusqu'à la Révolution de 1789*, XVIII (Belin-Leprieur 1829) 103.

10 R-J Pothier, *Traité de la procédure civile* (first published 1778, Tarlier 1831).

11 On this code see D Heirbaut, *Redefining Codification. A Comparative History of Civil, Commercial and Procedural Codes* (OUP 2024).

12 On this code see Heirbaut (n 11).

13 A Grilli, *Die französische Justizorganisation am linken Rheinufer (1797–1803)* (Peter Lang 1999).

procedural law. Here, however, it was originally not primarily Austria that was influenced by Germany, but vice versa, Germany by Austria; after all, the progressive Austrian procedural law of 1900, conceived by **Franz Klein (1854–1926)**, served as a model for reforms of German procedural law at the beginning of the 20th century. The result of these relationships is that one can currently rightly speak of a Germanic or German procedural law tradition.

#12 Although there are several traditions of civil procedural law on the European continent, their common basis in Romano-canonical procedural law provides a good starting point for harmonisation proposals. Fundamentally different seems to be the situation with respect to the procedural laws of the Common Law tradition. Indeed, the procedural laws belonging to this tradition are clearly different in character. Nevertheless, here too there is a relationship with the European continent's procedural laws and the Common Law. I limit myself in this contribution to the links of English procedural law with those of the European continent. It should be borne in mind that when I say England, I am referring to **England & Wales** only. **Scottish procedural law** has an entirely different character. Indeed, Scotland belongs to the so-called 'mixed legal systems', which is a consequence of the fact that in Scotland both Common Law and continental European law influences can be discerned. In Scotland, for example, procedural law terminology is surprisingly Romano-canonical in nature.

#13 In the English secular courts, the reception of Romano-canonical procedure in the Middle Ages took place on a much more limited scale than in the same courts on the European continent. A similar situation existed in terms of substantive law. This comes as no surprise, since English substantive law and procedural law were closely intertwined. Perhaps this also constitutes a (partial) explanation for the absence of a comprehensive reception of substantive Roman law in England, since on the Continent the reception of learned procedural law mostly preceded and facilitated the reception of substantive Roman law. In England, the so-called **forms of action**, or standard forms for commencing legal proceedings, dominated the legal landscape.

#14 In England the specific procedural rules to be followed were entirely determined by the procedural form used to commence the case. Only a limited number of forms of action were available. Although those familiar with the history of Roman formula litigation might be led to believe that English procedural law is akin to this procedural form, any similarity rests on coincidence; the English forms of action cannot be related to Roman legal sources.[14]

14 See however F Pringsheim, 'The Inner Relationship between English and Roman Law' [1935] CLJ 347.

#15 In the procedural law of the Common Law, only limited influence of the learned procedural law of the European continent could be detected.[15] In the field of **Equity** jurisprudence, however, more influences may be identified. Equity arose, as is well known, as a result of the fact that the Common Law with its rigid forms of action did not provide a satisfactory solution for certain factual situations. Traditionally, the emergence of Equity is associated with what one would nowadays call **trust law**.[16] For the sake of clarity, it should be noted that the simplest form of trust is created as follows (I will use civil law terminology for reasons of simplicity): A, the settlor, transfers an asset in 'ownership' to B, the trustee, who is instructed to 'hold' the asset for C, the beneficiary. Originally, the position of C, the beneficiary, was not very enviable, as C had no legal means to protect his position. Indeed, only B, the trustee, was considered a beneficiary under the Common Law. This situation was changed by the English king and his chancellor, who also granted C a 'property right', but now according to Equity. Consequently, in a trust construction, there are two 'owners', both B, the trustee, and C, the beneficiary.

#16 The Equity jurisdiction of the **Court of Chancery** developed quickly. Possibly because the Chancellor in the early period was a clergyman and consequently had knowledge of Roman and Canon law, including Romano-canonical procedure, we see that the procedural law of the Court of Chancery incorporated elements of this Romano-canonical procedure. Moreover, the procedural law of some other English courts was also influenced by the Romano-canonical procedure, such as the **Court of Admiralty**, which had jurisdiction in maritime matters, including maritime commerce.[17]

#17 The separate court systems for Common Law and Equity continued until the 19th century. However, they no longer worked properly during that period. Thus, in the field of procedural law and judicial organisation, the English legislature of the nineteenth century was extremely active. These activities peaked when the so-called ***Judicature Acts 1873–1875*** came into force.[18] This legislation introduced a streamlined court system, abolishing the distinction between Common Law and Equity in the field of procedural law. This did, however, not imply that the dis-

15 Some continental influence is discussed by M Macnair, *The Law of Proof in Early Modern Equity* (Duncker & Humblot 1999).

16 See R Helmholz and others (eds), *Itinera Fiduciae. Trust and Treuhand in Historical Perspective* (Duncker & Humblot 1998); CH van Rhee, 'Trusts, Trust-like Concepts and "Ius Commune"' [2000] ERPL 453.

17 A Wijffels, '"Ius Gentium" in the Practice of the Court of Admiralty Around 1600' in ADE Lewis and DJ Ibbetson (eds), *The Roman Law Tradition* (CUP 1994) 119; A Wijffels, 'Sir Julius Caesar and the Merchants of Venice' in F Battenberg and others (eds), *Geschichte der Zentraljustiz in Mitteleuropa* (Böhlau 1994) 195; A Wijffels, 'Arthur Duck et le "ius commune" européen' [1990] *Revue d'histoire des Facultés de Droit et de la Science Juridique* 193.

18 Y Wirth, *Common Law- und Equity-Gerichtsbarkeit in England und ihre Reform im 19. Jahrhundert* (Nomos 2025).

tinction was thereby also ended in the field of substantive law. This was most certainly not the case and the distinction lives on to this day.[19]

#18 Part of the Judicature Acts was, what was called, a '**uniform code of civil procedure and pleading**'. In this 'code', we do not find the old forms of action. The 'code' had only a general action to bring a lawsuit and thus English procedural law came closer to the procedural systems of the countries on the European continent, in which the same approach to initiating court action is found. This raises the question whether here too, as with regard to the similarity between the old forms of action and the Roman formula process, the similarity is coincidental or whether English procedure was influenced by the Continent's procedural law. To answer this question, we need to move to the other side of the Atlantic, to the United States of America. Indeed, developments in the US, more specifically those in the state of New York, provided a model for the English legislature of 1873–1875.

#19 In New York, the codification landscape was dominated by one person, namely **David Dudley Field (1805–1894)**. Field was a man very convinced of his own abilities. At the end of his life, when a number of his codification projects had been brought to a successful conclusion and these projects had also found emulation outside the US, he modestly declared:

> [. . .] [I]t is something to me that the work that I made, the scheme that I founded, which has gone already around the world; which is now the law of more than half of the English speaking people of the Globe! – Yes, sir; the words that I have written, the words that this hand has set down, are this moment the laws that encircle the whole globe. The sun does not shine in any of the twenty-four hours except upon some place of which the laws are written by me [. . .].[20]

#20 However, this was not yet the case in the period discussed here. In this period, much work had to be done by Field, work on a Civil Code, a Penal Code and a Code of Procedure, among others. The code of procedure was eventually the only code introduced in New York. This happened in 1848. Elsewhere in the US, Field was incidentally more successful.

#21 The distinction between Common Law and Equity in terms of procedural law lapsed in the **Field Code**, and this thus occurred before the Judicature Acts would accomplish the same in England. The procedure designed by Field combined elements of Common Law procedure and Equity. The new procedure emphasised the rules derived from Equity. In this light, it is not surprising that influences of Romano-canonical procedural law can be recognised in the Field Code since, as stated, Equity's procedure was significantly influenced by Roman-canon law. An-

19 J Jacob, 'The Judicature Acts 1873–1875, Vision and Reality' in *The Reform of Civil Procedural Law and Other Essays in Civil Procedure* (Sweet & Maxwell 1982) 301.
20 New York State Bar Association Reports II (1878) 135.

other reason for the influence of the learned procedure was that Field was inspired in his codification work by Louisiana procedural law, a so-called 'civil law jurisdiction'. The **1825 Louisiana procedural code** has been identified with a high degree of probability as a major source for Field's ideas on codification and civil procedure. Field thus drew on a procedural code that incorporated French, Spanish and Roman law elements (as well as, incidentally, elements from the common law tradition). Among others, the ***Corpus Iuris Civilis***, the ***Siete Partidas*** and the writings of **Jean Domat (1625–1696)** and **Robert-Joseph Pothier (1699–1772)** were consulted in the drafting of the Louisiana Code.[21]

#22 Although I have so far found only one reference to the Field Code in English parliamentary papers concerning the Judicature Acts, it still seems likely to me that it played a significant role in the creation of English procedural law, possibly, however, indirectly through codification attempts in the British overseas territories, for example in the **British East Indies**. Indeed, in **British India**, a procedural code was introduced in the 1850s.[22] In this codification, the American example played a significant role, and it cannot be ruled out that the Field Code, through British-India, eventually influenced the shaping of the new procedural law of (part of) the British motherland. And so the learned procedure reached the British Isles south of the River Tweed partly through a colony in the East Indies and former colonies in the West Indies. The result was that procedural law on the European continent and English procedural law came closer together.

#23 I will now discuss some examples of harmonisation or approximation of continental and English procedural law. I will first discuss examples of features that can be traced back to common sources of civil procedure in these parts of Europe. I will then turn to some commonalities whose origins have not yet been identified.

#24 According to the British legal historian **Theodore Plucknett (1897–1965)**, one of the key themes in European legal history is the ability to think substantive law apart from procedural law.[23] One already witnesses this development in Roman law, although it must be admitted that, despite of this, at a late stage in the development of Roman law, procedural law was still discussed as a more or less integrated part of substantive law. Even in the ***Corpus Iuris Civilis***, procedural law and substantive law are not treated separately. On the Continent, the separation of procedural and substantive law is to be credited to medieval jurists.[24] In Eng-

21 DS Clark, 'The Civil Law Influence on David Dudley Field's Code of Civil Procedure', in M Reimann (ed), *The Reception of Continental Ideas in the Common Law World (1820–1920)* (Duncker & Humblot 1993) 63.

22 W Macpherson (ed), The New Procedure of the Civil Courts of British India (4th edn, Lepaige 1860).

23 TFT Plucknett, *A Concise History of the Common Law* (5th edn, Little, Brown and Co. 1956) 381.

24 W Litewski, *Der römisch-kanonische Zivilprozess nach den älteren ordines iudiciarii* (2 vols, Wydawnictwo Universytetu Jagiellonskiego 1999).

land, there was a more gradual development. Only at a later date was a definitive separation of procedural and substantive law made, at least as far as the Common Law is concerned. Although first attempts are already found in the medieval tract that would become known as **Glanvill**,[25] as well as in the slightly later work of **Henry de Bracton (died 1268)**,[26] the first serious attempts only date from the eighteenth century. The inspiration for this came from outside. In the eighteenth century there was great interest in legal works by French and Dutch authors in England, and – as Theodore Plucknett argued – 'under this stimulus they (ie the jurists) attempted to think in terms of substantive law rather than merely procedure.'[27] **Blackstone**'s ***Commentaries on the Laws of England*** (first published 1765–1769) are a good example of this approach. However, only the reforms of English procedural law in the nineteenth century, in particular the abolition of the forms of action, made it effectively possible to separate procedural law and substantive law. These reforms, as stated, took place under the influence of systems of procedural law that went back to Romano-canonical procedure. The result of the developments described can still be seen today. At present, one finds separate procedural law as well as separate procedural textbooks in both England and on the Continent. Moreover, separate courses in procedural law are offered at almost all European universities although in England these are often optional, while in many continental countries they are a compulsory part of the curriculum.

#25 A further shared feature of continental and English procedural law can be observed with regard to the possibility of initiating legal proceedings. The Roman formula process, which I discussed earlier, had a more or less closed system of actions. A procedure could only be initiated if the complaint could be brought under one of the available *formulae*. English law with its forms of action had a similar approach. In Antiquity, however, the introduction of the **cognitio procedure** abolished the *formulae*, while Romano-canonical procedural law never knew the rigid approach of the formula process. After all, learned procedural law, like the continental European systems of procedural law based on this law, did not know separate procedural forms, but only a general legal action, although it must be admitted that in medieval learned literature the question of whether particular procedural forms were to be used is discussed. The same situation arose in England as a result of the **Judicature Acts**. The forms of action were abolished and replaced by a general procedural action. Striking is the similarity with the **Field Code** for New York, which also only speaks of one general action, the so-called 'civil action'.

---

25 *Tractatus de legibus et consuetudinibus regni Angliae* (1187–1189).

26 Henrici de Bracton, *De legibus et consuetudinibus Angliae*, vol 1–6 (T Twiss ed, CUP 2012) (before c. 1235).

27 Plucknett (n 23) 381–382.

#26 As regards counterclaims, approximation can be observed as well. A **counterclaim** was originally not permitted under the Common Law. The judge could only decide on the claim as it was instituted by the claimant. It was again the Judicature Acts that made the counterclaim generally possible in England. According to the Oxford legal historian **William Holdsworth (1871–1944)**, this change was based on the practice of the **ecclesiastical courts**.[28] Since the procedure of the ecclesiastical jurisdictions has a Romano-canonical origin, it seems obvious to assume that we are dealing here with the influence of learned procedural law on English procedure. Additionally, the influence of the Field Code needs to be examined. This then does not concern the original Field Code as it read in 1848, but the amended code from 1852, when a provision for the counterclaim was added.[29]

#27 Another example is pleading. **Pleading** is best described as the stage in the process in which the written complaint of the claimant, the answer of the defendant and further written arguments are submitted to the court. The **'pleadings'** can therefore be compared with, for example, the written 'conclusions' in French law. In modern English procedure, the pleadings are referred to generally as **'statements of case'**. In the English Judicature Acts 1873–1875, this stage of the process was shaped according to the practice of the English **Admiralty Court**.[30] The latter court had a procedure inspired by the Romano-canonical model. Furthermore, the rules of the Field Code may have exerted their influence. These rules were also based on Roman-canon law. Only four written pleadings were permitted called the **complaint**, **answer**, **reply** and **demurrer** (the latter term may be translated roughly as **'exception'** in continental procedural law; more about exceptions later). A reply was only allowed if the answer contained 'new matter'. The aim of this provision was to ensure that in many cases pleading was concluded after the answer of the defendant.

#28 Regarding **appeal**, too, one can witness a convergence between English and continental procedural law. Originally, the Common Law did not know of appeal in the sense of submitting the case to a higher court for a new decision. This was related to the fact that originally there was no hierarchical court system in England. Appeal became known in England through the ecclesiastical courts. It was not until the 19th century that appeal became generally available in English courts. The Judicature Acts introduced a system of appeal that was close to the system of the **Field Code**. Like the Field Code, these Acts abolished the old writ of error. This writ was a legal remedy intended to have the case examined by another judge because of errors in the handling of the case by the original judge, at

28 W Holdsworth, *A History of English Law* XV (Methuen & Co.; Sweet & Maxwell 1965) 135.
29 CE Clark, 'The Code Cause of Action' [1923–1924] YLR 823; SN Subrin, 'David Dudley Field and the Field Code: A Historical Analysis of an Earlier Procedural Vision' [1988] LHR 332.
30 Holdsworth (n 28) 134.

least, insofar as those errors were apparent from the court file. The new system of appeal included the cases that previously fell under the **writ of error**.[31]

#29 The examples I have discussed so far might give the impression that continental and English procedural law only began to show common features in the 18th and 19th centuries. That is not correct. A remarkable similarity between the procedural laws of the various European legal traditions, or at least between the procedural laws of France, the Low Countries and England which has since disappeared in most jurisdictions, can already be observed in the Middle Ages and the early modern period. The origin of this similarity, which is connected with the **default procedure**, has not been investigated yet. It concerns the so-called ***essoins***. Both according to the old English procedure and according to the procedural law on the Continent, a party could avoid the negative consequences of his absence from the court by sending a messenger in good time. This messenger's task was to convey *essoins*, that is to say valid excuses for absence. Valid excuses were, for example, the fact that the absentee was ill or abroad, on an official errand for the monarch, or could not reach the court because of a flood or a broken bridge. These grounds for absence gave the party concerned a claim to postponement of the hearing of the case.[32]

#30 Another common feature of procedural law in England and the Continent is the fact that the process in England as well as on the Continent was (and is) aimed at preventing **arbitrariness**. The rules of procedure are aimed at ensuring that a decision is made only after the facts have been carefully investigated. The process can therefore be understood both in England and on the Continent as a search for **truth** (whether the formal or the real truth). Both in England and on the Continent it is felt that this search is best accomplished if the process is **adversarial**. The adversarial nature of both English and continental procedural law is apparent from the fact that both systems of law frequently (but not in all stages of the process) leave the initiative to the parties. An example is the principle that the parties decide whether or not to initiate the action and also determine the particular procedural steps to be taken in their case. Moreover, the parties determine the content of the dispute: the judge is dependent on the parties in this respect and cannot, on his own initiative, take a different set of facts as the starting point for his decision or award more than is requested. That we are dealing here with views that are deeply embedded in European procedural law is clear from discussions held over the centuries about shortcomings in procedural law in England and on the European continent. These shortcomings are formed by the long dura-

31 Van Caenegem (n 8) 30–31; Plucknett (n 23) 388.

32 See on *essoins* in England: Plucknett (n 23) 384; in France A Tardif, *La procédure civile et criminelle aux XIIIe et XIVe siècles ou procédure de transition* (first published 1885; reprint Scientia 1974) 55f, and for the Low Countries CH van Rhee, *Litigation and Legislation. Civil procedure at first instance in the Great Council for the Netherlands in Malines (1522–1559)* (Archives générales du Royaume 1997) 290f.

tion and high costs of the proceedings. An obvious solution to this problem would be to increase the judge's powers in the procedure. The textbook example of legislation that sought to solve this problem is the Prussian legislation of **Frederick the Great (1712–1786)**. However, it was not successful since it did not correspond to the European views on the division of power between the judge and parties in litigation. This does not mean, however, that some changes could not be made in this respect. The **Judicature Acts**, for example, gave the judge more powers to influence the course of the lawsuit. Also the 1998 Woolf Reforms in England & Wales increased the powers of the judge. It is striking in this respect that **Lord Harry Woolf (1933)** as he then was, the spiritual father of the new **English civil procedure rules**, emphasises that although his rules give the judge more powers, this certainly does not mean that English procedural law will no longer be adversarial.[33]

C Attempts to design an efficient procedure

#31 I would now like to turn to the second way in which the history of procedural law can contribute to the shaping of a harmonised civil procedural law for Europe, namely by providing perspectives on the question of how an **efficient procedure** can be designed. In this context the history of the doctrine of exceptions will be discussed.

#32 In Continental law, **exceptions** can be described as defences that are not aimed at challenging the claim itself, but as arguments stating that the claim cannot be granted even if the claimant succeeds in proving the facts on which the claim is based.[34] Examples are the defence that the court has no jurisdiction or the defence that the claimant has summoned the wrong person as defendant in the proceedings. Exceptions originate in the Roman formula process, but there they fulfilled a different function. Since the formula process is not relevant in understanding the role of exceptions in modern procedural law, I will limit myself here to exceptions in the later Roman cognitio procedure, ie the standard procedure at the time of the **Emperor Justinian I (482–565)**. In the **cognitio procedure**, exceptions play a role that is comparable to their role in modern law, also with regard to the order in which they had to be presented in court.

---

33 *Access to Justice: Interim Report to the Lord Chancellor on the civil justice system in England and Wales* (HMSO, 1995); *Access to Justice: Final Report to the Lord Chancellor on the civil justice system in England and Wales* (HMSO, 1996).

34 CH van Rhee, 'The Role of Exceptions in Continental Civil Procedure', in P Brand, K Costello and WN Osborough (eds), *Adventures of the Law. Proceedings of the Sixteenth British Legal History Conference* (Four Courts Press 2005) 88.

#33 In the late **cognitio procedure**, exceptions were divided into three groups. There were procedural, dilatory and peremptory exceptions. In the cognitio procedure the situation was such that procedural exceptions had to be proposed and proven before the *litiscontestatio*, that is to say at the beginning of the procedure. As for **dilatory exceptions**, the rule was that they also had to be proposed before the ***litiscontestatio***, but that they only had to be proven after the claimant had provided evidence of his claim. **Peremptory exceptions** could be raised throughout the procedure. This arrangement was introduced in the civil procedural law of various European jurisdictions through Romano-canonical procedural law. In this procedural law, too, the main rule ultimately applied that the defences should be presented in a specific order. This order was: first the procedural exceptions (which were now classified as part of the larger group of dilatory exceptions and which were designated by their own name, namely as **declinatory exceptions**), then the (other) dilatory exceptions, then the peremptory exceptions and finally the **defence on the merits**. The idea was that this would prevent parties from wasting energy unnecessarily and thereby making the procedure a lengthy and costly event. After all, if the rules were that the entire defence had to be presented simultaneously, the parties would have to delve into all the ins and outs of the case, even if this subsequently turned out not to be necessary due to the success of a preliminary defence (exception). This prescribed order meant that points that logically had to be decided in advance, such as jurisdiction, should be addressed at the beginning of the lawsuit.

#34 In theory, the system described above worked well, but in practice the possibility of raising exceptions separately gave rise to serious abuse. After all, the various exceptions had to be decided separately as well, and the defendant could therefore seriously delay the lawsuit by endlessly proposing his exceptions, the one after the other, even if these exceptions had no chance of success. This tactic became known in later periods as 'exception-making'. There were numerous attempts to put a stop to this abuse. For example, it was decided early on that exceptions of the same kind had to be proposed together. Whether this measure provided the desired relief, however, is doubtful. In the Netherlands, for example, an attempt was made to tackle the matter drastically by stipulating that only a number of specifically named exceptions could be proposed prior to the defence on the merits, while all other exceptions, whether they had previously been qualified as declinatory, dilatory or peremptory, had to be combined with this defence. Since the **Dutch Code of Civil Procedure of 1838** did not follow this approach but closely followed the **French Code of Civil Procedure**, it should come as no surprise that at some point new measures were required to combat the abuse. These measures were taken by the so-called **Lex Hartogh** in 1897, which introduced changes to the procedural code of 1838. As a result of the Lex Hartogh, the Dutch Code of Civil Procedure stipulated that all exceptions must be combined with the (first) defence on the merits. Exceptions that had not been proposed at that time could not be introduced at a later date. It is striking that the original rule, whereby exceptions could be introduced separately, one after the other, originated from the desire to shorten the process, while in 1897 the opposite arrangement was chosen but with the explicit same objective.

#35 Incidentally, **Lex Hartogh** did not mean that the traditional division of exceptions into declinatory, dilatory and peremptory defences was a thing of the past. Shortly after the introduction of this law, the **Supreme Court of the Netherlands** had to decide on the question of whether peremptory exceptions were also subject to the rule of simultaneous introduction with the (first) defence on the merits. The Supreme Court decided that they were not, and effectively equated peremptory exceptions with a defence on the merits.[35] In practice, this decision meant that peremptory exceptions were subject to the rule that, insofar as any defence on the merits had initially been put forward, a further defence on the merits could always be proposed at a later time. As a result, the role of peremptory exceptions appeared to have been played out and they disappeared as a category from the textbooks. The distinction between declinatory and dilatory exceptions also faded into the background.

#36 Knowledge of the developments as regards exceptions in the Netherlands can provide useful points of view in the debate on the harmonisation of procedural law in Europe. For example, it is not advisable to maintain the distinction between categories of **exceptions** that is still made in other countries – I am thinking, for example, of the way in which the procedural law of Spain is interpreted.[36] This distinction only leads to confusion. Even a distinction between 'exceptions' in the sense of procedural defences and defences on the merits, as is known in Dutch procedural law, does not seem to be worth following. It is better to refrain from designating a specific group of defences with a generic name and simply to designate the defences for which special rules apply with their own, specific name (for example: 'defence of lack of jurisdiction'). This prevents classification problems. In addition, in the light of past developments, it is advisable to limit the number of defences that can be proposed separately. Theoretically speaking, the Romano-canonical rules on exceptions may have had their advantages, but in practice it has become apparent that these rules have not had the intended result.

---

35 HR 06-05-1904, W 8063.

36 Cf MA Fernández-Ballesteros López, JM Rifá Soler and JF Valls Gombau, *Comentarios a la nueva Ley de Enjuiciamiento Civil* (Iurgium 2001) Art. 405.

D Conclusion

#37 The present contribution shows that the history of procedural law may be relevant in attempts to harmonise or approximate civil procedural law in Europe. This is due to the fact that all civil procedural systems in Europe are siblings, based as they are on the Romano-canonical procedure of medieval and later times. It has been shown that Roman-canon influence was even present in the procedure of the Common Law, albeit that this influence was less profound than on the European Continent. Questions that may be addressed from an historical perspective are manifold. In the present contribution the questions discussed concern the historical relationship between the different systems of procedural law in Europe, and attempts to create an **efficient procedure** by studying the reasons for the success or failure of earlier reform attempts.

References

Access to Justice: Interim Report to the Lord Chancellor on the Civil Justice System in England and Wales (HMSO 1995).

Access to Justice: Final Report to the Lord Chancellor on the Civil Justice System in England and Wales (HMSO 1996).

Bracton de H, *De legibus et consuetudinibus Angliae*, vol 1–6 (T Twiss ed, CUP 2012).

Clark CE, 'The Code Cause of Action' [1923–1924] YLR 817.

Clark DS, 'The Civil Law Influence on David Dudley Field's Code of Civil Procedure' in M Reimann (ed), *The Reception of Continental Ideas in the Common Law World* (1820–1920) (Duncker & Humblot 1993) 63.

Drappatz T, *Die Überführung des internationalen Zivilverfahrensrechts in eine Gemeinschaftskompetenz nach Art. 65 EGV* (Mohr Siebeck 2002).

Fernández-Ballesteros López MA, Rifá Soler JM and Valls Gombau JF, *Comentarios a la nueva Ley de enjuiciamiento civil* (Iurgium 2001).

Grilli A, *Die französische Justizorganisation am linken Rheinufer (1797–1803)* (Peter Lang 1999).

Heirbaut D, *Redefining Codification. A Comparative History of Civil, Commercial and Procedural Codes* (OUP 2024).

Helmholz R and others (eds), *Itinera Fiduciae. Trust and Treuhand in Historical Perspective* (Duncker & Humblot 1998).

Holdsworth W, *A History of English Law*, vol XV (Methuen & Co; Sweet & Maxwell 1965).

Isambert F and others (eds), *Recueil général des anciennes lois françaises, depuis l'an 420 jusqu'à la Révolution de 1789*, vol XVIII (Belin-Leprieur 1829).

Jacob J, 'The Judicature Acts 1873–1875 – Vision and Reality' in *The Reform of Civil Procedural Law and Other Essays in Civil Procedure* (Sweet & Maxwell 1982) 301.

Litewski W, Der römisch-kanonische Zivilprozess nach den älteren ordines iudiciarii, 2 vols (Wydawnictwo Universytetu Jagiellonskiego 1999).

Macnair M, *The Law of Proof in Early Modern Equity* (Duncker & Humblot 1999).

Macpherson W (ed), *The New Procedure of the Civil Courts of British India* (4th edn, Lepaige 1860).

Plucknett TFT, A Concise History of the Common Law (5th edn, Little, Brown and Co 1956).

Pothier R-J, *Traité de la procédure civile* (first published 1778, Tarlier 1831).

Pringsheim F, 'The Inner Relationship between English and Roman Law' [1935] CLJ 347.

Rhee van CH, *Litigation and Legislation. Civil Procedure at First Instance in the Great Council for the Netherlands in Malines (1522–1559)* (Archives générales du Royaume 1997).

—— 'Civil Procedure: A European "Ius Commune"?' [2000] ERPL 589.

—— 'Trusts, Trust-like Concepts and "Ius Commune"' [2000] ERPL 453.

—— *European Traditions in Civil Procedure* (Intersentia 2005).

—— 'The Role of Exceptions in Continental Civil Procedure' in P Brand, K Costello and WN Osborough (eds), Adventures of the Law. Proceedings of the Sixteenth British Legal History Conference (Four Courts Press 2005) 88.

Storme M (ed), *Rapprochement du droit judiciaire de l'Union européenne/Approximation of Judiciary Law in the European Union* (Wolters Kluwer 1994).

Subrin SN, 'David Dudley Field and the Field Code: A Historical Analysis of an Earlier Procedural Vision' [1988] LHR 311.

Tardif A, *La procédure civile et criminelle aux XIIIe et XIVe siècles ou procédure de transition* (first published 1885; reprint Scientia 1974).

Wijffels A, 'Arthur Duck et le "ius commune" européen' [1990] Revue d'histoire des Facultés de Droit et de la Science Juridique 193.

—— '"Ius Gentium" in the Practice of the Court of Admiralty Around 1600' in ADE Lewis and DJ Ibbetson (eds), *The Roman Law Tradition* (CUP 1994) 119.

—— 'Sir Julius Caesar and the Merchants of Venice' in F Battenberg and others (eds), *Geschichte der Zentraljustiz in Mitteleuropa* (Böhlau 1994) 195.

Wirth Y, *Common Law- und Equity-Gerichtsbarkeit in England und ihre Reform im 19. Jahrhundert* (Nomos 2025).

Van Caenegem RC, *International Encyclopedia of Comparative Law* Volume 16: Civil Procedure, Chapter 2: History of European Civil Procedure (Brill 1973).

Matthias Weller

Chapter 4 Mutual Trust

A Introduction

#1 'Mutual trust' has advanced to one of the most fundamental principles of judicial cooperation in civil and commercial matters and as such of both European civil procedural law and European private international law. In a first step after the Treaty of Amsterdam 1999 mutual trust has established itself as an explanatory and interpretative principle in and for the relevant secondary law, not only for the procedural law on the cooperation in civil and commercial matters, but for all areas of judicial cooperation within the EU, including criminal and asylum matters. In a second step and in light of Article 2 TEU in particular, newly laid down by the Treaty of Lisbon 2009, the European Court of Justice has unfolded mutual trust to a powerful implicit and overarching principle of primary EU law in order to further pursue the EU's '*raison d'être*' – integration.[1] Thus, mutual trust must today be conceived as an integral element of the EU's '**constitutional identity**'.[2] On a doctrinal level, trust in – and residual control of – foreign judicial and legal acts as a condition for integrating foreign elements in one's own administration of justice, including foreign law ('**trust management**'), offers itself as a theory for private international law in its entirety, in particular in regard to its

1 Opinion 2/13 *Accession to the ECHR* (18 December 2014) ECLI:EU:C:2014:2454, para 172 in fine.
2 C-157/21 *Poland v Parliament and Council* (16 February 2022) ECLI:EU:C:2022:98, para 264: 'Article 2 TEU is not a mere statement of policy guidelines or intentions, but contains values which . . . are an integral part of the very identity of the European Union as a common legal order, values which are given concrete expression in principles comprising legally binding obligations for the Member States'. Similarly, Case C-156/21 *Hungary v Parliament and Council* (16 February 2022) ECLI:EU:C:2022:97, para 232. On the – controversial – concept of the EU's own constitutional identity see, affirmatively, A von Bogdandy, *Strukturwandel des öffentlichen Rechts, Entstehung und Demokratisierung der europäischen Gesellschaft* (Suhrkamp 2022) section 33, 180 et seq, on '*Europäische und nationale Identitäten*' (in translation): '[e]mergence of a European identity through European constititional law, in particular European principles'; see also eg T Drinóczi and P Faraguna, 'The Constitutional Identity of the EU as a Counterbalance for Unconstitutional Constitutional Identities of the Member States' European Yearbook of Constitutional Law 2022 (Springer 2023) 57.

Matthias Weller, Institute of German and International Civil Procedural Law, University of Bonn, Germany, e-mail: weller@jura.uni-bonn.de.

https://doi.org/10.1515/9783110781632-004

procedural areas.[3] It is the purpose of this Chapter to summarise briefly this remarkable history of mutual trust and to sketch its far-reaching impact today.

B First Conceptual Traces in the 19th Century

#2 The concept of mutual trust is by no means an invention of the European Union or its preceding Communities. Rather, traces of this notion can be found in a much earlier union, the **'German Union'** (*'Deutscher Bund'*), a union of many but not all German states in 1815 that was ultimately, in 1871, to become the **German Empire** (*'Deutsches Reich'*).[4] These German states found themselves, all of a sudden, in full sovereignty, after the **Holy Roman Empire of German Nation** had come to its end in 1806. Speaking in modern terms, the new German states started regulating their judicial cooperation in civil and commercial matters, and they did so in quite different ways. In this historical context, Paul Johann Anselm Feuerbach, an outstanding legal scholar mainly of criminal law, developed the so-called **'mirror principle'** (*'Spiegelbildprinzip'*)[5] to regulate indirect jurisdiction for the recognition and enforcement of foreign judgments: the foreign court should be regarded as having legitimately assumed jurisdiction if this was in accordance with the requested state's rules of direct jurisdiction had they applied to and by the foreign court. In other words: the requested state's rules on direct jurisdiction were to be projected ('mirrored') upon the state of origin to control its exercise of adjudicatory authority in international cases. Despite this intriguing concept, influential until today,[6] divergences remained in the legal orders. Therefore, the German Union sought to unify the rules on recognition and enforcement of foreign judgments. Originally, a very strict control of 'truly foreign' judgments was envisaged, ie foreign judgments from other than the German states that had been part of the Holy Roman Empire. Recognition and enforcement would only be allowed under the regime of a **bilateral treaty** with the state of

---

3 M Weller, '"Mutual Trust": A Suitable Foundation for Private International Law in Regional Integration Communities and Beyond?' in Collected Courses of the Hague Academy of International Law – Recueil des cours vol 423 (Brill 2022), 38, in particular at para 123.

4 ibid paras 337 et seq.

5 PJA Feuerbach, 'Über die Rechtskraft und Vollstreckung eines von einem auswärtigen Gerichte gesprochenen Erkenntnisses' in PJA Feuerbach, *Themis oder Beiträge zur Gesetzgebung*(Krüll 1812) 77; on this invention from today's perspective eg C Schärtl, *Das Spiegelbildprinzip im Rechtsverkehr mit ausländischen Staatenverbindungen* (Mohr Siebeck 2005) 59 et seq.

6 See eg Germany, s 328 (1) no. 1 German Code of Civil Procedure (*'Zivilprozessordnung'*); Austria, s 406 no 1 Act on the Enforcement of Judgments (*'Exekutionsordnung'*); (with slight variations) Italy, Article 64(1) Private International Law Act (*'Legge di Riforma del sistema italiano di diritto internazionale privato'*); Spain, Article 46(1)(c) (*'Ley de cooperación jurídica internacional en materia civil'*); since 2014 Japan, Article 118 Code of Civil Procedure ('民事訴訟法').

origin,[7] but more generous rules were to be applied to 'interstate' judgments, ie amongst those German states. The rationale for this distinction is obvious, as the legislative materials show: a lack of trust in 'international' judgments, as opposed to 'interstate' judgments.[8] Eventually, these drafts became obsolete when the German Empire (*'Deutsches Reich'*) came into being in 1871 and started unifying substantive and procedural law comprehensively on the imperial level. Thus, interstate recognition became entirely irrelevant, as the Empire imposed full trust in all judgments originating from courts within the Empire.

#3 Nevertheless, the example of the German Union shows that the question of how far mutual trust should reach and how far a residual control should stay in place, ie how **'trust management'** should be implemented, has been an issue within communities of states at least since the **19th century**. Contemporary comparative perspectives confirm that functionally, mutual trust plays a formative role in the set-up of judicial cooperation for all and any community of states, be it within a regional economic integration community, be it within a global treaty framework such as the HCCH Conventions,[9] no matter how little or deeply the respective community is integrated.[10]

#4 Even deeper roots of mutual trust can be identified in **Friedrich Carl von Savigny**'s private international law theory. The core of this theory is to select the law of the place where the legal relationship (*'Rechtsverhältnis'*) in question has its 'seat', ie to which the legal relationship has its **closest territorial connection**.[11] Such an approach presupposes an equivalence of all legal orders as adequate in principle to regulate the legal relation in question, despite differences in details. This precondition of a certain equivalence of all legal orders allows the law-selecting process to focus exclusively on localising the legal relation's seat in

---

7 Similarly, until today, eg Indonesia, based on Dutch law in its state of the early 20th century, see eg Article 436 (1) Code of Civil Procedure (*'RV – Rechtvordering'*). However, if fresh proceedings are instituted in Indonesia, courts can take the foreign judgment into account as evidence according to Article 436 (2) Code of Civil Procedure.

8 Protocolle der Commission zur Berathung einer allgemeinen Civilprozeßordnung für die deutschen Bundesstaaten, vol 13 (Sessions CCXLIX-CCLXXIV) (Keip 1865) Session CCLXX, 4908.

9 Which might lead to the conclusion that, as a matter of mutual trust (of a low degree), no anti suit injunctions amongst Contracting States of HCCH Convention on judicial cooperation in civil matters are admissible, as long as such measures aim at securing a 'better' application of the Convention, on this issue see eg M Ahmed and P Beaumont, 'Exclusive Choice of Court Agreements: Some Issues on the Hague Convention on Choice of Court Agreements and its Relationship with the Brussels I Recast Especially Anti-suit Injunctions, Concurrent Proceedings and the Implications of BREXIT' (2017) 13 Journal of Private International Law 386, 402, who in principle favour anti suit injunctions but concede that such 'second guessing' would 'create a rift'.

10 Weller (n 3) para 497.

11 FC v Savigny, *System des heutigen römischen Rechts*, vol VIII (Veit 1849) 10.

the space. Such an imperative of a purely **'spatial justice'** (*'räumliche Gerechtigkeit'*) in the law-selecting process necessitates a 'leap into the dark'[12] in respect to the contents of the selected foreign law.[13] Leaping into the dark is only rational if there is a basis for trust in principle and if there are sufficient tools for control ('trust management').[14] Indeed, 'the standpoint', v. Savigny explains, 'to which our considerations have lead us', 'is one of a community of interacting nations under public international law',[15] and this standpoint, we are informed, has received growing acceptance over time, partly under the influence of a 'common Christian civilization' (*'gemeinsame christliche Gesittung'*), partly driven by the evident mutual benefits arising therefrom 'for all involved'. Thus, the imperative of 'spatial justice', a justice in the law-selecting process irrespective, in principle, of the contents of the selected rules, presupposes a community of states that share common values and thereby are trusted in producing law that may differ in detail, but will principally appear equivalent to regulate the respective legal relationships. If we strip v. Savigny's standpoint from its religious overtones and translate it functionally into contemporary terms and notions of mutual trust and the management thereof, the structural parallels of v. Savigny's community of interacting nations under the public international law to the European Union on the basis of shared values are striking, in particular in light of Article 2 TEU. The more the law-selecting process emphasises the purely territorial connection, the more control will be necessary, before the domestic legal order may legitimately integrate the foreign law into its own by speaking out the 'applicatur'.[16]

C Slow Rise within the European Communities

#5 By the Treaty of Paris of 18 April 1951,[17] the **European Coal and Steel Community** (ECSC) began to unite European countries economically and politically in

---

12 L Raape, *Deutsches Internationales Privatrecht* (Franz Vahlen 1938) 59.

13 See also, much later, German Constitutional Court, Judgment of 4 May 1971, 1 BvR 636/68, BVerfGE 31, 58, 73, in relation to selecting foreign law: protection by fundamental rights must be guaranteed while 'leaping into the dark'.

14 Weller (n 3) para 36.

15 Savigny (n 11) 27: 'Der Standpunkt, auf den wir durch diese Erwägungen geführt werden, ist der einer völkerrechtlichen Gemeinschaft der mit einander verkehrenden Nationen, und dieser Standpunkt hat im Fortschritt der Zeit immer allgemeinere Anerkennung gefunden, unter dem Einfluß theils der gemeinsamen christlichen Gesittung, theils des wahren Vortheils, der daraus für alle Theile hervorgeht'.

16 The term 'applicatur' obviously mirrors the well-established term of 'exequatur', in order to underline the structural similarities in the process of integration the foreign into one's own, see Weller (n 3) paras 105 and 440.

17 Treaty establishing the European Coal and Steel Community, Paris, 18 April 1951.

order to secure lasting peace.[18] To this end, the production of coal and steel was pooled in a common market under a common High Authority. It cannot be overestimated that from the outset this initial community was attributed supranational powers.[19] The six founding States decided, with the **Treaties of Rome** of 25 March 1957,[20] entering into force on 1 January 1958, to set up a **European Atomic Energy Community (EAEC or Euratom)** and a **European Economic Community (EEC)**. Again, these communities were attributed **supranational powers** from the outset.[21] The EEC involved building a wider common market covering a large range of goods and services. Customs duties between the six countries were abolished on 1 July 1968.[22]

#6 In the same year, the then Member States agreed, as had been envisaged by Article 220 EEC,[23] to supplement the functioning of their economic community by the **Brussels Convention** on jurisdiction and the enforcement of judgments in civil and commercial matters.[24] This instrument entered into force on 1 February 1973. Functionally speaking, a quite far-reaching trust in judgments from other Member States was implemented, compared to partly very restrictive recognition and enforcement schemes in the national legal orders at the time.[25] Yet, there was no talk about mutual trust at all, although the **Jenard Report** had explained the prohibition of a *révision au fond* for the requested court by 'complete confidence' in the courts of the first State.[26] As Advocate General Spzunar has rightly observed recently, in his Opinion of 8 February 2024 in the case of *Real Madrid*,[27] when he deliberated on the emergence of the 'classic formula' of the public policy exception in the Brussels regime:

---

18 For context, see Weller (n 3) paras 34 et seq.

19 See eg G Thiemeyer, 'Supranationalität als Novum in der Geschichte der internationalen Politik der fünfziger Jahre' (1998) 4(2) Journal of European Integration History 5.

20 Treaty establishing the European Economic Community (hereafter 'EEC Treaty', but also known as TEEC or EEC) and Treaty establishing the European Atomic Energy Community (Euratom), Rome, 25 March 1957.

21 Eg M Gilbert, 'The Treaties of Rome' in E Jones, A Menon and S Weatherill (eds), *The Oxford Handbook of the European Union* (OUP 2012) 99.

22 W Ernst, 'The Free Movement of Goods and Services Within the European Economic Community in the Context of the World Economy' (1981) 137 Zeitschrift für die gesamte Staatswissenschaft 556, 563.

23 As laid down in the Treaty of Rome 1958, upheld in the Treaty of Maastricht 1993, renumbered as Article 293 EC Treaty by the Treaty of Amsterdam 1999, and deleted by the Treaty of Lisbon 2009.

24 [1972] OJ L299/32.

25 Jenard Report on the Convention of 27 September 1968 on jurisdiction and the enforcement of judgments in civil and commercial matters [1979] OJ C59/3.

26 ibid 46.

27 Case C-633/22 *Real Madrid v Le Monde* (8 February 2024) ECLI:EU:C:2024:127, Opinion of AG Szpunar, para 61.

> 'The reason why the reference to mutual trust does not appear in that classic formula is that, when it was given specific expression in the judgment in Krombach, neither EU law nor the Court had yet openly recognised the role played by such trust in the civil and commercial dimension of the area of freedom, security and justice.'

Krombach was decided on 28 March 2000.[28] Indeed, it took decades to unfold the principle of mutual trust.

#7 In 1977, Valery Giscard d'Estaing, then president of France, introduced the notion of a **'common judicial area'** (*'espace commun judiciaire'*) as a supplement to the common economic area.[29] This political intervention primarily presented itself as a means to combat more effectively cross-border criminality and organised crime,[30] also as an almost logical further step from economic towards **political integration** of the European Communities in general. In its conclusions for the European Council in Brussels from 5 and 6 December 1977, the then French Presidency 'noted with interest a communication from the President of the French Republic on development [sic!] of **judicial co-operation** between the Member States. It requested that active consideration be given to the proposals made in this respect'.[31] 'Judicial cooperation', today one of the most dynamic policies of the EU, was set in motion.

#8 In 1982, the European Parliament reinforced efforts to move on by its **Resolution on the European judicial area**[32] and held that:

> 'the creation of a European judicial area should relate to the establishment and safeguarding of the rights to which citizens are entitled, to the definition of the obligations incumbent upon them and to the manner in which the Member States will cooperate to ensure that those rights may be freely exercised, those obligations maintained and society protected against any attack on public order and security in the form of terrorist or other criminal activity perpetrated by individuals or groups of individuals'.

Obviously **judicial cooperation in civil matters** was not at the forefront but rather developed in the shadows of establishing **judicial cooperation in criminal matters** – which might be seen as a 'tactical advantage' for installing far-reaching judicial cooperation in civil matters.[33]

---

28 Case C-7/98 *Dieter Krombach v André Bamberski* (28 March 2000) ECLI:EU:C:2000:164.

29 Proposition de Valery Giscard d'Estaing sur la mise en place d'un espace judiciaire européen, Conseil européen, Bruxelles, 5 décembre 1977.

30 Eg L Menuet, "Le discours sur l'espace judiciaire européen: analyse du discours et sémantique argumentative linguistique", Université de Nantes (Université Libre de Bruxelles 2006) 41.

31 European Council, Conclusions of the Presidency, Brussels, 5 and 6 December 1977, sub VIII., 12, on: 'Judicial Co-operation' <https://www.consilium.europa.eu/en/european-council/conclusions/1992–1975/> accessed 5 February 2025.

32 Resolution on the European judicial area of 9 July 1982 [1982] OJ C238/83, 84.

33 B Hess, *Europäisches Zivilprozessrecht* (De Gruyter 2010) 32 para 6.

#9 Meanwhile, **economic integration** progressed. In a second major step, the **Single European Act** of 1986[34] aimed at removing remaining trade barriers by launching a 'single' or '**internal market**' by 1993, largely driven by a principle of mutual recognition: In order to avoid any further detailed harmonisation of regulatory issues by secondary law,[35] a **principle of mutual recognition** of the national exercise of regulatory power emerged in the case law of the ECJ, accompanied by the Commission on the policy level, first for the freedom of goods,[36] later for other freedoms. Over time, the logics and dynamics of deepening economic integration by ordering mutual recognition matched with and transgressed to judicial integration, in particular to the mutual recognition of Member State judgments.[37] But there was still a long way to go.

#10 The first time the term of mutual trust was employed to explain (largely) **automatic recognition** of Member States judgments by the ECJ seems to be the Opinion of **Advocate General Darmon** of 2 December 1992.[38] However, in respect to the notion of mutual trust, the AG did not make reference to the Jenard Report, but to French academic writing.[39] At the time, the ECJ did not take up the ball.

---

34 The Single European Act, signed at Luxembourg on 17 February 1986 and The Hague on 28 February 1986, entered into force on 1 July 1987; [1987] OJ L169.

35 In a first phase of the making of the internal market, harmonisation by secondary legislation came to its limits, both politically and practically, despite the specific head of competency of the EU for the harmonisation of law in (now) Article 114 of the Treaty on the Functioning of the European Union (TFEU) of 13 December 2007, OJ EU (2012) C 326/47.

36 See in particular Case C-120/*REWE-Zentral AG* v *Bundesmonopolverwaltung für Branntwein ('Cassis de Dijon')* (20 February 1979) ECLI:EU:C:1979:42, para 8. See also K Nicolaidis, 'Trusting the Poles? Constructing Europe through Mutual Recognition' (2007) 14 Journal of European Public Policy 682, proposing a better balance between trust and control by an approach that he calls 'managed mutual recognition'; from a global and economic perspective, see eg K Nicolaidis and G Shaffer, 'Transnational Mutual Recognition Regimes: Governance without Global Government' (2005) 68 Law and Contemporary Problems 263.

37 C Kohler, 'Vertrauen und Kontrolle im europäischen Justizraum für Zivilsachen' (2016) 19 Zeitschrift für europarechtliche Studien (ZEuS) 135, 136 et seq.

38 Case C-172/91 *Sonntag* v *Waidmann* (21 April 1993) ECLI:EU:C:1992:487, para 71.

39 ibid: 'The principle of the recognition of judgments is based on the Member States' mutual trust in their respective legal systems and judicial institutions', with reference to G Pluyette, 'La convention de Bruxelles et les droits de la défense' in *Etudes offertes a Pierre Bellet* (Litec 1991) 427.

D Fully Unfolding Mutual Trust in EU Secondary EU Law on Judicial Cooperation in Civil and Commercial Matters after 2002

#11 After the **European Council of Tampere** in 1999[40] had described mutual recognition as a '**cornerstone**' of judicial cooperation in the area of freedom, security and justice as introduced under the **Treaty of Amsterdam**,[41] the European Council's draft programme of measures then proposed **minimum procedural standards** and procedural guarantees as 'ancillary measures' for the 'strengthening of mutual trust'.[42] Most importantly, on the Commission's initiative,[43] mutual trust appeared in recitals 16 and 17 of the **Brussels I Regulation** (which later became recital 26 of the Brussels Ibis Regulation) to legitimise an even more facilitate recognition and enforcement mechanism of judgments from other Member States. That was the moment from which on mutual trust as a driver for deepening judicial cooperation, by interpreting the relevant secondary law, unfolded almost explosively to full practical effect in the case law of the ECJ.[44]

#12 The first decision in which the ECJ availed itself of the notion of mutual trust, now textually confirmed in the Brussels I Regulation (but not yet applicable to the case), was in ***Gasser***[45] where mutual trust was still used as one argument among others to reinforce an interpretation of EU secondary law against an implicit exception of the strict lis pendens rule – a result which could have easily been reached from the plain wording of the text, without any need to invoke mutual trust at all. The recourse to mutual trust shows that the ECJ considered this principle as underlying the relevant EU and EC law as well as related treaty law, before its expression in the texts of the European Council of Tampere and in the Brussels I Regulation.

---

40 Tampere European Council 15 and 16 October 1999, Presidency Conclusions, para 33.

41 Treaty of Amsterdam of 2 October 1997 amending the Treaty on European Union, the Treaties establishing the European Communities and certain related acts [1997] OJ C340/1.

42 Council, Draft programme of measures for implementation of the principle of mutual recognition of decisions in civil and commercial matters [2001] OJ C12/1, 5.

43 Commission, 'Proposal for a Council Regulation (EC) on jurisdiction and the recognition and enforcement of judgments in civil and commercial matters' COM (1999) 348 final [1999] OJ C376 E/1, Article 33 and recitals 17 and 18.

44 See also X Kramer, 'Cross-border Enforcement in the EU: Mutual Trust versus Fair Trial? Towards Principles of European Civil Procedure' (2011) 1 International Journal of Procedural Law 1 202, 221 et seq.; X Kramer, *Procedure Matters: Construction and Deconstructivism in European Civil Procedure* (Eleven international Publishing 2013) 17 et seq.

45 Case C-116/02 *Gasser* (9 December 2003) ECLI:EU:C:2003:657, paras 70 et seq.

#13 The next major decision, ***Turner***, started fleshing out mutual trust with a drive to deepen integration beyond black letter law (still under the Brussels Convention), in this case to exclude any review by the requested Member State court of the application of the common jurisdictional rules by the Member State court of origin and, as a consequence, **anti suit injunctions** amongst Member State courts (even though formally directed against the party rather than the court).[46] Thus, mutual trust served to pre-empt conflicting measures provided for under national procedural law and thereby broadened the scope of EU law.

#14 In ***Owusu***, mutual trust was invoked by Attorney General Léger only. In his Opinion, he confirmed two structural elements of the principle:[47] First, mutual trust had already governed the **Brussels Convention**. Second, the principle does not govern relations of a Member State with non-Member States. The ECJ did not feel urged to resort to mutual trust to explain the exclusion, similar to the case in *Gasser*, of an exception to the common distribution of jurisdiction amongst the Member States by a rule of national procedural law, in this case ***forum non conveniens***. At the time, mutual trust had mainly still the status of a supplementary optional argument.

#15 The next major decision came a couple of years later, in the case of ***West Tankers***.[48] The ECJ again pushed back national procedural law, once more **anti suit injunctions**; however, this time not directly in relation to a 'wrong' exercise of the common jurisdictional rules but in relation to the interpretation of the material scope of these rules, in particular of the arbitration exception in Aricle 1(2) Brussels I Regulation. Although structurally comparable to *Turner*, the inadmissibility of anti-suit injunctions in support of arbitral proceedings could no longer be based solely on a systematic interpretation of the black letter rules. Rather, in order to achieve its result, the ECJ had to overcome the unconditionally comprehensive wording of the arbitration exception. Arguably, this is the first instance in which mutual trust has played a decisive role in the development of EU civil procedural law, by way of a **'teleologically driven reduction'** (*'teleologische Reduktion'*) of an otherwise applicable rule. Later, in ***Gazprom***, the ECJ held that arbitral tribunals are not bound by these restrictions, as they do not form part of the mutual trust between the Member States on their respective administration of justice.[49] Thus, Member States remain free to recognise and enforce anti suit injunctions by an arbitral tribunal against state court proceedings in that Member State.

46 Case C-159/02 *Turner* (27 April 2004) ECLI:EU:C:2004:228, paras 25 et seq.

47 Case C-281/02 *Owusu* (14 December 2004) ECLI:EU:C:2004:798, Opinion of AG Léger, para 144.

48 Case C-185/07 *West Tankers* (10 February 2009) ECLI:EU:C:2009:69, para 30.

49 Case C-536/13 *Gazprom* (13 May 2015) ECLI:EU:C:2015:316, paras 37 et seq.

#16 An important first step in balancing mutual trust against competing principles marks the decision in ***Apostolides***:[50] The ECJ found it 'apparent from recitals 16 to 18' of the Brussels I Regulation that the system of appeals against recognition or enforcement of a judgment:

> 'aims to establish a fair balance between, on the one hand, mutual trust in the administration of justice in the Union, which justifies judgments given in a Member State being, as a rule, recognised and declared enforceable automatically in another Member State and, on the other hand, respect for the rights of the defence'.

This means, as the ECJ further explained, 'that the defendant should, where necessary, be able to appeal in an adversarial procedure against the declaration of enforceability if he considers one of the grounds for non-enforcement to be present'. The necessity for balancing mutual trust against (at least) **'rights of the defence'**, ie (at least some) fundamental rights was later confirmed eg in ***Trade Agency***.[51] In some other decisions, however, the ECJ abstained from expressly considering such balancing, although 'rights of defence' were in question.[52]

#17 In ***TNT Express Nederland***,[53] the Court reiterated,[54] more and more embedded in general conceptual explanations,[55] a core element of the principle of mutual trust: the court of the Member State addressed is never in a better position than the court of the State of origin to determine whether the latter was competent according to the common rules attributing jurisdiction. Accordingly, the Brussels I Regulation, apart from a few limited exceptions, does not authorise the jurisdiction of a court of a Member State to be reviewed by a court in another Member State.[56] While in *TNT Express Nederland* the prohibition to review the first court relates to a specified set of rules of EU secondary law that is governed by an express exclusion of a ***revision au fond***,[57] this prohibition will grow into much broader assumptions in other contexts, namely that mutual trust requires a Member State to assume that all other Member States will comply with fundamental

---

50 Case C-420/07 *Apostolides* (28 April 2009) ECLI:EU:C:2009:271, para 73.

51 Case C-619/10 *Trade Agency* (6 September 2012) ECLI:EU:C:2012:531, para 43.

52 Eg Case C-455/15 PPU *P v Q* (19 November 2015) ECLI:EU:C:2015:763, see below for further discussion.

53 Case C-533/08 *TNT Express Nederland* (4 May 2010) ECLI:EU:C:2010:243, paras 49 and 55.

54 See before Case C-185/07 *West Tankers* (10 February 2009) ECLI:EU:C:2009:69, para 30.

55 Case C-452/12 *Nipponka* (19 December 2013) ECLI:EU:C:2013:858, paras 38ff; see also, at a later stage, Case C-157/13 *Nickel & Goeldner Spedition* (4 September 2014) ECLI:EU:C:2014:2145, paras 39 et seq.; Case C-90/22 *Gjensidige* (21 March 2024) ECLI:EU:C:2024:252, para 46.

56 Similarly for the European Insolvency Regulation Case C-723/20 *GalapagosBid* (24 March 2022) ECLI:EU:C:2022:209, para 35.

57 On mutual trust as the basis of this prohibition see also Case C-139/10 *Prism Investments* (13 October 2011) ECLI:EU:C:2011:653, paras 30 et seq.

EU law[58] and even with all EU law.[59] Concretely, *TNT Express Nederland* extended the aforementioned element of mutual trust to 'specialised conventions' in the sense of the compatibility clause of Article 71 Brussels I Regulation (Article 71 Brussels Ibis Regulation), in the case at hand the CMR,[60] where such conventions distribute jurisdiction amongst the Member States, including lis pendens rules and with effect on special recognition and enforcement rules.[61] Thus, the ECJ undertook an interpretation of a treaty provision in light of overarching principles of EU law (mutual trust). In essence, this means that mutual trust has gained the status of a **principle of primary law**, beyond an interpretative principle of secondary law. This line of thought was confirmed in ***Nipponkoa***.[62] Thus, the ECJ, by way of interpreting the compatibility clause of Article 71 Brussels I Regulation, established a harmonised **minimum standard for jurisdiction**, parallel proceedings as well as for recognition and enforcement, governed inter alia by the notion of mutual trust.[63]

#18 In the cases of ***Povse*** and of ***Simone Pelz***, the ECJ, probably for the first time in European civil procedural law, pushed mutual trust to the maximum: In case of child abduction under the Brussels II Regulation, where time is of the essence, mutual trust serves as a conclusive presumption of the **sound administration of justice** of the competent court, even in regard to possible human rights violations (hearing of the child) in the judgment to be recognised.[64] Ordering **blind trust**, even in regard to fundamental rights, stands in direct opposition to ordering a balancing of mutual trust with '**rights of defence**'[65] and was hence overruled later by the ECJ[66] and the ECtHR.[67] However, these overruling decisions will relate to other transfers of persons within the common area of freedom, security and justice, namely in asylum and criminal procedural matters, and both the ECJ as well as the ECtHR were in a way reinventing a wheel of private international law

58 Opinion 2/13 *Accession to the ECHR* (18 December 2014) ECLI:EU:C:2014:2454, para 192, see also below.

59 Opinion 1/17 (30 April 2019) *CETA* ECLI:EU:C:2019:341, para 128; C-157/21 *Poland v Parliament and Council* (16 February 2022) ECLI:EU:C:2022:98, para 147.

60 Convention on the Contract for the International Carriage of Goods by Road (CMR) of 19 May 1956, UNTS 399, 189.

61 See Article 31 CMR, regulating jurisdiction, lis pendens and enforceability.

62 Case C-452/12 *Nipponkoa* (19 December 2013) ECLI:EU:C:2013:858, paras 38 et seq.

63 Case C-533/08 *TNT Express Nederland* (4 May 2010) ECLI:EU:C:2010:243, para 56.

64 C-211/10 PPU *Povse* (1 July 2010) EU:C:2010:400, para 70: 'no possibility of opposing . . . recognition'. C-491/10 PPU *Joseba Andoni Aguirre Zarraga v Simone Pelz* (22 December 2010) EU:C:2010:828, para 46.

65 Compare Case C-420/07 *Apostolides* (28 April 2009) ECLI:EU:C:2009:271, see above.

66 Opinion 2/13 *Accession to the ECHR* (18 December 2014) ECLI:EU:C:2014:2454, para 192, see also below.

67 *Avotiņš* v *Latvia* App no 17502/07 (ECtHR, 23 May 2016).

in that they develop a kind of public policy exception ('**exceptional circumstances**') for these latter two areas of (public) European procedural law.[68]

#19 In ***Gothaer Versicherung***,[69] the ECJ added another innovative element in that it ordered, as a matter of mutual trust, a binding effect to constitutive findings on the court's jurisdiction in the judgment of origin. In the case at hand, the ECJ held that the requested Member State court is bound by the finding of the Member State court of origin that there was in fact a valid **choice of court agreement** in favour of a third state (Iceland and as such a Contracting State to the Lugano Convention) because such a judgment by which the Member State court of origin declines assuming jurisdiction is a judgment within the scope of '**judgment**' in Article 32 Brussels I Regulation. Therefore, it must be recognised and enforced without a ***revision au fond***. In support of this proposition, the ECJ employed mutual trust as an interpretative principle to ensure a broad understanding of the concept of 'judgment'.[70] Moreover, the binding effect of the judgment of the Member State's court of origin extends even to findings 'made in the grounds of a judgment, which has since become final, declaring the action inadmissible', eg the existence and validity of the choice of court agreement designating a third state. The fact that Article 23 Brussels I Regulation on choice of court agreements did not apply, since a court of a third state was designated, was held to be irrelevant.

#20 In ***Salzgitter***,[71] the ECJ was confronted with the question whether the **ground of refusal** in Article 34(4) Brussels I Regulation applied, beyond its text, to a constellation where the judgment to be recognised in another Member State conflicted with an earlier judgment in the Member State of origin. It could come as a surprise that the ECJ rejected an extensive reading of a ground of refusal that confines itself to allow refusal if the judgment is in conflict with an earlier judgment of the requested Member State. Such an extension would have been nothing else but a plain ***révision au fond*** of the proceedings in the Member State of origin. It should have been an *acte claire* that this would not be admissible. To be on the safe side, the ECJ mobilised mutual trust as well, in order to back up its proposition that all grounds for refusal are to be interpreted narrowly. Given the mistakes of *Salzgitter* in the setting aside proceedings in the Member State of origin, the judgment appears conceptually convincing.

68 Weller (n 3) para 360.

69 Case C-456/11 *Gothaer Versicherung* (15 November 2012) ECLI:EU:C:2012:719, paras 28 et seq. See also, at a later stage, Case C-422/20 *RK* (9 September 2021) ECLI:EU:C:2021:718, paras 44 et seq., on binding effects from judgments by the Member State courts under the European Succession Regulation.

70 ibid para 28.

71 Case C-157/12 *Salzgitter* (26 September 2013) ECLI:EU:C:2013:597, para 36.

#21 In ***Lithuanian Airlines***,[72] the ECJ connected mutual trust and **public policy** for the first time. As a matter of mutual trust, the public policy exception needs to be interpreted narrowly, as all grounds for refusal. Thus, while it is in principle a matter for the Member States to concretise the public policy exception, the ECJ will control its outer limits. Therefore, recourse to the public policy clause can be envisaged only where recognition or enforcement of the judgment given in another Member State would be at variance to an unacceptable degree with the legal order of the State in which enforcement is sought inasmuch as it would infringe a fundamental principle. In order for the prohibition of any review of the substance of a judgment of another Member State to be observed, the infringement would have to constitute a manifest breach of a rule of law regarded as essential in the legal order of the State in which enforcement is sought or of a right recognised as being fundamental within that legal order. Thus, 'the concept of public policy is intended to prevent a manifest breach of a **rule of law** regarded as essential in the legal order of the State in which recognition is sought or of a right recognised as fundamental within that legal order'.[73]

#22 In ***Diageo Brands***,[74] the ECJ made clear that the violation of EU law as such does not constitute a **public policy violation**. Thus, EU law is of no distinct or 'higher' status for the purposes of mobilising the public policy defence than national law. In this context, the ECJ reiterated that:

> '[t]he principle of mutual trust between the Member States, which is of fundamental importance in EU law, requires, particularly with regard to the area of freedom, security and justice, each of those States, save in exceptional circumstances, to consider all the other Member States to be complying with EU law and particularly with the fundamental rights recognised by EU law[.]'

Consequently, the **public-policy clause** only applied where that error of law means that the recognition of the judgment concerned in the State in which recognition is sought would result in the manifest breach of an essential rule of law in the EU legal order and therefore in the legal order of that Member State.[75] This means, in essence, that 'safe in **exceptional circumstances**' mutual trust takes precedence over the correct application of secondary law that builds up and implements the mechanics of mutual recognition in the first place, unless such rules were to be considered as 'an essential rule of law in the EU legal order'. Whereas the principle itself is expressly held to be a fundamental principle of EU law, its implementing rules are apparently not. It would seem more convincing if blatant

72 Case C-302/13 *Lithuanian Airlines* (23 October 2014) ECLI:EU:C:2014:2319, para 45.

73 ibid para 55.

74 Case C-681/13 *Diageo Brands* (16 July 2015) ECLI:EU:C:2015:471, paras 40 et seq.

75 ibid para 50.

mistakes in the application of such rules would be considered as 'exceptional circumstance'.[76] Another incident of such exceptional circumstances may be seen in an intentional breach of EU law by the court of origin.[77] Such intention, however, is difficult to prove and is not proven by the mere fact that in a dissenting minority opinion a breach of EU law is argued but not followed by the majority.[78]

#23 In ***P v Q***,[79] the court of origin had blatantly infringed Article 15, and thereby Article 8, of the Brussels II Regulation in that it had assumed jurisdiction over a dispute about parental responsibility without receiving a request for assuming jurisdiction from the competent Member State court where the case was already pending. Nevertheless, the ECJ obliged the requested Member State Court to 'trust' the Member State court of origin and recognise and enforce the judgment, even though Article 15 was not mentioned in Article 24 Sentence 1 Brussel II Regulation prohibiting the review of assuming jurisdiction of the first court according to Articles 3–14. A factor of this decision certainly was that the judgment debtor did not fully appeal the judgment for error in law in the Member State of origin. Yet, **blatant mistakes** in applying the common core rules on attribution of jurisdiction should count as '**exceptional circumstance**'. In the background, lingering concerns about the factual foundations of 'mutual trust' were rising, given the volatile or low rankings of some Member States in rule of law and judicial independence surveys undertaken by the Commission, starting in 2013.[80] Yet, even strikingly low **rankings** of some Member States have so far never led the ECJ to allow or even impose an immediate suspension of mutual trust and its implementing rules of secondary law on judicial cooperation.

#24 In ***Meroni***,[81] the ECJ fully spelled out, following its decision in *Diageo Brands*,[82] the fundamental idea' of the Brussels I Regulation:

> 'that individuals are required, in principle, to use all the legal remedies made available by the law of the Member State of origin. Save where specific circumstances make it too difficult or impossible to make use of the legal remedies in the Member State of origin, the individuals concerned must avail themselves of all the legal remedies available in that Member State with a view to preventing a breach of public policy before it occurs'.

---

76 But compare Case C-455/15 PPU *P v Q* (19 November 2015) ECLI:EU:C:2015:763, see below. See also M Weller, 'Mutual Trust within the Judicial Cooperation in Civil Matters: A Normative Cornerstone – A Factual Chimera – A Constitutional Challenge' (2017) 35 Netherlands Journal of Private International Law 1; M Weller, 'Mutual Trust: In Search of the Future of Private International Law' (2015) 11 Journal of Private International Law 65.

77 Case C-681/13 *Diageo Brands* (16 July 2015) ECLI:EU:C:2015:471, arg. ex para 54.

78 ibid.

79 Case C-455/15 PPU *P v Q* (19 November 2015) ECLI:EU:C:2015:763.

80 The first of the European Commission's 'Justice Scoreboards' appeared in 2013.

81 Case C-559/14 *Meroni v Recoletos* (25 May 2016) ECLI:EU:C:2016:349, para 48.

82 Case C-681/13 *Diageo Brands* (16 July 2015) ECLI:EU:C:2015:471, at para 68.

As the requirement of a '**manifest breach**' of a '**fundamental principle**' of (national or EU) law is coupled with the requirement to exercise remedies in the Member State of origin, one is tempted to infer that in the case of breach of a 'truly' fundamental principle, this breach alone should suffice, whereas in the case of 'less' fundamental principles, the judgment debtor must have additionally made use of all available remedies in the state of origin before the public policy exception applies.

#25 In ***Ibrica Zulfikarpašić***[83] and ***Pula Parking***,[84] decided on the same day, the **notion of a 'court'** came under scrutiny:

> 'Compliance with the principle of mutual trust in the administration of justice in the Member States of the European Union which underlies that regulation requires, in particular, that judgments the enforcement of which is sought in another Member State have been delivered in court proceedings offering guarantees of independence and impartiality and in compliance with the principle of ***audi alteram partem***'.

Thus, as a matter of securing the basis for mutual trust, the notion of 'court' must be interpreted autonomously and strictly. Furthermore, in ***Achmea***,[85] the Court held that it is impossible for Member States to opt out (by **intra-EU bilateral investment treaties**) from the 'judicial system' as such, 'intended to ensure consistency and uniformity in the interpretation of EU law', in particular via **references for preliminary rulings** because such judicial system in turn ensures that the core values of the EU as laid down in Article 2 TEU are respected which 'implies and justifies the existence of mutual trust' in the first place.[86]

#26 In ***Liberato***,[87] the ECJ held, in respect to the Brussels II regime for **matrimonial matters**, parental responsibility or maintenance obligations, that a breach of the **lis pendens** rules does not amount to a ground for refusal of the judgment, even though these lis pendens rules certainly form part of the common core of rules allocating jurisdiction amongst the Member States. Yet, the rules generated directly from the principle of mutual trust that no court is better placed to apply these common rules than another does and that no court should review this application of another court prevailed. Thus, the principle of mutual trust is more and more detaching itself from securing its correct technical implementation – a problematic tension to the detriment of the acceptance of the principle.

---

83 Case C-484/15 *Ibrica Zulfikarpašić* (9 March 2017) ECLI:EU:C:2017:199, para 43.

84 Case C-551/15 *Pula Parking* (9 March 2017) ECLI:EU:C:2017:193, para 54.

85 Case C-284/16 *Slowakische Republik v Achmea* (6 March 2018) ECLI:EU:C:2018:158.

86 ibid para 34. See also, most recently, Case C-600/23 *Royal Football Club Seraing* (16 January 2025) ECLI:EU:C:2025:24, Opinion of AG Capeta, para 85: 'I understand the underlying rationale of *Achmea* to lie in the principle of mutual trust. Accepting the exclusion of certain disputes from the jurisdiction of Member State courts . . . sends the wrong message: that those courts might not be sufficiently independent and impartial to decide disputes brought by investors against Member States'.

87 Case C-386/17 *Liberato* (16 January 2019) ECLI:EU:C:2019:24.

#27 Further along these lines, in ***Agnes Weil***[88] and ***Salvoni***,[89] the ECJ held that the requested Member State court may not even review whether the judgment is within **the material scope of application of the Brussels I regime**, once the judgment is certified by the Member State of origin according to Arts. 54, 53(2) Brussels I Regulation – even if the court of origin, in the main proceedings, did not adjudicate on that issue. Both cases, and before *Trade Agency*,[90] were decided on questions by Member State courts expressly on the **scope of the principle of mutual trust**. Obviously, the Member States had accepted mutual trust as a legal principle of EU law by this point of time.[91]

#28 In ***H Limited***, the ECJ, as a matter of mutual trust, extended the concept of '**judgment**' to a decision by an **English court** on an action upon a judgment from a third state (Jordan),[92] because 'at the very least', that English decision was 'the subject of a **summary hearing**'.[93] The action upon judgment is the functional equivalent to an exequatur decision by a continental European court but is technically based on a new action upon the obligation created by the foreign judgment. The Court acknowledged the functional equivalence to exequatur decisions but nevertheless insisted on overcoming the principle of *exequatur sur exequatur ne vaut* by the principle of mutual trust, as long as there are some minimum adversarial elements in the proceedings that touch upon the underlying claim and subject to the general public policy control by the courts of the requested Member State (as curtailed by EU law). Such violation of a **public policy** would occur, the Court explained further, if the judgment debtor did not have any meaningful opportunity to contest the substance of the underlying claim in the proceedings on the action upon the foreign judgment in the Member State of origin.[94] It seems that this proposition puts Member States under the obligation to alter their exequatur proceedings in order to avoid public policy violations as soon as there is a minimal **adversarial element** in it. These results depart significantly from the Opinion of Advocate General Pikamäe who had approached the case as an issue of challenging a certificate wrongfully attesting the **enforceability** of a 'judgment' within the structures of Article 45 Brussels Ibis-Regulation by characterising the definition of 'judgment' in Article 2(a) of the Brussels Ibis Regulation as an 'essential rule' within the legal order of the European Union, in line with the criteria set out in ***Diageo***

---

88 Case C-361/18 Ágnes Weil (6 June 2019) ECLI:EU:C:2019:473, paras 33 et seq.

89 Case C-347/18 *Salvoni* (4 September 2019) ECLI:EU:C:2019:661, para 30.

90 Case C-619/10 *Trade Agency* (6 September 2012) ECLI:EU:C:2012:531.

91 See also the questions in Case C-262/21 PPU *A v B* (2 August 2021) ECLI:EU:C:2021:640, para 30.

92 Case C-568/20 *H Limited* (7 April 2022) ECLI:EU:C:2022:264, para 30.

93 ibid para 32.

94 To the surprise of many, the requested Member State court in the case at hand did not see such violation; Austrian Supreme Court (*Oberster Gerichtshof*, OGH), decision of 19 May 2022, 3 Ob 71/22w.

Brands[95] and by analogy to ***Eco Swiss***.[96] Thus, the Advocate General undertook to protect the foundations for mutual trust whereas the Court decided to the contrary, namely to stretch the principle beyond plausible limits.

#29 The same occurred in ***London Steamship***.[97] The case dealt with **parallel proceedings** between a Member State court (in Spain) and an **arbitral tribunal** whose award was confirmed by another Member State court (in the UK) that, according to its lex fori, produced a judgment identical to the award. Thus, the question arose whether such a judgment would bar recognition and enforcement of the judgment from Spain under Article 45(1) lit. c Brussels Ibis Regulation. This question was answered in the affirmative in principle, but the Court added that, as a matter of mutual trust, this would only be the case on condition that the **award** did not violate fundamental principles of EU law had it been rendered as a judgment by a Member State court. The Court found that such a hypothetical judgment would have infringed two such fundamental principles in the case at hand, namely the lis pendens rules of the Brussels Ibis Regulation and the principle of privity of **choice of jurisdiction agreements**, and came to the conclusion that therefore the Spanish judgment must be recognised and enforced, despite the affirming judgment upon the contradicting award rendered in the UK.

#30 Whereas *H Limited* and *London Steamship* must certainly appear as overly 'creative' and stretching the principle of mutual trust beyond reasonable limits, some more 'conservative' and more plausible judgments followed and further stabilised the concept. In ***Lufthansa Technik***,[98] the Court confirmed the prohibition of a **review of the jurisdiction of the first court** for Article 21(2) of the European Enforcement Order, in light of its recital 18. In ***BNP Paribas v TR***,[99] the Court confirmed the '**effects doctrine**', first developed in ***Hoffmann v Krieg***,[100] for judgments from other Member States according to which a judgment recognised under the Brussels I Regulation 'must in principle have the same effects in the State in which recognition is sought as it does in the State of origin'. In ***TT v AK***,[101] the Court reiterated its well established position that no Member State court may review the merits of a case or the jurisdiction of another Member State court for the (prospective) assessment under the '**better court**' provision of the Brussels IIbis Regulation. In ***Starlight Shipping***,[102] the ECJ considered damages for seizing the 'wrong' court (in violation of an **exclusive choice of court agree-**

---

95 Case C-681/13 *Diageo Brands* (16 July 2015) ECLI:EU:C:2015:471, see above.
96 Case C-126/97 *Eco Swiss* (1 June 1999) ECLI:EU:C:1999:269.
97 Case C-700/20 *London Steam-Shi*p (20 June 2022) ECLI:EU:C:2022:488.
98 Case C-393/21 *Lufthansa Technik* (16 February 2023) ECLI:EU:C:2023:104, para 46.
99 Case C-567/21 *BNP Paribas v TR* (8 June 2023) ECLI:EU:C:2023:452, paras 46 et seq.
100 Case C-145/86 *Hoffmann v Krieg* (4 February 1988) ECLI:EU:C:1988:61, para 11.
101 Case C-87/22 *TT* (13 July 2023) ECLI:EU:C:2023:571, para 63.
102 Case C-590/21 *Starlight Shipping* (7 September 2023) ECLI:EU:C:2023:633, para 39.

ment) as '**quasi-anti-suit injunctions**' and as such inadmissible under the Brussels system, as these were contrary to the underlying mutual trust rationale 'that every court is to rule on its own jurisdiction'. Another consequence of this strict interpretation, however, is that a remedy for the wrongful seizing of a Member State court can only be brought in the Member State of exactly that court. In ***Inkreal***,[103] the principle of mutual trust merely served as an additional argument to justify the application of the (now) Brussels Ibis-Regulation to constellations where there is no connection with another Member State except for a **forum selection clause** designating the court of another Member State. The normative force of this additional argument is questionable in this context,[104] while the result as such may well be justified,[105] although it was received with criticism.[106] In ***Gjensidige***,[107] the ECJ confirmed that (not even) the **violation of an exclusive choice of court agreement** allows mobilising the **public policy exception** – the violation of party autonomy does not count as an 'essential rule' in the sense of *Diageo Brands*[108] and despite *London Steamship*.[109] Rather, the principle of mutual trust applies and prohibits any review of the jurisdiction of the first Member State court, as long as disregarding Article 25 Brussels Ibis Regulation does not amount to a violation of the right to a fair trial.

#31 Most recently, in ***Real Madrid v Le Monde***,[110] the ECJ continued the 'classical' line of ***Apostolides*** in balancing mutual trust, 'of fundamental importance in EU law', requiring, 'save in **exceptional circumstances**, to consider all other Member States to be complying with EU law and particularly with fundamental rights recognised by EU law',[111] and **EU fundamental rights**, in particular 'respect for the **rights of defence**'[112] against recognition of judgments from other Member

---

103 Case C-566/22 *Inkreal* (8 February 2024) ECLI:EU:C:2024:123, para 35.

104 See Case C-566/22, Inkreal (12 October 2023) ECLI:EU:C:2023:768, Opinion of AG de la Tour, para 33: 'Even if that regulation forms part of a context of strengthening mutual trust and of unifying the conflict-of-law rules, it cannot have the effect of eliminating any distinction between the national and international rules of jurisdiction governed by EU law'.

105 Contrary to choice of law agreements selecting a foreign law, the choice of a foreign forum entails heavy factual consequences for the parties in conducting the future proceedings and therefore may well justify assuming a relevant cross-border element that pushes the case into the scope of the Brussels Ibis Regulation, see also M. Weller, 'The dialectics of delineating EU law from national Member State law: The latest from the CJEU on choice of court agreements (Inkreal, Lastre, Maersk)', in Yearbook of Private International Law 2025/2026 (Brill), forthcoming.

106 See eg the contributions to the online symposium of the EAPIL on *Inkreal*, <https://eapil.org/2024/02/25/online-symposium-on-inkreal/> accessed 5 February 2025.

107 Case C-90/22 *Gjensidige* (21 March 2024) ECLI:EU:C:2024:252.

108 Case C-681/13 *Diageo Brands* (16 July 2015) ECLI:EU:C:2015:471, paras 40 et seq.

109 Case C-700/20 *London Steam-Ship* (20 June 2022) ECLI:EU:C:2022:488.

110 Case C-633/22 *Real Madrid v Le Monde* (4 October 2024) ECLI:EU:C:2024:843, paras 42 et seq.

111 ibid para 42.

112 ibid para 31.

States. 'Accordingly', the Court concludes 'recourse to the public policy exception . . . can be envisaged only where recognition or enforcement . . . would be at variance to an unacceptable degree with the legal order of the Member State in which enforcement is sought inasmuch as it would infringe a fundamental principle'.[113] This conclusion runs into contradiction as it presupposes mutual trust, ie in particular compliance of the Member State of origin with the EU's fundamental rights, 'save in exceptional circumstances', but nevertheless allows a review of compliance with these fundamental rights, without further specifying which 'exceptional circumstances' were present or would be necessary in principle. To put it differently: Under this conception of mutual trust, cases like ***Krombach***[114] seem to be no longer possible, since mutual trust requires the requested Member State, safe in exceptional circumstances, to assume that the Member State of origin complies with EU law. It would be a self-contradicting argument to claim that such exceptional circumstances occur as soon as there is a public policy violation from the perspective of the requested Member State court.[115] Further, the Court does not clearly distinguish between the prohibition of a ***revision au fond*** and its limits for public policy control under the EU's secondary law[116] and the imposition of mutual trust, 'save in exceptional circumstances', under the **EU's primary law**. Whereas Attorney General Szpunar had submitted remarkable reflections on the connection between mutual trust and public policy at least on certain points,[117] thereby acknowledging the strong interaction between these two concepts of **primary and secondary law**, the Court, in essence, left this connection unresolved and simply followed the classical path of public policy control under EU's secondary law, while paying lip-service to the concept of mutual trust. However, primary law pre-empts secondary law. The question therefore remains how the mechanics of mutual trust as developed outside European civil procedural law interact and interfere with public policy exceptions of European secondary civil procedural law. In order to shed light on this question, it is necessary to have a closer look on how the concept of mutual trust established itself as a fundamental principle of primary EU law.

---

113 ibid para 37.

114 Case C-7/98 *Dieter Krombach v André Bamberski* (28 March 2000) ECLI:EU:C:2000:164, refusal of recognition of a French judgment violating the defendant's right to be heard.

115 On this contradiction see M Weller, 'Private International Law and Global Crisis – Protection of the Rule of Law: Enforcement and Mutual Trust' in European Association of Private International Law (EAPIL), *Private International Law and Global Crisis* (forthcoming).

116 Article 34(1) Brussels I Regulation/Article 45(1) lit. a Brussels Ibis Regulation.

117 Case C-633/22 *Real Madrid v Le Monde* (8 February 2024) ECLI:EU:C:2024:127, Opinion of AG Szpunar, paras 60 et seq.

E ECJ Opinion 2/13: Mutual Trust as Fundamental Principle of Primary EU law (Nuanced by Human Rights)

#32 In **Opinion 2/13** of the ECJ on the accession of the European Union to the ECHR,[118] the ECJ explained that:

> '[t]he principle of mutual trust between the Member States is of fundamental importance in EU law [. . .].[119] That principle requires [. . .] to consider all the other Member States to be complying with EU law and particularly with the fundamental rights recognised by EU law [. . .] Thus, when implementing EU law, the Member States may, under EU law, be required to presume that fundamental rights have been observed by the other Member States, so that not only may they not demand a higher level of national protection of fundamental rights from another Member State than that provided by EU law, but, save in exceptional cases, they may not check whether that other Member State has actually, in a specific case, observed the fundamental rights guaranteed by the EU'.[120]

Hence, the Court concluded that:

> '[i]n so far as the ECHR would, in requiring the EU and the Member States to be considered Contracting Parties not only in their relations with Contracting Parties which are not Member States of the EU but also in their relations with each other, including where such relations are governed by EU law, require a Member State to check that another Member State has observed fundamental rights, even though EU law imposes an obligation of mutual trust between those Member States, accession is liable to upset the underlying balance of the EU and undermine the autonomy of EU law'.[121]

This is why *(inter alia)* the ECJ held that **accession of the EU to the ECHR** would be inadmissible.

#33 However, in ***Avotiņš***,[122] the ECtHR rejected, once more,[123] but this time in the context of **judicial cooperation** in civil and commercial matters, the claim made by the ECJ in its Opinion 2/13 that mutual trust trumps human rights. In this case, the applicant was a defendant in **default proceedings** in Cyprus. The successful

---

118 Opinion 2/13 *Accession to the ECHR* (18 December 2014) ECLI:EU:C:2014:2454.

119 Confirmed, eg, by Case C-633/22 *Real Madrid v Le Monde* (4 October 2024) ECLI:EU:C:2024:843, para 42.

120 Opinion 2/13 *Accession to the ECHR* (18 December 2014) ECLI:EU:C:2014:2454, paras 191–192.

121 ibid para 194.

122 *Avotiņš* v *Latvia* App no 17502/07 (ECtHR, 23 May 2016).

123 Before, the ECtHR had already decided along these lines, albeit less explicitly, about the human rights implications of judicial cooperation between Greece and other Member States in asylum matters; *M.S.S.* v *Belgium and Greece* App no 30696/09 (ECtHR, 21 January 2011), para 338. Shortly afterwards, the ECJ adopted this line in its Judgment in Joined Cases C-411/10 and C-493/10 *NS v Secretary of State for the Home Department and ME et al. v Refugee Applications Commissioner and Minister for Justice* (21 December 2011) EU:C:2011:865.

claimant sought to get the judgment recognised and enforced in Latvia against the applicant under the Brussels I Regulation. The applicant argued that he had not been properly served with process in the proceedings in Cyprus and hence argued that recognition must be denied according to Article 34(2), of the Brussels I Regulation. The Latvian courts nevertheless granted recognition and enforcement. Thereupon, the applicant lodged a complaint against Latvia for violating Article 6(1) ECHR. The ECtHR observed:

> '[T]he Brussels I Regulation is based in part on mutual-recognition mechanisms which themselves are founded on the principle of mutual trust between the member States of the European Union . . . . The Court is mindful of the importance of the mutual-recognition mechanisms for the construction of the area of freedom, security and justice referred to in Article 67 of the TFEU, and of the mutual trust which they require . . . . Nevertheless, the methods used to create that area must not infringe the fundamental rights of the persons affected by the resulting mechanisms.'[124]

#34 Nonetheless, the Court held, in direct response to Opinion 2/13 of the ECJ, that:

> '[l]imiting to exceptional cases the power of the State in which recognition is sought to review the observance of fundamental rights by the State of origin of the judgment could, in practice, run counter to the requirement imposed by the Convention according to which the court in the State addressed must at least be empowered to conduct a review commensurate with the gravity of any serious allegation of a violation of fundamental rights in the State of origin, in order to ensure that the protection of those rights is not manifestly deficient'.[125]

Thus, a court must, under all circumstances, even within the scope of the **'Bosphorus presumption'**,[126]

124 ibid paras 113–114.

125 ibid para 114.

126 Even when applying EU law, the Contracting States to the ECHR remain bound by the obligations they freely entered into on acceding to the Convention. However, those obligations must be assessed in the light of the presumption established by the ECtHR in *Bosphorus* (*Bosphorus Hava Yolları Turizm ve Ticaret Anonim Şirketi* v *Ireland [GC]* App no 45036/98 (ECtHR, 30 June 2005)) and further developed in *Michaud* (*Michaud* v *France* App no 12323/11 (ECtHR 6 December 2012)): the protection of fundamental rights afforded by the legal system of the EU is in principle equivalent to that for which the Convention provided. Therefore, if EU law requires an EU Member State eg to recognise a judgment of another Member State without any margin of manoeuvre and if at the same time the full potential of the supervisory mechanism provided for by EU law is deployed in the Member State of origin, the strict obligation for the Member States of destination to apply EU law is compatible with the ECHR, even though EU law excludes the examination of the compatibility of the judgment with the ECHR. Arguably, the application of the public policy exception still provides for such a 'margin of manoeuvre' on behalf of the Member States, see eg G Cuniberti, Le fondement de l'effet des jugements étrangers, in Collected Courses of the Hague Academy of International Law – Recueil des cours, vol 394 (Brill 2019) 87, para 295.

'[v]erify that the principle of mutual recognition is not applied automatically and mechanically to the detriment of fundamental rights – which, the CJEU has also stressed, must be observed in this context. In this spirit, where the courts of a State which is both a Contracting Party to the Convention and a member State of the European Union are called upon to apply a mutual-recognition mechanism established by EU law, they must give full effect to that mechanism where the protection of Convention rights cannot be considered manifestly deficient. However, if a serious and substantiated complaint is raised before them to the effect that the protection of a Convention right has been manifestly deficient and that this situation cannot be remedied by European Union law, they cannot refrain from examining that complaint on the sole ground that they are applying EU law'.[127]

#35 Remarkably, and almost paradoxically, while mutual trust has reached the status of a **constitutional principle** of the highest rank as it enables and carries the *raison d'être* of the EU – integration –,[128] a high degree of mutual trust, resulting in far-reaching obligations to recognise and enforce, inter alia, juridical acts from other Member States, needs effective **human rights guarantees** in all participating states, but at the same time effective human rights guarantees exclude a maximisation of mutual trust – **'no blind trust'**.[129] Thus, residual control (**'trust management'**) is indispensable.

#36 In the following, this concept of **primary law** unfolded mainly in constellations of judicial cooperation in asylum and criminal matters where there were no express public policy exceptions. For example, in the recent case of ***X and Y*** concerning judicial cooperation under the **European Arrest Warrant** mechanism,[130] the ECJ explained:[131]

'When Member States implement EU law, they may, under EU law, be required to presume that fundamental rights have been observed by the other Member States, so that not only may they not demand a higher level of national protection of fundamental rights from another Member State than that provided by EU law, but also, save in exceptional cases, they may not check whether that other Member State has actually, in a specific case, observed the fundamental rights guaranteed by the European Union'.

127 *Avotiņš* v *Latvia* App no 17502/07 (ECtHR, 23 May 2016), para 116.

128 See once more Opinion 2/13 *Accession to the ECHR* (18 December 2014) ECLI:EU:C:2014:2454, para 172.

129 K Lenaerts (President of the Court of Justice of the European Union), 'La vie après l'avis: Exploring the Principle of Mutual Trust (Yet Not Blind Trust)' (2017) 54 Common Market Law Review 805.

130 Council Framework Decision No 2002/584/JHA of 13 June 2002 on the European Arrest Warrant and the Surrender Procedure Between Member States [2002] OJ L190/1; For an overview of the impact of mutual trust on EU judicial cooperation in criminal matters, starting from recognition of *ne bis in idem* in the Schengen Area, see C Cocq, *Mutual Trust in Regional and Interregional Cooperation on Counterterrorism* (Springer 2023) 82 et seq.

131 Joined Cases C-562/21 PPU and C-563/21 PPU *X and Y* (22 February 2022) ECLI:EU:C:2022:100, para 41.

As is known from earlier cases such as ***N.S.*** (asylum)[132] and ***Aranyosi*** (arrest warrant),[133] such 'exceptional cases' require a **'systemic deficiency'**.[134] Systemic deficiencies are, so far, not required in judicial cooperation in civil matters, in order to rely on the public policy exceptions in secondary law. Thus, **two different strands of judicial cooperation** have evolved in light of the principle of mutual trust, one for European civil procedural law and one for the other forms of judicial cooperation. It would seem necessary to reconcile these strands conceptually.[135] Since the 'systemic deficiency' requirement is an element of primary law, it appears likely that it will affect the secondary law of European civil procedural law, sooner or later.

F Conclusions

#37 Over time, mutual trust has elevated to one of the most fundamental principles of the European Union's civil procedural law on judicial cooperation in civil and commercial matters (and beyond). It rests on the assumption that each Member State will comply with the **fundamental values** laid down in Article 2 TEU, with the fundamental rights and principles of EU law as well as EU law in its entirety. In case of **violations**, mutual trust rests on the assumption that such violations can and must be corrected within the court system of the Member State affected, including, as a central element, the preliminary reference procedure to the ECJ under Article 267 TFEU. Thus, the proper functioning of each of the Member States' judiciaries in all of its dimensions is obviously crucial for upholding mutual trust. The reality is sometimes different.

#38 Nevertheless, the ECJ has transcended its initial status of an explanatory and interpretative principle of EU secondary law of judicial cooperation and has established it as an element of the **EU's constitutional identity**, 'safe in exceptional circumstances'. This exception operates functionally as a public policy defence against obligations to trust in principle (**'no blind trust'**) and attributes to the Member States a key function in exercising a residual control vis-à-vis each other.

---

132 Joined Cases C-411/10 and C-493/10 *NS v Secretary of State for the Home Department and ME et al. v Refugee Applications Commissioner and Minister for Justice* (21 December 2011) EU:C:2011:865, paras 83 et seq. in the meantime, this jurisprudence has found its way into Article 3(2) subsection 1 of the Regulation (EU) No 604/2013 (Dublin III) Establishing the Criteria and Mechanisms for Determining the Member State Responsible for Examining an Application for International Protection [2013] OJ L180/31.

133 Joined Cases C-404/15 and C-659/15 PPU *Aranyosi and Căldăraru* (5 April 2016) ECLI:EU:C:2016:198, para 89; see also Case C-216/18 PPU *LM* (25 July 2018) ECLI:EU:C:2018:586, para 61.

134 See also, most recently, German Constitutional Court, judgment of 24 January 2025, 2 BvR 1103/24 – Maja T (non-binary person), wrongfully transferred to Hungary.

135 See Weller (n 115).

In that mutual trust functions as a **meta-principle** for coordinating and integrating the Member States' judiciaries and legal systems in this manner, it has reached an importance that resembles other fundamental principles of EU law such as eg its **direct effect**. Furthermore, it will not be too far-fetched to claim a **reverse vertical effect** of the principle of mutual trust, grounded in Articles 4(2) and 4(3) TEU to the effect that the EU must, to a certain degree, trust its Member States as well, although this dimension of the principle of mutual trust has not been unfolded yet.

#39 At the same time, mutual trust has shaped and pushed the **secondary law** on judicial cooperation in civil and commercial matters in a multitude of aspects, sometimes beyond convincing limits. Based on structures of general international civil procedural law, in particular on a classical application of the public policy exception, the normative impositions of the principle of mutual trust have manifested themselves in a different way than in other fields of judicial cooperation. It is an open question whether these differences call for **consolidation** or are justified by different contexts. It seems that the EU has, largely unnoticed by herself, reinvented on the level of primary law a wheel ('safe in exceptional circumstances') functionally well-known from private international law ('public policy exception') for areas of judicial cooperation in **administrative and criminal law**.[136] Whereas each of these mechanisms of 'doing similarity in difference' operates under a logic of 'trust management' (far-reaching trust but residual control), the prognosis submitted here is that mutual trust as an element of EU primary law will continue turning the fundaments of the EU's secondary procedural law and private international law, although for the moment reconciling interpretations may still be possible.

References

Ahmed M and Beaumont P, 'Exclusive Choice of Court Agreements: Some Issues on the Hague Convention on Choice of Court Agreements and its Relationship with the Brussels I Recast Especially Anti-suit Injunctions, Concurrent Proceedings and the Implications of BREXIT' (2017) 13 Journal of Private International Law 386.

Cocq C, *Mutual Trust in Regional and Interregional Cooperation on Counterterrorism* (Springer 2023).

Cuniberti G, 'Le fondement de l'effet des jugements étrangers' in Collected Courses of the Hague Academy of International Law – Recueil des cours, vol 394 (Brill 2019) 87.

Drinóczi T and Faraguna P, 'The Constitutional Identity of the EU as a Counterbalance for Unconstitutional Constitutional Identities of the Member States' in European Yearbook of Constitutional Law 2022 (Springer 2023) 57.

136 And present in other constellations, again under a distinct label, see eg the relation between Article 2 TEU as the principal assumption and limited exceptions via the 'national identities' of the Member States, Article 4(2) TEU.

Ernst W, 'The Free Movement of Goods and Services Within the European Economic Community in the Context of the World Economy' (1981) 137 *Zeitschrift für die gesamte Staatswissenschaft* 556.

Feuerbach PJA, 'Über die Rechtskraft und Vollstreckung eines von einem auswärtigen Gerichte gesprochenen Erkenntnisses' in PJA Feuerbach, *Themis oder Beiträge zur Gesetzgebung* (Krüll 1812) 77.

Gilbert M, 'The Treaties of Rome' in E Jones, A Menon and S Weatherill (eds), *The Oxford Handbook of the European Union* (OUP 2012) 99.

Hess B, *Europäisches Zivilprozessrecht* (De Gruyter 2010).

Jenard P, *Report on the Convention of 27 September 1968 on Jurisdiction and the Enforcement of Judgments in Civil and Commercial Matters* [1979] OJ C59/3.

Kohler C, 'Vertrauen und Kontrolle im europäischen Justizraum für Zivilsachen' (2016) 19 Zeitschrift für europarechtliche Studien *(ZEuS)* 135.

Kramer X, 'Cross-border Enforcement in the EU: Mutual Trust versus Fair Trial? Towards Principles of European Civil Procedure' (2011) 1 International Journal of Procedural Law 202.

—— *Procedure Matters: Construction and Deconstructivism in European Civil Procedure* (Eleven International Publishing 2013).

Lenaerts K, 'La vie après l'avis: Exploring the Principle of Mutual Trust (Yet Not Blind Trust)' (2017) 54 Common Market Law Review 805.

Menuet L, *Le discours sur l'espace judiciaire européen: analyse du discours et sémantique argumentative linguistique* (Université Libre de Bruxelles 2006).

Nicolaidis K, 'Trusting the Poles? Constructing Europe through Mutual Recognition' (2007) 14 Journal of European Public Policy 682.

Nicolaidis K and Shaffer G, 'Transnational Mutual Recognition Regimes: Governance without Global Government' (2005) 68 Law and Contemporary Problems 263.

Pluyette G, 'La convention de Bruxelles et les droits de la défense' in *Etudes offertes à Pierre Bellet* (Litec 1991) 427.

Raape L, *Deutsches Internationales Privatrecht* (Franz Vahlen 1938).

Savigny FC von, *System des heutigen römischen Rechts*, vol VIII (Veit 1849).

Schärtl C, *Das Spiegelbildprinzip im Rechtsverkehr mit ausländischen Staatenverbindungen* (Mohr Siebeck 2005).

Thiemeyer G, 'Supranationalität als Novum in der Geschichte der internationalen Politik der fünfziger Jahre' (1998) 4(2) Journal of European Integration History 5.

Von Bogdandy A, *Strukturwandel des öffentlichen Rechts: Entstehung und Demokratisierung der europäischen Gesellschaft* (Suhrkamp 2022).

Weller M, 'Mutual Trust within the Judicial Cooperation in Civil Matters: A Normative Cornerstone – A Factual Chimera – A Constitutional Challenge' (2017) 35 Netherlands Journal of Private International Law 1.

—— 'Mutual Trust: In Search of the Future of Private International Law' (2015) 11 Journal of Private International Law 65.

—— '"Mutual Trust": A Suitable Foundation for Private International Law in Regional Integration Communities and Beyond?' in Collected Courses of the Hague Academy of International Law – Recueil des cours, vol 423 (Brill 2022).

—— 'Private International Law and Global Crisis – Protection of the Rule of Law: Enforcement and Mutual Trust' in European Association of Private International Law (EAPIL), *Private International Law and Global Crisis* (forthcoming).

Burkhard Hess*

Chapter 5
Access to Justice as a Fundamental Principle of European Union Procedural Law

A Access to Justice: Defining the Concept

I A Worldwide Movement in the 1970s and 1980s

#1 Access to civil justice was not a topic when the 1968 Brussels Convention was drafted in the 1960s. In 1973, when the Convention entered into force, ***Cappelletti* and *Garth*** had not yet published their multi-volume treatise on access to justice (1978–1979) that has garnered significant attention ever since its appearance.[1] *Cappelletti* and *Garth* did not refer to their project as a 'new doctrinal' approach, but rather a 'movement' to highlight its political dimension.[2] The 'access to justice' concept looked at barriers between justice-seekers and the justice system; from the very beginning, it focused on disadvantaged or vulnerable persons such as consumers or tenants; later, on indigenous persons, women and per se litigants. The multi-volume study edited by *Cappelletti* and *Garth* was not a homogenous doctrinal *corpus*, but rather a collection of articles on a multitude of topics related to civil justice, like legal aid, concentration of the proceedings, conciliation and collective litigation.[3] Against this background, the authors conceived a complex strategy to overcome barriers to justice in **three waves** or steps: the first aimed at developing and enlarging legal aid; the second looked at the representation/defence of 'diffuse interests' by collective litigation, through class ac-

---

1 M Cappelletti and B Garth (eds), *Access to Justice, vol I: A World Survey* (Sijthoff & Noordhoff 1978–1979) 6ff; B Hess, Dispute Resolution in the 21st Century, Recueil des Cours de l'Academie de La Haye (to be published in 2026), Chapter 2, paras 52ff.

2 In this regard, the project was very much 'a child of its time', that is to say, the welfare state of the late 1970s. Consequently, Cappelletti and Garth addressed legal aid as a means to overcome barriers to the justice system, cf M Cappelletti, B Garth and N Trocker, 'Access to Justice, Variations and Continuity of a World-Wide Movement' (1982) 46 RabelsZ 664.

3 M Cappelletti and B Garth (eds), *vol 1: Access to Justice, A World Survey*; *vol 2: Promising Institutions*; *vol 3: Emerging Issues and Perspectives*; *vol 4: Anthropological Perspective, Patterns of Conflict Management* (Giuffrè 1978–1979).

***Corresponding author: Burkhard Hess,** University of Vienna, e-mail: burkhard.hess@univie.ac.at

https://doi.org/10.1515/9783110781632-005

tions or actions of consumer organisation; the third wave proposed to simplify proceedings and to resort to conciliation (in today's terms: ADR).[4]

#2 Scientifically and practically, *Cappelletti* and *Garth's* project stood out for its novel perspective. It moved away from the classical approach of procedural law that addressed mostly institutional and technical questions of civil procedure (like: court structures, parties, elements of the lawsuit, res judicata, appeals, etc.) and instead considered the users of the system and their specific needs.[5] In addition, the applied methods were different, as the authors were open to techniques borrowed from social sciences, and especially to empirical and statistical research.[6] The project grew over time as new methods and more data became available. The increasing mechanisation and digitalisation of civil procedure facilitated the use of statistics; empirical research based on interviews generated qualitative data to be evaluated. **Legal sociology**[7] was the methodological angle backing the new approach.

II The Fourth 'Wave of the Movement'

#3 Today, the legal literature is discussing a '**fourth wave**' of access to justice. The debate has shifted to current barriers to access to justice such as lack of information, complicated legal language, parties' vulnerability and financial limitations.[8] These aspects are not entirely new, but they pose different challenges given the increasing digitalisation of dispute resolution processes. As such, the 'access to justice' movement is not restricted to being a phenomenon only of the late 20th century but is still on the current political agenda. In 2015, the UN endorsed it formally as self-standing Goal 16 in the Sustainable Goals for 2030.[9]

4 R Caponi and J Novak, 'Access to Justice' in B Hess and S Law (eds), *Implementing EU Consumer Law by National Procedural Law* (Beck/Hart 2019) 63, 63f.

5 R Macdonald, 'Access to Civil Justice' in P Cane and HM Kritzer (eds), *The Oxford Handbook of Empirical Legal Research* (OUP 2010) 492, 511ff; M Villamarín López, 'Access to Justice as a Fundamental Right' in B Hess and others (eds), *Comparative Procedural Law and Justice (Part III Chapter 2)*, paras 23ff <https://www.cplj.org/publications/3-2-access-to-justice-and-costs-of-litigation> accessed 5 March 2025.

6 Volume 1 was based on a questionnaire that had been sent to national reporters in different jurisdictions. In the questionnaire, the authors explicitly asked for statistical data.

7 The usual German expression of that time was '*Rechtstatsachenforschung*'. It should be mentioned here that the translation of 'access to justice' in some European languages proved difficult. One example is German, where '*Zugang zur Justiz*' has rather a physical connotation (access to the court building), '*Zugang zum Recht*' was one translation that excluded the justice system (which was meant, but the 'justice system' was missing). It retranslates as 'access to law'. Finally, some authors would not accept any translation.

8 Villamarín López (n 5) para 31ff with further references.

9 In 2023, the OECD adopted a 'Recommendation on Access to Justice and People-centered Justice', cf Villamarín López (n 5) para 33 with further references.

III The Constitutional Dimension

#4 There is a second layer of access to justice that derives from constitutional and human rights laws.[10] Here, the right to effective judicial protection is embracing 'access to justice' as a fundamental right. According to Article 6(1) of the European Convention on Human Rights, 'in the determination of his civil rights and obligations . . . everyone is entitled to a fair and public hearing within a reasonable time by an independent and impartial tribunal established by law'. Already in 1975, the ECtHR held in *Golder v UK*[11] that **Article 6 ECHR** includes the right to institute litigation. In 1979, the ECtHR extended said provision expressly to legal aid.[12] By way of consequence, the additional guarantees of Article 6 ECHR reinforce access to justice, especially the **right to timely and effective judicial protection,**[13] and the **right to enforcement of a judgment.**[14] Thus, **constitutionalisation** gave 'access to justice' additional appeal and influence.[15]

#5 A further development took place after the millennium. In order to combat structural deficiencies and delays in its Member States, the Council of Europe set up the **European Commission for the Efficiency of Justice (CEPEJ).**[16] CEPEJ collects and compares **statistical data** on the performance of justice systems in the Member States of the Council of Europe and regularly publishes surveys on the performance of the justice systems in Europe. However, the activities of CEPEJ are not limited to **benchmarking** and evaluating justice systems. It equally supports and advises the Member States of the Council of Europe on judicial reforms

---

10 *Cappelletti* and *Garth* also resorted to the human rights foundation of access to justice. They wrote: 'Effective access to justice can be seen as the most basic requirement – the most basic 'human right' – of a modern egalitarian legal system which purports to guarantee and not merely proclaim, the legal rights of all.' M Cappelletti and B Garth (eds), *Access to Justice*, Vol I (Giuffrè 1978) 6.

11 *Golder v United Kingdom* App no 4451/70 (ECtHR, 21 February 1975) ECLI:CE:ECHR:1975:0221JUD000445170, para 26ff.

12 *Airey v Ireland* (1980) 2 EHRR 305.

13 *Kudła v Poland* App no 30210/96 (ECtHR, 26 October 2000) ECLI:CE:ECHR:2000:1026JUD003021096, para 152.

14 *Hornsby v Greece* App no 18357/91 (ECtHR, 19 March 1997) ECLI:CE:ECHR:1997:0319JUD001835791, para 41; *Scordino v Italy* App no 36813/97 (ECtHR, 29 March 2006) ECLI:CE:ECHR:2006:0329JUD003681397, para 19.

15 T Domej, 'Constitutionalisation and Fundamentalisation of Access to Justice' in B Hess and others (eds), *Comparative Procedural Law and Justice (Part IV Chapter 2)*, para 48ff <cplj.org/a/4-2> accessed 5 March 2025.

16 B Hess, 'International Civil Litigation in the 21st Century', General Course at The Hague Academy of International Law (Recueil des Cours de l'Academie de La Haye – forthcoming 2026) Chapter 2.

by means of expert opinions, best practices and specific guides.[17] The collection of data permits lawmakers to assess the impacts of potential reforms.

#6 Since 2012, the **EU Justice Scoreboard** has provided even larger amounts of data regarding EU civil justice systems.[18] As a result, lawmaking in dispute resolution has changed. Legislators now frequently resort to statistical and social data when they prepare reforms. **Impact assessments** have become a new standard in lawmaking – especially in European Union law.[19] Comparative procedural law has also become much more sensitive to **empirical research**.

B Access to Justice in European Law in the 1980s and 1990s

#7 To properly look at the development of access to justice as a concept of European law, one needs to distinguish two different periods: before the Europeanisation of private international and procedural law by the Amsterdam Treaty (1998), and, additionally, after the entry into force of the Treaty of Lisbon (2009).

I The Brussels Regime

#8 For obvious reasons, the **Brussels Convention of 1968** could not address access to justice as such: the 'movement' started 10 years after its conception. However, the Convention already provided so-called protective heads of jurisdiction for insurance takers, employees and consumers. Their jurisdictional access to justice was facilitated in two ways: on the one hand, lawsuits against them could only be filed at their domicile. On the other hand, they could seize the courts of their place of domicile to sue their professional counterparty. Still, it is interesting to note that 'access to justice' as an underlying objective of the rules, has only been

17 Examples: CEPEJ, 'Guidelines on the Creation of Judicial Maps to Support Access to Justice within a Quality Judicial System' (21 June 2013); Council of Europe/CEPEJ, 'Guidelines on the Organisation and Accessibility of Court Premises' (12 December 2014); Council of Europe/CEPEJ, 'Checklist for Promoting the Quality of Justice and the Court' (3 July 2008) eg, at 19–25, including interpretation, access to information, accessibility of court judgments.

18 A Dori, *The Governance of EU Justice Reforms* (Nomos 2025) 152ff.

19 B Hess and M Requejo Isidro, 'El invisible colegio de juristas internacionales en el Derecho internacional privado de hoy' (2024) 16 Cuardernos de Derecho Transnacional 965.

mentioned once, and recently as 2024, in the case-law of the CJEU regarding these heads of jurisdiction.[20] However, functionally, the concept had already become a part of EC procedural law in cross-border settings.[21]

II Consumer Protection

#9 Direct references to 'access to justice' were originally found in the legislative activities concerning **consumer protection**. Since 1993, the European Communities had limited competences in consumer protection, as the Economic Community should 'contribute' to the promotion of consumer protection.[22] However, already in the 1980s, the Commission had published a concept paper on consumers' access to justice.[23] After the entry into force of the Maastricht Treaty, the Commission published a Green Paper on consumer access to justice and the settlement of consumer disputes in the internal market in 1993;[24] this was followed by a communication on an 'Action Plan on consumer access to justice and the settlement of consumer disputes in the internal market' in 1996.[25] Both programmes provided for far-reaching measures to improve judicial and extrajudicial redress in consumer cases. A tangible result was the Directive on representative actions (Directive 98/27/EC) providing for injunctive relief.[26] Since the mid-1990s, consumer policy has primarily focused on out-of-court dispute resolution. The Commission developed minimum standards for the implementation of **ADR procedures** and for bodies in charge of resolving consumer disputes, which the Council finally adopted as a (non-binding) recommendation.[27]

#10 This overview demonstrates that the main activities of the EU Commission in consumer protection remained limited to informal measures (as opposed to binding

20 Case C-774/22 *JX v FTI Touristik GmbH* ECLI:EU:C:2024:646, para 46; B Hess, *Europäisches Zivilprozessrecht* (2nd edn, de Gruyter 2021), para 6.118ff (addressing consumer protection).

21 It should be mentioned that the CJEU did not enlarge the protective heads of jurisdiction from individual claims to collective litigation. In *Schrems v Facebook* the Grand Chamber held that the EU lawmaker should decide upon the extension of collective redress under the head of jurisdiction of Article 18; Case C-498/16 *Schrems II* (18 January 2018) ECLI:EU:C:2018:37.

22 In practical terms, binding lawmaking requires an additional full competence (like Article 114 TFEU); under Article 169 TFEU, the Commission can only adopt (non-binding) recommendations; Hess (n 20) para 2.50.

23 M Tenreiro, 'L'accès du consommateur à la justice: une perspective européenne' in G Barrett (ed), *Creating a European Judicial Space* (ERA 2001) 111ff.

24 COM (1993) 576 final, cf PG Mayr and M Weber 'Europäische Initiativen zur Förderung der alternativen Streitbeilegung' (2007) 26 Zeitschrift für Rechtsvergleichung 163, 165, 167.

25 COM (1996) 13 final.

26 [1998] OJ L166/51ff, cf Hess (n 20) para 11.61ff.

27 Commission Recommendation of 30 March 1998 on the principles applicable to the bodies responsible for the out-of-court settlement of consumer disputes [1998] OJ L 115/31; Hess (n 20) para 12.17ff.

secondary Union law). Content-wise, however, the Commission was taking up the ideas of the 'access to justice' movement. Another area where the concept was implemented was environmental protection where the Union later ratified the **Aarhus Convention** that permits collective redress in administrative court proceedings.[28]

C Access to Justice under the Treaty of Amsterdam and the Lisbon Treaty

I Access to Justice as a Regulatory Concept in Legal Aid

#11 The legislative framework changed under the **Treaty of Amsterdam**. Article 65 of the Treaty conferred genuine **competences** in private international and procedural law to the Union. After 2000, the EC Commission embarked on wide-ranging legislative activities focused on cross-border litigation.[29] The term 'access to justice' was expressly mentioned in the proposal of the EC-Commission for the directive on legal aid. It stated:

> 'It is a corollary of the freedoms guaranteed by the EC Treaty that a citizen must be able, in order to resolve disputes arising from his activities while exercising any of those freedoms, to bring or defend actions in the courts of a Member State in the same way as nationals of that Member State. In many circumstances, such a right to access to justice can be effectively exercised only when legal aid is available under given conditions . . . In the absence of Community legislation, it is for each Member State's legal system to lay down detailed procedural rules to safeguard the rights which individuals derive from Community law, including those relating to legal aid. However, such rules may neither discriminate against those to whom Community law gives the right to equal treatment nor restrict the fundamental freedoms guaranteed by Community law'.[30]

#12 The Commission's proposal did not mature in a general instrument on legal aid but instead in Council **Directive 2003/8/EC** to improve access to justice in cross-border disputes – only[31] – by establishing minimum common rules relating to **legal aid** for such disputes.[32] By contrast, this Directive is not restricted to legal

28 Article 9 Aarhus Convention, ratified by Decision 2005/3701EC of the Council of 17 February 2005 [2005] OJ L124/1.

29 Hess (n 20) para 1.37ff.

30 EU Commission, 'Green Paper on Legal Aid in Civil Matters' COM (2000) 51 final, 4.

31 In 2015, the CJEU interpreted Directive (EC) 8/2003 in the light of Article 47 CFR and referred several times to its objective of granting access to justice; see Case C-670/15 *Šalplachta* (15 December 2015) ECLI:EU:C:2017:594, paras 25, 29 and 35.

32 [2003] OJ L26/41; Hess (n 20) para 8.85ff.

aid for consumers, but applies to all individual parties.[33] It establishes a kind of 'country of origin' approach as legal aid is granted to litigants before the courts of other Member States according to the standards of their countries of domicile. In any event, the practical importance of the Directive has remained limited, as legal aid is less and less available in the EU Member States.[34]

II Constitutional Dimensions

#13 The limited scope of application of Directive 2003/8/EC to cross-border situations stands inconsistently with Article 47(3) CFR, which guarantees **legal aid** in the EU Member States in all proceedings where Union rights are enforced.[35] In Case C-279/09 *DEB*,[36] however, the CJEU refrained from strengthening the fundamental guarantee of Article 47(3) CFR when it primarily referred to the **principle of proportionality** permitting a restriction of legal aid and left it to the national court:

> 'to ascertain whether the conditions for granting legal aid constitutes a limitation on the right of access to the courts which undermine the very core of that right; whether they pursue a legitimate aim; and whether there is a reasonable relationship of proportionality between the means employed and the legitimate aim which it is sought to achieve'.[37]

---

33 W Vandenbussche and P Taelman, 'Consumer Protection Proceedings' in B Hess and others (eds), *Comparative Procedural Law and Justice* (Part XII Chapter 6), para 225 <cplj.org/a/12-6> accessed 10 March 2025.

34 P Butler and S Menétrey, 'Public Funding (Legal Aid)' in B Hess and others (eds), *Comparative Procedural Law and Justice* (Part III Chapter 6), para 50ff <cplj.org/a/3-6> accessed 10 March 2025.

35 Pursuant to Article 47 CFR, 'legal aid should be made available to those who lack sufficient resources in so far as such aid is necessary to ensure effective access to justice'.

36 Case C-279/09 *DEB Deutsche Energiehandels- und Beratungsgesellschaft mbH v Bundesrepublik Deutschland* (22 December 2010) ECLI:EU:C:2010:811, para 60.

37 ibid para 61, the CJEU added: 'In making that assessment, the national court must take into consideration the subject-matter of the litigation; whether the applicant has a reasonable prospect of success; the importance of what is at stake for the applicant in the proceedings; the complexity of the applicable law and procedure; and the applicant's capacity to represent himself effectively. In order to assess the proportionality, the national court may also take account of the amount of the costs of the proceedings in respect of which advance payment must be made and whether or not those costs might represent an insurmountable obstacle to access to the courts. (62) With regard more specifically to legal persons, the national court may take account of their situation. The court may therefore take into consideration, inter alia, the form of the legal person in question and whether it is profit-making or non-profit-making; the financial capacity of the partners or shareholders; and the ability of those partners or shareholders to obtain the sums necessary to institute legal proceedings.'

#14 This notwithstanding, access to justice has become part of the constitutional guarantee of Article 47 CFR – in parallel with those afforded by Article 6 ECHR.[38] Here, access to justice is part of the fundamental **right to effective judicial protection** before an independent and impartial tribunal. In this regard, the CJEU has held that mandatory non-binding dispute settlement is permitted as long as litigation before state courts is possible.[39] Finally, at the constitutional level, litigation and **ADR** are not on the same footing since ADR cannot fully substitute for effective judicial protection by state courts.

III Access to Justice in the European Area of Justice

#15 For the practical implementation of access to justice, two instruments of judicial cooperation in civil matters are of the essence: the **European Small Claims Regulation**, and the **European Maintenance Regulation**. Both instruments improve access to justice in cross-border constellations, particularly in cases where the individual often lacks resources to initiate litigation. Each of them operates differently. The Small Claims Regulation provides for a self-standing, simplified procedure applicable to civil claims up to 5,000 EUR.[40] It is to be expected that digitalisation will make this procedure work more smoothly, and that, as a consequence, it is more broadly resorted to than today.[41] The Maintenance Regulation applies to the most vulnerable parties (often minors) in cross-border settings, where usually small amounts of money to be paid monthly are at stake.[42] The particularity of the mechanism involved lies with the fact that the plaintiffs are often represented or supported by public authorities. Interestingly, the facilitation of access to justice has been a recurring element in the CJEU's jurisprudence regarding the Maintenance Regulation.[43]

#16 The **Lisbon Treaty (2009)** strengthened access to justice as a foundational concept in several aspects. Reference to 'access to justice' is now found in two provi-

---

38 European Agency for Fundamental Rights and Council of Europe, *Handbook on European Law Relating to Access to Justice* (2016).

39 Joined Cases C-317/08 to C-320/08 *Rosalba Alassini v Telecom Italia SpA, Filomena Califano v Wind SpA, Lucia Anna Giorgia Iacono v Telecom Italia SpA* and *Multiservice Srl v Telecom Italia SpA* (18 March 2010), para 67.

40 Regulation (EC) 861/07 [2007] OJ L199/1 amended by Regulation (EU) 2421/2015 [2015] OJ L341/1; Hess (n 20) para 10.93 ff.

41 B Hess, 'Digital Judicial Cooperation' in M Fogt (ed), *Private International Law in an Era of Change* (Edward Elgar 2024) 155, 162ff.

42 Regulation (EC) 4/2009 [2009] OJ L7/1; Hess (n 20) para 7.141ff.

43 Case C-540/19 *Landkreis Harburg* (17 September 2020) ECLI:EU:C:2020:732, para 37; Cases C-400/13 and C-408/13 *Sanders* and *Huber* (18 December 2014) ECLI:EU:C:2014:2461, para 29 and Case C-41/19 *FX* (4 June 2020) ECLI:EU:C:2020:425, para 40.

sions of the TFEU itself. To start with, Article 67(4) TFEU describes the objectives of **judicial cooperation** in civil matters as follows: 'The Union shall facilitate access to justice, in particular through the principle of mutual recognition of judicial and extrajudicial decisions in civil matters'.[44]

#17 In addition, access to justice is mentioned in Article 81(2) lit c TFEU as one area of lawmaking falling within the remit of **EU competences** in (cross-border) civil justice. It should be noted, however, that the new wording of the Treaty has not led to an increase in the legislative activities under the enlarged head of competence. In legal commentaries, the concept has not gained interest either.[45]

IV Access to Justice in EU Consumer Law

#18 In fact, one could say that, quite to the contrary, the concept has lost much guiding influence, as **Directive (EU) 2013/11 on Alternative Resolution for Consumer Disputes**[46] demonstrates. The objectives of this legal instrument take up the idea of '**conciliation**' of the 'access to justice' movement.[47] The Regulation is based on Article 114 and Article 169 TFEU as it applies to domestic and cross-border disputes. However, access to justice is not mentioned therein – only the title of Article 5 requires Member States to 'facilitate the access of consumers to ADR procedures'. Against this background, it is difficult to claim that the Directive supports access to justice as a fundamental right including ADR.[48] It seems that the EU lawmaker's main concern was to establish a legal framework for consumer dispute resolution within the Internal Market.

#19 A similar observation must be made regarding **collective redress**. Consumers' access to justice was mentioned in the first documents and non-binding instruments regarding **representative actions**,[49] but it did not mature into a self-standing part of EU consumer policy. Later, collective redress was primarily discussed in cartel damage and in environmental law. However, the EU Commission faced considerable resistance from business interests in the Member States and their lobby representatives in Brussels. Collective redress appeared in the early programmes on consumer protection as part of consumers' access to justice.[50] The main arguments here derived nonetheless from '**private enforcement**', a concept originating in

44 Article 61 and Article 65 of the Treaty of Amsterdam did not refer to access to justice.

45 This result is explained by the fact that most commentators of these provisions are public law lawyers and, therefore, mainly interested in the first paragraphs of Article 67 TFEU.

46 [2013] OJ L165/63; Hess (n 20) para 12.23ff.

47 Supra text n 3–4.

48 Domej (n 15) para 129.

49 See supra text n 3–4.

50 Hess (n 20) para 11.88ff.

law and economics.[51] This approach is clearly visible in the **GDPR**, where private and public enforcement are combined.[52]

#20 In 2020, the Council finally adopted **Directive (EU) 2020/1828 on Consumer Collective Redress**, providing for **representative actions** brought by **qualified entities** on behalf of consumers. Again, one would have expected access to justice to be used as a central objective of the instrument. However, Article 1(1) describes the aims of the Directive as follows:

> 'This Directive sets out rules to ensure that a representative action mechanism for the protection of the collective interests of consumers is available in all Member States, while providing appropriate safeguards to avoid abusive litigation. The purpose of this Directive is, through the achievement of a high level of consumer protection, to contribute to the proper functioning of the internal market by approximating certain aspects of the laws, regulations and administrative provisions of the Member States concerning representative actions. To this end, this Directive also aims to improve consumers' access to justice.'

#21 This quote makes it difficult to regard access to justice as an overarching objective of the Directive. It appears as an additional or subsidiary objective of the instrument,[53] which is based on Article 114 TFEU and not on Article 81(2) lit c TFEU as the latter provision is limited to **cross-border settings**. It remains to be seen whether the CJEU will refer to Article 1(1) 3rd sentence when interpreting the Directive.[54] It is worth mentioning that the situation in environmental law is distinctively different, since the CJEU constantly refers to access to justice when interpreting collective redress in Article 9 of the **Aarhus Convention**.[55]

D Assessment: Limited Impacts of Access to Justice in EU Law

#22 Overall, 'access to justice' has per se been a concept of limited impact in EU procedural law. This is explained by the fact that **general principles** and methods of Union law, especially the concept of the efficient enforcement of EU (subjective) laws by the courts of the Member States have prevailed and become the **guiding principles** in lawmaking. They have replaced the right of access to justice despite

---

51 Domej (n 15) para 239ff.

52 Hess (n 20) para 11.93ff.

53 'It <u>also</u> aims . . .'.

54 During the last 10 years, the lawmaking activities of the EU in procedural law focused more and more on the competences regarding the Internal Market (Article 114 TFEU).

55 Research of the term in the CJEU database (on 10 March 2025) revealed 36 judgments where access to justice has been quoted. 26 out of them belong to environmental protection, 5 refer to the Maintenance Regulation.

the explicit insertion of the latter into the text of the Lisbon Treaty. What counts first, is 'redress', not 'access'.[56] The **constitutionalisation** of EU procedural law has entailed that access to justice is seen as a part of the right to effective judicial protection guaranteed by Article 47 CFR.

#23 It remains an open question whether access to justice may experience a resurgence in the context of **ADR**. Alternative dispute resolution mechanisms are increasingly present in the regulatory frame for **digital markets**. Here, access to justice may gain importance, together with the constitutional guarantees of Article 47 CFR. As of today, it is fair to state that, in terms of significance, access to justice cannot be compared to the principle of mutual recognition underlying the programmatic provision of Article 67 TFEU.

#24 Finally, the fundamental change of the access to justice movement has not been really adopted by the EU lawmaker. Its approach to the weak and vulnerable 'client' of the civil justice system is currently superseded by institutional perspectives in EU lawmaking. In its pursuit towards strengthening the **private enforcement** of EU subjective rights, the lawmaker does not primarily look at the users of the justice systems of EU Member States, but at the performance of the latter in the interest of EU law. Still, the focus on the users of the system is an important element of any assessment of civil justice. In this regard, the access to justice movement is still of considerable importance for the evaluation and reform of all civil justice systems – not only in Europe. In this regard, the **constitutionalisation** of civil procedure largely superseded the perspectives of the 'movement'.

References

Butler P and Menétrey S, 'Public Funding (Legal Aid)' in B Hess and others (eds), *Comparative Procedural Law and Justice* (Part III Chapter 6) <https://cplj.org/a/3-6> accessed 10 March 2025.

Caponi R and Novak J, 'Access to Justice' in B Hess and S Law (eds), *Implementing EU Consumer Law by National Procedural Law* (Beck/Hart 2019) 63.

Cappelletti M and Garth B (eds), *Access to Justice*, vol I: *A World Survey* (Sijthoff & Noordhoff 1978–1979).

Cappelletti M and Garth B (eds), *Access to Justice*, vols II–IV (*Promising Institutions*; *Emerging Issues and Perspectives*; *Anthropological Perspective, Patterns of Conflict Management*) (Giuffrè 1978–1979).

Cappelletti M, Garth B and Trocker N, 'Access to Justice, Variations and Continuity of a World-Wide Movement' (1982) 46 Rabels Zeitschrift für ausländisches und internationales Privatrecht (RabelsZ) 664.

Domej T, 'Constitutionalisation and Fundamentalisation of Access to Justice' in B Hess and others (eds), *Comparative Procedural Law and Justice* (Part IV Chapter 2) <https://cplj.org/a/4-2accessed>; 5 March 2025.

Dori A, *The Governance of EU Justice Reforms: The Role of the EU Justice Scoreboard and Country Specific Recommendations in Shaping National Judicial Systems* (Nomos 2025).

56 C. Hodges and S. Voet, *Delivering Collective Redress: New Technologies* (Hart 2018) 261ff.

European Agency for Fundamental Rights and Council of Europe, *Handbook on European Law Relating to Access to Justice* (2016).
Hess B, *Europäisches Zivilprozessrecht* (2nd edn, de Gruyter 2021).
—— 'Digital Judicial Cooperation' in M Fogt (ed), *Private International Law in an Era of Change* (Edward Elgar 2024) 155.
—— 'International Civil Litigation in the 21st Century', General Course at The Hague Academy of International Law (Recueil des Cours de l'Academie de La Haye – forthcoming 2026).
Hess B and Requejo Isidro M, 'El invisible colegio de juristas internacionales en el Derecho internacional privado de hoy' (2024) 16 *Cuadernos de Derecho Transnacional* 965.
Hodges C and Voet S, *Delivering Collective Redress: New Technologies* (Hart 2018) 261ff
Macdonald R, 'Access to Civil Justice' in P Cane and HM Kritzer (eds), *The Oxford Handbook of Empirical Legal Research* (OUP 2010) 492.
Mayr PG and Weber M, 'Europäische Initiativen zur Förderung der alternativen Streitbeilegung' (2007) 26 *Zeitschrift für Rechtsvergleichung* 163.
Tenreiro M, 'L'accès du consommateur à la justice: une perspective européenne' in G Barrett (ed), *Creating a European Judicial Space* (ERA 2001) 111.
Vandenbussche W and Taelman P, 'Consumer Protection Proceedings' in B Hess and others (eds), *Comparative Procedural Law and Justice* (Part XII Chapter 6) <https://cplj.org/a/12-6> accessed 10 March 2025.
Villamarín López M, 'Access to Justice as a Fundamental Right' in B Hess and others (eds), *Comparative Procedural Law and Justice* (Part III Chapter 2) <https://www.cplj.org/publications/3-2-access-to-justice-and-costs-of-litigation> accessed 5 March 2025.

Alain Ancery* and Bart Krans*

Chapter 6
EU Law and National Civil Procedural Law: A Much Greater Area than at First Glance

A Europe and Civil Procedural Law

#1 Over the past years, we have seen the amount of directives and regulations with civil procedural topics grow.[1] EU legislative products oblige or enable the Member States to amend parts of their national civil procedural systems. It is, however, not only EU legislative products that can impact national civil procedure.

#2 A less visible part of EU law, with arguably perhaps even more impact, are the **EU general principles** that impact civil procedure as well.[2] Several of those principles have been codified in the **Charter of Fundamental Rights of the Euro-**

1 Eg Regulation (EU) No 1215/2012 of the European Parliament and of the Council of 12 December 2012 on jurisdiction and the recognition and enforcement of judgments in civil and commercial matters (recast) [2012] OJ L351/1; Council Regulation (EC) No 805/2004 of the European Parliament and of the Council of 21 April 2004 creating a European Enforcement Order for uncontested claims [2004] OJ L143/15; Council Directive (EC) 2002/8/EC of 27 January 2003 to improve access to justice in cross-border disputes by establishing minimum common rules relating to legal aid for such disputes [2003] OJ L26/41; Council Regulation (EC) No 861/2007 of the European Parliament and of the Council of 11 July 2007 establishing a European Small Claims Procedure [2007] OJ L199/1; Council Regulation (EC) No 1896/2006 of the European Parliament and of the Council of 12 December 2006 creating a European order for payment procedure [2006] OJ L 399/1; Directive 2008/52/EC of the European Parliament and of the Council of 21 May 2008 on certain aspects of mediation in civil and commercial matters [2008] OJ L 136/3; Regulation (EU) 2020/1784 of the European Parliament and of the Council of 25 November 2020 on the service in the Member States of judicial and extrajudicial documents in civil or commercial matters (service of documents) (recast) [2020] OJ L405/40; Regulation (EU) 2020/1783 of the European Parliament and of the Council of 25 November 2020 on cooperation between the courts of the Member States in the taking of evidence in civil or commercial matters (taking of evidence) (recast) [2020] OJ L405/1; Council Regulation (EC) No 2201/2003 of 27 November 2003 concerning jurisdiction and the recognition and enforcement of judgments in matrimonial matters and the matters of parental responsibility, repealing Regulation (EC) No 1347/2000 [2003] OJ L338/1; Directive (EU) 2024/1069 of the European Parliament and of the Council of 11 April 2024 on protecting persons who engage in public participation from manifestly unfounded claims or abusive court proceedings ('Strategic lawsuits against public participation') [2024] OJ L16.4.2024/1–14; Corrigendum to Directive 2004/48/EC of the European Parliament and of the Council of 29 April 2004 on the enforcement of intellectual property rights [2004] OJ L157/45.

2 T Tridimas, *The General Principles of EU Law* (OUP 2006).

***Corresponding author: Alain Ancery**, Leiden University, e-mail: a.g.f.ancery@law.leidenuniv.nl
***Corresponding author: Bart Krans**, Leiden University, e-mail: h.b.krans@law.leidenuniv.nl

https://doi.org/10.1515/9783110781632-006

pean Union (also briefly addressed in section B), which are directly applicable in the national legal systems.[3] The non-codified principles have to be applied by national courts as well.[4] Such principles can have a decisive impact on whether a national provision of civil procedural law can be applied in an individual case.

#3 In this chapter, we briefly outline the various pillars of Europeanisation (Section II). However, the focus of this chapter is mainly on the initially less visible **significance of European law for national procedural law**. This pillar has become less and less invisible over the years and of great importance for national civil procedural law. We explain this below with reference to two elements of that pillar: **ex officio application and EU law** and the so-called **spontaneous harmonisation** at national level. Indeed, those two topics show that the **European dimension of civil procedural law** is larger than one might suspect at first sight. Moreover, they show that the **Europeanisation of procedural law** can have effects that can be quite unexpected. As far as national civil procedural law is concerned, the focus of this contribution is on Dutch law. Nevertheless, at several points, the law of other Member States will also be taken into consideration.

B Several Pillars of Europeanisation of Civil Procedural Law

#4 Aside from the regulations that directly impact national civil procedure, there are also less visible European principles or concepts that have a significant impact on national civil procedure. Examples of the first are the **European Convention on Human Rights (ECHR)**, the Charter of Fundamental Rights of the European Union, and the directly applicable EU regulations and the EU directives that require transposing efforts of national governments (Section B.I and B.II). Examples of the less visible concepts or principles are the provisions in directives impacting civil procedure and general principles (Section B.III).

I The First Pillar: ECHR and Charter of Fundamental Rights

#5 The European influence on national civil procedural law is not unilateral. We characterise the various ways in which European law is important, or at least

3 Cf Giesen, *Beginselen van burgerlijk procesrecht*, Asser Procesrecht/Giesen 1/33 (Wolters Kluwer 2015).

4 Case C-144/04 *Mangold* (22 November 2005) ECLI:EU:C:2005:709.

relevant, for national civil procedure as 'pillars'.[5] The Europeanisation of national civil procedural law consists of several pillars.

#6 The first field, or pillar, of this process is the ECHR. This field of European influence does not need any further introduction. It governs, *inter alia*, access to court, a fair trial, and the impartiality of the judge. A commentator has noted that the important dimension of Article 6 of the ECHR has undoubtedly contributed to denormalisation of Dutch civil procedural law.[6] The meaning of Article 6 of the ECHR has been the topic of many publications.[7] In addition to the ECHR, the Charter of the EU Fundamental Rights became binding.[8] This Charter can also play a role in procedures before national courts. Several decisions taken by the Court of Justice of the European Union (hereinafter the 'CJEU') on **Article 47** of the Charter regarding the right to an effective remedy and to a fair trial have played a role.[9]

II The Second Pillar: Crossroads of Civil Procedural Law and Private International Law

#7 A second pillar of the European influence on civil procedure is the growing number of European regulations. The European legislator has produced many regulations with impressive speed on various subjects concerning the crossroads of civil procedural law and private international law. It has likewise created many Regulations concerning European procedure law in civil matters. Since the year 2000, a large number of regulations on various topics of a cross-border procedural nature have been established within the framework of judicial cooperation between the Member States, among which, the Brussels Regulation, the Brussels IIbis Regulations, the Service Regulation, the Evidence Regulation, the Regulations creating a European enforcement order, the Regulation creating a European

5 On this, see B Krans, 'EU Law and National Civil Procedure law: An Invisible Pillar' (2015) 23 ERPL 567; some parts in this chapter are based on or taken from parts of that contribution.

6 A Hammerstein, 'De invloed van art. 6 EVRM op het burgerlijk procesrecht' in G Corstens and P Haak (eds), *Europeanisering van Nederlands recht* (Kluwer 2004) 221–222.

7 See for the impact of the ECHR on sixteen national legal systems, H Keller and A Stone Sweet (eds), *A Europe of Rights, Assessing the Impact of the ECHR on National Legal Systems* (OUP 2008) and concerning Article 6 ECHR, for Belgium J Vande Lanotte and Y Haeck, *Handboek EVRM, Deel 1, Algemene beginselen* (Intersentia 2005) and J Vande Lanotte and Y Haeck (eds), *Handboek EVRM, Deel 2, Artikelsgewijs Commentaar*, vol I (Intersentia 2004), for the Netherlands P Smits, *Artikel 6 EVRM en de civiele procedure* (Kluwer 2008).

8 For the current version: OJ [2012] 326/391-407.

9 Case C-386/10 C*halkor AE Epexergasias Metallon v European Commission* (8 December 2011) ECLI:EU:C:2011:815; Case C-272/09 *KME Germany AG v European Commission I* (8 December 2011) ECLI:EU:C:2011:816; and Case C-389/10 *KME Germany AG v European Commission II* (8 December 2011) ECLI:EU:C:2011:810.

order for payment procedure, and the Regulation establishing a European small claims procedure.[10] This type of the Europeanisation of procedural law concerns procedural matters in cases with a cross-border dimension. This form of supranational interference can be considered as moving towards a European civil procedural law, at least for cross-border issues. The report of the Storme Commission has played an important role in the process towards uniformity of European civil procedural law and its academic foundation.[11] The same applies for the initiative that led to the ELI – UNIDROIT Model European Rules of Civil Procedure.[12]

#8 As with the other pillars (or types) of Europeanisation of procedural law, in this pillar case law is important, or even decisive. For example, in the Dutch decision in the *Kalimijnen* case, the CJEU decided that the location of the event that gives rise to liability in tort delict or quasidelict does not necessarily have to be the same location as where the damage takes place. In these cases, the expression 'place where the harmful event occurred', in Article 5(3) of the Brussels Convention, now replaced by Article 7(2) of the Brussels I-bis Regulation,[13] must be understood as being intended to cover both the location where the damage occurred and the location of the event giving rise to liability.[14] More recently, the CJEU's decision in the two joined cases *eDate Advertising GmbH/X en Martinez/MGN Limited* concerned a jurisdictional matter for a damage claim resulting from a publication on the internet. In which country does the claim have to be filed? The CJEU ruled that Article 5(3) of this regulation must be interpreted as meaning that, in the event of an alleged infringement of personality rights by means of content placed on an internet website, the person who considers that his rights have been infringed has the option of bringing an action for liability, in respect of all the damage caused, either before the courts of the Member State in which the publisher of that content is established or before the courts of the Member State in which the centre of his interests is based. That person may also, rather than taking action for liability in respect

10 Cf n 1.

11 M Storme (ed), *Rapprochement du Droit Judiciaire de l'Union européenne; Approximation of Judiciary Law in the European Union* (Kluwer 1994).

12 ELI – UNIDROIT Model European Rules of Civil Procedure. From Transnational Principles to European Rules of Civil Procedure <https://www.unidroit.org/english/principles/civilprocedure/eli-unidroit-rules/200925-eli-unidroit-rules-e.pdf> accessed 18 February 2025.

13 Regulation (EU) No 1215/2012 of the European Parliament and of the Council of 12 December 2012 on jurisdiction and the recognition and enforcement of judgments in civil and commercial matters, OJ [2012] L351/1; See: Convention of 27 September 1968 on jurisdiction and the enforcement of judgments in civil and commercial matters [1972] OJ L299/32.

14 Case C-21/76 *Handelskwekerij G.J. Bier BV v Mines de potasse d'Alsace SA* (30 November 1976) ECLI: EU:C:1976:166; Case C-68/93 *Fiona Shevill, Ixora Trading Inc., Chequepoint SARL and Chequepoint International Ltd v Presse Alliance SA* (7 March 1995) ECLI:EU:C:1995:61.

of all the damage caused, bring his action before the courts of each Member State in the territory where the content was placed online is or was accessible.[15]

#9 Another development in this pillar of the Europeanisation of procedural law is the European Account Preservation Order[16] to facilitate cross-border debt recovery in civil and commercial matters. Difficulties in cross-border debt recovery were the reason for this proposal. It introduces a European account preservation order that can be obtained following an *ex parte* procedure. According to this proposal, creditors can prevent debtors from withdrawing money from their bank account or transferring money within the EU. The proposal has received a great deal of attention from scholars.[17]

#10 It is tempting to dive into a number of interesting and varying topics on this pillar of Europeanisation of civil procedural law; however, this contribution will focus on what we refer to as the invisible pillar.

III The Third Pillar: Less and Less Invisible

#11 What is the invisible pillar of the Europeanisation of procedural law? It is, of course, not really invisible, but simply much less visible than the first two pillars of Europeanisation. This pillar concerns two aspects.

#12 The first part of this invisible pillar follows from the role of national civil procedural law in enforcing EU law. EU law finds its way to European citizens through national civil procedural law. EU law therefore, needs national civil procedural law to be enforced. In the words of Keus, national law is the 'vehicle' that transports EU law.[18] It is settled case law of the European Court of Justice that Member States have **procedural autonomy**.[19] The European Court leaves the procedural law to the national courts.

#13 At the same time, the national legislator must ensure that EU law has full effect. This is also referred to as the **principle of loyalty**.[20] The result of this combina-

15 Case C-509/09 *eDate Advertising GmbH v X and Olivier Martinez and Robert Martinez v MGN Limited* (25 October 2011) ECLI:EU:C:2011:685.

16 Regulation (EU) No 655/2014 of the European Parliament and of the Council of 15 May 2014 establishing a European Account Preservation Order procedure to facilitate cross-border debt recovery in civil and commercial matters [2014] OJ L189/59.

17 See *inter alia* B Krans and P Ribbers, 'The European Account Preservation Order in Dutch Practice' in M Deguchi (ed), *Effective Enforcement of Creditors' Rights* (Springer 2022) 121. Just to mention a few sources for the Netherlands (in Dutch): BJ Van Het Kaar, 'Conservatoir (derden)beslag niet langer territoriaal?' [2011] WPNR 6905, 903; JM Atema and EC Netten, 'Het Europees bankbeslag: een ruwe diamant' [2012] MvV 1, 11; and NWM van den Heuvel and MLSWE de Lange, 'Het Europees bankbeslag' [2011] BER 32.

18 LAD Keus, *Europees privaatrecht. Een bonte lappendeken* (Koninklijke Vermande 1993) 35.

19 Case C-265/78 *H. Ferwerda BV v Produktschap voor Vee en Vlees* (5 March 1980) ECLI:EU:C:1980:66, para 10.

20 Article 4(3) Treaty on the European Union [2012] OJ L326/13ff.

tion is that the national courts have to apply their procedural law in accordance with the so-called ***Rewe/Comet*** rule.[21] The *Rewe/Comet* rule comes down to the well-known **principles of effectiveness and equivalence**. The requirement of effectiveness means that the exercise of EU rights must not be made virtually impossible or excessively difficult. From the requirement of equivalence, it follows that the procedures and remedies may not be less favourable than those regarding rules applicable to similar actions based on domestic law. These two minimum requirements can have direct consequences for the enforcement of European private Law.

#14 The second area of the invisible pillar concerns procedural rules in Directives. European Directives can contain rules that are specifically procedural, even if the nature of the Directive is mainly substantive. A close look at European Directives reveals that the list of procedural topics touched upon by Directives is far from small. These Directives contain procedural rules relevant for various *capita* of civil procedural law of the Member States.

#15 The European influence in this invisible pillar concerns several procedural topics. We address below, as mentioned, two parts of this increasingly pillar that is less and less invisible. In the following, we will deal only with ex officio application and spontaneous harmonisation. This is because these are two topics that, in our view, illustrate that the European dimension of civil procedural law is larger than may appear at first sight.

C Application of EU Law by National Courts

I General

#16 One element of the invisible pillar via which the effectiveness of EU law is ensured by the ECJ is the ex officio application of EU law. Case law on the ex officio application of EU law has developed rapidly since the early 90s of the last century. It is also a much-debated topic in legal doctrine. Usually, a distinction is made between the **ex officio application of EU consumer law**, and ex officio application of other provisions with an EU law origin. We will also discuss both matters separately, because the impact of the ex officio application on national civil procedures tends to be greater than the impact of the ex officio application of other provisions with an EU law origin.

21 Case C-33/76 *Rewe-Zentralfinanz eG and Rewe-Zentral AG v Landwirtschaftskammer für das Saarland* (16 December 1976) ECLI:EU:C:1976:188; Case C-45/76 *Comet BV v Produktschap voor Siergewassen* (16 December 1976) ECLI:EU:C:1976:191; Case C-473/00 *Cofidis SA v Jean-Louis Fredout* (21 November 2002) ECLI:EU:C:2002:705.

#17 As a general starting point, we advocate determining if there is a conflict between EU law and national law. Do national provisions prevent EU law from being effectuated? If the answer is yes, the following question should be whether this conflict is of a direct or a more indirect nature.[22] A **direct conflict between EU rules and national rules** is characterised by opposing rules on the same matter, while an indirect conflict does not so much comprise diverging provisions on the same matter, but a national provision that make the effectuation of rights derived from EU law more burdensome or impossible.[23] A direct conflict between EU law and national law can have no other outcome than that the conflicting national provisions should be disregarded by the national court.[24]

#18 For indirect conflicts between provisions of EU law and provisions of national law, the outcome is more nuanced and can differ from case to case. The CJEU acknowledges that EU law needs to be enforced in a national procedural environment, with its inherent restrictions. It is therefore not generally excluded that EU law is subject to, for example, national rules entailing limitation periods. As a matter of fact, the CJEU considers national procedural autonomy the basis for the application of EU law by national courts. Without further restrictions, such an approach could easily stand in the way of enforcing one's rights before a national court, and for that reason, the CJEU applies some rules of thumb to this principle of national procedural autonomy. Enforcing your rights derived from EU law should be possible in an equal manner compared to enforcing your rights derived from national law. In addition, national provisions should not make the enforcement of EU rights extremely difficult or virtually impossible.[25] A safety pin is on top of that provided for by the **principle of effective judicial protection**. Even if the national procedural environment treats rights derived from EU law equally to those derived from national law, the absence of an effective judicial remedy for those seeking to enforce their rights could make the CJEU decide to set rules of national law aside.[26]

#19 Direct conflicts between EU law and national law are perhaps less common than cases in which the enforcement of rights derived from EU law is blocked by restrictions derived from national law. Most, if not all, procedural restrictions are

22 A Ancery, *Ambtshalve toepassing van EU-recht* (Kluwer 2012) 103ff.

23 ibid.

24 Case C-106/77 *Amministrazione delle Finanze dello Stato v Simmenthal SpA* (9 March 1978) ECLI:EU:C:1978:49, paras 14–24.

25 Case C-33/76 *Rewe-Zentralfinanz eG and Rewe-Zentral AG v Landwirtschaftskammer für das Saarland* (16 December 1976) ECLI:EU:C:1976:188; Case C-45/76 *Comet BV v Produktschap voor Siergewassen* (16 December 1976) ECLI:EU:C:1976:191.

26 Case C-222/84 *Marguerite Johnston v Chief Constable of the Royal Ulster Constabulary* (15 May 1986) ECLI:EU:C:1986:206. Cf Krans (n 5); and P Sirena, M Ginestri and E Valletta, 'National Procedural Rules and the New Boundaries of ECJ's Control in the Light of Directive 93/13' (2024) 32 ERPL 549, 551, referring to Article 19 TEU.

there for good reasons. If the application of those procedural restrictions, however, would unjustifiably disregard rights derived from EU law, it is up to the national court to prevent that from happening. In this regard, EU law also indirectly influences the procedural and legal relationship between the parties.[27]

#20 An example of such indirect effect is the case law of the CJEU on ex officio application of EU law. We will start with the ex officio application of EU consumer law, and end with the ex officio application of EU law in general.

II Ex Officio Application of EU Consumer Law

#21 Over the past years, the case law of the CJEU on ex officio application of EU consumer law spread like an oil stain from the ex officio application of parts of rights derived from the **Unfair Terms Directive** to (almost) the entire EU consumer law corpus.[28] When referring to the entire EU consumer law corpus, we mean the whole body of consumer-protective provisions deriving from EU consumer-protective legislative products, mostly EU directives.

#22 Consumers are in a weaker position vis-à-vis their professional counterpart. They have fewer (legal) knowledge and are in a weaker financial position. Without some additional efforts on the procedural side, there is a real and inherent risk that consumers will not be able to enforce their consumer rights in civil proceedings. This would also affect the **effectiveness of EU consumer law**.[29]

#23 As mentioned previously, as a basic principle, those who are attributed rights by substantive law should also be in the possession of an **effective judicial remedy** to enforce those rights.[30] In cases involving a consumer and a professional party, the so-called **B2C** cases, there is a risk that a consumer would not be able to enforce their rights due to an inherent inequality in the legal relationship between those parties. This would leave the consumer with rights that he is unable to en-

27 Cf A Hartkamp, *Europees recht en Nederlands vermogensrecht*, Asser/Hartkamp [2023] 3–1/8ff (Wolters Kluwer).

28 Cf W Vandenbussche, 'Zijn afwijkende procedureregels voor consumenten steeds nodig?' 2023 (40) NTBR 289.

29 Case C-51/17 *OTP Bank and OTP Faktoring Követeléskezelő v Teréz Ilyés and Emil Kiss* (20 September 2018) ECLI:EU:C:2018:750, para 88; A van Duin and C Leone, 'Ambtshalve toetsing van Europees consumentenrecht en instrumentalisering van burgerlijk procesrecht: reactie op Bert van Schaick' [2023–4] TCR 127; Vandenbussche (n 28) 290–291.

30 Case C-222/84 *Marguerite Johnston v Chief Constable of the Royal Ulster Constabulary* (15 May 1986) ECLI:EU:C:1986:206. This principle applied to EU consumer law: Case C-32/14 *ERSTE Bank Hungary v Attila Sugár* (1 October 2015) ECLI:EU:C:2015:637; Case C-377/14 *Radlinger and Radlingerová v Finway* (21 April 2016) ECLI:EU:C:2016:283; Case C-598/15 *Banco Santander v Sánchez López* (7 December 2017) ECLI:EU:C:2017:945; Case C-483/16 *Sziber v ERSTE Bank Hungary* (31 May 2018) ECLI:EU:C:2018:367.

force, hence without an effective judicial remedy. To ensure he has one, the CJEU has developed the doctrine of the ex officio application of EU consumer law.[31]

#24 The starting point for applying EU consumer law remains national civil procedure.[32] National courts should be mindful of the fact that a rigid application of the rules of national civil procedure could deprive the consumer from an effective judicial remedy. Most national procedural systems rely on the principle that the court applies the applicable provisions of substantive law, ie the rights to which parties are entitled, but the parties themselves are responsible for providing the courts with the necessary factual information to substantiate their claims or defences. In fact, national courts are generally not allowed to go beyond the factual information that parties have presented.[33]

#25 Clearly, this approach would not work in B2C cases. Consumers are generally not aware of their rights. Most of them do not even appear in court. If courts were required to rely solely on the factual basis brought together by the professional party,[34] it would most likely almost never be able to apply consumer-protective provisions. For that reason, the CJEU introduced the obligation for national courts to ex officio apply consumer-protective provisions deriving from **EU consumer-protective directives**. This obligation exists regardless of the national procedural system[35] and regardless of whether the specific consumer meets the general characteristics that the CJEU attributed to consumers.[36] As said, the case law of the CJEU started with a part of the Unfair Terms Directive,[37] spreading to the entire Unfair Terms Directive,[38] and then to the entire **EU consumer-protective corpus.**[39] This makes complete sense as the rationale for the ex officio application of EU consumer law is not restricted to the Unfair Terms Directive, but applies to all EU consumer-protective directives.

31 van Duin and Leone (n 29).

32 A Beka, *The Active Role of Courts in Consumer Litigation* (Intersentia 2018) 24–25.

33 V Zeno-Zencovich and MC Paglietti, 'Le droit processuel des consommateurs' (2014) 66 Revue de droit internationale et de droit compare 321.

34 The trader, the seller, the supplier, the party operating in a professional capacity.

35 A Ancery, 'Ambtshalve toepassing van consumentenbeschermend EU-recht' [2013] MvV 12/330.

36 H Schulte-Nolke, 'The Objectives of Directive 93/13/EEC on Unfair Contract Terms: An Overview after 30 Years of Case Law' (2024) 32 ERPL 315, 317.

37 Joined Cases C-240/98 to C-244/98 *Océano Grupo Editorial SA v Roció Murciano Quintero and Salvat Editores SA v José M. Sánchez Alcón Prades, José Luis Copano Badillo, Mohammed Berroane and Emilio Viñas Feliú* (27 June 2000) ECLI:EU:C:2000:346.

38 Case C-473/00 *Cofidis SA v Jean-Louis Fredout* (21 November 2002) ECLI:EU:C:2002:705, para 33; Case C-168/05 *Mostaza Claro v Centro Móvil Milenium* (26 October 2006) ECLI:EU:C:2006:675, para 28.

39 Case C-429/05 *Max Rampion and Marie-Jeanne Godard, née Rampion v Franfinance SA and K par K SAS* (4 October 2007) ECLI:EU:C:2007:575; Case C-227/08 *Eva Martín Martín v EDP Editores SL* (); Case C-32/12 *Soledad Duarte Hueros v Autociba SA and Automóviles Citroën España SA* (3 October 2013) ECLI:EU:C:2013:637; Case C-497/13 *Froukje Faber v Autobedrijf Hazet Ochten BV* (4 June 2015) ECLI:EU:C:2015:357.

#26 Three remarks. One could argue that this rationale is also not confined to consumer law. It is not just consumers who are in a weaker position vis-à-vis their counterparts. One could imagine that the same applies to employees vis-à-vis their employers, and tenants vis-à-vis the owners, to name a few examples. In financial law, the invasion of the ex officio application of EU consumer law can sometimes already be noticed,[40] which is not just a matter of protecting the weaker party but also to ensure a good and orderly functioning level playing field on the internal market.[41]

#27 Secondly, although the case law of the CJEU affects the entire EU consumer-protective corpus, that does not mean that all provisions of the EU consumer-protective directives – more specifically, the provisions by which they are transposed into national law – should at all times be applied ex officio outside the **ambit of the dispute**. A case that led to a ruling of the Dutch Supreme Court of 12 November 2021 could illustrate this.[42] That case concerned information duties following from the **Consumer Rights Directive**, which were transposed into national law. The Dutch Supreme Court considered that the case law of the CJEU on the ex officio application of EU consumer law does not imply that all provisions of EU consumer law need to be applied ex officio. Specifically for the information duties of the Consumer Rights Directive, the Dutch Supreme Court considers that there are three types of **information duties**: the ones that are sanctioned by law, the ones that are essential to consumers, and all the other ones. For the first two types of information duties courts should ex officio assess if the duties have been complied with, and if not, give due effect to all the consequences following from such a non-compliance. The approach to be taken is described in the following paragraphs. For the third type of information duty such an obligation does not exist, also because is not essential for the **effectiveness of consumer protection**.[43]

#28 Thirdly, although national courts are generally required to ensure the effectiveness of EU consumer law, not all **procedural restrictions** following from national procedural law need to be set aside. Rules regarding limitation periods and *res judicata*, to name two examples, are there for a good reason. They contribute to the proper functioning of the judicial system.[44] In so far, they comply with the

40 A Ancery, 'Ambtshalve toepassing van EU-recht: ook financieel toezichtrecht?' [2018] MvV 94–99; Case C-419/18 and C-483/18 *Profi Credit Polska v Wlostowska* (7 November 2019) ECLI:EU:C:2019:930, paras 26–28. On this matter as well: D Busch, 'De toekomst van de bijzondere zorgplicht in de financiële sector' (2020) 95 NJB 452, 454, 462 and 466.

41 A Ancery, 'Consumer Credit Contracts and *Ex Officio* Application: A Dutch Perspective' (2021) 10 Journal of European Consumer and Market Law 160.

42 *Intrum Nederland* (12 November 2021) ECLI:NL:HR:2021:1677.

43 ibid.

44 Cf Case C-483/16 *Sziber v ERSTE Bank* (31 May 2018) ECLI:EU:C:2018:367.

principles of effectiveness and equivalence, those rules can be maintained, even if this means that EU consumer law cannot be applied ex officio.[45]

#29 Circling back to what this means for national civil procedure. In the past, we asked ourselves if the national court would still be allowed to confine itself to the ambit of the dispute, as determined by the parties, or if the CJEU would require the national court to go further to ensure the effective judicial protection of consumers.[46] We now know it is the latter. With hindsight bias, one could state the logic in that. If we truly believe in the importance of the effectiveness of the consumer-protective EU law corpus, we should put our money where our mouth is. Without national courts going beyond the ambit of the dispute, if needed, the effectiveness of consumer protection remains a utopia. For the professional party, there would be no incentive to provide the national court with the factual basis needed to apply consumer-protective provisions. Consumers would have such an incentive, but do not have the knowledge or financial means to enforce their rights in court.

#30 The CJEU considered in its ***Pannon*** ruling that courts are required to ensure the effectiveness of the consumer protection intended to be given. Consequently, the national court should ex officio examine the possible application of consumer-protective provisions, where it has available to it the legal and factual elements necessary for that task.[47] In its ***Pénzügyi*** ruling the CJEU clarified this matter as follows:

> the national court must investigate of its own motion whether a term conferring exclusive territorial jurisdiction in a contract concluded between a seller or supplier and a consumer, which is the subject of a dispute before it, falls within the scope of the Directive and, if it does, assess of its own motion whether such a term is unfair.[48]

With this ruling, the CJEU turns the ex officio application of consumer-protective EU into a two-step approach. National courts should first determine if the matter falls within the scope of a consumer-protective EU provision/directive. In that stage, the national court is required to **investigate** itself whether this is the case. Once confirmed, stage two entails the national court to ex officio apply consumer-protective provisions, where it has available to it the legal and factual elements necessary for that task. What the CJEU expects from the national courts in stage two is further clarified in the ***Profi Credit Polska*** ruling:

45 C Pavillon, 'Ignorance is Bliss – How *Ex Officio* Control Became the *Raison d'Être* of the UCTD' (2024) 32 ERPL 519, 527–528.

46 A Ancery and B Krans, 'Ambtshalve toepassing van Europees consumentenrecht' [2009] RM Themis 191–200.

47 Case C-243/08 *Pannon GSM Zrt. v Erzsébet Sustikné Győrfi* (4 June 2019) ECLI:EU:C:2009:350, para 32.

48 Case C-137/08 *VB Pénzügyi Lízing Zrt. v Ferenc Schneider* (9 November 2010) ECLI:EU:C:2010:659, para 56.

(. . .) It follows that, where a national court is hearing an application based on a promissory note which was initially left blank when issued and subsequently completed and is intended to secure a debt arising under a consumer credit agreement, and that court has serious doubts as to the merits of that application, Articles 6(1) and 7(1) of Directive 93/13 require that that court be able to demand the production of the documents on which that application is based, including the promissory note agreement, where under national law such an agreement constitutes a precondition for the issuance of such a promissory note.[49]

A court therefore, can be required to make use of its powers to issue instruction measures. An interesting element of this ruling is that the CJEU explicitly addresses the criticism that such an approach would infringe upon the principle that civil courts remain passive when it comes to establishing the factual basis required for the application of legal provisions.[50] The CJEU disagrees with this criticism:

It must also be noted that the considerations above do not contravene the principle, referred to by the referring court, that the subject matter of an action is to be defined by the parties. The national court's requirement that the applicant produce the content of the document or documents on which his application is based simply forms part of the evidential framework of the proceedings, since the purpose of such a request is merely to verify the basis of the action.[51]

In France, for example, this topic is also approached from an **equality of arms** perspective, which would make it easier to accept the more active approach of a court.[52] **Instruction measures** are therefore part of the toolkit of the national courts to ensure that it has available to it the **legal and factual elements** necessary for the ex officio application of EU consumer law. When a national court determines that an infringement was made on consumer rights, it is obliged to give due effect to all the consequences under national law resulting from such an infringement without waiting for the consumer to make an application to that effect, provided always that the principle of ***audi alteram partem*** has been complied with.[53]
#31 Interestingly enough, this follows exactly what the Dutch Supreme Court ruled in its ***Heesakkers/Voets*** ruling in 2013.[54] The Dutch Supreme Court considered that

49 *Profi Credit Polska v Wlostowska* (n 40) paras 64, 66–67.
50 A clear representative of this criticism: B van Schaick, 'Instrumentalisering van burgerlijk procesrecht. Over de inzet van burgerlijk procesrecht om buiten het burgerlijk procesrecht gelegen doelen te realiseren' [2023–3] TCR 70–73. Cf as well Schulte-Nolke (n 36) 332.
51 *Profi Credit Polska v Wlostowska* (n 40) para 68.
52 G Biardeaud and P Flores, 'L'office du juge et le crédit à la consommation' [2009] Le Dalloz 2227–2228; G Poisonnier, 'Office du juge en droit de la consommation, une clarification bienvenue' [2008] Le Dalloz 1290–1291.
53 *Profi Credit Polska v Wlostowska* (n 40) para 69 and *Radlinger and Radlingerová v Finway* (n 30) para 71.
54 *Heesakkers v Voets* (13 December 2013) ECLI:NL:HR:2013:691.

if the court has available to it the legal and factual elements necessary to substantiate a suspicion that the matter falls within the scope of a consumer-protective EU directive, and a consumer-protective provision is infringed upon, it is required to investigate both if the matter falls within the scope of the directive, as well as if a consumer-protective provision needs to be ex officio applied.[55] Well ahead of the CJEU, the Dutch Supreme Court already ruled in *Heesakkers/Voets* that when the national court determined that an infringement was made on consumer rights, it is obliged to give due effect to all the consequences under national law resulting from such an infringement without waiting for the consumer to make an application to that effect, provided always that the principle of *audi alteram partem* has been complied with.[56]

#32 This ruling of the Dutch Supreme Court did not come as a surprise.[57] At the time when the case law of the CJEU reached its peak the Dutch civil procedural system found itself in a transition phase, seeking a new balance with regard to the **role of civil courts** vis-à-vis the parties, and was therefore perhaps more susceptible for change.[58] When the CJEU came out with several rulings on the ex officio application of EU consumer law, Dutch courts of first instance took matters in their own hands and developed a practical toolkit on how to deal with this doctrine. This toolkit has been refined a few times and is currently considered as an important source on how to deal with the ex officio application of EU consumer law.[59]

#33 The **toolkit** provides for the steps to be taken by courts in order to determine if a consumer-protective provision needs to be applied, and if so, how to best do that. As per the case law of the CJEU and the Dutch Supreme Court, the court should determine in B2C cases if the matter falls within the **scope of a consumer-protective EU directive**. Where necessary, the court should investigate this matter.[60] Once the court determines that the B2C matter falls within the scope of a consumer-protective EU directive, the court has to determine whether it has **available to it the necessary legal and factual elements to ex officio apply consumer-protective provisions**. If that is not the case, but the court nonetheless suspects that provisions of consumer law are infringed upon, it should investigate if this is the case. At all times the principle of *audi alteram partem* needs to be complied with.[61]

55 ibid para 3.9.1.

56 ibid para 3.7.3.

57 In this line as well: *Lindorff* (12 February 2016) ECLI:NL:HR:2016:236, following *Lindorff v Statia* (13 June 2014) ECLI:NL:HR:2014:1385; Dutch Supreme Court (10 February 2023) ECLI:NL:HR:2023:198, paras 3.7–3.8.5.

58 D Asser, B Groen, J Vranken and I Tzankova, *Uitgebalanceerd. Eindrapport Fundamentele herbezinning Nederlands Burgerlijk Procesrecht* (Boom 2006).

59 Ambtshalve toetsing III – Herzien rapport van de redactieraad van het LOVCK&T (rechtspraak.nl) accessed 18 February 2025).

60 ibid 23.

61 ibid 20–23.

#34 This is all still very much in line with what the CJEU and the Dutch Supreme Court have ruled. The toolkit however also contains **practical guidance**, ie what should a court do when the required factual elements are missing in the case file? In that case the toolkit advises the court to render an interlocutory judgment in which the professional party is assigned with the task to substantiate the missing factual elements, provided that the professional party substantiated its claim/defence to a certain extent. If that was not the case, the court should immediately render judgment and dismiss the claim/defence of the professional party. In case the claim/defence was substantiated to a certain extent a standard interlocutory judgment was developed in legal doctrine and in practice used by Dutch courts.[62] If, in the second round, the professional party still provides too little factual elements, the toolkit advises the court to dismiss the claim/defence of the professional party.[63] The same approach applies if a court is asked to grant an exequatur for an arbitral award of if the court is asked to quash such an award.[64]

III Ex Officio Application of EU Law In Non-Consumer Cases

#35 The case law on the ex officio application of EU law outside consumer law has less impact on national civil procedure. Not because this part of EU law does not need to be applied ex officio, but because the rationale that brought the CJEU to the doctrine of the ex officio application of EU consumer law is not there. The inherent imbalance between parties in a B2C relationship – which could affect other legal relationships with an inherent imbalance as well – is not generally there in civil proceedings. For those general cases, the CJEU more or less follows the format of national civil procedure.

#36 In most civil procedural systems courts remain within the ambit of the dispute, unless the **public interest** is at stake. It is therefore not a surprise that in the non-consumer cases the focus of the CJEU was mostly on the question if the public interest was at stake,[65] or if other restricting procedural provisions meet the principles of equality and effectiveness.

---

62 C Seinen and A Ancery, 'Vorderingen in b2c-verstekken: toetsen of toewijzen?' [2015–3] TCR 77.

63 Ambtshalve toetsing III (n 59) 50–51.

64 *Intermaris* (8 November 2019) ECLI:NL:HR:2019:1731; *Mostaza Claro v Centro Móvil Milenium* (n 38); Case C-40/08 *Asturcom Telecomunicaciones SL v Cristina Rodríguez Nogueira* (6 October 2009) ECLI:EU:C:2009:615. A topic that is relevant for, in particular, Spanish courts. Cf on this: A van Duin, *Effective Judicial Protection in Consumer Litigation* (Intersentia 2022).

65 Case C-8/08 *T-Mobile Netherlands BV, KPN Mobile NV, Orange Nederland NV and Vodafone Libertel NV v Raad van bestuur van de Nederlandse Mededingingsautoriteit* (4 June 2009) ECLI:EU:C:2009:343, para 49; Joined Cases C-222/05 to C-225/05 *J. van der Weerd and Others v Minister van Landbouw, Natuur en Voedselkwaliteit* (1 March 2007) ECLI:EU:C:2007:124; Joined Cases C-295/04 to C-298/04 *Vincenzo Manfredi v Lloyd Adriatico Assicurazioni SpA, Antonio Cannito v Fondiaria Sai SpA and Nicolò Tricar-*

D Spontaneous Harmonisation

#37 The second sub-topic we consider here, albeit somewhat briefly, is so-called spontaneous harmonisation. EU law prescribes to Member States the requirements that civil procedural law must meet in certain areas. Those European rules often have a more or less defined scope, such as intellectual property rights or competition law. However, Member States can decide to **extend the European rules** to parts of their national procedural law that are not governed by the relevant European rules. This sounds more abstract than it is. We explain it using an example.

#38 The preamble to the Directive on the **enforcement of intellectual property rights** (hereinafter the Enforcement Directive) notes the need to ensure that substantive intellectual property law, now largely part of the acquis communautaire, is effectively applied in the Community. In this context, the means of enforcing intellectual property rights are of paramount importance for the success of the internal market.

#39 This Enforcement Directive led to the introduction of a separate section in the Dutch Code of Civil Procedure containing procedural mechanisms for the enforcement of intellectual property rights.[66] This includes a provision on so-called **seizure of evidence.**[67] According to the Enforcement Directive, Member States must ensure that the judicial authorities may, at the request of the applicant, order the seizure or extradition of goods suspected of infringing an intellectual property right in order to prevent those goods from entering or moving about in trade. There was no such provision in Dutch procedural law, neither for intellectual property cases nor for other civil law cases. Thus, since the implementation of the Enforcement Directive (entered into force as of May 2007), Dutch procedural law has included the possibility of seizing evidence for intellectual property cases.

#40 However, this did not clarify whether that possibility also existed for other civil law cases. An explicit statutory provision was lacking, and judges in courts of fact ruled differently on that question. This therefore led to a lack of clarity. Moreover, there was thus a possible difference in procedural possibilities between intellectual property cases and other cases. This could lead to the situation that, for example, the victim of a traffic accident, has fewer rights the entitled party in an intellectual property case.[68]

---

ico and Pasqualina Murgolo v Assitalia SpA (13 July 2006) ECLI:EU:C:2006:461, para 58; Case C-38/98 *Régie nationale des usines Renault SA v Maxicar SpA and Orazio Formento* (11 May 2000) ECLI:EU:C:2000:225; Case C-126/97 *Eco Swiss China Time Ltd v Benetton International NV* (1 June 1999) ECLI:EU:C:1999:269; Joined Cases C-430/93 and C-431/93 *Jeroen van Schijndel and Johannes Nicolaas Cornelis van Veen v Stichting Pensioenfonds voor Fysiotherapeuten* (14 December 1995) ECLI:EU:C:1995:441.

66 Book 4, Titel 4, Dutch Code of Civil Procedure (Articles 1019 -1019i).

67 Article 1019b DCCP.

68 Cf B Krans, *Nederlands burgerlijk procesrecht en materieel EU-recht* (Kluwer 2010), inter alia para 7.1.

#41 The preliminary relief judge in Amsterdam referred questions to the Supreme Court on the seizure of evidence in (national) preliminary relief proceedings. In a preliminary ruling in September 2013, the Supreme Court considered that it would have been preferable if the legislator had weighed up and chosen in connection with the seizure of evidence. Since that had not been done by then, the Supreme Court cut the Gordian knot itself: the possibility of seizing evidence exists. To substantiate this decision, the Supreme Court considered that the national provisions on the seizure of evidence in intellectual property cases apply mutatis mutandis in other civil law cases.[69] A similar ruling was provided by the Belgian Cour de cassation which was inspired by the ruling of the Dutch Supreme Court.[70]

#42 Following the Supreme Court, the legislature has now also introduced a statutory regime for the attachment of evidence. As of 2015, as part of the then revamped civil evidence law, section 205 new CCP will provide the option of evidence attachment. The parliamentary documents accompanying that legislation have more than once referred to the regime of evidence seizure in IP cases. Thus, where the scope of the Enforcement Directive is limited to intellectual property cases, spontaneous harmonisation at the national level has extended the scope of part of that directive.

#43 There are also examples from other areas of law. For example, Vedder wrote in 2004 that almost all Member States have modelled their competition law on EC competition law. In doing so, they have incorporated substantive rules and some of the procedural rules deriving from that law into their own national procedural rules.[71]

#44 Spontaneous harmonisation, then, is not a phenomenon that has its basis in European law. As has been noted: it is a phenomenon that occurs entirely **without a legal basis in the Treaties.**[72] It is, however, a consequence of European interference in a particular area.

E Final Remarks

#45 Europeanisation of procedural law does not take place through one line but through several pillars. One pillar that initially seemed less visible has increasingly stepped out of the shadows in recent decades. Ex officio application has become a key element in several Member States, including those not discussed

69 DSC (13 September 2013) ECLI:NL:HR:2013:BZ9958, *NJ* 2013/455, with case note B Krans.

70 Belgian Cour de Cassation (Cass.) 4 januari 2024, AR C.22.0373.N.

71 H Vedder, 'Spontaneous Harmonisation of National (Competition) Laws in the Wake of the Modernisation of EC Competition Law' (2004) 1 The Competition Law Review 1, 20. He describes spontaneous harmonisation as 'the convergence of rules of the Member States following the example of comparable rules in the European Union without any express harmonising activity of the Union' (at 5)

72 F Amtenbrink and H Vedder, *Recht van de Europese Unie* VI-25 (7th edn, BJU 2022).

here. It has also led to various questions around delimitation. Spontaneous harmonisation, moreover, underlines that the Europeanisation of procedural law not only goes further than one might suspect at first glance, but can also resolve certain imbalances at the national level. We suspect that the Europeanisation of civil procedural law has by no means come to an end.

References

Amtenbrink F and Vedder H, *Recht van de Europese Unie* VI-25 (7th edn, BJU 2022).
Ancery A, *Ambtshalve toepassing van EU-recht* (Kluwer 2012).
—— 'Ambtshalve toepassing van consumentenbeschermend EU-recht' [2013] MvV 12/330.
—— 'Ambtshalve toepassing van EU-recht: ook financieel toezichtrecht?' [2018] MvV 94.
—— 'Consumer Credit Contracts and Ex Officio Application: A Dutch Perspective' (2021) 10 Journal of European Consumer and Market Law 160.
Ancery A and Krans B, 'Ambtshalve toepassing van Europees consumentenrecht' [2009] RM Themis 191.
Atema JM and Netten EC, 'Het Europees bankbeslag: een ruwe diamant' [2012] MvV 1.
Asser D, Groen B, Vranken J and Tzankova I, *Uitgebalanceerd. Eindrapport Fundamentele herbezinning Nederlands Burgerlijk Procesrecht* (Boom 2006).
Beka A, *The Active Role of Courts in Consumer Litigation* (Intersentia 2018).
Biardeaud G and Flores Ph, 'L'office du juge et le crédit à la consommation' [2009] Le Dalloz 2227.
Busch D, 'De toekomst van de bijzondere zorgplicht in de financiële sector' (2020) 95 NJB 452.
Duin van A, *Effective Judicial Protection in Consumer Litigation* (Intersentia 2022).
Giesen I, *Beginselen van burgerlijk procesrecht*, Asser Procesrecht/Giesen 1/33 (Wolters Kluwer 2015).
Hammerstein A, 'De invloed van art. 6 EVRM op het burgerlijk procesrecht' in G Corstens and P Haak (eds), *Europeanisering van Nederlands recht* (Kluwer 2004) 221.
Hartkamp A, *Europees recht en Nederlands vermogensrecht*, Asser/Hartkamp 3-1/8ff (Wolters Kluwer 2023).
Keller H and Stone Sweet A (eds), *A Europe of Rights: Assessing the Impact of the ECHR on National Legal Systems* (OUP 2008).
Keus LAD, *Europees privaatrecht. Een bonte lappendeken* (Koninklijke Vermande 1993).
Krans B, *Nederlands burgerlijk procesrecht en materieel EU-recht* (Kluwer 2010).
—— 'EU Law and National Civil Procedure Law: An Invisible Pillar' (2015) 23 ERPL 567.
Krans B and Ribbers P, 'The European Account Preservation Order in Dutch Practice' in M Deguchi (ed), Effective Enforcement of Creditors' Rights (Springer 2022) 121.
Leone C and van Duin A, 'Ambtshalve toetsing van Europees consumentenrecht en instrumentalisering van burgerlijk procesrecht: reactie op Bert van Schaick' [2023–4] TCR 127.
Pavillon C, 'Ignorance is Bliss – How Ex Officio Control Became the Raison d'Être of the UCTD' (2024) 32 ERPL 519.
Poisonnier G, 'Office du juge en droit de la consommation, une clarification bienvenue' [2008] Le Dalloz 1290.
Schaick van B, 'Instrumentalisering van burgerlijk procesrecht. Over de inzet van burgerlijk procesrecht om buiten het burgerlijk procesrecht gelegen doelen te realiseren' [2023–3] TCR 70.
Schulte-Nölke H, 'The Objectives of Directive 93/13/EEC on Unfair Contract Terms: An Overview after 30 Years of Case Law' (2024) 32 ERPL 315.
Seinen C and Ancery A, 'Vorderingen in b2c-verstekken: toetsen of toewijzen?' [2015–3] TCR 77.
Sirena P, Ginestri M and Valletta E, 'National Procedural Rules and the New Boundaries of ECJ's Control in the Light of Directive 93/13' (2024) 32 ERPL 549.

Smits P, *Artikel 6 EVRM en de civiele procedure* (Kluwer 2008).
Storme M (ed), *Rapprochement du Droit Judiciaire de l'Union européenne; Approximation of Judiciary Law in the European Union* (Kluwer 1994).
Tridimas T, *The General Principles of EU Law* (OUP 2006).
Van den Heuvel NWM and de Lange MLSWE, 'Het Europees bankbeslag' [2011] BER 32.
Van Het Kaar BJ, 'Conservatoir (derden)beslag niet langer territoriaal?' [2011] WPNR 6905, 903
Vande Lanotte J and Haeck Y, *Handboek EVRM, Deel 1, Algemene beginselen* (Intersentia 2005).
—— (eds), *Handboek EVRM, Deel 2, Artikelsgewijs Commentaar, Volume I* (Intersentia 2004).
Vandenbussche W, 'Zijn afwijkende procedureregels voor consumenten steeds nodig?' (2023) 40 NTBR 289.
Vedder H, 'Spontaneous Harmonisation of National (Competition) Laws in the Wake of the Modernisation of EC Competition Law' (2004) 1 The Competition Law Review 1.
Zeno-Zencovich V and Paglietti MC, 'Le droit processuel des consommateurs' (2014) 66 Revue de droit internationale et de droit comparé 321.

Anna Nylund*

Chapter 7
Innovation and Digitalisation

A Introduction

#1 Innovation encompasses a broad range of regulatory, conceptual, and technological novelties. Often, innovation *per se* is not the primary goal of EU law; rather, it is a byproduct of addressing current challenges, handling issues arising in a cross-border multi- and supra-national context, improving access to justice, and leveraging the advantages of novel technologies. Interplay between national and European law often drives the process. Digitalisation has been a core EU policy to facilitate and expedite access to justice, particularly in cross-border cases. The pathways to and mechanisms underpinning innovation and digitalisation in EU law mirror the complex structure of the Union and the legal bases for civil procedure harmonisation. This chapter discusses three broad, intersecting categories of innovation in EU civil procedure law: innovative regulatory techniques (part B), innovations promoting access to justice (part C), and innovations advancing the digitalisation of civil justice (part D). Finally, part E discusses the implementation of EU law in national law, which is vital for proliferating innovations across Europe.

B Regulatory innovations

#2 The regulatory innovations in the EU fall within three broad categories: international law as a vehicle for developing EU law, the sectoral or substantive approach in which innovations are introduced in a specific sector rather than as general measures, and using soft law tools to promote harmonisation.

I Utilising international law as a regulatory tool

#3 The 1968 **Brussels Convention on jurisdiction and the enforcement of civil and commercial matters,**[1] which was the predecessor of the Brussels Ibis Reg-

1 OJ L299/ 1972, p. 32–42.

***Correspondeing author: Anna Nylund,** University of Bergen, e-mail: anna.nylund@uib.no

https://doi.org/10.1515/9783110781632-007

ulation,[2] marked the genesis of EU civil procedure law. In the absence of a legal basis for civil justice cooperation,[3] the Member States concluded an international convention to create 'the fifth freedom' – the free circulation of civil judgments – to supplement and support the four freedoms. This technique of expanding competence through international conventions was continued when the Luxembourg Protocol[4] was signed in 1971. This integrated 'the fifth freedom' and the Brussels Convention into what was then community law, by enshrining the right to interpret the Convention to the European Court of Justice.

#4 This innovative regulatory technique has since been used in different forms on several occasions. One of the first palpable steps towards the 1995 enlargement of the EU was accomplished in 1988 through the **Lugano Convention**,[5] which, in essence, extended the Brussels regime to the EFTA States. In this way, the then-EFTA States achieved the fifth freedom – the free movement of judgments – before joining the single market. This manifests the centricity of effective and equal access to the vindication of rights, particularly in a cross-border setting, which permeates EU civil procedure law.

#5 The intimate ties between the 2007 **Hague Maintenance Convention**[6] and its Protocol[7] and the Maintenance Regulation[8] are another, more recent example of the interaction between EU law and international law. The EU decided to develop its internal rules on the choice of law and recognition and enforcement of family maintenance in parallel with the negotiation at the Hague Conference, which resulted in two parallel regimes with identical or very similar rules and approaches.[9]

---

2 European Parliament and Council Regulation (EU) 1215/2012 of 12 December 2012 on jurisdiction and the recognition and enforcement of judgments in civil and commercial matters (recast) [2012] OJ L351/1.

3 See E Storskrubb, *Civil Procedure and EU Law: A Policy Area Uncovered* (OUP 2008); E Storskrubb, Chapter 2; CH van Rhee, Chapter 3.

4 Protocol concerning the interpretation by the Court of Justice of the convention of 27 September 1968 on jurisdiction and the enforcement of judgments in civil and commercial matters – signed in Luxembourg on 3 June 1971 [1990] OJ C189/25.

5 Convention on jurisdiction and the enforcement of judgments in civil and commercial matters – Done at Lugano on 16 September 1988 [1988] OJ L319/9.

6 Convention of 23 November 2007 on the International Recovery of Child Support and Other Forms of Family Maintenance.

7 Protocol of 23 November 2007 on the Law Applicable to Maintenance Obligations.

8 Council Regulation (EC) No 664/2009 of 7 July 2009 establishing a procedure for the negotiation and conclusion of agreements between Member States and third countries concerning jurisdiction, recognition and enforcement of judgments and decisions in matrimonial matters, matters of parental responsibility and matters relating to *maintenance* obligations, and the law applicable to matters relating to *maintenance* obligations [2009] OJ L200/46.

9 P Beaumont, 'International Family Law in Europe–the Maintenance Project, the Hague Conference and the EC: A Triumph of Teverse Subsidiarity' (2009) 73 Rabels Zeitschrift für ausländisches und internationales Privatrecht 509; V Lipp, 'Maintenance and Multi-level Harmonisation: A European Union

#6 The Unified Patent Court is the apex of the approach of using international law as a tool in EU civil procedure law. The **Agreement on a Unified Patent Court**[10] is a momentous innovation: it is a cross-jurisdictional court with jurisdiction in the participating Member States. It comprises judges from all participating Member States based at their local court, forming local lower divisions, regional lower divisions for Member States that so desire, a central lower division with two seats, and a Court of Appeal. In addition, there are two Patent and Arbitration Centres. Despite some criticism of unclear rules and competencies,[11] the UPC has been enormously successful: during the first 11 months of operation, 341 cases were filed.[12] It is an example of overcoming the limits of sufficient legal basis and the reluctance to engage in deep-level integration on behalf of some Member States.

II The sectoral – or substantive law – approach

#7 Although the competence of the EU has been palpably widened since the late 1960s, the legal basis for civil justice – the Treaty of the Functioning of the European Union[13] Article 81 – is limited to civil matters having cross-border implications, not civil justice in general. Article 114 on the approximation of laws has a broader scope – the functioning of the internal market in general – and provides a legal basis for appropriate measures in civil justice. However, using Article 114 rather than Article 81 as the legal basis entails linking civil procedure to a specific problem in the internal market and, consequently, to a specific sector of law. The measures to promote alternative dispute resolution (ADR) illustrate this: the ambit of the **EU Mediation Directive**[14] is limited to cross-border cases, whilst the **Consumer ADR Directive**[15] applies to all consumer cases, including purely domestic cases. In fact, Article 81 has turned out to be mostly a paper tiger. The dis-

Perspective' in A Nylund and M Strandberg (eds), *Civil Procedure and the Harmonisation of Law* (Intersentia 2019) 193.

10 Agreement on a Unified Patent Court [2013] OJ C175/1.

11 H Ullrich, 'The Unified Patent Court' (2023) 42 Yearbook of European Law 135.

12 <www.unified-patent-court.org/en/news/case-load-court-start-operation-june-2023-update-end-april-2024> accessed 1 June 2024.

13 Consolidated version of the Treaty on the Functioning of the European Union [2012] OJ C326/47.

14 European Parliament and Council Directive 2008/52/EC of 21 May 2008 on certain aspects of mediation in civil and commercial matters [2008] OJ L136/3.

15 European Parliament and Council Directive 2013/11/EU of 21 May 2013 on alternative dispute resolution for consumer disputes and amending Regulation (EC) No 2006/2004 and Directive 2009/22/EC (Directive on consumer ADR) [2013] OJ L165/63.

tinct European processes for cross-border cases, such as the European Enforcement Order,[16] the European Order for Payment Procedure,[17] the European Small Claims Procedure,[18] and the aforementioned Mediation Directive, which sprouted in the early 2000s, have only to a limited degree been embraced by Europeans, whilst the **sectoral approach** has had a tangible impact on civil procedure across Europe.[19]

#8 Examples of innovations in sectoral rules include rules on access to evidence through **disclosure** in the IPR Enforcement Directive,[20] the Antitrust Damages Directive,[21] and the Product Liability Directive;[22] mechanisms for **collective redress** in the Representative Actions Directive;[23] and **alternative dispute resolution** in the Consumer ADR Directive. The CJEU case law on the obligation of courts to apply EU consumer law in their own motion is another – case law-driven – facet of the sectoral approach.[24] The sectoral approach allows the introduction of innovations 'through the backdoor', limited to a specific sector and specific types of cases.[25]

#9 The sectoral approach is associated with a tangible drawback, namely the national **fragmentation** of civil procedure law. Instead of general rules that are applicable to all civil cases, there are increasingly special rules and procedures that are applicable only to a specific category of cases, such as consumer disputes. This is the opposite of the ideal of coherence that has dominated civil procedure

---

16 European Parliament and Council Regulation (EC) No 805/2004 of 21 April 2004 creating a European Enforcement Order for uncontested claims [2004] OJ L143/15.

17 European Parliament and Council Regulation (EC) No 1896/2006 of 12 December 2006 creating a European order for payment procedure [2006] OJ L399/1.

18 European Parliament and Council Regulation (EC) No 861/2007 of 11 July 2007 establishing a European Small Claims Procedure [2007] OJ L199/1. See also E D'Alessandro, Chapter 16.

19 Eg, X Kramer, 'European Procedures on Debt Collection: Nothing or Noting? Experiences and Future Prospects' in B Hess, M Bergström and E Storskrubb (eds), *EU Civil Justice: Current Issues and Future Outlook* (Hart 2016) 97; C Oro Martinez, 'The Small Claims Regulation: On the Way to an Improved European Procedure?' in B Hess, M Bergström and E Storskrubb (eds), *EU Civil Justice: Current Issues and Future Outlook* (Hart 2016) 123.

20 European Parliament and Council Directive 2004/48/EC of 29 April 2004 on the enforcement of intellectual property rights [2004] OJ L157/45.

21 European Parliament and Council Directive 2014/104/EU of 26 November 2014 on certain rules governing actions for damages under national law for infringements of the competition law provisions of the Member States and of the European Union [2014] OJ L349/1.

22 European Parliament and Council Directive 2024/2853/EU of 23 October 2024 on liability for defective products and repealing Council Directive 85/374/EEC [2024] OJ L2853.

23 European Parliament and Council Directive (EU) 2020/1828 of 25 November 2020 on representative actions for the protection of the collective interests of consumers and repealing Directive 2009/22/EC [2020] OJ L409/1. See E Lein, Chapter 21.

24 See A Ancery and B Krans, Chapter 6.

25 See part E below.

thinking,[26] as it increases complexity and opacity, and creates friction between rules that are applicable to different types of cases. Why should access to evidence be far better in a dispute on intellectual property rights than in a personal injury case? Why should one have far better protection in a dispute on the furniture one has bought for one's home than in a dispute concerning the lease of one's home?

#10 The lack of coordination among EU instruments exacerbates the fragmentation of rules. Two examples illustrate this problem. Rules on the standard of evidence do not use coherent language or a coherent approach.[27] Consequently, determining the standard of proof is difficult. Rules on the disclosure of and access to evidence are not consistent across the IPR Directive, the Antitrust Damages Directive, and the Product Liability Directive. Even when there are distinct, uniform European proceedings in place, the rules piggyback on national procedural rules, the result of which is not a single uniform regime but one for each Member State. Two examples from the Brussels Ibis Regulation illustrate this. As Aleš Galič has noted, when the Regulation abolished the relatively uniform regime for **exequatur** in favour of direct recognition unless an interested party applies for refusal of the recognition, the differences in the procedural systems of the Member States were augmented. This also applies to other aspects of the enforcement, such as suspension of enforcement.[28] Similarly, the estoppel effects of a judgment under the Regulation depend on the rules in the court that rendered the ruling.[29] Given that understanding the intricacies of *res judicata* in some 30 jurisdictions is an insurmountable task, judges can hardly be expected to comply with this rule fully. This lack of uniformity and foreseeability explains why the distinct European procedures have never gained popularity.

---

26 P Collin, 'Einfürung: Europäische Entwicklungslinien gerichtlicher und aussergerichtligcher Konfliktlösung im 19. und 20. Jahrhundert' in P Collin (ed), *Konfliktlösung im 19. Und 20. Jahrhundert* (Springer 2021) 1.

27 Eg, W Hau, 'A German Perspective on the Waning Procedural Autonomy in Civil Matters: Who Is Afraid of European Civil Procedure?' in B Krans and A Nylund (eds), *Procedural Autonomy Across Europe* (Intersentia 2020) 81, 91–99. For an overview of different regimes for evidence, see A Stadler and M Strandberg, '(Rules 87–110, 128–129) General and Procedural Issues' in A Stadler, V Smith and F Gascón Inchausti (eds), *European Rules of Civil Procedure: A Commentary on the ELI/UNIDROIT Model* Rules (Edward Elgar 2023) 252.

28 A Galič, 'Procedural Autonomy between EU Law and the Slovenian Law of Civil Procedure' in B Krans and A Nylund (eds), *Procedural Autonomy Across Europe* (Intersentia 2020) 165, 171–172.

29 Case C-567/21 *BNP Paribas SA v TR* (8 June 2023) ECLI:EU:C:2023:452, paras 49–55; Case C-456/11 *Gothaer Allgemeine Versicherung AG, ERGO Versicherung AG, Versicherungskammer Bayern-Versicherungsanstalt des öffentlichen Rechts, Nürnberger Allgemeine Versicherungs-AG, Krones AG v Samskip GmbH* (15 November 2012) ECLI:EU:C:2012:719. See also W Voss, 'Article 36' in M Requejo Isidro (ed), *Brussels I Bis. A Commentary on Regulation (EU) No 1215/2012* (Edward Elgar 2022), 548, 551–554.

III Soft law as a regulatory tool

#11 **Soft law** is another, often remarkably efficient pathway to the harmonisation – or, at least, approximation – of law, which the EU has used extensively.[30] One form is in recommendations and codes of conduct, such as the European Code of Conduct for Mediators[31] and Collective Redress Framework,[32] which some Member States utilise as a benchmark and source of inspiration for (possible) legislative reforms. The **EU Justice Scoreboard** and the European Commission for the Efficiency of Justice (**CEPEJ**) *Evaluation Report of European Judicial Systems*, discussed in part C below, could also be regarded as a form of soft law in that they could be regarded as containing direct and indirect recommendations. However, these tools are only effective when the Member State and stakeholders in the Member State take an interest in developing their justice system – be it using mediation, collective redress, or something else – but they have virtually no impact when these conditions are not met.

#12 The **European Law Institute** (ELI)[33] should be mentioned as a novel regulatory technique, although it is an independent body that is not formally associated with the EU, beyond being co-funded by the EU. The ELI/UNIDROIT European Model Rules of Civil Procedure[34] demonstrate how to reconcile the need for the approximation and modernisation of laws and the freedom of the Member States to form their civil justice systems. In creating a comprehensive and coherent set of rules based on best practices, they create a benchmark, a common frame of reference, and shared terminology and concepts on which discussions of civil procedure law – nationally and on a European level – can be based.[35] The rules form a terminological, conceptual, and regulatory foundation for future procedural rules in EU law, many of which are enacted as part of regulations that aim to harmonise substantive law and thus regulate only specific parts of court proceedings.

#13 Examples of a combination of soft law and **sectoral law** form an incremental regulatory technique in which soft law instruments are the first step taken before a regulation or directive is enacted. The recommendation on collective redress and the newly enacted Consumer Representative Actions Directive illustrate how this

30 See E Jeuland, Chapter 24.

31 European Code of Conduct for Mediators, Brussels 2 July 2004. Available at <https://e-justice.europa.eu/63/EN/eu_rules_on_mediation> accessed 1 June 2024.

32 Commission Recommendation of 11 June 2013 on common principles for injunctive and compensatory collective redress mechanisms in the Member States concerning violations of rights granted under Union Law [2013] OJ L201/60.

33 <www.europeanlawinstitute.eu/> accessed 1 June 2024.

34 <www.europeanlawinstitute.eu/projects-publications/publications/eli-unidroit-model-european-rules-of-civil-procedure/> accessed 1 June 2024.

35 See also A Stadler, V Smith and F Gascón Inchausti (eds), *European Rules of Civil Procedure. A Commentary on the ELI/UNIDROIT Model Rules* (Edward Elgar 2023).

incremental approach is used to entice recalcitrant Member States to accept collective redress as an indispensable tool for ensuring access to justice.

C Conceptual innovations to promote access to justice

#14 Conceptual innovations to improve access to justice in European civil procedure law fall into three broad categories: effective enforcement of rights deriving from EU law, **judicial cooperation**, and benchmarking.

I Effective enforcement of rights deriving from EU law

#15 The effective enforcement of rights, particularly effective judicial protection, epitomises the conceptual innovations of European civil procedure law.[36] Efficient court proceedings are not just a technical matter but a core prerequisite for the rule of law, democracy, and economic prosperity. Without access to effective remedies, EU law will never be implemented and practised as intended. The requirement for equivalent and efficient vindication of rights arising from EU law and access to expedient court proceedings has shifted the focal point from procedural formalities to how procedural rules and practices might hamper the effectiveness of EU law. In the seminal *Comet* and *Rewe* rulings,[37] the CJEU articulated what has become known as the **principles of equivalence and effecti**veness, which require that rights derived from EU law must have equal protection as rights based on national law, and that the courts of the Member States set aside 'a national procedural provision [that] renders application of Community law impossible or excessively difficult . . .'.[38] This line of case law also marks the genesis of the doctrine of **procedural autonomy**, whereby 'in the absence of Community rules on this subject, it is for the domestic legal system of each Member State . . . to determine the procedural conditions governing actions at law intended to ensure the protection of the rights which citizens have from the direct effect of Community law'[39] unless national law does not meet the abovementioned principles.

---

36 See A Ancery and B Krans, Chapter 6.

37 Case C-45/76 *Comet BV v Produktschap voor Siergewassen* (16 December 1976) ECLI:EU:C:1976:191; Case C-33/76 *Rewe-Zentralfinanz eG and Rewe-Zentral AG v Landwirtschaftskammer für das Saarland* (16 December 1976) ECLI:EU:C:1976:188.

38 Joined Cases C-430/93 and C-431/93 *Jeroen van Schijndel and Johannes Nicolaas Cornelis van Veen v Stichting Pensioenfonds voor Fysiotherapeuten* (14 December 1995) ECLI:EU:C:1995:441, para 19.

39 Case C-33/76 *Rewe* (n 37), para 5; Case C-45/76 *Comet* (n 37), para 13.

#16 Some years after *Rewe*, in the *Von Colson* and *Johnston* cases,[40] the Court introduced the principle of **effective judicial protection**, which derives from the Member States' constitutional traditions and Articles 6 and 13 of the European Convention for the Protection of Human Rights and Fundamental Freedoms. However, the distinction between the *Rewe*-effectiveness principle and the principle of effective judicial protection has often been blurred; it is not entirely clear whether the two are separate principles or whether the principle of effective judicial protection could rather be regarded as a meta-principle encompassing all aspects of the right to an effective remedy,[41] or as a broad fundamental, constitutional principle of EU law.[42] If the latter is the case, then the contrast between the principles is relatively sharp. As noted by Fernando Pastor-Merchante, '[t]he rationale of the principle of effectiveness is strongly instrumental, in that is . . . primarily concerned with . . . ensuring compliance with Union law',[43] and therefore, it is not an expression of a fundamental right.

#17 Similarly, the principle or doctrine of procedural autonomy remains ambiguous. It was formulated when EU civil procedure law was still nascent, but in the increasingly dense landscape of European rules, courts often operate in the (partial) presence of EU procedural law, not in its absence.[44] In addition, the fundamental

40 Case C-14/83 *Sabine von Colson and Elisabeth Kamann v Land Nordrhein-Westfalen* (1984) ECLI:EU:C:1984:153; Case C-222/84 *Marguerite Johnston v Chief Constable of the Royal Ulster Constabulary* (15 May 1986) EU:C:1986:206.

41 A Arnull, 'The Principle of Effective Judicial Protection in EU Law: An Unruly Horse?' (2011) 36 European Law Review 51; S Prechal and R Widdershoven, 'Redefining the Relationship between "Rewe-effectiveness" and Effective Judicial Protection' (2011) 4 Review of European Administrative Law 31; S Prechal and K Cath, 'The European Acquis of Civil Procedure: Constitutional Aspects' (2014) 19 Unified Law Review 179; J Krommendijk, 'Is There Light on the Horizon? The Distinction between "Rewe Effectiveness" and the Principle of Effective Judicial Protection in Article 47 of the Charter after Orizzonte' (2016) 53 Common Market Law Review 1395; M Eliantonio and E Muir, 'The Principle of Effectiveness: Under Strain?' (2019) 12 REALaw 255; F Pastor-Merchante, 'The Overlap between the Principles of Effectiveness and Effective Judicial Protection in Union Law' in C Izquierdo–Sans, C Martínez–Capdevila and M Nogueira–Guastavino, *Fundamental Rights Challenges: Horizontal Effectiveness, Rule of Law and Margin of National Appreciation* (Springer 2021) 211. See also Joined Cases C-317/08 to C-320/08 *Rosalba Alassini and Others v Telecom Italia SpA and Others* (18 March 2010) ECLI:EU:C:2010:146, where the Court discussed both principles in parallel.

42 M Bonelli, 'Effective Judicial Protection in EU Law: An Evolving Principle of a Constitutional Nature' (2019) 12 Review of European Administrative Law 35; Pastor-Merchante (n 41); G Gentile, 'Effective Judicial Protection: Enforcement, Judicial Federalism and the Politics of EU Law' (2023) 2 European Law Open 128.

43 Pastor-Merchante (n 41) 214.

44 M Bobek, 'Why There Is No Principle of "Procedural Autonomy" of the Member States' in B de Witte and H Micklitz (eds), *The European Court of Justice and Autonomy of the Member States* (Intersentia 2011); B Krans and A Nylund, 'Aspects of Procedural Autonomy' in B Krans and A Nylund (eds), *Procedural Autonomy Across Europe* (Intersentia 2020) 1; B Krans and A Nylund, 'Comparative Insights

principles of EU civil procedure law[45] – notably effective judicial protection – diminish the leeway for Member States to shape their civil procedure rules.

II Mutual trust, mutual recognition, and direct judicial cooperation

#18 **Mutual trust**[46] is a pivotal conceptual innovation that paves the way for direct judicial cooperation. Turning the presumption from suspicion towards foreign courts and proceedings to an acceptance of them because they abide by standards comparable to those in one's own jurisdiction results in receiving courts asking how, rather than whether, to comply with requests from and to enforce rulings handed down by foreign courts. Direct judicial cooperation without involving Central Authorities expedites proceedings because the requesting court may contact the receiving court directly, thus reducing communication from three steps (requesting court to **Central Authority** 1, **Central Authority** 1 to Central Authority 2, and Central Authority 2 to receiving court) to only one (requesting court to receiving court).

#19 However, although the concept of mutual trust is important, creating real trust is an arduous endeavour that cannot only be mandated from the 'top-down' but also needs to be created from the 'bottom-up'.[47] Trust needs to be built at the institutional level by ensuring that all courts fulfil minimum fair trial standards, and that there are appropriate and trust-instilling methods of, and practices for, communication between courts. It also needs to be built personally through judicial training sessions and other opportunities for relationship-building and first-hand knowledge-sharing across Member States. The **European Judicial Network** and **European Judicial Training Network** are thus of paramount importance.[48]

on Procedural Autonomy' in B Krans and A Nylund (eds), *Procedural Autonomy Across Europe* (Intersentia 2020) 227.

45 See B Hess, Chapter 5.

46 See M Weller, Chapter 4.

47 T Wischmeyer, 'Generating Trust Through Law? Judicial Cooperation in the European Union and the "Principle of Mutual Trust"' (2016) 17 German Law Journal 339; E Mak, N Graaf and E Jackson, 'The Framework for Judicial Cooperation in the European Union: Unpacking the Ethical, Legal and Institutional Dimensions of Judicial Culture' (2018) 34 Utrecht Journal International and European Law 24, 40–43.

48 M Claes and M de Visser, 'Are you Networked Yet? On Dialogues in European Judicial Networks' (2012) 8 Utrecht Law Review 100. See also <https://e-justice.europa.eu/public_html/index_en.htm> and <https://ejtn.eu/> both accessed 1 June 2024.

III Benchmarking and rankings

#20 **Benchmarking** and '**judicial competition**' are strategies that deserve attention for producing innovation and enhancing efficiency. The 2004 inaugural CEPEJ Evaluation Report[49] of European judicial systems under the Council of Europe marks the genesis of the present European regime. The report contained data on the number of incoming cases, case disposition times and rates, the number of courts and judges, court budgets, and so forth, based on information obtained from national correspondents using a questionnaire. Since then, the CEPEJ has published reports biannually. In 2013, the EU launched the EU Justice Scoreboard,[50] which is based on data retrieved from CEPEJ combined with data from other sources, notably the European Network of Councils for the Judiciary, the European Judicial Training Network, the Council of Bars and Law Societies of Europe, a group of contact persons, and the Eurobarometer.

#21 Benchmarking rests on the assumption that 'rankings' not only generate information on the relative performance of European judiciaries but also drive them to seek to increase their relative performance to avoid 'finishing last'. Moreover, rankings allow European bodies to monitor judiciaries for compliance with the rule of law and other shared European values and goals, and to make recommendations accordingly.[51] The factors measured communicate facets of civil procedure that are found to be of particular importance, such as the **digitalisation** of proceedings, which has been added to the measurements to communicate its importance. However, there is limited evidence that bench-marking fuels **regulatory competition** in civil justice.[52] The reason for this is that states receive no direct income from attracting disputants to use their dispute resolution system, and the indirect benefits of modifying rules with an eye on international competition are hardly perceptible and incidental.

#22 Whilst numerical data gives an air of accuracy, it can also be very misleading. One problem is that the data collected from different legal systems is often incom-

49 Council of Europe, *European Judicial Systems 2002. Facts and Figures on the Basis of a Survey Conducted in 40 Council of Europe Member States.* European Commission for the Efficiency of Justice (CEPEJ) (Council of Europe Publishing 2004).

50 European Commission, *The 2024 EU Justice Scoreboard*, Communication from the Commission to the European Parliament, the Council, the European Central Bank, the European Economic and Social Committee and the Committee of the Regions COM(202) 950, European Union [2024].

51 A Jakab and L Kirchmair, 'How to Develop the EU Justice Scoreboard into a Rule of Law Index: Using an Existing Tool in the EU Rule of Law Crisis in a More Efficient Way' (2021) 22 German Law Journal 936.

52 S Vogenauer, 'Regulatory Competition Through Choice of Contract Law and Choice of Forum in Europe: Theory and Evidence' in H Eidenmüller (ed), *Regulatory Competition in Contract Law and Dispute Resolution* (Beck/Hart/Nomos 2013) 272–273.

mensurable.[53] For example, some justice systems are court-centred; in other systems, many cases are resolved by other dispute resolution bodies and processes. This influences the number of cases, the average workload associated with each case, and case processing times. In court-centred systems, most of the justice system is covered by the data; in other countries, the information only covers part of the system. Moreover, it is likely that the categories used will differ from national law, leaving room for interpretation and discretion. For instance, the notion of a judge is basic yet ambiguous.[54]

#23 Because judiciaries are benchmarked and ranked, they have incentives to report data selectively and strategically to put them in an advantageous light.[55] For instance, the data on the number of incoming cases that the Nordic countries report does not match the data found in their judiciaries' annual reports, yet no explanation is given for this deviation.[56]

#24 The relevance and the operationalisation of key concepts are unclear. Although the number of incoming cases and case disposition times are easily measured, their relation to the quality of justice is unclear; it depends on the caseload composition. Expenditure on courts could be misleading depending on how court-centred the system is, which bodies are included in the numbers, the level of court fees, the availability of **legal aid**, and the division of labour between the court and the parties, and so forth. Given that many of the concepts measured, such as the quality of justice, are elusive, obtaining reliable measurements is chal-

53 C Kern, *Justice between Simplification and Formalism* (Mohr Siebeck 2007); EA Ontanu, F Contini and M Velicogna, 'How Many Cases? Assessing the Comparability of EU Judicial Datasets' in CA d'Alessandro and C Marchese (eds), *Ius Dicere in a Globalized World*, vol. 2 (Roma TrE-Press 2018); A Dori, 'In Data We Trust? Quantifying the Costs of Adjudication in the EU Justice Scoreboard' [2021–4] Erasmus Law Review 281.

54 M Fabri, 'Comparing the Number of Judges and Court Staff across European Countries' (2019) 26 International Journal of the Legal Profession 5.

55 R Mohr and F Contini, 'Conflict and Commonalities in Judicial Evaluation' (2014) 4 Oñati Socio-Legal Series 843; A Uzelac, 'Harmonised Civil Procedure in a World of Structural Divergences? Lessons Learned from the CEPEJ Evaluations' in X Kramer and CH van Rhee (eds), *Civil Litigation in a Globalising World* (Springer 2012) 175; M Fabri, 'Methodological Issues in the Comparative Analysis of the Number of Judges, Administrative Personnel, and Court Performance Collected by the Commission for the Efficiency of Justice of the Council of Europe' (2017) 7 Oñati Socio-Legal Series 616; C Kern, 'Statistical Methods in Comparative Civil Procedure: Chances and Risks' in L Cadiet, B Hess and M Requejo Isidro (eds), *Approaches to Procedural Law: The Pluralism of Methods* (Nomos 2017) 121; A Nylund, 'Comparing the Efficiency and Quality of Civil Justice in Scandinavia: The Role of Structural Differences and Definitions of Quality' (2019) 38 Civil Justice Quarterly 427; EA Ontanu and M Velicogna, 'The Challenge of Comparing EU Member States Judicial Data' (2021) 11 Oñati Socio-Legal Series 446.

56 Nylund (n 55).

lenging.[57] Often, no information is given on how key concepts are defined and operationalised, such as how '**artificial intelligence** applications' are defined and what 'child-friendly' information and participation entails.

#25 Because the methods for gathering and analysing the data and the raw data are not made available for all sources, the reliability and validity of the data and the outcomes of the analysis are questionable.[58] For instance, it is unclear based on whose assessments and based on which materials, the 'child-friendliness' of each jurisdiction has been measured. Similarly, it is not clear whether the availability of technologies rather than their usage has been decisive for scoring. Stakeholders might have unconscious biases that skew the views they report, such as interpreting the Justice Scoreboard to rest on a presumption of the inherent value of technological innovations, which would lead them to give high scores to technological applications that are seldom used rather than based on whether the technologies implemented have increased the efficiency and quality of court proceedings.

#26 Despite the innovative approach, given the methodological weaknesses, the quality of the conclusions drawn on the state of the European judiciaries, their development, and the recommendations made are equally questionable. They can serve as an impetus for some policy changes nationally and supranationally, but could also lead governments to direct resources to measures with insubstantial effects on quality and efficiency, while foregoing those that could have a tangible impact.[59] The technocratic paradigm inherent in benchmarking treats courts as producers of quick and cheap judgments, which reduces them to rubberstamps, and not as indispensable for enforcing **substantive law**[60] and vital organs for the rule of law, which the doctrine of effective judicial protection requires. Considering these weaknesses, Member States' endeavours to position themselves strategically to spread innovations, concepts, and regulatory models emanating from their legal system are likely to be relatively unfruitful.

---

57 C Dallara, 'The Definition of "Best Judicial Practices" by Judicial and Legal Expert Networks and Commissions' in A Vauchez (ed), *The Fabric of International Jurisprudence. An Interdisciplinary Encounter* (EUI-RSCAS Working Papers 2012/51, EUI 2012) 21; D Kosar and S Spac, 'Conceptualization(s) of Judicial Independence and Judicial Accountability by the European Network of Councils for the Judiciary: Two Steps forward, One Step back' (2018) 9 International Journal of Court Administration 37.

58 M Fabri, 'Pitfalls in Data Gathering to Assess Judiciaries' (2018) 9 International Journal for Court Administration 67.

59 A Dori, 'The Supply and Demand of Justice: What Policy Implications from the EU Justice Scoreboard?' in E Storskrubb (ed), *YSEC Yearbook of Socio-Economic Constitutions 2022 – Funding of Justice* (Springer 2023) 53.

60 G Wagner, 'Dispute Resolution as a Product: Competition between Civil Justice Systems' in H Eidenmüller (ed), *Regulatory Competition in Contract Law and Dispute Resolution* (Beck/Hart/Nomos 2013) 347, 374–376. See also G Wagner, 'Legal Origin, Civil Procedure, and the Quality of Contract Enforcement' (2010) 166 Journal of Institutional and Theoretical Economics 171, 175–176.

D Digitalisation and technological innovations

#27 Digitalisation and digital justice efforts can be approached in several ways, such as through their potential functions in the justice system: administrative, communication-related, and substantive functions.[61] In a cross-country context, digitalisation has a fourth dimension that, in many contexts, is equally important as the three other dimensions: access to digital systems across borders.[62] However, because all functions fall primarily under the competence of the Member States, technological advances hinge on the technological and regulatory solutions in place in each Member State.

#28 The futile effort to promote access to justice for consumers through **the Consumer Online Dispute Resolution (ODR) Regulation**[63] demonstrates how the complications of the technological leap should not be underestimated. It highlights the costs of building a reliable, user-friendly, trustworthy system that delivers justice for disputants.[64] Creating awareness of online proceedings and incentives to use them is essential for attracting users.

I Infrastructure for cross-border digital communication

#29 The e-Justice Communication via Online Data Exchange **(e-CODEX)**[65] is a decentralised, interoperable system that allows communication between national digital judicial systems. The European Union Agency for the Operational Management of Large-Scale IT Systems in the Area of Freedom, Security and Justice **(eu-LISA)** operates the e-CODEX.[66] It was introduced as a transformational digital infra-

61 N Ebner and EE Greenberg, 'Strengthening Online Dispute Resolution Justice' (2020) 63 Washington University Journal of Law and Policy 65, 71–72.

62 See also E Steigenga and M Velicogna, 'Envisioning the Next Step in e-Justice: In Search of the Key to Provide Easy Access to Cross-border Justice for All Users' in B Hess and X Kramer (eds), *From Common Rules to Best Practices in European Civil Procedure* (Nomos/Hart 2017) 243; E Storskrubb, 'E-Justice, Innovation and the EU' in B Hess and X Kramer (eds), *From Common Rules to Best Practices in European Civil Procedure* (Nomos/Hart 2017) 271.

63 European Parliament and Council Regulation No 524/2013 of 21 May 2013 on online dispute resolution for consumer disputes and amending Regulation (EC) No 2006/2004 and Directive 2009/22/EC [2013] OJ L165/1., which will be withdrawn.

64 P Cortes and AR Lodder, 'Consumer Dispute Resolution Goes Online: Reflections on the Evolution of European Law for Out-of-Court Redress' (2014) 21 Maastricht Journal of European and Comparative Law 14. See also E van Gelder, Chapter 20.

65 European Parliament and Council Regulation 2022/850 of 30 May 2022 on a computerised system for the cross-border electronic exchange of data in the area of judicial cooperation in civil and criminal matters (e-CODEX system), and amending Regulation 2018/1726 [2022] OJ L150/1.

66 European Parliament and Council Regulation 2018/1726 of 14 November 2018 on the European Union Agency for the Operational Management of Large-Scale IT Systems in the Area of Freedom, Se-

structure to resolve the problem of cross-border access to case management or filing systems. It allows the transformation of data and information across different systems. When a public authority or officer needs to serve a document in another Member State, it sends it electronically to the competent authority or officer in the receiving Member State. The receiving agency then acknowledges the receipt of the document, serves it in accordance with local rules, and finally issues a certificate of service. Documents served through this mechanism must be accepted, even if national law would not recognise electronic documents. When technological solutions enable it, individuals and businesses may file claims directly with the competent authority in another Member State. However, such functionality requires that each Member State establishes a sufficiently secure electronic identification system that forms the European Digital Identity Wallet for each natural and legal person across the EU.[67] The IT systems used must also be compliant with the **General Data Protection Regulation (GDPR)**.[68]

#30 The Digital Justice or **e-Justice Regulation**[69] that was adopted in December 2023 is a substantial step towards cross-border digitalisation and a step towards a comprehensive digital infrastructure for European judiciaries. Once the system has been fully rolled out, which is expected to be by 2031, the European infrastructure, the e-CODEX, shall be the primary method for communication between judicial authorities, pursuant to Article 3. Other methods shall only be used when there is a system failure or similar incident. More importantly, it allows individuals to communicate electronically with authorities and courts across borders through 'European electronic access points'. With the consent of the users or their legal representatives, the service of documents and other types of communication will be performed electronically under Article 4. The system is intended to enable the filing of cases and documents directly through the portal. Functions in current systems, such as information on legal aid, will be transferred to the new

curity and Justice (eu-LISA), and amending Regulation (EC) No 1987/2006 and Council Decision 2007/533/JHA and repealing Regulation (EU) No 1077/2011 [2018] OJ L295/99.

67 European Parliament and Council Regulation 2024/1183 of 11 April 2024 amending Regulation (EU) No 910/2014 as regards establishing the European Digital Identity Framework [2024] OJ L2024/1183; European Parliament and Council Regulation No 910/2014 of 23 July 2014 on electronic identification and trust services for electronic transactions in the internal market and repealing Directive 1999/93/EC [2014] OJ L257/73.

68 European Parliament and Council Regulation 2016/679 of 27 April 2016 on the protection of natural persons with regard to the processing of personal data and on the free movement of such data, and repealing Directive 95/46/EC [2016] OJ L119/1.

69 European Parliament and Council Regulation 2023/2844 of the European Parliament and of the Council of 13 December 2023 on the digitalisation of judicial cooperation and access to justice in cross-border civil, commercial and criminal matters, and amending certain acts in the field of judicial cooperation [2024] OJ L2023/2844.

system. The new system applies to EU law instruments mentioned in the Digital Justice Regulation, whereas new instruments will have their own arrangements, most of which are expected to utilise the e-CODEX infrastructure.

II Digitalisation of administration, communication, and substance

#31 For the administration of justice, the fully rolled-out e-CODEX structure marks a transition to digital case filing, delivery of documents, and access to the case file of a pending case. However, as it hinges on national judicial infrastructure, the extent to which cross-border proceedings are digitalised hinges on the level and nature of digitalisation of the judiciary in each Member State. This includes developing automated case monitoring and scheduling processes, fully digitised (paperless) case files, and so forth. The **Service Regulation** recast[70] has already implemented the possibility of serving documents by email to recipients who have consented.

#32 Similarly, communication-related functions also hinge on the digitalisation of national judiciaries, whether they provide infrastructure for fully or partly remote hearings, remote witness (and expert) examinations, remote mediation, platforms for electronic (and even computer-assisted) negotiation, and so forth. The **Evidence Regulation** recast[71] contains rules for examining witnesses, experts, and so forth remotely. This can be done either directly, where the person giving evidence is in direct contact with the court hearing the case, or indirectly, where the person appears in person at a court that has established a digital connection with the court hearing the case.

#33 Digital substantive functions, such as technology-assisted or technology-conducted party education, suggesting or evaluating options for a solution or the likely judicial outcome, identifying relevant statutory and case law, and automated decision-making, have thus far not been directly regulated in EU law. However, the Artificial Intelligence Act[72] restrains how AI can be implemented to automate and facilitate decision-making. Another guiding document is ***Opinion 26: Moving forward: use***

70 European Parliament and Council Regulation 2020/1784 of 25 November 2020 on the service in the Member States of judicial and extrajudicial documents in civil or commercial matters (recast) OJ L405/40 Article 19. See also W Kennett, Chapter 8.

71 European Parliament and Council Regulation 2020/1783 of 25 November 2020 on cooperation between the courts of the Member States in the taking of evidence in civil or commercial matters (taking of evidence) (recast) [2020] OJ L405/1. See also J Van Doninck and W Vandenbussche, Chapter 11.

72 Regulation (EU) 2024/1689 of the European Parliament and of the Council of 13 June 2024 laying down harmonised rules on artificial intelligence and amending Regulations (EC) No 300/2008, (EU) No 167/2013, (EU) No 168/2013, (EU) 2018/858, (EU) 2018/1139 and (EU) 2019/2144 and Directives 2014/90/EU, (EU) 2016/797 and (EU) 2020/1828 (Artificial Intelligence Act) [2024] OJ L2024/1689.

of modern technologies in the judiciary,[73] which was adopted by the Consultative Council of European Judges in December 2023 and explicates many of the same concerns, situating them in the context of the judiciary and judicial proceedings. ELI has initiated a project developing principles for the digitisation of civil justice systems.[74]

#34 The restrictions imposed by data protection on e-discovery or **e-disclosure** and data protection are important when (prospective) parties may request access to evidence pursuant to national or EU law. In these situations, prospective parties might need to process (sensitive) personal data to establish whether they have a claim. For instance, to establish an infringement of competition law, a party might request access to customer information from a company selling medical devices (eg blood sugar monitors). To establish a contractual obligation, a party could request access to e-mail correspondence that might contain personal data. Parties must also be able to share documents containing personal data with the other party and the court. If a (prospective) party may request disclosure of information under EU or national law, there might be broad access to personal data, including sensitive data, and a need to export it to a provider of e-discovery tools in a third country.[75] GDPR Article 9(2)(f) enshrines exceptions for handling sensitive data to establish, exercise, and defend legal claims.[76] The extent of the exceptions, particularly for e-disclosure, is unclear, including the limits that apply to exporting the data to third countries for processing.[77]

E Implementation of EU civil procedure law

#35 The indirect effects of EU procedural law should not be underestimated. Given that EU civil procedure law is often sectoral, it is not unsurprising that Member States sometimes **'over-implement'** the rules by extending their reach into other areas of law.[78] Although some Member States are reluctant to implement rules

73 Consultative Council of European Judges (CCJE), CCJE Opinion No. 26 (2023): Moving forward: The Use of Assistive Technology in the Judiciary. CCJE(2023)3 Strasbourg, 1 December 2023.

74 See <https://www.europeanlawinstitute.eu/projects-publications/current-projects/current-projects/eli-digitalisation-of-civil-justice-systems-in-europe/> accessed 1 June 2025.

75 M Surguy, *International E-Discovery* (2nd edn, Globe Law and Business Limited 2021).

76 See also recitals 20, 52, and 97. See also L Georgieva and C Kuner, 'Article 9' in C Kunder, LA Bygrave and C Docksey (eds), *The EU General Data Protection Regulation (GDPR): A Commentary* (OUP 2020) 365, 379; A Jóri, 'Art. 9' in I Speicker gen. Döhmann and others (eds), *General Data Protection Regulation. Article-by-Article Commentary* (Hart/Beck/Nomos 2023) 400, 417.

77 See recital 115.

78 See A Nylund and B Krans (eds), *The European Union and National Civil Procedure* (Intersentia 2016); B Krans and A Nylund (eds), *Procedural Autonomy Across Europe* (Intersentia 2020).

that give (prospective) litigants opportunities to gain access to evidence in possession of the opposite party and third parties, they might be willing to do so for specific types of cases, such as intellectual property right infringements and competition cases, and then, either immediately or later on, extend the reach of the rules on disclosure to other types of cases as well. By extending the scope of the rules through over-implementation, novel mechanisms trickle down to national rules. The sectoral approach of EU law functions in essence as a 'Trojan horse' – a vehicle to introduce new elements incrementally, realm by realm – thus allowing for a way to overcome initial scepticism and consider introducing similar national legislation on a broader or even general basis.

#36 Nevertheless, one should not overestimate **'indirect' harmonisation**. On the contrary, divergences in the implementation – and interpretation – of EU law result in dissimilarities between EU Member States, which the diverse legal contexts of the Member States augment.[79] When applying EU law, lawyers naturally start with the legal concepts and institutions that they know – those that they are familiar with. This is natural, and deficient knowledge of EU law amplifies this challenge. The quality of EU civil procedure law – how well-chosen the legal-technical and conceptual solutions are and the clarity of the language used – influences the quality of the implementation and the extent of divergences between Member States. As has been discussed above, the regulatory technique employed in the Small Claims Regulation, strongly piggybacking on national law,[80] is a quintessential example of a regulatory technique that augments differences among Member States and consequently reduces the efficacy of the instrument.

#37 The challenges associated with implementing EU civil procedure law decelerate the uptake of innovations in EU law. They might remain unutilised due to a lack of awareness, the (potential) friction with national law, or a lack of perceived added value compared to existing national mechanisms. Digitalisation strongly depends on each Member State's judiciaries having user-friendly, reliable technological solutions.

#38 Given the different factors impacting the implementation of EU law, it is hardly surprising that EU civil procedure law makes uneven progress regarding the extent to which it influences civil procedure law in the Member States and on the European level.

79 See Nylund and Krans (n 78); Krans and Nylund (n 78).

80 Oro Martinez (n 19) 134–136.

References

Arnull A, 'The Principle of Effective Judicial Protection in EU Law: An Unruly Horse?' (2011) 36 European Law Review 51.

Beaumont P, 'International Family Law in Europe – the Maintenance Project, the Hague Conference and the EC: A Triumph of Teverse Subsidiarity' (2009) 73 Rabels Zeitschrift für ausländisches und internationales Privatrecht 509.

Bobek M, 'Why There Is No Principle of "Procedural Autonomy" of the Member States' in B de Witte and H Micklitz (eds), The European Court of Justice and Autonomy of the Member States (Intersentia 2011).

Bonelli M, 'Effective Judicial Protection in EU Law: An Evolving Principle of a Constitutional Nature' (2019) 12 Review of European Administrative Law 35.

Claes M and de Visser M, 'Are you Networked Yet? On Dialogues in European Judicial Networks' (2012) 8 Utrecht Law Review 100.

Collin P, 'Einfürung: Europäische Entwicklungslinien gerichtlicher und aussergerichtligcher Konfliktlösung im 19. und 20. Jahrhundert' in P Collin (ed), *Konfliktlösung im 19. Und 20. Jahrhundert* (Springer 2021) 1.

Cortés P and Lodder AR, 'Consumer Dispute Resolution Goes Online: Reflections on the Evolution of European Law for Out-of-Court Redress' (2014) 21 Maastricht Journal of European and Comparative Law 14.

Dallara C, 'The Definition of "Best Judicial Practices" by Judicial and Legal Expert Networks and Commissions' in A Vauchez (ed), *The Fabric of International Jurisprudence. An Interdisciplinary Encounter* (EUI-RSCAS Working Papers 2012/51, EUI 2012) 21.

Dori A, 'In Data We Trust? Quantifying the Costs of Adjudication in the EU Justice Scoreboard' [2021–4] Erasmus Law Review 281.

—— 'The Supply and Demand of Justice: What Policy Implications from the EU Justice Scoreboard?' in E Storskrubb (ed), *YSEC Yearbook of Socio-Economic Constitutions 2022 – Funding of Justice* (Springer 2023) 53.

Ebner N and Greenberg EE, 'Strengthening Online Dispute Resolution Justice' (2020) 63 Washington University Journal of Law and Policy 65.

Eliantonio M and Muir E, 'The Principle of Effectiveness: Under Strain?' (2019) 12 Review of European Administrative Law 255.

Fabri M, 'Methodological Issues in the Comparative Analysis of the Number of Judges, Administrative Personnel, and Court Performance Collected by the Commission for the Efficiency of Justice of the Council of Europe' (2017) 7 Oñati Socio-Legal Series 616.

—— 'Pitfalls in Data Gathering to Assess Judiciaries' (2018) 9 International Journal for Court Administration 67.

—— 'Comparing the Number of Judges and Court Staff across European Countries' (2019) 26 International Journal of the Legal Profession 5.

Galič A, 'Procedural Autonomy between EU Law and the Slovenian Law of Civil Procedure' in B Krans and A Nylund (eds), *Procedural Autonomy Across Europe* (Intersentia 2020) 165.

Gentile G, 'Effective Judicial Protection: Enforcement, Judicial Federalism and the Politics of EU Law' (2023) 2 European Law Open 128.

Georgieva L and Kuner C, 'Article 9' in C Kunder, LA Bygrave and C Docksey (eds), *The EU General Data Protection Regulation (GDPR): A Commentary* (OUP 2020) 365.

Hau W, 'A German Perspective on the Waning Procedural Autonomy in Civil Matters: Who Is Afraid of European Civil Procedure?' in B Krans and A Nylund (eds), Procedural Autonomy Across Europe (Intersentia 2020) 81.

Jakab A and Kirchmair L, 'How to Develop the EU Justice Scoreboard into a Rule of Law Index: Using an Existing Tool in the EU Rule of Law Crisis in a More Efficient Way' (2021) 22 German Law Journal 936.

Jóri A, 'Art. 9' in Speicker gen. Döhmann I and others (eds), *General Data Protection Regulation. Article-by-Article Commentary* (Hart/Beck/Nomos 2023) 400.
—— (eds), *Procedural Autonomy Across Europe* (Intersentia 2020).
Krans B and Nylund A, 'Aspects of Procedural Autonomy' in B Krans and A Nylund (eds), *Procedural Autonomy Across Europe* (Intersentia 2020) 1.
—— 'Comparative Insights on Procedural Autonomy' in B Krans and A Nylund (eds), *Procedural Autonomy Across Europe* (Intersentia 2020) 227.
Krans B and Nylund A, Procedural Autonomy Across Europe (Intersentia 2020)
Kern C, *Justice between Simplification and Formalism* (Mohr Siebeck 2007).
—— 'Statistical Methods in Comparative Civil Procedure: Chances and Risks' in L Cadiet, B Hess and M Requejo Isidro (eds), *Approaches to Procedural Law: The Pluralism of Methods* (Nomos 2017) 121.
Kosar D and Spac S, 'Conceptualization(s) of Judicial Independence and Judicial Accountability by the European Network of Councils for the Judiciary: Two Steps Forward, One Step Back' (2018) 9 International Journal of Court Administration 37.
Kramer X, 'European Procedures on Debt Collection: Nothing or Noting? Experiences and Future Prospects' in B Hess, M Bergström and E Storskrubb (eds), *EU Civil Justice: Current Issues and Future Outlook* (Hart 2016) 97.
Krommendijk J, 'Is There Light on the Horizon? The Distinction between "Rewe Effectiveness" and the Principle of Effective Judicial Protection in Article 47 of the Charter after Orizzonte' (2016) 53 Common Market Law Review 1395.
Lipp V, Maintenance and Multi-level Harmonisation: A European Union Perspective' in Anna Nylund & Magne Strandberg (eds), Civil Procedure and the Harmonisation of Law (Intersentia 2019) 193.
Mak E, Graaf N and Jackson E, 'The Framework for Judicial Cooperation in the European Union: Unpacking the Ethical, Legal and Institutional Dimensions of Judicial Culture' (2018) 34 Utrecht Journal of International and European Law 24.
Mohr R and Contini F, 'Conflict and Commonalities in Judicial Evaluation' (2014) 4 Oñati Socio-Legal Series 843.
Nylund A, 'Comparing the Efficiency and Quality of Civil Justice in Scandinavia: The Role of Structural Differences and Definitions of Quality' (2019) 38 Civil Justice Quarterly 427.
Nylund A and Krans B (eds), *The European Union and National Civil Procedure* (Intersentia 2016).
Ontanu EA, Contini F and Velicogna M, 'How Many Cases? Assessing the Comparability of EU Judicial Datasets' in CA d'Alessandro and C Marchese (eds), *Ius Dicere in a Globalized World*, vol 2 (Roma TrE-Press 2018).
Ontanu EA and Velicogna M, 'The Challenge of Comparing EU Member States Judicial Data' (2021) 11 Oñati Socio-Legal Series 446.
Oro Martinez C, 'The Small Claims Regulation: On the Way to an Improved European Procedure?' in B Hess, M Bergström and E Storskrubb (eds), *EU Civil Justice: Current Issues and Future Outlook* (Hart 2016) 123.
Pastor-Merchante F, 'The Overlap between the Principles of Effectiveness and Effective Judicial Protection in Union Law' in C Izquierdo-Sans, C Martínez-Capdevila and M Nogueira-Guastavino (eds), *Fundamental Rights Challenges: Horizontal Effectiveness, Rule of Law and Margin of National Appreciation* (Springer 2021) 211.
Prechal S and Cath K, 'The European Acquis of Civil Procedure: Constitutional Aspects' (2014) 19 Unified Law Review 179.
Prechal S and Widdershoven R, 'Redefining the Relationship between "Rewe-effectiveness" and Effective Judicial Protection' (2011) 4 Review of European Administrative Law 31.
Stadler A and Strandberg M, '(Rules 87–110, 128–129) General and Procedural Issues' in A Stadler, V Smith and F Gascón Inchausti (eds), *European Rules of Civil Procedure: A Commentary on the ELI/UNIDROIT Model Rules* (Edward Elgar 2023) 252.

Steigenga E and Velicogna M, 'Envisioning the Next Step in e-Justice: In Search of the Key to Provide Easy Access to Cross-border Justice for All Users' in B Hess and X Kramer (eds), *From Common Rules to Best Practices in European Civil Procedure* (Nomos/Hart 2017) 243.

Storskrubb E, *Civil Procedure and EU Law: A Policy Area Uncovered* (OUP 2008).

—— 'E-Justice, Innovation and the EU' in B Hess and X Kramer (eds), *From Common Rules to Best Practices in European Civil Procedure* (Nomos/Hart 2017) 271.

Surguy M, *International E-Discovery* (2nd edn, Globe Law and Business Limited 2021).

Ullrich H, 'The Unified Patent Court' (2023) 42 Yearbook of European Law 135.

Uzelac A, 'Harmonised Civil Procedure in a World of Structural Divergences? Lessons Learned from the CEPEJ Evaluations' in X Kramer and CH van Rhee (eds), *Civil Litigation in a Globalising World* (Springer 2012) 175.

Vogenauer S, 'Regulatory Competition Through Choice of Contract Law and Choice of Forum in Europe: Theory and Evidence' in H Eidenmüller (ed), *Regulatory Competition in Contract Law and Dispute Resolution* (Beck/Hart/Nomos 2013) 272.

Voss W, 'Article 36' in M Requejo Isidro (ed), Brussels I Bis: A Commentary on Regulation (EU) No 1215/ 2012 (Edward Elgar 2022) 548.

Wagner G, 'Legal Origin, Civil Procedure, and the Quality of Contract Enforcement' (2010) 166 Journal of Institutional and Theoretical Economics 171.

—— 'Dispute Resolution as a Product: Competition between Civil Justice Systems' in H Eidenmüller (ed), *Regulatory Competition in Contract Law and Dispute Resolution* (Beck/Hart/Nomos 2013) 347.

Wischmeyer T, 'Generating Trust Through Law? Judicial Cooperation in the European Union and the "Principle of Mutual Trust"' (2016) 17 German Law Journal 339.

Part II: **Litigating and Other Means of Dispute Resolution in Europe**

Wendy Kennett

Chapter 8
Getting Started: Service of Documents

A Introduction

#1 The service of documents plays a foundational role in ensuring that a judgment is capable of enforcement. It was therefore one of the first areas in which European legislation was adopted,[1] and the effectiveness of that legislation has been kept under review since.[2] The current iteration of the European legislation on service is **Regulation 2020/1784 (**ESR 2020),[3] which is principally concerned with the mechanisms of **cross-border transmission of documents** for service, rather than with general principles relating to service.[4]

1 The recently proposed amendments are the fourth iteration of the European rules. The earliest EU measure adopted was the 1997 Convention on the service in the Member States of the European Union of judicial and extrajudicial documents in civil or commercial matters, which pre-dated the changes in EU competence in relation to judicial co-operation in civil matters introduced by the Treaty of Amsterdam (1998) and was strongly influenced by the 1965 Hague Service Convention. This was followed by Regulations 1348/2000 and 1393/2007. The amendments to the rules have gradually reduced possible reservations, improved technical co-operation, and brought the legislation into conformity with significant rulings of the ECtHR and CJEU. There has also been additional partial regulation of service in the context of the EU Regulations on recognition and enforcement of judgments, which has proved influential in shaping the development of the law on service, in particular through the rulings of the CJEU.
2 For significant reviews of Regulation 1393/2007 and preparing for Regulation 2020/1784 (available online from the Publications Office of the European Union: POEU) see eg Mainstrat and University of the Basque Country, *Study on the Application of Council Regulation (EC) No 1393/2007 on the Service of Judicial and Extrajudicial Documents in Civil and Commercial Matters* (European Commission 2014) (hereafter, *Mainstrat Study*); Directorate-General for Justice and Consumers (European Commission) and Max Planck Institute, *An Evaluation Study of National Procedural Laws and Practices in Terms of Their Impact on the Free Circulation of Judgments and on the Equivalence and Effectiveness of the Procedural Protection of Consumers under EU Consumer Law* (European Commission 2017) (hereafter, *Luxembourg MPI Study*). See also Commission Staff Working Document, Impact Assessment SWD(2018) 287 final (hereafter, *Impact Assessment*) and the annexed *Evaluation Report* and A Simoni and G Pailli, *Study on the Service of Documents: Comparative Legal Analysis of the Relevant Laws and Practices of the Member States. Final Report.* No JUST/2014/JCOO/PR/CIVI/0049 (European Commission 2016) (hereafter, Simoni and Pailli).
3 Regulation (EU) 2020/1784 of the European Parliament and of the Council of 25November 2020 on the service in the Member States of judicial and extrajudicial documents in civil or commercial matters (service of documents) (recast).
4 At the same time as the ESR 2020 was being negotiated, UNIDROIT and the European Law Institute were developing model European rules of civil procedure (ERCP) which set out general principles re-

Wendy Kennett, Cardiff University, e-mail: KennettW@cardiff.ac.uk

https://doi.org/10.1515/9783110781632-008

B Factors Influencing the Rules on Service

#2 National approaches to the regulation of **service of documents** are strongly influenced by broad considerations of legal, social and political culture. At one extreme, there may be a culture of transparency, trust and compliance, with low scores on indexes of power/distance and uncertainty avoidance.[5] In such Member States there is a willingness to accept quite informal contacts between administration and citizens. In Sweden, for example, it appears that defendants regularly acknowledge **postal service**, and that courts may also telephone a defendant to check whether documents have been received. At the other extreme, there may be a culture of distrust, formality and distance. In such a context, formal methods of service have an enhanced role to play, **fictitious service** may play a more important role and there may be less willingness to cure defects in service.

#3 Another important factor is the approach taken by individual legal systems towards the **balance between the interests of parties**. Some systems may prioritise the claimant's interest in the ease and low cost of commencement of proceedings. Others may place a higher value on the protection of the defendant and the extent to which a right to a hearing is guaranteed. Moreover, service of documents has also long been perceived by states as linked to their **sovereignty**. A comparative study of national approaches to the service of documents, funded by the European Commission as part of the groundwork for the ESR 2020, comments that:

> [T]he link that exists between service and jurisdiction (between service and a State's *imperium*), has long justified the hostility showed toward service by foreign agents in another sovereign territory, forcing parties and foreign courts to face high hurdles before being able to serve documents abroad.[6]

#4 In the specific context of litigation, responsibility for service is allocated to different actors in different Member States, in accordance with the organisation of judicial and other procedural institutions in each State. This complicates discussion of methods of service, since there is no shared understanding of the status and functions of the actors who may be involved. Service may be undertaken by **Judicial Officers,**[7] **court bailiffs**, employees of an administrative agency, agents of the post

---

lating to service. Although the following discussion is primarily concerned with the ESR 2020, footnote reference will be made to complementary or contrasting provisions found in the ERCP.

5 G Hofstede, *Cultures and Organizations: Software of the Mind* (McGraw-Hill 1991).

6 Simoni and Pailli (n 2) 2.

7 In this paper the term 'Judicial Officer' is used to designate an independent regulated professional such as a *Commissaire de justice* or *gerechtsdeurwaarder*. Such professionals are distinguished by the fact that they have primary responsibility for the execution of judgments, but they may also have much wider functional competences, depending on the jurisdiction in question: see further W Ken-

office, police officers or **private bailiffs**.[8] The COVID pandemic also gave impetus to the use of **electronic methods of service**, which may or may not require the involvement of traditional process servers.

#5 An example of the way that procedures for service of documents are embedded in legal culture is the exclusive competence of a Judicial Officer for **formal service of documents (*signification*)** in France, Belgium the Netherlands and Luxembourg. Formal service is required at certain points in civil litigation and notably to initiate proceedings. The exclusive competence of Judicial Officers is rooted in the historical development of the profession and remains fiercely protected. By contrast, in many jurisdictions postal service is commonly used – whether initiated by the claimant or by the court.[9] **Certain formalities for postal service** are intended to provide a greater guarantee that the documents for service are actually received by the defendant. Thus, in most jurisdictions service must take place via **registered mail**, and in some jurisdictions a specially marked envelope is used to emphasise the significance of correct delivery.

#6 There may also be significant differences in relation to how far the institution with responsibility for service may have **privileged access to information** in order to locate the defendant. Furthermore, Member States take different approaches to the question whether individuals have a responsibility to notify public authorities about any change in address. And there may or may not be a presumption that service at the registered address constitutes due service. Where a defendant proves difficult to locate, some jurisdictions entrust service to the police, or other municipal officers who may be well placed to identify an address. In this respect, legal cultures differ considerably. Judicial Officers in Eastern Europe have been heard to complain that prior to the privatisation of their role, it was common for the police to assist them with service in difficult cases, but cooperation in this public task has diminished since they became part of an independent profession.

#7 National responses to **digitalisation** are a further important consideration in this context, and these have an impact on issues relating to service well beyond the mere addition of a new method of communication. For example, digitalisation has led to changes in the territorial jurisdiction of courts and judicial officers,

---

nett, *Civil Enforcement in a Comparative Perspective: A Public Management Challenge* (Intersentia 2021). In legal writing more generally the term 'judicial officer' tends to be used to translate a variety of different types of legal personnel – from bailiffs to court administrators (as in Case C-223/14 *Tecom Mican* (11 November 2015) ECLI:EU:C:2015:744) – which confuses comparisons.

8 For further detail, see Simoni and Pailli (n 2) 30 ff.

9 Simoni and Pailli (n 2) 31 note the 'two-fold nature' of postal operators who may be understood as process servers if they can be approached directly by the initiator (eg the party's lawyer), and as mere means of transmission if the executor (eg a court or bailiff) uses the postal service for delivery of the document.

and changes in the functional competences and degree of specialisation of institutions involved in service. It is also altering the relationship between citizens and state, with greater state awareness of the location and actions of citizens. Evidence from Member States indicates the widespread introduction of new strategies to allow service of documents via email or via a designated digital platform, but there are great variations in approach.[10] The ESR 2020 have attempted to facilitate these changes, while at the same time recognising that states are moving at different speeds.[11]

C Scope of the ESR 2020

#8 The Regulation applies to **judicial documents** and **extra-judicial documents**. According to Article 21 ESR 2020 the same principles apply to both, although most of the emphasis in case law is understandably on the service of the document instituting judicial proceedings. Historically there has been heavy reliance on **'fictitious' service** in cross-border cases in Europe – such as service by publication of the relevant information in a specified location or through a specified channel in the State of origin. The 1965 Hague Convention on Service of Documents did not address this issue since it does not apply when the address of the defendant is unknown. In principle the same approach has been followed in the European rules on service, including Article 1(2) ESR 2020,[12] even though Member States have ways of locating the defendant in comparable domestic cases.[13] Evidence of the difficulty sometimes experienced in locating the defendant[14] has, however, led to a new Article 7 that provides for **cross-border assistance** in identifying the defendant's address. It identifies several methods of assistance for locating the addressee that may be sought from the state addressed and it requires Member States to notify the Commission as to which method they will provide and the relevant contact details. Under Article 7(1) assistance may take the form of:

---

10 These differences of approach are explored in Simoni and Pailli (n 2) 94–121. For more recent data, see the <https://e-justice.europa.eu/38580/EN/serving_documents_recast> accessed 14 February 2025 and the reports on service of documents from the DG JUST funded project 'Digital Communication and Safeguarding the Parties' Rights: Challenges for European Civil Procedure (DIGI-GUARD)', available at <https://pf.um.si/en/acj/projects/pr10-digi-guard/results/national-reports/> accessed 11 April 2025.

11 This is also true of the ERCP.

12 In spite of a proposed amendment to the previous rule (Article 1(1) ESR 2007) to the effect that the Regulation would apply to the service of judicial documents on persons domiciled in a Member State other than the one where the judicial proceedings take place.

13 Luxembourg MPI Study (n 2) 73; Impact Assessment (n 2) 17–18.

14 See Evaluation Study (n 2) 22–23; Impact Assessment (n 2), 11; Simoni and Pailli (n 2) 121–129 and 261; Luxembourg MPI Study (n 2) 56.

a. **Access to information** through official channels (between a transmitting agency and a designated authority in the State addressed);
b. Direct access to publicly accessible databases in the State addressed via a standard form available on the European e-Justice Portal; or
c. Provision of detailed information, through the European e-Justice Portal, on how to find the addresses of persons to be served.

#9 But in addition, the authorities of the Member State addressed responsible for effecting service are required to communicate via the **e-Justice Portal** whether they submit requests for address information to the relevant domestic databases on their own initiative if the information in a request for service is incorrect (Article 7(2)(c)).[15]

D Structure of the ESR 2020

#10 Chapter I of the Regulation contains general provisions. After defining the scope of the Regulation and certain terms used, it deals with the establishment of **transmitting agencies** and **receiving agencies** in each Member State and the means of communication between those agencies (Chapter I, Arts 3–6 and Chapter II, Section 1, Arts 8–15). Under Article 5 a **central authority**[16] is also designated to provide relevant information to transmitting agencies and resolve problems that arise.

#11 The Preamble explains the relevance of the transmitting and receiving agencies as follows:

> **Efficiency and speed in judicial proceedings** in civil matters require that judicial and extrajudicial documents be transmitted directly and by rapid means between local bodies designated by the Member States. Member States should be able to designate separate transmitting agencies and receiving agencies or to designate one or more agencies to perform both functions . . . [17]

---

15 According to the e-Justice Portal, the following Member States provide access to information through official channels and the authorities entrusted with service check addresses of their initiative (Article 7(1)(a) and (2)(c): Belgium, Bulgaria, Czechia, Denmark, Croatia, Greece, Luxembourg, Netherlands, Portugal, Slovenia, Slovakia, Spain. Although Finland and Sweden instead offer information about how to access address data (Article 7(1)(c)), as very open societies they provide access to the same data available to official process servers. Cyprus, Hungary, Italy, Lithuania, Malta and Romania state that they will provide access to address information through official channels (Article 7(1)(a)) but do not commit their authorities to checking incorrect addresses. The other Member State provide varying amounts of information on how to access relevant registers. Germany also states that receiving agencies will normally endeavour to check incorrect addresses. Ireland regards all address checks as the responsibility of the party seeking to effect service. This is also it's domestic position, but in the event that an address is hard to establish an application may be made for 'substituted service' by which is meant service using a method of last resort such as publication.

16 More than one central authority may be designated in federal states.

17 Recital 9.

#12 Documents to be served can be sent by a transmitting agency in the State of origin to the relevant receiving agency in the State addressed, with service then being effected under the rules applicable in the State addressed. Although significant attention is devoted to these agencies, the Regulation also permits other cross-border methods of service as specified in Ch II Section 2 of the Regulation:[18]

i) Diplomatic or consular channels (Article 17)
ii) Registered mail (Article 18)
iii) Electronic means (Article 19)
iv) 'Direct service' (Article 20)

#13 The alternative methods in Árticles 18–20 permit a document to be served 'directly' on the addressee. For example, the service initiator[19] may be able to use postal service from the State of origin to the addressee or may be able to approach a process server in the State addressed without going via the transmitting and receiving agencies. Permission to use electronic means of service is a further possibility, seen as an important innovation introduced by the recast regulation.

#14 The particular significance of transmitting and receiving agencies arises from the different ways in which proceedings are commenced in different Member States.[20] Taking a standard first instance action as an example, proceedings may be commenced when the **document instituting the proceedings is filed with the competent court and responsibility for the service of procedural documents lies with that court.** Alternatively, it may be that court proceedings do not start with the filing of the claim with the court[21] – **rather the claimant must first serve the document instituting the proceedings on the defendant and afterwards file the claim with the court.** This is the position in countries which have traditionally required formal service of the document instituting the proceedings by a Judicial Officer.[22] And some legal systems in which service is normally undertaken by the

18 Article 16, located in this Section, is concerned with the transmission of documents via diplomatic or consular channels to a receiving agency in the State addressed for onward service, but the other provisions are concerned with direct service on the addressee.

19 Depending on the jurisdiction, service may be initiated by a party or their legal representative, or by a court or other authority.

20 This is not to overlook the fact that the Regulation applies to service of documents in a wide range of contexts, or the pragmatic reasons for transmitting and receiving agencies, such as confidence in the source of the documents, consistency of approach, centralisation of expertise, and under the ESR 2020 improved channels of communication.

21 Reference is made here to a claimant commencing proceedings

22 France, Belgium, Luxembourg and the Netherlands. This approach to the commencement of proceedings is also adopted in Italy (Arts 163–165, 137 CPC). In Cyprus and Ireland, the document instituting the proceedings is issued by the court to the claimant or their representative and served by them. The defendant either then enters an appearance (through lodging the appropriate form at the competent court) or leaves the way open for the claimant to apply for a default judgment. In each case, the validity of service is nevertheless subject to court scrutiny.

court may also, on request, permit the claimant to arrange for service.[23] In the following discussion, reference will be made to **court-initiator jurisdictions** and **party-initiator jurisdictions** in order to reflect these distinctions.[24]

#15 The role of the courts in service of documents is significant to the mechanisms by which cross-border service can be facilitated. If service of the document instituting the proceedings is seen as part of the court's **exercise of jurisdiction**, this reduces the scope for introducing flexibility into procedures for service, including the scope for a claimant in the State of origin to approach the authority competent to effect service in the State addressed. At the same time, the arrangements for cross-border service are not an instance of cooperation between courts.[25] The introduction of transmitting and receiving agencies provides a formal solution.

#16 Typically, transmitting and receiving agencies are either courts or **Judicial Officers**,[26] although other solutions exist, and in some states that know the institution of Judicial Officer it is nevertheless the court that is responsible for service of documents in ordinary proceedings. Moreover, the role of transmitting and receiving agency may be given to all local courts, or there may be a central or regional court that is given this responsibility. In some Member States these roles may be given to two different authorities. For example, in Denmark courts are transmitting agencies, but the Ministry of Justice is the receiving agency and in Latvia courts are transmitting agencies, but the Council of Sworn Bailiffs[27] is the receiving agency.

E Service under Chapter II, Section 1

I Communication Between Transmitting and Receiving Agencies

#17 Reviews of the operation of the ESR 2007[28] found that communication between agencies was in many cases undesirably slow and that modern channels of communication were not used 'partly due to old habits, partly due to legal obstacles, and partly due to the lack of interoperability of the national IT systems.[29] The

23 See Simoni and Pailli (n 2) 30 (but most of the examples here relate to service after proceedings have commenced).

24 This terminology is used by Simoni and Pailli (n 2).

25 Cf the approach adopted in Regulation 2020/1783 on taking of evidence.

26 Note that the entry for Spain in the e-Justice Portal says that Judicial Officers are the transmitting and receiving agencies. In this case, Judicial Officers are senior court administrators. Under Spanish court reforms, such administrators may be located in administrative centre separate from the court.

27 Using the terminology adopted here this is the national chamber of Judicial Officers.

28 Impact Assessment (n 2) 14–15 and 19; Evaluation Report (n 2) 30–31; Simoni and Pailli (n 2) 242.

29 Explanatory Memorandum to the proposal for a Regulation amending the ESR 2007 (COM(2018) 379 final) 3.

compulsory use of electronic communication between transmitting and receiving agencies was an obvious and pressing development and the Article 5(1) ESR 2020 requires all communications to be transmitted through **a secure and reliable decentralised IT system**. That decentralised IT system shall be based on an interoperable solution such as **e-CODEX**.

#18 Article 2 of the Regulation defines a 'decentralised IT system' as a 'network of national IT systems and interoperable access points, operating under the individual responsibility and management of each Member State, that enables the secure and reliable cross-border exchange of information between national **IT** systems'. The technical specifications for this system and other requirements for implementation have been laid down in Commission Implementing Regulations under Article 25 ESR 2020.[30] Arrangements for governance and management of the e-CODEX system were established by **Regulation 2022/850 on a computerised system for the cross-border electronic exchange of data** in the area of judicial cooperation in civil and criminal matters (e-CODEX system), with management being entrusted to **eu-LISA**.[31]

#19 The decentralised IT system as an obligatory means of communication for the transmission and receipt of requests for service and related documentation will apply as from 1 May 2025.[32] It remains to be seen how far implementation is timely. The introduction of computerised systems in various Member States has faced many technical and resource problems.[33] Simoni and Pailli also commented that in some Member States receiving agencies lacked adequate knowledge of the rules on service and did not have appropriate language skills.[34]

#20 As with other EU procedural regulations, there are a number of **standard forms** annexed to the ESR 2020 to ease communication across multiple languages and ensure that transmitting agencies are informed about the progress of the request for service, including where relevant requests for further information and notification that the request has been sent to the wrong agency and has been forwarded on.[35]

30 Commission Implementing Regulations (EU) 2022/422 and 2022/423.

31 The European Union Agency for the Operational Management of Large-Scale IT Systems in the Area of Freedom, Security and Justice, established by Regulation 2018/1726.

32 The first day of the month following the period of three years after the date of entry into force of the implementing regulations (as specified in Article 37(2) ESR 2020).

33 See, for example, for Italy, D Carnevali and A Resca, 'The Case of Trial On-Line in Italy' in GF Lanzara and F Contini (eds), *Building Interoperability for European Civil Proceedings Online* (CLUEB 2013) 273, and with respect to the general problems of implementing the ESR 2007 and the implications for ESR 2020 see R Amato and M Velicogna, 'Cross-Border Document Service Procedures in the EU from the Perspective of Italian Practitioners: The Lessons Learnt and the Process of Digitalisation of the Procedure through e-CODEX' (2022) 11(6) Laws 81, 21. See also MD Barišin, 'Cross-Border Service of Documents in EU Going Online: Implementation and Implications' (2023) 7 ECLIC 267, 275.

34 Simoni and Pailli (n 2) 242.

35 Notably regulated in Arts 10, 11, 12 and 14 ESR 2020.

II Service of Documents

#21 **Service itself is effected on the addressee of service in accordance with the law of the Member State addressed (Article 11).** This may be undertaken by the receiving agency itself (for example if the receiving agency is a Judicial Officer) or may be arranged by the receiving agency (for example, a court may arrange for postal service, or a centralised receiving agency may remit the documents to the local competent authority). If the transmitting agency requests a particular method of service, the receiving agency will comply unless the requested method is 'incompatible' with the law of the State addressed. According to Article 13 ESR 2020, the **date of service** is the date 'on which the document was served **in** accordance with the law of the Member State addressed'. To ensure that the applicant for service is not unduly disadvantaged by delays over which they have no control, however, Article 13(2) ensures that where the law of the Member State of origin requires a document be served within a particular period, the date to be taken into account with respect to the applicant is the date determined by that law.

#22 Once the formalities for service of the document are completed, the receiving agency must send a **certificate of service** to the transmitting agency (or alternatively certify non-service where relevant) using the appropriate form annexed to the Regulation.

III Service on an Authorised Representative

#23 Article 1(3) of the ESR 2020 deals with the situation where a person to be served has authorised a representative for service in the forum state. The Regulation does not apply to service on that representative, but Recital 6 to the Regulation highlights the fact that the Regulation should apply 'to the service of any document on a party in another Member State if such service is required under the law of the forum Member State, irrespective of whether the document has been served on the party's representative'. The Regulation thus does not take up a position on whether parties to proceedings should be required to appoint a representative for service in the forum state but leaves it to national law.[36] In addition, there is no clarity as to the scope of the term 'authorised representative', which is not defined in the Regulation. While an autonomous meaning of this term may

36 This contrasts with the Commission's proposal for the recast regulation, which would have imposed an obligation to appoint a representative for service, or in the alternative to provide an address for electronic service. The consequence of failure to comply with this obligation would have been the permissibility of fictitious service. See A Stein, 'The European Service Regulation: Introduction' in A Anthimos and M Requejo Isidro (eds), *The European Service Regulation* (Edward Elgar 2023) 1, 16–17.

emerge in time from the case law of the CJEU, the contours of such a meaning will only gradually become apparent. Nevertheless, the existing case law of the CJEU[37] suggests that the powers of an insurance claims representative must include the authority validly to accept service of the judicial documents necessary for proceedings, and thus an **'authorised representative'** should not be taken to refer solely to a representative *ad litem*.[38] In practice, service between lawyers once proceedings have been initiated is very commonly permitted by the laws of the Member States.

IV Translation Requirements

#24 Article 8 of the ESR 2007 permitted the addressee of service to refuse to accept the document to be served if it was not written in, or accompanied by a translation into, 'a language which the addressee understands' or an official language of the Member State addressed (and more specifically of the place where service was to be effected). This provision, and the further details for giving effect to it, gave rise to a number of difficulties in practice.[39] While maintaining the same basic principle, the ESR 2020 has therefore introduced significant changes to the procedures for securing its effective implementation.

#25 First of all, in contrast to the position under ESR 2007, the addressee of service need only be informed of the right to refuse service if the document to be served is not in the relevant official language of the Member State addressed (Article 12 (2)).[40] Where the **right to refuse service** does need to be communicated to the addressee, Article 12(2) sets out the information to be provided in a standard form annexed to the Regulation.[41] The form should be in an official language of

---

37 Case C-306/12 *Spedition Welter GmbH v Avanssur* SA (10 October 2013) ECLI:EU:C:2013:650; Case C-25/19 *Corporis Sp.z.o.o. v Gefion Insurance A/S* (27 February 2020) ECLI:EU:C:2020:126.

38 It does not, however, automatically include a subsidiary of the addressee of service: Case C-632/22 *Volvo AB v Transsaqui SL* (11 July 2024) ECLI:EU:C:2024:601. See also A Anthimos, 'Article 1 – Scope' in A Anthimos and M Requejo Isidro (eds), *The European Service Regulation: A Commentary* (Edward Elgar Publishing 2023) 27, 41–43.

39 The studies reviewing the operation of the Regulation produced mixed conclusions on the significance of these difficulties: see Evaluation Report (n 2) 51, which noted the contrasting results of an online public consultation and the Luxembourg MPI Study as to how far service was proving problematic. See also the Impact Assessment (n 2) 13.

40 The obligation to inform the addressee of the right to refuse service in every case was stated by the CJEU in Case C-519/13 *Alpha Bank Cyprus* (16 September 2015) ECLI:EU:C:2015:603 and confirmed in Case C-354/15 *Henderson* (2 March 2017) ECLI:EU:C:2017:157, and with respect to an order for payment in Case C-21/17 *Catlin Europe SE* (6 September 2018) ECLI:EU:C:2018:675.

41 Following the same process as used in the ESR 2007.

the State of origin and of the State addressed,[42] but in addition '[i]f there is an indication that the addressee understands an official language of another Member State [the form] shall also be provided in that language'. Stein notes that although this latter obligation may be well-intentioned as a means of protecting the interests of the addressee, '[i]t is unclear what the threshold for such indications is and what the consequences of non-compliance would be'.[43] Given that the addressee is expected to accept a document in the language of the State addressed without being informed of the right to refuse service, it would be odd if a failure to provide the form in a third language, when it is provided in an official language of the place where service is to be effected, was regarded as a defect in service.

#26 Under Article 12(3), the addressee may **refuse to accept the document** to be served at the time of service, but they are also given a further two weeks within which they may communicate their refusal to the receiving agency. This can be done either by returning the relevant form or by providing a separate written declaration. This approach encompasses the two methods of communication adopted in practice by addressees. It thus sensibly conforms the law to practice, since either approach meets the objective of the provision. The time permitted by the State of origin for entering an appearance in the proceedings must take account of this two-week period.[44]

#27 Service may be remedied in such a case by reserving the document concerned with the correct translation. Although for most purposes the date of service will be the date of this corrected service, Article 12(5) provides that if 'the law of a Member State requires a document to be served within a particular period, the date to be taken into account with respect to the applicant shall be the date of the service of the initial document'. Like Article 13(2) it thus seeks to strike a balance between the rights of the parties.

#28 It is only if the **refusal to accept the document** is verified as well founded that service is recognised as defective and needing to be remedied by means of a new attempt at service with the required translation of the document. Although the ESR 2020 does not include any formal regulation of this issue, recital 26 to the Regulation does identify factors that should be taken into account in determining whether the refusal to accept the document is justified. The court or authority considering the matter[45] should 'take into account all the relevant information on the file' to determine the addressee's language skills. Such information might in-

---

42 Further precision is given for the situation where either or both these States have more than one official language.

43 Stein n (36) 12.

44 Case C-7/21 *LKW WALTER Internationale Transportorganisation AG* (7 July 2022) ECLI:EU:C:2022:527.

45 This approach makes particular sense where the transmitting agency is the court hearing the proceedings. A decision that renewed service is not required is more problematic if service takes place before the case is filed with a court.

clude documents written by the addressee in the language concerned, the addressee's profession, and whether the addressee is a citizen of the State of origin or resided there for an 'extended period of time'. In the event of a decision not to reserve, the court or authority should 'consider an appropriate way of informing the addressee of that decision in accordance with national law'.

#29 More generally, in Case C-443/03, *Leffler*[46] the CJEU observed that the rules in the service regulation[47] on reservice did not 'call into question the importance of national law and the role of national courts' in the case of a lacuna in the EU rules. In addition to safeguarding the rights of the addressee of service, the rights of the service initiator should be respected. The latter should not be obliged to suffer 'in urgent proceedings where the defendant fails to appear, the adverse consequences of a refusal to accept an untranslated document which purely seeks to delay matters and manifestly constitutes an abuse, when it can be proved that the addressee of that document understands the language of the Member State of transmission in which the document is written'. Nevertheless, national rules should be interpreted with due concern for the cross-border dimension of the proceedings and should not 'compromise the raison d'etre and objective of the Regulation'.

#30 Although Article 12(1)–(5) are drafted with reference to service via transmitting and receiving agencies, Article 12(6) makes it clear that the rules with respect to the right to refuse to accept a document also apply in the case of direct service.

F Service under Chapter II, Section 2

#31 Section 2 provides for a variety of methods of service that do not require the use of the system of transmitting and receiving agencies. Articles 16 and 17 ESR 2020 preserve traditional but rarely used methods of service of documents: the use of **diplomatic or consular channels** to transmit documents to receiving agencies or central authorities (thus avoiding the use of transmitting agencies), and service without the use of coercive methods via **diplomatic or consular agents.**[48] Articles 18 to 20 regulate certain **'direct' methods of service** that are of more practical relevance: postal service, electronic service and direct service via 'judicial officers, officials or other competent persons' in the State addressed.

46 Case C-443/03 *Götz Leffler v Berlin Chemie AG* (8 November 2005) ECLI:EU:C:2005:665, paras 49–52.
47 In that case Regulation 1348/2000.
48 In this latter case, Member States may restrict such service to service on the nationals of the State of origin.

#32 Although the use of transmitting and receiving agencies is presented first and regulated in detail, the CJEU has made it clear that there is no hierarchy of methods of service:[49] the initiator of service has a free choice.

I Postal Service (Article 18 ESR 2020)

#33 The service of foreign process on their soil via the post was long seen by many EU Member States as an infringement of sovereignty but changing EU rules are progressively altering that position.[50] The use of postal channels is a usual domestic method of service by courts in court-initiator jurisdictions, and in practice **postal service** is now also widely used in cross-border cases, particularly low value cases where the cost of **formal service** would be disproportionate. Article 18 ESR 2020 provides, laconically: 'The service of judicial documents[51] may be effected directly by postal services on persons present in another Member State by registered letter with acknowledgement of receipt or equivalent.' This wording leaves open the possibility that postal service may be party initiated as well as court initiated, a point that was ambiguous in the ESR 2007. Moreover, Recital 29 indicates that the relevant postal service providers may be public or private entities.

#34 The Regulation does not seek to harmonise the method of proof of service through a standard form of acknowledgement of receipt.[52] Nor does it regulate the approach to be taken if the addressee is not found at the given address.[53] But Recital 30, picking up one of the Commission's proposals that did not find its way into the main text of the Regulation, emphasises the approach of the CJEU in permitting **substituted service** in such circumstances.[54] According to Recital 30:

> direct service by postal service under this Regulation should be considered to be validly effected, even if the document was not delivered to the addressee in person, where it was served at the addressee's home address on an adult person who is living in the same household as the addressee or who is employed there by the addressee and who has the ability and is willing to accept the document, unless the law of the forum Member State only allows the service of that document on the addressee in person.

---

49 Case C-473/04 *Plumex v Young Sports NV* (9 February 2006) ECLI:EU:C:2006:96; Case C-325/11 *Alder* (19 December 2012) ECLI:EU:C:2012:824; C-223/14 *Tecom Mican* (11 November 2015) ECLI:EU:C:2015:744; C-354/15 *Henderson* (2 March 2017) ECLI:EU:C:2017:157.

50 For the incremental change, see V Richard, 'Article 18 – Service by Postal Services' in A Anthimos and M Requejo Isidro (eds), *The European Service Regulation: A Commentary* (Edward Elgar 2023) 168, 169.

51 The provision also covers extra-judicial documents by virtue of Article 21 ESR 2020.

52 The Commission proposed the use of a standard form, but this idea was not adopted in the final act.

53 See Richard (n 50) 173.

54 Case C-354/15 *Henderson* (2 March 2017) ECLI:EU:C:2017:157.

This wording combines elements from several sources. While adopting the reasoning of the CJEU in Case C-354/15, *Henderson*, it also draws on Regulations 805/2004 and 1896/2006, replacing a reference to 'members of the family' with 'person living in the same household'.[55]

II Electronic means of service under the ESR 2020

1 Overview of Article 19

#35 Although electronic means of communication between transmitting and receiving agencies are accorded great importance under the ESR 2020, such communication is not a means of service.[56] Service is undertaken by the receiving agency under the rules applicable in the state addressed. Article 19 is, however, concerned with possibility of direct service on the addressee via electronic means. Thus, according to Article 19(1):

> The service of judicial documents may be effected directly on a person who has a known address for service in another Member State by any electronic means of service available under the law of the forum Member State for the domestic service of documents, provided that:
> (a) the documents are sent and received using qualified electronic registered delivery services within the meaning of Regulation (EU) No 910/2014[57] and the addressee gave prior express consent to the use of electronic means for serving documents in the course of legal proceedings; or
> (b) the addressee gave prior express consent to the court or authority seised of the proceedings or to the party responsible for service of documents in such proceedings to the use of email sent to a specified email address for the purpose of serving documents in the course of those proceedings and the addressee confirms receipt of the document with an acknowledgement of receipt, including the date of receipt.

The ESR 2020 thus does not impose on Member States an obligation to recognise electronic service but rather makes such service available in cross-border situa-

55 It largely aligns with the wording of ERCP Rule 78 on alternative methods of service.

56 And indeed para 11 of the Preamble specifically states that (without prejudice to future developments) the decentralised IT system used for communication between transmitting and receiving agencies 'should not be understood to necessarily constitute a qualified electronic registered delivery service' as defined by Regulation 910/2014.

57 Regulation 910/2014 on electronic identification and trust services for electronic transactions in the internal market, as modified by Regulation (EU) 2024/1183 (the eIDAS Regulation) was adopted with a view to ensuring that electronic identities, signatures, seals and stamps – all of which have been introduced in purely domestic settings – could be used in cross-border cases. As Member States have responded to the need for digitalisation in different ways and at different speeds their solutions are not directly interoperable. The eIDAS Regulation sought to develop a 'circle of trust' so that confidence could be placed in electronic identification and authentication mechanisms adopted in other Member States.

tions only where it is already 'available under the law of the forum Member State for the domestic service of documents'.[58]

#36 In fact, three different approaches are adopted in relation to electronic service of documents in the Member States, with the potential for more than one method to be used in a given Member State, depending on the situation. First, **electronic platforms** may be developed by the state. These may be specifically for communications between legal and judicial professionals or may be designed for wider use. For example, in Italy legal professionals, legal persons, commercial undertakings and public bodies are required to include their certified electronic mail address (PEC) on relevant registers for official use. In Estonia, more extensive use of electronic communication has been introduced for communication between state and citizens, widening the scope for electronic service. Such platforms require user pre-registration and secure log-in credentials. Safety and authenticity may be ensured by using encryption protocols, e-signature and other certificates. But they may not technically meet the requirements to be a qualified electronic registered delivery service.

#37 A second possible approach to electronic service of documents is the use of a (public or private sector) **qualified electronic registered delivery service (QERDS)** provider within the meaning of the eIDAS Regulation, which will provide for Europe-wide authentication of the recipient of the document and security of delivery. Such providers may well provide business services without being authorised for the service of documents in the forum state but may be recognised by the state as a relevant partner for electronic service.[59]

#38 A final possibility is the use of ordinary **email communication**. In this case, the standard of security is much lower, and reliance is placed on acknowledgement of delivery by the addressee.[60]

#39 These different approaches should be borne in mind when looking at the detail of Article 19.

---

58 This is clarified by Recital 31.

59 For example, the e-Justice portal entry for Czechia specifies that 'a court, at the addressee's request, may serve a document to an electronic address specified by the addressee, provided that the addressee has asked the court to serve the document by this means, or gave their consent to this type of service, and provided they appointed an accredited certification service provider who issued its qualified certificate and maintains a record thereof, or has presented a valid qualified certificate'. Valid service is further subject to confirmation by the addressee.

60 For further explanation of these different approaches, see D Tsikrikas and W Kennett, 'Chapter 11: (Rules 68–86, 134) Service and Notice of Proceedings' in A Stadler, V Smith and F Gascon Inchausti (eds), *European Rules of Civil Procedure – A Commentary on the ELI/UNIDROIT Model Rules* (Edward Elgar 2023) 219.

2 Article 19(1)(a)

#40 The characteristics of a qualified electronic registered delivery services, mentioned in Article 19(1)(a), are established by the **eIDAS Regulation**[61] and are usefully summarised by Onțanu:

> the transmissions of data by electronic means, such as forms of certified emails or accounts, are able to provide evidence related to the transmission of the data (including proof of sending and receiving data), secured by an advanced electronic signature identifying the party from which it emanates, include a qualified electronic time stamp certifying the date and time of transmission and receipt, and protect the data by advanced electronic seal against the risk of loss, damage, theft or unauthorised modifications.[62]

#41 It is evident that Article 19(1)(a) only applies to certain categories of litigants since the documents must be both sent and received using the platforms provided by qualified electronic registered delivery services and **prior agreement to use of this means of service** 'in the course of legal proceedings' must be secured.[63] In business contexts this means that it should be relatively straightforward, in principle, to obtain agreement to electronic service for disputes arising out of a legal relationship. The question of how far that agreement can be implemented under the relevant national laws is more complex.

#42 The wording of Article 19 is ambiguous as to the scope of the rules on **electronic service**, and whether they can include service of the document instituting proceedings. The wording of Recital 32 indicates that 'general consent' may be given for the service of documents by electronic means in the course of [future] legal proceedings. In practice, however, the electronic platforms created by Member States for the service of documents are national in scope and do not appear to provide for or permit the registration on that platform of legal or natural persons from other Member States.[64] Provision for electronic service of the document in-

---

61 Regulation (EU) 910/2014 on electronic identification and trust services for electronic transactions in the internal market, recently amended by Regulation (EU) 2024/1183.

62 EA Onțanu, 'The Digitalisation of European Union Procedures: A New Impetus Following a Time of Prolonged Crisis' (2023) 5 Law, Technology and Humans 93, 100.

63 See A Anthimos, 'Article 19 – Electronic Service' in A Anthimos and M Requejo Isidro (eds), *The European Service Regulation: A Commentary* (Edward Elgar 2023 177; for discussion of the scope of the phrase 'in the course of legal proceedings'. Anthimos highlights a number of ambiguities in the text of Article 19 that could lead to it being given a very narrow interpretation. He also notes the need for protection of weaker parties against imposed agreement.

64 This is, for example, explicitly stated on the European e-justice portal in relation to service of documents by Italy, and seems to be implicit in relevant regulations of other Member States. It should also be noted that service via an e-justice or other e-government platform may not be eIDAS compliant, having been designed with domestic considerations in mind, and in some cases prior to the adoption of the eIDAS Regulation: see Tsikrikas and Kennet (n 60) 219. The ERCP provide for service via such platforms, but leaves open any question of cross-border application.

stituting proceedings outside the scope of these platforms exists – for example, Member State courts may permit the claimant to arrange for service – but it is not immediately evident how far this option is used, how far it might include electronic service, and whether electronic service could be used in an international context.[65]

#43 It is more likely that provisions relating to electronic service during the course of proceedings may be interpreted, or revised, to facilitate cross-border service. But in addition, it is increasingly likely that an authorised representative in the forum state (for the purposes of Article 1(3) ESR 2020) may be under an obligation to register on an electronic platform, in a professional capacity, in order to receive service.

3 Article 19(1)(b)

#44 Article 19(1)(b), which does not require the same technical standards to be met, clearly has a narrower scope. It is limited to situations where a court or authority is seised of proceedings, and so to service of documents other than the document instituting the proceedings. There is double protection for the addressee: prior consent to use this method of service and **acknowledgment of receipt** of the document. The requirement of acknowledgement of receipt, while understandable for the protection of parties who are not regular users of email, puts severe limits on the utility of email service in dealings with parties who have an interest in delaying proceedings.[66]

#45 In addition, Article 19(2) provides for Member States to be able to specify additional conditions under which they will accept **electronic service by email**. It is clear that this is to encourage the use of Article 19 by Member States that would not normally allow service by email or would only do so under stricter conditions. Recital 33 suggests that such conditions could address issues such as the identification of the sender and the recipient, the integrity of the documents sent and the protection of the transmission against outside interference. Since, however, the recital also specifically says that such electronic service is 'without the use of qualified electronic registered delivery services' any additional conditions might further complicate the already fragmented approach to security issues noted above.[67]

65 The position in Estonia, for example, is not very clear under § 311ff of the Code of Civil Procedure and in particular § 316(1). Similarly, § 45ff of the Czech Code of Civil Procedure (including § 50j) could be open to varying interpretations.

66 Consider, for example, the decision of the Irish Court of Appeal in *Permanent TSB v Skoczylas* [2020] IECA 152.

67 At Section F.II.1. See also Onțanu (n 62) 101.

4 Translation Requirements

#46 The procedure outlined in Article 12 also applies to electronic service. Article 12(7) ESR 2020 provides that the authority or person responsible for electronic service must inform the addressee that they may refuse to accept the document. In case of refusal, the relevant form annexed to the Regulation or a written declaration of refusal must be sent to that authority or person.

III Direct Service (Article 20 ESR 2020)

#47 The text of Article 20(1) ESR 2020 states:

> Any person with an interest in particular judicial proceedings may effect the service of judicial documents directly through the judicial officers, officials or other competent persons of the Member State in which the service is sought, provided that such direct service is permitted under the law of that Member State.

#48 **'Direct service'** is the designation given to the possibility for the service initiator (party or court) directly to approach a process server (referred to in Article 20 as '**judicial officers**, officials or other competent persons') in the State addressed. Its principal field of operation – although not specified in the wording of Article 20 – has been where the state addressed is a party-initiator jurisdiction, since it is less likely in these states that service will be regarded as an exercise of sovereignty reserved to the courts.[68] Thus, in the case of cross-border litigation where the parties involved are located in party-initiator states, direct service is in principle unproblematic. A party in France, for example, may approach a Judicial Officer in Belgium, the Netherlands or Luxembourg to effect service. Cyprus and Ireland also permit direct service under Article 20 through local process servers. The legal stance of the state addressed is the key question.[69] Most court-initiator states will not permit a direct approach to a process server within their territory.[70] But some do accept this method of service.[71]

---

68 Although there may be regulatory restrictions on the persons competent to serve documents.
69 See P Franzina, 'Article 20 – Direct Service' in A Anthimos and M Requejo Isidro (eds), *The European Service Regulation: A Commentary* (Edward Elgar 2023) 191 for a more nuanced approach.
70 The responses to the Mainstrat Study (n 2) indicated that many respondents did not understand what was meant by 'direct service'. Direct service is discussed in the study at 56–63. The range of comments indicates that the concept is interpreted in a variety of different ways by different respondents.
71 The Evaluation Report (n 2) found that only 12 Member States explicitly allowed 'direct service', although it might be possible in others (some interviewees did send documents to eg lawyers or judicial officers to effect service). Overall, the position was unclear (at 33). Among court-initiator states, according to the e-Justice Portal, Malta, Romania, Finland, and Sweden allow direct service under Arti-

#49 The Commission unsuccessfully proposed an **amendment to the ESR 2007** that would have effected more radical change. It would have required all Member States to permit direct service and would have extended the scope of the existing article by abandoning the requirement that the initiator should be a 'person interested in a judicial proceeding', so that transmitting agencies and courts seised with the proceedings could also have used this method of service.[72]

#50 As required by Article 20(2), the **e-Justice Portal** provides information about the countries that allow direct service in their territories and the professions or competent persons who are permitted to effect service.

G Defendant Not Entering Appearance

#51 The ESR 2020 largely preserves the previous rules concerning the position where a defendant does not enter an appearance, which were modelled on Article 15 of the 1965 Hague Service Convention.[73]

#52 The scope of the relevant provision (now Article 22) remains essentially unchanged under the ESR 2020. It applies when 'a document instituting proceedings or its equivalent has had to be transmitted to another Member State for the purpose of service under this Regulation and the defendant has not entered an appearance'.[74] Although the question regularly arises as to when such a document has to be transmitted to another Member State, more clarity exists on this point than under previous iterations of the Regulation in the light of Arts 1(2) and 7 (see Section C).

#53 In essence, Article 22(1) provides that judgment should not be entered in proceedings falling within Article 22 unless it can be shown that there has been **due and**

---

cle 20, and Germany allows such service in certain circumstances (largely in relation to the service of a judgment and enforcement matters).

72 Greater use of direct methods of service is explicitly recommended by Simoni and Pailli (n 2) 255 and 265. Franzina (n 69) 195 argues that 'nothing in the Regulation appears to prevent a Member State from providing that direct service in its territory is also available when a request to that effect is made by a court or other authority in the State of origin'.

73 Some changes in wording have been introduced to clarify certain points of interpretation (eg 'writ of summons' becomes 'document instituting the proceedings'

74 See A Anthimos, 'Article 22 – Defendant Not Entering an Appearance' in A Anthimos and M Requejo Isidro (eds), *The European Service Regulation: A Commentary* (Edward Elgar 2023) 205, 222–225 for a discussion of the scope of Article 22 and the significance of the word 'transmitted'. The interpretation adopted, reserving Article 22 for cases involving transmitting and receiving agencies, seems to be unduly narrow. 'Transmission' can reasonably refer to the process of conveying the document to the place where it is served.

timely service or delivery of the document instituting the proceedings.[75] In the scheme of this paragraph, service is effected under the rules of the State addressed via the transmitting and receiving agencies (Article 11), and delivery may take place via one of the methods of direct service (Article 18–20).[76]

#54 Article 22 (2) nevertheless provides that a Member State may, under certain circumstances, give judgment 'even if no certificate of service or delivery of the document instituting the proceedings or its equivalent has been received'. The document must have been transmitted using one of the methods provided for in the Regulation[77] and, despite every reasonable effort, 'no certificate of any kind' has since been received after an adequate time has elapsed to allow for this.[78] Although Article 22(2) refers only to the absence of a **'certificate of service'**, this should be interpreted as also including a certificate of non-service or equivalent document – particularly since Article 22(2)(c) provides for judgment to be given when 'no certificate of any kind has been received' in spite of every reasonable effort to obtain one.[79] With respect to the methods of service in Arts 18–20, it is reasonable to expect that in the absence of an acknowledgement of receipt of postal service an alternative method of service would be attempted. On the other hand, in the case of electronic service (if it is permitted for the document instituting the proceedings), the use of a qualified electronic registered delivery service would provide a guarantee of whether or not service had been received. And in the case of direct service, it might be expected that the Judicial Officer or other process server would be able to certify the outcome of attempted service, with information about attempts made, which could factor into a decision on whether or not to give judgment.

#55 The Regulation does not have any specific provision relating to the curing of **defects in service**, but the observations of the CJEU in Case C-443/03, *Leffler*[80] suggest that national rules intended to prevent abusive avoidance by an addressee of service of the proceedings against them may be applicable.

#56 The Commission made a number of proposals for amendments to what is now Article 22, but only minor amendments were accepted. In particular, it was sought to include a new paragraph 3 stating:

75 Anthimos (n 74) 216–217 notes that to date, determination of the timeliness of service tends to be calculated in accordance with the rules of the forum state, although the development of an autonomous, European approach by the CJEU might be more appropriate.

76 This may also encompass a 'particular method' of service requested by the transmitting agency (Article 11(1)).

77 See n 71.

78 The adequacy of time is to be determined by the court in the particular case and should be not less than six months (Article 22(2)(b)).

79 See to the same effect Anthimos (n 74) 224.

80 Above at #29.

> Where the conditions set out in paragraph 2 are met, reasonable efforts shall be made to inform the defendant through any available channels of communication, including means of modern communication technology, for which an address or an account is known to the court seised, that court proceedings have been instituted against him or her.[81]

#57 This proposal was rejected largely on the grounds of its ambiguity. The rejection potentially leaves a defendant less well protected, since notifying them of proceedings via a social media account, for example, could be seen as to their advantage.[82] Nevertheless, the rapid development of privileged access by competent authorities to information about a defendant's address is reducing the need to rely on means of service of last resort and on Article 22(2).

#58 Article 22(4) preserves the court's power to 'relieve the defendant from the effects of the expiry of the time for appeal from the judgment'. Thus, if judgment has been given in the absence of a certificate of service and it later emerges that the defendant did not know about the document in sufficient time to enter a defence, or did not know about the judgment in time to appeal, under certain circumstances the defendant may be permitted to appeal against the judgment out of time. There are four cumulative conditions:

(i) The defendant's lack of knowledge must not be the result of their own fault;
(ii) They must have a prima facie defence to the action on the merits;
(iii) The defendant must seek this relief within a reasonable time after learning of the judgment; and
(iv) The defendant must seek this relief before any deadline imposed by the forum Member State.[83]

#59 Article 22 contains two provisos as to its scope. First, it does not prevent a court from granting **provisional or protective measures** in urgent cases (Article 22(3) 22 (3)) and second, Article 22(4) does not apply to judgments concerned with the **status or capacity of persons**.

---

81 This approach aligned with the ERCP, Article 80 of which includes as a method of service of final resort 'publication in electronic registers accessible to the public' and adds in Comment 3 to Article 80 that this is wording that is broad enough to cover social media. In the development of the ERCP, the European Parliament was keen to electronic service and electronic communication in the case of methods of service of last resort, but the Council of the EU has proved less enthusiastic.

82 Attitudes of Member States towards email and social media contacts with defendants vary markedly, which largely correlates with their score on power/distance indexes.

83 This deadline must not be less than one year after judgment (Article 22(4)). Member States' choices in this respect can be found via the e-Justice Portal and range from one year (eg Belgium) to no deadline at all (eg Czechia).

H Concluding Remarks

#60 Ensuring the proper service of documents is both an essential task in constructing a European judicial area and a technically difficult problem. This is partly because of differences in legal culture but also because of historic choices about the specific structure of legal institutions and procedural rules and also choices made in other areas such as IT infrastructure or the regulation of postal services.

#61 The ESR 2020 was adopted at a time of rapid change in domestic rules on service as a result of digitalisation – later accelerated by the demands of the COVID pandemic. Further digitalisation has the potential to resolve many of the problems associated with cross-border service by facilitating communication between different legal and IT systems, but legal systems are moving at different speeds and with different degrees of acceptance of digital procedures and this tension is reflected in the text of the Regulation. As experience with digital communication in judicial proceedings grows, the extent to which confidence in such communication is justified will become more apparent.

#62 The digitalisation of judicial cooperation is an important objective for the EU, and further progress towards this objective can be found in **Regulation 2023/2844 on the digitalisation of judicial cooperation and access to justice** in cross-border civil, commercial and criminal matters. Although a major purpose of this Regulation is to extend communication using e-CODEX to a wider range of procedures – and so the ESR 2020 is excluded from its scope since it already provides for such communication – an innovation introduced is a **European electronic access point** for communication between 'natural or legal persons or their representatives and competent authorities'. Communication via the electronic access point, when it comes into operation,[84] is specified to depend on 'prior express consent . . . specific to the procedure in which it is given' (Article 4(6) and so remains similarly narrow in scope to the Article 19 ESR 2020,[85] but it has the capacity to be given a more extensive role. Just as a range of legal persons, public bodies and professionals are being required to register on domestic electronic platforms for the receipt of judicial documents, it is conceivable that a similar obligation might be created on an EU-wide basis. Certain categories of persons and entities might eventually be required to register with the e-Justice Portal to accept the secure service of documents.[86]

84 This requires a series of implementing regulations for different procedures, each with its own two-year implementing period on a timescale extending up to 2031: Arts 10 and 26 of Regulation 2023/2844.

85 Indeed Article 19(1)(a) ESR 2020 is arguably wider in scope than this.

86 See above at #35. See also the ERCP Article 74(1)(b) and similar suggestions by F Gascón Inchausti, 'The New Regulation on the Digitalisation of Judicial Cooperation in the European Union: Something

References

Amato R and Velicogna M, 'Cross-Border Document Service Procedures in the EU from the Perspective of Italian Practitioners: The Lessons Learnt and the Process of Digitalisation of the Procedure through e-CODEX' (2022) 11(6) Laws 81.

Anthimos A, 'Article 1 – Scope' in A Anthimos and M Requejo Isidro (eds), *The European Service Regulation: A Commentary* (Edward Elgar Publishing 2023) 27.

—— 'Article 19 – Electronic Service' in A Anthimos and M Requejo Isidro (eds), *The European Service Regulation: A Commentary* (Edward Elgar 2023 177.

—— 'Article 22 – Defendant Not Entering an Appearance' in A Anthimos and M Requejo Isidro (eds), *The European Service Regulation: A Commentary* (Edward Elgar 2023) 205.

Barišin MD, 'Cross-Border Service of Documents in EU Going Online: Implementation and Implications' (2023) 7 ECLIC 267.

Carnevali D and Resca A, 'The Case of Trial On-Line in Italy' in GF Lanzara and F Contini (eds), Building Interoperability for European Civil Proceedings Online (CLUEB 2013) 273.

Directorate-General for Justice and Consumers (European Commission) and Max Planck Institute, *An Evaluation Study of National Procedural Laws and Practices in Terms of Their Impact on the Free Circulation of Judgments and on the Equivalence and Effectiveness of the Procedural Protection of Consumers under EU Consumer Law* (European Commission 2017).

Franzina P, 'Article 20 – Direct Service' in A Anthimos and M Requejo Isidro (eds), *The European Service Regulation: A Commentary* (Edward Elgar 2023) 191.

Gascón Inchausti F, 'The New Regulation on the Digitalisation of Judicial Cooperation in the European Union: Something Old, Something New, Something Borrowed and Something Blue' (2023) 24 ERA Forum 535.

Hofstede G, *Cultures and Organizations: Software of the Mind* (McGraw-Hill 1991).

Kennett W, *Civil Enforcement in a Comparative Perspective: A Public Management Challenge* (Intersentia 2021).

Mainstrat and University of the Basque Country, *Study on the Application of Council Regulation (EC) No 1393/2007 on the Service of Judicial and Extrajudicial Documents in Civil and Commercial Matters* (European Commission 2014).

Onțanu EA, 'The Digitalisation of European Union Procedures: A New Impetus Following a Time of Prolonged Crisis' (2023) 5 Law, Technology and Humans 93.

Richard V, 'Article 18 – Service by Postal Services' in A Anthimos and M Requejo Isidro (eds), *The European Service Regulation: A Commentary* (Edward Elgar 2023) 168.

Rieländer F, 'Digitalisierung des Grenzüberschreitenden Zivilprozesses' RabelsZ Online First 2/2025, 1.

Simoni A and Pailli G, *Study on the Service of Documents: Comparative Legal Analysis of the Relevant Laws and Practices of the Member States. Final Report.* No JUST/2014/JCOO/PR/CIVI/0049 (European Commission 2016).

Stein A, 'The European Service Regulation: Introduction' in A Anthimos and M Requejo Isidro (eds), *The European Service Regulation: A Commentary* (Edward Elgar 2023) 1.

Tsikrikas D and Kennett W, 'Chapter 11: (Rules 68–86, 134) Service and Notice of Proceedings' in A Stadler, V Smith and F Gascon Inchausti (eds), *European Rules of Civil Procedure – A Commentary on the ELI/UNIDROIT Model Rules* (Edward Elgar 2023) 219.

Old, Something New, Something Borrowed and Something Blue' (2023) 24 ERA Forum 535, 544; F Rieländer, 'Digitalisierung des Grenzüberschreitenden Zivilprozesses' RabelsZ Online First 2/2025, 1, 44.

Geert van Calster

Chapter 9
International Jurisdiction: Fundamental Issues and 'Principles' of EU Private International Law

#1 In this chapter, I intend to discuss the key issues and the general framework for international jurisdiction in Europe and the EU. The Chapter serves as a foundational exploration, preparing the groundwork for Chapter 10 on civil and commercial matters and Chapter 14 on family matters. The primary focus of this chapter is to offer a conceptual understanding of the pivotal issues concerning international jurisdiction in Europe and the EU.

A The Overall Direction of EU Private International Law and its Legal Basis

#2 Its **'legal basis'** is the be all and end all of all European law and policy. No EU initiative can unfold without a clear legal basis in the European Treaties: a Head of Power which specifically gives the EU institutions the right to take an initiative in the area concerned, and which at the same time prescribes the limits to such power. That is the result of the EU being a 'centripetal' 'federal'[1] system as opposed to a centrifugal regime. All legislative and regulatory power exercised by the EU and its institutions originally rested with its constituent Member States. Only those powers expressly delegated by those States to the EU therefore, may be exercised by the latter and if so exercised, only within the conditions and constraints imposed by that delegation of power. This principle is known as the prin-

---

1 I use 'federal' here simply as shorthand for the EU's hybrid form as an intergovernmental and supranational system. I do not intend to wade into the more theoretical debate of what a 'federation' entails and whether the EU is one. On the specific issue of federal systems, the EU and private international law, see J Heymann, *Le Droit International Privé à l'Epreuve du fédéralisme européen* (Economica 2010) and, briefly, D Lasok and P Stone, *Conflict of Laws in the European Community* (Professional Books 1987) 17ff.

Geert van Calster, University of Leuven (KU Leuven), e-mail: gavc@law.kuleuven.be

https://doi.org/10.1515/9783110781632-009

ciple of attributed powers or the principle of 'conferral', expressed in Article 5 of the Treaty on European Union.[2]

#3 In a broad interpretation of 'conflict of laws', engaging with the hierarchy between European law and the national laws of its Member States, conflict of laws may be said to have received a tremendous amount of attention from the very beginning of the European Treaties, crystallising in the pivotal cases by the Court of Justice of the European Union ('CJEU') concerning **primacy and direct effect**.[3] Similarly, (now) Article 268 of the Treaty on the Functioning of the European Union – TFEU which allocates exclusive jurisdiction to the CJEU for **actions in damages invoking the non-contractual liability of the Union**,[4] and (now) Article 272 TFEU, which makes contractual liability subject to parties' choice of court, with the possibility however to assign the CJEU as the arbitrator, can be said to be private international law provisions included in the very first European Treaties.

#4 In the case of private international law in the more narrow sense (which readers will appreciate by the time they reach current chapter in this volume, comprises rules on jurisdiction, applicable law and recognition and enforcement of judgments), the **original legal basis** in the relevant Treaty was **Article 220 of the Treaty establishing the European Economic Community – EEC**:

Member States shall, so far as is necessary, enter into negotiations with each other with a view to securing for the benefit of their nationals:

- the protection of persons and the enjoyment and protection of rights under the same conditions as those accorded by each State to its own nationals,
- the abolition of double taxation within the Community,
- the mutual recognition of companies or firms within the meaning of the second paragraph of Article 48, the retention of legal personality in the event of trans-

2 'Under the principle of conferral, the Union shall act only within the limits of the competences conferred upon it by the Member States in the Treaties to attain the objectives set out therein. Competences not conferred upon the Union in the Treaties remain with the Member States'.

3 Lasok and Stone (n 1) 24ff.

4 'The Court of Justice of the European Union shall have jurisdiction in disputes relating to compensation for damage provided for in the second and third paragraphs of Article 340'. Article 340 TFEU in turn reads 'The contractual liability of the Union shall be governed by the law applicable to the contract in question. In the case of non-contractual liability, the Union shall, in accordance with the general principles common to the laws of the Member States, make good any damage caused by its institutions or by its servants in the performance of their duties. Notwithstanding the second paragraph, the European Central Bank shall, in accordance with the general principles common to the laws of the Member States, make good any damage caused by it or by its servants in the performance of their duties. The personal liability of its servants towards the Union shall be governed by the provisions laid down in their Staff Regulations or in the Conditions of Employment applicable to them'. See for more on Articles 268 and 272 TFEU, B Schima, 'Article 268 TFEU' in M Kellerbauer, M Klamert and J Tomkin (eds), *The EU Treaties and the Charter of Fundamental Rights: A Commentary* (OUP 2019) 1841; B Schima, 'Article 272 TFEU' in M Kellerbauer, M Klamert and J Tomkin (eds), *The EU Treaties and the Charter of Fundamental Rights: A Commentary* (OUP 2019) 1854.

fer of their seat from one country to another, and the possibility of mergers between companies or firms governed by the laws of different countries,
– the simplification of formalities governing the reciprocal recognition and enforcement of judgments of courts or tribunals and of arbitration awards.

#5 Article 220 EEC, in instructing the Member States to 'enter into negotiations with each other',[5] confined any co-operation mentioned in it to the means of classic instruments of public international law.

#6 It is likely that the Member States did not need the 'go ahead' of Article 220 EEC to be able to conduct the negotiations which later led to the relevant Conventions in the area. Only a most extensive reading of a duty of co-operation between the (then) European Economic Community and its Member States, a notion now referred to as 'Bundestreue' or '**federal loyalty**',[6] would suggest that the Member States ought to have refrained from multilateral co-operation among themselves in the area of private international law, in the absence of European initiatives in the area. Such interpretation, which I do not support, would suggest Article 220 gave the Member States the necessary cover to be able to conduct their consultations in good faith.

#7 Article 220 EEC clearly deferred to initiatives of a public international law nature rather than a 'European' nature, entrusted to the (now) EU institutions. This was not or perhaps not merely a nod to the then very infant European institutions recognising a need to prioritise certain policy areas over others, and leaving the development of accompanying policies to the Member States coming together in initiatives of a public international law nature. It was arguably[7] decided that instruments of public international law would be better suited to disentangling the spaghetti bowl of bilateral and multilateral treaties which pre-dated the creation of the European Economic Communities. This was all the more so considered attractive

5 Note the use in French of the 'indicatif futur': PE Partsch, *Le droit international privé européen – De Rome à Nice* (Larcier 2003) 46; Member States' recognition of an instruction to act in the 'Jenard Report', which accompanies the initial Brussels Convention of 1968 and counts as its most important interpretative instrument [see its very first introductory remark: 'By Article 220 of the Treaty establishing the European Economic Community, the Member States *agreed to enter into negotiations with each other*, so far as necessary, with a view to securing for the benefit of their nationals the simplification of formalities governing the reciprocal recognition and enforcement of judgments of courts or tribunals and of arbitration awards', emphasis added, P Jenard, 'Report on the Convention on Jurisdiction and the Enforcement of Judgments in Civil and Commercial Matters' [1979] OJ C59/1 <https://tinyurl.com/56wr522e> accessed 15 March 2025; see also the CJEU in Case C-12/76 *Industrie Tessili Italiana Como* v *Dunlop AG* (6 October 1976) ECLI:EU:C:1976:133, particularly its original, French version, para 9: 'Attendu qu'aux termes de l'article 220 . . . .les Etats Membres *sont tenus d'engager* entre eux, en tant que de besoin, des négotiations . . .', emphasis added: 'Member States are *bound* to enter into negotiations' (my translation).

6 See for more on the issue, G de Baere and T Roes, 'EU Loyalty as Good Faith' (2015) 64 ICLQ 829; M Klamert, *The Principle of Loyalty in EU Law* (OUP 2014).

7 Partsch (n 5) 42ff.

as these Treaties often engaged non-EU Member States, too. These Treaties not only regulated the issue of recognition and enforcement of judgments, but also for instance double taxation Treaties which are included in the Article 220 EEC list.[8]

#8 Article 220 EEC did not provide a legal basis for any *European Economic Community* initiative in the area. Rather it encouraged Member States to enter into classic, Treaty negotiations, and in doing so at the least condoned but more precisely encouraged the Member States to hold such negotiations. It also expressed the broad brushes of what kind of ends the Member States ought to have in mind with such negotiations. The most immediate expression of this became first the 1968 Brussels Convention, and later the 1980 Rome Convention.

#9 Of additional note is that the original Treaties constituting what we now call the EU, did not offer any *explicit* accommodation, policy let alone tailored legal basis for the **harmonisation of *private* law**.[9] The foundational Treaties assumed that the Member States would continue to employ diverging sets of substantive private law rules, hence requiring conflict of laws solutions to manage the ensuing difficulties.[10] Unification or harmonisation of substantive laws themselves is often discussed as a means to overcome the limits to and difficulties associated with the competition between legal regimes expressed by private international law, in particular its applicable law leg,[11] and unification of European private law or the creation of a European 'civil code' may be said to be the 'dream and vision'[12] of many private law professors across the EU. However as Article 220 EEC above shows, the original Treaty did envisage co-ordination by the Member States in the area of private international law.

---

8 See on the tax issue A Huet, 'Article 220' in V Costantinesco and others (eds), *Traité instituant la C.E.E., Commentaire article par article* (Economica 1992) 1377ff.

9 See also M Fallon, *Les conflits de lois et de juridictions dans un espace économique intégré – L'expérience de la Communauté Européenne* (Martinus Nijhoff 1995) 27.

10 See also W-H Roth, 'Der Einfluß des Europäisches Gemeinschaftsrechts auf das Internationale Privatrecht' (1991) 55 RabelsZ 623, 643: 'Der EWG-Vertrag geht hingehen von der Existenz konkurrierender Privatrechtsordnungen and damit von der Notwendigkeit ihrer kollisionsrechtlichen Vermittlung aus'.

11 See more in G Van Calster, 'On the Role of Borders in European Conflict of Laws' in M Piers, H Storme and J Verhellen (eds), *Liber Amicorum Johan Erauw* (Intersentia 2014) 219 and G Van Calster, 'To Unity and Beyond? The Boundaries of European Private International Law and the European Ius Commune' in A Verbeke and others (eds), *Liber Amicorum Walter Pintens* (Intersentia 2012) 1459. See also Lasok and Stone (n 1) 82ff.

12 HJ Thue, 'European Private International Law as the European Solution, and the European Economic Area (EEA/EWR) Problem' in G Reichelt (ed), *Europäisches Gemeinschaftsrecht und IPR: Ein Beitrag zur Kodifikation der allgemeinen Grundsätze des Europäischen Kollisionsrechts. Symposium Wien 1. Dezember 2006 aus Anlass des 10-jährigen Bestehens des Ludwig Boltzmann Institutes für Europarecht* (Manz 2007) 93.

#10 The Article's reference to 'recognition and enforcement of judgments'[13] is the clearest reference in the original Treaties to private international law. Article 220's instruction (Member States 'shall enter into negotiations') is often referred to as the Treaty's ambition to achieve a **free movement of judgments**. However this is not the only part of Article 220 impacting on private international law. Much of Article 220 EEC touches upon private international law, seeing as it refers inter alia to non-discrimination in personal status and cross-border implications of (change in) corporate seat.

#11 Arguably the prime perhaps even exclusive focus of EU private international law until the new millennium was its link with cross-border business, and its ambition to employ predictable rules on jurisdiction, applicable law and recognition and enforcement of judgments to facilitate the core free movement agenda of the European project. This was the case right up to the 1997 **Treaty of Amsterdam** when a wider private international law agenda was included in what was then **Article 65 of the Treaty Establishing the European Community** ('EC'). Similarly, the recognition of personal rights across the European Member States arguably was not seen an end in its own right. Rather it was considered instrumental in supporting the economics-driven free movement of establishment,[14] and of workers (now often mistakenly called the free movement of 'persons'). The foundational European principles of non-discrimination, loyalty, and the four freedoms were yardsticks against which national private international rules were measured, usually in the context of hard core economic freedoms.[15]

B An Area of Freedom, Security and Justice

#12 At a broader level, the overall agenda for private international law in the EU is embedded in the **'Area of Freedom, Security and Justice'** – **AFSJ**, often also referred to as a 'common judicial area'.

#13 The **common judicial area** was arguably first mooted by Valéry Giscard d'Estaing, then French President, in Brussels on 5 December 1977. President Giscard d'Estaing squarely had a common European approach to addressing criminality in mind when he issued his proposal for a common judicial area, more specifically a

13 And of arbitration awards. The European Institutions later chose to abandon any effort to regulate arbitration in favour of the system provided for by the New York Convention. This was a decision which later ricocheted into considerable European case-law and extensive amounts of scholarship.

14 See also R Savatier, 'Le Marché commun au regard du droit international privé' [1959] Rev.Crit.DIP 237, 253.

15 Compare the extensive discussion in Partsch (n 5).

system of near-automated extradition in cases involving terrorism and serious crimes.[16]

#14 Giscard d'Estaing's suggestion built on the findings of the intergovernmental **'TREVI' group**, formed during the Rome December 1971 European Council meeting. The acronym is said to stand for *Terrorisme, Radicalisme, Extrémisme et Violence Internationale*.[17] It was the cooperation in TREVI which led to the 1990 Schengen Convention.

#15 TREVI itself subsumed into the third 'pillar', **'Justice and Home Affairs' – JHA**, of the 1992 **Treaty of Maastricht**. That pillar, in Article K.1 listed 9 fields of cooperation in the fields of justice and home affairs,[18] of which 'judicial cooperation in civil matters' — the natural domain for EU cooperation on private interna-

---

16 Proposition de Valéry Giscard d'Estaing sur la mise en place d'un espace judiciaire européen (Centre Virtuel de de la Connaissance sur l'Europe-CVCE 1977) <https://tinyurl.com/3ucmrw3y> accessed 14 March 2025. GDE's proposal took place with fresh memories of Palestine's 'Black September's terrorist attack against the 1972 Munich Olympics and ETA, and IRA terrorism among others.

17 R Coolseat, 'EU Counterterrorism Strategy: Value Added or Chimera?' (2010) 86 International Affairs 857. Obviously the acronym is also a reference to Rome's TREVI fountain, where the group's first meeting was held, and chaired by the Dutchman Jacques Fonteijn, 'fontein' meaning 'fountain' in Dutch. See ia T Bunyan, *Statewatching the New Europe: Handbook on the European State* (Statewatch 1993) 11.

18 ARTICLE K Cooperation in the fields of justice and home affairs shall be governed by the following provisions.

ARTICLE K.1

For the purposes of achieving the objectives of the Union, in particular the free movement of persons, and without prejudice to the powers of the European Community, Member States shall regard the following areas as matters of common interest:

1. asylum policy;
2. rules governing the crossing by persons of the external borders of the Member States and the exercise of controls thereon;
3. immigration policy and policy regarding nationals of third countries;
   (a) conditions of entry and movement by nationals of third countries on the territory of Member States;
   (b) conditions of residence by nationals of third countries on the territory of Member States, including family reunion and access to employment;
   (c) combating unauthorized immigration, residence and work by nationals of third countries on the territory of Member States;
4. combating drug addiction in so far as this is not covered by 7 to 9;
5. combating fraud on an international scale in so far as this is not covered by 7 to 9;
6. judicial cooperation in civil matters;
7. judicial cooperation in criminal matters;
8. customs cooperation;
9. police cooperation for the purposes of preventing and combating terrorism, unlawful drug trafficking and other serious forms of international crime, including if necessary certain aspects of customs cooperation, in connection with the organization of a Union-wide system for exchanging information within a European Police Office (Europol).

tional law — was only one. Yet its inclusion in the far more contentious (compared to conflict of laws) JHA areas such as visa, migration, police cooperation etc meant that EU private international law got caught up in the maelstrom of Member States' opposition to further co-operation in this area. In the institutional arrangements on the further harmonisation of EU private international law,[19] the UK, like Ireland, secured a flexible **'opt-in'**. This means that in principle it was not bound by further EU PIL instruments unless it notified, by 'simple' letter to the EU Institutions, that it did wish to be so subject to the EU law at issue. By use of this flexible mechanism, the UK was bound of its own volition inter alia by the successors to the Brussels Convention: the Brussels I and Brussels Ia Regulations;[20] the commercially highly relevant Rome I and II Regulations on applicable law for contractual and non-contractual obligations; and the Insolvency Regulation. Overall, the UK was subject to 12 of the core 18 EU law instruments in the area of private international law[21] when it left the EU in January 2020. Denmark 'secured' a more inflexible opt-in (effectively a hard **opt-out**):[22] any participation by Denmark in EU private international law can only take place via a tailored, subject-matter specific Treaty between Denmark and the EU. This amounts to a very rigid system which effectively has kept Denmark out of the vast majority of EU private international law.[23]

#16 Arguably, the UK's (and Ireland and Denmark's) principal exclusion of EU private international law was not the result of an objection against the very area of harmonisation in private international law. Rather, private international law instruments were seen as part and parcel of the **'area of freedom, security and justice'** – **AFSJ** which the Member States adopted as an aspiration in the Treaty of Maastricht. The focus of that Title of the Treaty, Title IV, was on 'Visas, asylum, immigration and other policies related to free movement of persons'. It was the

---

19 Specifically, in Article 3 of the Protocol on the position of the United Kingdom and Ireland annexed to the 1992 Treaty on European Union and the Treaty establishing the European Communities [2006] OJ C321/E, 198–200.

20 Regulation 1215/2012 on jurisdiction and the recognition and enforcement of judgments in civil and commercial matters [2012] OJ L351/1.

21 M Poesen, 'Civil and Commercial Private International Law in Times of Brexit: Managing the Impact, and Fostering Prospects for a Future EU–UK Cooperation' in M Sacco (ed), *Brexit and EU Law: A Way Forward* (Vernon Press 2019) 255, 257, n 10, referring to J Ungerer, 'Brexit von Brüssel und den anderen Verordnungen zum Internationalen Privat- und Verfahrensrecht' in M Kramme, C Baldus and M Schmidt-Kessel (eds), *Brexit und die Juristischen Folgen* (Nomos 2017) 296, 306.

22 Compare J von Hein, 'EU Competence to Legislate in the Area of Private International Law and Law Reforms at the EU Level' in P Beaumont and others (eds), *Cross-border Litigation in Europe* (Bloomsbury/Hart 2017) 19.

23 M Fogt, 'Denmark' in J Basedow and others (eds), *Encyclopedia of Private International Law* (Edward Elgar 2017); see also J Monar, 'The Area of Freedom, Security and Justice' in A von Bogdandy and J Bast (eds), *Principles of European Constitutional Law* (Bloomsbury/Hart 2011) 551.

prospective of further co-operation on migration policies which these States did not wish to adhere to. The resulting complexity for private international law arguably was collateral damage.

#17 At this point it is also important to point out that other Member States have hesitated to extend the reach of EU harmonisation in those areas of **family law** which touch upon core societal choices, such as marriage and divorce. It is no coincidence that the area of private international law is the biggest single user so far of the EU's '**enhanced co-operation**' mechanism, a procedure where a minimum of nine Member States may establish advanced integration or co-operation in an area within EU structures but without the other EU countries being involved, let alone bound.

#18 The AFSJ's objectives are currently set out in Article 3(2) of the Treaty on European Union and further specified in Title V of the TFEU, Articles 67 to 89. The **AFSJ's objectives** are listed in Article 67 TFEU.[24] Only the last element of these objectives ('The Union shall facilitate access to justice, in particular through the principle of mutual recognition of judicial and extrajudicial decisions in civil matters') concerns private international law.

#19 The introduction and subsequent development of the AFSJ (also referred to as the **European Judicial Area**, echoing Giscard d'Estaing's 'common judicial area' [#13 above] is a key development in both the direction and pace of European private international law. The Treaty of Maastricht had brought private international law within the EU's three pillar structure, rather than leaving it outside it, as a pure instrument of public international law [see #7]. However private international law was still not part of the 'Community' pillar.[25] The Treaty of Amsterdam by

---

24 'The Union shall constitute an area of freedom, security and justice with respect for fundamental rights and the different legal systems and traditions of the Member States; It shall ensure the absence of internal border controls for persons and shall frame a common policy on asylum, immigration and external border control, based on solidarity between Member States, which is fair towards third-country nationals. For the purpose of this Title, stateless persons shall be treated as third-country nationals; The Union shall endeavour to ensure a high level of security through measures to prevent and combat crime, racism and xenophobia, and through measures for coordination and cooperation between police and judicial authorities and other competent authorities, as well as through the mutual recognition of judgments in criminal matters and, if necessary, through the approximation of criminal laws; The Union shall facilitate access to justice, in particular through the principle of mutual recognition of judicial and extrajudicial decisions in civil matters'.

25 The 'Community pillar' is the EU's fully-fledged 'supranational pillar' (F Laursen and S Vanhoonacker, 'The Maastricht Treaty: Creating the European Union' in *Oxford Research Encyclopedia of Politics* (OUP 2019) <https://oxfordre.com/politics/view/10.1093/acrefore/9780190228637.001.0001/acrefore-9780190228637-e-1067> accessed 14 March 2025). 'In a nutshell, the Community method provides a means to move European integration forward by passing different interests through three successive filters: (a) the general European interest at the level of the independent European Commission; (b) democratic representation of people and the Member States, at the level of the European Parliament and the Council of Ministers that together form the EU's legislature; and (c) judicial control at the

contrast integrated the subject matter into the EU's core institutional framework. This changed the nature and scope of European private international law to such considerably extent that the Treaty of Amsterdam is seen as the proper birthdate of European Private International Law,[26] with the preceding 'intergovernmental' period (1957–1999) only a prelude to the deeper nature of integration currently developing. The Treaty of Amsterdam also triggered the development of a whole series of EU Regulations on private international law, consistent interpretation of which is not always guaranteed nor warranted.[27]

#20 The initial drive for the development of 'European' private international law as noted was the support which a coordinated approach to the issues could give to the **objective of the internal market**. These internal market credentials of European private international law have clearly not been dropped from the judicial area agenda. The flagship Brussels Ia, Rome I and Rome II Regulations which are discussed in other chapters of this volume, continue to be an important driver accompanying the completion of the EU's Internal Market. They most certainly comprise an important part of litigation before both national courts and the CJEU in the private international area. This part of the EU private international law agenda can be said to encourage the mobility of EU citisens, alongside that of corporations,[28] as part of the broader agenda of mobility of resources, human and otherwise, in the EU.

#21 However initially alongside and arguably currently overpowering the internal market, economic agenda of EU private international law, the focus is now more

---

level of the European Court of Justice. The system combines supranational aspects with negotiation between the States that make up the Union': Y Devuyst, 'The European Union's Community Method: Foundations and Evolution' in *Oxford Research Encyclopedia of Politics* (OUP 2020) <https://oxfordre.com/politics/view/10.1093/acrefore/9780190228637.001.0001/acrefore-9780190228637-e-153> accessed 14 March 2025).

26 L Pailler and C Nourissat (eds), *Un système de droit international privé de l'Union européenne? Bilan et perspectives de 20 ans de coopération judiciaire en matière civile* (Larcier Intersentia 2023). See also E Farnoux, 'Regard historique sur la construction de la coopération judiciaire en matière civile' in L Pailler and C Nourissat (eds), *Un système de droit international privé de l'Union européenne? Bilan et perspectives de 20 ans de coopération judiciaire en matière civile* (Larcier Intersentia 2023) 49 noting at 50 the relatively young phenomenon of the EU's judicial cooperation namely 'vingt ans, comme le suggèrent les organisateurs du colloque' and at 55 citing the Treaty of Amsterdam as the 'birth of European private international law'.

27 See D Draguiev and G Van Calster, 'The EU Regulations on Jurisdiction and Applicable Law in Cross-border Insurance Disputes and their Interaction' in M Walachowska, M Fras and P Marano (eds), *Insurance and Private International Law* (Springer 2024) 3; J Guillaumé, 'La cohérence des interprétations du droit international privé de l'Union' in L Pailler and C Nourissat (eds), *Un système de droit international privé de l'Union européenne? Bilan et perspectives de 20 ans de coopération judiciaire en matière civile* (Larcier Intersentia 2023) 313); M Szpunar, 'EU Private International Law: Consistency of the Scopes of Application and/or of the Solutions' in B Hess and K Lenaerts (eds), *The 50th Anniversary of the European Law of Civil Procedure* (Bloomsbury /Hart 2020) 71.

28 Compare J Basedow, *EU Private Law* (Intersentia 2021), Part X in particular, discussing the use of conflicts rules to promote the EU's trade agenda.

on the **EU *citizen*** as primary recipient of justice, rather than as a means to and reflection of internal market-related mobility.[29]

#22 It is clear that EU private international law plays a role in securing the **right to an effective remedy**, guaranteed by Article 47 of the Charter of Fundamental Rights of the European Union – EUCFR.[30] However it is not in my view the current state of affairs that EU private international law centres upon that ambition. This is not to say that it might not establish it as its central objective in future, and it is certainly the case that **sound administration of justice** (distinct nota bene from 'access to justice'[31]) does currently play a role in (some of) the EU's private international law rules.[32] The flagship EU Regulation on private international law, the Brussels Ia Regulation, only really happenstance mentions the 'sound administration of justice' as a consideration of its jurisdictional matrix, it does not in my view posit it as a core goal.[33] What 'sound administration of justice' actually means is not even defined by it.

#23 Before saying a little more on what one could posit as the or more likely some of the principles of EU private international law, it is worth recalling a crucial moment in the development of EU private international law, one which arguably continues to drive many of the characteristics of the sector, and certainly the driver of the CJEU approach to the interpretation of the relevant instruments. The initial Brussels Convention, now the Brussels Ia Regulation, and the Lugano Convention are so-called '**traités doubles**'. These are treaties that not only facilitate

29 An interesting illustration is the entire absence other than for one out of 29 chapters, of civil and commercial private international law in a recent book celebrating the 'Area of Freedom, Security and Justice': K Lenaerts and others (eds), *Shaping a Genuine Area of Freedom, Security and Justice: Liber Amicorum Vice-President Bay Larsen* (Bloomsbury/Hart 2024). Compare even before the current focus on asylum and migration, S Poillot-Peruzzetto, 'La priorité de Liberté, de Sécurité et de Justice et l'élaboration d'un code européen de droit international privé' in M Fallon, P Lagarde and S Poillot-Peruzzeto (eds), *Quelle architecture pour un code européen de droit international privé?* (Peter Lang 2011) 51, 53ff.

30 Compare P Beaumont and M Danov, 'The EU Civil Justice Framework and Private Law' (2015) 22 Maastricht Journal of European and Comparative Law 706.

31 See M Barba, 'L'accès à la justice en droit international privé européen' in Pailler and Nourissat (eds), *Un système de droit international privé de l'Union européenne? Bilan et perspectives de 20 ans de coopération judiciaire en matière civile* (Larcier Intersentia 2023) 279.

32 Including for instance some instruments adopted in the early 2000s, such as Council Directive 2003/8/EC of 27 January 2003 to improve access to justice in cross-border disputes by establishing minimum common rules relating to legal aid for such disputes [2003] OJ L26/41.

33 Contra eg P Beaumont and M Danov, 'Introduction: Research Aims and Methodology' in P Beaumont and others (eds), *Cross-border Litigation in Europe* (Bloomsbury/Hart 2017) 1 with reference to recital 16 Brussels Ia (which in fact addresses special jurisdictional rules and which links 'sound administration of justice' specifically to predictability and reasonable foreseeability).

recognition and enforcement but also provide for direct jurisdictional rules.[34] Indeed the direct harmonisation of jurisdictional rules is key to the Brussels regime's almost automatic recognition and enforcement of judgments from the courts of other Member States. It is precisely because the jurisdictional rules are harmonised that swift recognition and enforcement is possible. I have referred to that elsewhere as 'mission creep' in the sense that the negotiators went beyond what Article 220 instructed them to do, although on less of a soundbite approach to the issue, I also explain that the negotiators of the 1968 Convention saw the harmonisation of jurisdictional rules as the only avenue to achieve what they had been formally instructed with: the smooth recognition and enforcement of judgments across the (then) European Economic Community.[35]

C Principles of EU Private International Law

I Legal Certainty and Predictability

#24 **Legal certainty and predictability** are arguably the main drivers for EU private international law, particularly in the context of the civil and commercial claims that find their home in Brussels Ia. Both of course are laudable objectives and they are clearly influenced by the internal market credentials of early, and continuing EU private international law: if uncertainty as to the three steps of private international law is an obstacle to corporations and individuals doing business across the EU, then certainty viz those steps evidently will act as a lubricant to the internal market.

#25 In the CJEU's approach viz the Brussels Ia Regulation, predictability and legal certainty are intimately bound up with the Regulation's, and the Court's, solid emphasis on its stated core jurisdictional gateway of **'actor sequitur forum rei'**, included in Article 4: as a matter of course and firm principle, a claim should be brought in the defendant's home. As a result, any and all other jurisdictional rules in the Regulation, in the Court's firmly established approach, must be **interpreted restrictively** and solely with their intended aim in mind.[36]

---

34 See eg European Commission Communication, 'Assessment on the Application of the United Kingdom of Great Britain and Northern Ireland to Accede to the 2007 Lugano Convention' COM (2021) 222.

35 G van Calster, *EU Private International Law: Commercial Litigation in the EU* (4th edn, Bloomsbury/Hart 2024) para 2.6. See similarly Lasok and Stone (n 1) 150: '(the Convention goes) far beyond what the Treaty apparently 'envisaged'.

36 Ex multi, Case C-464/01 *Johann Gruber v Bay Wa AG* (20 January 2005) ECLI:EU:C:2005:32, para 32: 'First of all, within the scheme of the Brussels Convention, the jurisdiction of the courts of the Contracting State in which the defendant is domiciled constitutes the general principle enshrined in the first paragraph of Article 2, and it is only by way of derogation from that principle that the Convention

#26 The CJEU arguably equates 'legal certainty' with 'predictability' and its approach as just noted is closely linked to it giving paradigm status to the Article 4 actor sequitur forum rei rule, whose predictable effect vis-à-vis defendants is held to be the core purpose of the Regulation. '(T)he purpose of [the Brussels Ia] regulation . . . is to guarantee, to the greatest extent possible, the protection of defendants who are domiciled in the European Union'.[37]

#27 Legal certainty also has an impact on the extent to which courts should entertain jurisdictional issues before engaging with the merits: 'It is also consonant with that aim of legal certainty that the court seised should be able readily to decide whether it has jurisdiction on the basis of the rules of the Convention, without having to consider the substance of the case.'[38]

II Proximity

#28 Proximity is often mentioned in on breath with predictability as a guiding principle of EU private international law. However Brussels Ia itself does not mention 'proximity' as an axiomatic rule indeed it does not use the words at all. Only a number of jurisdictional rules are said, including by the CJEU, to be either explained[39] or must be interpreted[40] with 'proximity' in mind.

#29 Proximity however comes in many forms.

#30 In its simplest expression it suggests that those courts with a territorial link with the case should have jurisdiction. This is indeed clearly reflected in exclusive jurisdictional rules that are linked to '**comity**' and the avoidance of conflict with foreign jurisdictions, in particular in the universally accepted **Moçambique rule** (after *British South Africa Co v Companhia de Moçambique* [1893] AC 602) in which the House of Lords confirmed that an English court will not, as a matter of its own limits to jurisdiction, determine matters by and large of title to foreign land. This rule echoes in

provides for an exhaustive list of cases in which the defendant may or must be sued before the courts of another Contracting State. As a consequence, the rules of jurisdiction which derogate from that general principle are to be strictly interpreted, so that they cannot give rise to an interpretation going beyond the cases envisaged by the Convention (see, in particular, *Bertrand*, paragraph 17; *Shearson Lehman Hutton*, paragraphs 14, 15 and 16; *Benincasa*, paragraph 13, and *Mietz*, paragraph 27)'.

37 Case C-327/10 *Hypoteční banka as v Udo Mike Lindner* (17 November 2011) ECLI:EU:C:2011:745, para 31ff.

38 Case C-269/95 *Francesco Benincasa v Dentalkit Srl* (3 July 1997) ECLI:EU:C:1997:337, para 27.

39 Article 24(1)'s exclusive jurisdictional rule for proceedings which have as their object rights in rem in immovable property or tenancies of immovable property: See Jenard Report (n 5), 35 and Case 73/77 *Theodorus Engelbertus Sanders v Ronald van der Putte* [1977] ECR 238.

40 Ex multi, Case C-21/76 *Handelskwekerij GJ Bier BV v Mines de potasse d'Alsace SA* (30 November 1976) ECLI:EU:C:1976:166; Case C-147/12 *ÖFAB, Östergötlands Fastigheter AB v Frank Koot and Evergreen Investments BV* (18 July 2013) ECLI:EU:C:2013:490.

other exclusive heads of jurisdiction such as those over the life and deaths of corporations, and the validity of a number of intellectual property rights.

#31 The CJEU's approach to Brussels Ia's special jurisdictional rule for tort, too, is a clear expression of proximity seeing as the court(s) where the damage occurred were held to be particularly well placed to judge the case, from the point of evidence and the conduct of the proceedings.

#32 In a more conceptual approach to proximity, the concept links to **Friedrich Von Savigny**'s focus on the *Sitz* or 'seat' of a relationship in law: which legal order has the closest connection to the specific facts at issue, where lies the nexus of the case, which legal order *connects* predominantly to the case. This approach has the obvious inconvenience that 'distance by itself is not a meaningful connection for either the normative expectations of the parties or the intentions maintained by lawmakers when legislating an issue. Distance has to be combined with a value judgment on the significance of certain aspects of a legal relation and on the weight accorded to some interests involved as compared with others . . . .'[41]

III Uniformity, Including Autonomous Interpretation

#33 'Unification of the rules of conflict of jurisdiction in civil and commercial matters' has been held by the CJEU to be the overall objective of the Brussels Ia Regulation.[42] It is settled law[43] that, in principle,[44] the CJEU interprets the terms of Brussels Ia and with it, of EU private international law generally, 'autonomously' so as to ensure that it is fully effective. That **autonomous interpretation** alone is said to be capable of ensuring uniform application of the Brussels regime, so as to avoid as far as possible the multiplication of the bases of jurisdiction in relation to one and the same legal relationship and to reinforce the legal protection available to persons established in the EU.

#34 In reality there are many factors leading to a lack of uniformity in practice, related among others to lack of systematic publication of case-law in many Member States; the differing nature of application proprio motu of private international law by the courts; differing practices of treating foreign law as fact that needs to

41 Basedow and others (n 23) 317.

42 Case C-185/07 *Allianz v West Tankers* (10 February 2009) ECLI:EU:C:2009:69 para 24.

43 Ex multi and verbatim, Case C-383/95 *Petrus Wilhelmus Rutten v Cross Medical Ltd* (9 January 1997) ECLI:EU:C:1997:7, paras 12–13.

44 See eg Case 12/76 *Industrie Tessili Italiana Como v Dunlop AG* [1976] ECR 1473, para 14]: 'Having regard to the differences between national laws of contract and to the absence at this stage of legal development of any unification in the substantive law applicable, it does not appear possible to give any more substantial guide to the interpretation of . . . 'place of performance' of contractual obligations. This is all the more true since the determination of the place of performance of obligations depends on the contractual context to which these obligations belong'.

be proven cq law with which the court seized is supposed to be familiar (ius novit curia) etc.[45]

#35 The initial CJEU approach to the issue of **autonomy** was to resort to a comparative tour de table of the interpretation of particular legal concepts in the national law of the Member States, a **'ius commune'** exercise such as in the pivotal case of *Eurocontrol*, on the notion of 'civil and commercial': the CJEU held that 'the concept in question must be regarded as independent and must be interpreted by reference, first, to the objectives and scheme of the Convention, and, secondly, to the general principles which stem from the corpus of the national legal systems.'[46] That comparative approach has arguably[47] been abandoned in favour of an approach engaging with the text and travaux of the European statutes themselves.

IV Mutual Trust

#36 The **mutual trust** principle in EU private international law is an expression, in the specific private international law context, of a wider EU law principle. This general principle requires each Member State, save in exceptional circumstances, to consider all other Member States to be complying with EU law and particularly with the fundamental rights recognised by EU law.[48] A subset of the principle is precisely the mutual recognition by the Member States, of each other's judicial decisions, said to be the cornerstone for the creation of a genuine judicial area.[49]

#37 The consequences of the 'mutual trust' principle particularly impacted the United Kingdom, specifically in the insistence by the CJEU that the genesis of the jurisdictional rules in the Brussels Convention (see my 'mission creep' remark above, #23), implied a strict respect for lis pendens rules even when the court first seized was one in a Member State well known for its tardy proceedings, or where a court other than that clearly identified in a choice of court agreement was seized so as to 'tor-

45 See extensively J von Hein, E-M Kieninger and G Rühl (eds), *How European is European Private International Law?* (Intersentia 2019).

46 Case C-29/76 *LTU Lufttransportunternehmen GmbH & Co. KG v Eurocontrol* (14 October 1976) ECLI: EU:C:1976:137, para 3.

47 See M Audit, 'Uniformité des notions autonomes' in Pailler and Nourissat (eds), *Un système de droit international privé de l'Union européenne? Bilan et perspectives de 20 ans de coopération judiciaire en matière civile* (Larcier Intersentia 2023) 297, 298.

48 Case C-216/18 PPU *Minister for Justice and Equality (Deficiencies in the system of justice)* (25 July 2018) ECLI:EU:C:2018:586, para 36.

49 Case C-454/19 *ZW intervener Staatsanwaltschaft Heilbronn* (19 November 2020) ECLI:EU:C:2020:947, para 49.

pedo' the prompt assessment of the claim in the prorogated court.[50] The Court's inflexibility[51] (turning a positively phrased 'mutual trust' into an inflexible insistence on deference to the implementation of the Brussels regime by the court seised, even in the light of tardy proceedings and /or disrespect for contractual party autonomy), at best has rendered the CJEU 'impopular'[52] and is even said to have led to the 'systematic dismantling'[53] of the common law approach to conflict of laws.

#38 The mutual trust principle finds specific expression in the near-automated **mutual recognition of judgments**, which at the **Tampere Council** was formally said to be a 'cornerstone of judicial co-operation in both civil and criminal matters within the Union.'[54] Mutual trust has found its way into the recitals of the Brussels Ia Regulation as a justification for mutual recognition of judgments[55] however the principle itself is not defined in any way in the Regulation. In CJEU case-law it is referred to justify the strict approach to the lis pendens rule, referred to #37.

V Party Autonomy

#39 **Party autonomy** has a 'legitimate, prominent position within the individualistic European conflict of laws of the 21st century'.[56] Even in private international law in family matters, long the domain of State-imposed territorially decided rules, the EU has more recently firmly chosen the party autonomy route, first via an

---

50 A particularly potent torpedoing mechanism since rendered harmless to some degree by the Brussels Ia Regulation; See van Calster (n 35) para 2.539.

51 Case C-116/02 *Erich Gasser GmbH v MISAT Srl* (9 December 2003) ECLI:EU:C:2003:657, para 72: '[I]t must be borne in mind that the Brussels Convention is necessarily based on the trust which the Contracting States accord to each other's legal systems and judicial institutions. It is that mutual trust which has enabled a compulsory system of jurisdiction to be established, which all the courts within the purview of the Convention are required to respect, and as a corollary the waiver by those States of the right to apply their internal rules on recognition and enforcement of foreign judgments in favour of a simplified mechanism for the recognition and enforcement of judgments'.

52 Farnoux (n 26) 59.

53 TC Hartley, 'The European Union and the Systematic Dismantling of the Common Law of Conflict of Laws' (2005) 54 ICLQ 813.

54 Tampere European Council of 15 and 16 October 1999, Presidency Conclusions, 33 <https://www.europarl.europa.eu/summits/tam_en.htm> accessed 17 March 2025.

55 Recital 26: 'Mutual trust in the administration of justice in the Union justifies the principle that judgments given in a Member State should be recognised in all Member States without the need for any special procedure. In addition, the aim of making cross-border litigation less time-consuming and costly justifies the abolition of the declaration of enforceability prior to enforcement in the Member State addressed. As a result, a judgment given by the courts of a Member State should be treated as if it had been given in the Member State addressed'.

56 H-P Mansel, 'Party Autonomy, Legal Doctrine on Choice of Law, and the General Section of the European Conflict of Laws' in S Leible (ed), *General Principles of European Private International Law* (Wolters Kluwer 2016) 131, 133.

extensive interpretation of the Treaty rules on free movement, subsequently more explicitly in statutory instruments.[57] The CJEU has put party autonomy on a pedestal in recent authorities for instance on the flexibility with which parties may construct 'asymmetric' choice of court,[58] and on the possibility for parties to 'internationalise' an otherwise purely domestic contract simply by choosing a foreign court,[59] or foreign applicable law.[60] While party autonomy has been an established principle in contractual conflict of laws for some time, including in European private international law, its wide acceptance is much more recent.[61]

VI Value Neutrality or the 'Purely Technical' Nature of EU Private International Law

#40 Finally, **value neutrality** is an important current characteristic of EU private international law if not so much a 'principle' perhaps. The EU system is not alone in its apparent disinterest, at its outset, in the substantive consequences of its private international law rules.

#41 Value neutrality is often also referred to as the **'purely technical nature' of private international law rules**. It is so much part of the contemporary approach to private international law that 'classic private international law' is defined by a leading scholar as 'broadly defined in technical terms, classical private international law is generally understood by both courts and scholars to define the competent court, applicable law, and status of foreign judgments in transnational settings without regard for the final result in terms of individual rights and obligations or indeed of wider policy concerns.'[62] Arguably because the focus of private international law since the 17th century has been on ringfencing what is called 'parochial jurisdiction': excessive exercise of jurisdiction at the expense of other States.[63]

57 A Faucon Alonso, *The EU and Party Autonomy in Private International Family Law* (Doctoral thesis, KU Leuven 2020) on file with the author.

58 Case C-537/23 *Società Italiana Lastre SpA (SIL) v Agora Sarl*, (27 February 2025) ECLI:EU:C:2025:120. See B Marshall, 'CJEU on Substantive Validity and on Asymmetric Clauses: What We Now Know, and What We (Still) Don't' (www.gavclaw.com, 7 March 2025) <https://tinyurl.com/pw4n67a7> accessed 17 March 2025.

59 Case C-566/22 *Inkreal s.r.o. v Dúha reality s.r.o.*, (8 February 2024) ECLI:EU:C:2024:123. This case in fact is an excellent illustration of many of the principles discussed here, seeing as the Court refers to party autonomy, effectiveness, predictability, legal certainty, mutual trust and increased access to justice.

60 Case C-54/16 *Vinyls Italia SpA, in liquidation v Mediterranea di Navigazione SpA*, (8 June 2017) ECLI: EU:C:2017:433.

61 F Wilke, *A Conceptual Analysis of European Private International Law* (Intersentia 2019) 195.

62 H Muir Watt, 'Theorizing Private International Law' in A Orford and F Hoffmann (eds), *The Oxford Handbook of the Theory of International Law* (OUP 2016) 862, 863.

63 A Mills, 'The Public History of Private International Law' (2006) 55 ICLQ 1.

#42 Of course, whether to define EU private international law as hitherto 'value neutral' depends very much on one's definition of 'values' and 'neutrality'. All of the 'principles' discussed in the previous headings may be said to reflect a 'value', in particular the use of private international law as a mechanism of support for the Internal Market. Likewise, while EU private international law may be said ostensibly not to consider international competitiveness,[64] it may well in effect be 'efficient' and supportive of an EU economic agenda.[65]

#43 More generally, over and above the traditional implications of the ordre public exception in private international law, and the application of overriding mandatory laws (also known as lois de police or in Belgian French-speaking scholarship and practice as 'lois d'application immédiate'[66]), a variety of more or less traditional mechanisms both within and outside EU private international law have recognised the values recognised by, sought by, enviseaged and supported by either the design and /or the functioning of private international law.[67] This includes favor negotis rules (rules for instance in Rome I which encourage the validity of contract by offering a myriad of potentially applicable rules to save a contract from formal invalidity), rules to protect vulnerable parties such as employees and consumers, varying approaches to renvoi etc.

#44 Nevertheless it is true that in the EU like elsewhere, an *explicit* recognition of the societal values which can and may be supported by private international law, is more recent.[68]

---

64 For instance in *Gasser* (n 51) where the United Kingdom specifically put forward the argument that the Brussels Convention had to be interpreted taking into account the needs of international trade, a suggestion not much entertained by the CJEU.

65 See in particular G Rühl, *Statut und Effizienz* (Mohr Siebeck 2011) 811; and G Rühl, 'The Role of Economic Efficiency' in Leible S (ed), *General Principles of European Private International Law* (Wolters Kluwer 2016) 45.

66 This last shorthand explaining exactly what they stand for: laws of the forum which 'immediately' apply regardless of any diverging choice of law.

67 Wilke (n 61) 289ff.

68 See eg the rule of Article 7 of the Rome II Regulation, giving claimants choice of law for non-contactual liability in environmental matters (G Van Calster, 'Lex Ecologia. On Applicable Law for Environmental Pollution, A Pinnacle of Business and Human Rights as well as Climate Change Litigation' [2022] IPRax 441); the attention to 'sound administration of justice' and relevant reference to i.a. the rule of law in Brussels Ia's forum non conveniens-type regime of its Articles 33–34 (G Van Calster, 'Lis Pendens and Third States: The Origin, DNA and Early Case-Law on Articles 33–34 of the Brussels Ia Regulation's 'Forum Non Conveniens- Light' Rules' (2022) 18 Journal of Private International Law 363); the fairly recent phenomenon of sophisticated international law firms recognising the relevance of private international law, and employing that for forum shopping and applicable law shopping (E Aristova, *Tort Litigation Against Transnational Corporations: The Challenge of Jurisdiction in English Courts* (OUP 2024); E Aristova and U Grusic (eds), *Civil Remedies and Human Rights in Flux* (Bloomsbury/Hart 2022); R Meeran (ed), *Human Rights Litigation Against Multinationals in Practice* (OUP 2021); G Van Calster, 'Climate Justice Litigation and Private International Law' [2023] Lex&Forum 583; and the excellent scholarly effort to link the UN Sustainable Development goals – SDGs to private interna-

References

Aristova E, *Tort Litigation Against Transnational Corporations: The Challenge of Jurisdiction in English Courts* (OUP 2024).
Aristova E and Grusic U (eds), *Civil Remedies and Human Rights in Flux* (Bloomsbury/Hart 2022).
Audit M, 'Uniformité des notions autonomes' in L Pailler and C Nourissat (eds), *Un système de droit international privé de l'Union européenne? Bilan et perspectives de 20 ans de coopération judiciaire en matière civile* (Larcier Intersentia 2023) 297.
Baere de G and Roes T, 'EU Loyalty as Good Faith' (2015) 64 ICLQ 829.
Barba M, 'L'accès à la justice en droit international privé européen' in L Pailler and C Nourissat (eds), *Un système de droit international privé de l'Union européenne? Bilan et perspectives de 20 ans de coopération judiciaire en matière civile* (Larcier Intersentia 2023) 279.
Basedow J, *EU Private Law* (Intersentia 2021).
Beaumont P and Danov M, 'The EU Civil Justice Framework and Private Law' (2015) 22 Maastricht Journal of European and Comparative Law 706.
—— 'Introduction: Research Aims and Methodology' in P Beaumont and others (eds), *Cross-border Litigation in Europe* (Bloomsbury/Hart 2017) 1.
Bunyan T, *Statewatching the New Europe: Handbook on the European State* (Statewatch 1993).
Coolseat R, 'EU Counterterrorism Strategy: Value Added or Chimera?' (2010) 86 International Affairs 857.
Devuyst Y, 'The European Union's Community Method: Foundations and Evolution' in *Oxford Research Encyclopedia of Politics* (OUP 2020) <https://oxfordre.com/politics/view/10.1093/acrefore/9780190228637.001.0001/acrefore-9780190228637-e-153> accessed 14 March 2024.
Draguiev D and Van Calster G, 'The EU Regulations on Jurisdiction and Applicable Law in Cross-border Insurance Disputes and their Interaction' in M Walachowska, M Fras and P Marano (eds), *Insurance and Private International Law* (Springer 2024) 3.
Fallon M, *Les conflits de lois et de juridictions dans un espace économique intégré – L'expérience de la Communauté Européenne* (Martinus Nijhoff 1995).
Farnoux E, 'Regard historique sur la construction de la coopération judiciaire en matière civile' in L Pailler and C Nourissat (eds), *Un système de droit international privé de l'Union européenne? Bilan et perspectives de 20 ans de coopération judiciaire en matière civile* (Larcier Intersentia 2023) 49.
Faucon Alonso A, *The EU and Party Autonomy in Private International Family Law* (Doctoral thesis, KU Leuven 2020).
Fogt M, 'Denmark' in J Basedow and others (eds), *Encyclopedia of Private International Law* (Edward Elgar 2017).
Giscard d'Estaing V, 'Proposition sur la mise en place d'un espace judiciaire européen' (Centre Virtuel de la Connaissance sur l'Europe-CVCE 1977) <https://tinyurl.com/3ucmrw3y> accessed 14 March 2025.
Guillaumé J, 'La cohérence des interprétations du droit international privé de l'Union' in L Pailler and C Nourissat (eds), *Un système de droit international privé de l'Union européenne? Bilan et perspectives de 20 ans de coopération judiciaire en matière civile* (Larcier Intersentia 2023) 313.
Hartley TC, 'The European Union and the Systematic Dismantling of the Common Law of Conflict of Laws' (2005) 54 ICLQ 813.
Heymann J, *Le Droit International Privé à l'Epreuve du fédéralisme européen* (Economica 2010).
Huet A, 'Article 220' in V Costantinesco and others (eds), *Traité instituant la C.E.E., Commentaire article par article* (Economica 1992) 1377.

tional law by R Michaels, V Ruiz Abou-Nigm and H van Loon (eds), *The Private Side of Transforming Our World – UN Sustainable Development Goals 2030 and the Role of Private International Law* (Intersentia 2021).

Jenard P, 'Report on the Convention on Jurisdiction and the Enforcement of Judgments in Civil and Commercial Matters' [1979] OJ C59/1 <https://tinyurl.com/56wr522e> accessed 15 March 2025.

Klamert M, *The Principle of Loyalty in EU Law* (OUP 2014).

Laursen F and Vanhoonacker S, 'The Maastricht Treaty: Creating the European Union' in *Oxford Research Encyclopedia of Politics* (OUP 2019) <https://oxfordre.com/politics/view/10.1093/acrefore/9780190228637.001.0001/acrefore-9780190228637-e-1067> accessed 15 March 2025.

Lasok D and Stone P, *Conflict of Laws in the European Community* (Professional Books 1987).

Lenaerts K and others (eds), *Shaping a Genuine Area of Freedom, Security and Justice: Liber Amicorum Vice-President Bay Larsen* (Bloomsbury/Hart 2024).

Mansel H-P, 'Party Autonomy, Legal Doctrine on Choice of Law, and the General Section of the European Conflict of Laws' in S Leible (ed), *General Principles of European Private International Law* (Wolters Kluwer 2016) 131.

Marshall B, 'CJEU on Substantive Validity and on Asymmetric Clauses: What We Now Know, and What We (Still) Don't' (www.gavclaw.com, 7 March 2025) <https://tinyurl.com/pw4n67a7> accessed 17 March 2025.

Meeran R (ed), *Human Rights Litigation Against Multinationals in Practice* (OUP 2021).

Michaels R, Ruiz Abou-Nigm V and van Loon H (eds), *The Private Side of Transforming Our World – UN Sustainable Development Goals 2030 and the Role of Private International Law* (Intersentia 2021).

Mills A, 'The Public History of Private International Law' (2006) 55 ICLQ 1.

Monar J, 'The Area of Freedom, Security and Justice' in A von Bogdandy and J Bast (eds), *Principles of European Constitutional Law* (Bloomsbury/Hart 2011) 551.

Muir Watt H, 'Theorizing Private International Law' in A Orford and F Hoffmann (eds), *The Oxford Handbook of the Theory of International Law* (OUP 2016) 862.

Pailler L and Nourissat C (eds), *Un système de droit international privé de l'Union européenne? Bilan et perspectives de 20 ans de coopération judiciaire en matière civile* (Larcier Intersentia 2023).

Partsch PE, *Le droit international privé européen – De Rome à Nice* (Larcier 2003).

Poesen M, 'Civil and Commercial Private International Law in Times of Brexit: Managing the Impact, and Fostering Prospects for a Future EU–UK Cooperation' in M Sacco (ed), *Brexit and EU Law: A Way Forward* (Vernon Press 2019) 255.

Poillot-Peruzzetto S, 'La priorité de Liberté, de Sécurité et de Justice et l'élaboration d'un code européen de droit international privé' in M Fallon, P Lagarde and S Poillot-Peruzzetto (eds), *Quelle architecture pour un code européen de droit international privé?* (Peter Lang 2011) 51.

Rühl G, *Statut und Effizienz* (Mohr Siebeck 2011).

—— 'The Role of Economic Efficiency' in S Leible (ed), General Principles of European Private International Law' (Wolters Kluwer 2016) 45.

Roth W-H, 'Der Einfluß des Europäisches Gemeinschaftsrechts auf das Internationale Privatrecht' (1991) 55 RabelsZ 623.

Savatier R, 'Le Marché commun au regard du droit international privé' [1959] Rev.Crit.DIP 237.

Schima B, 'Article 268 TFEU' in M Kellerbauer, M Klamert and J Tomkin (eds), *The EU Treaties and the Charter of Fundamental Rights: A Commentary* (OUP 2019) 1841.

—— 'Article 272 TFEU' in M Kellerbauer, M Klamert and J Tomkin (eds), *The EU Treaties and the Charter of Fundamental Rights: A Commentary* (OUP 2019) 1854.

Szpunar M, 'EU Private International Law: Consistency of the Scopes of Application and/or of the Solutions' in B Hess and K Lenaerts (eds), *The 50th Anniversary of the European Law of Civil Procedure* (Bloomsbury/Hart 2020) 71.

Thue HJ, 'European Private International Law as the European Solution, and the European Economic Area (EEA/EWR) Problem' in G Reichelt (ed), *Europäisches Gemeinschaftsrecht und IPR: Ein Beitrag zur Kodifikation der allgemeinen Grundsätze des Europäischen Kollisionsrechts. Symposium Wien 1. Dezember*

2006 aus Anlass des 10-jährigen Bestehens des Ludwig Boltzmann Institutes für Europarecht (Manz 2007) 93.

Ungerer J, 'Brexit von Brüssel und den anderen Verordnungen zum Internationalen Privat- und Verfahrensrecht' in M Kramme, C Baldus and M Schmidt-Kessel (eds), *Brexit und die Juristischen Folgen* (Nomos 2017) 296.

Van Calster, 'To Unity and Beyond? The Boundaries of European Private International Law and the European Ius Commune' in A Verbeke and others (eds), *Liber Amicorum Walter Pintens* (Intersentia 2012) 1459.

—— 'On the Role of Borders in European Conflict of Laws' in M Piers, H Storme and J Verhellen (eds), *Liber Amicorum Johan Erauw* (Intersentia 2014) 219.

—— 'Lex Ecologia. On Applicable Law for Environmental Pollution, A Pinnacle of Business and Human Rights as well as Climate Change Litigation' [2022] IPRax 441.

—— 'Lis Pendens and Third States: The Origin, DNA and Early Case-Law on Articles 33–34 of the Brussels Ia Regulation's "Forum Non Conveniens-Light" Rules' (2022) 18 Journal of Private International Law 363.

—— 'Climate Justice Litigation and Private International Law' [2023] Lex&Forum 583.

von Hein J, 'EU Competence to Legislate in the Area of Private International Law and Law Reforms at the EU Level' in P Beaumont and others (eds), *Cross-border Litigation in Europe* (Bloomsbury/Hart 2017) 19.

von Hein J, Kieninger E-M and Rühl G (eds), *How European is European Private International Law?* (Intersentia 2019).

Pietro Franzina

Chapter 10
International Jurisdiction in Civil and Commercial Matters

#1 Regulation (EU) No 1215/2012 of the European Parliament and of the Council of 12 December 2012,[1] known as the **Brussels I-bis Regulation**, performs two interrelated functions. Some of its provisions deal with the **international jurisdiction** of the courts of EU Member States to rule on cross-border cases. Others concern the **free movement of judgments** from one Member State to another. This contribution is concerned with the former group of rules.[2]

A General Features of the Brussels I-bis Regulation

I Scope

#2 The Brussels I-bis Regulation applies in 'civil and commercial matters'. The term covers the whole spectrum of private law, but some areas, such as maintenance, succession, arbitration and insolvency, are explicitly excluded from the scope of the Regulation pursuant to Article 1(2).

#3 Matters involving a **public authority** come with the purview of the Regulation unless the authority in question acted in the exercise of its powers, *ie* outside the scope of the rules applicable to relationships between private individuals.[3] Similarly, the Regulation does not apply where the remedies sought by the public

1 [2012] OJ L351/1.
2 See W Hau, Chapter 13 for a discussion of the rules on recognition and enforcement. The Regulation applies in all EU Member States, including Denmark, although the latter does not take part in the development of the European 'area of freedom, security and justice'. An agreement between the European Community, as it was then, and Denmark, concluded on 19 October 2005, extended to Denmark the effects of the rules that now appear in the Brussels I *bis* Regulation: see [2005] OJ L299/62.
3 Case 29/76, *LTU Lufttransportunternehmen GmbH & Co KG v Eurocontrol* (14 October 1976) ECLI:EU:C:1976:137LTU, para 4.

Pietro Franzina, Catholic University of the Sacred Heart, Milan, e-mail: pietro.franzina@unicatt.it

https://doi.org/10.1515/9783110781632-010

party, or the opportunities it enjoys in respect of the proceedings (eg, as regards the collection of evidence), differ from those available to private individuals.[4]

#4 An **international element** must exist to trigger the operation of the Brussels I-bis Regulation. As regards jurisdiction, this may result from the location of the defendant's domicile or from the subject matter of the proceedings, provided that that situation is such as to raise questions before a court of a Member State relating to the determination of international jurisdiction.[5] In fact, any meaningful connection between the proceedings or the substantive relationship concerned and a State other than the forum State would suffice, no matter whether the Regulation would regard that connection as a ground of jurisdiction.[6] The situation does not need to involve two or more Member States. The involvement of a Member State and a **third country** is sufficient.[7]

#5 The Regulation is solely concerned with proceedings instituted on or after 10 January 2015 (Article 66).

II Origin, Evolution, Legal basis and Context

#6 The Brussels I-bis Regulation is the latest incarnation of a body of rules of international civil procedure whose roots are in the **Brussels Convention** of 27 September 1968 on jurisdiction and the enforcement of judgments in civil and commercial matters.[8] The layout of the Brussels I-bis Regulation and several of its provisions correspond, in substance, to the layout and provisions of the Convention. The case law of the Court of Justice relating to the previous versions of the Brussels I regime – that is, the Convention itself and Regulation (EC) No 44/2001 of 22 December 2000,[9] ie the immediate predecessor of the current text – remains relevant, in principle, to this day.[10]

#7 The Brussels I regime, as embodied in Regulation (EC) No 44/2001, is mirrored in the **Lugano Convention** of 30 October 2007 on jurisdiction and the recognition

---

4 Cf Case C-73/19 *Belgische Staat and Directeur-Generaal van de Algemene Directie Controle en Bemiddeling van de FOD Economie, K.M.O., Middenstand en Energie v Movic BV and Others* (16 July 2020) ECLI: EU:C:2020:568, paras 35 et seq.

5 Case C-339/22 *BSH Hausgeräte GmbH v Electrolux AB* (25 February 2025) ECLI:EU:C:2025:108, para 59.

6 Thus, a case is international, inter alia, where the defendant is a national of a State other than the forum, despite the fact that no weight is accorded in the Regulation to the nationality of the parties as a possible ground of jurisdiction: Case C-327/10 *Hypoteční banka a.s. v Udo Mike Lindner* (17 November 2011) ECLI:EU:C:2011:745, para 31 et seq.

7 Case C-281/02 *Andrew Owusu v N. B. Jackson, trading as "Villa Holidays Bal-Inn Villas" and Others* (1 March 2005) ECLI:EU:C:2005:120, para 26.

8 For the latest consolidated version, see [1998] OJ C27/1.

9 [2001] OJ L12/1.

10 Recital 34 of the Brussels I-bis Regulation.

and enforcement of judgments in civil and commercial matters.[11] The Convention is in force for the Union in its relations with Iceland, Norway and Switzerland. The case law concerning the Convention, notably by the Court of Justice, provides guidance also in respect of the Brussels I-bis Regulation.

#8 Enacted on the basis of Article 81 TFEU, the Regulation is part of the Union's acquis on '**judicial cooperation in civil matters**', or private international law broadly understood.[12] This entails, inter alia, that in interpreting the Regulation regard should be had, where appropriate, to other pertinent legislative measures in this field. One such measure is Regulation (EC) No 593/2008 of 17 June 2008 (Rome I) on the law applicable to **contractual obligations**.[13]

III Relationship with Other Instruments

#9 The international agreements to which the Union is a party take precedence over the Brussels I-bis Regulation in accordance with Article 216 TFEU. However, some multilateral agreements concluded by the EU, such as the Hague Convention of 30 June 2005 on exclusive **choice of court** agreements,[14] come with a disconnection clause whereby Member States' courts are permitted to rely on EU rules in situations that are solely or essentially connected with two or more Member States, subject to the conditions specified in the conventions themselves.[15]

#10 Pursuant to Article 71, the Brussels I-bis Regulation does not affect any conventions to which a Member State is a party, insofar as they deal with jurisdiction or the recognition and enforcement of judgments in 'particular matters'. That is the case, inter alia, of the Geneva Convention of 19 May 1956 on the contract for the international carriage of goods by road (**CMR**).[16] For this purpose, pre-existing conventions must nevertheless be consistent with the principles underlying the Brussels I regime, meaning, inter alia, that their rules must be highly predictable, enable the risk of concurrent proceedings to be minimised, and ensure the move-

---

11 [2009] OJ L147/5.

12 The Regulation is in fact a fundamental component of the Union's acquis in this area, both due to its broad scope and to the influence that the previous incarnations of the Brussels I regime exerted on the development of the European legislation on international civil procedure: U Magnus, 'Introduction' in U Magnus and P Mankowski (eds), *Brussels Ibis Regulation* (2nd edn, Otto Schmidt 2023) 6, 13 et seq.

13 [2008] OJ L177/6.

14 Council Decision 2009/397/EC of 26 February 2009 on the signing on behalf of the European Community of the Convention on choice of court agreements [2009] OJ L133/1.

15 In the case of the Hague Convention mentioned above, the clause at issue is found in Article 26.

16 Convention on the Contract for the International Carriage of Goods by Road (CMR) (adopted 19 May 1956, entered into force 2 July 1961) 399 UNTS 189.

ment of judgments from one State to another under conditions at least as favourable as those contemplated under EU rules.[17]

#11 The Regulation is without prejudice to provisions contained in EU instruments, like the General Data Protection Regulation (**GDPR**),[18] or in domestic legislation harmonised thereunder.

B The Rules Dealing with Jurisdiction: An Overview

#12 The Brussels I-bis Regulation deals with jurisdiction in Chapter II. The thirty or so provisions in that chapter can be divided into three groups, based on their task. The first group consists of **jurisdictional rules** proper, *ie* rules the purpose of which is to set out the grounds on which the courts of a Member State may entertain a case and decide it on its merits (Sections 1–7). The rules in the second group are concerned with **parallel litigation**, which occurs where the courts of two or more States are seised of identical or related proceedings (Section 9). Finally, the rules in the third group address some of the procedural issues that may arise in the operation of jurisdiction-conferring provisions, such as whether the court before which the matter is brought must declare that it lacks jurisdiction *ex officio* or should only do so upon a request by the defendant (Section 8).

#13 Only the first two groups of rules will be examined in this chapter. Before doing so, it is expedient to present the common features of the rules of the Regulation and illustrate their relationship with the domestic rules of the Member States.

I Common Features

#14 The Brussels I-bis Regulation is an instrument of **regional integration**. It aims to enhance legal certainty in international litigation as a means to encourage market actors to deploy their activity across borders, thereby exploiting the potential of the freedoms enshrined in the European Treaties.[19]

#15 The rules in the Regulation build on the high degree of trust that the Member States owe to each other. One corollary of **mutual trust** is that litigation in one Member State is regarded as equivalent to litigation in another. Procedural rules

17 Case C-533/08 *TNT Express Nederland BV v AXA Versicherung AG* (4 May 2010) ECLI:EU:C:2010:243, para 47 et seq.

18 Regulation (EU) 2016/679 of the European Parliament and of the Council of 27 April 2016 on the protection of natural persons with regard to the processing of personal data and on the free movement of such data, and repealing Directive 95/46/EC [2016] OJ L119/1; see, in particular, Article 79(2).

19 Cf A Mills, 'La Convention de Bruxelles de 1968: un code et un concept' [2018] Revue critique de droit international privé 503, 506 et seq.

vary from one Member State to another, and so do the efficiency of the judicial systems. Yet, the courts of one Member State cannot use the peculiarities of the law or practice of another Member State as an excuse for not cooperating with the courts of the latter State as prescribed by the Regulation.[20] By the same token, and for stronger reasons, the courts in a Member State must refrain from affecting by their measures the way in which the courts of other States discharge their functions (eg, through **anti-suit injunctions**),[21] and should rather regard as binding the determinations made by the latter as to their own jurisdiction.[22]

#16 Consistent with the above premises, the jurisdiction-conferring rules of the Regulation share three inter-connected features.

#17 Structurally, they take the form of abstract provisions that predetermine the grounds of jurisdiction that Member States' courts are permitted (and required) to rely upon. According to Article 7, point 2, for example, proceedings in matters relating to tort or delict may be brought in the courts for the place where the harmful event occurred or may occur. To assess its jurisdiction, a court must merely determine whether the place of the event lies within its territory. The approach is meant to enhance **predictability**, ensure the issue of jurisdiction can be dealt with rapidly and efficiently, and facilitate the uniform application of the Regulation across Member States, thereby ensuring that market actors enjoy the same rights and opportunities as regards access to justice, whatever the Member State in which they are established or operate.

#18 Functionally, the rules in the Brussels I-bis Regulation do not content themselves with providing the courts of a Member State with the power to adjudicate a case. They also require that the designated courts exercise such power, if requested, regardless of whether the courts of another State may appear to be better placed to do so. This way, the Regulation bestows a right on the plaintiff to have the claim adjudicated by the court specified under its provisions. This is meant to enhance legal certainty and reduce the risk of positive and negative conflicts of jurisdiction, the prospect of which might discourage **businesses, consumers** and **employees** from entering into cross-border relations.

#19 Operationally, the Regulation, at the same time as it confers jurisdiction on the courts of one or more Member States, also prevents the courts of the other Member States from ruling on the matter. While domestic rules on jurisdiction operate in a binary fashion, in the sense that they only determine whether the courts of the forum may adjudicate the dispute, but fail to indicate, in the negative,

---

20 Case C-116/02 *Erich Gasser GmbH v MISAT Srl* (9 December 2003) ECLI:EU:C:2003:657, para 70 et seq.

21 Case C-185/07 *Allianz SpA and Generali Assicurazioni Generali SpA v West Tankers Inc* (10 February 2009) ECLI:EU:C:2009:69, para 28 et seq.

22 Case C-456/11 *Gothaer Allgemeine Versicherung AG and Others v Samskip GmbH* (15 November 2012) ECLI:EU:C:2012:719, para 29 et seq.

whether the courts of another State have the power to do so, the rules in the Regulation effectively allocate jurisdiction among the Member States of the EU. This enables the parties to determine at once, based on a single set of uniform rules, whether the courts of a Member State would be available to hear a claim or would rather dismiss it for want of jurisdiction.

II Relationship with Domestic Rules

#20 The Brussels I-bis Regulation takes precedence over domestic rules on jurisdiction in accordance with the **principle of primacy of EU law**. The assertion calls for two qualifications. Depending on the circumstances, the rules of the forum are either be free to fill the gaps left by the Regulation or are rather charged by the Regulation to deal with specific situations within its scope.

1 Domestic Law Applied as a Gap Filler

#21 Situations exist within the scope of the Regulation which the Regulation itself fails to address. In principle, nothing prevents Member States from dealing with those situations under their own rules. Should Member States refrain from doing so in circumstances where this would undermine, indirectly as the case may be, the effectiveness of the Regulation? The issue arises, in particular, in two scenarios.

#22 As explained below in more detail, Article 25 of the Regulation provides that the parties may agree that the courts of a Member State are to have jurisdiction to rule on their disputes. Nothing is said in the Regulation as regards the agreements that designate a court, or the courts, of a third State. It is generally accepted that Member States' courts can fall back on their **domestic rules** in this scenario.[23] This means that, apart from cases governed by an international convention to which the Union is a party, a court sitting in a Member State, seised of a matter within the scope of the parties' agreement, may dismiss the case for lack of jurisdiction where the private international law rules of the forum provide that the agreement should be enforced. This approach, however, if followed unreservedly, entails that, where the choice points to the courts in a third country, the jurisdictional rules of the Member State of the forum effectively exclude the jurisdiction of the courts of that Member State *in any event*, including where the courts of the forum, or those of another Member State, would be entitled to entertain the claim

23 Case C-387/98 *Coreck Maritime GmbH v Handelsveem BV and Others* (9 November 2000) ECLI:EU:C:2000:606, para 19 et seq.

pursuant to other provisions in the Regulation (eg, the general rule in Article 4, whereby jurisdiction lies with the courts of the Member State of the domicile of the defendant). Whether the Regulation permits an unrestricted reliance on domestic rules in the latter circumstances remains a subject of debate.[24]

#23 The rules of exclusive jurisdiction laid down in Article 24 have, for a long time, raised similar doubts. As discussed below in more detail, matters within the scope of those rules may only be litigated before the courts of the Member State with which the case features a given connection, as specified in the Regulation. No other provisions in the Regulation is available to the parties in such cases. This applies, for instance, to disputes over rights in rem in immoveable property, which are subject to the exclusive jurisdiction of the Member State where property is located. What if the property at issue is in a third State? Of course, Article 24 cannot be relied upon as a jurisdiction-conferring rule in this case, since the relevant circumstances (the situs of the immoveable) do not materialise in a Member State. Rather, one may wonder whether Member States' courts are free in this scenario to turn to the jurisdictional rules of the forum. Should they be permitted to do so, or should they rather rely on the other rules in the Regulation (ie the rules the operation of which would be excluded, if the **immoveable property** in question were within the EU)? Or should Article 24 be understood to have a **'reflexive' effect**, meaning that, in view of the rationale of Article 24, the courts of the Member States should be permitted (if not required) to refrain from hearing a dispute of this kind, because of its qualified ties with a third State? In *BSH Hausgeräte*, a case decided in 2025 relating to the alleged infringement of a patent, the Court of Justice discussed the possibility that Article 24(4), which confers exclusive jurisdiction over the validity of patents on the courts of the Member State of registration, could exclude 'reflexively' the jurisdiction of a Member State's courts where the patent in question is one granted in a third State. The Court replied in the negative, as a matter of principle. It held that, without prejudice to such international conventions as may apply in the relations with the third country concerned (and without prejudice to Articles 33 and 34, on extra-EU ***lis pendens*** and **related actions**), the courts of the Member State of the domicile of the defendant have jurisdiction under Article 4(1) to rule on an infringement action brought against that defendant by the holder of a patent granted in a third State.[25] Rather, having recalled that Article 24(4) confers jurisdiction on the courts of the Member State of registration 'irrespective of whether the issue [of the validity of the **patent**] is raised by way of an action or as a defence', the Court went on to assess the restrictions that general international law may impose on Member States' courts as regards the exercise of their jurisdiction where the validity

---

24 See generally G Van Calster, *European Private International Law* (4th edn, Hart 2024) 153 et seq.
25 Case C-339/22 *BSH Hausgeräte GmbH* (n 5) para 61.

of a third country patent is at issue. Relying on the principle of non-interference in another State's internal affairs, the Court observed that where a judicial decision annulling a patent affects the existence or, in the event of annulment in part, the content of those exclusive rights, only the courts having jurisdiction in that State may give such a decision.[26] Thus, only the courts of the third State in which a patent is granted have jurisdiction to declare that patent invalid by a decision that may cause the national register of that State to be amended as regards the existence or content of that patent. Instead, nothing prevents the court of the Member State of the domicile of the defendant from relying on Article 4(1) of the Brussels I-bis Regulation to rule on an infringement action in the context of which the issue of the validity of a patent granted in a third State is raised merely as a defence.[27]

2 Application of Domestic Rules by Virtue of the Regulation

#24 The Brussels I-bis Regulation provides that jurisdiction over certain matters falling within its scope is to be assessed, in each Member State, in accordance with the domestic rules of that State. Specifically, pursuant to Article 6(1), domestic rules apply, with some exceptions, to proceedings against persons domiciled in a non-Member State.

#25 The rationale of the provision may be summarised as follows. Some of the jurisdictional rules in the Brussels I-bis Regulation explicitly limit their applicability to proceedings against persons domiciled in a Member State of the Union (hereinafter, 'European defendants').[28] This is true, inter alia, of the rules of special jurisdiction in Articles 7 and 8. Other provisions, instead, including Article 24 on **exclusive jurisdiction** and Article 25 on **choice of court agreements**, take care of clarifying that they apply 'regardless of the domicile of the parties'. In addition, rules exist that take the former approach as a basis but deviate from it in some respects. The protective regime for **employment disputes**, among others, features a deviation of this kind. The rule in Article 21(2), according to which the employee may sue the employer before the courts for the place where he habitually

26 ibid para 73.

27 ibid para 74.

28 Several authors consider that the applicability of the Regulation's jurisdictional rules is contingent on the defendant being domiciled in a Member State: see, inter alia, Van Calster (n 24) 33. A better view, it is contended, is that the operation of the Regulation is not restricted, in general, to proceedings against persons domiciled in the Union. Indeed, certain provisions in the Regulation feature such a restriction, but they do not speak for the Regulation as a whole. The latter view is corroborated by the finding of the Court of Justice in Opinion 1/03, discussed below.

carries out his work, applies irrespective of whether the employer is domiciled in a Member State.

#26 By limiting the operation of certain of its rules to proceedings against European defendants, the Regulation creates a sort of imbalance. On the one hand, litigation against persons domiciled in the Union is dealt with by the Regulation through an elaborate set of jurisdictional rules designed to take account of a broad range of situations and offering balanced and nuanced solutions. The cases involving non-European defendants, instead, form the object of a small selection of harmonised rules (Articles 24 and 25, etc.). If it were only for the latter provisions, the expectations and practical needs of those willing to suing a third State domiciliary in Europe would largely remain unanswered. To redress this situation, the Regulation provides that, where the defendant is domiciled outside the Union, the courts of each Member State may assert their jurisdiction whenever the (unharmonised) rules in force in the forum so provide. Domestic rules are meant to perform, here, a **'residual' function**.

#27 Member States' courts are permitted to rely in these cases on rules that significantly depart from the policies and style of the Union's rules. Persons domiciled in a third State may in fact be sued in a Member State, via Article 6(1), on grounds that the provisions of the Regulation regard as unsuitable to found jurisdiction, such as the nationality of the plaintiff or the presence in the forum of assets belonging to the defendant. Reliance on **'exorbitant' grounds** is proscribed vis-à-vis EU defendants (and against those domiciled in contracting States of the Lugano Convention), while it is tolerated, and actually endorsed, as concerns non-European defendants. The Regulation adopts, here, a double standard.[29] The differentiation is even more significant considered that judgments based on a ground of jurisdiction that only exists in national law benefit from the Regulation's rules on recognition and enforcement in the same way as any other judgment emanating from a Member State.

#28 As clarified by the Court of Justice in Opinion 1/03, the rule whereby Member States are to apply their own domestic rules against non-European defendants 'forms part of the system' of the Regulation, since it resolves a situation that the Regulation itself is meant to address 'by reference to the legislation of the Member State before whose court the matter is brought'.[30] In other terms, domestic law applies to proceedings against persons domiciled in a third country not because those proceedings are regarded as falling outside the scope of the Regulation, but because the Regulation entrusts Member States with dealing with such proceedings in accordance with their own rules.

---

29 See further P Franzina, 'L'universalisation partielle du régime européen de la compétence en matière civile et commerciale dans le règlement Bruxelles I *bis*: une mise en perspective' in E Guinchard (ed), *Le nouveau règlement Bruxelles I bis* (Bruylant 2014) 39, 58 et seq.

30 Opinion 1/03 (7 February 2006) ECLI:EU:C:2006:81, para 148.

C The Rule of General Jurisdiction

#29 The jurisdiction-conferring rules in the Regulation are arranged to form a system. The cornerstone of the system is the rule of general jurisdiction in Article 4: 'persons **domiciled** in a Member State shall, whatever their **nationality**, be sued in the courts of that Member State'.

#30 The rule is general in the sense that it applies, save for relatively few exceptions, to any matter within the scope of the Regulation. As stated in Recital 15, jurisdiction is always available on this ground, 'save in a few well-defined situations in which the subject-matter of the dispute or the autonomy of the parties warrants a **different connecting factor**'. The central place occupied by Article 4 entails that the provisions that contemplate other connecting factors may not be interpreted extensively. The latter provisions should even be disregarded altogether in cases where their application would result in an unjustified departure from Article 4, that is, in case where the advantages that would normally warrant such a departure fail to materialise.[31]

#31 For the purposes of the Regulation, a company or other legal person is deemed to be domiciled in the State where it has its statutory seat, its central administration or its principal place of business (Article 63). The three locations are listed alternatively, meaning that an entity whose statutory seat is in State X should be deemed to be domiciled, at the same time, in State Y if the key decisions regarding its management are taken in Y or its activity is primarily being carried out there.[32]

#32 A different approach is followed for natural persons. Pursuant to Article 62, the court seised must apply its own internal law (provided this does not undermine the effectiveness of EU law)[33] to determine whether a natural person is domiciled in the forum State. If that person is not domiciled in the forum, and the issue arises of whether their domicile is in another Member State, the law of that other Member State applies.

---

31 The Court found, for example, that the special rule on matters relating to a contract, which assigns jurisdiction on the courts of the place of performance of the obligation in question, does not apply to a dispute concerning a contractual obligation to refrain from doing something, where the latter is not subject to any geographical limit and is therefore characterised by an unlimited multiplicity of places of performance. Reliance on the said rule would not serve, then, the goals of proximity and predictability underlying the special rule. It is in view of those goals that the Brussels I regime enables, in this area, a derogation from the general rule in Article 4. Case C-256/00 *Besix SA v Wasserreinigungsbau Alfred Kretzschmar GmbH & Co. KG (WABAG) and Planungs- und Forschungsgesellschaft Dipl. Ing. W. Kretzschmar GmbH & KG (Plafog)* (19 February 2002) ECLI:EU:C:2002:99, para 35.

32 See further A Briggs, *Civil Jurisdiction and Judgments* (6th edn, Informa Law 2015) 199 et seq.

33 Case C-222/23 *'Toplofikatsia Sofia' EAD* (16 May 2024) ECLI:EU:C:2024:405, para 55 et seq.

D Special Jurisdiction

#33 Various rules of **special jurisdiction**, mainly laid down in Articles 7 and 8, operate alongside Article 4. They are special in the sense that each is concerned with a given set of homogeneous matters, such as matters relating to a contract, or to a tort.

#34 Jurisdiction conferred pursuant to special rules is concurrent in nature, meaning that those rules do not affect the operation of such other jurisdiction-conferring rules as may apply in the circumstances, notably Article 4. For example, since Article 7, point 2, confers concurrent jurisdiction in tort on the courts of the place of the harmful event, a person seeking reparation following a tort may bring proceedings, at his choice, at the place where the harmful event occurred or in the courts of the Member State where the defendant is domiciled.

#35 Based on the policies they serve, the rules of special jurisdiction fit into two broad categories.

#36 Some of them chiefly underlie a concern for proximity. They rest on the assumption that a close connection exists in some cases between the subject matter of the dispute and a given State, and that it is expedient, in these circumstances, to enable the claimant to bring proceedings in that State. Article 7, point 2, follows this pattern. The idea is that litigation at the place where the cause of action arose can prove particularly efficient, both because evidence is likely to be found there and because local courts are presumably in a good position to assess the legal aspects of, and the social and economic background to, the dispute. In addition, litigating in the State with which the claim is objectively connected is highly predictable for the parties and does not involve, as such, a preferential treatment for any of the litigants.

#37 Other rules of special jurisdiction aim to promote **consistency** in the resolution of complex disputes. They are used in cases involving multiple parties or multiple causes of action and are designed to reduce the risk that litigation may be dispersed across different States. One such rule is found in Article 8, point 1. It applies to proceedings against **multiple defendants**, as it occurs, for example, where the plaintiff seeks a determination of their joint liability. The provision enables the plaintiff to attract all the defendants in one court, namely the court of the place where any of them is domiciled. Article 8, point 2, to name just one more example, stipulates that a person may be sued as a third party in an action on a warranty or guarantee in the court seised of the original proceedings, subject to certain conditions. The jurisdiction conferred under the latter provision displays a 'derivative' character, since the power to rule on the claim against the third party is a sort of extension of the jurisdiction of the court seised of the main claim.

#38 Only two rules of special jurisdiction will be analysed here in more detail: the rule in Article 7, point 1, on matters relating to a contract, and the rule in Article 7, point 2, on torts.

I Special Jurisdiction on Matters Relating to a Contract

#39 Article 7, point 1, sets out a rule of concurrent jurisdiction that applies in 'matters relating to a contract'.[34] The provision consists of three parts, each identified by a letter. Pursuant to (a), a person domiciled in a Member State may be sued in another Member State in the courts of the **'place of performance** of the obligation in question'. The rule comes with two specifications, found in (b). Unless otherwise agreed, the place of performance of the obligation in question is, in the case of the sale of goods, the place in a Member State where the goods were delivered or should have been delivered under the contract (first indent), and, in the case of the provision of services, the place in a Member State where the services were provided or should have been provided (second indent). As stated in (c), where the special rules in (b) do not apply, then the general rule in (a) applies. In practice, the rule in (a) is applicable where the dispute relates to a contract that is neither a sale of goods nor a provision of services, and where the dispute is about a sale or a provision of services but the place of delivery of the goods or the place of supply of the services lies outside the EU.

1 Scope

#40 The Brussels I-bis Regulation fails to define the term **'contract'**. The only indication offered by the text of the Regulation is that matters relating to specific types of contracts fall outside the scope of Article 7, point 1, as they form the object of dedicated jurisdictional rules. Reference is made to insurance contracts (Articles 10 to 16), **consumer contracts** (Articles 17 to 19), individual **employment contracts** (Articles 20 to 23) and **tenancies** (Article 24, point 1).

#41 The notion of contract must be construed autonomously. The rich case law of the Court of Justice on this topic can be condensed into three main statements.

#42 First, a matter cannot be deemed to relate to a contract unless an obligation was freely undertaken by one party towards the other.[35] This has two implications. Article 7, point 1, is only available in disputes that oppose parties bound by a di-

34 On this provision see generally P Mankowski, 'Article 7' in U Magnus and P Mankowski (eds), *Brussels Ibis Regulation* (2nd edn, Otto Schmidt 2023) 108, 147 et seq.

35 Case C-26/91 *Jakob Handte & Co. GmbH v Traitements Mécano-chimiques des Surfaces SA* (17 June 1992) ECLI:EU:C:1992:268, para 15.

rect relationship. In *Handte*, the Court excluded on this basis that an action brought by a sub-buyer of goods against the manufacturer of those goods, rather than the seller, could be classified as contractual, noting that there was no direct relationship between the claimant and the defendant, and that the manufacturer had not undertaken any obligation specifically towards the sub-buyer.[36] The Court stressed that the rule now in Article 7, point 1, must be interpreted in such a way as to enable a normally well-informed defendant reasonably to determine in advance the State before whose courts he could be sued.[37] The second implication of the above statement is that Article 7, point 1, can only be relied upon where the obligation at issue was undertaken voluntarily by the party concerned, as opposed to being imposed by the law. In *Tacconi*, the Court held that an action founded on the **pre-contractual liability** of the defendant, specifically on the ground that the latter had withdrawn from negotiations, does not constitute a contractual matter, because the claim rests on the defendant's alleged failure to comply with duties imposed by a source external to the parties, ie the general duty to act in good faith in pre-contractual dealings. The implementation of the above findings proves difficult where the liability of the defendant can be seen as arising both from a breach of a freely undertaken obligation and from the infringement of a legal duty. In *Brogsitter* the Court asserted that a claim is contractual in nature where the conduct complained of may be considered a breach of the terms of the contract, explaining that that will *a priori* be the case where the interpretation of the contract between the parties 'is indispensable to establish the lawful or, on the contrary, unlawful nature of the conduct complained of' by the applicant.[38] The nature of the rules relied upon by the plaintiff in his application, the Court elaborated in a later ruling, also have an impact on this assessment.[39]

#43 The second of the three statements summarising the views of the Court of Justice on the notion of contract is that Article 7, point 1, does not require, as such, the conclusion of a contract.[40] The rule also applies, for example, where the applicant seeks to enforce a unilateral promise.[41] On a more general note, the alleged liability of a party does not have to be grounded on a specific agreement between the parties, even less an agreement concluded in writing or in another particular

---

36 ibid para 16 et seq.

37 ibid para 18.

38 Case C-548/12 *Marc Brogsitter v Fabrication de Montres Normandes EURL and Karsten Fräßdorf* (13 March 2014) ECLI:EU:C:2014:148, para 25.

39 Case C-59/19 *Wikingerhof GmbH & Co. KG v Booking.com BV* (24 November 2020) ECLI:EU:C:2020:950, para 29 et seq.

40 Case C-334/00 *Fonderie Officine Meccaniche Tacconi SpA v Heinrich Wagner Sinto Maschinenfabrik GmbH (HWS)* (17 September 2002) ECLI:EU:C:2002:499, para 22.

41 Case C-27/02 *Petra Engler v Janus Versand GmbH* (20 January 2005) ECLI:EU:C:2005:33, para 50 et seq.

form. In *Granarolo*, the Court ruled that an action for damages founded on an abrupt termination of a **long-standing business relationship** must be viewed as a matter relating to a contract whenever a tacit **contractual relationship** existed between the parties, as may be evidenced, inter alia, by the regularity of the transactions between the parties and their development over time.[42]

#44 The third statement condensing the views of the Court of Justice on the concept of **contract** goes as follows. Although contractual matters are defined by reference to a (freely undertaken) obligation of one party towards the other, Article 7, point 1, is not only concerned with claims that relate directly to such obligations, but extends to proceedings that involve, or even have as their object, a determination as to the existence and validity of a contractual relationship between the parties. The Court made in clear in *Effer* that the special rule on matters relating to a contract can be invoked even when the existence of a contract is in dispute between the parties: if that were not the case, the Court explained, the rule would be deprived of its effect, since it would be sufficient for one party to claim that the contract does not exist to defeat the operation of the rule.[43] In *Feniks*, the Court endorsed an even broader reading of Article 7, point 1, by stating that the latter provision applies to an *actio pauliana* aimed at safeguarding a contractual right, that is, an action aimed to shield the creditor from the effects of the fraudulent transfers made by the debtor to a third person with a view to preventing the creditor himself from seizing the transferred assets.[44] By an action of this kind, the Court observed, the creditor seeks a declaration that the transfers caused detriment to rights that correspond with the obligations freely consented to by the debtor. Thus, the cause of this action 'lies essentially in the breach of these obligations', which is enough to characterise the matter as contractual.[45]

2 The General Rule in Article 7, point 1, (a)

#45 Unlike Article 4, which confers jurisdiction on the courts of a given Member State, considered globally, Article 7, point 1, identifies the particular court, within the Member State concerned, that has jurisdiction to rule on the matter.[46] The provision, in other terms, is not merely concerned with international jurisdiction of a State's courts, but also has implications for **territorial jurisdiction**. The do-

---

42 Case C-196/15 *Granarolo SpA v Ambrosi Emmi France SA* (14 July 2016) ECLI:EU:C:2016:559, para 24 et seq.

43 Case 38/81 *Effer SpA v Hans-Joachim Kantner* (4 March 1982) ECLI:EU:C:1982:79, para 7 et seq.

44 Case C-337/17 *Feniks Sp. z o.o. v Azteca Products & Services SL* (4 October 2018) ECLI:EU:C:2018:805, para 44.

45 ibid para 43.

46 Case C-30/20 *RH v AB Volvo and Others* (15 July 2021) ECLI:EU:C:2021:604, para 33 et seq.

mestic rules of local jurisdiction they cannot be relied upon where they would undermine the *effet utile* of Article 7, point 1. The described peculiarity, which is common to other rules in the Regulation, basically reflects a concern for proximity.

#46 As observed above, jurisdiction under (a) lies with the courts of the place of performance of the obligation in question. The obligation 'in question' is the one that serves as a basis for the claim. For instance, if the plaintiff complains that the defendant failed to perform a given obligation, jurisdiction belongs to the courts of the place where the latter obligation ought to be performed.

#47 One corollary of this approach is that disputes relating to contracts that provide for multiple obligations, each with its own place of performance, could be heard by different courts, all of which would be able to assert their jurisdiction based on Article 7, point 1, (a) of the Regulation. This would frustrate procedural efficiency and increase the likelihood of reaching inconsistent judgments. To mitigate these shortcomings, the Court of Justice held in *Shenavai* that, where various obligations are at issue, 'it will be the principal obligation which will determine its jurisdiction'.[47] In other terms, the court of the place where the defendant should have performed one of the obligations that form the basis of the plaintiff's claim may also entertain claims that relate to other obligations, as long as they are ancillary to the former obligation.

#48 As explained in *Tessili*, the court seised of the proceedings must identify the place of performance of the obligation in question in two stages. It should begin by determining the law (or the rules of law) that govern the substance of the contract. The seised court will normally rely for this on the **conflict-of-laws rules** of the forum, ie those in the Rome I Regulation (unless the latter is displaced by a convention in force in the forum State, pursuant to its Article 25). The court should then turn to the rules that identify, under the said law, the place of performance of the obligation concerned. Suppose, for example, that the plaintiff complains that the defendant owes him money under a contract. It is for the law applicable to the contract to determine whether, for the purposes of jurisdiction, payment is due at the domicile of the creditor (as required, inter alia, by Italian and Swiss law), or at the domicile of the debtor (as it is the case, among other, under Spanish law).[48] If the parties agreed on the place where the obligation in question ought to be performed, substantively, then the agreed place will also be the place of performance of the obligation in question for the purposes of Article 7, point 1, (a), provided the agreement is valid under the law governing the contract.[49]

---

47 Case 266/85 *Hassan Shenavai v Klaus Kreischer* (15 January 1987) ECLI:EU:C:1987:11, para 19.

48 For further references, see P Franzina, 'Place of Performance' in J Basedow and others (eds), *Encyclopedia of Private International Law* (Edward Elgar 2017) 1360, 1362.

49 Case 56/79 *Siegfried Zelger v Sebastiano Salinitri* (17 January 1980) ECLI:EU:C:1980:15, para 5.

3 The special Rules in Article 7, point 1, (b)

#49 The *Tessili* approach, which the Court of Justice devised in one of the first rulings concerning the **Brussels Convention**, attracted two main criticisms. The detour through the *lex causae*, some argued, makes it unduly complicated for the parties to predict which court, or courts, may have jurisdiction to rule on a given matter. In addition, reliance on the law applicable to the contract means that jurisdiction ends up depending on rules that, on top of lacking **uniformity**, do not reflect the concerns that underlie jurisdiction here, namely proximity and **predictability**. This is especially true of pecuniary obligations, as recourse to criteria designed for substantive law involves the risk of jurisdiction being conferred on the courts of a place with which the case fails to display any meaningful connection.

#50 At the time of replacing the Brussels Convention with **Regulation (EC) No 44/2001**, the decision was taken (not to delete, but rather) to complement the old rule, which was to become the general rule in (a), with two new rules, built on an entirely different logic. The latter rules, now found in (b), apply, as observed, to sales of goods and provisions of services. Despite being presented as mere specifications of the old rule, they depart in fact from the latter in two crucial respects. First, the obligation whose place of performance defines jurisdiction is not, under (b), the obligation that serves as a basis for the claim, but rather the **characteristic obligation** of the contract, ie the obligation to deliver the goods and supply the services, respectively. In practice, jurisdiction is to be determined, according to (b), with reference to one and the same obligation whatever the ground on which the claim is based and regardless of the party bringing the proceedings. This avoids at the outset the risk of a proliferation of fora. The second innovation concerns the determination of the place of performance of the pertinent obligation. No room is left in proceedings within the scope of (b) to the law applicable to the contract. The place of performance, where it was not agreed upon by the parties, must be assessed factually, based on the circumstances of the case.

#51 Two main groups of issues have been raised regarding the operation of the rules in (b). The issues in the first group are about the material scope of those rules. The terms 'sale of goods' and 'provision of services' must be understood **autonomously**. The Court held that the former encompasses the sale of goods to be manufactured and produced,[50] while the latter presupposes that that one party carries out a particular activity in return for remuneration.[51] Arrangements that involve both the **transfer of goods** and a **provision of services** fall either under the former special rule or under the latter depending on which obligation charac-

---

50 Case C-381/08 *Car Trim GmbH v KeySafety Systems Srl* (25 February 2010) ECLI:EU:C:2010:90, para 43.

51 Case C-533/07 *Falco Privatstiftung and Thomas Rabitsch v Gisela Weller-Lindhorst* (23 April 2009) ECLI:EU:C:2009:257, para 29.

terises the contract at issue.[52] Contractual relationships that are neither sales of goods nor provisions of services in the sense outlined above, such as IP licence agreements[53] or donations,[54] remain subject to the general rule in (a).

#52 The second group of issues surrounding the rules in Article 7, point 1, (b) relate to the determination of the **place of delivery** and the **place of provision of services** absent an agreement of the parties. In the case of sale of goods, where the goods are to be transported by one or more independent carriers, the issue arises of where, precisely, 'delivery' should be deemed to occur, ie whether regard should be had to the place where the goods are handed over to the first carrier or to the place where the goods reach the buyer at their final destination. The Court of Justice endorsed the latter reading in *Car Trim*, noting that, in the absence of agreement between the parties, the solution that consists in referring to the place where the goods were physically transferred or should have been physically transferred to the purchaser at their final destination is consistent with the two key objectives of the rule of special jurisdiction in matters relating to a contract.[55] As to the provision of services, the issue arose, in particular, of services that the provider is required to supply in two or more States. In *Wood Floor Solutions*, a case concerning a commercial **agency contract**, the Court held that regard should be had to the place of the main provision of services, as it appears from the provisions of the contract or, in the absence of such provisions, the actual performance of that contract or, where it cannot be established on that basis, the place where the agent is domiciled.[56]

II Special Jurisdiction in Matters Relating to Tort or Delict

#53 Article 7, point 2, of the Brussels I-bis Regulation stipulates that a person domiciled in a Member State may be sued in another Member State, 'in matters relating to tort, delict or quasi-delict, in the courts for the place where the harmful event occurred or may occur'.[57]

---

52 Case C-9/12 *Corman-Collins SA v La Maison du Whisky SA* (19 December 2013) ECLI:EU:C:2013:860, para 33 et seq.

53 Case C-533/07 *Falco Privatstiftung* (n 51), para 30 et seq.

54 Case C-417/15 *Wolfgang Schmidt v Christiane Schmidt* (16 November 2016) ECLI:EU:C:2016:881, para 38.

55 Case C-381/08 *Car Trim* (n 50), para 60.

56 Case C-19/09 *Wood Floor Solutions Andreas Domberger GmbH v Silva Trade SA* (11 March 2010) ECLI:EU:C:2010:137, para 36 et seq.

57 On Article 7 point 2, see generally E Lein, 'Jurisdiction in Matters Reating to Tort' Delict or Quasi-Delict' in A Dickinson and E Lein (eds), *The Brussels I Regulation Recast* (OUP 2015) 155.

1 Scope

#54 The terms **'tort'**, **'delict'** and 'quasi delict' go undefined in the Regulation. According to the Court of Justice in *Kalfelis* the above expressions, which should be given an independent meaning, cover all actions which seek to establish the liability of a defendant and do not relate to a 'contract' within the meaning of what is now Article 7, point 1.[58] In *Hrvatske Šume*, the Court stressed that Article 7, point 2, applies where a party is alleged to have committed an act or omission contrary to a duty or prohibition imposed by law, and concluded on this basis that an action for restitution on grounds of unjust enrichment, where it is not based on an unlawful act or omission by a party, falls outside the scope of the latter special rule.[59]

2 The Place of the Harmful Event

#55 As indicated by the Court in *Mines de Potasse*, the expression **'place of the harmful event'** refers both to the place where the damage occurred and to the place of the event giving rise to it.[60] The ruling originated in proceedings brought in Rotterdam by a local undertaking engaged in horticulture against a company based in France concerning the pollution of the waters of the Rhine caused by the discharge of saline waste from the operations of the defendant. The plaintiff complained that the high salt content of the waters, which it used for irrigation, caused damage to the plantations. The Court considered that the place of the event giving rise to the damage (the discharge of saline waste, in France) no less than the place where the damage occurred (the damage to the Dutch plantations) can 'constitute a significant connecting factor from the point of view of jurisdiction', noting that litigation at either one location or the other may be 'helpful from the point of view of the evidence and of the conduct of the proceedings'.[61] In practice, the plaintiff has an option to sue the defendant either at the place where the damage occurred or at the place of the event giving rise to it, in addition to relying on Article 4.

#56 The described approach entails, in practice, an advantage for the victim of the alleged tort, who is normally the plaintiff in proceedings relating to tort. It lies, how-

---

58 Case 189/87 *Athanasios Kalfelis v Bankhaus Schröder, Münchmeyer, Hengst and Co. and Others* (27 September 1988) ECLI:EU:C:1988:459, para 17.

59 Case C-242/20 *Hrvatske Šume d.o.o., Zagreb v BP Europa SE* (9 December 2021) ECLI:EU:C:2021:985, para 53 et seq.

60 Case 21/76 *Handelskwekerij G.J. Bier BV v Mines de Potasse d'Alsace SA* (30 November 1976) ECLI:EU:C:1976:166.

61 ibid para 17.

ever, on considerations of proximity and predictability, and does not reflect a concern for the victim as a weaker party. In *Folien Fischer* the Court ruled on this basis that the above understanding of Article 7, point 2, equally applies to proceedings brought by the alleged author of the tort to obtain a declaration of non-liability.[62]

#57 The Court of Justice took care of clarifying that the term 'place where the harmful event occurred' cannot be understood to cover the place where the victim claims to have suffered financial damage following upon initial damage arising and suffered by him in another State.[63] If the rule were to be given such a broad reading, proximity and predictability would be defeated, and the plaintiff would almost systematically be permitted to seise the courts of his own domicile, which would run against the logic of Article 4. The Court similarly excluded that the rule in Article 7, point 2, allows an action in tort to be initiated in the courts of the place where the tort caused prejudice to an indirect victim, as in the case of damage suffered by a parent company through **financial losses** sustained by a subsidiary.[64]

3 The Operation of the Rule in Special Settings

#58 The rule of special jurisdiction in tort, delict and quasi-delict applies to a range of diverse situations. The contribution of the Court of Justice to the understanding of the rule largely consists of judgments that reflect the specific features of tort liability in particular areas, such as product liability,[65] liability for the infringement of **intellectual property rights**,[66] **prospectus liability**,[67] and liability for the violation of **competition law**,[68] among others. In one area, namely **defamation** and the infringement of **personality rights**, the Court's rulings resulted in an interpretation of the rule that departs rather significantly from its own text.

#59 In *Shevill*, the Court held that the victim of a libel by a newspaper article distributed in several Member States may bring an action for damages against the pub-

---

62 Case C-133/11 *Folien Fischer AG and Fofitec AG v Ritrama SpA* (25 October 2012) ECLI:EU:C:2012:664, para 44 et seq.

63 Case C-364/93 *Antonio Marinari v Lloyds Bank plc and Zubaidi Trading Company* (19 September1995) ECLI:EU:C:1995:289, para 15.

64 Case C-220/88 *Dumez France SA and Tracoba SARL v Hessische Landesbank and Others* (11 January 1990) ECLI:EU:C:1990:8.

65 Case C-189/08 *Zuid-Chemie BV v Philippo's Mineralenfabriek NV/SA* (16 July 2009) ECLI:EU:C:2009:475.

66 Among various rulings, see Case C-523/10 *Wintersteiger AG v Products 4U Sondermaschinenbau GmbH* (19 April 2012) ECLI:EU:C:2012:220, and Case C-441/13 *Pez Hejduk v EnergieAgentur.NRW GmbH* (22 January 2015) ECLI:EU:C:2015:28.

67 Case C-709/19 *Vereniging van Effectenbezitters v BP plc* (12 May 2021) ECLI:EU:C:2021:377.

68 See, among others, Case C-352/13 *Cartel Damage Claims (CDC) Hydrogen Peroxide SA v Evonik Degussa GmbH and Others* (21 May 2015) ECLI:EU:C:2015:335.

lisher either before the courts of the Member State of the place where the publisher is established, which have jurisdiction to award damages for all the harm caused by the defamation, or before the courts of each Member State in which the publication was distributed and where the victim claims to have suffered injury to his reputation, with the clarification that, in the latter case, the jurisdiction of the court seised is limited to the harm caused in the State of that court.[69] The Court of Justice later acknowledged in *eDate* that the above reading should not extend to the **placing of defamatory content on-line**, as that content may be consulted instantly by an unlimited number of users throughout the world, irrespective of any intention on the part of the person who placed it in regard to its consultation beyond that person's Member State of establishment and outside of that person's control.[70] In these circumstances, reliance on the *Shevill* formula would frustrate proximity and predictability. The Court concluded that the rule now in Article 7, point 2, should be interpreted as meaning that a person who considers that his rights have been infringed has the option of bringing an action for liability, in respect of all the damage caused, either before the courts of the Member State in which the publisher of the content is established or before the courts of the Member State in which the centre of his interests is based, ie where he has fixed his habitual residence.[71]

E Prorogation of Jurisdiction

#60 **'Prorogation'** occurs where jurisdiction is conferred on a court outside the cases where it would exist on objective grounds, eg because the defendant is domiciled in the forum, or because the harmful event occurred there. The Brussels I-bis Regulation contemplates two forms of prorogation: explicit prorogation, or prorogation by agreement, and tacit prorogation.

I Prorogation by Agreement

#61 Pursuant to Article 25, the parties to a dispute may agree that a court or the courts of a Member State are to have jurisdiction to rule on or more of their disputes.[72]

---

69 Case C-68/93 *Fiona Shevill, Ixora Trading Inc., Chequepoint SARL and Chequepoint International Ltd v Presse Alliance SA* (7 March 1995) ECLI:EU:C:1995:61, para 29 et seq.

70 Joined Cases C-509/09 and C-161/10 *eDate Advertising GmbH and Others v X and Société MGN Limited* (25 October 2011) ECLI:EU:C:2011:685, para 45.

71 ibid para 48 et seq.

72 On choice of court agreements see extensively U Magnus, 'Article 25' in U Magnus and P Mankowski (eds), *Brussels Ibis Regulation* (2nd edn, Otto Schmidt 2023) 580.

Subject to the conditions set forth in the Regulation, jurisdiction lies with the chosen court and is exclusive unless the parties agree otherwise. A choice of court agreement may relate to a dispute that has already arisen or to such disputes as may arise in connection with a particular legal relationship. The rule applies irrespective of the domicile of the parties. An agreement whereby the parties to a contract, established in the same Member State, confer jurisdiction on the courts of another Member State also comes with the purview of Article 25.[73]

#62 The parties can choose any court they wish, including a court sitting in a State with which the dispute has neither an objective nor a personal connection. The parties may thus confer jurisdiction on the courts of a given State merely on the ground that they regard that State as a convenient venue for litigation, eg, because of the efficiency of the court system, the peculiar features of the law of procedure in force in that State or the expertise of local magistrates in the area of law concerned.

1 Rationale

#63 **Choice of court agreements** are tools for managing litigation. They avoid the uncertainties surrounding the operation of the objective rules of the Regulation and ensure, in principle, that the issue of jurisdiction is dealt with rapidly and efficient by the seised court. All this increases the efficiency of proceedings featuring a cross-border element.

#64 More generally, choice of court agreements provide the parties with an opportunity to make reliable predictions as to the outcome of such proceedings as may be brought in connection with their activity. When it comes to matters with an international element, the venue of litigation is hardly a neutral factor. The costs and length of litigation can vary greatly from one State to another, and so do the rules that govern that conduct of proceedings. Knowing in advance the State where the dispute is to be tried ultimately contributes to the efficient management of the substantive relationships at issues. The availability of instruments that enable the parties to plan for litigation makes business intercourse more efficient and enhances the functioning of the market.

#65 Few situations exist within the scope of the Brussels I-bis Regulation in which the benefits of party autonomy are outweighed by other considerations. There is notably no room for choice of court agreements in respect of claims for which Article 24 confers **exclusive jurisdiction** on the courts of a Member State. As regards matters within the purview of special protective regimes, agreements conferring jurisdiction are subject to additional conditions set out in the relevant regime.

73 Case C-566/22 *Inkreal v Dúha reality* (8 February 2024) ECLI:EU:C:2024:123.

2 Separability

#66 As observed above, a choice of court agreement may concern disputes that have not yet arisen, provided they relate to 'a particular legal relationship'. In fact, most agreements take the form of a choice court clause included in a contract and cover such disputes as may arise in connection with the contract in question. A clause of this kind, despite forming part of a contract, must be treated as an agreement independent of the other terms of the contract. As specified in Article 25(5), this implies that the validity of the agreement cannot be contested solely on the ground that the contract is not valid. The parties may thus have different views on the validity of the contract, and even disagree on whether a contract was in fact concluded between them, but this does not affect as such the enforceability of the parties' choice of forum. The existence and validity of the latter may only be challenged on grounds that specifically relate to the choice itself, as separate from the contract to which it belongs.

#67 The only purpose of the **principle of separability** is to avoid the risk that the **choice of court** made by the parties might be deprived of its effect for reasons that do not relate to the choice itself but rather refer to the contract where the choice is featured. Nothing prevents a court from relying on the ties between a choice of court clause and the contract in which the clause itself is included for other purposes. This may occur, for example, where the need arises to determine the objective scope of the clause (to see whether it covers a given dispute, or not), insofar as the interpretation of the parties' agreement on jurisdiction requires that reference be made to its context, which would obviously include the contract as a whole.

3 Formal Validity

#68 Agreements conferring jurisdiction are not enforceable under the Regulation unless they meet the requirements set out for this purpose in Article 25(1). The agreement must either be: (a) in writing or evidenced in writing; (b) in a form which accords with practices which the parties have established between themselves, which presupposes the parties have been entertaining mutual relations for some time, and have consistently regarded choices made or evidenced otherwise that in writing as being valid; or (c) in international trade or commerce, in a form which accords with a usage of which the parties are or ought to have been aware and which in such trade or commerce is widely known to, and regularly observed by, parties to contracts of the type involved in the particular trade or commerce concerned. Member States' courts cannot make the enforcement of a choice of court agreement contingent on compliance with the additional formal requirements, if any, prescribed by domestic law.

#69 The purpose of the above formal requirements is to ensure that the consensus between the parties is in fact established.[74] The Court of Justice often stressed that, in view of the effects that arise from a jurisdictional agreement – that is, the exclusion, in principle, of both the general rule in Article 4 and the special rules in Articles 7 and 8 – the said requirements should be strictly construed.

#70 The latter concern has shaped, inter alia, the approach followed by the Court of Justice towards choice of court clauses included in general conditions prepared by one party, where it is unclear whether the other party, which agreed on the contract, also agreed, in fact, on the clause in question. The Court displayed a cautious attitude in most of its early rulings on this subject. It held in *Estasis Salotti* that, where a choice of court clause appears in the general conditions of one party, the requirement that the agreement be in writing cannot be deemed to be fulfilled unless the contract signed by both parties contains an express reference to such conditions.[75] With the advent of electronic communications, the Court reassessed its approach. Crucial to this development was a provision introduced with Regulation (EC) No 44/2001, according to which communication by electronic means must be deemed to be equivalent to in writing, as long as a durable record of the agreement is provided. In *Jaouad El Madjoub* the Court considered a case where the general conditions of the defendant were included in a webpage that did not open automatically when a user registered in the party's website. Rather, a box appeared in the registration page which invited the user to read the general conditions and provided a hypertext link to the page containing such conditions (**'click wrapping'**). The Court held that the above method constitutes a communication by electronic means which provides a durable record of the agreement, and is thereby equivalent to in writing, whenever the user is given the possibility to print and save the text of the conditions prior to concluding the contract.[76] More recently, in *Tilman*, the Court of Justice held that a jurisdiction clause is validly concluded where it is contained in the **general conditions** to which a contract concluded in writing refers to by the inclusion of a link to a website: for this, however, the wbsite must allow the parties to access those conditions prior to that contract being signed, it being immaterial whether the user was formally asked to accept those general conditions by ticking a box on that website.[77]

---

74 Case 25/76 *Galeries Segoura SPRL v Société Rahim Bonakdarian* (14 December 1976) ECLI:EU:C:1976:178, para 6.

75 Case 24/76 *Estasis Salotti di Colzani Aimo e Gianmario Colzani s.n.c. v Rüwa Polstereimaschinen GmbH* (14 December 1976) ECLI:EU:C:1976:177, para 10.

76 Case C-322/14 *Jaouad El Majdoub v CarsOnTheWeb.Deutschland GmbH* (21 May 2015) ECLI:EU:C:2015:334, para 40.

77 Case C-358/21 *Tilman SA v Unilever Supply Chain Company AG* (24 November 2022) ECLI:EU:C:2022:923, para 59.

4 Substantive Validity

#71 Agreements that purport to confer jurisdiction on the courts of a Member State must be denied effect where they are null and void as to their substantive validity under the law of the State of the chosen courts (*lex fori prorogati*). As clarified in Recital 20, the latter law must be understood to include the conflict-of-laws rules in force therein. Suppose a court in Member State A is seised of a matter within the scope of a clause conferring jurisdiction on the courts of Member State B, and the substantive validity of the clause is challenged by one party on the ground that that party was led to agree on the clause by a fraudulent representation by the other party. The substantive standards against which the former court must assess the challenge are those set out in the law specified pursuant to the conflict-of-laws rules of State B, which may be, depending on the circumstances, the law of a State other than B. The goal, here, is to ensure that the issue of the substantive validity of the agreement is decided in accordance with the same standards no matter which court, within the European judicial area, is called upon to rule on that issue. The notion of an agreement being 'null and void as to its substantive validity' must be given an autonomous interpretation. It covers the general causes of nullity of a contract, such as those which vitiate consent, including error, deceit, violence or fraud, and incapacity to contract.[78]

#72 Situations exists where the effectiveness of an agreement may be called into question (for reasons unrelated to its form) without the *lex fori prorogati* playing any role. By stating that the parties must have 'agreed' on the jurisdiction of a court, or the courts, of a Member State, Article 25 includes a requirement of precision in order for the agreement to be valid. The latter requirement must be examined having regard not to the criteria set out in the law of the court chosen, but to autonomous criteria which are derived from Article 25 itself, as interpreted by the Court of Justice.[79] Similar remarks apply to the issue whether the validity of an agreement can be challenged in view of its **asymmetry**, as it occurs where the one of the parties to the agreement may only bring proceedings before the court designated thereunder, whereas the other party is also permitted to bring proceedings before any other competent court. A choice of court agreement, the Court of Justice ruled, cannot be deemed to be invalid merely because of its asymmetry. Agreements conferring jurisdiction on the courts of one or more Member States (or contracting States of the Lugano Convention) should be enforced insofar as they meet the above requirement of precision, are not contrary to the provisions on explicit prorogation in matters relating to consumer contracts, employ-

---

78 Case C-537/23 *Società Italiana Lastre SpA (SIL) v Agora SARL* (27 February 2025) ECLI:EU:C:2025:120, para 36.

79 ibid para 44.

ment contracts or **insurance matters**, and do not derogate from an exclusive jurisdiction pursuant to Article 24.[80]

II Tacit Prorogation

#73 **Tacit prorogation** or **tacit submission** arises, according to Article 26, where the defendant enters an appearance but fails to contest the jurisdiction of the seised court. Subject to certain limitations, the latter court is then entitled, on this ground, to rule on the matter. Article 26 is of no avail if the defendant enters an appearance to contest the jurisdiction of the court, no matter whether he also submits his defences on the merits of the case, as he might have to do to comply with the procedural rules of the forum.

#74 Jurisdiction may not be asserted based on Article 26 to defeat exclusive jurisdiction on the ground of Article 24.

F Protective Regimes on Insurance Matters and Consumer and Employment Contracts

#75 Three special jurisdictional regimes operate in the context of the Brussels I-bis Regulation. They respectively concern insurance matters (Articles 10–16), matters relating to consumer contracts (Articles 17–19) and matters regarding individual employment contracts (Article 20–23).[81]

#76 Each regime reflects a concern for the protection of the **weaker party**, that is, the insured, the policyholder or the beneficiary of the insurance, the consumer, the employee. The three regimes operate independently from the rest of the Regulation.

#77 Various techniques are employed under the three regimes to enhance the protection of the weaker party.

#78 First, a distinction is made based on whether the proceedings are brought by, or against, the weaker party. The options accorded to the weaker party, where he acts as a plaintiff, are broader than those available to insurers, traders and employers, respectively. As regards employment matters, for example, Article 22(1) stipulates that the employer may only bring proceedings in the courts of the

80 ibid para 55 et seq.

81 For an analysis of the three regimes see, among others, T Hartley, *Civil Jurisdiction and Judgments in Europe* (OUP 2017) 171 et seq.

Member State in which the employee is domiciled, whereas, pursuant to Article 21, the employee may choose to sue the employer either before the courts of the Member State of the employer's domicile or before the courts for the place where he habitually carries out his work. If the employee does not carry out his work in any one country, jurisdiction lies instead with the courts of the place where the business which engaged the employee was situated.

#79 Secondly, the admissibility of choice of court agreements that purport to derogate from the above rules is limited. The rules on employment matters, for example, may be departed from by agreement, as stated in Article 23, only in two cases: where the agreement is entered into after the dispute has arisen (it is safe to assume that the employee would then be in a position to make an informed choice on the agreement itself), and where the agreement provides that the employee may bring proceedings in courts other than those having jurisdiction on objective grounds (in other words, where the agreement is meant to extend, not to restrict, the options available to the weaker party).

#80 Finally, tacit prorogation does not work against the weaker party, i.e., in proceedings where he acts as a defendant, unless the court is satisfied that he was informed of his right to contest the jurisdiction of the court and of the consequences of entering or not entering an appearance.

G Exclusive Jurisdiction

#81 It has already been observed that the Regulation includes (special) rules conferring exclusive jurisdiction. These are found in Article 24 and apply regardless of the domicile of the parties. Jurisdiction under Article 24 is exclusive in the sense that disputes within the scope of the rules in that provision may be litigated, in Europe, only in the courts specified in the rules themselves. Article 24, point 1, for instance, provides that proceedings which have as their object rights in rem in, or tenancies of, immovable property are subject to the exclusive jurisdiction of the courts of the Member State where the property is situated. Neither the courts of the Member State where the defendant is domiciled, nor the courts chosen by the parties or any other courts may entertain the case. Similarly, pursuant to Article 24, point 4, proceedings concerned with the registration or validity of **patents** and other **IP rights** required to be deposited or registered, may only be brought in the courts of the Member State in which the deposit or registration has been applied for, has taken place or is deemed to have taken place under the applicable rules.

#82 Generally, the conferral of **exclusive jurisdiction** reflects one or more of the following considerations.

#83 First, exclusive jurisdiction refers to disputes that are so closely connected with one State, factually and legally, that it would not be in the interest of a sound administration of justice to allow the courts of other States to rule on such disputes. The Court of Justice relied on this reasoning to explain the rationale of the rule currently laid down in Article 24, point 1. In *Sanders*, it observed that actions concerning **rights in rem in immovable property** are to be judged according to the rules of the State in which the property is situated, stressing that disputes in this area frequently involve checks, inquiries and expert assessments which must be carried out on the spot, with the result that the assignment of exclusive jurisdiction satisfies the need for a proper administration of justice.[82] Tenancies of immovable property, the Court added, are generally governed by special rules and it is preferable, in the light of their complexity, that they be applied by the courts of the States in which they are in force.[83] Referring to the rule of exclusive jurisdiction of Article 24, point 4, on IP rights, the Court noted that the courts of the State where the registers are kept may rule, applying their own national law, on the validity and effects of the patents which have been issued in that State, adding that this concern for the sound administration of justice becomes all the more important in the field of patents since, given the specialised nature of this area, several States have set up a system of specific judicial protection, to ensure that these types of cases are dealt with by **specialised courts**.[84]

#84 Second, situations exist in the realm of private law which States have a particularly strong interest in regulating, substantively and through their judicial authorities. The State with which a situation of this kind is closely connected should then, in principle, be able to shape it through its rules and the decisions of its courts, without any external interference. The remarks made above concerning Article 24, point 1, are again of interest here, from a slightly different angle: it is commonly accepted that the State where immoveable property is located has a special interest in shaping, both by its rules and by its courts, any **proprietary rights** in such property. The rule in Article 24, point 5, whereby proceedings concerned with the **enforcement of judgments** lie with the exclusive jurisdiction of courts of the Member State in which the judgment has been or is to be enforced, warrants similar considerations. The enforcement of judicial decisions is one of the most typical prerogatives of sovereignty, and a tangible expression of a State authority over its own territory. Jurisdiction over the enforcement of judgments could not be shared between the State of enforcement and one or more other States without resulting in a dilution of the political status of the former.

---

82 Case 73/77 *Theodorus Engelbertus Sanders v Ronald van der Putte* (14 December 1977) ECLI:EU:C:1977:208, para 13.

83 ibid para 14.

84 Case C-4/03 *Gesellschaft für Antriebstechnik mbH & Co. KG v Lamellen und Kupplungsbau Beteiligungs KG* (13 July 2006) ECLI:EU:C:2006:457, para 20 et seq.

#85 Finally, there areas of law in which conflicting decisions would be particularly harmful, as they would defeat the effectiveness of a State's policies. One way to prevent this risk from arising consists in conferring jurisdiction on the courts of one State, at the exclusion of all others. In *Nicole Hassett*, the Court considered that the rule of exclusive jurisdiction in Article 22, point 2, on proceedings which have as their object the validity of the constitution, the nullity or the dissolution of companies or the validity of the decisions of their organs reflects precisely a concern for centralising jurisdiction (with the courts of the Member State in which the company has its seat) in order to avoid conflicting judgments being given in the said matters.[85] Analogous remarks apply to the point 3, according to which proceedings which have as their object the validity of entries in public registers are subject to the exclusive jurisdiction of the courts of the Member State in which the register is kept. Public registers are meant to ensure the highest possible reliability of certain legal information. That goal would be frustrated if the courts of two or more States were permitted to rule on the validity of the register's entries.

#86 A particularly narrow reading is mandated for the rules of exclusive jurisdiction, since they result in depriving the parties of the choice of forum which would otherwise be theirs and may result in their being brought before a court which is not that of the domicile of any of them.[86]

H Jurisdiction to Grant Interim Relief

#87 The Brussels I-bis Regulation is not merely concerned with the adjudication of disputes. It also deals with **provisional measures**, ie measures that are intended to preserve a factual or legal situation to safeguard the rights of the applicant.[87] Jurisdiction to grant provisional, including protective, measures is inherent in a court's power to rule on the substance of the matter. However, as stated in Article 35, application may be made to the courts of a Member State for such provisional measures as may be available under the law of that State even if those courts lack jurisdiction regarding the substance of the case. As the Court of Justice made clear in *Van Uden*, the granting of provisional measures by a court without sub-

85 Case C-372/07 *Nicole Hassett v South Eastern Health Board and Cheryl Doherty v North Western Health Board* (2 October 2008) ECLI:EU:C:2008:534, para 20.

86 For an illustration, see, among other rulings, Case C-518/99 *Richard Gaillard v Alaya Chekili* (5 April 2001) ECLI:EU:C:2001:209, para 14 et seq.

87 Case C-261/90 *Mario Reichert, Hans-Heinz Reichert and Ingeborg Kockler v Dresdner Bank AG* (26 March 1992) ECLI:EU:C:1992:149, para 34. As regards the approach of the Brussels I regime to provisional measures see generally A Nuyts, 'Provisional Measures' in A Dickinson and E Lein (eds), *The Brussels I Regulation Recast* (OUP 2015) 357.

stantive jurisdiction over the case is conditional on the existence of a real connecting link between the subject-matter of the measures sought and the State before which courts those measures are sought.[88] This condition is typically met where provisional measures are sought in the State where the measures themselves are meant to be implemented (eg, if they consist in the seizing of assets, the State where the assets are located).

I Parallel Proceedings

#88 Situations arise where the courts of different States are simultaneously seised of proceedings concerning the same or related claims. **Parallel litigation** entails a risk of conflicting judgments, since the findings of one court may differ from those of the other. This risk is particularly high where the courts of different States are involved, because each court is bound by its own rules of civil procedure and, possibly, its own rules on conflicts of laws, meaning that the case will not necessarily be decided by the various courts in question based on the same evidence or in accordance with the same substantive standards. The Brussels I-bis Regulation deals with parallel proceedings in Articles 29 to 34.[89]

#89 Conflicting judgments challenge the very purpose of judicial integration. Within an integrated judicial area, judgments should move freely across borders, unless strong reasons exist that require otherwise. One such reason arises where the recognition of a judgment would result in **irreconcilable judgments** being in force at once in the legal order of the State addressed. As stated in Article 45(1)(c) and (d) of the Brussels I-bis Regulation, a conflict of this kind is in fact one of the grounds on which a judgment emanating from a Member State may be denied recognition and enforcement in another. The rules on parallel litigation aim to prevent such conflicts from happening. They do so by ensuring that only one set of proceedings, among those simultaneously pending before the courts of different States, will eventually result in a ruling on the merits.

#90 The Regulation distinguishes the case of *lis pendens* from that of related actions. *Lis pendens* occurs where proceedings involving the same cause of action and between the same parties are brought in the courts of different States. The Court of Justice has understood the latter condition rather liberally. In *Gubisch*, it held that if a party applies in one State for a declaration that a contract is inoperative, whilst the other party seeks the enforcement of that contract in a different State, the two proceedings must be deemed to be identical, personally and objectively,

88 Case C-391/95 *Van Uden Maritime BV, trading as Van Uden Africa Line v Kommanditgesellschaft in Firma Deco-Line and Another* (17 November 1998) ECLI:EU:C:1998:543, para 40.

89 See generally on these provisions Van Calster (n 24) 243 et seq.

and the scenario should accordingly be classified as one of *lis pendens*.[90] A case of related actions arises, instead, where the courts of different States are seised of actions that, while not identical as to their respective cause of action and/or the parties involved, are so closely interconnected that it is expedient to hear and determine them together to avoid the risk of irreconcilable judgments resulting from separate proceedings (Article 30(3)).

#91 From a different angle, the Brussels I-bis Regulation treats parallel litigation involving the courts of different Member States in a different way than parallel litigation involving a court sitting in a Member State and a court in a third country. Intra-EU cases may be dealt with under rules that bind both courts. Instead, cases involving a court in a third State are addressed under EU legislation in a unilateral fashion, that is, from the standpoint of the Union alone, and with effects limited to the Member States concerned. In addition, while the management of intra-EU parallel litigation benefits from the mutual trust that exists between the Member States, and can accordingly build on highly effective rules leaving no discretion to the courts concerned, cases involving third countries involve an assessment of the circumstances of the case and require a dose of caution.

#92 Intra-EU ***lis pendens*** cases are dealt with under Article 29. The latter provision requires the court second seised to stay its proceedings, of its own motion, until such time as the jurisdiction of the court first seised is established. If the court first seised determines that it has the power to rule on the case, then the court second seised must decline jurisdiction in favour of that court. The scheme is simple and easy to implement. The courts involved are required to identify the Member State where litigation started first. Uniform rules are provided in the Regulation to determine the moment when a court should be deemed to be seised, and the courts are required to inform each other, upon request, of the date of their seisin (Article 32).

#93 The priority accorded under Article 29 to the court first seised comes with a significant exception. The latter applies where the courts seised of the parallel proceedings include a court on which the parties agreed to confer exclusive jurisdiction in accordance with Article 25. Pursuant to Article 31(2), 'any court of another Member State shall stay the proceedings until such time as the court seised on the basis of the agreement declares that it has no jurisdiction under the agreement'. If the court agreed upon by the parties establishes jurisdiction in accordance with the agreement, then, pursuant to Article 31(3), any other courts must decline jurisdiction. In practice, when it comes to parallel litigation involving a court chosen by the parties, priority is accorded to the latter court, not to the court first seised. The rule, which is meant to reinforce the effectiveness of **party autonomy** and

90 Case 144/86 *Gubisch Maschinenfabrik KG v Giulio Palumbo* (8 December 1987) ECLI:EU:C:1987:528, para 15 et seq.

enhance the operation of Article 25, represent a (partial) response to a delaying tactic known as the Italian Torpedo. This consists, for one party, in bringing proceedings in a Member State where proceedings normally suffer considerable delays, with the aim of preventing the other party, under Article 29, from obtaining a ruling on the substance through a later application in a different Member State. The rule in Article 31(2) makes the tactic useless whenever the parties concluded an exclusive choice of court agreement.

#94 Extra-EU *lis pendens* is governed by Article 33. The court of a Member State, if seised second, may stay its proceedings following a two-fold assessment. To begin with, it must establish whether the judgment that the court of the third State will give would, in due course, be capable of recognition in the forum. If this were not the case, there would be no risk of conflicts, and accordingly no reasons for a stay. In the second place, the court of the Member State must be satisfied that, in the circumstances, a stay would be 'necessary for the proper administration of justice'. The latter condition would hardly be fulfilled, for example, if proceedings in the third State were likely to take significantly longer to complete, compared with those in the Member State, or if most of the evidence were located in the latter State rather than in the third country. In any case, a stay under Article 33 is not permitted, inter alia, where the court of the Member State concerned has exclusive jurisdiction pursuant to Article 24 or is the court (or one of the courts) chosen by the parties in accordance with Article 25.

#95 The rules on extra-EU *lis pendens* depart rather significantly from those regarding intra-EU cases. Unlike Article 29, which goes as far as to require the court second seised to dismiss the case if the jurisdiction of the court first seised is established, Article 33 only makes provision for a stay of proceedings, and clarifies that proceedings in the Member Stay may resume at any time, including as a result of the reassessment of the grounds on which the stay was ordered in the first place. On a different note, Article 33 contemplates an optional stay of proceedings, while Article 29 requires that proceedings be stayed where the relevant conditions are met.

#96 The approach to **related actions**, both in intra-EU and in extra-EU cases, differs from the approach to *lis pendens* in various respects. As to intra-EU cases, the court second seised is permitted (not required), under Article 30, to stay its proceedings. It may also decline its jurisdiction, but subject to conditions that are stricter than those provided for *lis pendens*. In fact, a risk exists that the dismissal of the later proceedings, out of a concern for coordination, may end up in a denial of justice. To avoid this, a dismissal by the court second seised is only permitted, inter alia, if the jurisdiction of the court first seised extends to the various actions that need coordination, provided the consolidation of all actions is possible under the procedural law of that State. An even stricter scrutiny is contemplated for extra-EU cases. In the latter scenario, by the way, coordination may result, at best, in a stay of proceedings, not a dismissal.

J Future Developments

#97 The Brussels I regime is a living body of rules. Although the key principles enshrined in the Brussels Convention have largely remained the same, the operation of the regime's rules has significantly evolved over the decades, not only through formal amendments but also, and sometimes prominently, through the work of the Court of Justice. Since 1976, the latter gave more than 300 rulings that are either chiefly concerned with, or relate to, the successive incarnations of the regime.

#98 The renewal of the Brussels I regime is, of course, an ongoing concern. At the time of writing this chapter, discussions had been launched, essentially in academia, concerning the upcoming review of the Regulation. Several improvements have been suggested, regarding both the rules on jurisdiction and those on the recognition and enforcement of judgments. It would not be appropriate to examine the said suggestions in detail. It is worth mentioning, however, that alongside several relatively small (but often practically important) improvements, the suggested changes include wide-ranging innovations that would modify significantly, if adopted, the general layout of the Brussels I regime.

#99 Specifically, reference is made to the idea of reconsidering, at least in part, if not entirely, the traditional distinction between defendants domiciled inside and outside the EU.[91] The discussion is not new, but the proposal would seem to enjoy, today, a broad consensus among experts and practitioners,[92] and is further justified by the development of EU jurisdictional rules in other areas, most of which fail to distinguish between European and non-European defendants and, more importantly, leave no room for the residual application of domestic rules.[93] A step into that direction would involve more than suppressing the rule currently laid down in Article 6 of the Brussels I-bis Regulation. The current scheme of the rules on jurisdiction would need to be complemented by new rules (including, most likely, a provision on *forum necessitatis*), and probably be reviewed in various respects in light of this significant innovation.

---

91 See extensively on this topic the contributions in T Lutzi, E Piovesani and D Zgrabljic Rotar (eds), *Jurisdiction Over Non-EU Defendants* (Hart 2023).

92 B Hess and others, 'The Reform of the Brussels Ibis Regulation – Academic Position Paper' (2024) Vienna Research Paper, 16 *et seq* <https://ssrn.com/abstract=4853421> accessed 7 April 2025.

93 See, inter alia, Regulation (EU) No 650/2012 of 4 July 2012 on jurisdiction, applicable law, recognition and enforcement of decisions and acceptance and enforcement of authentic instruments in matters of succession and on the creation of a European Certificate of Succession [2012] OJ L201/107, and Regulation (EU) 2016/1103 of 24 June 2016 implementing enhanced cooperation in the area of jurisdiction, applicable law and the recognition and enforcement of decisions in matters of matrimonial property regimes [2016] OJ L183/1.

#100 It remains to be seen whether the political institutions of the Union will be available to engage in a challenging reassessment of the *status quo*, or will rather content themselves with refining the operation of the existing rules.

References

Briggs A, *Civil Jurisdiction and Judgments* (6th edn, Informa Law 2015).

Franzina P, 'L'universalisation partielle du régime européen de la compétence en matière civile et commerciale dans le règlement Bruxelles I bis: une mise en perspective' in E Guinchard (ed), *Le nouveau règlement Bruxelles I bis* (Bruylant 2014) 39.

—— 'Place of Performance' in J Basedow and others (eds), *Encyclopedia of Private International Law* (Edward Elgar 2017) 1360.

Hartley T, *Civil Jurisdiction and Judgments in Europe* (OUP 2017).

Hess B and others, 'The Reform of the Brussels Ibis Regulation – Academic Position Paper' (2024) Vienna Research Paper <https://ssrn.com/abstract=4853421> accessed 7 April 2025.

Lein E, 'Jurisdiction in Matters Relating to Tort, Delict or Quasi-Delict' in A Dickinson and E Lein (eds), *The Brussels I Regulation Recast* (OUP 2015) 155.

Lutzi T, Piovesani E and Zgrabljic Rotar D (eds), *Jurisdiction Over Non-EU Defendants* (Hart 2023).

Magnus U, 'Article 25', in U Magnus and P Mankowski (eds), *Brussels Ibis Regulation* (2nd edn, Otto Schmidt 2023) 580.

—— 'Introduction' in U Magnus and P Mankowski (eds), *Brussels Ibis Regulation* (2nd edn, Otto Schmidt 2023) 6.

Mankowski P, 'Article 7' in U Magnus and P Mankowski (eds), *Brussels Ibis Regulation* (2nd edn, Otto Schmidt 2023) 108.

Mills A, 'La Convention de Bruxelles de 1968: un code et un concept' [2018] Revue critique de droit international privé 503.

Nuyts A, 'Provisional Measures' in A Dickinson and E Lein (eds), *The Brussels I Regulation Recast* (OUP 2015) 357.

Van Calster G, *European Private International Law* (4th edn, Hart 2024).

Jachin Van Doninck and Wannes Vandenbussche

Chapter 11
Taking of Evidence

A Introduction

#1 *Idem est non esse aut non probari.*[1] International litigation is also familiar with the adage. Since the effective access to evidence is generally outcome determinative, quick and efficient procedures to obtain evidence abroad are indispensable. At the same time, States are wary to renege on the sovereignty involved in the acts of evidence gathering performed on their territory. Evidence gathering abroad needs to strike a balance between those competing interests.[2] The question then arises how the cross-border taking of evidence can be organised. The Hague Convention of 1 March 1954 on Civil Procedure[3] used the system of letters of request for that purpose, whereby foreign judicial authorities were requested through diplomatic channels to carry out acts of investigation. That regime was relaxed by the Hague Convention of 18 March 1970 on the Taking of Evidence Abroad in Civil or Commercial Matters.[4] The latter convention replaced the diplomatic channel with the use of national Central Authorities.[5] A EU-wide relaxation came about through Council Regulation (EC) No 1206/2001 of 28 May 2001 on cooperation between the courts of the Member States in the taking of evidence in civil or commercial matters, in short the **Evidence Regulation**, which was revised in 2020.[6] The Evidence Regulation

1 What is not proven does not exist (J Carbonnier, *Droit civil* (Presses Universitaires de France, first published 1955, 2017) 334, n° 174).

2 A Nuyts and J Sepulchre, 'Cross-Border Taking of Evidence in the European Judicial Area' (2005) 4(2) Tijdschrift voor Internationaal Privaatrecht 79, 81.

3 <https://www.hcch.net/en/instruments/conventions/full-text/?cid=33> accessed 31 March 2025.

4 <https://www.hcch.net/en/instruments/conventions/full-text/?cid=82> accessed 31 March 2025.

5 For a recent overview of both instruments with reference to case law, see G Payan, *Conventions et protocoles de La Haye annotés* (Bruylant 2020) 29ff and 133ff respectively.

6 [2001] OJ L174/1. Entered into force on 1 July 2001 and applicable since 1 January 2004 in all EU Member States except Denmark. As revised by Regulation (EU) 2020/1783 of the European Parliament and of the Council of 25 November 2020 on cooperation between the courts of the Member States in the taking of evidence in civil or commercial matters (taking of evidence) (recast) [2020] OJ L405/1.

Note: The first author would like to acknowledge the co-authorship of Karolien Emmerechts in Jachin Van Doninck and Karolien Emmerechts, "Internationale bewijsverkrijging na de herziene Bewijsverordening" in Jachin Van Doninck, Wannes Vandenbussche, Max De Schryver and Karolien Emmerechts, *Grensoverschrijdende betekening en bewijsvoering* (Larcier-Intersentia 2024) 1ff, on which part B. of this chapter draws.

Jachin Van Doninck, Vrije Universiteit Brussel, e-mail: jachin.van.doninck@vub.be
Wannes Vandenbussche, Ghent University, e-mail: wannes.vandenbussche@ugent.be

https://doi.org/10.1515/9783110781632-011

seeks to improve the effectiveness and speed of judicial proceedings by simplifying and streamlining the mechanisms for cooperation in the taking of evidence in cross-border proceedings, while at the same time helping to reduce delays and costs for individuals and businesses.[7] The use of modern communications technology is one of the means of attaining that goal (see #3 and #11).[8]

#2 The chapter will begin by briefly explaining the operation of the Evidence Regulation, before shedding light on the Evidence Regulation's interaction with possible *fora* for evidence taking, and ending with the growing impact of EU law on the national rules of evidence.

B Cross-border Taking of Evidence

I The Evidence Regulation

1 Scope of Application

#3 On 1 July 2022, the revised Evidence Regulation[9] **entered into force**, with the exception of Article 7 which shall only apply from the first day of the month following the period of 3 years after the date of entry into force of the implementing acts referred to in Article 25, ie 1 May 2025.[10] Article 7 provides for the transmission of requests and other communications through a secure and reliable decentralised IT system. In this context, the European Commission first needed to adopt certain implementing acts establishing such a decentralised IT system. The use of this decentralised IT system in the context of the Evidence Regulation is in line with the stated ambition to ensure the speedy transmission of requests and com-

7 Recital 3 of the revised Evidence Regulation, earlier in the same sense Recitals 7 and 8 of the original Evidence Regulation. On that *ratio legis* also Case C-283/09 *Artur Weryński v Mediatel 4B spółka z o.o* (17 February 2011) ECLI:EU:C:2011:85, paras 58 and 62 ('*Weryński*').

8 Recital 7 Evidence Regulation.

9 Unless mentioned otherwise, all references hereafter are to the revised edition of the Evidence Regulation.

10 Article 35(1) in conjunction with 35(3) Evidence Regulation. The Commission Implementing Regulation (EU) 2022/422 of 14 March 2022 laying down the technical specifications, measures and other requirements for the implementation of the decentralised it system referred to in Regulation (EU) 2020/1783 of the European Parliament and of the Council ([2022] OJ L87/1), referred to in the Evidence Regulation, entered into force on the 20th day following its publication in the Official Journal of 15 March 2022, making Article 7 applicable from 1 May 2025 (<https://online-forms.e-justice.europa.eu/online-forms/taking-of-evidence-forms_en> accessed 31 March 2025).

munications between Member States for the purposes of taking of evidence by using any appropriate modern communications technology.[11]

#4 The Evidence Regulation applies **geographically** in all European Union member states except Denmark.[12] In the relationship between EU Member States other than Denmark,[13] the Evidence Regulation replaces the Hague Convention of 1 March 1954 on Civil Procedure as well as the Hague Convention of 18 March 1970 on the Taking of Evidence Abroad in Civil and Commercial Matters. In principle, relations with third countries are not governed by the Evidence Regulation.[14]

#5 The Evidence Regulation applies in **civil and commercial matters**, a concept to be interpreted autonomously in the light of the objectives of the Evidence Regulation.[15] Alignment can be sought with the interpretation of that concept in the Brussels Ibis Regulation.[16]

#6 The notion of **the taking of evidence** in the Evidence Regulation should be given an autonomous and broad interpretation, precisely because the purpose of the simplified mutual assistance mechanism of the Evidence Regulation is only served by being applicable to as many evidentiary measures as possible.[17] Article 1(2) of the Evidence Regulation ('A request shall not be made to obtain evidence which is not intended for use in judicial proceedings that have already commenced or are being contemplated') clarifies that the Evidence Regulation can also be given effect with a view to a contemplated proceeding. Measures to protect and obtain evidence such as a descriptive seizure thus fall within the scope of the Evidence Regulation.[18]

---

11 Recital 7 Evidence Regulation; J von Hein, 'Digitalisierungsaspekte der neuen Europäischen Beweisaufnahmeverordnung' in P Reuß and J Laß (eds), *Göttinger Kolloquien zur Digitalisierung des Zivilverfahrensrechts* (Universitätsverlag Göttingen 2024) 25ff.

12 Recital 38 Evidence Regulation.

13 Between Denmark and the other Member States the Convention of 1970 applies, see <https://online-forms.e-justice.europa.eu/online-forms/taking-of-evidence-forms_en> accessed 31 March 2025. Between Belgium and Denmark, the The Hague Convention of 1 March 1954 on Civil Procedure still applies though.

14 V Nekrošius, 'The Taking of Evidence in Civil Proceedings of the European Union' (2020) *Teka Komisji Prawniczej PAN Oddział W Lublinie* 299, 302; P de Vareilles-Sommières, 'Le règlement communautaire sur l'obtention de preuves à l'étranger et les rapports avec les Etats tiers' in A Nuyts and N Watté (eds), *International Civil Litigation in Europe and Relations with Third States* (Bruylant 2010) 281, 286.

15 European Commission, *Practice Guide for the Application of the Regulation on the Taking of Evidence* (Commission Services 2011), para 7 <https://e-justice.europa.eu/fileDownload.do?id=dec18da1-6842-47b3-a142-d0e0c236fcbc> accessed 27 May 2024 ('*Practice Guide*').

16 M Lebois, 'Le Règlement (CE) n°1206/2001 du Conseil du 28 mai 2001 relatif à la coopération entre les juridictions des Etats membres dans le domaine de l'obtention des preuves en matière civile ou commerciale' in M Storme and G de Leval (eds), *Le Droit Processuel & Judiciaire Européen / The European Judicial & Procedural Law* (die Keure 2003) 271, 280, para 14; Nekrošius (n 14) 301; See also G Van Calster, Chapter 9.

17 For this overarching rationale see Case C-175/06 *Alessandro Tedesco v Tomasoni Fittings Srl and RWO Marine Equipment Ltd.*, Opinion of AG Kokott (18 July 2007) ECLI:EU:C:2007:451, para 43 ('*Tedesco*').

18 *Tedesco*, Opinion of AG Kokott (n 17) paras 94 and 113.

#7 The request for the taking of evidence must emanate from **a court**. This term is defined for the first time in the revised Evidence Regulation as:

> Courts and other authorities in Member States as communicated to the Commission under Article 31(3), that exercise judicial functions, that act pursuant to a delegation of power by a judicial authority or that act under the control of a judicial authority, and which are competent under national law to take evidence for the purposes of judicial proceedings in civil or commercial matters.[19]

Member States must notify the European Commission of which 'courts' fall within the scope. The list of these can be consulted via the European e-Justice Portal.[20]

2 Methods of Evidence Taking

a) General

#8 The Evidence Regulation provides **two main**[21] **methods** of evidence taking:

- the taking of evidence by the requested court, following a request transmitted directly from the requesting court to the requested court, also known as the indirect method (Section 3 of the Evidence Regulation)
- the direct taking of evidence by the requesting court (Section 4 of the Evidence Regulation)

In the first case, the requested court has the responsibility over the taking of the evidence procedure, in the second case, the requesting court.[22] The direct taking of evidence by the requesting court requires the authorisation of the Member State in which the evidence is to be taken and can only be carried out on a voluntary basis without the use of coercive measures.[23] In both cases, evidence can be taken through local and distant means (such as through a videoconference).[24] Before elaborating on both methods, some general issues on the transmission and receipt of requests will be addressed.

---

19 Article 2(1) Evidence Regulation.

20 See more specifically <https://e-justice.europa.eu/38581/NL/taking_evidence_recast?init=true> accessed 27 May 2024.

21 We do not elaborate on the taking of evidence by diplomatic or consular officials (see Article 21 Evidence Regulation).

22 Practice Guide (n 15) 8, para 14.

23 Article 19(1) and 19(2) Evidence Regulation.

24 Article 12(4) and Article 20 Evidence Regulation.

b) Transmission and execution of requests

#9 A request for the taking of evidence must be submitted using a **standard form**: either Form A in the case of a request from the requesting court to the requested court or Form L in the case of a request for direct taking of evidence.[25] The Evidence Regulation excludes the need for authentication or any equivalent formality.[26]

#10 The **language** of the request shall be the official language of the requested Member State. The request may also be made in another language which the Member State has declared that it will accept. To this end, Member States have had to communicate to the Commission which official language(s) other than their own they accept.[27] In view of the difficulties that the language barrier may entail for judges, it is up to the interested party to arrange for a translation by an external translator, if necessary, after which the costs may ultimately qualify as court costs and thus be borne by the losing party.[28] The Evidence Regulation does not clarify in which language the documents resulting from the execution of the request for the taking of evidence must be drawn up. Here, the requested court evidently has a choice between the official language of the requesting or the requested court.[29] These documents may, where appropriate, be translated after transmission to the requesting court.[30]

#11 The biggest innovation in the revised Evidence Regulation concerns the transmission of requests and communications between Member States **via a secure and reliable decentralised IT system**.[31] Although the Evidence Regulation refers to e-CODEX ('e-Justice Communication via Online Data Exchange'),[32] it is mindful of possible technological advances and leaves the option of using another system.[33] The e-CODEX system facilitates secure electronic communication in civil and criminal proceedings.[34] The system does not aim to unify the IT infrastructure of

25 These are attached under Annex I to the Evidence Regulation. The online forms are available on <https://online-forms.e-justice.europa.eu/online-forms/taking-of-evidence-forms_en> accessed 24 May 2024.

26 Article 5(2) Evidence Regulation.

27 Article 6 Evidence Regulation <https://e-justice.europa.eu/38581/NL/taking_evidence_recast?init=true> accessed 31 March 2025, allows for consultation on a country-by-country basis.

28 I Couwenberg, 'Bewijsvergaring in de Europese Unie' in S Rutten and B Vanlerberghe (eds), *Het bewijs in het burgerlijke proces / La preuve dans le procès civil* (die Keure 2015) 71, 89, n° 39.

29 Nuyts and Sepulchre (n 2) 92.

30 ibid.

31 Article 7(1) Evidence Regulation.

32 Article 7(1) Evidence Regulation.

33 Recital 7 Evidence Regulation.

34 Recital 7 Evidence Regulation; Regulation (EU) 2022/850 of the European Parliament and of the Council of 30 May 2022 on a computerised system for cross-border electronic data exchange in the field of judicial cooperation in civil and criminal matters (e-Codex), and amending Regulation (EU) 2018/1726 (e-Codex Regulation) [2022] OJ L150/1; see also A Nylund, Chapter 7.

the courts of different Member States, but rather to ensure secure communication and interaction between those national systems. The Evidence Regulation does, however, leave room for situations where the decentralised IT system is or cannot be used for transmission.[35] More specifically, such transmission may not be possible due to (1) the disruption of the decentralised IT system, (2) the nature of the evidence in question (such as DNA or blood samples) or (3) exceptional circumstances. Exceptional circumstances include the situation where converting voluminous documentation into electronic form would impose a disproportionate administrative burden on the competent authorities or where the original document in paper form is needed to assess its authenticity.[36] In these three cases, transmission will have to use the fastest, most convenient alternative means that also ensure reliability and security.[37] Documents that are transmitted through the decentralised IT system shall not be denied legal effect or considered inadmissible as evidence in the proceedings solely on the grounds that they are in electronic form.[38] This leaves some discretion to Member States.[39]

#12 Within seven days of **receiving a request**, the requested competent court should send an acknowledgement of receipt to the requesting court using standard Form B.[40] If the requested court does not have jurisdiction to execute the request, it must forward the request to the court in the same Member State that does have jurisdiction.[41] If the request is incomplete, the requested court shall be notified without delay and at the latest within 30 days of receipt of the request.[42] Where the taking of evidence requires an expert opinion, the requested court may ask the requesting court for an adequate deposit or advance towards the anticipated costs. In that case, the requested court may await the deposit or advance before executing the request for the taking of evidence.[43]

---

35 Article 7(4) Evidence Regulation.

36 Recital 12 Evidence Regulation.

37 Article 7(4) Evidence Regulation and Recital 12 Evidence Regulation.

38 Article 8 Evidence Regulation.

39 V Richard, 'La refonte du règlement sur l'obtention des preuves en matière civile' (2021-1) Revue critique de droit international privé 67, 70.

40 Article 9(1) Evidence Regulation. The online forms are available on <https://online-forms.e-justice.europa.eu/online-forms/taking-of-evidence-forms_en> accessed 31 March 2025.

41 Article 9(2) Evidence Regulation.

42 Article 10(1) Evidence Regulation.

43 Article 21(3) Evidence Regulation.

3 Taking of evidence by the requested court

a) General

#13 The basic principle for the taking of evidence by the requested court is that the **requested court** shall execute the request for the taking of evidence in accordance with its national law.[44] The requesting court may, however, ask that the taking of evidence be performed in accordance with a special procedure provided for by the law of the Member State of the requesting court.[45] That confrontation with foreign procedural law[46] may be avoided only if such a form of the taking of evidence is not compatible with national law or is not possible due to major practical difficulties.[47] The observation that public policy is missing as a ground for refusal here,[48] does not take away from the fact that the public policy exception provides a good yardstick for interpreting that incompatibility test.[49] In any event, as a less far-reaching remedy than the bare refusal to do so, the requested court should seek to implement the requested measure in such a modified form that national concerns are met, in accordance with the mutual assistance-friendly philosophy of the Evidence Regulation.

b) Grounds for refusal

#14 Refusal to execute a request should be the exception.[50] The Evidence Regulation provides four **general grounds for refusal**. First, the request may be refused if it does not fall within the scope of the regulation. This is also the case if the execution of the request is not within the jurisdiction of the judiciary under the law of the Member State of the requested court. Furthermore, a refusal is possible if the requesting court does not comply with the requested court's request to complete the request for the taking of evidence within 30 days.[51] Should the court deliver a supplemented request to the requested court after 30 days, this may be considered a new request. The requested court may therefore immediately proceed with the execution of this new request.[52] Finally, if necessary, the requested court

---

44 Article 12(2) Evidence Regulation.
45 Article 12(3) Evidence Regulation.
46 *Dixit Tedesco*, Opinion of AG Kokott (n 17) para 58.
47 Article 12(3) Evidence Regulation.
48 B-J van het Kaar, *IPR-bewijsrecht en bewijsverkrijging* (Wolters Kluwer 2008) 182f.
49 *Tedesco*, Opinion of AG Kokott (n 17) para 96.
50 Recital 16 Evidence Regulation; *Weryński* (n 7) para 53; Practice Guide (n 15) para 43.
51 Although it is not specified, this time limit reasonably begins to run from the receipt of the notification following an incomplete request in accordance with Article 10(1) Evidence Regulation, see van het Kaar (n 48) 181).
52 Couwenberg (n 28) 90 and there n 94; van het Kaar (n 48) 182.

may refuse the request if the requested deposit or advance has not been made within 60 days of the requested court's request.[53] Although the Evidence Regulation sets several deadlines, only non-compliance with the two deadlines mentioned is sanctioned through the grounds for refusal. The refusal does not prevent the requesting court from making a **new evidence request**.[54]

#15 The Evidence Regulation also provides for a **specific ground for refusal** that can be invoked **in the event of a request to hear a person**. Such a request will not be executed if the person concerned invokes the right not to testify or is prohibited from giving evidence under the law of the Member State of the requested court or the law of the Member State of the requesting court. In the latter case, that right not to testify or the prohibition on giving evidence must be indicated in the request or, failing that, confirmed by the requesting court after questioning by the requested court.[55] The requested court does not have to check whether such a right actually exists under the law of the Member State of the requesting court.[56] Despite the wording used (*"a request for the examination of a person"*), the ground for refusal also applies where the requested court does not proceed to question the person but seeks to obtain documentary evidence from him.[57] Unlike under the 1970 Hague Convention on Evidence, reliance on a right to privilege or prohibition to testify based on the law of a third state appears to be excluded. Nevertheless, it has been said that the person may also invoke a right to privilege or a prohibition to testify based on the law of a third state if the law of the Member State of the requested court or of the Member State of the requesting court allows the person to invoke such a right or prohibition.[58]

#16 The requested court may not refuse the request solely because under its national law another court of its country has **exclusive jurisdiction** over the matter at issue in that case. Nor may the requested court refuse the request solely because the law of the requested court does not allow a **right of action** on that matter.[59] Whether the refusal is amenable to any remedy is for the Member States to determine in accordance with their national law.[60]

53 Article 16(2) Evidence Regulation.

54 On the refusal in case of non-payment of the deposit or advance within 60 days: R Jansen, *Legal Privilege and Transnational Evidence-Taking. A Comparative Study on Cross-Border Disclosure, Evidence-Shopping and Legal Privilege* (Intersentia 2022) 63 and there n 308. On refusal in the absence of supplementary application: van het Kaar (n 48) 176.

55 Article 16(1) Evidence Regulation; Nuyts and Sepulchre (n 2) 98.

56 Nekrošius (n 14) 304.

57 Jansen (n 54) 63 (and there n 309); Nekrošius (n 14) 310.

58 Jansen (n 54) 63.

59 Article 16(3) Evidence Regulation.

60 Practice Guide (n 15) 15f, para 43; Nekrošius (n 14) 311.

c) Presence and participation of the parties and/or representatives of the requesting court in the taking of evidence

#17 The parties, and possibly their representatives, have the **right to be present** at the taking of evidence by the requested court to the extent that they have this right under their own national law. In this way, it is as if the evidence is taken in the Member State of the requesting court.[61]

#18 To the extent compatible with the law of the Member State of the requesting court, the **representatives of the requesting court** have the right to be present during the taking of evidence by the requested court. Indeed, this should enable them to better assess the evidence.[62] These so-called 'representatives' are the judicial personnel or other persons (such as experts) appointed by the requesting court in accordance with its national law.[63]

d) Costs

#19 Legal assistance under the Evidence Regulation is, in principle, **free of charge.**[64] **Only in three cases** will the requested court nevertheless be able to seek **reimbursement of taxes or costs** following the execution of a request for the taking of evidence, in particular for (1) fees paid to experts and interpreters, (2) costs pursuant to the use of a special procedure and (3) costs caused by the use of specified communications technology. Following a request for reimbursement, the requesting court shall ensure reimbursement without delay. The national law of the requesting court shall then govern the obligation of the parties to bear the fees or costs.[65]

#20 As mentioned above, the requested court may ask the requesting court for an **adequate deposit or advance** for the expected costs of the **expert opinion** when the opinion of an expert is required for the execution of the request for the taking of evidence. If the law of the Member State of the requesting court so provides, the parties will make a deposit or advance payment.[66] Only when an expert opinion is required may a deposit or advance be a condition for the execution of a request.[67] Accordingly, a court may not postpone the execution of a request until the costs due to the use of a special procedure or for using specified communication technology are reimbursed.

---

61 Article 13(1) and Recital 18 Evidence Regulation; Nekrošius (n 14) 309.

62 Article 14(1) and Recital 19 Evidence Regulation.

63 Article 14(2) Evidence Regulation.

64 Article 22(1) Evidence Regulation.

65 Articles 22(1) and 22(2) Evidence Regulation.

66 Article 22(3)(2) Evidence Regulation.

67 Article 22(3)(1) Evidence Regulation. See also *Weryński* (n 7), in which the Court ruled that a requesting court cannot be required to make an advance payment of witness fees to the requested court or to refund fees paid to a witness heard.

4 Direct taking of evidence by the requesting court

a) General

#21 In the case of the direct taking of evidence, as said on a **voluntary** basis **without** the use of **coercive measures**,[68] the taking of evidence will be carried out by a member of the judicial staff or other person, such as an expert, designated for this purpose in accordance with the **national law of the requesting court**.[69] If the request has been accepted by the central body or competent authority of the requested Member State, the conditions for doing so in accordance with the law of the requested Member State will be communicated.[70] In all other regards, the requesting court will carry out the direct taking of evidence in accordance with its national law.[71] The latter should improve the efficiency of the execution of the request.[72]

b) Grounds for refusal

#22 The central body or the competent authority of the requested Member State may refuse a request only if (1) the request does not fall within the **scope** of the Evidence Regulation, (2) the request does not contain all of the necessary **information** referred to in Article 5 or (3) the requested taking of evidence is contrary to fundamental principles of law (amounting to a conflict with **public policy**)[73] of the requested Member State.[74] However, the added value of the latter ground for refusal is questioned, since the central body will be able to attach conditions to the acceptance of the request to avoid such a conflict with public policy.[75]

c) Participation and practical assistance in the taking of evidence by a court of the requested Member State

#23 The central body or the competent authority may decide that a court of its Member State should participate in the direct taking of evidence to ensure the proper application of the rules on the direct taking of evidence and compliance with the

---

68 Article 19(2) Evidence Regulation.
69 Article 19(3) Evidence Regulation.
70 Article 19(4) Evidence Regulation.
71 Article 19(8) Evidence Regulation.
72 B Allemeersch and A-S Houtmeyers, 'De Bewijsverordening' in B Allemeersch and T Kruger (eds), *Handboek Europees Burgerlijk Procesrecht* (Intersentia 2015) 253, 272f (para 36); Jansen (n 54) 64; van het Kaar (n 48) 184.
73 J Valdhans and D Sehnálek, 'The 1970 Hague Evidence Convention, the European Union and the 2001 EU Evidence Regulation – Interfaces' in CH van Rhee and A Uzelac (eds), *Evidence in Contemporary Civil Procedure. Fundamental Issues in a Comparative Perspective* (Intersentia 2015) 337, 358.
74 Article 19(7) Evidence Regulation.
75 Jansen (n 54) 65; van het Kaar (n 48) 185.

conditions imposed by the requested Member State.[76] It may, for instance, require that a judicial officer of its court is present while the evidence is taken.[77]

II The Most Performant Route of Taking Evidence

#24 A principle that should contribute to the proper functioning of the Evidence Regulation is the freedom to choose the most performant route of taking evidence.

1 At the Forum of the Merits

#25 The court with international jurisdiction to hear the case on the merits also has **jurisdiction to order the taking of evidence**. The CJEU was clear on this when interpreting[78] what is now the Brussels I*bis* Regulation.[79] How does this international jurisdiction on the merits – which for the sake of clarity may also have a different basis – interact with the Evidence Regulation?

#26 In the Netherlands, aggrieved *Fortisbank* investors requested that its former directors provide clarification through a preliminary witness examination. Some directors requested that this examination take place in Belgium, country of their residence, by letter of request. Their demand was rejected by the Dutch court, eventually resulting in a preliminary reference to the CJEU: should the Evidence Regulation be interpreted as meaning that a court wishing to hear a witness who resides in another Member State must always use the methods provided for in that Regulation in order to obtain that form of evidence, or is it entitled to use the methods provided for in its own national procedural law, such as summoning the witness to appear before it? In *Lippens*, the CJEU ruled that **the Evidence Regulation does not have any exclusive effect**, holding that it does not contain any provision governing or excluding the possibility for the court in one Member State of summoning a party residing in another Member State to appear and

76 Article 19(4)(2) Evidence Regulation.

77 Jansen (n 54) 65.

78 Case C-391/95 *Van Uden Maritime BV, trading as Van Uden Africa Line v Kommanditgesellschaft in Firma Deco-Line and Another* (17 November 1998) ECLI:EU:C:1998:543, paras 19 and 22 ('*Van Uden*').

79 Regulation (EU) No 1215/2012 of the European Parliament and of the Council of 12 December 2012 on jurisdiction and the recognition and enforcement of judgments in civil and commercial matters (recast, here abbreviated as the Brussels I*bis* Regulation) [2012] OJ L351/1. Geographically, the Brussels I*bis* Regulation applies in all EU Member States, substantively, the autonomous interpretation of the concept of civil and commercial matters is the starting point, and formally the Brussels I*bis* Regulation applies if the defendant is domiciled in an EU Member State, unless the domicile-independent criteria apply (the exclusive jurisdiction rules of Article 24; the forum clause of Article 25 and the case of plaintiff-consumer or plaintiff-employee; see Articles 5 and 6 of the Brussels I*bis* Regulation).

make a witness statement directly before it.[80] Thus, if that **national route** to bring the evidence before it[81] proves simpler, more efficient and quicker, it may be used: 'The competent court of a Member State has the power to summon as a witness a party residing in another Member State and to hear him in accordance with the law of the Member State in which that court is situated.'[82]

#27 What if that **party refuses to give evidence**? The court may then attach to a party's failure to appear as a witness any consequences provided for by the law of the Member State of that court, provided that they are applied in compliance with EU law.[83] It is important to recognise that this is the situation of a court having international jurisdiction on the substance in which an investigative measure was sought against a party.[84] Application of national law is thereby the starting point when coercive measures are issued, general principles of Union law – such as the principle of proportionality – can at most play a corrective role here.[85]

#28 What if the taking of evidence is required from **a third party**? Precisely because the court does not assume international jurisdiction over that third party – after all, it is not a party: to the proceedings – the power to issue coercive measures does not extend to that third party.[86] If the aim is to be able to enforce the measure of taking evidence, recourse to the Evidence Regulation will still be necessary for that reason.[87]

#29 Not much later, the CJEU had another opportunity to delineate the scope of the Evidence Regulation.[88] The case involved a goods train accident in Amsterdam on

---

80 Case C-170/11 *Maurice Robert Josse Marie Ghislain Lippens and Others v Hendrikus Cornelis Kortekaas and Others* (6 September 2012) ECLI:EU:C:2012:540, para 27 ('*Lippens*').

81 One author aptly speaks in this context of '*faire venir à lui*' (C Besso, 'Cooperation in the Taking of Evidence: The European Attitude' (2012) 2 International Journal of Procedural Law 68, 75).

82 *Lippens* (n 80) para 37.

83 ibid para 38.

84 ibid emphasis at para 36; Case C-170/11 *Maurice Robert Josse Marie Ghislain Lippens and Others v Hendrikus Cornelis Kortekaas and Others*, Opinion AG Jääskinen (24 May 2012) ECLI:EU:C:2012:311, para 65.

85 *Lippens*, Opinion AG Jääskinen (n 84) para 55. The AG did not elaborate on the idea. It draws us into the field of the constitutionalisation of national civil procedure, eg through the lens of the ECHR or the Charter of Fundamental Rights of the European Union (on the latter most recently J Gerards, 'Het EU-Grondrechtenhandvest: een crashcourse' in *Waarde, werking en potentie van het EU-Grondrechtenhandvest in de Nederlandse rechtsorde* (Wolters Kluwer 2024) 5ff). On this paragraph of the opinion of the AG also A Galic, 'Open Issues Concerning the Non-Mandatory character of the Cross-Border Taking of Evidence Regulation' (2017) 18 ERA Forum 213, 219.

86 *Lippens*, Opinion AG Jääskinen (n 80) para 65.

87 A Nuyts, 'Les arrêts Lippens et ProRail: retour sur l'exclusivité de la réglementation européenne de collecte des preuves' [2014] Journal des Tribunaux 557, 559f, para 11.

88 Case C-332/11 *ProRail BV v Xpedys NV and Others* (21 February 2013) ECLI:EU:C:2013:87 ('*ProRail*').

which an expert opinion was ordered by the judge in summary proceedings in Belgium. In *ProRail*, the CJEU confirmed the insights of the LIPPENS judgment,[89] but also ruled that the court expert who travels abroad to carry out the expertise there must satisfy himself that:

> the investigation which has been entrusted to him, (. . . .) might, in certain circumstances, affect the powers of the Member State in which it takes place, in particular where it is an investigation carried out in places connected to the exercise of such powers or in places to which access or other action is, under the law of the Member State in which the investigation is carried out, prohibited or restricted to certain persons.[90]

If **public authority** is at stake when the expertise is carried out abroad, the court expert will have to have the Evidence Regulation applied.[91]

2 At the Forum of Provisional or Protective Measures

#30 The Evidence Regulation only regulates the modalities (the 'how') of the taking of evidence abroad if the court requests it,[92] it does not have any fundamental blocking effect on extraterritorial evidence orders (#26 above) nor does it prevent a party from obtaining the evidence where it lies.[93] If the courts of another Member State have international jurisdiction to hear the case on the substance,[94] then **Article 35 of the Brussels *Ibis* Regulation** offers the court an alternative. According to that provision, provisional or protective measures provided for by the law of a Member State may be applied for in the courts of that State even if a court of another Member State has jurisdiction to hear the substance of the case. As such, Article 35 does not yet provide a basis for international jurisdiction, the law of the forum State will have to determine whether the court has jurisdiction.[95] Thus, if the national law of the forum State is the starting point for the

89 ibid para 49.
90 ibid paras 47f.
91 ibid para 48.
92 Article 1 Evidence Regulation; cf von Hein (n 11) 29.
93 Jansen (n 54) 12 and 143ff.
94 Irrespective of whether that jurisdiction on the merits is founded on the Brussels *Ibis* Regulation (see H Gaudemet-Tallon and C Kessedjian, 'La refonte du règlement Bruxelles I' (2013) 3 Revue trimestrielle de droit européen 435, 447, para 39; A Nuyts, 'Les mesures provisoires dans le Règlement Bruxelles *Ibis*' (2013) 5 Tijdschrift voor Belgisch Handelsrecht/Revue de Droit Commercial belge 348, 354), is exclusive under the Brussels *Ibis* Regulation (Case C-616/10 *Solvay SA v Honeywell Fluorine Products Europe BV and Others* (12 July 2012) ECLI:EU:C:2012:445
('*Solvay*')) or is subject to arbitration (*Van Uden* (n 78) paras 24f.
95 This may include the so-called 'exorbitant grounds of jurisdiction', the application of which the revised Brussels I Regulation and its predecessors exclude in principle; *Van Uden* (n 78) para 42).

application of Article 35 (the court reviews *its* jurisdiction and *its* provisional or protective measures), the CJEU has nevertheless felt the need to specify the operation of that forum for provisional or protective measures. In *Reichert*, the Court held that provisional or protective measures are to be understood as those intended to preserve a factual or legal situation so as to safeguard rights the recognition of which is sought elsewhere from the court having jurisdiction as to the substance of the matter.[96]

#31 Applying the same *Reichert* criteria, the Court's judgment in *St Paul Dairy*[97] shook the consensus that court proceedings seeking to preserve evidence undoubtedly also qualify as such a provisional or protective measure. At the request of the Dutch Supreme Court, the CJEU ruled in *St Paul Dairy* that a measure ordering the hearing of a witness for the purpose of enabling the applicant to decide whether to bring a case, determine whether it would be well founded and assess the relevance of evidence which might be adduced in that regard is not covered by the notion of 'provisional, including protective, measures'.[98]

#32 Legal doctrine has interpreted the judgment to mean that the CJEU's intention in *St Paul Dairy* WAS merely to close the door on **fishing expeditions**, ie claims that merely seek to estimate the chances of trial.[99] The revision of the Brussels I*bis* Regulation resorted to a recital to secure the qualification of the taking of evidence as a provisional or protective measure.[100] It would seem desirable however to rediscover to the principle already contained in the 1968 Brussels Convention on Jurisdiction and the Enforcement of Judgments in Civil and Commercial Matters[101]: 'As regards the measures which may be taken, reference should be made to the internal law of the country concerned'.[102] To this extent, the provision also implies **a conflicts of law rule**: the question of whether provisional or protective measures are possible, and if so, which ones, is decided by domestic law.[103] It would enhance the predictability and thus the systematisation of the forum of

96 Case C-261/90 *Mario Reichert, Hans-Heinz Reichert and Ingeborg Kockler v Dresdner Bank AG* (26 March 1992) ECLI:EU:C:1992:149, paras 34f ('*Reichert*').

97 Case C-104/03 *St. Paul Dairy Industries NV v Unibel Exser BVBA* (28 April 2005) ECLI:EU:C:2005:255 ('*St Paul Dairy*').

98 ibid para 25.

99 A Nuyts, 'Cross-Border Provisional Measures: Stepping Backwards in the Brussels I Recast' in G Van Calster and J Falconis (eds), *European Private International Law at 50. Celebrating and Contemplating the 1968 Brussels Convention and its Successors* (Intersentia 2018) 83, 102.

100 Recital 25 Brussels I*bis* Regulation.

101 Consolidated version published in [1998] OJ C27/1.

102 P Jenard, 'Report on the Convention on Jurisdiction and the Enforcement of Judgments in Civil and Commercial Matters' [1979] OJ C59/1, 42.

103 In this sense already HE Ras, 'De betekenis van het EEG-executieverdrag voor de rechter van het land waar een onder het Verdrag vallende zaak wordt aangebracht' (1975) 4 Tijdschrift voor Privaatrecht 851, 907.

provisional or protective measures if the diversity of provisional or protective measures in the national legal order were again taken as the starting point for delimiting the provisional or protective nature of the measure.[104]

#33 It also follows from the *Van Uden* judgment that, as an additional condition of EU law, the authorisation of provisional or protective measures depends on **a real connecting link** between the subject-matter of the measures sought and the territorial jurisdiction of the Contracting State of the requested court.[105] Specifically, this means that in the case of provisional measures, the condition of a real connecting link is fulfilled when the forum requested is also the place of execution of the measure, ie *forum acti*, also known as *forum arresti* or *forum loci*.[106]

#34 That leaves the question whether Article 35 of the Brussels I*bis* Regulation provides a forum when the **proceedings on the substance are pending** before a court of another Member State. The view that only the latter court has jurisdiction to do so, and at least that the *lis pendens rule* prevents parallel proceedings to obtain provisional or protective measures, has since been contradicted by the CJEU in the ***TOTO*** judgment.[107] In order to secure obligations entered into in the context of a public contract concluded in Poland for the construction of a section of a motorway, the construction companies awarded the contract had provided the Polish contracting authority with a number of guarantees, insured by a Bulgarian insurer. Some years later, those construction companies unsuccessfully applied to the Polish court, with exclusive jurisdiction under a forum clause, for interim or conservatory measures that would prohibit the contracting authority from making use of those guarantees. The contractors made a similar request to the Bulgarian court, which rejected the request at first instance and granted it on appeal. On cassation appeal by the Polish contracting authority, the Bulgarian cassation court referred the matter to the CJEU for a preliminary ruling. The CJEU holds that a court of a Member State before which an application for provisional or protective measures has been brought under Article 35 of the Brussels I*bis* Regulation is not required to decline jurisdiction where the court of another Member State, which has jurisdiction on the substance of the case, has already ruled on an

104 Hess earlier also advocated such affirmation of national procedural law, albeit not on the basis of the wording of the Treaty provision, in B Hess and C Zhou, 'Beweissicherung und Beweisbeschaffung im europäischen Justizraum' [2007] IPrax 183, 189 under 'Bejahung der Nationalen Ausgangsqualifikationen'; cf X Kramer, 'Harmonisation of Provisional and Protective Measures in Europe' in M Storme (ed), *Procedural Laws in Europe. Towards Harmonisation* (Maklu 2003) 305, 314, para 6.1 *in fine*.

105 *Van Uden* (n 78) para 40.

106 H Born, M Fallon and J-L Van Boxstael, *Droit judiciaire international. Chronique de jurisprudence 1991-1998* (Larcier 2001) 484, para 242.

107 Case C-581/20 *Skarb Państwa Rzeczypospolitej Polskiej reprezentowany przez Generalnego Dyrektora Dróg Krajowych i Autostrad v TOTO SpA - Costruzioni Generali and Vianini Lavori SpA* (6 October 2021) ECLI:EU:C:2021:808, paras 4, 12 ('*TOTO*').

application concerning the same subject-matter, based on the same cause of action and between the same parties. According to the CJEU, Article 35 must be interpreted as meaning that an application for provisional or protective measures must be examined in the light of the law of the Member State of the court seized and that it does not preclude national legislation which does not allow summary proceedings to be brought concerning a pecuniary claim against the State or a public body. Much of the controversy provoked by this judgment[108] ceases to exist if it is recognised that the obtaining of provisional or protective measures constitutes a dispute of an entirely different nature, which cannot be equated with a dispute on the merits.[109] Well-intentioned calls for greater coordination cannot detract from this.[110]

C The Impact of EU Law on the National Rules of Evidence

#35 Beyond the cross-border context, the EU is increasingly influencing **national rules of evidence**. This is done primarily by direct means, where EU legislation itself contains rules of evidence (see I). In adopting such rules applicable in a wide range of civil and commercial cases, including in purely domestic cases, the EU legislator relies on its general and specific powers, such as those to enact rules for the functioning of the internal market (Article 114 TFEU), to take measures to combat discrimination (Article 19 TFEU) or to ensure uniform protection of intellectual property rights (Article 118 TFEU). In addition, the EU indirectly influences national evidence law through the jurisprudence of the CJEU, for example by applying the principle of effectiveness or by relying on horizontally applicable EU law, such as the GDPR (see Section C.II).

108 See G Cuniberti, 'CJEU Rules on Parallel Interim Litigation' (*The EAPIL Blog*, 7 October 2021) <https://eapil.org/2021/10/07/cjeu-rules-on-parallel-interim-litigation/> accessed 29 May 2024); C Santaló Goris, 'C-581/20, TOTO: A Missed Opportunity to Cast Light on Article 35 of the Brussels I Bis Regulation?' (2022) 1 Cuadernos de Derecho Transnacional 915.

109 J Van Doninck, 'De expertise in het internationaal privaatrecht: een moeilijk huwelijk?' (2020) 33 Rechtskundig Weekblad 1283, 1291 and 1295; A Nuyts, 'L'arrêt 'TOTO': retour sur les mesures provisoires dans les litiges transfrontières européens' (2023) 66 Tijdschrift voor Belgisch Handelsrecht/ Revue de Droit Commercial belge 66, 72, paras 11 and 74, para 14 and para 21.

110 See B Hess' suggestion for coordination during the colloquium devoted by the Max Planck Institute for Procedural Law Luxembourg to the envisaged evaluation of the Brussels *Ibis* Regulation in M Weller, 'Conference Report from Luxembourg: On the Brussels Ibis Reform' (*Conflict of Laws.net*, 12 September 2022) https://conflictoflaws.net/2022/conference-report-from-luxemburg-on-the-brussels-ibis-reform (accessed 29 May 2024).

#36 While the Europeanisation of civil procedure has been extensively explored in the legal literature,[111] studies specifically addressing the EU dimension of civil law of evidence remain relatively scarce.[112] This does not mean that evidence law has been completely neglected. Evidence law studies are often part of larger examinations of European civil procedure.[113] This inherent link between evidence law and civil procedure is also reflected in the **ELI-Unidroit Model Rules of European Civil Procedure**, Part VII of which deals with 'Access to Information and Evidence'. Nevertheless, evidence law has unique features that distinguish it from other procedural issues. These include its closer ties with substantive law, its importance in establishing the facts and the sometimes wide discretion granted to judges in the assessment of evidence.

#37 Given the scope of this handbook, it is not possible to explore these nuances in depth or to provide a comprehensive overview of all EU interventions in the law of civil evidence. Instead, the aim is to outline the main issues and highlight notable trends in this area.

I EU Legislation

#38 A first observation regarding EU legislative activity is the increasing importance of the law of evidence. Comparing earlier directives with more recent ones including newly adopted directives, it is striking that the rules of evidence have become more numerous, have become more far-reaching, and are much more detailed.

#39 Early EU legislation was often limited to a single provision on the **easing of the burden of proof**, typically of an optional nature. It was left up to the discretion of Member States to decide whether or not to reverse the burden of proof. Several directives adopted between 1997 and 2005 in the field of consumer law (such as

---

111 See among others B Hess, *Europäisches Zivilprozessrecht* (2nd edn, De Gruyter 2020) 1026; F Gascón Inchausti and B Hess (eds), *The Future of the European Law of Civil Procedure: Coordination or Harmonisation* (Intersentia 2016) 290; A Nylund and B Krans (eds), *The European Union and National Civil Procedure* (Intersentia 2016); E Storskrubb, *Civil Procedure and EU Law: A Policy Area Uncovered* (OUP 2008) 521. See also A Ancery and B Krans, Chapter 6.

112 One example is of course, V Rijavec, T Ivanc and T Keresteš, *Dimensions of Evidence in European Civil Procedure* (Kluwer Law International 2016) 410. However, contrary to what the title suggests, this work is still primarily comparative in nature. See also K Jansen, 'Europa en de instrumentalisering van het bewijsrecht' (2023) 3 Tijdschrift voor Civiele Rechtspleging 83; B Krans, 'Europees recht en Nederlands Burgerlijk Bewijsrecht' in A Hartkamp and others (eds), *De invloed van het Europese recht op het Nederlandse privaatrecht* (Kluwer 2014) 923.

113 See among others E Vallines Garcia, 'Harmonising Access to Information and Evidence' in F Gascon Inchausti and B Hess (eds), *The Future of the European Law of Civil Procedure: Coordination or Harmonisation* (Intersentia 2016) 124.

those on the protection of consumers in respect of **distance contracts**,[114] on the **distance marketing** of consumer financial services[115] and on **payment services**[116]) provided that Member States 'may' stipulate that the burden of proof regarding the fulfilment of information obligations may lie with the professional or trader. In the field of **anti-discrimination** law, where the EU legislator has essentially codified the case law of the CJEU[117] since 1997,[118] this restrained approach means that the plaintiff does not automatically benefit from any adjustment of the burden of proof. It is only once a claimant has established a *prima facie* case of discrimination that the burden of proof shifts to the respondent, who must then prove that there has been no discrimination.[119]

#40 In more recent EU legislation, and in particular in the revisions of the above-mentioned directives, the evolution from a permissive 'may' to a mandatory 'the burden of proof shall be on the trader' is striking.[120] In addition, there is now much more focus on rules of evidence. A prime example is the recast of the **Product Liability Directive**. This directive includes an extensive provision on **disclosure of evidence**.[121] This was already provided for in earlier directives[122], but the

---

114 Directive 97/7/EC on the protection of consumers in respect of distance contracts [1997] OJ L144/19, Article 11(3)(a).

115 Directive 2002/65/EC concerning the distance marketing of consumer financial services and amending Council Directive 90/619/EEC and Directives 97/7/EC and 98/27/EC [2002] OJ L271/16, Article 15(1).

116 Directive 2007/64/EC on payment services in the internal market amending Directives 97/7/EC, 2002/65/EC, 2005/60/EC and 2006/48/EC and repealing Directive 97/5/EC [2007] OJ L319/1, Article 33.

117 See Case C-109/88 *Handels- og Kontorfunktionærernes Forbund I Danmark v Dansk Arbejdsgiverforening, acting on behalf of Danfoss* (17 October 1989) ECLI:EU:C:1989:383, para 14 ('*Danfoss*'); Case C-127/92 *Dr. Pamela Mary Enderby v Frenchay Health Authority and Secretary of State for Health* (27 October 1993) ECLI:EU:C:1993:859, para 18 ('*Enderby*').

118 Council Directive 97/80/EC on the burden of proof in sex discrimination cases [1998] OJ L14/6, Article 4. See also among others Directive 2000/43/EC implementing the principle of equal treatment between persons irrespective of racial or ethnic origin [2000] OJ L180/22, Article 8; Directive 2000/78/EC establishing a general framework for equal treatment in employment and occupation (Employment Equality Directive) [2000] OJ L303/16, Article 13.

119 For a more in-depth discussion, see J Ringelheim, 'The Burden of Proof in Anti-Discrimination Proceedings. A focus on Belgium, France and Ireland' (2019) 2 European Equality Law Review 49.

120 Directive 2011/83/EU on consumer rights, amending Council Directive 93/13/EEC and Directive 1999/44/EC of the European Parliament and of the Council and repealing Council Directive 85/577/EEC and Directive 97/7/EC [2011] OJ L304/64, Article 6(9); Directive 2023/2673 amending Directive 2011/83/EU as regards financial services contracts concluded at a distance and repealing Directive 2002/65/EC [2023] OJ L2023/2673, Article 1; Directive 2015/2366 on payment services in the internal market, amending Directives 2002/65/EC, 2009/110/EC and 2013/36/EU and Regulation (EU) No 1093/2010, and repealing Directive 2007/64/EC [2015] OJ L337/35, Article 41.

121 Directive 2024/2853 on liability for defective products [2024] OJ L18/11/2024, Article 9.

122 Such as Directive 2004/48/EC on the enforcement of intellectual property rights [2004] OJ L157/54, Article 6; Directive 2014/104/EU on certain rules governing actions for damages under national law for infringements of the competition law provisions of the Member States and of the European Union

recast of the Product Liability Directive now goes a step further by empowering national courts to require the evidence to be presented in an easily accessible and easily understandable manner. This could mean that manufacturers are required to compile or produce documents summarising the available evidence.[123] Furthermore, the directive introduces several new rules to alleviate the claimant's burden of proof, by specifying situations or conditions in which the defectiveness of the product and/or the causal link between the defectiveness and the damage are presumed.[124]

#41 This shift probably reflects the EU's increased awareness of the phenomenon of **evidentiary deficiency**, which can particularly occur in certain areas where the EU has regulatory powers (such as consumer protection, anti-discrimination and environmental issues). Evidentiary deficiency implies that the party bearing the burden of proof is often unable to provide the necessary evidence due to an imbalance in factual or technical knowledge.[125]

#42 A second observation is that EU law does not cover the whole field of evidence law, but proceeds in a fragmented manner. This is logical, as the EU must respect the principle of subsidiarity and the principle of conferral of competences.[126] Consequently, EU rules of evidence are always designed to address a specific problem (they are functional) and are usually limited to a single policy area (they are sectoral).

#43 As suggested above, provisions regarding the alleviation of the burden of proof (including various types of legal presumptions) and the disclosure of evidence constitute a significant part of the EU body of legislation on evidence, as such provisions are found in multiple EU instruments. Additionally, there are rules concerning the **evidentiary effect of final decisions** of public authorities[127] or courts[128], rules that allow judges to take measures to preserve confidential information (either in the context of disclosure of evidence or during legal proceedings

---

[2014] OJ L349/1, Article 5 and Directive 2020/1828 on representative actions for the protection of the collective interests of consumers and repealing Directive 2009/22/EC [2020] OJ L409/1, Article 18.

123 M De Ridder, 'Het bewijs van gebrekkigheid en causaal verband bij complexe producten in het voorstel voor een nieuwe productaansprakelijkheidsrichtlijn' (2023) 9 NTBR 356, 358.

124 Directive 2024/2853 on liability for defective products OJ L2024/2853, Article 10.

125 For a more extensive study of this phenomenon, see W Vandenbussche, 'Dealing With Evidentiary Deficiency in Tort Law' (2019) 9 International Journal of Procedural Law 53, 59.

126 JT Nowak, 'Considerations on the Impact of EU Law on National Civil Procedure: Recent Examples from Belgium' in V Lazic and S Stuij (eds), *International Dispute Resolution. Short Studies in Private International Law* (TMC Asser Press 2018) 30.

127 Directive 2014/104/EU on certain rules governing actions for damages under national law for infringements of the competition law provisions of the Member States and of the European Union [2014] OJ L349/1, Article 9.

128 Directive 2020/1828 on representative actions for the protection of the collective interests of consumers and repealing Directive 2009/22/EC [2020] OJ L409/1, Article 15.

relating to the unlawful acquisition, use, or disclosure of **trade secrets**[129]), rules that restrict the freedom of the parties to enter into contractual arrangements concerning the taking of evidence[130], and rules regulating the probative value of **electronic signatures.**[131]

#44 A third observation is that the specific formulation and design of the EU rules of evidence are often very different. This is, of course, a consequence of the functional and sectoral approach of EU legislation. The varying rules on the relaxation of the burden of proof are a notable example. Even within the field of consumer protection, the EU legislator sometimes chooses to adjust the allocation of the burden of proof (eg for **misleading advertising**[132] and **unfair commercial practices**[133]), or to adopt a rebuttable presumption (eg for the pre-existence of the lack of conformity in **the sale of consumer goods**[134]) or sometimes even to completely reverse the burden of proof (eg for the fulfilment of information duties vis-à-vis consumers). In the context of the implementation of this EU legislation by Member States, this sometimes leads to confusion about the precise scope of the EU rules of evidence, in particular about who has to prove what.[135]

II CJEU Case Law

#45 When examining the impact of the CJEU's case law on the national rules of evidence, the crucial role of the **principle of effectiveness** stands out.[136] This princi-

129 Directive 2016/943 on the protection of undisclosed know-how and business information (trade secrets) against their unlawful acquisition, use and disclosure [2016] OJ L157/1, Article 9.

130 Council Directive 93/13/EEC on unfair terms in consumer contracts [1993] OJ L95/29, annex 1.

131 Regulation 910/2014 on electronic identification and trust services for electronic transactions in the internal market and repealing Directive 1999/93/EC [2014] OJ L257/73, Article 25.

132 Directive 2006/114/EC concerning misleading and comparative advertising [2006] OJ L376/21, Article 7.

133 Directive 2005/29/EC concerning unfair business-to-consumer commercial practices in the internal market [2005] OJ L149/22, Article 12.

134 Directive 2019/771 on certain aspects concerning contracts for the sale of goods [2019] OJ L136/28, Article 11.

135 For instance, the CJEU had to clarify, in the context of the presumption in the sale of consumer goods, that consumers still have to prove the existence of the defect, although they do not have to prove the cause of this lack of conformity or that its origin is attributable to the seller (Case C-497/13 *Froukje Faber v Autobedrijf Hazet Ochten BV* (4 June 2015) ECLI:EU: C:2015:357, paras 71-75.

136 In this respect, the law of evidence is no different from other areas of law, since the principle of effectiveness is generally considered to be the most important principle in the development and expansion of European private law; AS Hartkamp, *European Law and National Private Law – Effect of EU Law and European Human Rights Law on Legal Relationships between Individuals* (Intersentia 2016) 98; See also A Ancery and B Krans, Chapter 6.

ple dictates that national procedural rules must not render the exercise of EU law impossible or excessively difficult.[137] In decisions across various policy domains (such as consumer protection, customs duties[138], and waste and hazardous materials[139]), the Court assesses national rules of evidence in het light of this principle of effectiveness. If the Court finds that these rules impede the exercise of EU law, the consequences vary from case to case. For instance, in a 2014-case concerning the copy of a **community design**, the CJEU held that the national court is required, in order to ensure observance of the principle of effectiveness, to use all procedures available to it under national law where appropriate, including rules of national law which provide for the burden of proof to be adjusted or lightened.[140] In *Sanofi Pasteur*, where the existence of a causal link between a defect attributed to a vaccine and the appearance of a nerve disease was at issue, the Court suggested to **lower the standard of proof**, arguing that a high standard would make it excessively difficult or impossible for consumers to establish product liability, thus undermining the effectiveness of the EU Directive.[141] In addition, there are also two notable cases concerning proof of compliance with consumer information obligations.[142] In a 2014-case, the Court hinted at a **reversal of the burden of proof** by ruling that compliance with the principle of effectiveness would be undermined if the burden of proving the non-performance of the creditor's information obligations were to lie with the consumer.[143] This was made more explicit in 2021, when the Court held that consumer protection may only be ensured where the seller or supplier is, in principle, required to prove the fulfilment of its pre-contractual and contractual obligations.[144]

---

137 Case C-33/76 *Rewe-Zentralfinanz eG and Rewe-Zentral AG v Landwirtschaftskammer für das Saarland* (16 December 1976) ECLI:EU:C:1976:188, para 6 ('*Rewe*').

138 Case 199/82 *Amministrazione delle Finanze dello Stato v SpA San Giorgio* (9 November 1983) ECLI:EU:C:1983:318, para 14.

139 Case C-113/12 *Donal Brady v Environmental Protection Agency* (3 October 2013) ECLI:EU:C:2013:627, paras 62-65.

140 Case C-479/12 *H. Gautzsch Großhandel GmbH & Co. KG v Münchener Boulevard Möbel Joseph Duna GmbH* (13 February 2014) ECLI:EU:C:2014:75, para 43.

141 Case C-621/15 *N. W and Others v Sanofi Pasteur MSD SNC and Others* (21 June 2017) ECLI:EU:C:2017:484, para 43.

142 See G Straetmans and J Werbrouck, 'Cases VB and Others v. BNP Paribas Personal Finance SA and AV and Others v. BNP Paribas Personal Finance SA and Procureur de la République (C-776/19 to C-782/19): New Jurisprudential Levers to Combat Unfair Terms in B2C contracts' (2022) 2 European Journal of Consumer Law 183, 195f.

143 Case C-449/13 *CA Consumer Finance SA v Ingrid Bakkaus and Others* (18 December 2014) ECLI:EU:C:2014:2464, para 27f.

144 Cases C-776/19 to C-782/19 *VB and Others v BNP Paribas Personal Finance SA and AV and Others v BNP Paribas Personal Finance SA and Procureur de la République* (10 June 2021) ECLI:EU:C:2021:470, para 89.

#46 Finally, it should be noted that the **GDPR** has impacted many areas of (procedural) law, and evidence law is no exception.[145] This was further emphasised in *Norra Stockholm Bygg*. First, the Court confirmed that the production of evidence (in this case, a register of employees containing personal data of third parties, collected mainly for the purpose of tax control) constitutes a processing of data within the meaning of the GDPR. Therefore, the GDPR's conditions for lawful processing are indeed applicable to an investigative measure in the context of civil proceedings. When ordering the production of a document containing personal data, the national court must take into account the interests of the data subjects concerned and balance them up according to the circumstances of the case, the type of proceeding at issue and duly taking into account the requirements arising from the principle of proportionality as well as, in particular, those resulting from the principle of data minimisation.[146] This last point in particular may represent a significant shift in certain Member States where the decision to produce documents was primarily inspired by concerns of access to evidence.[147]

References

Allemeersch B and Houtmeyers A-S, 'De Bewijsverordening' in B Allemeersch and T Kruger (eds), *Handboek Europees Burgerlijk Procesrecht* (Intersentia 2015) 253.

Besso C, 'Cooperation in the Taking of Evidence: The European Attitude' (2012) 2 International Journal of Procedural Law 68.

Born H, Fallon M and Van Boxstael J-L, *Droit judiciaire international. Chronique de jurisprudence 1991-1998* (Larcier 2001).

Carbonnier J, *Droit civil* (Presses Universitaires de France, first published 1955, 2017).

Couwenberg I, 'Bewijsvergaring in de Europese Unie' in S Rutten and B Vanlerberghe (eds), *Het bewijs in het burgerlijke proces / La preuve dans le procès civil* (die Keure 2015) 71.

Cuniberti G, 'CJEU Rules on Parallel Interim Litigation' (*The EAPIL Blog*, 7 October 2021) <https://eapil.org/2021/10/07/cjeu-rules-on-parallel-interim-litigation/> accessed 29 May 2024.

De Ridder M, 'Het bewijs van gebrekkigheid en causaal verband bij complexe producten in het voorstel voor een nieuwe productaansprakelijkheidsrichtlijn' (2023) 9 NTBR 356.

European Commission, *Practice Guide for the Application of the Regulation on the Taking of Evidence* (Commission Services 2011) <https://e-justice.europa.eu/fileDownload.do?id=dec18da1-6842-47b3-a142-d0e0c236fcbc> accessed 27 May 2024.

145 See also A Nylund, Chapter 7.

146 Case C-268/21 *Norra Stockholm Bygg AB* (2 March 2023) ECLI:EU:C:2023:145, paras 56-58.

147 Comp. Rule 100 ELI-UNIDROIT Model European Rules of Civil Procedure: 'When making orders under the Rules in this Part the court will give effect to the following principles: (b) in response to a party's application, under Rule 101, seeking access to evidence, the court will, if the application is granted, direct the production of relevant, non privileged, and sufficiently identified evidence held or controlled by another party or, if necessary, by a non-party, even if such production might be adverse to that person's interests'.

Galic A, 'Open Issues Concerning the Non-Mandatory Character of the Cross-Border Taking of Evidence Regulation' (2017) 18 ERA Forum 213.

Gascón Inchausti F and Hess B (eds), *The Future of the European Law of Civil Procedure: Coordination or Harmonisation* (Intersentia 2016).

Gaudemet-Tallon H and Kessedjian C, 'La refonte du règlement Bruxelles I' (2013) 3 Revue trimestrielle de droit européen 435

Gerards J, 'Het EU-Grondrechtenhandvest: een crashcourse' in *Waarde, werking en potentie van het EU-Grondrechtenhandvest in de Nederlandse rechtsorde* (Wolters Kluwer 2024).

Hartkamp AS, *European Law and National Private Law – Effect of EU Law and European Human Rights Law on Legal Relationships between Individuals* (Intersentia 2016).

Hess B and Zhou C, 'Beweissicherung und Beweisbeschaffung im europäischen Justizraum' [2007] IPrax 183.

Hess B, *Europäisches Zivilprozessrecht* (2nd edn, De Gruyter 2020).

Jansen K, 'Europa en de instrumentalisering van het bewijsrecht' (2023) 3 Tijdschrift voor Civiele Rechtspleging 83.

Jansen R, *Legal Privilege and Transnational Evidence-Taking. A Comparative Study on Cross-Border Disclosure, Evidence-Shopping and Legal Privilege* (Intersentia 2022).

Jenard P, 'Report on the Convention on Jurisdiction and the Enforcement of Judgments in Civil and Commercial Matters' [1979] OJ C59/1.

Kaar van het BJ, *IPR-bewijsrecht en bewijsverkrijging* (Wolters Kluwer 2008).

Kramer X, 'Harmonisation of Provisional and Protective Measures in Europe' in M Storme (ed), *Procedural Laws in Europe. Towards Harmonisation* (Maklu 2003) 305.

Krans B, 'Europees recht en Nederlands Burgerlijk Bewijsrecht' in A Hartkamp and others (eds), *De invloed van het Europese recht op het Nederlandse privaatrecht* (Kluwer 2014) 923.

Lebois M, 'Le Règlement (CE) n°1206/2001 du Conseil du 28 mai 2001 relatif à la coopération entre les juridictions des Etats membres dans le domaine de l'obtention des preuves en matière civile ou commerciale' in M Storme and G de Leval (eds), *Le Droit Processuel & Judiciaire Européen / The European Judicial & Procedural Law* (die Keure 2003) 271.

Nekrošius V, 'The Taking of Evidence in Civil Proceedings of the European Union' (2020) *Teka Komisji Prawniczej PAN Oddział W Lublinie* 299.

Nowak JT, 'Considerations on the Impact of EU Law on National Civil Procedure: Recent Examples from Belgium' in V Lazic and S Stuij (eds), *International Dispute Resolution. Short Studies in Private International Law* (TMC Asser Press 2018) 30.

Nuyts A and Sepulchre J, 'Cross-Border Taking of Evidence in the European Judicial Area' (2005) 4(2) Tijdschrift voor Internationaal Privaatrecht 79.

Nuyts A, 'Les arrêts Lippens et ProRail: retour sur l'exclusivité de la réglementation européenne de collecte des preuves' [2014] *Journal des Tribunaux* 557.

—— 'Cross-Border Provisional Measures: Stepping Backwards in the Brussels I Recast' in G Van Calster and Jura Falconis (eds), *European Private International Law at 50. Celebrating and Contemplating the 1968 Brussels Convention and its Successors* (Intersentia 2018) 83.

—— 'L'arrêt 'TOTO': retour sur les mesures provisoires dans les litiges transfrontières européens' (2023) 66 Tijdschrift voor Belgisch Handelsrecht/Revue de Droit Commercial belge 66.

Nylund A and Krans B (eds), *The European Union and National Civil Procedure* (Intersentia 2016).

Payan G, *Conventions et protocoles de La Haye annotés* (Bruylant 2020).

Ras HE, 'De betekenis van het EEG-executieverdrag voor de rechter van het land waar een onder het Verdrag vallende zaak wordt aangebracht' (1975) 4 Tijdschrift voor Privaatrecht 851.

Richard V, 'La refonte du règlement sur l'obtention des preuves en matière civile' (2021) 1 Revue critique de droit international privé 67.

Rijavec V, Ivanc T and Keresteš T, *Dimensions of Evidence in European Civil Procedure* (Kluwer Law International 2016).

Ringelheim J, 'The Burden of Proof in Anti-Discrimination Proceedings. A Focus on Belgium, France and Ireland' (2019) 2 European Equality Law Review 49.

Santaló Goris C, 'C-581/20, TOTO: A Missed Opportunity to Cast Light on Article 35 of the Brussels I Bis Regulation?' (2022) 1 Cuadernos de Derecho Transnacional 915.

Storskrubb E, *Civil Procedure and EU Law: A Policy Area Uncovered* (OUP 2008).

Straetmans G and Werbrouck J, 'Cases VB and Others v. BNP Paribas Personal Finance SA and AV and Others v. BNP Paribas Personal Finance SA and Procureur de la République (C-776/19 to C-782/19): New Jurisprudential Levers to Combat Unfair Terms in B2C Contracts' (2022) 2 European Journal of Consumer Law 183.

Valdhans J and Sehnálek D, 'The 1970 Hague Evidence Convention, the European Union and the 2001 EU Evidence Regulation – Interfaces' in CH van Rhee and A Uzelac (eds), *Evidence in Contemporary Civil Procedure. Fundamental Issues in a Comparative Perspective* (Intersentia 2015) 337.

Vallines Garcia E, 'Harmonising Access to Information and Evidence' in FG Inchausti and B Hess (eds), *The Future of the European Law of Civil Procedure: Coordination or Harmonisation* (Intersentia 2016) 124.

Van Doninck J, 'De expertise in het international privaatrecht: een moeilijk huwelijk?' (2020) 33 *Rechtskundig Weekblad* 1283.

Vandenbussche W, 'Dealing With Evidentiary Deficiency in Tort Law' (2019) 9 International Journal of Procedural Law 53.

Vareilles-Sommières de P, 'Le règlement communautaire sur l'obtention de preuves à l'étranger et les rapports avec les Etats tiers' in Arnaud Nuyts and Nadine Watté (eds), *International Civil Litigation in Europe and Relations with Third States* (Bruylant 2010) 28.

von Hein J, 'Digitalisierungsaspekte der neuen Europäischen Beweisaufnahmeverordnung' in P Reuß and J Laß (eds), *Göttinger Kolloquien zur Digitalisierung des Zivilverfahrensrechts* (Universitätsverlag Göttingen 2024) 25.

Weller M, 'Conference Report from Luxembourg: On the Brussels Ibis Reform' (*Conflict of Laws.net*, 12 September 2022) <https://conflictoflaws.net/2022/conference-report-from-luxemburg-on-the-brussels-ibis-reform> accessed 29 May 2024.

Fernando Gascón Inchausti

Chapter 12
Recognition and Enforcement: Fundamental Issues

A Recognition, Declaration of Enforceability and Enforcement

#1 Even if a dispute does not in principle have a cross-border element, it is possible for one of the parties to seek to have the decision which has ended it produce its effects in a different Member State. One of the objectives of European civil procedural law (hereinafter ECPL) is to regulate this cross-border **effectiveness** of judgments[1] (including that of certain instruments equivalent to judgments, such as **authentic instruments** and court-approved transactions).

#2 These potential cross-border effects undoubtedly include **enforceability**, which operates when the use of force or authority may be necessary to render them effective: eg, when the defendant's seizable assets or the property to be delivered are located in another Member State, or if the performance ordered in the judgment must be carried out, in whole or in part, abroad.

#3 The (extraterritorial) effects of a court decision also include **res judicata**, which may be necessary for a party who is a defendant in a Member State despite the fact that proceedings with the same subject-matter and between the same parties have already been decided by a court in another Member State (res judicata plea, which would release them from such new proceedings). And it may also be in the litigant's interest when part of the subject-matter of a pending proceeding has already been decided by a court of another State in a previous proceeding between the same parties and with a related scope, if they want the court in the second proceeding to be bound by the decision in the first one (positive or prejudicial effect of res judicata). The existence of a cross-border res judicata has been acknowledged by the Court of Justice. In *De Wolf/Cox*,[2] the CJEU held that a new action could not be brought where the matter had already been decided in a previous procedure before the courts of another Member State – enforcement of the

1 W Voss, 'Article 36' in M Requejo Isidro (ed), *Brussels I bis. A Commentary on Regulation (EU) No 1215/2012* (Edward Elgar 2022) 548, paras 36-10 to 36-18; P Franzina, 'The Recognition and Enforcement of Member States Judgments' in A Dickinson and E Lein (eds), *The Brussels I Regulation Recast* (OUP 2015) 373, paras 13.07-13.19.

2 Case C-42/76 *De Wolf/Cox* (30 November 1976) ECLI:EU:C:1976:168.

Fernando Gascón Inchausti, Complutense University of Madrid, e-mail: fgascon@ucm.es

https://doi.org/10.1515/9783110781632-012

judgment would then be possible. In *Gothaer*,[3] the CJEU attributed res judicata effects to the decision by which a Belgian court declared that it lacked **international jurisdiction** to hear a dispute due to the effectiveness of a choice of court agreement in favour of the courts of Iceland and, consequently, it established that the German court before which the same plaintiffs sought to bring a similar claim (and covered by the same agreement) was bound by the Belgian decision and should also decline jurisdiction. It thus constructed a sort of **'European res judicata'** concerning procedural matters.[4]

#4 A litigant may also need a merely **declaratory or constitutive judgment** to be effective in another Member State (beyond its res judicata), so that it can be binding and be taken into account by public authorities or individuals in that State (as is the case, for example, when a contract has been annulled or a divorce has been decreed and registration in the civil register of another Member State is required).[5]

#5 The approach may be different in the case of the so-called **evidentiary effects** of judgments, expressly provided for by some European legislation,[6] and to their **factual effects**: these are not inherent effects of judgments, but rather the consequence of specific legal provisions; it is up to the procedural law of the forum or to the specific European provisions to decide the weight they are granted to these purposes.[7]

#6 Judicial decisions are rendered in the exercise of jurisdictional power and draw their force from the **sovereignty** of the State. For this reason, States tend to make the effectiveness in their territory of **foreign judments** subject to **prior control**, the passing of which determines their **recognition** (which must be understood as synonymous with acceptance). The levels of control to which recognition is made conditional usually consist of requirements and/or the absence of grounds for re-

3 Case C-456/11 *Gothaer Allgemeine Versicherung* (15 November 2012) ECLI:EU:C:2012:719.

4 H Roth, 'Europäischer Rechtskraftbegriff im Zuständigkeitsrecht?' [2014] IPRax 163; D Dalfino, 'Un giudicato «europeo» sulla competenza giurisdizionale?' [2013/2014] Int'l Lis 16; E Torralba Mendiola and E Rodríguez Pineau, 'Two's a Company, Three's a Crowd: Jurisdiction, Recognition and *Res Judicata* in the European Union' (2014) 10 Journal of Private International Law 403. At national level, see Spanish Supreme Court 8 September 2023 ECLI:ES:TS:2023:3608.

5 This is the case of Article 30(2) Brussels II II-ter for updating the civil-status records of a Member State on the basis of a decision relating to divorce, legal separation or marriage annulment given in another Member State, and against which no further appeal lies under the law of that Member State.

6 Pursuant to Article 9(2) of Directive 2014/104 in antitrust damages claims, '[t]he decision by a court establishing an infringement of competition law may be presented before the courts of other Member States as at least prima facie evidence'. In a similar vein, Article 15 of Directive 2020/1828 establishes for collective proceedings in the interest of consumers that 'the final decision of a court of any Member State concerning the existence of an infringement harming collective interests of consumers can be used by all parties as evidence in the context of any other action to seek redress measures against the same trader for the same practice'.

7 Franzina (n 1) paras 13.12–13.13.

fusal. They may also vary from a procedural point of view, as an express prior control may be required or it may be decided to presume that the requirements for recognition are met and to allow, where appropriate, an **ex-post control** in case of non-conformity. The requirements and the way to articulate them, moreover, may be different depending on the type of effects at stake: it is usual to treat differently and more rigorously foreign decisions intended to be enforced.[8] Nor is it unusual for differences to be established according to the subject matter: certain more sensitive matters may require stricter controls or, on the contrary, greater flexibility for the sake of expediency.

#7 In the current state of development of ECPL, the general rule is that the **recognition of foreign decisions is automatic, except when they are intended to be enforced.** The automatic nature of recognition means that a foreign judicial decision unfolds its effects – except for its enforceability – in the other Member State without further ado. Automatic, however, does not mean compulsory: the legal instruments of ECPL envisage as a rule the possibility for the party affected by the recognition to seek its refusal, on the basis of some specific grounds. This challenge can be made within the framework of the proceedings in which the effectiveness of the foreign decision is invoked, which will force the court to rule on its recognition: this is referred to as **incidental recognition**. And it is also possible to bring ad hoc proceedings requesting the court to establish that there are not grounds for refusing to recognise a decision (recognition as a main point).

#8 Where **enforcement** is sought, on the other hand, the scrutiny may be higher, as the effects are considered to be more serious.[9] The general rule in *International* civil procedural law is the need for a prior **exequatur procedure**, which entails the **declaration of enforceability** of the foreign decision (or of other non-judicial titles). The granting of exequatur usually also entails the recognition of the other effects of the judgments ('who can do more, can do less'). In *European*

8 This difference in treatment can lead to paradoxical results, as the recognition of effects other than the executive can also have serious consequences: consider, for example, the plea of res judicata, which circulates automatically because it is subject to recognition and can deprive a litigant of the right of access to the courts.

9 It may sometimes be debatable whether or not the enforceability of a judgment is at stake and whether it is therefore necessary to obtain its prior declaration of enforceability - where it is still applicable - in order to achieve its effectiveness. This was the issue at stake in Case C-92/12 PPU *Health Service Executive* (26 April 2012) ECLI:EU:C:2012:255, in the field of parental responsibility: a decision of a court of a Member State ordering the placement of a child in closed care in an institution in another Member State was to be made enforceable. In the CJEU's view, recognition in this case is not sufficient, but a declaration of enforceability is necessary, since enforcement of the judgment entails the use of force. It is a different matter whether, because of its scope and content, the effectiveness of this judgment benefited from the system of enforcement without exequatur provided for by Brussels II-bis; since this was not the case, the CJEU required in return that the exequatur should be swift and that appeals should not have suspensive force.

civil procedural law, however, exequatur has been progressively abolished, and it is thus possible that the granting of enforceability is subject to the ordinary rule of automatism. Once a decision has been declared enforceable – also, of course, when such a declaration is not necessary – it is possible to apply to the relevant authority for enforcement, which will be subject to the procedural rules of the State where it is to be carried out. There is thus a dual level of regulation: ECPL is concerned with establishing the conditions under which foreign decisions can be effective in Member States; **national procedural law** regulates their enforcement and the way in which their other effects are to be displayed (eg, how their res judicata is to be invoked). The interplay between these two levels is constant and must be properly handled by legal practitioners.

B The Abolition of Exequatur in the European Area of Justice

#9 The implementation of recognition and enforcement of foreign decisions is directly associated with the level of mutual trust that exists between the judicial systems involved. The EU has made the greatest progress in this area thanks to the degree of legal integration triggered by the building of the European Area of Justice. Promoting the **free circulation of judicial decisions** has been, from the outset, one of the goals pursued by the European institutions. This 'fifth freedom' was initially conceived as a tool in the service of the construction of a common market, which required the circulation of judicial decisions settling disputes relating to persons, goods, capital or services which, previously, also circulated freely between the Member States. Subsequently, it gained autonomy as one of the basic elements on which to turn the EU into an **area of freedom, security and justice,** at the service of the protection of rights [Article 67(4) TFEU] and in connection with the other European goals [Article 81(2) TFEU].

#10 In the **1968 Brussels Convention** system, the circulation of judicial decisions and extrajudicial titles was based on a clear distinction between recognition and declaration of enforceability. While recognition of non-executory effects was automatic, a special **exequatur procedure** was necessary to make enforcement possible. The Convention enshrined the prohibition of review as to the substance of the foreign decision and established a single list of grounds for refusing recognition and exequatur (overcoming ambiguous categories, such as reciprocity). It also provided for a rather flexible mechanism for deciding on the granting of exequatur at first instance, without hearing the party against whom enforcement was sought, although with a possible ex officio review of the existence of the grounds for refusal. On the other hand, a double recourse was introduced, which prevented enforcement in the proper sense (but not the taking of protective measures) and delayed the full satisfaction of the cross-border creditor.

#11 The transformation of the Brussels Convention into the **Brussels I Regulation** as a result of the Amsterdam Treaty (1997) and the Tampere European Council (1999) maintained this scheme, but the granting of exequatur at first instance was automated, as any ex officio review of the grounds for refusal was eliminated.

#12 The European Commission, however, considered that the subsistence of **exequatur** was not compatible with the clear commitment to mutual recognition as the cornerstone of the system of judicial cooperation in the EU and promoted a plan to abolish it. This objective became one of the leitmotifs of ECPL during the early 2000s and materialised in two different ways: abolishing it in the instruments governing judicial cooperation in civil matters and making it unnecessary in the so-called second generation instruments.

I Abolition of Exequatur in Intra-European Judicial Cooperation Instruments

#13 A first line of action aimed at abolishing, in whole or in part, exequatur in the instruments governing judicial cooperation in the EU. The first step was taken in 2003 with the **Brussels II-bis Regulation**, which abolished exequatur for the cross-border enforcement of judgments relating to rights of access and for those relating to the international return of children, ie decisions where the time factor is more essential and where exequatur delays were more unacceptable. In 2019, with the **Brussels II-ter Regulation**, the abolition of exequatur was generalised to all decisions on parental responsibility, but a more privileged status was given to the direct enforcement of decisions on access and return orders.

#14 In 2009, the **Maintenance Regulation** abolished exequatur for decisions rendered in Member States that were party to the 2007 Hague Protocol (Article 17): the application of its conflict rules allows to presume a reasonable equivalence of results and to abolish pre-enforcement review of judgments in an area where speed is also of the essence.

#15 The most important objective, in any case, was the **abolition of exequatur** at a general level, ie transforming the Brussels I Regulation into the **Brussels I-bis Regulation.**[10] This was the most prominent proposal when the Commission

10 Its efficiency, however, did not seem to be subject to much criticism in practice: B Hess, T Pfeiffer and P Schlosser, *Report on the Application of Regulation Brussels I in the Member States (Study JLS/C4/ 2005/03)* <http://ec.europa.eu/civiljustice/news/docs/study_application_brussels_1_en.pdf> accessed 1 June 2024; Also G Cuniberti, 'Some Remarks on the Efficiency of Exequatur' in H Kronke and K Thorn (eds), *Grenzen überwinden - Prinzipien bewahren: Festschrift für Bernd von Hoffmann* (Gieseking 2011) 568.

launched its initiative to reform it,[11] seeking a balance between mutual trust, speed and safeguards for the rights of defence.[12] The end result was an abolition of exequatur as a procedure, but not as a control. Article 39 Brussels I-bis states that a judgment given in a Member State which is enforceable in that Member State shall be enforceable in the other Member States without any declaration of enforceability being required. Consequently, anyone seeking to enforce a judgment from a Member State in another Member State will simply make an application for enforcement on the same terms as they would have to do if the judgment had been given by a national court, providing as an additional document the certificate issued under Article 53 by the court of origin attesting to the enforceability of the judgment. By applying for enforcement, the creditor triggers enforcement proceedings in accordance with the procedural rules of the forum. In the course of such enforcement the debtor may, in addition to the grounds of opposition provided for in the lex fori, raise the **grounds of opposition** provided for in the Regulation itself, which had hitherto served as grounds for refusal of exequatur. A review of the original judgment is therefore still possible: the difference is the procedural context in which it is to be made operational. It will be the debtors' burden to defend themselves, in the context of enforcement proceedings already in progress, by pleading the grounds on which they consider enforcement to be improper (although taking into account that Brussels I-bis itself defines and rates the grounds of defence that can be raised arising from the cross-border nature of the enforcement).

#16 The **2012 Regulation on Succession** did not follow the path and maintained the traditional schemes and the exequatur procedure – in the terms of BR-I – for attributing enforceability to most judgments (Articles 43 et seq.): the great diversity of substantive regimes possibly explains this option. A major innovation, however, was the introduction of a special system of circulation without exequatur for a specific document, the 'European Certificate of Succession', which may be of

11 COM (2010) 748 final.

12 Among many others, see P Beaumont and E Johnston, 'Can *Exequatur* Be Abolished in Brussels I whilst Retaining a Public Policy Defence?' (2010) 6 Journal of Private International Law 249; P Biavati, 'Judicial Cooperation in Europe: Is *Exequatur* Still Necessary?' (2011) 2 International Journal of Procedural Law 403; M De Cristofaro, 'The Abolition of Exequatur Proceedings: Speeding Up the Free Movement of Judgments while Preserving the Rights of the Defense' (2011) 2 International Journal of Procedural Law 432; X Kramer, 'Cross-Border Enforcement in the EU: Mutual Trust *versus* Fair Trial? Towards Principles of European Civil Procedure' (2011) International Journal of Procedural Law 202; LJ Timmer, 'Abolition of Exequatur under the Brussels I Regulation: Ill Conceived and Premature?' (2013) 9 Journal of Private International Law 129; T Domej, 'Die Neufassung der EuGVVO. Quantensprünge im europäischen Zivilprozessrecht' (2014) 78 RabelsZ 508; A Frackowiak-Adamska, 'Time for a European "Full Faith and Credit Clause"' (2015) 52 Common Market Law Review 191.

judicial origin (eg because it is drawn up at the end of contentious or voluntary proceedings).

#17 The exequatur procedure has also been maintained in **2016** as necessary to achieve cross-border enforcement in the area of **matrimonial property regimes** and in that of the **property consequences of registered partnerships** (Regulations 1103/2016 and 1104/2016, Article 42 et seq.): here too, the lack of substantive harmonisation explains the situation, as shown by the European legislator's concern for respect for fundamental rights and the principle of non-discrimination (cf Article 38).

#18 The most recent initiative under way to draw up a **Parenthood Regulation (2022)**[13] remains undefined, because in this area decisions are of a declaratory or constitutive nature, so that it is not necessary to consider whether it would be possible to dispense with exequatur. The creation of a 'European Certificate of Parenthood' is being proposed, which would circulate without intermediate procedures, along the lines of the European Certificate of Succession.

II The Abolition of Exequatur in the Second-Generation Instruments

#19 In parallel, the European legislator has promoted the so-called second-generation instruments, designed to overcome the difficulties of cross-border litigation through the creation of genuinely **European procedures**, at the end of which decisions are given that are automatically recognised and directly enforceable in all Member States, without the need for exequatur.

#20 The starting point was set by the creation of the **European Enforcement Order** in 2004 (Article 5 EEO-Regulation), which abolished the exequatur procedure for uncontested claims if service on the defendant in the proceedings of origin had met certain minimum safeguards, provided that the national law of the State of origin offers adequate means of review in the event of involuntary default of the defendant.

#21 In the **European order for payment procedure** (2006) (EOP) direct enforceability – without the need for exequatur – is also attributed to the European order for payment (Article 19 EOP-Regulation) in a similar way as it is the case for judgments rendered at the end of a **European small claims procedure** (2007) (Article 20(1) ESCP-Regulation). In both cases, the abolition of exequatur is directly linked to the prior conduct of the (order for payment or small claims) procedure in accordance with

13 Commission, 'Proposal for a Council Regulation on jurisdiction, applicable law, recognition of decisions and acceptance of authentic instruments in matters of parenthood and on the creation of a European Certificate of Parenthood,' COM (2022) 695 final.

the rules created by the European legislator itself. The same formula was followed in 2014 with the **European account preservation order** (EAPO), directly enforceable in any Member States where there are bank assets (Article 22 EAPO-Regulation): the harmonisation of the requirements and the procedure for the adoption of the protective measure is the basis for granting it immediate enforceability.[14]

C Mutual Recognition and Mutual Trust

I Broad, But Not Absolute, Scope of Mutual Recognition

#22 The abolition of exequatur is a step forward that has only been possible in the European Area of Justice: in less integrated environments exequatur is still a preliminary step for access to enforcement, although its granting may be more or less automated in the first instance, as evidenced by the Hague Convention of 2019.[15] The development achieved by the ECPL is based on the **principle of mutual recognition** as the cornerstone of the system (Articles 67(4) and 81(1) TFEU), which in turn is underpinned by a generic rule of mutual trust.[16] The option for mutual recognition represented a legislative policy strategy: to coordinate national procedural systems, refraining from harmonising them.[17] The second generation instruments mark a turning point, as they create genuine European procedures applicable before national courts and which, as far as the effectiveness of decisions is concerned, also benefit from the idea of mutual recognition.

14 E D'Alessandro and F Gascón Inchausti (eds), *The European Account Preservation Order. A Commentary on Regulation (EU) No 655/2014* (Edward Elgar 2022) I.11 and 22.1–22.10.

15 Hague Conference on Private International Law, Convention (41) of 2 July 2019 on the Recognition and Enforcement of Foreign Judgments in Civil or Commercial Matters <https://www.hcch.net/en/instruments/conventions/full-text/?cid=137> accessed 1 June 2024.

16 M Weller, 'Mutual Trust: In Search of the Future of European Union Private International Law' (2015) 11 Journal of Private International Law 64; P Hovaguimian, 'The Enforcement of Foreign Judgments under Brussels I bis: False Alarms and Real Concerns' (2015) 11 Journal of Private International Law 212, 244-248; X Kramer, 'Cross-Border Enforcement and the Brussels I-Bis Regulation: Towards a New Balance Between Mutual Trust and National Control over Fundamental Rights' (2013) 60 Netherlands International Law Review 343, 364-367; M Zilinsky, 'Trust and Cross-Border Enforcement of Judgments in Civil Matters in the EU: Does the Step-by-Step Approach Work?' (2017) 64 Netherlands International Law Review 115.

17 The regulations on judicial cooperation have contributed to align some aspects of national procedural legislation, although not significantly; see A Nylund and B Krans (eds), *The European Union and National Civil Procedure* (Intersentia 2016); F Gascón-Inchausti, 'Have the EU Regulations on Judicial Cooperation Fostered Harmonisation of National Procedures?' in F Gascón Inchausti and B Hess (eds), *The Future of the European Law of Civil Procedure: Coordination or Harmonisation?* (Intersentia 2020) 91.

#23 **Mutual recognition** is a principle of relative value in ECPL. Understood absolutely, as initially formulated by the Court of Justice in 1979 in *Cassis de Dijon*, it should lead to a 'full **equivalence** of outcomes', without controls in the State of destination. This is not, however, what has occurred in all the European regulatory instruments developed as implementations of the principle of mutual recognition. Most **'sectoral' regulations** maintain exequatur as a preliminary procedure. Brussels I-bis, despite dispensing with exequatur, maintains a system of 'control at destination' over the judgment and over the originating procedure, although procedurally relocated in enforcement phase. The same applies to EEOs (Article 21(1) EEO-R), EOPs (Article 22 (1 EOP-R),[18] judgments given at the end of a ESCP (Article 22(1)),[19] judgments in maintenance matters in a State bound by the Hague Protocol (Article 21(2) Maint-R), EAPOs (Article 34 EAPO-R) or privileged judgments on rights of access and the return of children under BR-IIb (Article 50): although they are very few in number, there are still certain grounds which may **prevent** their **enforcement** due to their cross-border nature – notably **irreconcilability** with a decision previously given in the State of enforcement or already effective there; **public policy**, however, has been removed from that list, except in the case of the EAPO.

#24 There are, therefore, **different degrees of intensity** in the assumption of mutual recognition. And, of course, there is no imperative European mandate 'of maximums': keeping exequatur in some contexts is reasonable; so is the existence of grounds to oppose a posteriori a recognition or enforcement regulated as automatic.

II Mutual Trust and European Civil Procedural Law

#25 This relative or flexible character of mutual recognition is explained by its link to the principle of **mutual trust**. Even within the EU context there are factors that condition the level of trust which, in turn, underpins the greater or lesser ease with which decisions circulate. The scope of proceedings is undoubtedly one of them. It is easier to make progress in mutual recognition in property and commercial matters, with more harmonised substantive rules (cf consumer affairs, intellectual and industrial property, competition). It is also justified in sectors for which European society itself demands a speed that is incompatible with a priori controls (maintenance, family visits and the return of children). On the other hand, reluctance is more understandable in other aspects of legal life that have a less homogeneous substantive regulation and are not harmonised by European law, such as succession and family law matters.

---

18 In case C-119/13 *eco cosmetics and Raiffeisenbank St. Georgen* (4 September 2014) ECLI:EU:C:2014:2144, the CJEU insisted in the need for control to be performed in the Member State of origin, not in that of destination.

19 Control on recognition, however, is completely excluded (Articles 19 EOP-R and 20(1) ESCP-R).

#26 The level of confidence in the **proper functioning** of domestic judicial systems also plays a role, albeit in a somewhat more hidden way. In the area of criminal cooperation, also governed by the principle of mutual recognition, the case law of the CJEU has had to assume that certain systemic shortcomings (such as poor prison conditions[20] or lack of judicial independence[21]) can become obstacles to mutual recognition whenever there are elements foreseeable to affect the individual concerned in particular (similar displays of mistrust have occurred in the area of asylum).[22] This approach could also be transposed to the civil field, especially in highly sensitive areas (eg the risks for children in the event of enforcement of a return order or an order for the placement of a child in a closed facility in another Member State).[23]

#27 The effectiveness of the **CFREU** and the adherence of all Member States to the **ECHR** is a relevant factor that allows to presume (i) the proper functioning of judicial systems, (ii) an adequate level of respect for procedural safeguards and (iii) the existence of effective corrective mechanisms at the domestic level in the event of infringement of those safeguards. The ECtHR has clearly indicated that the mechanisms for recognition and enforcement of decisions in force in the EU, with a high degree of automatism – both 'with' and 'without' exequatur – benefit from the **presumption of compliance** with the Convention, condensed in the 'Bosphorus doctrine'.[24] This presumption applicable to EU law contrasts with the ECtHR's approach when the extraterritorial effectiveness of decisions from States that are not members of the Council of Europe is at stake:[25] in these cases the ECtHR does not consider itself competent to assess whether procedural rights are respected in the State of origin, but to what extent the courts of a Contracting State, called upon to decide on the recognition and enforcement of those decisions, have applied a standard of control or review of what happened in origin that is compatible with the standards of the Convention.

#28 Beyond a general presumption of respect for fundamental rights, the European institutions are concerned with increasing trust between the judicial systems of

20 Case C-216/18 PPU *LM/Minister for Justice and Equality (Défaillances du système judiciaire)* (25 July 2018) ECLI:EU:C:2018:586.

21 Cases C-404/15 and C-659/15 PPU *Aranyosi and Căldăraru* GC (5 April 2016) ECLI:EU:C:2016:198; Case C-220/18 PPU *Generalstaatsanwaltschaft Bremen* (25 July 2018) ECLI:EU:C:2018:589; Case C-128/18 *Dorobantu* GC (15 October 2019) ECLI:EU:C:2019:857.

22 Cases C-411/10 *N.S. v Secretary of State for the Home Department* and C-493/10 *M.E. and others v Refugee Applications Commissioner* and *Minister for Justice, Equality and Law Reform* GC (21 December 2011) ECLI:EU:C:2011:865; Case C-163/17 *Abubacarr Jawo v Bundesrepublik Deutschland* (19 March 2019) ECLI:EU:C:2019:218.

23 As in *Health Service Executive* (n 9).

24 *Povse v Austria* App no 3890/11 (ECtHR, 18 June 2013); *Avotiņš v Latvia* App no 17502/07 (ECtHR, 23 May 2016).

25 *Dolenc v Slovenia* App no 20256/20 (ECtHR, 20 October 2022); *Pellegrini v Italy* App no 30882/96 (ECHR, 20 July 2001).

Member States from a more **functional perspective**, that of their effectiveness and efficiency, as this is the key to sustaining the system and making progress in integration. For this reason, European institutions monitor the functioning of national justice systems through various tools: the most relevant is the **EU Justice Scoreboard**, which has been consolidated for more than a decade[26] and serves to analyse the indicators that are considered relevant. In some cases, the focus is on issues affecting efficiency (caseload, estimated length of proceedings, resolution rates, among others); but also on the quality of justice (in terms of access to courts and **ADR** methods, financial resources, number of judges per inhabitant or **digitalisation**) and **judicial independence** (in 2024 and 2025, eg, with a clear concern for how companies perceive the independence of judges and courts and its impact on the effectiveness of investment protection). These factors also have an impact on the trust that is needed to legitimise a deepening of mutual recognition. Regarding the latter, a specific tool has also been developed, the Rule of Law mechanism and the Rule of Law Reports. The results of such monitoring serve to formulate **recommendations** for improvements, especially in the European Semester, but also in the evaluation of 'Resilience and Next Generation' plans. The ultimate goal of enhancing mutual trust is also promoted by significantly funding projects and action grants to improve the functioning of national justice systems, with a particular emphasis, in recent years, on digitisation (only extensive national digitisation will make European plans to digitise intra-European **judicial cooperation** possible).[27]

D Limits to Mutual Recognition and Mutual Trust: Grounds for Refusal, Prohibition of Review on the Merits and Decisions Capable of Recognition

#29 Except in very specific cases, ECPL makes the validity of mutual recognition compatible with the establishment of a list of **grounds for refusal** of recognition, ex-

---

26 A Dori, 'The EU Justice Scoreboard – Judicial Evaluation as a New Governance Tool' [2015] *MPILux Working Paper* 2; A Dori, 'The Supply and Demand of Justice: What Policy Implications from the EU Justice Scoreboard?' in E Storskrubb (ed), *YSEC Yearbook of Socio-Economic Constitutions 2022 – Funding of Justice* (Springer 2023) 53; A Dori, 'The Methodological Influence of European Private International Law on Domestic Legal Systems: A Downstream Analysis' in X Kramer and L Carballo Piñeiro (eds), *Research Methods in Private International Law. A Handbook on Regulation, Research and Teaching* (Edward Elgar 2024) 200 (esp. at 206–208 and 209–213); A Dori, *The Governance of EU Justice Reforms. The Role of the EU Justice Scoreboard and Country-Specific Recommendations in Shaping National Judicial Systems* (Nomos 2025).
27 European E-Justice Strategy 2024-2028 (15509/2023). Cf F Gascón Inchausti, 'The New Regulation on the Digitalisation of Judicial Cooperation in the European Union: Something Old, Something New, Something Borrowed and Something Blue' (2023) 24 ERA Forum 535.

equatur and/or enforcement – where there is no exequatur. Where enforceability is at stake and the exequatur subsists, the concurrence of one of these grounds may prevent the decision from being declared enforceable. In other cases, it is the burden of the affected party to assert that the foreign judgment should not be effective because of a ground for non-recognition or non-enforcement. These grounds thus represent the filters that States impose on the effectiveness of foreign decisions: they are the limits to mutual recognition and the boundaries to its automaticity. Each instrument contains its own catalogue of grounds for refusal: their greater or lesser extent depends on the instrument's approach, as well as on the subject matter. They are more numerous in cooperation than in second-generation instruments; and, among the former, they are also more numerous in **family law** than in patrimonial matters. The choice of mutual recognition as a principle has two consequences: (i) the list is closed, so no grounds for refusal of recognition other than those provided for by the relevant instrument may be applied;[28] (ii) the interpretation of the grounds for refusal of recognition must be restrictive.

#30 Within this catalogue, the infringement of the **public policy** of the requested Member State is usually granted a specific value, considering it as an **'emergency brake'**.[29] The European legislator has not been able to avoid the inertia of including it, except sporadically (it does not operate in the second generation instruments, with the exception of the EAPO). Its practical application, however, is very limited,[30] partly because the CJEU has repeatedly pointed out that it is a ground that can only be invoked exceptionally, in cases where the recognition or enforcement of the judgment given in another Member State clashes in an unacceptable manner with the legal order of the requested Member State, by undermining a **fundamental principle**[31] and assuming that the general rule is the debtors' burden to defend themselves in the Member State of origin.[32] The Court is also torn between the general proclamation that an autonomous definition of public policy is not possible and the need to give full effect to the objectives pursued by ECPL itself.[33]

---

28 Case C-139/10 *Prism Investments* (13 October 2011) ECLI:EU:C:2011:653; Case C-386/17 *Liberato* (16 January 2019) ECLI:EU:C:2019:24.

29 M Hazelhorst, *Free Movement of Civil Judgments in the European Union and the Right to a Fair Trial* (Springer/Asser 2017) 279–343.

30 B Hess and T Pfeiffer, *Interpretation of the Public Policy Exception as Referred to in EU Instruments of Private International and Procedural Law*, European Parliament Study PE 453.189 (2011).

31 Case C-7/98 *Krombach* (28 March 2000) ECLI:EU:C:2000:164, para 37; Case C-38/98 *Renault* (11 May 2000) ECLI:EU:C:2000:225, para 30; Case C-420/07 *Apostolides* (28 April 2009) ECLI:EU:C:2009:271, para 59; Case C-633/22 *Real Madrid Club de Fútbol* (4 October 2024) ECLI:EU:C:2024:843, para 37.

32 Case C-681/13 *Diageo Brands* (16 July 2015) ECLI:EU:C:2015:471; Case C-559/14 *Meroni* (25 May 2016) ECLI:EU:C:2016:349, paras 47-50.

33 Very recently, in Case C-590/21 *Charles Taylor Adjusting* (7 September 2023) ECLI:EU:C:2023:633, the Court considered (para 39) that 'quasi anti suit injunctions' (ie, decisions ordering to pay provisional damages for infringement of a choice of court agreement) violate mutual trust and, thus, public policy:

#31 The existence of 'limits to limits' must also be taken into account. The clearest is the **prohibition of review on the merits**, which is present in all instruments[34] and which is a basic and classic rule in matters of international (not only European) civil procedure: the controls imposed on foreign decisions may under no circumstances entail an assessment of the quality of the decisions.[35] Similarly, the court of the State in which enforcement is sought cannot review the accuracy of the findings of law or fact made by the court of the State of origin.[36] This point is reminiscent of the times when these matters were subject to rules of reciprocity and comity. Some instruments, in fact, go even further and expressly prohibit refusing recognition on the grounds that, under the law of the requested Member State, the result would have been different (Article 70 Brussels II-ter). The CJEU itself constantly warns that the public policy test cannot become a formula for circumventing the prohibition of review on the merits.

#32 Another way of imposing limits has also been developed, through the determination of what is meant by **'decision'** for the purposes of recognition and enforcement. Even if, for many purposes, arbitral awards are equivalent to judgments, they are not included here, even if the arbitration was developed in a Member State and according to that Member State's statutes: arbitration does not lie within the scope of ECPL instruments and, hence, the mutual trust underpinning them does not apply to arbitral awards. This was recalled by the CJEU in its decision *London Steamship Owners' Mutual Insurance* (see also further in text #34). The legal texts and/or the case law of the CJEU have excluded certain types of decisions from the scope of the relevant regulation and their recognition will, where appropriate, be subject to the internal legal regime. The reasons for the exclusion – imposing limits on recognition – are linked to the incompatibility with the values and principles of the ECPL.

#33 The formula is well visible in connection with **provisional and protective measures**. In *Denilauler*[37] and *Mærsk Olie & Gas*[38] the CJEU held that provisional measures taken without a prior hearing and without subsequent service on the debtor were not decisions that could circulate under the Brussels Convention. Later, in *Mietz*[39] and *Purrucker*,[40] it also excluded from this legal notion of a decision those taken by a court without jurisdiction as to the merits of the case (ie by virtue of the rule currently contained in Articles 35 Brussels I-bis, 15(1) Brussels II-ter, 14

even if it is not an autonomous notion of public policy, the Court has created a specific example of public policy infringement applicable in all Member States.

34 Articles 52 BR-Ia, 71 BR-IIb, 42 Maint-R, 41 Succ-R, 40 MPR-R, 40 PCRP-R, 21(2) EEO-R, 22(2) ESCP-R or 22(3) EOP-R.

35 *Renault* (n 31) para 33; *Diageo Brands* (n 32) paras 48-52; *Real Madrid Club de Fútbol* (n 31) para 36.

36 *Apostolides* (n 31) para 58; *Real Madrid Club de Fútbol* (n 31) para 36.

37 Case C-125/79 *Denilauler v Couchet Frères* (21 May 2000) ECLI:EU:C:1980:130.

38 Case C-39/02 *Mærsk Olie & Gas* (4 October 2004) ECLI:EU:C:2004:615, paras 48–51.

39 Case C-99/96 *Hans-Hermann Mietz v Intership Yachting Sneek BV* (27 April 1999) ECLI:EU:C:1999:202.

40 Case C-256/09 *Purrucker* (15 July 2010) ECLI:EU:C:2010:437, in matrimonial and parental responsibility matters.

Maint-R, 19 Succ-R, 19 MPR-R and 19 PCRP-R). These rulings have subsequently been given legal status (Article 2 a) BR-Ibis and Article 2.1 b) Brussels II-ter; Article 131 Regulation 2017/1001 on EU trade mark).

#34 It has also pointed out that **decisions that merely approve a settlement** between the parties are not decisions for these purposes (*Solo Kleinmotoren*);[41] this exclusion would perhaps be more questionable if the settlement has been subject to a thorough judicial review for approval.[42] In a related vein, the CJEU has considered in *H Limited* as a decision, for the purposes of EU-circulation, an order for payment issued on the basis of final judgments rendered in a third State[43]; the Court has also ruled in *London Steamship Owners' Mutual Insurance* that a judgment entered in the terms of an arbitral award can be regarded as a judgment impeding recognition and enforcement of an irreconcilable decision given in another Member State.[44]

#35 These decisions are closely connected with an additional limit, the **prohibition of double exequatur** (*exequatur sur exequatur ne vaut*), which excludes the circulation of judgments whose scope and content is limited to proclaiming the recognition or declaring the enforceability of a different decision originating from a third State. The CJEU rulings in *H Limited* and *London Steam-Ship Owners' Mutual Insurance* have been criticised for this very reason, since the judgments considered in these cases were not given on the merits after a self-standing examination by a court of a Member State.[45]

E Effects of Recognition and of the Declaration of Enforceability

I General Rules: Extension of Effects and Adaptation

#36 Both **recognition** and, where necessary, **declaration of enforceability** of a judgment enable it to produce effects in other Member States. It is often discussed whether the effects of the judgment in the State of origin are transferred or ex-

41 Case C-414/92 *Solo Kleinmotoren/Boch* (2 June 1994) ECLI:EU:C:1994:221.

42 B Hess and others, *The Reform of the Brussels Ibis Regulation – Academic Position Paper* (2024) Vienna Research Paper, 3 <https://ssrn.com/abstract=4853421> accessed 1 June 2024.

43 Case C-568/20 *H Limited* (7 April 2022) ECLI:EU:C:2022:264. The judgment is a little Kafkaesque, however, as it points to the possibility of opposing enforcement on grounds of breach of public policy if the rights of the defence have been seriously infringed in the third State that issued the final decisions that form the basis for the one now being enforced. It is interesting to note how the Court rejects any restrictive interpretation of the notion of judgment, in line with the restrictive nature of everything that entails a limit to circulation (paras 29f).

44 Case C-700/20 *London Steam-Ship Owners'Mutual Insurance Association Limited* (22 June 2022) ECLI:EU:C:2022:488.

45 Hess and others (n 42) 22-24.

tended through recognition and, if necessary, exequatur (extension or *Wirkungserstreckung*), or whether recognition serves to 'equate' the foreign judgment with a possible equivalent judgment given in the State of destination (assimilation, *Gleichstellung* or *Nostrifizierung*). The debate is complex and nuanced. In ECPL it must be considered settled by the CJEU in favour of the notion of **extension**, which stated in *Hoffmann*[46] that '[a] foreign judgment which has been recognised by virtue of Article 26 of the Convention must in principle have the same effects in the State in which enforcement is sought as it does in the State in which the judgment was given' This view has been confirmed in subsequent decisions,[47] although the wording of the regulations on this issue remains mostly 'neutral', referring in a generic way to the recognition of judgments (but not to their effects) or to their enforceability (without specification). Exceptionally, Article 11 EEO-R (for European enforcement orders) and Article 47(5) Brussels II-ter (for privileged decisions on access and return) are more openly in favour of the extension of effects, stating that certificates 'shall take effect only within the limits of the enforceability of the judgment'.

#37 What the proper **effects of a decision** are is a matter for the procedural law of the State of origin, since the regulations on cooperation do not determine the conditions under which judgments are to be enforceable,[48] have the force of res judicata or have other effects.[49] Something similar happens with **second generation instruments**: part of the effects of judgments is regulated by European law (eg the provisional enforceability of judgments given in a ESCP: Article 15(1)), but the rest is covered by the generic reference to national procedural law. It should be possible, therefore, that recognition attaches effects to foreign judgments that are not associated with equivalent national judgments (eg, if a non-final judgment is enforceable in the State of origin but would not be enforceable if it had been delivered in the State of enforcement); the CJEU, however, seems reluctant to accept this conclusion without restrictions.[50]

46 Case C-145/86 *Hoffmann/Krieg* (4 February 1988) ECLI:EU:C:1988:61. See Franzina (n 1) 13.20–13.56; B Hess, *Europäisches Zivilprozessrecht* (2nd edn, DeGruyter 2020) 436-439.

47 Among others, *Apostolides* (n 31); *Prism Investments* (n 28); *Gothaer* (n 3); *Health Service Executive* (n 9) in parental responsibility matters; more recently, case C-567/21 *BNP Paribas* (8 June 2023) ECLI:EU:C:2023:452.

48 Cases C-208/20 and C-256/20 *Toplofikatsia Sofia* (9 September 2021) ECLI:EU:C:2021:719, para 37: 'As that regulation does not determine the conditions in which judicial decisions become enforceable or the conditions governing the validity of those decisions, those conditions, therefore, fall within the procedural autonomy of the Member States'.

49 In *BNP Paribas* (n 47) para 50, the CJEU addressed the preclusive effect linked to a national rule on the centralisation of claims, requiring the parties to centralise all their claims relating to the same legal relationship within a single set of proceedings, failing which they will be inadmissible. In the Court's view such a rule 'is not intended to govern the authority and effectiveness accorded to a judgment in the Member State in which it was given' and is not therefore subject to recognition. See also French *Cour de Cassation* 19 June 2024 pourvoi n° 19-23-298, ECLI:FR:CCASS:2024:C100342.

50 *Apostolides* (n 31) para 66: 'although recognition must have the effect, in principle, of conferring on judgments the authority and effectiveness accorded to them in the Member State in which they

#38 Since national procedural systems are different, the rule of extension of effects may be problematic when it comes to recognising and/or enforcing a foreign judgment containing a **measure or order that does not exist in the requested State**. This may be the case with provisional and protective measures;[51] with certain decisions on the merits, such as injunctions in personam and injunctions in rem; with coercive measures, such as *astreintes*, that may not exist in the State of enforcement or operate differently – depending on whether the beneficiary is the enforcing party or the State; and, at least in some jurisdictions, even with monetary judgments, if the precise amount to be paid is not concretised in the judgment itself (similarly to what is established in Article 54 Brussels II-ter).[52]

#39 For this type of situation, Article 54 BR-Ibis contains a mandate for **adaptation**, which seeks to prevent legal disparities from becoming obstacles to the free circulation of judgments.[53] Specifically, the measure or order which is unknown in the legal system of the requested Member State shall be adapted to the extent possible to a measure or order known in the law of that State which has equivalent effects and pursues similar aims and interests. As a limit, the adaptation shall not result in effects going beyond those provided for in the law of the Member State of origin. This combination of extension of effects and assimilation is not established in the other regulations, but the criterion underlying Article 54 BR-Ibis is a

were given (see Hoffmann, paragraphs 10 and 11), there is however no reason for granting to a judgment, when it is enforced, rights which it does not have in the Member State of origin (see the Jenard Report on the Convention on Jurisdiction and the Enforcement of Judgments in Civil and Commercial Matters (OJ 1979 C 59, p. 48) or *effects that a similar judgment given directly in the Member State in which enforcement is sought would not have.*' Also in case C-379/17 *Società Immobiliare Al Bosco* (4 October 2018) ECLI:EU:C:2018:806, para 40 and in *BNP Paribas* (n 47) para 52.

51 Spanish authorities rejected the registration in the Land Registry of an *inscription hypothécaire judiciaire provisoire* ordered by a French *tribunal de commerce*, stressing that this protective measure was alien to the Spanish legal and registry system, despite its obvious similarities with the *anotación preventiva de embargo* (cf Decision of the *Dirección General de los Registros y del Notariado* of 12 May 1992, RAJ 1992/4847). The same happened with a *Sicherungshypothek* grantes by a German court (Decision of the *Dirección General de los Registros y del Notariado* of 23 February 2004, RJ 2004 \5295).

52 See also Hovaguimian (n 16) 230f. As described in Hess and others (n 42) 45–47, this lack of concretisation may amount to an obstacle for enforcement in some Member States. They suggest, therefore, to a provision to Article 54 BR-Ia allowing the authorities competent for enforcement or the courts of the Member State of enforcement to concretise the operational part of the judgment, if the necessary concretisations have not at all or have not sufficiently been made by the courts of the Member State of origin, provided the essential elements of this decision are respected.

53 It originates from case C-235/09 *DHL Express France* (12 April 2011) ECLI:EU:C:2011:238, concerning difficulties arising from the enforcement of a French *astreinte* in another Member State. See also E Vallines García, 'Article 54' in M Requejo Isidro (ed), *Brussels I bis. A Commentary on Regulation (EU) No 1215/2012* (Edward Elgar 2022) 735; J Fitchen, 'The Recognition and Enforcement of Member State Judgments' in A Dickinson and E Lein (eds), *The Brussels I Regulation Recast* (OUP 2015) 505, paras 13.482 ff.

standard of ECPL: national differences must not become obstacles to proper interaction and coordination of the judicial systems and to achieving the maximum level of cross-border **effectiveness** of judicial decisions.

II Limitation Periods

#40 The rule of the extension of effects may also cause problems as regards the **limitation periods** of the enforcement action. There are striking divergences in the legal systems of Member States as to the time margin available to the successful party in civil proceedings to seek enforcement.[54] What to do when enforcement is not time barred under the law of origin but would be time barred under the law of destination, or vice versa?

#41 The question has been raised on several occasions and has not received a homogeneous answer at the domestic level. The Swiss Federal Court, in a judgment of 2 August 2022,[55] considered that the law governing the time limit to enforce a foreign judgment is that of the State of origin; if enforcement of the judgment is time barred in its state of origin, it should not be enforceable abroad, either. This solution is consistent with the extension of effects doctrine, because the enforceability of judgments is established by the procedural law of the issuing State. The Spanish Supreme Court, in a judgment of 16 October 2014,[56] had opted to apply the national limitation period of five years to a Finnish judgment, despite the fact that Finnish law does not impose such a time limitation.[57] Also in a different way,

---

54 In some cases procedural rules establish specific time limits (eg, 5 years in Spain), in others the general limitation periods for the rights at stake in the merits of the case apply: 30 years in Austria; 10 years in Belgium; 2 years in Bulgaria; 15 years in Finland (20 if the creditor is a natural person); 10 years in France; 30 years in Germany; 20 years in Greece; 12 years in Ireland (may be reduced to 6); 3 years in Romania; 10 or 30 years in Luxembourg (depending on whether the case is civil or commercial); 10 years in Malta; 6 years in the United Kingdom; and indefinitely in Portugal. See F Gascón Inchausti and M Requejo Isidro, 'A Classic Cross-border Case: The Usual Situation in the First Instance' in B Hess and P Ortolani (eds), *Impediments of National Procedural Law to the Free Movement of Judgments. Luxembourg Report on European Procedural Law. Volume I* (Hart/Nomos/Beck 2019) 143.

55 BGE 148 III 420ff.

56 ECLI: ES:TS:2014:4838.

57 The rule has in fact, been incorporated into the Spanish Act on International Legal Cooperation in Civil Matters (Article 50.2), which is not applicable to the circulation of decisions from the European Area of Justice. The Spanish Supreme Court found it shocking that foreign judgments were enforced, which, had they been Spanish, would have already had their enforceability time-barred. To avoid this apparently discriminatory result, it decided to apply the domestic rule, arguing that a period of five years is more than sufficient to apply for enforcement. This reasoning, however, is not necessarily valid in a cross-border context (who knows how long the creditor had been trying to enforce the judgment in Finland or other countries before discovering that there were attachable assets in Spain?).

the French *Cour de Cassation* confirmed in its judgment of 11 January 2023[58] that the 10-year time limit laid down in the *Code des procédures d'exécution* applies to foreign decisions, arguing that what is actually enforced is the French decision granting enforceability to the foreign decision (an argument, however, more difficult to sustain for decisions that do not need exequatur to be enforced). The possible loss of enforceability due to the passage of time in the State of origin, according to French case law, creates a problem of standing for the creditor to apply for enforcement, but not of time limits (again, questionable).[59] The CJEU, finally, seems to consider that procedural rules of the Member State of enforcement are applicable and that 'the courts of that Member State are not required to apply any provisions of the national legislation of the Member State of origin which, in respect of the enforcement of decisions given by the courts of the Member State of origin, lay down time limits which differ from those laid down by the law of the Member State in which enforcement is sought.'[60]

#42 Given the divergences, **harmonising action** at European level would make sense, since the disparity of time limits and criteria can undermine the reasonable expectations of creditors in possession of fully effective enforceable titles under the law of their State of origin. The only specific European provision is Article 21(2) Maint-R, that proposes the application of the longest time limit, to the benefit of the maintenance creditor.[61]

III Potential or Actual Loss of Effects in Member States of Origin

#43 It is equally possible that a judgment, already recognised, declared enforceable or even enforced in another Member State, **loses its effects in the State of origin** as a result of an appeal or some extraordinary mechanism of review. It may therefore be necessary to address the impact on recognition and enforcement of the loss at origin of the effects that a judgment is already having at destination. The ECPL offers a partial solution to this type of situation.

58 Pourvoi n° 21-21.168, ECLI:FR:CCASS:2023:C100073.

59 See G Cuniberti, 'Time Limitations Affecting Foreign Judgments' [2024] IPRax 1.

60 *Società Immobiliare Al Bosco* (n 50) para 36. It is important to note, however, that the decision at stake was not a judgment on the merits, but a preventive attachment order; the function of deadlines to enforce such orders is subject to a very different rationale, compared to that of judgments on the merit. Critically, see G Chiapponi, 'Article 39' in M Requejo Isidro (ed), *Brussels I bis. A Commentary on Regulation (EU) No 1215/2012* (Edward Elgar 2022) 577, para 39.22.

61 More specifically, it provides for refusal of enforcement 'if the right to enforce the decision of the court of origin is extinguished by the effect of prescription or the limitation of action, either under the law of the Member State of origin or under the law of the Member State of enforcement, whichever provides for the longer limitation period'.

#44 It does so, firstly, when two circumstances concur simultaneously: (i) the decision has not yet lost its effectiveness at origin, but there is a risk that it will lose it, because it has been challenged; and (ii) the judicial proceedings in which the effects of the decision are sought to be deployed are still in progress, whether these are declaratory proceedings, proceedings for the declaration of enforceability or enforcement proceedings. In these circumstances, the court may **stay the proceedings** at hand pending the outcome in the State of origin.[62] Thus, declaratory proceedings in which the res judicata, evidentiary or declaratory effect of a final foreign judgment is sought to be asserted may be stayed pending the challenge in the State of origin. And it is also possible to stay the exequatur proceedings or the enforcement proceedings whose enforceable title was the foreign judgment affected by the challenge in its State of origin. The stay is not imposed but is a possibility offered to the court, depending on the circumstances of the case. Once the challenge in the State of origin has been concluded the suspended proceedings in the State of destination will be resumed or discontinued depending on the outcome. In the case of the enforcement of an EEO, an EOP or a judgment in an ESCP the stay of enforcement is an exceptional option, to be used only if it is not possible or sufficient to limit the enforcement procedure to **protective measures** or to make it subject to the **provision of security**.[63] In the case of an EAPO, and given the inherent provisional nature of the situation, the relevant factor is not the original challenge but the loss of enforceability of the judgment whose enforcement the creditor sought to secure by means of the order: in such a case, moreover, the consequence will not be the suspension of the enforcement of the order but its immediate termination.[64]

#45 Except for the latter cases, there is no express solution in the European instruments when the judgment has **already lost its effectiveness** in the State of origin, because it has been revoked in the context of an ordinary appeal or an extraordinary mechanism of review that has taken place after its enforcement or after final conclusion of the proceedings in which its effects were asserted in the State of destination. In these cases, the specific rules for this type of situation of the State of destination – where the judgment unfolded its effects – will have to be applied: eg, promoting the review of the judgment rendered on the basis of the res judicata of the foreign decision, which later lost it; claiming compensation for the debtor who endured enforcement based on a foreign title that was later revoked. Paradoxically, judgments given in the Member State of origin that determine the final loss of effectiveness of the original judgment will in turn be recognised, insofar as they are the basis for obtaining the corresponding remedies.

62 See Articles 38, 44(2) and 51 Brussels I-bis; Articles 33(a), 44, 56(2) and 63 Brussels II-ter; Articles 21(3), 25 and 35 Maint-R; Articles 42 and 53 Succ-R; Articles 41 and 52 MPR-R; and Articles 41 and 52 PCRC-R.

63 Articles 23 EEO-R, EOP-R and ESCP-R.

64 Article 34(1)(b)(iii) EAPO-R.

#46 Nonetheless, a few instruments foresee for these situations a **specific mechanism** to demonstrate that the judgment has lost its effectiveness, as a way of facilitating the reversal of effects or the equivalent remedy that may be appropriate. Article 6(2) EEO-R provides for a certificate to attest that the judgment previously certified as a EEO has ceased to be enforceable or that its enforceability has been suspended or limited. The same is done by Article 49 Brussels II-ter for the 'privileged' decisions granting rights of access and on the **return of children**.

References

Beaumont P and Johnston E, 'Can Exequatur Be Abolished in Brussels I whilst Retaining a Public Policy Defence?' (2010) 6 Journal of Private International Law 249.

Biavati P, 'Judicial Cooperation in Europe: Is Exequatur Still Necessary?' (2011) 2 International Journal of Procedural Law 403.

Chiapponi G, 'Article 39' in M Requejo Isidro (ed), *Brussels I bis: A Commentary on Regulation (EU) No 1215/2012* (Edward Elgar 2022) 577.

Cuniberti G, 'Some Remarks on the Efficiency of Exequatur' in H Kronke and K Thorn (eds), *Grenzen überwinden – Prinzipien bewahren: Festschrift für Bernd von Hoffmann* (Gieseking 2011) 568.

—— 'Time Limitations Affecting Foreign Judgments' [2024] IPRax 1.

D'Alessandro E and Gascón Inchausti F (eds), *The European Account Preservation Order: A Commentary on Regulation (EU) No 655/2014* (Edward Elgar 2022).

Dalfino D, 'Un giudicato «europeo» sulla competenza giurisdizionale?' [2013/2014] Int'l Lis 16.

De Cristofaro M, 'The Abolition of Exequatur Proceedings: Speeding Up the Free Movement of Judgments while Preserving the Rights of the Defense' (2011) 2 International Journal of Procedural Law 432.

Dickinson A and Lein E (eds), *The Brussels I Regulation Recast* (OUP 2015)

Domej T, 'Die Neufassung der EuGVVO. Quantensprünge im europäischen Zivilprozessrecht' (2014) 78 RabelsZ 508.

Dori A, 'The EU Justice Scoreboard – Judicial Evaluation as a New Governance Tool' [2015] *MPILux Working Paper* 2.

—— 'The Supply and Demand of Justice: What Policy Implications from the EU Justice Scoreboard?' in E Storskrubb (ed), *YSEC Yearbook of Socio-Economic Constitutions* [2022] 53

—— 'The Methodological Influence of European Private International Law on Domestic Legal Systems: A Downstream Analysis' in X Kramer and L Carballo Piñeiro (eds), *Research Methods in Private International Law. A Handbook on Regulation, Research and Teaching* (Edward Elgar 2024) 200.

—— The Governance of EU Justice Reforms. The Role of the EU Justice Scoreboard and Country-Specific Recommendations in Shaping National Judicial Systems, (Nomos 2025).

Fitchen J, 'The Recognition and Enforcement of Member State Judgments' in A Dickinson and E Lein (eds), *The Brussels I Regulation Recast* (OUP 2015) 505–510.

Frackowiak-Adamska A, 'Time for a European «full faith and credit clause»' (2015) 52 Common Market Law Review 191.

Franzina P, 'The Recognition and Enforcement of Member States Judgments' in A Dickinson and E Lein (eds), *The Brussels I Regulation Recast* (OUP 2015) 373.

Gascón Inchausti F and Hess B (eds), *The Future of the European Law of Civil Procedure: Coordination or Harmonisation?* (Intersentia 2020).

Gascón Inchausti F and Requejo Isidro M, 'A Classic Cross-border Case: The Usual Situation in the First Instance' in B Hess and P Ortolani (eds), *Impediments of National Procedural Law to the Free Movement of Judgments. Luxembourg Report on European Procedural Law. Volume I* (Hart/Nomos/Beck 2019) 143.

Gascón Inchausti F, 'The New Regulation on the Digitalisation of Judicial Cooperation in the European Union: Something Old, Something New, Something Borrowed and Something Blue' (2023) 24 ERA Forum 535.

—— 'Have the EU Regulations on Judicial Cooperation Fostered Harmonisation of National Procedures?' in Fernando Gascón Inchausti and Burkhard Hess (eds), *The Future of the European Law of Civil Procedure: Coordination or Harmonisation?* (Intersentia 2020) 91.

Hazelhorst M, *Free Movement of Civil Judgments in the European Union and the Right to a Fair Trial* (Springer/Asser 2017).

Hess and others, *The Reform of the Brussels Ibis Regulation – Academic Position Paper* (2024) Vienna Research Paper <https://ssrn.com/abstract=4853421> accessed 1 June 2024.

Hess B and Pfeiffer T, *Interpretation of the Public Policy Exception as Referred to in EU Instruments of Private International and Procedural Law*, European Parliament Study PE 453.189 (2011).

Hess B, Pfeiffer T and Schlosser P, *Report on the Application of Regulation Brussels I in the Member States* (Study JLS/C4/2005/03) <http://ec.europa.eu/civiljustice/news/docs/study_application_brussels_1_en.pdf> accessed 1 June 2024.

Hess B, *Europäisches Zivilprozessrecht* (2nd edn, De Gruyter 2020).

Hovaguimian P, 'The Enforcement of Foreign Judgments under Brussels I bis: False Alarms and Real Concerns' (2015) 11 Journal of Private International Law 212.

Kramer X, 'Cross-Border Enforcement in the EU: Mutual Trust versus Fair Trial? Towards Principles of European Civil Procedure' (2011) International Journal of Procedural Law 202.

—— 'Cross-Border Enforcement and the Brussels I-Bis Regulation: Towards a New Balance Between Mutual Trust and National Control over Fundamental Rights' (2013) 60 Netherlands International Law Review 343.

Nylund A and Krans B (eds), *The European Union and National Civil Procedure* (Intersentia 2016).

Requejo Isidro M (ed), *Brussels I bis: A Commentary on Regulation (EU) No 1215/2012* (Edward Elgar 2022).

Roth H, 'Europäischer Rechtskraftbegriff im Zuständigkeitsrecht?' [2014] IPRax 2.

Timmer LJ, 'Abolition of Exequatur under the Brussels I Regulation: Ill Conceived and Premature?' (2013) 9 Journal of Private International Law 129.

Torralba Mendiola E and Rodríguez Pineau E, 'Two's a Company, Three's a Crowd: Jurisdiction, Recognition and Res Judicata in the European Union' (2014) 10 Journal of Private International Law 403.

Vallines García E, 'Article 54' in M Requejo Isidro (ed), *Brussels I bis: A Commentary on Regulation (EU) No 1215/2012* (Edward Elgar 2022) 735.

Voss W, 'Article 36' in M Requejo Isidro (ed), *Brussels I bis: A Commentary on Regulation (EU) No 1215/2012* (Edward Elgar 2022) 548.

Weller M, 'Mutual Trust: In Search of the Future of European Union Private International Law' (2015) 11 Journal of Private International Law 64.

Zilinsky M, 'Trust and Cross-Border Enforcement of Judgments in Civil Matters in the EU: Does the Step-by-Step Approach Work?' (2017) 64 Netherlands International Law Review 115.

Wolfgang Hau*

Chapter 13
Recognition and Enforcement of Civil and Commercial Judgments

A Introduction

#1 A common market cannot function without **free movement of civil and commercial judgments**. What seems self-evident today was already clear to the six Contracting States of the Treaty of Rome establishing the European Economic Community of 1957, when they agreed to facilitate the recognition and enforcement of court decisions and arbitration awards (Article 220 EEC Treaty). The resulting **Brussels Convention of 1968**[1] was groundbreaking in its endeavour to achieve orderly cross-border cooperation and coordination in civil and commercial matters: This visionary instrument did not simply order 'mutual trust' between the national courts involved, but, together with the mostly wise interpretation by the ECJ, has contributed to the development of this trust over the years. The Brussels Convention was later replaced by the **Brussels I Regulation 44/2001**,[2] which in turn has been superseded by the **Brussels I-bis Regulation 1215/2012**,[3] as applicable since 10 January 2015.[4] Compared to the Brussels Convention, the Brussels I Regulation already limited the grounds for refusal of recognition and further accelerated the exequatur procedure; the Brussels I-bis Regulation then abolished the exequatur requirement and functionally replaced it with a new review procedure (for details, see # 33 ff).[5]

1 Original version: [1972] OJ L299/32; consolidated version: [1998] OJ C27/1.

2 [2001] OJ L12/1.

3 [2012] OJ L351/1.

4 On the temporal scope of application, see Article 66 Brussels I-bis Regulation and below # 26.

5 For further reading on the principles, background and details of the Brussel I-bis rules on recognition and enforcement, refer to: M Berglund, *Cross-Border Enforcement of Claims in the EU: History, Present Time and Future* (2nd edn, Wolters Kluwer 2014); G Cuniberti, 'Making Cross-Border Enforcement More Efficient for Creditors' in J von Hein and T Kruger (eds), *Informed Choices in Cross-Border Enforcement* (Intersentia 2021) 413; F Gascón Inchausti, 'Ensuring Adequate Protection in Cross-Border Enforcement for Debtors, Especially Consumers', in J von Hein and T Kruger T (eds), *Informed Choices in Cross-Border Enforcement* (Intersentia 2021) 429; P Hovaguimian, 'The Enforcement of Foreign Judgments under Brussels I bis: False Alarms and Real Concerns' (2015) 11 Journal of Private International Law 212; X Kramer, 'Cross-border Enforcement and the Brussels I-Bis Regulation: Towards a New Balance Between Mutual Trust and National Control Over Fundamental Rights' (2013) Netherlands Inter-

***Corresponding author: Wolfgang Hau**, Ludwig Maximilian University of Munich,
e-mail: wolfgang.hau@lmu.com

https://doi.org/10.1515/9783110781632-013

#2 The material scope of the Brussels I-bis Regulation (and, correspondingly, this chapter) is limited to **civil and commercial matters** as defined in Article 1.[6] While the following presentation will mainly focus on the recognition and enforcement of **judgments** (see Article 2(a)), it shall be mentioned from the outset that the Brussels I-bis Regulation also provides for rules on enforceable **authentic instruments** (Articles 2(c) and 58) and **court settlements** (Articles 2(b) and 59). Special chapters in this book examine the recognition and enforcement of provisional and protective measures (including account preservation orders), European orders for payment, and judgments resulting from the European small claims procedure.[7]

#3 While the Brussels I-bis Regulation deals with the relevance of parallel or related actions pending in Member States (Articles 29–32) and in third countries alike (Articles 33 and 34), its Articles 36 ff only apply to the recognition and enforcement of **judgments from other Member States** (ie all EU States, including Denmark[8]). In this respect, however, it is not relevant whether the judgment was given against a person domiciled in a Member State (see Recital 27[9]) and whether the court of the Member State of origin has based its international jurisdiction on the Regulation or on its national rules. Contrary to demands from the academic community,[10] the reform of the Brussels I Regulation was not used to introduce unified rules for the free movement of **non-EU judgments**.[11] What EU law does pro-

---

national Law Review 343; G Mäsch G and M Peiffer, 'New Enforcement Regime under the Brussels Ibis Regulation: Does the Paradigm Shift Help Judgment Creditors?' in J von Hein and T Kruger (eds), *Informed Choices in Cross-Border Enforcement* (Intersentia 2021) 31; M Requejo Isidro, 'The Enforcement of Monetary Final Judgments Under the Brussels Ibis Regulation (A Critical Assessment)' in V Lazić and S Stuij (eds), *Brussels Ibis Regulation: Changes and Challenges of the Renewed Procedural Scheme* (Asser 2017) 71; LJ Timmer, 'Abolition of Exequatur under the Brussels I Regulation: Ill Conceived and Premature?' (2013) 9 Journal of Private International Law 1293.

6 For details, see Chapter 10. On recognition and enforcement in family and succession matters and insolvency proceedings, which are excluded from the scope of application of the Brussels I-bis Regulation (Article 1(2)), see Chapters 14, 15 and 18.

7 See chapters 16 and 17.

8 See [2013] OJ L79/4 and [2014] OJ L240/1.

9 Articles 4–6 only define the scope of application of the Brussels I-bis Regulation's rules on international jurisdiction.

10 See the European Group for Private International Law's proposal to amend the Brussels I Regulation in order to apply it to external situations <https://gedip-egpil.eu/wp-content/uploads/2010/10/gedip-Bergen.pdf> accessed 17 September 2025.

11 For details, see W Hau, 'Unified European Rules on the Recognition and Enforceability of Third-Country Judgments' in Liber Amicorum Piet Taelman (Wolters 2025) 467; D Martiny, 'The Recognition and Enforcement of Court Decisions Between the EU and Third States' in A Trunk and N Hatzimihail (eds), *EU Civil Procedure Law and Third Countries* (Nomos 2021) 127; D Tsikrikas, 'The Recognition of the Effects of Foreign Judgments Between the EU and Third States' in A Trunk and N Hatzimihail (eds), *EU Civil Procedure Law and Third Countries* (Nomos 2021) 147.

vide for, however, are rules stipulating that Member States may not recognise and enforce judgments from third countries in certain cases.[12]

#4 The **Lugano Convention of 30 October 2007**[13] is an important addition to the EU rules for judgments, authentic instruments, and court settlements obtained in Iceland, Norway, or Switzerland; its provisions on recognition and enforcement (Articles 33 ff) essentially correspond to those of the Brussels I Regulation. Furthermore, the EU has ratified the **Hague Choice of Court Convention of 30 June 2005**[14] and the **Hague Judgments Convention of 2 July 2019.**[15] Even between EU Member States, the Brussels I-bis Regulation, at least in principle, does not affect rules on the recognition and enforcement provided for in **special multilateral treaties** (Article 71), such as Article 31 of the Geneva Convention of 19 May 1956 on the international carriage of goods by road.[16] However, within its scope of application, the Brussels I-bis Regulation supersedes bilateral agreements concluded between its Member States (Article 69) and arguably also national rules, even if these are exceptionally more favourable to recognition and enforcement than the Regulation itself.

B Recognition

I Recognition as Extension of Effects

#5 The centrepiece of Chapter III of the Brussels I-bis Regulation is its Article 36(1), which sets out the Member States' **obligation to recognise judgments** given in other Member States. In this context, recognition requires the extension of the effects that the judgment has in its 'Member State of origin' (cf Article 2(d)) to the territory of the other Member States (cf Article 2(e): the 'Member State addressed' or second state).

---

12 See Article 48 of the Regulation (EU) 2016/679 of 27 April 2016 on the protection of natural persons with regard to the processing of personal data [2016] OJ L119/1; Article 16 of the Directive (EU) 2024/1069 of 11 April 2024 on protecting persons who engage in public participation from manifestly unfounded claims or abusive court proceedings [2024] OJ L2024/1069.

13 [2007] OJ L339/3.

14 [2009] OJ L133/3. As of September 2025, this is relevant for judgments and judicial settlements from Albania, Bahrein, Mexico, the Republic of Moldova, Montenegro, North Macedonia, Singapore, Switzerland, Ukraine, and the United Kingdom.

15 [2022] OJ L187/4. As of September 2025, this is relevant for judgments and judicial settlements from Albania (from 1 March 2026 onwards), Andorra (from 1 June 2026 onwards), Montenegro (from 1 March 2026 onwards), Ukraine, the United Kingdom, and Uruguay.

16 Cf Case C-90/22 *Gjensidige* (21 March 2024) ECLI:EU:C:2024:252, paras 39ff.

#6 A significant consequence of this concept of recognition is that the effects of a foreign judgment can go beyond those that would apply under the procedural law of the second state to a judgment issued there. In principle (ie if the second state's public policy is not affected), the extension of such **'strong effects'** is to be accepted, because it is exactly these effects that the parties in the first state proceedings leading to the judgment could expect. This aspect is neglected by the less recognition-friendly 'cumulation theory', which denies that a foreign judgment can have more far-reaching effects than the second state would attach to a comparable domestic judgment. According to the prevailing opinion, the principle of the extension of effects is to be applied within the Brussels I-bis Regulation. However, the ECJ suggests a strange differentiation: It emphasises this concept as regards **recognition as such**, but departs from this line (and tacitly leans towards the 'cumulation theory') when free movement of judgments is particularly important in practice, namely when it comes to **enforceability**: "while recognition must have the effect, in principle, of conferring on foreign judgments the authority and effectiveness accorded to them in the Member State in which they were given, this is not the case when that judgment is being enforced on the ground that, during that stage, there is no reason for granting to a judgment rights which it does not have in the Member State of origin or effects that a similar judgment given directly in the Member State addressed would not have".[17]

#7 Sometimes the effects of a foreign judgment under its law of origin fall short of those under the law of the second state (**'weak effects'**). In this constellation, it would be incompatible with the right to be heard and a fair trial to insist on 'equivalence' of foreign and domestic judgments and thus impute effects to the foreign judgment in the Member State addressed that the parties did not expect in the foreign court proceedings. Regarding a specific question, but generalisable, the second subparagraph of Article 54(1) underlines that recognition cannot achieve an effect not envisaged in the Member State of origin.

II Recognisable Judgments and Recognisable Effects

#8 The Brussels I-bis Regulation deals with the recognition of judgments issued by **state courts**, as opposed to awards by (private or state) arbitration tribunals. The designation of the judgment provided for by the law of the Member State of origin

17 See Case C-567/21 *BNP Paribas v TR* (8 June 2023) ECLI:EU:C:2023:452, para 52 and the further case law cited there. For a critical assessment of this questionable distinction between recognition and enforceability, see H Linke and W Hau, *Internationales Zivilverfahrensrecht* (9th edn, Otto Schmidt 2024), paras 12.6ff.

is irrelevant (Article 2(a)).[18] Decisions issued by **non-judicial authorities** can also be recognised and enforced in so far as provided for in Article 3 Brussels I-bis Regulation; however, this provision (unlike Article 62 of the Lugano Convention) is exhaustive and therefore cannot be extended by analogy.[19]

#9 Recognition normally relates to the **merits of the foreign judgment**, such as the defendant's obligation to pay a certain amount of money to the successful plaintiff. But judgments dismissing an action and thereby denying the plaintiff's claim can also be recognised. In contrast, **mere 'procedural judgments'**, such as interim decisions on the admissibility or inadmissibility, are not recognisable. This, however, does not necessarily follow from the nature of such decisions, but rather from the fact that they normally have no effects relevant to recognition beyond the forum state.

#10 Foreign **judgments on the issue of international jurisdiction** deserve special attention. If, for example, a Japanese court renders a decision that the Japanese courts have exclusive international jurisdiction, this does not bind a court seised in a Member State. Conversely, if the Japanese court has dismissed the action because it only considers the Member States' courts to have international jurisdiction (eg based on a jurisdiction agreement), this decision should of course be considered, but it is not binding within the EU. In both constellations, an EU court must independently examine the question of jurisdiction and may reach another conclusion than the Japanese court. It has become doubtful, however, whether the same applies if the first judgment was given in another Member State. According to the ECJ, a German court must deny its international jurisdiction if the same action was previously dismissed in Belgium because the Belgian court assumed that only the courts of Iceland were competent to hear the case due to a valid jurisdiction agreement.[20] In its (rather questionable) reasoning, the ECJ referred to an autonomous and broad interpretation of the term 'judgment' (today: Article 2(a) Brussels I-bis Regulation), the principle of mutual trust and the fundamental prohibition of a review as to the merits, particularly in circumstances where the court in the first state has ruled that it had jurisdiction (today: Article 45(3) Brussels I-bis Regulation).[21]

#11 According to the traditional view, there is **no double exequatur:** a judgment that declares a judgment from another country to be recognisable or enforceable cannot be recognised or enforced as such. If, for example, a Canadian court has ruled that a US judgment is recognisable in Canada, but the US judgment is not recognis-

18 On default judgments, see Case C-619/10 *Trade Agency v Seramico Investments* (6 September 2012) ECLI:EU:C:2012:531.

19 Case C-551/15 *Pula Parking v Sven Klaus Tederahn* (March 2017) ECLI:EU:C:2017:193.

20 Case C-456/11 *Gothaer Allgemeine Versicherung* v *Samskip* (15 November 2012) ECLI:EU:C:2012:719.

21 For a new reference for a preliminary ruling in this context, see Bundesgerichtshof (Federal Court of Germany), Order of 24 October 2024 – Case VII ZR 199/22, ECLI:DE:BGH:2024:241024BVIIZR199.22.0.

able under the German rules, then no indirect recognition or enforcement of the US judgment takes place in Germany by recognising the Canadian decision. Recently, the ECJ has deviated from this traditional understanding: If a court of a Member State (in casu, before Brexit: the UK) has issued a payment order on the basis of a third-country judgment (in casu: from Jordan) in adversarial proceedings on the basis of a summary examination, according to the ECJ, the UK payment order incorporating the Jordanian judgment constitutes a judgment within the meaning of Article 2(a), which therefore is to be recognised and enforced in the other Member States (Articles 36(1) and 39).[22] This seems highly doubtful, because the ECJ, without plausible reasons, departs from the traditional autonomous definition of 'judgment' and undermines each Member State's competence to determine the requirements for the recognisability of judgments given in third states. Contrary to the ECJ, these concerns are not allayed by the fact that the public policy clause (Article 45(1)(a)) may limit the obligation to recognise in extreme cases.

#12 The main recognisable effect of a foreign judgment is **res judicata**: the decision becomes binding between the parties and the claim cannot be retried in the Member State of origin or, as a result of recognition, in any other forum.[23] Under the principle of extension of effects (see # 5 ff), the scope of res judicata (who is bound and how far-reaching are the binding effects?) is determined in accordance with the law of the Member State of origin. At least in principle (subject to Article 45(1)(a), ie the public policy of the Member State addressed), the same holds true for **preclusion effects** foreseen in the law of origin, which exclude the presentation of facts not relied upon in the first proceedings or which prevent the plaintiff from asserting further damages in separate proceedings.[24] Furthermore, **third-party related effects** are also recognisable. This becomes particularly evident in Article 65(2), which prescribes the recognition and enforcement of judgments given in actions on a warranty or guarantee or in other third-party proceedings (as mentioned in Article 8(2)).

22 Case C-568/20 *J v H limited* (7 April 2022) ECLI:EU:C:2022:264. For a critical analysis, see B Hess, 'Exequatur sur Exequatur (Ne) Vaut?' [2022] 42 IPRax 349.

23 For details on the concepts of res judicata, preclusion and similar binding effects of judgments, see O Chase and others, *Civil Litigation in Comparative Context* (2nd edn, West Academic 2017) 563ff (chapter 9).

24 However, the position taken here is not entirely in line with Case C-567/21 *BNP Paribas v TR* (8 June 2023) ECLI:EU:C:2023:452, where the ECJ suggests that such a preclusive effect is not necessarily recognisable under the Brussels I-bis rules even if it is provided for in the procedural law of both the Member State of origin and the Member State addressed. For a critical analysis, see W Hau, 'Having Two Bites at the Same Cherry?' [2024] IPRax 41.

III Procedure

#13 According to Article 36(1), a judgment given in a Member State shall be recognised in the other Member States **without any special procedure** being required. In other words, in order to facilitate EU-wide free movement of judgments, recognition comes about automatically (or 'ipso iure'). The **documents** to be produced by the party invoking recognition are set out in Article 37 (for the required certificate, see Article 53 and Annex I).

#14 If the outcome of proceedings in a court of a Member State depends on the refusal of recognition of another Member State's judgment, the court shall have jurisdiction over that **incidental issue** (Article 36(3)). Notwithstanding the ipso-iure principle and Article 36(3), the Regulation also provides for special procedures to clarify the question of eligibility for recognition: Article 36(2) allows an application for a **(positive) declaratory decision** stating that there are no grounds for refusal of recognition as referred to in Article 45. While this is relevant for 'any interested party' (ie any party interested in the recognition of the foreign judgment), the other party can apply for a **(negative) refusal of recognition** pursuant to Article 45 (for the procedural details, Article 45(4) refers to Articles 47 ff; see below # 36 ff). If both a positive recognition procedure (Article 36(2)) and a negative refusal procedure (Article 45) are initiated before different courts in the same Member State, it is supposed that the proceedings initiated later should be stayed and that the decision issued first becomes binding. Less clear is the relation between the positive recognition procedure or the negative refusal procedure on the one hand, and the incidental examination according to Article 36(3) on the other hand. The wide wording of the latter provision indicates that the incidental examination can lead to a positive or to a negative result as regards recognisability. However, the court dealing only incidentally with the issue should suspend its proceedings in accordance with Article 38(b) if either a positive recognition procedure or a negative refusal procedure is already pending.

C Grounds for Refusal of Recognition

I Basics

#15 As its wording already shows, Article 45(1) does not specify (positive) requirements for recognition, but rather grounds for refusal of recognition. Since this regulatory technique is no coincidence but was chosen with care, a default rule can be deduced from Articles 36(1) and 45(1): In principle, foreign decisions are to be perceived as recognisable, whereas **non-recognition is the exception** rather than the rule. In line with that, the ECJ interprets the grounds for refusal restrictively, because they constitute an obstacle to one of the main objectives of the Brussels I-bis Regulation, namely "to maintain and develop an area of freedom, security and justice by facilitating the free movement of judgments".[25] If full recognition fails, it is generally assumed that **partial recognition** should still be considered,[26] although this is not explicitly stated in the Brussels I-bis Regulation (but, for example, in Article 53 of the Brussels II-ter Regulation and Article 9 of the Hague Judgments Convention 2019).

II Review of Jurisdiction

#16 In principle, the question whether the court of the Member State of origin had jurisdiction either under the Regulation's own rules or via Article 6 under the national rules is not to be reviewed in the Member State addressed. Article 45(1)(e) lists only a few exceptions to this prohibition.[27] But even when a review of jurisdiction takes place, the court in the second state is bound by the **findings of fact** on which the court of origin based its jurisdiction (Article 45(2)). This clearly reflects the mutual trust that the courts in all Member States fulfil their obligation under Article 28 to examine their own jurisdiction.

#17 According to Article 45(1)(e)(i), the rules of jurisdiction in **insurance, consumer and employment matters** as foreseen in Sections 3 to 5 of Chapter II are subject to review, but this only applies in favour of the protected party (namely the policyholder, the consumer, or the employee). Moreover, Article 45(1)(e)(ii) mentions Section 6 of Chapter II (ie the heads of **exclusive jurisdiction** pursuant to Article 24), but remarkably not Article 25; in consequence, refusal of recognition cannot be based on the assumption that the foreign court was addressed in breach of an exclusive **jurisdiction agreement**.[28] Article 45(3) clarifies that in cases not mentioned in Article 45(1)(e), the prohibition of review must not be circumvented by recourse to the **public policy** clause (Article 45(1)(a)).[29] This applies even if the court in the Member State of origin clearly misunderstood the Regulation's juris-

25 See, eg, Case C-302/13 *flyLAL-Lithuanian Airlines* (23 October 2014) ECLI:EU:C:2014:2319, para 27.

26 Cf P Wautelet, 'Article 36 Brussels Ibis' in U Magnus and P Mankowski (eds), *Brussels Ibis Regulation Commentary* (2nd edn, Otto Schmidt 2023) para 35.

27 Article 72 should also be mentioned but becomes very rarely relevant.

28 Case C-90/22 *Gjensidige* (21 March 2024) ECLI:EU:C:2024:252, paras 49ff.

29 Therefore, it is at least highly misleading (and hopefully a soon forgotten lapse) that the ECJ mentions public policy as an exception to the prohibition of review of the foreign court's jurisdiction; see Case C-590/21 *Charles Taylor Adjusting v Starlight Shipping* (7 September 2023) ECLI:EU:C:2023:633, para 24.

diction rules or failed to comply with Article 5 when relying on its national rules.[30]

III The Right to Be Heard

#18 Violations of the defendant's right to be heard when **initiating proceedings** in the Member State of origin can trigger a ground for non-recognition pursuant to Article 45(1)(b), whereas similar violations of parties' rights of participation occurring in the further course of the foreign proceedings can be reviewed under the general public policy clause (Article 45(1)(a)).

#19 Article 45(1)(b) only applies to **judgments given in default of appearance**, if the defendant was not served with the document which instituted the foreign proceedings[31] (or with an equivalent document) in sufficient time and in such a way as to enable him to arrange for his defence. In this respect, it is important that the defendant was not only able to declare his willingness to defend or to appear at the scheduled hearing, but that they also had a reasonable chance to prepare an effective defence; not crucial, however, is the formal correctness of the service. The certificate pursuant to Article 53 must state the date on which the document had been served, but this does not obviate the need for an examination pursuant to Article 45(1)(b) if the defendant claims that the document was not served.[32] The defendant cannot insist on a refusal of recognition if they had failed to take action against the judgment in the Member State of origin. In this respect, the term 'proceedings to challenge a judgment' in Article 45(1)(b) is to be interpreted broadly.[33]

IV Conflicts of res judicata and lis pendens

#20 Problems can arise if a foreign judgment is not compatible with another (domestic or foreign) judgment which, in the view of the second state, should take precedence. Within the scope of application of the Brussels I-bis Regulation, Article 45 (1)(c) and (d) states the extent to which such **incompatibility of decisions** can result in a refusal of recognition. It seems remarkable that recognition cannot be

30 Case C-7/98 *Krombach v Bamberski* (28 March 2000) ECLI:EU:C:2000:164; Case C-234/04 *Kapferer v Schlank & Schick* (16 March 2006) ECLI:EU:C:2006:178.

31 For details on the minimum requirements for the documents initiating proceedings, see Case C-343/22 *PT v VB* (30 March 2023) ECLI:EU:C:2023:276.

32 Case C-619/10 *Trade Agency v Seramico Investments* (6 September 2012) ECLI:EU:C:2012:531.

33 Case C-70/15 *Lebek v Domino* (7 July 2016) ECLI:EU:C:2016:524.

denied solely because the foreign court has disregarded Articles 29 ff and therefore ignored the earlier pendency of proceedings in the second state.[34] In principle, notwithstanding Article 1(2)(d), a judgment of the second state that confirms an arbitration award can be a judgment within the meaning of Article 45(1)(c) and (d), and as such prevent the recognition of an incompatible foreign judgment. However, in a highly controversial decision, the ECJ defined the applicability of Article 45(1)(c) and (d) very narrowly in such cases.[35]

V Public Policy

#21 At the heart of the provisions on recognition is the idea that the free movement of judgments contributes to orderly cross-border cooperation and that all legal and court systems should initially be regarded as equivalent – but unfortunately also as equally prone to error. Therefore, as a rule, foreign judgments should be recognised, even at the risk that they might be incorrect from the perspective of the second state. This explains why the second state is barred from reviewing the foreign judgment 'as to its substance'. This prohibition of a ***révision au fond*** ('review on the merits'), as stated in Article 52, encompasses two aspects: firstly, recognition may not be refused solely because the law applied by the foreign court deviates from the law that would have been applied in the second state; secondly, it shall not to be examined whether the foreign court has assessed the case correctly in law and in fact.[36]

#22 Nevertheless, contrary to the Commission's original proposal for a reform of the Brussels I regime,[37] Article 45(1)(a) Brussels I-bis Regulation still acknowledges that recognition may be refused by invoking the **public policy** of the Member State addressed.[38] This is meant as an 'emergency brake' for extreme cases only: The re-

---

34 The ECJ has clarified this in the context of maintenance and custody cases, see Case C-386/17 *Liberato v Grigorescu* (16 January 2019) ECLI:EU:C:2019:24.

35 Case C-700/20 *London Steam-Ship Owners' Mutual Insurance Association v Kingdom of Spain* (20 June 2022) ECLI:EU:C:2022:488.

36 See eg Case C-568/20 *J v H limited* (7 April 2022) ECLI:EU:C:2022:264, para 43.

37 Cf COM(2010) 748 final.

38 For details and examples, see T Domej, 'Regionalism in the Recognition and Enforcement of Foreign Titles: Implications for Public Policy Scrutiny' (2019) 9 International Journal of Procedural Law 235; P Mostowik and E Figura-Góralczyk, 'Ordre Public and Non-Enforcement of Judgments in Intra-EU Civil Matters: Remarks on Some Recent Polish-German Cases' (2022) 18 Journal of Private International Law 317; Z Witek, 'Trust, but Verify: Loss of Mutual Trust as a Ground for Non-Recognition in the Area of Freedom, Security and Justice' in B Hess and K Lenaerts (eds), *The 50th Anniversary of the European Law of Civil Procedure* (Nomos 2020) 507.

quirement of a 'manifest' conflict with public policy emphasises the exceptional nature of the reservation clause.[39] The Brussels I-bis Regulation does not provide an autonomous definition of public policy, leaving this in principle to the law of the Member State addressed. However, the ECJ claims its competence to monitor the limits within which national courts may use public policy as an obstacle to recognition.[40] Although this is not explicitly emphasised in the Brussels I-bis Regulation (unlike, eg, in Article 33 of the European Insolvency Regulation 2015[41]), compatibility with fundamental rights and prohibitions of discrimination is an important aspect of public policy,[42] whereas not every infringement of national or even EU law can justify refusal of recognition.[43]

#23 If the foreign judgment was reached in a way that deviates from **mandatory procedural provisions** of the second state, this does not yet preclude recognition; even significant procedural differences must be accepted. The public policy clause can only come into consideration if the foreign proceedings deviate from essential principles to such an extent that the foreign decision can no longer be regarded as the result of an orderly and fair procedure. An important procedural aspect of public policy is the **right to be heard**;[44] in this respect, as already mentioned (# 18), Article 45(1)(a) supplements Article 45(1)(b). Article 64, following earlier case law of the ECJ,[45] allows refusal specifically for decisions in civil actions before criminal courts that are issued in the absence of the defendant. The loosing party's right to a **fair trial** is also of importance for recognition. In particular, the ECJ derives from

39 The exceptional nature is highlighted by the ECJ again and again. For a recent statement, see Case C-590/21 *Charles Taylor Adjusting v Starlight Shipping* (7 September 2023) ECLI:EU:C:2023:633.

40 See eg Case C-681/13 *Diageo Brands BV v Simiramida-04 EOOD* (16 July 2015) ECLI:EU:C:2015:471; Case C-568/20 *J v H limited* (7 April 2022) ECLI:EU:C:2022:264, para 42.

41 [2015] OJ L141/19.

42 Case C-619/10 *Trade Agency v Seramico Investments* (6 September 2012) ECLI:EU:C:2012:531. For a recent example, see Case C-633/22 *Real Madrid Club de Fútbol v Société Éditrice du Monde* (4 October 2024) ECLI:EU:C:2024:843, stating that the enforcement of a judgment ordering a newspaper publishing house and one of its journalists to pay damages by way of compensation for the non-material damage suffered by a sports club and one of the members of its medical team due to harm caused to their reputation by the publication of information about them must be refused where it would give rise to a manifest breach of the freedom of the press, as enshrined in Article 11 of the Charter of Fundamental Rights, and thus an infringement of public policy in the Member State in which enforcement is sought.

43 See eg Case C-681/13 *Diageo Brands BV v Simiramida-04 EOOD* (16 July 2015) ECLI:EU:C:2015:471.

44 See, eg, Case C-394/07 *Marco Gambazzi v DaimlerChrysler Canada* (2 April 2009) ECLI:EU:C:2009:219; Case C-568/20 *J v H limited* (7 April 2022) ECLI:EU:C:2022:264, paras 45ff.

45 Case C-7/98 *Krombach v Bamberski* (28 March 2000) ECLI:EU:C:2000:16.

this that judicial decisions normally should contain a statement of reasons.[46] Similar to Article 45(1)(b), the defence of public policy remains irrelevant if the party asserting an infringement has not done everything reasonably possible in the Member State of origin to remedy alleged procedural errors.[47]

D Enforceability

I Basics

#24 The interest of a winning party is not only that the judgment is recognised outside the Member State of origin, but also that it can be enforced in other Member States. While the effects of judgments are normally recognised ipso iure (Article 36(1); see # 13) and thus extended to the territory of other Member States, there has traditionally been a significant exception for enforceability: this must first be conferred by a special act (the so-called **declaration of enforceability** or **exequatur**) for the territory of the second state before its enforcement authorities carry out enforcement. Both the Brussels Convention and the Brussels I Regulation understood this as a necessary instrument to protect the interests of the second state and the judgment debtor. In this respect, the Brussels I-bis Regulation proves to be a huge step forward: it abolishes the exequatur requirement but maintains that the judgment debtor should still have a remedy in the Member State of enforcement if they assume that the foreign judgment is not recognisable. Conceptually, the traditional requirement to formally bring about enforceability in the second state has been replaced by **recognising enforceability** as soon as it occurs in the first state.

#25 The rules on the free movement of judgments were created primarily in the interests of judgment creditors who depend on enforcing their titles abroad because enforcement in the state of origin proves impossible or illusory. However, a well-informed and well-advised creditor may, when considering the factual circumstances as well as the applicable law, procedural and cost aspects, come to the conclusion that state A would be the ideal forum for the action, but that state B would then offer the most effective enforcement options. **Enforcement shopping** can therefore be added to the well-known phenomenon of forum shopping. In principle, this appears to be neither illegal nor illegitimate, provided that the creditor only takes advantage of the free circulation of judgments and the remaining legal differences in national enforcement laws.

---

46 Case C-619/10 *Trade Agency v Seramico Investments* (6 September 2012) ECLI:EU:C:2012:531; Case C-302/13 *flyLAL-Lithuanian Airlines AS v Starptautiskā lidosta Rīga VAS and Air Baltic Corporation AS* (23 October 2014) ECLI:EU:C:2014:2319.

47 Case C-559/14 *Meroni v Recoletos* (25 May 2016) ECLI:EU:C:2016:349.

II Background: From the Brussels I Model to the Second-Generation Regulations

1 Brussels I Regulation

#26 When the Brussels I Regulation replaced the Brussels Convention in 2002, Articles 38 ff Brussels I Regulation maintained the traditional **requirement of a declaration of enforceability** but designed the procedure for obtaining exequatur and the appeal system to be more creditor-friendly and efficient. Since the Brussels I-bis Regulation came into force on 10 January 2015, the Brussels I exequatur procedure has only applied to judgments issued in proceedings instituted, to authentic instruments formally drawn up or registered, and to court settlements approved or concluded before that date (Article 66(2) Brussels I-bis Regulation). Nevertheless, the Brussels I rules are briefly outlined below, not only because, in practice, they still apply ratione tempori in many cases, but also because they served as a model for the Lugano Convention of 2007 (Articles 38 ff; see # 4) and for some recent EU Regulations in the field of family law[48] and succession law.[49] Moreover, the special features of the new exequatur-free models can be understood better against the historical backdrop of the old rules.

#27 The Brussels I exequatur procedure is initiated by any interested party (normally: the judgment creditor) filing an **application for a declaration of enforceability** (Article 38(1) Brussels I Regulation). According to Article 40(3) Brussels I Regulation, the application must be accompanied by the documents referred to in Article 53 Brussels I Regulation. The local jurisdiction for the exequatur procedure is based either on the place of domicile of the judgment debtor or the place of enforcement (Article 39(2) Brussels I Regulation). If the **formal requirements** are met and the foreign judgment is already enforceable under the rules of the Member State of origin, the exequatur judge does not examine whether there are grounds for refusal of recognition (as it was still required under the Brussels Convention): According to sentence 1 of Article 41 Brussels I Regulation, such a review of the grounds for refusal is neither a prerequisite for a declaration of enforceability nor permissible; even the public policy of the second state must not be

---

48 See Articles 42ff of the Regulation (EU) 2016/1103 of 24 June 2016 implementing enhanced cooperation in the area of jurisdiction, applicable law and the recognition and enforcement of decisions in matters of matrimonial property regimes, [2016] OJ L 183/1; Articles 42ff of the Regulation (EU) 2016/1104 of 24 June 2016 implementing enhanced cooperation in the area of jurisdiction, applicable law and the recognition and enforcement of decisions in matters of the property consequences of registered partnerships [2016] OJ L183/30.

49 See Articles 43ff of the Regulation (EU) 650/2012 of 4 July 2012 on jurisdiction, applicable law, recognition and enforcement of decisions and acceptance and enforcement of authentic instruments in matters of succession and on the creation of a European Certificate of Succession [2012] OJ L201/107.

taken into account at this stage of the exequatur proceedings. Rather, the exequatur judge must declare enforceability immediately without hearing the debtor (Article 41 Brussels I Regulation). The decision on the application is brought to the notice of the applicant and served on the debtor (Article 42 Brussels I Regulation).

#28 A review of the grounds for refusal of recognition only takes place if the debtor[50] brings **appeal proceedings against the declaration of enforceability** within the time limit prescribed in Article 43(5) Brussels I Regulation.[51] The details of the appeal procedure are left to the rules of the Member State addressed (Article 43 (3) Brussels I Regulation).[52] According to Article 45 Brussels I Regulation, the appeal court may only revoke the declaration of enforceability based on one of the grounds set out in Articles 34 and 35 Brussels I Regulation (which largely correspond to today's Article 45 Brussels I-bis Regulation, see # 15 ff).[53] A **further appeal** may be available if provided for under national law (Article 44 Brussels I Regulation).

2 Second-generation Regulations

#29 Even after the Brussels I Regulation had simplified the more cumbersome provisions of the old Brussels Convention, consideration was given to how the cross-border enforcement of titles could be made even easier within the EU. The obvious solution was to dispense with the requirement of a declaration of enforceability altogether. In civil and commercial matters, the Regulation (EC) 805/2004 of 21 April 2004 creating a European Enforcement Order for uncontested claims **(EEO Regulation)**[54] has already moved away from the traditional exequatur model: The EEO Regulation allows EU-wide enforcement if the creditor has obtained a title that has been confirmed in the Member State of origin as a European Enforcement Order.

#30 For the purposes of the EEO Regulation, the title must relate to a **claim for payment of a specific sum of money** (Article 4(2) EEO Regulation) and the claim

50 A competing creditor of the debtor is not entitled to this option, see Case C-167/08 *Draka NK Cables* (23 April 2009) ECLI:EU:C:2009:263.

51 See Case C-3/05 *Verdoliva v Van der Hoeven* (16 February 2006) ECLI:EU:C:2006:113.

52 For the significance of proper service on the debtor for the commencement of the time limit, see Case C-433/18 *ML v Aktiva Finants* (12 December 2019) ECLI:EU:C:2019:1074.

53 The ECJ emphasises that the reference in Article 45 to Articles 34 and 35 Brussels I Regulation is exhaustive and leaves no room for the examination of further defences against the claim within the exequatur procedure (such as a debtor's alleged payment); however, the ECJ assumes that the debtor can bring an action to defend against enforcement in the second state. See Case C-139/10 *Prism Investments BV v Van der Meer* (13 October 2011) ECLI:EU:C:2011:653.

54 [2004] OJ L143/15.

must be **uncontested** within the meaning of Article 3(1) EEO Regulation.[55] Confirmation requires an application by the creditor, which is not subject to a time limit (Article 6(1) EEO Regulation). The further preconditions for the certification are determined for court decisions in Articles 6 ff EEO Regulation[56] and for court settlements and authentic instruments in Articles 24 ff EEO Regulation. Particular mention should be made of the procedural safeguards stated in Articles 6(1)(c) and 12 ff[57] and the extensive consumer protection as regards international jurisdiction pursuant to Article 6(1)(d) EEO Regulation.[58]

#31 A judgment certified as a **European Enforcement Order** shall be enforced under the same conditions as a judgment given in the Member State of enforcement (Article 20(1) EEO Regulation); the same applies to certified court settlements and authentic instruments (Articles 24(2) and 25(2) EEO Regulation). Article 5 EEO Regulation underlines that enforcement does not require a declaration of enforceability. The enforcement procedure as such is governed by the law of the second state (Article 20(1) EEO Regulation). The only **ground for refusal of enforcement** is irreconcilability of the judgment certified as a European Enforcement Order and an earlier judgment given in any Member State or in a third country (Article 21(1) EEO Regulation). Article 21(2) EEO Regulation expressly prohibits the enforcement authorities from reviewing the substance of the judgment; a public policy clause was deliberately not included in the Regulation. An enforcement refusal procedure pursuant to Article 45 ff Brussels I-bis Regulation (see below # 34, 36 ff) does not take place within the scope of application of the EEO Regulation. Instead, debtors can only take action against the European Enforcement Order in the Member State of origin, insofar as this is still possible (see Articles 6(2), 10 and 19 EEO Regulation). If they do so, enforcement in the second state can be suspended or restricted in accordance with Article 23 EEO Regulation. However, as the ECJ emphasises, a stay under Article 23(c) EEO Regulation can only be considered in exceptional circumstances and cannot be combined with measures pursuant to Article 23(a) or (b).[59]

#32 In summary, it can be said that the EEO Regulation is remarkably creditor-friendly: It is characterised on the one hand by the possibility of EU-wide enforcement without a declaration of enforceability and on the other hand by a concentration of legal protection for the debtor in the Member State of origin. Both aspects differ considerably from the Brussels I Regulation, which introduced a few

55 For details, see Case C-511/14 *Pebros Servizi v Aston Martin Lagonda* (16 June 2016) ECLI:EU:C:2016:448; ECJ, Case C-484/15 *Zulfikarpašić v Gajer* (9 March 2017) ECLI:EU:C:2017:199.

56 On the confirmation procedure, see Case C-300/14 *Imtech Marine Belgium v Radio Hellenic* (17 December 2015) ECLI:EU:C:2015:825.

57 See Case C-289/17 *Collect Inkasso v Aint* (28 February 2018) ECLI:EU:C:2018:133.

58 On the inapplicability of Article 6(1)(d) EEO Regulation in the event of a dispute between two consumers, see Case C-508/12 *Vapenik v Thurner* (5 December 2013) ECLI:EU:C:2013:790.

59 Case C-393/21 *Lufthansa Technik AERO Alzey* (16 February 2023) ECLI:EU:C:2023:104.

procedural simplifications compared to the Brussels Convention, but still corresponded to its traditional exequatur model. In contrast, the abolition of the exequatur transfers the burden of instituting court proceedings from the creditor to the debtor (so-called *inversion du contentieux*). The second-generation model, which was originally designed in the EEO Regulation only for uncontested money claims, was later also applied to the enforcement of titles issued in the **European order for payment procedure** and the **European small claims procedure**.[60]

III The Compromise Model of the Brussels I-bis Regulation

#33 In view of the instruments described so far, the question arose as to why the exequatur requirement should be retained for general (contentious) civil and commercial matters within the meaning of the Brussels I Regulation. The **Commission's proposal for the Brussels I reform** presented in 2010 denied any reason for this and advocated the abolition of the declaration of enforceability.[61] In the further discussion, this seemed reasonable or at least acceptable to many, but not the drastic reduction of grounds for refusal of recognition that would have been associated with it according to the original proposal.

#34 Not surprisingly, the Commission was unable to push through its far-reaching plans. At the end of 2012, the **compromise solution of today's Brussels I-bis Regulation** finally emerged, which is mostly seen as a fair balance between creditor and debtor interests. According to Article 39, judgments given in a Member State (as well as authentic instruments and court settlements, Articles 58 ff) are enforceable in all other Member States without exequatur as soon as they are enforceable in the Member State of origin. It is hoped that the **abolition of the exequatur procedure** will, above all, reduce the time and costs involved (Recital 26). However, the foreign judgment remains subject to a certain degree of review in the Member State addressed: This difference to the second-generation Regulations results from the **new enforcement refusal procedure** pursuant to Articles 46 ff. The review is essentially carried out on the basis of the same grounds for refusal of recognition as in the Brussels I Regulation (Article 45 Brussels I-bis Regulation; see # 15 ff).

#35 The **enforcement proceedings** as such are governed by the national rules of the Member State addressed (Article 41(1); see # 41). In principle, this also includes the provisions on refusal or suspension of enforcement (Article 41(2)) and on taking precautionary measures (Article 40). The Member State addressed must not

60 For details, see Chapter 16.
61 Cf COM (2010) 748 final.

require the creditor to have a postal address or an authorised representative in this State, unless representation is mandatory irrespective of nationality and domicile (Article 41(3)). The documents to be submitted by the creditor to initiate enforcement are listed in Article 42(1). The **certificate** provided for in Article 53 and Annex I, which is to be issued in the Member State of origin, plays a special role. This is because, in normal cases, enforcement should take place simply based on the information on this form without further examination. In particular, this should also prevent another examination in the Member State addressed whether the matter is within the material scope of application of the Brussels I-bis Regulation pursuant to Article 1.[62] However, it seems questionable whether the courts of the other Member States in this respect are bound by the certificate as issued in the Member State of origin[63] or rather remain authorised to carry out an independent examination. Although the enforcement authority can request a **translation** of the certificate (Article 42(3)), it can only exceptionally request a translation of the foreign judgment if this appears indispensable (Article 42(4)). However, under certain circumstances, the debtor may insist on a translation (Article 43(2)). Insofar as a translation is required, Article 57 applies.

#36 The **enforcement refusal procedure** is set out in Articles 46 ff. It is initiated on the **application** by the person against whom enforcement is sought (ie the debtor) to the competent court (see Article 47(2)). Recital 30 indicates that the law of the Member State in which enforcement is sought may provide for a time-limit for the initiation of the enforcement refusal procedure. According to Article 46, the **grounds for refusal** referred to in Article 45 are the standard of review; of course, the prohibition of a révision au fond applies (Article 52; see # 21). The court must issue its decision without delay (Article 48). If the debtor succeeds, the court removes enforceability of the foreign judgment with effect ex tunc, but only for the Member State in which the refusal procedure has taken place.

#37 An **appeal** is available against the decision on the application for refusal of enforcement (Article 49) and, if necessary, a further appeal under the law of the Member State (Article 50). For the court's discretion to **stay the enforcement refusal procedure**, see Article 51(1). If a refusal of enforcement has been applied for, the court in the Member State addressed can make provisional orders as set

62 For the necessary examination of this point in the Member State of origin, see Case C-361/18 *Weil v GulácsiK* (6 June 2019) ECLI:EU:C:2019:473; Case C-579/17 *Bauarbeiter-Urlaubs- und Abfertigungskasse v Gradbeništvo Korana* (28 February 2019) ECLI:EU:C:2019:162.

63 This was suggested, albeit only obiter and without further explanation, by ECJ, Case C-361/18 *Weil v GulácsiK* (6 June 2019) ECLI:EU:C:2019:473, para 35. For a reference for a preliminary ruling in this context, see Bundesgerichtshof (Federal Court of Germany), Order of 5 June 2025 – Case V ZB 15/24, ECLI:DE:BGH:2025:050625BVZB15.24.0.

out in Article 44(1). In contrast, Article 44(2) deals with the case that enforceability has been suspended in the Member State of origin. With regard to the concept of extension of effects (see # 5 ff) and the wording of Article 39, it seems obvious that a judgment that has already lost its enforceability in its Member State of origin can likewise no longer be enforced in other Member States.[64] If the debtor nevertheless fears enforcement measures in a Member State, Article 44(2) alone does not provide sufficient help. Rather, it is suggested that in this case they can make an application by analogy with Articles 46 ff.

#38 The **relationship between a recognition refusal procedure and an enforcement refusal procedure** is not entirely clear. It seems as if the Brussels I-bis Regulation assumes that these instruments do not have the same subject matter. However, it is unlikely to be meant that, after recognition has already been refused in a Member State, a subsequent application for refusal of enforcement in the same Member State can be rejected based on a different assessment of Article 45(1). Nor does it seem sensible that, after enforcement has been refused, it is still possible to hold in subsequent proceedings that the foreign judgment should at least be recognised as res judicata. To avoid such discrepancies, the court hearing an application for refusal should endeavour from the outset to ensure that it relates to both recognition and enforcement.

#39 To be distinguished from the enforcement refusal procedure is the issue of whether and how debtors can assert outside the Member State of origin that they have already paid their debts or that the creditor is no longer the holder of the claim to be enforced. According to the ECJ, a debtor can assert such **substantive defences** in a procedure in accordance with the national law of the Member State addressed; the international jurisdiction for this should arise from Article 24 (5).[65] However, in view of the prohibition of a révision au fond (Article 52), it is suggested that only those defences that could not already have been raised in the original proceedings leading to the judgment in the Member State of origin can be taken into account.

#40 An **assessment of the Brussels I-bis model** leads to an ambivalent result. The compromise basically brings about a **shift in the burden of procedural initiative**. Under the Brussels I Regulation, it was on the creditor to initiate the exequatur procedure and then on the debtor to raise any grounds for refusal by means of an appeal. Now the creditor can directly proceed with enforcement and the debtor must counter this by initiating the enforcement refusal procedure. In the first few years since the entering into force of the Brussels I-bis Regulation, court

---

64 This was taken for granted, eg, in Case C-420/07 *Apostolides v Orams* (28 April 2009) ECLI:EU:C:2009:271, para 66.

65 See Case C-139/10 *Prism Investments BV v Van der Meer* (13 October 2011) ECLI:EU:C:2011:653.

practice, at least in Germany, has shown that debtors defend themselves much less frequently under the new rules than under the old Brussels I rules. However, the Brussels I-bis Regulation also gives rise to a new opportunity for the debtor: Whereas, under the Brussels I Regulation, a debtor could only react after the creditor had already obtained exequatur in a Member State, now, based on Articles 46 ff Brussels I-bis Regulation, debtors can bring about a decision on their own initiative if they wish to oppose enforcement before the creditor has even taken any steps towards enforcement.

E Enforcement Measures

#41 Even if the enforceability of a foreign judgment is governed by EU law, the procedure for the enforcement as such is generally governed by the rules applicable in the Member State addressed. This is stated in sentence 1 of Article 41(1) Brussels I-bis Regulation, which in turn leads to the question of the extent to which the **lex loci executionis** or the lex causae applies.[66] In principle, the latter is important for the manners in which the debtor's obligation is extinguished, whereas the lex loci executionis will determine, eg, the enforcement authorities, enforcement measures, objects of enforcement, and remedies. Furthermore, it can be problematic whether the law of the enforcement state or the law of the judgment state is decisive.[67] Another question is the international jurisdiction of the Member State addressed to issue enforcement measures. This is not explicitly dealt with in the Brussels I-bis Regulation; in particular, this is not what Article 24(5) is about. Rather, it follows from the principle of territoriality that **'jurisdiction to enforce'** results from the location of assets in the state of enforcement (which can cause difficulties regarding intangible assets). Finally, it should be noted that Articles 29 ff do not apply to enforcement proceedings, which means that the Brussels I-bis Regulation fails to provide a suitable solution if the creditor pursues enforcement in several Member States simultaneously.

---

66 For details, see R Garnett, *Substance and Procedure in Private International Law* (OUP 2012), paras 6.78ff.

67 On the (doubtful) relevance of a time-limit for enforcement as foreseen in the second state but not in the first state, see ECJ, Judgment of 4 October 2018 – Case C-379/17 (*Società Immobiliare Al Bosco*), ECLI:EU:C:2018:806.

References

Beaumont P and Walker WD, 'Recognition and Enforcement of Judgments in Civil and Commercial Matters in the Brussels I Recast and Some Lessons from It and the Recent Hague Conventions for the Hague Judgments Project' (2015) 11 Journal of Private International Law 31.

Berglund M, *Cross-Border Enforcement of Claims in the EU: History, Present Time and Future* (2nd edn, Wolters Kluwer 2014).

Biavati P and Lupoi MA, *European Judicial Cooperation in Cross-Border Litigation* (Bologna UP 2024).

Calvo Caravaca A-L and Carrascosa González J 'Free Movement of Judgments in Civil Matters in the European Union' in A-L Calvo Caravaca and J Carrascosa González (eds), *European Private International Law* (Comares 2022) 415.

Chase O and others, *Civil Litigation in Comparative Context* (2nd edn, West Academic 2017).

Cuniberti G, 'Making Cross-Border Enforcement More Efficient for Creditors' in J von Hein and T Kruger (eds), *Informed Choices in Cross-Border Enforcement* (Intersentia 2021) 413

Domej T, 'Regionalism in the Recognition and Enforcement of Foreign Titles: Implications for Public Policy Scrutiny' (2019) 9 International Journal of Procedural Law 235

Franzina P, Kramer X and Fitchen J, 'The Recognition and Enforcement of Member State Judgments' in A Dickinson and E Lein (eds), *The Brussels I Regulation Recast* (OUP 2015) 373.

Garnett R, *Substance and Procedure in Private International Law* (OUP 2012).

Gascón Inchausti F, 'Does EU Law Ensure an Adequate Protection of Debtors in Cross-Border Enforcement?' (2020) Rivista di diritto internazionale privato e processuale 255.

——, 'Ensuring Adequate Protection in Cross-Border Enforcement for Debtors, Especially Consumers' in J von Hein and T Kruger (eds), *Informed Choices in Cross-Border Enforcement* (Intersentia 2021) 429.

Goddard D and Beaumont P, 'Recognition and Enforcement of Judgments in Civil or Commercial Matters' in P Beaumont and J Holliday (eds), *A Guide to Global Private International Law* (Bloomsbury 2022) 407.

Hau W, 'Having Two Bites at the Same Cherry?' [2024] IPRax 41.

——, 'Unified European Rules on the Recognition and Enforceability of Third-Country Judgments', in *Liber Amicorum Piet Taelman* (Wolters Kluwer 2025) 467.

Hess B, 'Exequatur sur Exequatur (Ne) Vaut?' [2022] IPRax 349.

Hovaguimian P, 'The Enforcement of Foreign Judgments under Brussels I bis: False Alarms and Real Concerns' (2015) 11 Journal of Private International Law 212.

Kramer X, 'Cross-Border Enforcement and the Brussels I-Bis Regulation: Towards a New Balance Between Mutual Trust and National Control Over Fundamental Rights' (2013) Netherlands International Law Review 343.

Linke H and Hau W, *Internationales Zivilverfahrensrecht* (9th edn, Otto Schmidt 2024).

Linton M, 'Abolition of Exequatur, All in the Name of Mutual Trust' in B Hess, M Bergström and E Storskrubb (eds), *EU Civil Justice: Current Issues and Future Outlook* (Hart 2016) 257.

Lupoi MA, 'Jurisdiction and Recognition and Enforcement of Judgments in Civil and Commercial Matters: Regulation No. 1215 of 2012' in P Biavati and MA Lupoi (eds), *European Judicial Cooperation in Cross-Border Litigation* (Bologna UP 2024).

Mankowski P and Pein L, 'Recognition and Enforcement' in V Lazić and P Mankowski (eds), *The Brussels I-Bis Regulation: Interpretation and Implementation* (Edward Elgar 2023) 395.

Mäsch G and Peiffer M, 'New Enforcement Regime under the Brussels Ibis Regulation: Does the Paradigm Shift Help Judgment Creditors?' in J von Hein and T Kruger (eds), *Informed Choices in Cross-Border Enforcement* (Intersentia 2021) 31.

Martiny D, 'The Recognition and Enforcement of Court Decisions Between the EU and Third States' in A Trunk and N Hatzimihail (eds), *EU Civil Procedure Law and Third Countries* (Nomos 2021) 127.

Mostowik P and Figura-Góralczyk E, 'Ordre Public and Non-Enforcement of Judgments in Intra-EU Civil Matters: Remarks on Some Recent Polish-German Cases' (2022) 18 Journal of Private International Law 317.
Requejo Isidro M, 'On the Abolition of Exequatur' in B Hess, M Bergström and E Storskrubb (eds), *EU Civil Justice: Current Issues and Future Outlook* (Hart 2016) 283.
——, 'The Enforcement of Monetary Final Judgments Under the Brussels Ibis Regulation (A Critical Assessment)' in V Lazić and S Stuij (eds), *Brussels Ibis Regulation: Changes and Challenges of the Renewed Procedural Scheme* (Asser 2017) 71.
Rijavec V and others (eds), *Remedies Concerning Enforcement of Foreign Judgements: Brussels I Recast* (Wolters Kluwer 2018).
Schramm D, 'Enforcement and the Abolition of Exequatur under the 2012 Brussels I Regulation' (2013/2014) 15 Yearbook of Private International Law 143.
Storskrubb E, 'Mutual Recognition as a Governance Strategy for Civil Justice' in B Hess, M Bergström and E Storskrubb (eds), *EU Civil Justice: Current Issues and Future Outlook* (Hart 2016) 299.
Timmer LJ, 'Abolition of Exequatur under the Brussels I Regulation: Ill Conceived and Premature?' (2013) 9 Journal of Private International Law 129.
Tsikrikas D, 'The Recognition of the Effects of Foreign Judgments Between the EU and Third States' in A Trunk and N Hatzimihail (eds), *EU Civil Procedure Law and Third Countries* (Nomos 2021) 147.
Vogel L, *Jurisdiction and Recognition of Judgments since the Brussels Regulation Recast* (2nd edn, Bruylant 2020).
Wautelet P, 'Article 36 Brussels Ibis' in U Magnus and P Mankowski (eds), *Brussels Ibis Regulation Commentary* (2nd edn, Otto Schmidt 2023) 794
Witek Z, 'Trust, but Verify: Loss of Mutual Trust as a Ground for Non-Recognition in the Area of Freedom, Security and Justice' in B Hess and K Lenaerts (eds), *The 50th Anniversary of the European Law of Civil Procedure* (Nomos 2020) 507.

Apostolos Anthimos

Chapter 14
International Jurisdiction and Recognition and Enforcement in Family Matters and Maintenance

A Introduction

#1 The two key regulations dealing with family law matters in the EU are: (1) Council Regulation 2019/111 on jurisdiction, the recognition and enforcement of decisions in matrimonial matters and the matters of **parental responsibility**, and on international **child abduction** (recast), generally referred to **as Brussels II-bis**; and (2) Council Regulation (EC) No 4/2009 on jurisdiction, applicable law, recognition and enforcement of decisions and cooperation in matters relating to **maintenance obligations** (Maintenance Regulation). This chapter will focus on the operation of the rules on international jurisdiction and recognition and enforcement of the Brussels II-ter Regulation (see Sections B-H) and the Maintenance Regulation (see Section I). The chapter is based on the case law on these instruments, in particular the extensive case law of the Court of Justice of the European Union (CJEU) on the Brussels II-ter Regulation. As all case law so far concerned its predecessor, the Brussels II-bis Regulation, reference is made to provisions in both instruments as far as the numbering or content differs.

B Brussels II-ter Regulation

#2 Since 1 August 2022, matrimonial matters and matters of parental responsibility are governed by EU Regulation 2019/111 (Brussels II-ter).[1] This Regulation is the fruit of lengthy efforts by the competent EU bodies and academics,[2] and forms

1 [2019] OJ L178/1.

2 See TM de Boer, 'What We Should Not Expect from a Recast of the Brussels IIbis Regulation' (2015) 33 Nederlands Internationaal Privaatrecht 10; C González Beilfuss, 'What's New in Regulation (EU) No 2019/1111?' (2020/2021) 22 Yearbook of Private International Law 95; E Rodríguez Pineau, 'La refundición del Reglamento Bruselas II bis: de nuevo sobre la función del Derecho internacional privado europeo' (2017) 69(1) Revista Española de Derecho Internacional 139; T Kruger and L Samyn, 'Brussels II bis: Successes and Suggested Improvements' (2016) 12 J. Priv. Int. Law 132; M NÍ Shúilleabháin, 'An

Apostolos Anthimos, CITY College, University of York Europe Campus, e-mail: apostolos.anthimos@gmail.com

https://doi.org/10.1515/9783110781632-014

the recast of the previous Regulation nr. 2201/2003 (Brussels II-bis),[3] which was preceded by Regulation nr. 1347/2000.[4] The Brussels II-ter Regulation is founded upon the structure of the previous Regulations. At the same time, it has extended its scope to core issues, such as **child abduction**, direct recognition and enforcement of foreign judgments, and increased cooperation between Member States.[5]

#3 The Regulation consists of nine chapters, which are covering the following issues: Scope of the Regulation (Articles 1–2); jurisdiction (Articles 3–21); International child abduction (Articles 22–29); recognition and enforcement (Articles 30–75); cooperation (Articles 76–84);[6] general provisions (Articles 85–91); delegated acts (Articles 92–93); relations with other instruments (Articles 94–99);[7] final provisions (Articles 100–105).

C Scope of Application and Definitions

#4 The Regulation applies to matters of **divorce**, legal separation, marriage annulment, and **parental responsibility** cases, including custody, contact rights, guardianship, curatorship, designation of a person having charge of a child, placement of children in institutional foster care, and measures for child protection (Article (1 & 2). A catalogue of cases where the Regulation does not apply is to be found under Article 1(4).

Overview of the Principal Reforms in Regulation (EU) 2019/1111' (2020/2021) 22 Yearbook of Private International Law 117.

3 In detail C Althammer (ed), *Brussels IIa – Rome III* (Hart/Beck/Nomos 2019); U Magnus and P Mankowski (eds), *European Commentaries on Private International Law. ECPIL Commentary Volume IV Brussels IIbis Regulation* (Otto Schmidt 2017). See also C Honorati and MC Baruffi, *EU Private International Law in Family Matters, Legislation and CJEU Case Law* (Intersentia 2022). A full list of pertinent case law is embedded in the text of the Brussels II-bis Regulation, ibid 73 et seq.

4 M Jänterä-Jareborg, 'A European Family Law for Cross-border Situations – Some Reflections Concerning the Brussels II Regulation and its Planned Amendments' (2002) 3 Yearbook of Private International Law 67.

5 In detail N Lowe, C Honorati and M Hellner, *Brussels II-ter – Cross-border Marriage Dissolution, Parental Responsibility Disputes and Child Abduction in the EU* (Intersentia 2024); C González Beilfuss and others (eds), *Jurisdiction, Recognition and Enforcement in Matrimonial and Parental Responsibility Matters. A Commentary on Regulation 2019/1111 (Brussels IIb)* (Edward Elgar 2023); MA Lupoi, *La crisi matrimoniale e genitoriale nello spazio di giustizia europeo Giurisdizione, circolazione delle decisioni e sottrazione internazionale di minori* (Pacini Editore Srl 2022).

6 Ad hoc D Martiny, 'New Efforts in Judicial Cooperation in European Child Abduction Cases' [2021] Polski Proces Cywilny 501; M Župan, C Hoehn and U Kluth, 'Central Authority Cooperation under the Brussels II ter Regulation' (2020/2021) 22 Yearbook of Private International Law 183.

7 See O Bobrzyńska, 'Brussels II ter Regulation and the 1996 Hague Convention on Child Protection – The Interplay of the European and Hague Regimes in the Matters of Parental Responsibility [2021] Polski Proces Cywilny 593, referring to Article 97.

#5 In spite of the provision's detailed text, and the list of definitions hosted in Article 2, the CJEU was repeatedly called to interpret the scope of the Regulation.[8] Initially, the Court ruled that Article 1 is to be interpreted to the effect that a single decision ordering a child to be taken into care and placed outside his original home in a foster family is covered by the term **'civil matters'**, where that decision was adopted in the context of public law rules relating to child protection.[9] Along the same lines, the Court ruled that a decision ordering that a child be immediately taken into care and placed outside his original home is covered by the term 'civil matters', where that decision was adopted in the context of public law rules relating to child protection.[10] On the same topic, the CJEU ruled that the judgment of a Member State court which orders the placement of child in a secure institution providing therapeutic and educational care situated in another Member State, and which entails that, for her own protection, the child is deprived of her liberty for a specified period, falls within the material scope of the Regulation.[11]

#6 In the field of **guardianship**, the Court decided that the approval of an agreement for the sharing-out of an estate concluded by a 'guardian ad litem' on behalf of minor children, constitutes a measure relating to the exercise of parental responsibility within the meaning of Article 1(1)(b); thus, it is not a measure relating to succession within the meaning of Article 1(4)(f), excluded from the scope thereof.[12]

---

8 See also A Borrás, 'The Substantive Scope of Application of European Instruments in Matrimonial Matters' in B Hess, E Jayme and HP Mansel (eds), *Europa als Rechts- und Lebensraum. Liber Amicorum für Christian Kohler zum 75. Geburtstag* (Gieseking 2018) 23.

9 Case C-435/06 *C* (27 November 2007) ECLI:EU:C:2007:714. See comments by M Andrae, 'On the Applicability of the Brussels II a Regulation to State Measures for the Protection of the Child' [2008] The European Legal Forum 189, and A Quiñones Escámez, '¿Cuándo se aplica el Reglamento Bruselas II bis? El TJCE se pronuncia sobre su ámbito de aplicación' (2008) 12 Revista de Derecho Comunitario Europeo 457. See also S Dominelli, 'Cross-Border Placement of Children within the European Judicial Space: First Thoughts on the Recast Brussels IIa Regulation in Light of the German Experience' [2016] The European Legal Forum 113.

10 Case C-523/07 *A* (2 April 2009) ECLI:EU:C:2009:225. See comments by J Pirrung, 'Der gewöhnliche Aufenthalt des Kindes in internationalen Sorgerechtssachen' in O Sandrock and others (eds), *Festschrift für Gunther Kühne zum 70. Geburtstag* (Recht und Wirtschaft 2009) 843, and S Marino, 'Nuovi criteri interpretativi per la determinazione della giurisdizione in materia di responsabilità genitoriale: la nozione di residenza abituale dei minori in una recente sentenza della Corte di giustizia CE' (2010] 65 Rivista di diritto processuale 467.

11 Case C-92/12 PPU *Health Service Executive v S.C. and A.C.* (26 April 2012) ECLI:EU:C:2012:255. See comments by A Borrás and C Pellisé, 'Jurisprudencia del Tribunal de Justicia de la Unión Europea – Cooperación judicial en materia civil – Sentencia de 26 de abril de 2012, Asunto C-92/12 PPU, Health Service Executive c. S.C., A.C.' [2012] Revista Jurídica de Catalunya 273, and K Kroll-Ludwigs, 'Anmerkung zu EuGH, Urt. v. 26. April 2012, Rs. C-92/12 PPU – Health Service Executive' (2013) 10 GPR 46.

12 Case C-404/14 *Proceedings brought by Marie Matoušková* (6 April 2015) ECLI:EU:C:2015:653. See comments by K Hilbig-Lugani, 'Anmerkung zu EuGH, Urt. v. 26. April 2012, Rs. C-92/12 PPU – Health Service Executive' (2016) 13 GPR 199, and V Darmois, 'La procédure de contrôle du partage successoral conclu

#7 With respect to travel arrangements of children, the Court ruled that an action in which one parent asks the court to remedy the lack of agreement of the other parent to their child travelling outside his Member State of residence, and a passport being issued in the child's name is within the material scope of the Regulation, even though the decision in that action will have to be taken into account by the authorities of the Member State, of which the child is a national, in the administrative procedure for the issue of that passport.[13]

#8 Issues of annulment of marriage and contact rights of third persons appeared at a later stage of the Regulation's application. In regards to the former, the Court ruled that an action for annulment of marriage brought by a third party, following the death of one of the spouses, falls within the scope of Regulation under Article 1(1)(a).[14] The same position was taken concerning contact rights of grandparents: The Court clarified that the concept of 'rights of access' referred to in Article 1(2)(a), Article 2(7) and Article 2(10), must be interpreted as including rights of access of grandparents to their grandchildren.[15]

#9 Article 2 contains a list of definitions, but these did not always suffice, resulting in additional preliminary references to the CJEU. The Court was called to interpret Article 2(11) three times so far.

#10 At first, it ruled that the Regulation does not preclude a Member State from providing by its law that the acquisition of rights of custody by a child's father, where he is not married to the child's mother, is dependent on the father's obtaining a judgment from a national court with jurisdiction awarding such rights to

pour le compte d'enfants mineurs relève du champ d'application du Règlement Bruxelles II bis' [2016] Gazette du Palais 87.

13 Case C-215/15 *Vasilka Ivanova Gogova v Ilia Dimitrov Iliev* (21 October 2015) ECLI:EU:C:2015:710. See comments by P Orejudo Prieto de los Mozos, 'Sentencia TJEU (Sala 4.ª), de 15 de octubre de 2015, asunto c-215/15, *Vasilka Ivanova Gogova y Ilia Dimitrov Iliev*' (2016) 68(1) Revista Española de Derecho Internacional 175, and F Koechel, 'Art. 12 III Brüssel IIa-VO: Zustimmung zu Reise und Passerteilung für bulgar. Kind' [2016] FamRZ 438.

14 Case C-294/15 *Edyta Mikołajczyk v Marie Louise Czarnecka and Stefan Czarnecki* (13 October 2016) ECLI:EU:C:2016:772. See comments by S Corneloup, 'L'action en annulation du mariage intentée par un tiers après le décès d'un epoux' [2017] Revue critique de droit international privé 291, and F Berner, 'Familien- und Erbrecht. Anmerkung zu EuGH, Urt. v. 13.10.2016 – C-294/15 (Mikołajczyk)' (2017) 14 GPR 131.

15 Case C-335/17 *Neli Valcheva v Georgios Babanarakis* (31 May 2018) ECLI:EU:C:2018:359. See comments by MI de la Iglesia Monje, 'El derecho de visita transfronterizo de los abuelos a sus nietos a la luz del TJUE' [2018] Revista crítica de Derecho Inmobiliario 2671, and H Péroz, 'Champ d'application du réglement Bruxelles II bis élargi au droit de visite des grands-parents' (2018) 93 La Semaine Juridique 1376.

him, on the basis of which the removal or the retention of the child by its mother may be considered wrongful, within the meaning of Article 2(11).[16]

#11 Following a second preliminary request, the Court ruled that where the removal of a child has taken place in accordance with a judgment which was provisionally enforceable and was thereafter overturned by a judgment which fixed the residence of the child at the home of the parent living in the Member State of origin, the court of the Member State to which the child was removed, seised of an application for the return of the child, must determine, by undertaking an assessment of all the circumstances of fact specific to the individual case, whether the child was still habitually resident in the Member State of origin immediately before the alleged wrongful retention. As part of that assessment, it is important that account be taken of the fact that the judgment authorising the removal could be provisionally enforced and that an appeal had been brought against it.[17]

#12 The issue was once again sent to Luxembourg, where the CJEU ruled that no wrongful removal or retention has taken place where one of the parents, without the other parent's consent, removes the child from his or her Member State of **habitual residence** to another Member State pursuant to a decision to transfer taken by the first Member State in application of Regulation 604/2013, establishing the criteria and mechanisms for determining the Member State responsible for examining an application for international protection lodged in one of the Member States by a third-country national or a stateless person, then remains in the second Member State after the decision to transfer has been annulled without the authorities of the first Member State deciding to take back the persons transferred or authorise their residence.[18]

#13 The concept of **'parental responsibility'** has been also a matter under dispute. By order of the CJEU it was ruled that parental responsibility, as defined by Article 2(2)7, must be interpreted as covering decisions relating to custody of the child and the child's place of habitual residence, but it does not include parental contributions towards the costs of the child's care and upbringing, which is covered by the concept of 'maintenance obligations' under Regulation 4/2009.[19]

#14 Finally, the CJEU was called to define the term 'judgment' under Article 2(4) Brussels II-bis, now 'decision' under Article 2(1) Brussels II-ter, and ruled that this must be interpreted as meaning that a divorce decree drawn up by a civil regis-

16 Case C-400/10 PPU *J. McB. v L. E.* (5 October 2010) ECLI:EU:C:2010:582. See comments by M Krausenboeck, 'No Luck for Fathers of Children Born out of Wedlock' [2010] European Law Reporter 352, and J Pirrung, 'Kein Hinderungsgrund aus der Brüssel IIa-VO, wenn Mitgliedstaaten den Erwerb des Sorgerechts durch den nicht mit der Mutter verheirateten Vater von einer gerichtlichen Entscheidung abhängig machen' (2011) 19 ZEuP 901.

17 Case C-376/14 PPU *C v M.* (9 October 2014) ECLI:EU:C:2014:2268.

18 Case C-262/21 PPU *A v B* (2 August 2019) ECLI:EU:C:2021:640.

19 Case C-759/18 *OF v PG* (3 October 2019) ECLI:EU:C:2019:816.

trar of the Member State of origin, containing a divorce agreement concluded by the spouses and confirmed by them before that registrar in accordance with the conditions laid down by that Member State legislation, constitutes a 'judgment' under Article 2(4) Brussels II-bis.[20]

D International Jurisdiction in Matrimonial Matters

#15 Chapter II on international jurisdiction in matrimonial matters is the most important part of the Regulation, which is the reason why a great number of preliminary requests were submitted to the Court's registry, primarily emanating from divorce proceedings. Section I covers the ambit of divorce, legal separation and marriage annulment (Articles 3–6).[21] The provisions deal with general jurisdiction (Article 3), counterclaim (Article 4), conversion of legal separation to divorce (Article 5), and **residual jurisdiction** matters (Article 6).

#16 A number of issues have been examined by the CJEU concerning the habitual residence under Article 3(a) Brussels II-ter.[22] The court ruled that a spouse who divides his/her time between two Member States may have his/her habitual residence in only one of those; hence, only the courts of the Member State in which that habitual residence is situated have jurisdiction to rule on the application for divorce.[23]

---

20 Case C-646/20 *Senatsverwaltung für Inneres und Sport* (15 November 2022) ECLI:EU:C:2022:879.

21 Ad hoc M Ní Shúilleabháin, *Cross-Border Divorce Law Brussels II Bis* (OUP 2011). See also K Boele-Woelki, 'For Better or for Worse: The Europeanization of International Divorce Law' (2010) 12 Yearbook of Private International Law 1.

22 Ad hoc B Hess, 'Towards a Uniform Concept of Habitual Residence in European Procedural and Private International Law?' [2021] Polski Proces Cywilny 523. See also T Kruger, 'Finding a Habitual Residence' in I Viarengo and F Villata (eds), *Planning the Future of Cross Border Families: A Path Through Coordination* (Hart 2020) 117; K Hilbig-Lugani, 'Divergenz und Transparenz: Der Begriff des gewöhnlichen Aufenthalts der privat handelnden natürlichen Person im jüngeren EuIPR und EuZVR' (2014) 11 GPR 8; A Limante, 'Establishing Habitual Residence of Adults under the Brussels IIa Regulation: Best Practices from National Case-Law' (2018) 14 J. Priv. Int. Law 160; R Lamont, 'Habitual Residence and Brussels IIbis: Developing Concepts for European Private International Family Law (2007) 3 J. Priv. Int. Law 261; A Zanobetti, '*La residenza abituale nel diritto internazionale privato: spunti di riflessione*' in *Liber Amicorum Angelo Davì La vita giuridica internazionale nell'età della globalizzazione*, vol II0 (Editoriale Scientifica 2019) 1361.

23 Case C-289/20 *IB v FA* (25 November 2021) ECLI:EU:C:2021:955: Article 3(1)(a) Regulation. See comments by J Sagot-Duvauroux, 'Précisions sur la notion de résidence habituelle en matière de divorce' (2022) 58 Revue trimestrielle de droit européen 193, and SL Gössl, 'Rechtsaktbezogene Einzigartigkeit und subjektive Komponenten: einige Notizen zum gewöhnlichen Aufenthalt im europäischen Kollisions- und Verfahrensrecht: zu EuGH, 25.11.2021' [2022] IPRax 489.

#17 In addition, the CJEU clarified that Article 3(a) must be interpreted as meaning that the status of the spouses concerned as members of the contract staff of the E.U. working in the latter's delegation to a third country, and in respect of whom it is claimed that they enjoy diplomatic status in that State, is not capable of constituting a decisive factor for the purposes of determining habitual residence.[24]

#18 With respect to the fifth and sixth indents of Article 3(1)(a), the CJEU ruled that a person other than one of the spouses who brings an action for annulment of marriage may not rely on those grounds of jurisdiction.[25]

#19 Focusing on the last indent of Article 3(vi) Brussels II-ter (former Article 3(1) Brussels II-bis), and taking into account the **principle of non-discrimination** on grounds of **nationality**, enshrined in Article 18 TFEU, the CJEU interpreted the rule as not precluding a situation in which the jurisdiction of the courts of the Member State in the territory of which the habitual residence of the applicant is located, is subject to the applicant being resident for a minimum period immediately before making his or her application, which is six months shorter than that provided for in Article 3(v) Brussels II-ter, on the ground that the person concerned is a national of that Member State.[26] The Court clarified that the provision aforementioned makes the jurisdiction of the court subject to the condition that the applicant, who is a national of that Member State, provides evidence that he or she has acquired a habitual residence in that Member State for at least six months immediately prior to the application's submission.[27]

#20 In regards to spouses of common **nationality**, the CJEU ruled that where the applicant brings proceedings before a court of the Member State of the spouses' common nationality, although their habitual residence is in another Member State, that court has jurisdiction pursuant to Article 3(b). As the defendant is not required to give consent, it is not necessary to examine whether a failure of the defendant to raise an objection that the court lacks jurisdiction, constitutes tacit consent to the court seised.[28] In the course of the same preliminary reference, the CJEU clarified that according to Articles 3(1) and 18 Brussels II-ter (Article 18 Brussels II-bis), the fact that the couple seeking dissolution of their marriage have a minor child is irrelevant for the purposes of determining the court's jurisdiction to rule on the divorce application. Since the above court has jurisdiction to rule

24 Case C-501/20 *M P A* (1 August 2022) ECLI:EU:C:2022:619.

25 Case C-294/15 *Edyta Mikołajczyk v Marie Louise Czarnecka and Stefan Czarnecki* (13 October 2016) CLI:EU:C:2016:772.

26 Case C-522/20 *OE v VY* (10 February 2022) ECLI:EU:C:2022:87. See comments by W Hau, 'Internationale Zuständigkeit kraft Staatsangehörigkeit im Europäischen Familienverfahrensrecht: [zu EuGH, 10.2.2022, Rs. C-522/20: OE./. VY]' [2022] IPRax 342, and D Martin, 'Quelques observations sans intérêt sur la notion de discrimination [2022] Revue des affaires européennes 153.

27 Case C-462/22 *BM* (6 July 2023) ECLI:EU:C:2023:553.

28 Case C-759/18 *OF v PG* (3 October 2019) ECLI:EU:C:2019:816.

on that application under Article 3(b), it cannot raise an objection that it lacks international jurisdiction.

#21 Finally, the Court underlined that where both spouses hold the nationality of the same two Member States, Article 3(b) precludes the jurisdiction of the courts of one of those Member States from being rejected on the ground that the applicant does not put forward other links with that State. Therefore, the courts of those Member States have jurisdiction and the spouses may seise the court of the Member State of their choice.[29]

#22 In yet another preliminary reference founded upon the same provision, it was ruled that the court with jurisdiction to hear an application for divorce between two spouses who are nationals of that Member State, does not have jurisdiction to rule on rights of custody and access in respect of the spouses' child in the case where, at the time when the court is seised, that child is habitually resident in another Member State. The conditions for such jurisdiction are not satisfied by that court, unless that court has jurisdiction under Articles 9, 10 or 15 of the Regulation.[30]

#23 Article 6 (previously Article 7 Brussels II-bis) grants the right to establish **international jurisdiction** on the grounds of domestic legislation (residual jurisdiction). The matter has been brought twice before the CJEU: In the first case, the Court ruled that where, in divorce proceedings, a respondent is not habitually resident in, and not a national of a Member State, the courts cannot base their jurisdiction to hear the petition on their national law, if the courts of another Member State have jurisdiction under Article 3.[31] In the second case, it was ruled that, where no court of a Member State has jurisdiction to rule on an application for the dissolution of matrimonial ties, the fact that the respondent is a national of a Member State other than that of the court seised, prevents the application of the clause relating to residual jurisdiction to establish the jurisdiction of that court without, however, preventing the courts of the Member State of which the respondent is a national from having jurisdiction to hear such an application pursuant to the latter Member State's national rules.[32]

29 Case C-168/08 *Laszlo Hadadi (Hadady) v Csilla Marta Mesko, épouse Hadadi (Hadady)* (16 July 2009) ECLI:EU:C:2009:474. See comments by W Hau, 'Doppelte Staatsangehörigkeit im europäischen Eheverfahrensrecht' [2010] IPRax 50, and S Álvarez González, 'La doble nacionalidad comunitaria en materia matrimonial – Comentario a la STJCE de 16 de julio de 2009' [2011] Noticias de la Unión Europea 89.

30 Case C-604/17 *PM v AH* (16 January 2018) ECLI:EU:C:2018:10.

31 Case C-68/07 *Kerstin Sundelind Lopez v Miguel Enrique Lopez Lizazo* (29 November 2007) ECLI:EU:C:2007:740. See comments by A Borrás Rodríguez, '"Exclusive" and "Residual" Grounds of Jurisdiction on Divorce in the Brussels IIbis Regulation [2008] IPRax 233, and F Garau Sobrino, 'Sentencia Tribunal de Justicia de las Comunidades Europeas (Sala Tercera), de 29 de noviembre de 2007, en el asunto C-68/07 (Sundelind López)' (2007) 59(2) Revista Española de Derecho Internacional 763.

32 Case C-501/20 M P A (1 August 2022) ECLI:EU:C:2022:619.

E International Jurisdiction in Parental Responsibility Matters

I Overview

#24 The core rule for establishing international jurisdiction in matters of parental responsibility is Article 7 Brussels II-ter (previously Article 8 Brussels II-bis). A significant number of preliminary requests has shed light to the proper interpretation of the provision, most notably on the issue of the child's habitual residence.[33] Beyond this article, Section 2 of Chapter II contains a series of important provisions, such as continuing jurisdiction in relation to access rights (Article 8), Jurisdiction in cases of the wrongful removal or retention of a child (Article 9), Choice of court (Article 10), Jurisdiction based on presence of the child (Article 11),transfer of jurisdiction to a court of another Member State (Article 12), request for transfer of jurisdiction by a court of a Member State not having jurisdiction (Article 13), and residual jurisdiction (Article 14) and provisional and protective measures (Article 15).

II General Jurisdiction and Habitual Residence

#25 The CJEU ruled that the concept of 'habitual residence' that is central in these jurisdiction rules must be interpreted as meaning that such residence corresponds to the place which reflects some degree of integration by the child in a social and family environment. To that end, where the situation concerned is that of an infant who has been staying with her mother only a few days in a Member State — other than that of her habitual residence — to which she has been removed, the factors which must be taken into consideration include, first, the duration, regularity, conditions and reasons for the stay in the territory of that Member State and for the mother's move to that State and, second, with particular reference to the child's age, the mother's geographic and family origins and the family and social connections which the mother and child have with that Member State. It is for the national court to establish the habitual residence of the child. If the application of the abovementioned tests cannot establish the child's habitual residence, the matter would have to be determined on the basis of the criterion of the child's presence under Article 11 Brussels II-ter (Article 13 Brussels II-bis).[34]

33 See GP Romano, 'Conflicts Between Parents and Between Legal Orders in Respect of Parental Responsibility' (2014/2015) 16 Yearbook of Private International Law 129.

34 Case C-497/10 PPU *Barbara Mercredi v Richard Chaffe* (22 December 2010) ECLI:EU:C:2010:829. See comments by P Mankowski, 'Der gewöhnliche Aufenthalt eines verbrachten Kindes unter der Brüssel

#26 In addition, the CJEU clarified that the courts of the Member State which made a decision that has become final concerning parental responsibility with regard to a minor child no longer have jurisdiction to decide on an application for variation of the provisions ordered in that decision, inasmuch as the habitual residence of the child is in another Member State. The courts of the Member State of habitual residence have jurisdiction to decide on that application.[35]

#27 In yet another preliminary reference, the Court underlined that a child's place of habitual residence is the place which, in practice, is the centre of that child's life. National courts will have to determine where that centre was located at the time the application was submitted. The following, taken together, are decisive factors: the fact that, from its birth until its parents' separation, the child generally lived with those parents in a specific place; the fact that the parent who, in practice, has had custody of the child since the couple's separation continues to stay in that place with the child on a daily basis and is employed there under an employment contract of indefinite duration; and the fact that the child has regular contact there with its other parent, who is still resident in that place. By contrast, the following cannot be regarded as decisive: the stays which the parent who, in practice, has **custody** of the child has spent in the past with that child in the territory of that parent's Member State of origin in the context of leave periods or holidays; the origins of the parent in question, the cultural ties which the child has with that Member State as a result, and the parent's relationships with family residing in that Member State, and any intention the parent has of settling in that Member State with the child in the future.[36]

#28 The Court was given the chance to interpret the notion of habitual residence even deeper: a child must have been physically present in a Member State in order to be regarded as habitually resident in that State. Circumstances, such as, first, the fact that the father's coercion of the mother had the effect of her giving birth to their child in a third country where she has resided with that child ever since,

IIa-VO – Anmerkung zu EuGH, Urt. v. 22.12.2010 – Rs. C-497/10 PPU' (2011) 8 GPR 209, and L Pailler, 'La portée de l'obligation de reconnaître une décision relative à la garde d'un enfant émanant de la juridiction de l'État membre dans lequel l'enfant a été déplacé en application du réglement n° 2201/2003 "Bruxelles II bis"' [2016] Journal du droit international 593.

35 Case C-499/15 *W and V v X* (15 February 2017) ECLI:EU:C:2017:118. See comments by C Nourissat, 'Encore et toujours la résidence habituelle de l'enfant' [2017–4] Procédures 24, and J Wißling, 'Kind von Welt beim EuGH. Anmerkung zu EuGH-Urteilen C-499/15 und C-283/16' (2017) 14 GPR 255.

36 Case C-512/17 *Proceedings brought by HR* (28 June 2018) ECLI:EU:C:2018:513. See comment by L Idot, 'Notion de résidence habituelle' (2018) 28(8–9) Europe 48, and UP Gruber, 'Der gewöhnliche Aufenthalt von Säuglingen und Kleinkindern' [2018] IPRax 217.

and, secondly, the breach of the mother's or the child's rights, do not have any bearing in that regard.[37]

#29 In search of connecting factors determining a child's habitual residence, the CJEU ruled that the mother's nationality and her residence prior to the marriage in the Member State of the court seised of an application relating to parental responsibility is irrelevant, whereas the fact that the minor children were born in that Member State and hold the nationality of that Member State is insufficient.[38]

#30 The CJEU also ruled that a national court hearing a dispute relating to parental responsibility does not retain jurisdiction to rule on that dispute, where the habitual residence of the child has been lawfully transferred, during the proceedings, to the territory of a third State that is a party to the 1996 Hague Convention.[39]

#31 With respect to Article 8(1) Brussels II-ter (previously Article 9(1) Brussels II-bis), the CJEU held the three-month period during which the courts of the Member State of the child's former habitual residence retain jurisdiction to hear an application for modification of a final judgment concerning access rights, begins on the day following that on which that child actually moved to the Member State of the new habitual residence.[40]

III Wrongful Removal or Retention

#32 Article 9 Brussels II-ter (previously Article 10 Brussels II-bis) is dealing with the thorny issue of determining international Jurisdiction in cases of wrongful removal or retention of a child. It is therefore not a surprise that the CJEU was called time and again to interpret the content of this provision.

#33 Initially, the Court ruled that in a case, in which a child who was habitually resident in a Member State was wrongfully removed to another Member State, the courts of the latter do not have jurisdiction to rule on an application relating to custody, in the absence of any indication that the other parent consented to his removal or did not bring an application for the return of that child.[41]

#34 In addition, the Court clarified that the provision is not applicable to a situation where a finding is made that a child has, at the time when an application relating

37 Case C-393/18 PPU *UD v XB* (17 October 2018) ECLI:EU:C:2018:835. See comments by É Viganotti, 'La notion de "résidence habituelle" de l'enfant selon la CJUE' [2018] Gazette du Palais n° 40 Jur. 24, and C Thomale, 'Der gewöhnliche Aufenthalt im Europäischen Kindschaftsrecht' (2019) 16 GPR 173.

38 Case C-501/20 M P A (1 August 2022) ECLI:EU:C:2022:619.

39 Case C-572/21 *CC* (14 July 2022) ECLI:EU:C:2022:562.

40 Case C-372/22 *CM* (27 April 2023) ECLI:EU:C:2023:364.

41 Case C-85/18 PPU *CV v DU* (10 April 2018) ECLI:EU:C:2018:220.

to parental responsibility is brought, acquired his or her habitual residence in a third State following abduction to that State. In that situation, the jurisdiction of the court seised will have to be determined in accordance with the applicable international conventions, or, in the absence of such conventions, in accordance with Article 14.[42]

#35 A further prerequisite for applying the rule has been established by the CJEU, which ruled that a provisional measure does not constitute a 'judgment on custody that does not entail the return of the child', and cannot be the basis of a transfer of jurisdiction to the courts where the child has been unlawfully removed.[43] Recently, the CJEU held that Article 9(b)(i) Brussels II-ter (previously 10 (b)(i) Brussels II-bis) must be interpreted as meaning that that provision does not cease to be applicable on the sole ground that a request was made to the central authority of a third country for proceedings to be commenced for the return of a child under the 1980 Hague Convention, and that those proceedings have failed. In addition, the Court ruled that the same provision must be interpreted as meaning that the concept of 'request for return' does not cover either an application for the return of the child to a State other than the Member State in which that child was habitually resident immediately before the wrongful removal or retention, or an application for custody of that child brought before the courts of that Member State. Finally, Article 29(3, 5 & 6) Brussels II-ter (formerly 11(6) to (8) Brussels II-bis) must be interpreted as not applying when proceedings for the return of a child under the 1980 Child Abduction have commenced between a third country and a Member State on the territory of which that child is present following a wrongful removal or retention.[44]

42 Case C-603/20 PPU *SS v MCP* (24 March 2021) ECLI:EU:C:2021:231. See comments by M González Marimón, 'Competencia judicial internacional ante un caso de sustracción internacional de menores de un estado miembro de la UE a un estado tercero: La STJUE de 24 de marzo de 2021'[2021] Revista General de Derecho Europeo 229, and E Gallant, 'Inapplicabilité de l'article 10 du règlement Bruxelles II bis en cas d'acquisition d'une résidence habituelle dans un État tiers' [2023] Revue critique de droit international privé nº 1 127.

43 Case C-211/10 PPU *Doris Povse v Mauro Alpago* (1 July 2010) ECLI:EU:C:2010:400. See comments by V Lazić, 'Family Private International Law Issues Before the European Court of Human Rights: Lessons to Be Learned from Povse v. Austria in Revising the Brussels IIa Regulation, Fundamental Rights in International and European Law' in C Paulussen and others (eds), *Fundamental Rights in International and European Law* (Asser 2016) 161, and MH Zoeteweij-Turhan, 'Brussels II bis: The Right of the Child to be Heard in International Proceedings' [2015] Pravnik: revija za pravno teorijo in prakso 861.

44 Case C-35/23 *Greislzel* (20 June 2024) ECLI:EU:C:2024:532. See comments by L Idot, 'Règlement « bruxelles II bis » – Déplacement illicite d'enfant' (2024) 34(8–9) Europe 336.

IV Choice of Court

#36 Article 10 Brussels II-ter provides a limited possibility to make a choice of court. This provision uses the term 'choice of court', which differs from the initial formulation, **prorogation** of jurisdiction in Article 12 Brussels II-bis.[45]

#37 Jurisdiction which has been prorogued in favor of a Member State court, before which proceedings have been brought by mutual agreement by the holders of parental responsibility, ceases following a final judgment in those proceedings.[46]

#38 The provision must be interpreted as allowing the jurisdiction of a Member State court, which is not that of the child's habitual residence, to be established even where no other proceedings are pending before the court chosen; it cannot be considered that the jurisdiction of the court seised by one party has been 'accepted expressly or otherwise in an unequivocal manner by all the parties, where the defendant in those first proceedings subsequently brings a second set of proceedings before the same court and, on taking the first step required of him in the first proceedings, pleads the lack of jurisdiction of that court.[47]

#39 In a situation, where the parents of a minor child, habitually resident with the latter in a Member State, have lodged, in the name of that child, an application for permission to renounce an inheritance before the courts of another Member State, Article 10(1) Brussels II-ter, must be interpreted as meaning, (1) that the joint lodging of proceedings by the parents before the courts of their choice is an unequivocal acceptance of that court. A prosecutor who, according to national law, has the capacity of a party to the proceedings commenced by the parents, is a party to the proceedings within the meaning of the Regulation; (2) opposition by that party to the choice of jurisdiction made by the parents after the date on which the court was seised, precludes the acceptance of prorogation by all the parties to the proceedings at that date from being established. In the absence of

45 See MA Lupoi, 'Between Parties' Consent and Judicial Discretion: Joinder of Claims and Transfer of Cases in Regulation (EU) 2019/1111' [2021] Polski Proces Cywilny 543; GP Moreno, 'Crisis matrimoniales internacionales y autonomía de la voluntad' [2013] Cursos de derecho internacional y relaciones internacionales de Vitoria-Gasteiz 451; O Feraci, 'Party Autonomy and Conflict of Jurisdictions in the EU Private International Law on Family and Succession Matters (2014/2015) 16 Yearbook of Private International Law 105.

46 Case C-436/13 *E. v B.* (1 October 2014) ECLI:EU:C:2014:2246. See comments by M-C de Lambertye-Autrand 'Le prononcé de la décision épuise la prorogation du for' [2016] Revue critique de droit international privé 174, and M Andrae, 'Erste Entscheidungen des EuGH zu Art. 12 Abs. 3 EuEheVO' [2015] IPRax 212.

47 Case C-656/13 *L v M* (2 November 2014) ECLI:EU:C:2014:2364. See comments by M Andrae, 'Erste Entscheidungen des EuGH zu Art. 12 Abs. 3 EuEheVO' [2015] IPRax 212, and C Nourissat, 'Prorogation volontaire de compétence en matière de responsabilité parentale' [2015–1] Procédures 41.

such opposition, the agreement of that party may be regarded as implicit and the condition of unequivocal acceptance of prorogation by all parties may be held to be satisfied; (3) the fact that the residence of the deceased at the time of his death, his assets, and the liabilities of the succession were situated in the Member State of the chosen courts leads, in the absence of matters that might demonstrate that the prorogation was liable to have a prejudicial impact on the child's position, to the conclusion that that prorogation is in the best interests of the child.[48]

V Transfer of Jurisdiction

#40 Article 12 Brussels II-ter (previously Article 15 Brussels II-bis Regulation) allows the transfer of jurisdiction to a court of another Member State under certain conditions. The previous title of the provision referred to the transfer to a court *better placed* to hear the case.[49] The wording triggered a flood of preliminary requests to the CJEU.[50]

#41 Article 12 is applicable where a child protection application brought under public law by the competent authority of a Member State concerns the adoption of measures relating to parental responsibility, where it is a necessary consequence of a court of another Member State assuming jurisdiction that an authority of that other Member State thereafter commence proceedings that are separate from those brought in the first Member State, pursuant to its own domestic law and possibly relating to different factual circumstances.[51]

#42 Article 12(1) must be interpreted as meaning that, in order to determine that a court of another Member State with which the child has a particular connection is better placed, the court having jurisdiction in a Member State must be satisfied that the transfer of the case to that other court is such as to provide genuine and specific added value to the examination of that case, taking into account the rules of procedure applicable in that other Member State. In order to determine that

48 Case C-565/16 *Alessandro Saponaro and Kalliopi-Chloi Xylina* (19 April 2018) ECLI:EU:C:2018:265:

49 See G Cuniberti and C Camara, 'The EU Forum Non Conveniens Rule in Child Care Proceedings Cases Involving Public Bodies' (2016/2017) 18 Yearbook of Private International Law 431.

50 See also M Szpunar, 'Forum of Necessity in Family Law Matters Within the Framework of EU and International Law' [2021] Polski Proces Cywilny 563.

51 Case C-428/15 *Child and Family Agency v J. D.* (27 October 2016) ECLI:EU:C:2016:819. See comments by J Pirrung, 'Forum (non) conveniens – Art. 15 EuEheVO Vor zwei obersten Common law-Gerichten (zu EuGH, 27.10.2016 – Rs. C-428/15 – Child and Family Agency /. J. D., unten S. 610, Nr. 45)' [2017] IPRax 562, and L Idot, 'Précisions tant sur le champ d'application que sur les conditions de mise en oeuvre de l'article 15 du règlement qui permet le renvoi à une juridiction d'un autre État membre mieux placée' (2016) 26(12) Europe 46.

such a transfer is in the best interests of the child, the court having jurisdiction must be satisfied, that that transfer is not liable to be detrimental to the situation of the child.[52]

#43 A court having jurisdiction in a Member State must not take into account, when applying that provision, either the effect of a possible transfer of that case to a court of another Member State on the right of freedom of movement of persons concerned other than the child in question, or the reason why the mother of that child exercised that right, prior to that court being seised, unless those considerations are such that there may be adverse repercussions on the situation of that child.[53]

#44 Article 12 Brussels II-ter must be interpreted as not applying in circumstances, in which both courts seised have jurisdiction as to the substance of the matter under Article 10 (Article 12 Brussels II-bis) and Article 7 (Article 8 Brussels II-bis), respectively.[54]

#45 Article 12(1) Brussels II-ter establishes an exception to the general rule of jurisdiction.[55] If one or more of the alternative criteria are satisfied, the court having jurisdiction has the option to transfer the case to a court which it considers to be better placed to deal with the dispute, but is not obliged to do so. If the court having jurisdiction reaches the conclusion that the relations which link the child to the Member State of her habitual residence are stronger than those which link her to another Member State, that conclusion is sufficient to rule out the application of Article 12.[56] The existence of differences between the rules of law, in particular the rules of procedure, of a Member State having jurisdiction as to the substance of a case and those of another Member State with which the child has a particular connection, such as the examination of cases in camera by specialist judges, does not constitute a relevant criterion, in light of the best interests of the child. The court having jurisdiction may take those differences into consideration only if they provide genuine and specific added value with respect to the decision to be taken, as compared with the possibility of the case remaining before that court.[57]

#46 A Member State court, which has jurisdiction to rule on the substance (under Article 7), may exceptionally request the transfer of that case to a Member State court to which the child has been wrongfully removed.[58] The only conditions are those expressly set out in Article 12. When examining those conditions in respect of, first, the existence in the latter Member State of a court better placed to hear

52 ibid.
53 ibid.
54 Case C-478/17 *IQ v JP* (4 October 2018) ECLI:EU:C:2018:812.
55 Case C-530/18 *EP v FO* (10 July 2019) ECLI:EU:C:2019:583.
56 ibid.
57 ibid.
58 Case C-87/22 *TT v AK* (13 July 2023) ECLI:EU:C:2023:571.

the case and, second, the best interests of the child, the court of the first Member State must take into consideration the existence of proceedings for the return of that child which have been instituted pursuant to Article 8 of the 1980 Hague Convention, and in which a final decision has not yet been delivered in the Member State to which that child was wrongfully removed.[59]

#47 The court of the Member State of the child's former habitual residence, which has jurisdiction as to the substance of the matter, may exercise the option of transferal to the court of the Member State of that child's new habitual residence, provided that the conditions laid down in Article 12 are satisfied.[60]

VI Residual Jurisdiction

#48 Where no court of a Member State has jurisdiction to rule on an application relating to parental responsibility, Article 14 must be interpreted as meaning that the fact that the respondent in the main proceedings is a national of a Member State other than that of the court seised does not preclude the application of the clause relating to **residual jurisdiction** laid down in Article 14.[61]

VII Provisional Measures

#49 **Provisional measures** are regulated in Article 15.[62] The rule must be interpreted as not allowing a court to take a provisional measure in parental responsibility matters granting custody of a child who is in the territory of that Member State to one parent, where a court of another Member State, which has jurisdiction as to the substance of the dispute relating to custody, has already delivered a judgment provisionally giving custody to the other parent, and that judgment has been declared enforceable in the territory of the former Member State.[63]

---

59 ibid.

60 Case C-372/22 CM (27 April 2023) ECLI:EU:C:2023:364.

61 Case C-501/20 *M P A* (1 August 2022) ECLI:EU:C:2022:619.

62 See I Pretelli, 'Provisional Measures in Family Law and the Brussels IIter Regulation' (2018/2019) 20 Yearbook of Private International Law 113; M Requejo Isidro, 'El artículo 20 Reglamento (CE) número 2201/2003 ante el TJCE' [2010] Diario La Ley, N° 7479, Sección Tribuna, 30 Sep. 2010; A Carratta, 'Tre Provvedimenti urgenti a tutela dei minori e sottrazione internazionale (2017) 71 Rivista Trimestrale Di Diritto E Procedura Civile 1257.

63 Case C-403/09 PPU *Jasna Detiček v Maurizio Sgueglia* (23 December 2009) ECLI:EU:C:2009:810. See comments by M Requejo Isidro, 'El artículo 20 Reglamento (CE) número 2201/2003 ante el TJCE' [2010] Diario La Ley N° 7479, and U Janzen and V Gärtner, 'Kindschaftsrechtliche Spannungsverhältnisse im Rahmen der EuEheVO – die Entscheidung des EuGH in Sachen Detiček [2011] IPRax 158.

F Common Provisions

I Seising of a Court

#50 Article 17 deals with the seising of the court. The CJEU has ruled that this provision must be interpreted to the effect that the 'time when the document instituting the proceedings or an equivalent document is lodged with the court', is the time when that document is lodged with the court concerned, even if under national law lodging that document does not of itself immediately initiate proceedings.[64]

II Examination as to Jurisdiction

#51 Article 3(1) on general jurisdiction in divorce cases and Article 18 regarding the examination of jurisdiction must be interpreted as meaning that, the fact that the couple seeking dissolution of their marriage have a minor child is irrelevant for the purposes of determining the court having jurisdiction. Since the court of the Member State of the spouses' common nationality, seised by the applicant, has jurisdiction to rule on that application under Article 3(1)(b), that court cannot, even where there is no agreement between the parties on the matter, raise an objection that it lacks international jurisdiction.[65]

III Lis Pendens and Dependent Actions

#52 Article 20 deals with lis pendens and dependent actions.[66] As a ground rule it lays down the 'first seised' rule, meaning that the court second seised shall of its own motion stay its proceedings until the first court establishes its jurisdiction. The CJEU has ruled that this provision does not apply where a court of a Member State first seised for the purpose of obtaining measures in matters of parental responsibility is seised only for the purpose of its granting provisional measures, and where a court of another Member State which has jurisdiction as to the substance of the matter is seised second of an action directed at obtaining the same measures, whether on a provisional basis or as final measures.[67]

---

64 Case C-173/16 *M.H. v M.H.* (22 June 2016) ECLI:EU:C:2016:542.

65 Case C-759/18 *OF v PG* (3 October 2019) ECLI:EU:C:2019:816.

66 Ad hoc S Ziino, 'La giurisdizione sulle cause matrimoniali e sulle domande connesse secondo la normativa europea (2014) 68 Rivista Trimestrale Di Diritto e Procedura Civile 537.

67 Case C-296/10 *Bianca Purrucker v Guillermo Vallés Pérez* (9 November 2010) ECLI:EU:C:2010:665. See comments by L Idot, 'Déplacement illicite d'enfant et reconnaissance d'une décision de mesures provisoires (2010) 20(10) Europe 42, and E Rodriguez Pineau, 'STJ (Sala 2.ª) de 9 de noviembre de 2010,

#53 The fact that a court of a Member State is seised in the context of proceedings to obtain interim relief or that a judgment is handed down in the context of such proceedings, and there is nothing in the action brought or the judgment handed down which indicates that the court seised for the interim measures has jurisdiction, does not necessarily preclude the possibility that there may be an action as to the substance of the matter which is linked to the action to obtain interim measures, and in which there is evidence to demonstrate that it has jurisdiction.[68]

#54 In the case of judicial separation and divorce proceedings brought between the same parties before the courts of two Member States, the main proceedings in which the proceedings before the court first seised expired after the second court was seised, the criteria for ***lis pendens*** are no longer fulfilled and, therefore, the jurisdiction of the court first seised must be regarded as not being established.[69]

#55 Where in a matrimonial matter or parental responsibility dispute, the court second seised delivers a judgment which becomes final, the rules preclude the courts of the Member State first seised from refusing to recognise that judgment solely for that reason. That breach cannot justify non-recognition of a judgment on the ground that it is manifestly contrary to public policy.[70]

G International Child Abduction

#56 Chapter III is a regulatory novelty, compared to the predecessor of this Regulation.[71] A special chapter is dedicated exclusively to international child abduction cases,[72]

Bianca Purrucker c. Guillermo Vallés Pérez' (2010) 62(2) Revista Española de Derecho Internacional 244.

68 ibid.

69 Case C-489/14 *A v B* (6 October 2015) ECLI:EU:C:2015:654. See comments by C Chalas, 'Litispendance et décalage horaire dans le contentieux du divorce en Europe [2016] Revue critique de droit international privé 387, and K Hilbig-Lugani, 'Anmerkung zu EuGH, Urt. vom 6.10.2015 – C-489/14 (A v B)' (2016) 13 GPR 132.

70 Case C-386/17 *Stefano Liberato v Luminita Luisa Grigorescu* (16 January 2019) ECLI:EU:C:2019:24. See comments by H Muir Watt, 'Sanctionner ou circuler? Les conséquences sur le terrain des effets des jugements de la méconnaissance par le juge second saisi des règles relatives à la litispendance [2019] Revue critique de droit international privé 495, and J von Hein and N Grohmann, 'Anmerkung zu EuGH, C-386/17 (Liberato./. Grigorescu)' [2019] FamRZ 1164.

71 For the latter, see F Gascón Inchausti, 'International Child Abduction in the Case Law of the Court of Justice of the European Union: Learning from the Past and Looking to the Future' [2021] Polski Proces Cywilny 617; C Honorati, 'Sottrazione Internazionale Dei Minori e Diritti Fondamentali (2013) 49 Rivista di diritto internazionale privato e processuale 5.

72 See in this respect K Trimmings, '*Child Abduction within the European Union* (Hart 2013); AS de Sousa Gonçalves, 'A Deslocação Ou Retenção Ilícitas De Crianças No Regulamento N.º 2201/2003 (BRUXELAS II BIS)' (2014) 6 Cuadernos de Derecho Transnacional; S Tonolo, 'La Sottrazione Dei Minori Nel

extending to Articles 22–29, and covering crucial matters, such as the return of the child under the 1980 Hague Convention (Article 22), case management issues between competent state authorities (Articles 23–24), ADR[73] (Article 25), and the manifestation of children rights to express their views in return proceedings (Article 26).[74]

#57 Important issues, such as the procedure for the return of the child, the enforcement of decisions ordering the return of a child, and the procedure following a refusal to return the child under point (b) of Article 13(1) and Article 13(2) of the Convention, are thoroughly covered under Articles 27–29. A matter frequently discussed in legal scholarship is also the relationship between the Regulation and the ECHR in this context.[75]

I Return of the Child Under the 1980 Hague Convention

#58 According to Article 22, the return of a child in breach of rights of custody under the 1980 Hague Convention is complemented by the provisions of the Regulation. The CJEU has ruled in relation to its predecessors, Articles 2(11) and 11 Brussels II-bis that this provision must be interpreted as meaning that where the removal of a child has taken place in accordance with a judgment which was provisionally enforceable and was thereafter overturned by a judgment which fixed the **residence** of the child at the home of the parent living in the Member State of origin, the court of the Member State to which the child was removed, seised of an application for the return of the child, must determine whether the child was still habitually resident in the Member State of origin immediately before the alleged wrongful retention. It is important that the judgment authorising the removal could be provisionally enforced, and an appeal had been brought against it.[76]

#59 In addition Article 22 (Article 11(1) Brussels II-bis), must be interpreted as meaning that, where a child was born and has lived continuously with her mother for sev-

Diritto Processuale Civile Europeo: Il Regolamento Bruxelles Ii-Bis E La Convenzione Dell'aja Del 1980 A Confronto' (2011) 47 Rivista di Diritto Internazionale Privato e Processuale 81.

73 Ad hoc S Vigers, *Mediating International Child Abduction Cases: The Hague Convention* (Hart 2011).

74 In depth K Lenaerts, 'The Best Interests of The Child Always Come First: The Brussels Ii Bis Regulation and the European Court of Justice' (2013) 2020 Jurisprudence 1302. See also O Lopes Pegna, 'L'interesse Superiore Del Minore Nel Regolamento N. 2201/2003' (2013) 49 Rivista di diritto internazionale privato e processuale 357; EC Tuo, 'Superiore interesse del minore e regolamenti UE di diritto internazionale privato della famiglia (2020) 36 NGCC 676; G Biagioni and L Carpaneto, 'Children under Brussels II ter Regulation (2020–21) 22 Yearbook of Private International Law 139.

75 See N Lowe, 'Strasbourg in Harmony with The Hague and Luxembourg over Child Abduction?' in K Hilbig-Lugani and others (eds), *Zwischenbilanz – Festschrift für Dagmar Coester-Waltjen zum 70. Geburtstag* (Gieseking 2015) 543.

76 Case C-376/14 PPU *C v M* (9 October 2014) ECLI:EU:C:2014:2268.

eral months, in accordance with the joint wishes of her parents, in a Member State other than that where those parents were habitually resident before her birth, the initial intention of the parents with respect to the return of the mother, together with the child, to the latter Member State cannot allow the conclusion that that child was 'habitually resident' there. Consequently, the refusal of the mother to return together with the child cannot be considered to be a 'wrongful removal or retention'.[77]

#60 For the purposes of Article 29(6) Brussels II-ter (Article 11(8) Brussels II-bis), a judgment of the court with jurisdiction ordering the return of the child falls within the scope of that provision, even if it is not preceded by a final judgment of that court relating to custody rights.[78]

II Expeditious Court Proceedings

#61 Article 24 Brussels II-ter (formerly Article 11(3) Brussels II-bis) requires expeditious court proceedings in case of the application for the return of a child under Article 22. The CJEU has ruled that this provision, read in the light of Article 47 of the Charter of Fundamental Rights, precludes national legislation which confers on non-judicial authorities the power to obtain automatic suspension, for a period of at least two months, of the enforcement of a return decision handed down on the basis of the 1980 Hague Convention, without having to provide reasons for that suspension.[79]

III Procedure Following a Decision Refusal the Return of the Child

#62 Article 29 lays down rules in case the a decision refusing the return of a child to another Member State is based solely on point (b) of Article 13(1) and Article 13(2) of the 1980 Hague Convention. These deal with the situation that 'the person, institution or other body having the care of the person of the child was not actually exercising the custody rights at the time of removal or retention' or that there is a 'grave risk that his or her return would expose the child to physical or psychological harm or otherwise place the child in an intolerable situation'. The CJEU ruled in relation to Article 11(7) and (8) Brussels II-bis, now Article 29(5 and 6) Brussels II-ter, that these provisions do not preclude a Member State from allocating to a

77 Case C-111/17 PPU *OL v PQ* (8 June 2017) ECLI: ECLI:EU:C:2017:436.
78 Case C-211/10 PPU *Doris Povse v Mauro Alpago* (1 July 2010) ECLI:EU:C:2010:400.
79 Case C-638/22 PPU *Rzecznik Praw Dziecka and Others* (16 February 2023) ECLI:EU:C:2023:103.

specialised court the jurisdiction to examine questions of return or custody with respect to a child, even where proceedings on the substance have already, separately, been brought before a court or tribunal.[80]

H Recognition and Enforcement

#63 The entire concept of the system for the recognition and enforcement of foreign judgments has been reshaped in the Brussels II-ter Regulation.[81] It spreads over 5 sections, regulating general provisions on recognition and enforcement (Articles 30–41), the recognition and enforcement of certain privileged decisions (Articles 42–50), common provisions on enforcement (Articles 51–63), **authentic instruments** and agreements (Articles 64–68), and finally, other provisions (Articles 69–75), most notably the prohibition of review of jurisdiction of the court of origin (Article 69), the prohibition of the revision on the merits of the case (Article 71), and the right to seek legal aid (Article 74).

#64 The most important amendment is the **abolition of exequatur** proceedings. Case law produced under Articles 28–36 Brussels II-bis Regulation is not anymore relevant.[82]

I Recognition of a Decision and Grounds of Refusal in Matrimonial Matters

#65 As regards the meaning of the term ‘decision’ used in Article 30 and further, the CJEU has ruled that it covers divorce decree drawn up by a civil registrar of the Member State of origin, containing a divorce agreement concluded by the spouses and confirmed by them before that registrar in accordance with the conditions laid down by legislation of that State.[83] See also #14 above.

80 Case C-498/14 PPU *RG v SF* (9 January 2015) ECLI:EU:C:2015:3. See comments by C Azcárraga Monzonís, ‘Sentencia del Tribunal de Justicia (Sala 4.ª) de 9 de enero de 2015, asunto C-498/14, *David Bradbrooke c. Anna Aleksandrowicz*’ (2015) 67(2) Revista Española de Derecho Internacional 202, and C Nourissat, ‘Des juridictions spécialisées en matière d'enlèvement d'enfant’ [2015–3] Procédures 24.

81 Ad hoc V Lazić and I Pretelli, ‘Revised Recognition and Enforcement Procedures in Regulation Brussels II ter’ [2020–2021] 22 Yearbook of Private International Law 155.

82 See for example Joined Cases C-325/18 PPU, and C-375/18 PPU *Hampshire County Council v C.E. and N.E.* (19 November 2018) ECLI:EU:C:2018:739.

83 Case C-646/20 *Senatsverwaltung für Inneres und Sport, Standesamtsaufsicht, v TB* (15 November 2022) ECLI:EU:C:2022:879.

#66 Article 38 features the grounds for refusal of recognition of decisions in matrimonial matters. It includes the grounds common in EU Regulations, including: (a) if the decision was manifestly against public policy of the Member State in which recognition is sought; (b) if it was given in default of appearance and the respondent was not served in sufficient time and in a way to arrange for the defence; or (c) if it is irreconcilable with a decision given in that Member State; or (d) an earlier decision given in another country that is recognised in that country. The classic obstacle is perpetually the public policy defence, which is often invoked, however rarely granted.[84]

II Grounds for Refusal in Matters of Parental Responsibility

#67 The grounds of refusal in regard of decisions in matters of parental responsibility are laid down in Article 39, and add a number of other grounds of refusal to those relating to matrimonial matters, including if it was given without the person claiming whose parental responsibility is infringed an opportunity to be heard (sub c). As regards public policy under sub a, the CJEU ruled that in the absence of a manifest breach, having regard to the best interests of the child, of a rule of law regarded as essential in the legal order of a Member State or of a right recognised as being fundamental within that legal order, this provision does not allow a Member State court, which considers that it has jurisdiction, to refuse to recognise a judgment of a court of another Member State which has ruled on the custody of that child.[85]

III Recognition and Enforcement of Certain Privileged Decisions

#68 Article 42–50 Brussels II-ter deal with the enforcement of privileged decisions within the meaning of Article 42. According the CJEU, the court with jurisdiction in the Member State of enforcement cannot oppose the enforcement of a certified judgment, ordering the return of a child wrongfully removed, on the ground that

84 S Marinai, 'Matrimonial Matters and the Harmonization of Conflict of Laws: A Way to Reduce the Role of Public Policy as a Ground for Non-Recognition of Judgments' (2011) 13 Yearbook of Private International Law 255.

85 Case C-455/15 PPU *P v Q* (19 November 2015) ECLI:EU:C:2015:763. See comments by S Álvarez González, 'Tribunal de Justicia: Espacio de libertad, seguridad y justicia – Reconocimiento y ejecución de resoluciones: Reglamento 2201/2003 – Responsabilidad parental [. . .] Sentencia del TJUE de 19 de noviembre de 2015, asunto C-455/15 PPU, P y Q' (2016) 68 Revista española de Derecho Internacional 84, and B Rentsch and M-P Weller, 'Urteilsanerkennung im Internationalen Sorgerecht: Regelungsebenen der EuEheVO gegen Wertungsebenen des ordre public' [2017] IPRax 262.

the court of origin may have infringed Article 43 interpreted in accordance with Article 24 of the **Charter of Fundamental Rights**, since the assessment of whether there is such an infringement falls exclusively within the jurisdiction of the courts of the Member State of origin.[86]

#69 Privileged decisions, i.e., decisions ordering the return of the child, which are rendered notwithstanding a previous refusal by the court of the Member State to which the child has been re moved or retained, are exempted from the cumbersome exequatur proceedings (Article 46 para 1).[87]

IV Enforcement Procedure

#70 The enforcement procedure is regulated in Articles 51–63 Brussels II-ter Regulation. Under the Brussels II-bis Regulation the CJEU ruled that a judgment delivered subsequently by a court in the Member State of enforcement which awards provisional rights of custody and is deemed to be enforceable under the law of that State cannot preclude enforcement of a **certified judgment** delivered previously by the court which has jurisdiction in the Member State of origin, ordering the return of the child.[88]

#71 Enforcement of a certified judgment cannot be refused in the Member State of enforcement, because it might be seriously detrimental to the best interests of the child. Such a change must be pleaded before the court which has jurisdiction in the Member State of origin, which should also hear any application to suspend enforcement of its judgment.[89]

#72 Recovery of a **penalty payment** forms part of the same scheme of enforcement as the judgment concerning the rights of access that the penalty safeguards and the latter must therefore be declared enforceable in accordance with the rules of the Regulation. A foreign judgment ordering a periodic penalty payment is enforceable in the State in which enforcement is sought only if the amount of the payment has been finally determined by the courts of the Member State of origin.[90]

---

86 Case C-491/10 PPU *Joseba Andoni Aguirre Zarraga v Simone Pelz* (22 December 2010) ECLI:EU:C:2010:828. See comments by MH Zoeteweij-Turhan, 'Brussels II bis: The Right of the Child to be Heard in International Proceedings' [2015] Pravnik: revija za pravno teorijo in prakso 861, and H Muir Watt, 'Enlèvement international d'enfant et ordre de retour: compétence et vie privée' [2012] Revue critique de droit international privé 172.

87 See also CM Caamiña Domínguez, 'La «supresión» del exequátur en el Reglamento 2201/2003' (2011) 3 Cuadernos de Derecho Transnacional 63.

88 Case C-211/10 PPU *Doris Povse v Mauro Alpago* (1 July 2010) ECLI:EU:C:2010:400.

89 ibid.

90 Case C-4/14 *Christophe Bohez v Ingrid Wiertz* (9 September 2015) ECLI:EU:C:2015:563. See comments by K Kroll-Ludwigs, 'Anmerkung zu EuGH, Urteil vom 9.9.2015 – C-4/14' (2016) 13 GPR 255, and L Esteve

#73 Once a non-return decision has been taken and brought to the attention of the court of origin, it is irrelevant, for the purposes of issuing the certificate of 43 (Article 42 Brussels II-bis) that that decision has been suspended, overturned, set aside or, in any event, has not become res judicata or has been replaced by a decision ordering return, in so far as the return of the child has not actually taken place. Since no doubt has been expressed as regards the authenticity of that certificate and since it was drawn up in accordance with the standard form set out in the Regulation, opposition to the recognition of the decision ordering return is not permitted and it is for the requested court only to declare the enforceability of the certified decision and to allow the immediate return of the child.[91]

V Authentic Instruments and Agreements

#74 Articles 64–68 cover issues of recognition and enforcement of authentic instruments and agreements, by specifying the particulars for the issuance of a certificate, which may be rectified, or even refused enforcement, if certain conditions are not met. A relatively novel point is the enforceability of extrajudicial agreements, which triggers the interest of legal scholars.[92]

I The Maintenance Regulation

I Introduction and Scope

#75 Since 18 June maintenance matters are governed by the EU Regulation nr. 4/2009.[93] The Regulation consists of nine chapters, which are covering the following

González, 'Sentencia del TJUE (Sala Primera) de 9 de septiembre de 2015, asunto C-4/14, Christophe Bohez c. Ingrid Wiertz' (2016) 68 Revista española de Derecho Internacional 181.

91 Case C-195/08 PPU *Inga Rinau* (11 July 2008) ECLI:EU:C:2008:406. See comments by MH Zoeteweij-Turhan, 'Brussels II bis: The Right of the Child to be Heard in International Proceedings' [2015] Pravnik 861, and UP Gruber, 'Effektive Antworten des EuGH auf Fragen zur Kindesentführung' [2009] IPRax 413.

92 C Honorati and S Bernasconi, 'L'efficacia Cross-Border Degli Accordi Stragiudiziali In Materia Familiare Tra I Regolamenti Bruxelles Ii-Bis E Bruxelles Ii-Ter' [2020–2] Freedom, Security & Justice: European Legal Studies 22.

93 See in detail P Beaumont and others (eds), *The Recovery of Maintenance in the EU and Worldwide* (Hart 2014), where the following contributions are to be found: P Beaumont and L Walker, 'Introduction to Part Two (International) and Part Three (International and EU)' 17; B Hess and S Spancken, 'Setting the Scene-The EU Maintenance Regulation' 331; L Walker and P Beaumont, 'Empirical Study on the Early Operation of the EU Maintenance Regulation' 337; B Hess and S Spancken, 'The Effective Operation of the EU Maintenance Regulation in the Member States' 385; M Abendroth, 'Choice of Court

points: Scope of the Regulation and definitions (Articles 1–2); jurisdiction (Articles 3–14); applicable law (Article 15),[94] recognition and enforcement (Articles 16–43), access to Justice (Articles 44–47), court settlements and authentic instruments (Article 48), cooperation (Article 49–63), public bodies (Article 64), general and final provisions (Articles 65–76).[95] The primary objective of this Part is to present briefly the major issues and challenges of the Regulation's implementation, as reflected in the case law produced by the CJEU, namely, the topics of international jurisdiction, and the mechanism for recognition and enforcement of foreign judgments.[96]

#76 Article 1 stipulates that maintenance obligations must arise from a family relationship, parentage, marriage or affinity, whereas Article 2 contains a lengthy list of definitions. So far, no request was addressed to the CJEU concerning the above matters.

II International Jurisdiction

#77 Matters of international jurisdiction are almost monopolising the legal discourse. This chapter covers general provisions (Article 3), choice of court (Article 4), jurisdiction based on the appearance of the defendant (Article 5), subsidiary jurisdictions (Article 6), **forum necessitatis** (Article 7), limit of proceedings (Article 8), fixation of the time of filing (Article 9), examination of jurisdiction and admissibility (Articles 10–11), lis pendens and related actions (Articles 12–13). Provisional measures are also falling under the scope of the same chapter (Article 14).

#78 Article 3 is the undisputed protagonist. It contains a list of four grounds for international jurisdiction, namely, the habitual residence of the defendant (lit. a) or the creditor (lit. b), or the court having jurisdiction concerning the status of a person (lit. c), or the court having jurisdiction concerning parental responsibility (lit. d). There is no hierarchy between the grounds of jurisdiction; it is for the claimant to choose between them.[97] The CJEU was repeatedly called to interpret the provision. In particular, the Court ruled as follows:

---

in Matters Relating to Maintenance Obligations' 459; I Viarengo, 'The Enforcement of Maintenance Decisions in the EU: Requiem for Public Policy? Family Relationships and the (Partial) Abolition of Exequatur' 473; D Martiny, 'Jurisdiction, Recognition and Enforcement in Cases of Reimbursement Claims by Public Bodies' 485.

94 Matters of applicable law are not falling under the scope of this chapter. See, however, Case C-83/17 *KP v LO* (7 June 2018) ECLI:EU:C:2018:408, concerning Article 15 and the 2007 Hague Protocol.

95 See A Bonomi, 'The Hague Protocol of 23 November 2007 on the Law Applicable to Maintenance Obligations' (2008) 10 Yearbook of Private International Law 333, focusing on Article 69.

96 L Walker, *Maintenance and Child Support in Private International Law* (Hart 2015).

97 European Commission (Directorate-General for Justice and Consumers) and C Honorati, *Practice Guide on the Application of Regulation No 4/2009 on Maintenance Obligations* (Publications Office of the European Union 2023) 25 ('*Practice Guide Regulation 4/2009*').

(1) *Territorial jurisdiction.* Article 3(b) precludes national legislation which establishes a centralisation of jurisdiction in cross-border maintenance matters in favour of a first instance court which has jurisdiction for the seat of the appeal court, except where that rule helps to achieve the objective of a proper administration of justice and protects the interests of maintenance creditors, while promoting the effective recovery of such claims, which is a matter for the referring courts to verify.[98]
(2) *Ancillary claims.* Article 3(c) and (d) must be understood as meaning that, in the event that a court of a Member State is seised of proceedings involving separation or dissolution of a marital link between the parents of a minor child and a court of another Member State is seised of proceedings in matters of parental responsibility involving that same child, an application relating to maintenance concerning that child is ancillary only to the latter proceedings.[99] In addition, where a court of the Member State of the spouses' common nationality, seised by the applicant, has jurisdiction to rule on divorce proceedings, it does not have jurisdiction under Article 3(d) Regulation 4/2009 to rule on issues relating to maintenance obligations.[100]
(3) *Application to modify child support judgment.* Article 3 must be interpreted as meaning that the courts of the Member State which made a decision that has become final concerning parental responsibility and maintenance obligations with regard to a minor child no longer have jurisdiction to decide on an application for variation of the provisions ordered in that decision, inasmuch as the habitual residence of the child is in another Member State. It is the courts of the Member State of habitual residence that have jurisdiction to decide on that application.[101]
(4) *Habitual residence of the defendant.* Article 3(a) and (d) and Article 5 must be interpreted as meaning that where there is an action before a Member State court which includes three claims concerning divorce of the parents of a minor child, parental responsibility, and maintenance obligations with regard to the child, the court ruling on the divorce, which has de-

98 Joined Cases C-400/13 *Sophia Marie Nicole Sanders, represented by Ms Marianne Sanders, v David Verhaegen* and C-408/13 *Barbara Huber v Manfred Huber* (18 December 2014) ECLI:EU:C:2014:2461. See comments by M Andrae, 'Erste Entscheidungen des EuGH zu Art. 12 Abs. 3 EuEheVO [2015] IPRax 212, and C Nourissat, 'Prorogation volontaire de compétence en matière de responsabilité parentale [2015–1] Procédures 41.

99 Case C-184/14 *A v B* (16 July 2015) ECLI:EU:C:2015:479. See a summary of the case in the Practice Guide Regulation 4/2009 (n 97) 28, and comments by S Hamou, 'La demande relative à une obligation alimentaire concernant un enfant est accessoire à l'action relative à la responsabilité parentale' [2016] Gazette du Palais n° 1 74, and T Rauscher, 'Unterhaltzuständigkeit zwischen Sorgerechts- und Ehesachenverbund' [2016] IPRax 215.

100 Case C-759/18 *OF v PG* (3 October 2019) ECLI:EU:C:2019:816.

101 Case C-499/15 *W, V v X* (15 February 2017) ECLI:EU:C:2017:118.

clared that it has no jurisdiction to rule on the claim concerning parental responsibility, nevertheless has jurisdiction to rule on the claim concerning the maintenance obligation, where it is also the court for the place where the defendant is habitually resident or the court before which the defendant entered an appearance, without contesting the jurisdiction of that court.[102]

(5) *Public body acting as maintenance creditor.* A public body which seeks to recover sums paid in place of maintenance to a maintenance creditor, and to which the claims against the maintenance debtor have been transferred by way of subrogation, may validly invoke the jurisdiction of the court for the place where the creditor is habitually resident, as provided in Article 3(b).[103]

(6) *Child abduction.* In a case in which a child who was habitually resident in a Member State was wrongfully removed to another Member State, the courts of that other Member State do not have jurisdiction to rule on an application relating to custody or maintenance with respect to that child, in the absence of any indication that the other parent consented to his removal or did not bring an application for the return of that child.[104]

#79 **Forum necessitatis** did also reach the CJEU,[105] which ruled that, where the habitual residence of all the parties is not in a Member State, jurisdiction founded on the forum necessitatis may be established if no court of a Member State has jurisdiction under Articles 3 to 6, if the proceedings cannot reasonably be brought or conducted in the third State with which the dispute is closely connected, or proves to be impossible, and there is a sufficient connection between the dispute and the court seised. In order to find that proceedings cannot be brought or conducted in a third State, it is important that, following an analysis of available evidence, access to justice in that third State is, in law or in fact, hindered, in particular by the application of procedural conditions that are discriminatory or contrary to the fundamental guarantees of fair trial, without there being any requirement that the party relying on Article 7 demonstrate that he or she has been

102 Case C-468/18 *R v P* (5 September 2019) ECLI:EU:C:2019:666. For a summary of the case, see Practice Guide Regulation 4/2009 (n 97) 26.

103 Case C-540/19 *WV v Landkreis Harburg* (17 September 2020) ECLI:EU:C:2020:732. See F Rieländer, 'Die Wahlfreiheit zwischen den Aufenthaltszuständigkeiten nach Art. 3 lit. a und b EuUntVO im Unterhaltsregressverfahren: Anmerkung zu EuGH, Urt. v. 17.9.2020 – C-540/19, WV/Landkreis Harburg' (2021) 18 GPR 33, and G Payan, 'Chronique Espace judiciaire européen en matière civile – Obligations alimentaires: compétence juridictionnelle et recours subrogatoire d'un organisme public [2021] Revue trimestrielle de droit européen 407.

104 Case C-85/18 PPU *CV v DU* (10 April 2018) EU:C:2018:220.

105 Practice Guide Regulation 4/2009 (n 97) 32.

unsuccessful in bringing or has attempted to bring the proceedings in question before the courts of the third State concerned. In order to consider that a dispute must have a sufficient connection with the Member State of the court seised, it is possible to rely on the nationality of one of the parties.[106]

III Lis Pendens

#80 A preliminary request for the interpretation of Article 12 gave recently the chance to the Court to examine and interpret the lis pendens provision. The Court ruled, that the conditions for recognition of a situation of lis pendens are not satisfied when, at the time a claim is brought before a court of one Member State by a child – who has in the meantime become an adult – for payment of maintenance from his or her mother, a claim has already been brought before a court of another Member State by the mother seeking compensation from the child's father for accommodation and maintenance of that child, since the applicants' actions do not have the same end in view and do not relate to the same period. The absence of a situation of lis penden does not preclude the application of Article 13, if the actions at issue are sufficiently closely connected for them to be regarded as related within the meaning of Article 13(3), with the result that, where it is not the court first seised, the referring court may stay the proceedings.[107]

IV Recognition and Enforcement

#81 Chapter IV regulates extensively the area of recognition and enforcement. Following a general provision on the scope of application (Article 16), three sections are setting the stage: Section 1 (Articles 17–22) is referring to decisions given in a member state bound by the 2007 Hague Protocol, whereas Section 2 (Articles 23–38) refers to decisions given in a member state not bound by the 2007 Hague Protocol. Finally, Section 3 features common provisions for both sections 1 and 2 (Articles 39–43). Taking into account that all Member States are now bound by the Hague Protocol, Section 2 is slowly becoming obsolete, with rare exceptions of a transitional nature.

106 Case C-501/20 *MPA v LCDNMT* (1 August 2022) ECLI:EU:C:2022:619.

107 Case C-381/23 *ZO v JS* (6 June 2024) ECLI:EU:C:2024:467. See short comment by L Idot, 'Règlement « obligations alimentaires » – Exception de litispendance' (2024) 34 (8–9) Europe 337.

#82 A maintenance creditor who obtained an order in one Member State and wishes to enforce it in another Member State, may make an application directly to the competent authority of the latter State, such as a specialised court, and cannot be required to submit the application to that court through the **Central Authority** of the State of enforcement.[108] Member States are required to give full effect to the right laid down in Article 43(1) Brussels II-ter (Article 41(1) Brussels II-bis) by amending their rules of procedure. It is for the national court to apply this provision, if necessary, refusing to apply any conflicting provision of national law and to allow a maintenance creditor to submit her application directly to the competent authority of the Member State of enforcement, even if national law does not make provision for such an application.[109]

#83 *Remedies against enforcement.* An application opposing enforcement against a decision given by a court of the State of origin, which has a close link with the procedure for enforcement, falls within its scope and is within the international jurisdiction of the courts of the Member State of enforcement.[110] It is for the court of the State of enforcement to adjudicate on the admissibility and the validity of the evidence adduced by the maintenance debtor, seeking to support the submission that he has predominantly discharged his debt.[111]

V Transitional Provisions, The 2007 Hague Protocol and Convention

#84 *Non application of the Regulation.* Taking into account that all Member States have ratified the 2007 Hague Protocol, transitional issues will hardly arise in the future. However, a request for a preliminary ruling was addressed to the Court, which ruled that Article 75 (2)(a) must be interpreted as applying only to decisions given by national courts in States which were already members of the European

108 Case C-283/16 *M. S. v P. S.* (9 February 2017) ECLI:EU:C:2017:104.
109 ibid. See comments by N Joubert, 'L'exécution des décisions entre autonomie procédurale des Etats membres et pleine efficacité du règlement Aliments' [2017] Revue critique de droit international privé 568, and OL Knöfel, 'Die Rolle der zentralen Behörden bei der grenzüberschreitenden Vollstreckung von Unterhaltstiteln in der Europäischen Union' [2018] IPRax 487.
110 Case C-41/19 *FX v GZ* (4 June 2020) ECLI:EU:C:2020:425. See L Idot, 'Règlement « Obligations alimentaires » – Action en opposition à exécution' (2020) (30) Europe 285; J Wolber, 'Die internationale Zuständigkeit für den Vollstreckungsabwehrantrag im europäischen Unterhaltsrecht: Rs. C-41/19: FX./. GZ' [2021] IPRax 450.
111 ibid.

Union on the date of adoption of those decisions. No provision enables decisions in maintenance matters given in a State before its accession to the European Union and before the date of application of that Regulation, to be recognised and enforced, after that State's accession to the EU, in another Member State.[112]

#85 *2007 Hague Convention.* In a second request, the Court was called to interpret provisions of the 2007 Hague Convention, for which it has powers, given that the convention has been approved by the EU, and applies meanwhile to all Member States. The CJEU ruled that Articles 27 and 30 of the Convention, must be interpreted as meaning that, in the case of lis pendens, the date on which a mandatory conciliation procedure was lodged before a conciliation authority under Swiss law is the date on which a 'court' is deemed to be seised.[113]

References

Abendroth M, 'Choice of Court in Matters Relating to Maintenance Obligations' in P Beaumont and others (eds), *The Recovery of Maintenance in the EU and Worldwide* (Hart 2014) 459.

Althammer C (ed), *Brussels IIa – Rome III* (Hart/Beck/Nomos 2019).

Álvarez González S, 'La doble nacionalidad comunitaria en materia matrimonial – Comentario a la STJCE de 16 de julio de 2009' [2011] Noticias de la Unión Europea 89.

—— 'Tribunal de Justicia: Espacio de libertad, seguridad y justicia – Reconocimiento y ejecución de resoluciones: Reglamento 2201/2003 – Responsabilidad parental [. . .] Sentencia del TJUE de 19 de noviembre de 2015, asunto C-455/15 PPU, P y Q' (2016) 68 Revista española de Derecho Internacional 84.

Andrae M, 'On the Applicability of the Brussels II a Regulation to State Measures for the Protection of the Child' [2008] The European Legal Forum 189.

—— 'Erste Entscheidungen des EuGH zu Art. 12 Abs. 3 EuEheVO' [2015] IPRax 212.

Azcárraga Monzonís C, 'Sentencia del Tribunal de Justicia (Sala 4.ª) de 9 de enero de 2015, asunto C-498/14, *David Bradbrooke c. Anna Aleksandrowicz*' (2015) 67(2) Revista Española de Derecho Internacional 202.

Beaumont P and others (eds), *The Recovery of Maintenance in the EU and Worldwide* (Hart 2014).

Beaumont P and Walker L, 'Introduction to Part Two (International) and Part Three (International and EU)' in Beaumont P and others (eds), *The Recovery of Maintenance in the EU and Worldwide* (Hart 2014) 17.

Berner F, 'Familien- und Erbrecht. Anmerkung zu EuGH, Urt. v. 13.10.2016 – C-294/15 (Mikołajczyk)' (2017) 14 GPR 131.

Biagioni G and Carpaneto L, 'Children under Brussels II ter Regulation (2020–21) 22 Yearbook of Private International Law 139.

112 Case C-729/19 *TKF v Department of Justice for Northern Ireland* (15 April 2021) ECLI:EU:C:2021:275. The case refers to a Polish judgment issued before Poland's accession to the EU.

113 Case C-467/16 *Brigitte Schlömp v Landratsamt Schwäbisch Hall*) (20 December 2017) ECLI:EU:C:2017:993. See comments by AR Markus, 'Rechtshängigkeit und Schlichtungsverfahren nach EuGH – C-467/16, Schlömp' (2019) 16 GPR 60, and W Hau, 'Rechtshängigkeitssperre durch obligatorische ADR-Verfahren im europäischen Zivilprozessrecht' [2019] ZEuP 384.

Bobrzyńska O, 'Brussels II ter Regulation and the 1996 Hague Convention on Child Protection – The Interplay of the European and Hague Regimes in the Matters of Parental Responsibility [2021] Polski Proces Cywilny 593.
Boele-Woelki K, 'For Better or for Worse: The Europeanization of International Divorce Law' (2010) 12 Yearbook of Private International Law 1.
Boer de TM, 'What We Should Not Expect from a Recast of the Brussels IIbis Regulation' (2015) 33 Nederlands Internationaal Privaatrecht 10.
Bonomi A, 'The Hague Protocol of 23 November 2007 on the Law Applicable to Maintenance Obligations' (2008) 10 Yearbook of Private International Law 333, focusing on Article 69.
Borrás A and Pellisé C, 'Jurisprudencia del Tribunal de Justicia de la Unión Europea – Cooperación judicial en materia civil – Sentencia de 26 de abril de 2012, Asunto C-92/12 PPU, Health Service Executive c. S.C., A.C.' [2012] Revista Jurídica de Catalunya 273.
Borrás A, 'The Substantive Scope of Application of European Instruments in Matrimonial Matters' in B Hess, E Jayme and HP Mansel (eds), *Europa als Rechts- und Lebensraum. Liber Amicorum für Christian Kohler zum 75. Geburtstag* (Gieseking 2018) 23.
Borrás Rodríguez A, '"Exclusive" and "Residual" Grounds of Jurisdiction on Divorce in the Brussels IIbis Regulation [2008] IPRax 233.
Caamiña Domínguez CM, 'La «supresión» del exequátur en el Reglamento 2201/2003' (2011) 3 Cuadernos de Derecho Transnacional 63.
Carratta A, 'Tre Provvedimenti urgenti a tutela dei minori e sottrazione internazionale (2017) 71 Rivista Trimestrale Di Diritto E Procedura Civile 1257.
Chalas C, 'Litispendance et décalage horaire dans le contentieux du divorce en Europe [2016] Revue critique de droit international privé 387.
Corneloup S, 'L'action en annulation du mariage intentée par un tiers après le décès d'un epoux' [2017] Revue critique de droit international privé 291.
Cuniberti G and Camara C, 'The EU Forum Non Conveniens Rule in Child Care Proceedings Cases Involving Public Bodies' (2016/2017) 18 Yearbook of Private International Law 431.
Darmois V, 'La procédure de contrôle du partage successoral conclu pour le compte d'enfants mineurs relève du champ d'application du Règlement Bruxelles II bis' [2016] Gazette du Palais 87.
de la Iglesia Monje MI, 'El derecho de visita transfronterizo de los abuelos a sus nietos a la luz del TJUE' [2018] Revista crítica de Derecho Inmobiliario 2671
de Lambertye-Autrand M-C, 'Le prononcé de la décision épuise la prorogation du for' [2016] Revue critique de droit international privé 174.
de Sousa Gonçalves AS, 'A Deslocação Ou Retenção Ilícitas De Crianças No Regulamento N.° 2201/2003 (BRUXELAS II BIS)' (2014) 6 Cuadernos de Derecho Transnacional.
Dominelli S, 'Cross-Border Placement of Children within the European Judicial Space: First Thoughts on the Recast Brussels IIa Regulation in Light of the German Experience' [2016] The European Legal Forum 113.
Esteve González L, 'Sentencia del TJUE (Sala Primera) de 9 de septiembre de 2015, asunto C-4/14, Christophe Bohez c. Ingrid Wiertz' (2016) 68 Revista española de Derecho Internacional 181.
European Commission (Directorate-General for Justice and Consumers) and Honorati C, *Practice Guide on the Application of Regulation No 4/2009 on Maintenance Obligations* (Publications Office of the European Union 2023).
Feraci O, 'Party Autonomy and Conflict of Jurisdictions in the EU Private International Law on Family and Succession Matters (2014/2015) 16 Yearbook of Private International Law 105.
Gallant E, 'Inapplicabilité de l'article 10 du règlement Bruxelles II bis en cas d'acquisition d'une résidence habituelle dans un État tiers' [2023] Revue critique de droit international privé n° 1 127.

Garau Sobrino F, 'Sentencia Tribunal de Justicia de las Comunidades Europeas (Sala Tercera), de 29 de noviembre de 2007, en el asunto C-68/07 (Sundelind López)' (2007) 59(2) Revista Española de Derecho Internacional 763.
Gascón Inchausti F, 'International Child Abduction in the Case Law of the Court of Justice of the European Union: Learning from the Past and Looking to the Future' [2021] Polski Proces Cywilny 617.
González Beilfuss C and others (eds), *Jurisdiction, Recognition and Enforcement in Matrimonial and Parental Responsibility Matters. A Commentary on Regulation 2019/1111 (Brussels IIb)* (Edward Elgar 2023).
González Beilfuss C, 'What's New in Regulation (EU) No 2019/1111?' (2020/2021) 22 Yearbook of Private International Law 95.
González Marimón M, 'Competencia judicial internacional ante un caso de sustracción internacional de menores de un estado miembro de la UE a un estado tercero: La STJUE de 24 de marzo de 2021' [2021] Revista General de Derecho Europeo 229.
Gössl SL, 'Rechtsaktbezogene Einzigartigkeit und subjektive Komponenten: einige Notizen zum gewöhnlichen Aufenthalt im europäischen Kollisions- und Verfahrensrecht: zu EuGH, 25.11.2021' [2022] IPRax 489.
Gruber UP, 'Effektive Antworten des EuGH auf Fragen zur Kindesentführung' [2009] IPRax 413.
Hamou S, 'La demande relative à une obligation alimentaire concernant un enfant est accessoire à l'action relative à la responsabilité parentale' [2016] Gazette du Palais n° 1 74.
Hau W, 'Doppelte Staatsangehörigkeit im europäischen Eheverfahrensrecht' [2010] IPRax 50.
—— 'Rechtshängigkeitssperre durch obligatorische ADR-Verfahren im europäischen Zivilprozessrecht' [2019] ZEuP 384.
—— 'Internationale Zuständigkeit kraft Staatsangehörigkeit im Europäischen Familienverfahrensrecht: [zu EuGH, 10.2.2022, Rs. C-522/20: OE./. VY] [2022]' IPRax 342.
Hess B and Spancken S, 'Setting the Scene-The EU Maintenance Regulation' in P Beaumont and others (eds), *The Recovery of Maintenance in the EU and Worldwide* (Hart 2014) 331.
—— 'The Effective Operation of the EU Maintenance Regulation in the Member States' in P Beaumont and others (eds), *The Recovery of Maintenance in the EU and Worldwide* (Hart 2014) 385.
Hess B, 'Towards a Uniform Concept of Habitual Residence in European Procedural and Private International Law?' [2021] Polski Proces Cywilny 523.
Hilbig-Lugani K, 'Divergenz und Transparenz: Der Begriff des gewöhnlichen Aufenthalts der privat handelnden natürlichen Person im jüngeren EuIPR und EuZVR' (2014) 11 GPR 8.
—— 'Anmerkung zu EuGH, Urt. v. 26. April 2012, Rs. C-92/12 PPU – Health Service Executive' (2016) 13 GPR 199.
—— 'Anmerkung zu EuGH, Urt. vom 6.10.2015 – C-489/14 (A v B)' (2016) 13 GPR 132.
Honorati C and Baruffi NC, *EU Private International Law in Family Matters, Legislation and CJEU Case Law* (Intersentia 2022).
Honorati C and Bernasconi S, 'L'efficacia Cross-Border Degli Accordi Stragiudiziali In Materia Familiare Tra I Regolamenti Bruxelles Ii-Bis E Bruxelles Ii-Ter' [2020–2] Freedom, Security & Justice: European Legal Studies 22.
Honorati C, 'Sottrazione Internazionale Dei Minori e Diritti Fondamentali (2013) 49 Rivista di diritto internazionale privato e processuale 5.
Idot L, 'Déplacement illicite d'enfant et reconnaissance d'une décision de mesures provisoires (2010) 20(10) Europe 42.
—— 'Précisions tant sur le champ d'application que sur les conditions de mise en oeuvre de l'article 15 du règlement qui permet le renvoi à une juridiction d'un autre État membre mieux placée' (2016) 26(12) Europe 46.
—— 'Notion de résidence habituelle' (2018) 28(8–9) Europe 48, and UP Gruber, 'Der gewöhnliche Aufenthalt von Säuglingen und Kleinkindern' [2018] IPRax 217.
—— 'Règlement « Obligations alimentaires » – Action en opposition à exécution' (2020) (30) Europe 285.

—— 'Règlement « bruxelles II bis » – Déplacement illicite d'enfant' (2024) 34(8–9) Europe 336.
—— 'Règlement « obligations alimentaires » – Exception de litispendance' (2024) 34 (8–9) Europe 337.
J Wolber, 'Die internationale Zuständigkeit für den Vollstreckungsabwehrantrag im europäischen Unterhaltsrecht: Rs. C-41/19: FX./. GZ' [2021] IPRax 450.
Jänterä-Jareborg M, 'A European Family Law for Cross-border Situations – Some Reflections Concerning the Brussels II Regulation and its Planned Amendments' (2002) 3 Yearbook of Private International Law 67.
Janzen U and Gärtner V, 'Kindschaftsrechtliche Spannungsverhältnisse im Rahmen der EuEheVO – die Entscheidung des EuGH in Sachen Detiček [2011] IPRax 158.
Joubert N, 'L'exécution des décisions entre autonomie procédurale des Etats membres et pleine efficacité du règlement Aliments' [2017] Revue critique de droit international privé 568.
Knöfel OL, 'Die Rolle der zentralen Behörden bei der grenzüberschreitenden Vollstreckung von Unterhaltstiteln in der Europäischen Union' [2018] IPRax 487.
Koechel F, 'Art. 12 III Brüssel IIa-VO: Zustimmung zu Reise und Passerteilung für bulgar. Kind' [2016] FamRZ 438.
Krausenboeck M, 'No Luck for Fathers of Children Born out of Wedlock' [2010] European Law Reporter 352.
Kroll-Ludwigs K, 'Anmerkung zu EuGH, Urt. v. 26. April 2012, Rs. C-92/12 PPU – Health Service Executive' (2013) 10 GPR 46.
—— 'Anmerkung zu EuGH, Urteil vom 9.9.2015 – C-4/14' (2016) 13 GPR 255.
Kruger T and Samyn L, 'Brussels II bis: Successes and Suggested Improvements' (2016) 12 J. Priv. Int. Law 132.
Kruger T, 'Finding a Habitual Residence' in I Viarengo and F Villata (eds), *Planning the Future of Cross Border Families: A Path Through Coordination* (Hart 2020) 117.
Lamont R, 'Habitual Residence and Brussels IIbis: Developing Concepts for European Private International Family Law (2007) 3 J. Priv. Int. Law 261.
Lazić V and Pretelli I, 'Revised Recognition and Enforcement Procedures in Regulation Brussels II ter' [2020–2021] 22 Yearbook of Private International Law 155.
Lazić V, 'Family Private International Law Issues Before the European Court of Human Rights: Lessons to Be Learned from Povse v. Austria in Revising the Brussels IIa Regulation, Fundamental Rights in International and European Law' in C Paulussen and others (eds), *Fundamental Rights in International and European Law* (Asser 2016) 161
Lenaerts K, 'The Best Interests of The Child Always Come First: The Brussels Ii Bis Regulation and the European Court of Justice' (2013) 2020 Jurisprudence 1302.
Limante A, 'Establishing Habitual Residence of Adults under the Brussels IIa Regulation: Best Practices from National Case-Law' (2018) 14 J. Priv. Int. Law 160.
Lopes Pegna O, 'L'interesse Superiore Del Minore Nel Regolamento N. 2201/2003' (2013) 49 Rivista di diritto internazionale privato e processuale 357.
Lowe N, 'Strasbourg in Harmony with The Hague and Luxembourg over Child Abduction?' in K Hilbig-Lugani and others (eds), *Zwischenbilanz – Festschrift für Dagmar Coester-Waltjen zum 70. Geburtstag* (Gieseking 2015) 543.
Lowe N, Honorati C and Hellner M, *Brussels II-ter – Cross-border Marriage Dissolution, Parental Responsibility Disputes and Child Abduction in the EU* (Intersentia 2024).
Lupoi MA, 'Between Parties' Consent and Judicial Discretion: Joinder of Claims and Transfer of Cases in Regulation (EU) 2019/1111' [2021] Polski Proces Cywilny 543.
—— *La crisi matrimoniale e genitoriale nello spazio di giustizia europeo Giurisdizione, circolazione delle decisioni e sottrazione internazionale di minori* (Pacini Editore Srl 2022).
Magnus U and Mankowski P (eds), *European Commentaries on Private International Law. ECPIL Commentary Volume IV Brussels IIbis Regulation* (Otto Schmidt 2017).

Mankowski, 'Der gewöhnliche Aufenthalt eines verbrachten Kindes unter der Brüssel IIa-VO – Anmerkung zu EuGH, Urt. v. 22.12.2010 – Rs. C-497/10 PPU' (2011) 8 GPR 209.
Marinai S, 'Matrimonial Matters and the Harmonization of Conflict of Laws: A Way to Reduce the Role of Public Policy as a Ground for Non-Recognition of Judgments' (2011) 13 Yearbook of Private International Law 255.
Marino S, 'Nuovi criteri interpretativi per la determinazione della giurisdizione in materia di responsabilità genitoriale: la nozione di residenza abituale dei minori in una recente sentenza della Corte di giustizia CE (2010] 65 Rivista di diritto processuale 467.
Markus AR, 'Rechtshängigkeit und Schlichtungsverfahren nach EuGH – C-467/16, Schlömp' (2019) 16 GPR 60.
Martin D, 'Quelques observations sans intérêt sur la notion de discrimination [2022] Revue des affaires européennes 153.
Martiny D, 'Jurisdiction, Recognition and Enforcement in Cases of Reimbursement Claims by Public Bodies' in P Beaumont and others (eds), *The Recovery of Maintenance in the EU and Worldwide* (Hart 2014) 485.
—— 'New Efforts in Judicial Cooperation in European Child Abduction Cases' [2021] Polski Proces Cywilny 501.
Moreno GP, 'Crisis matrimoniales internacionales y autonomía de la voluntad' [2013] Cursos de derecho internacional y relaciones internacionales de Vitoria-Gasteiz 451.
Muir Watt H, 'Enlèvement international d'enfant et ordre de retour: compétence et vie privée' [2012] Revue critique de droit international privé 172.
—— 'Sanctionner ou circuler? Les conséquences sur le terrain des effets des jugements de la méconnaissance par le juge second saisi des règles relatives à la litispendance [2019] Revue critique de droit international privé 495.
Ní Shúilleabháin M, *Cross-Border Divorce Law Brussels II Bis* (OUP 2011).
—— 'An Overview of the Principal Reforms in Regulation (EU) 2019/1111 (2020/2021) 22 Yearbook of Private International Law 117.
Nourissat C, 'Des juridictions spécialisées en matière d'enlèvement d'enfant' [2015–3] Procédures 24.
—— 'Prorogation volontaire de compétence en matière de responsabilité parentale' [2015–1] Procédures 41.
—— 'Encore et toujours la résidence habituelle de l'enfant' [2017–4] Procédures 24, and J Wißling, 'Kind von Welt beim EuGH. Anmerkung zu EuGH-Urteilen C-499/15 und C-283/16' (2017) 14 GPR 255.
Orejudo Prieto de los Mozos P, 'Sentencia TJEU (Sala 4.ª), de 15 de octubre de 2015, asunto c-215/15, *Vasilka Ivanova Gogova y Ilia Dimitrov Iliev*' (2016) 68(1) Revista Española de Derecho Internacional 175
Pailler L, 'La portée de l'obligation de reconnaître une décision relative à la garde d'un enfant émanant de la juridiction de l'État membre dans lequel l'enfant a été déplacé en application du réglement n° 2201/2003 "Bruxelles II bis"' [2016] Journal du droit international 593.
Payan G, 'Chronique Espace judiciaire européen en matière civile – Obligations alimentaires: compétence juridictionnelle et recours subrogatoire d'un organisme public [2021] Revue trimestrielle de droit européen 407.
Péroz H, 'Champ d'application du réglement Bruxelles II bis élargi au droit de visite des grands-parents' (2018) 93 La Semaine Juridique 1376.
Pirrung J, 'Der gewöhnliche Aufenthalt des Kindes in internationalen Sorgerechtssachen' in O Sandrock and others (eds), *Festschrift für Gunther Kühne zum 70. Geburtstag* (Recht und Wirtschaft 2009) 843.
—— 'Kein Hinderungsgrund aus der Brüssel IIa-VO, wenn Mitgliedstaaten den Erwerb des Sorgerechts durch den nicht mit der Mutter verheirateten Vater von einer gerichtlichen Entscheidung abhängig machen' (2011) 19 ZEuP 901.
—— 'Forum (non) conveniens – Art. 15 EuEheVO Vor zwei obersten Common law-Gerichten (zu EuGH, 27.10.2016 – Rs. C-428/15 – Child and Family Agency /. J. D., unten S. 610, Nr. 45)' [2017] IPRax 562.

Pretelli I, 'Provisional Measures in Family Law and the Brussels IIter Regulation' (2018/2019) 20 Yearbook of Private International Law 113.
Quiñones Escámez A, '¿Cuándo se aplica el Reglamento Bruselas II bis? El TJCE se pronuncia sobre su ámbito de aplicación' (2008) 12 Revista de Derecho Comunitario Europeo 457.
Rauscher T, 'Unterhaltzuständigkeit zwischen Sorgerechts- und Ehesachenverbund' [2016] IPRax 215.
Rentsch B and Weller M-P, 'Urteilsanerkennung im Internationalen Sorgerecht: Regelungsebenen der EuEheVO gegen Wertungsebenen des ordre public' [2017] IPRax 262.
Requejo Isidro M, 'El artículo 20 Reglamento (CE) número 2201/2003 ante el TJCE' [2010] Diario La Ley, N° 7479, Sección Tribuna, 30 Sep. 2010.
Rieländer F, 'Die Wahlfreiheit zwischen den Aufenthaltszuständigkeiten nach Art. 3 lit. a und b EuUntVO im Unterhaltsregressverfahren: Anmerkung zu EuGH, Urt. v. 17.9.2020 – C-540/19, WV/Landkreis Harburg' (2021) 18 GPR 33.
Rodriguez Pineau E, 'STJ (Sala 2.ª) de 9 de noviembre de 2010, Bianca Purrucker c. Guillermo Vallés Pérez.' (2010) 62(2) Revista Española de Derecho Internacional 244.
—— 'La refundición del Reglamento Bruselas II bis: de nuevo sobre la función del Derecho internacional privado europeo' (2017) 69(1) Revista Española de Derecho Internacional 139.
Romano GP, 'Conflicts Between Parents and Between Legal Orders in Respect of Parental Responsibility' (2014/2015) 16 Yearbook of Private International Law 129.
Sagot-Duvauroux J, 'Précisions sur la notion de résidence habituelle en matière de divorce' (2022) 58 Revue trimestrielle de droit européen 193.
Szpunar M, 'Forum of Necessity in Family Law Matters Within the Framework of EU and International Law' [2021] Polski Proces Cywilny 563.
Thomale C, 'Der gewöhnliche Aufenthalt im Europäischen Kindschaftsrecht' (2019) 16 GPR 173.
Tonolo S, 'La Sottrazione Dei Minori Nel Diritto Processuale Civile Europeo: Il Regolamento Bruxelles Ii-Bis E La Convenzione Dell'aja Del 1980 A Confronto' (2011) 47 Rivista di Diritto Internazionale Privato e Processuale 81.
Trimmings K, '*Child Abduction within the European Union* (Hart 2013).
Tuo EC, 'Superiore interesse del minore e regolamenti UE di diritto internazionale privato della famiglia (2020) 36 NGCC 676.
Viarengo I, 'The Enforcement of Maintenance Decisions in the EU: Requiem for Public Policy? Family Relationships and the (Partial) Abolition of Exequatur' in P Beaumont and others (eds), *The Recovery of Maintenance in the EU and Worldwide* (Hart 2014) 473.
Viganotti É, 'La notion de "résidence habituelle" de l'enfant selon la CJUE' [2018] Gazette du Palais n° 40 Jur. 24.
Vigers S, *Mediating International Child Abduction Cases: The Hague Convention* (Hart 2011).
von Hein J and Grohmann N, 'Anmerkung zu EuGH, C-386/17 (Liberato./. Grigorescu)' [2019] FamRZ 1164.
Walker L and Beaumont P, 'Empirical Study on the Early Operation of the EU Maintenance Regulation' in P Beaumont and others (eds), *The Recovery of Maintenance in the EU and Worldwide* (Hart 2014) 337.
Walker L, *Maintenance and Child Support in Private International Law* (Hart 2015).
Zanobetti A, '*La residenza abituale nel diritto internazionale privato: spunti di riflessione*' in *Liber Amicorum Angelo Davì La vita giuridica internazionale nell'età della globalizzazione*, vol II0 (Editoriale Scientifica 2019) 1361.
Ziino S, 'La giurisdizione sulle cause matrimoniali e sulle domande connesse secondo la normativa europea' (2014) 68 Rivista Trimestrale Di Diritto e Procedura Civile 537.
Zoeteweij-Turhan MH, 'Brussels II bis: The Right of the Child to be Heard in International Proceedings' [2015] Pravnik: revija za pravno teorijo in prakso 861.
Župan M, Hoehn C and Kluth U, 'Central Authority Cooperation under the Brussels II ter Regulation' (2020/2021) 22 Yearbook of Private International Law 183.

Anna Wysocka-Bar

Chapter 15 International Jurisdiction and Recognition and Enforcement in Matters of Property Regimes and Succession

A Introduction

I Setting the Scene

#1 The **Succession Regulation**[1] provides for the rules on jurisdiction, choice-of-law, recognition and enforcement of decisions and court settlements in succession matters, as well as on the acceptance and enforcement of authentic instruments in matters of **succession** between EU Member States (MS). It also covers a number of other aspects of international civil procedure, including legal aid. It has established a new instrument titled **European Certificate of Succession** (ECS), governs the procedure of the issuance of an ECS in an EU MS, as well as the effects of an ECS in other EU MS.

#2 The **Matrimonial Property Regimes Regulation** and **Property Regimes of Registered Partnerships Regulation**[2] (Twin Regulations) similarly to the Succession Regulation, cover a wide range of matters of judicial cooperation. They provide for rules on jurisdiction, choice-of-law, recognition and the enforcement of decisions and **court settlements** in – respectively – matrimonial property matters and property matters of **registered partnerships**, as well as on the acceptance and enforcement of authentic instruments in such matters between MS. As with the Succession Regulation, they also cover other aspects of international civil procedure, for example, legal aid. These Twin Regulations are adopted within the

1 Regulation (EU) 650/2012 of the European Parliament and of the Council of 4 July 2012 on jurisdiction, applicable law, recognition and enforcement of decisions and acceptance and enforcement of authentic instruments in matters of succession and on the creation of a European Certificate of Succession [2012] OJ L201/107.

2 Council Regulation (EU) 2016/1103 of 24 June 2016 implementing enhanced cooperation in the area of jurisdiction, applicable law and the recognition and enforcement of decisions in matters of matrimonial property regimes [2016] OJ L183/1 and Council Regulation (EU) 2016/1104 of 24 June 2016 implementing enhanced cooperation in the area of jurisdiction, applicable law and the recognition and enforcement of decisions in matters of the property consequences of registered partnerships [2016] OJ L183/30.

Anna Wysocka-Bar, Licensed attorney-at-law in Poland, Assistant Professor in Private International Law, Jagiellonian University in Kraków (Poland), e-mail: anna.wysocka@uj.edu.pl

https://doi.org/10.1515/9783110781632-015

procedure of enhanced cooperation.[3] Hence, they are applicable only in certain MS.

#3 As Matrimonial Property Regimes Regulation and Property Regimes of Registered Partnerships Regulation contain many rules which are either identical or similar, they will be referred to as Twin Regulations and commented on jointly. In any case of a difference between the provisions of these regulations, this will be clearly signaled. As certain provisions of Twin Regulations are identical or similar to their counterparts in the Succession Regulation, a given institution will be commented on the example of the Succession Regulation (as this was enacted earlier than the Twin Regulations) and the existence of identical provisions in the Twin Regulations will only be signaled. As this Handbook is devoted to international civil procedure, choice-of-law rules contained in the regulations will be omitted (unless they need to be mentioned due to their impact on jurisdiction).

#4 The general structure of all three regulations is similar: Chapter I deals with scope and definitions, Chapter II – with jurisdiction, Chapter III – with applicable law, Chapter IV – with recognition, enforceability and the enforcement of decisions, Chapter V – with **authentic instruments** and **court settlements**. Chapter VI of the Succession Regulation is devoted to ECS, whereas Chapter VI of the Twin Regulations contain already general and final provisions. The latter provisions are included in the Succession Regulation in its Chapter VII. All three regulations are preceded by long preambles.

II Scopes of Application

1 Material Scope

#5 Pursuant to Article 1(1) Succession Regulation, it applies to **succession** to the estates of deceased persons.[4] Succession means 'succession to the estate of a deceased person and covers all forms of transfer of assets, rights and obligations by reason of death, whether by way of a voluntary transfer under a disposition of property upon death or a transfer through intestate succession' (Article 3(1)(a)).

Article 1(2) Succession Regulation lists matters excluded from its scope. One of the examples includes the formal validity of dispositions of property upon death made orally (Article 1(2)(f)).

---

3 Council Decision (EU) 2016/954 of 9 June 2016 authorising enhanced cooperation in the area of jurisdiction, applicable law and the recognition and enforcement of decisions on the property regimes of international couples, covering both matters of matrimonial property regimes and the property consequences of registered partnerships [2016] OJ L 159/16.

4 C Azcárraga Monzonís, 'Succession' in I Viarengo and F Villata (eds), *Planning the Future of Cross Border Families. A Path Through Coordination* (Hart 2020) 93.

#6 Pursuant to Article 1(1) Twin Regulations, they apply – respectively – to **matrimonial property** regimes and to matters of the **property consequences of registered partnerships.**[5] Matrimonial property regime is defined as 'a set of rules concerning the property relationships between the spouses and in their relations with third parties, as a result of marriage or its dissolution' (Article 3(1)(a) Matrimonial Property Regimes Regulation). A **registered partnership** is defined as 'the regime governing the shared life of two people which is provided for in law, the registration of which is mandatory under that law and which fulfils the legal formalities required by that law for its creation' (Article 3(1)(a) Property Regimes of Registered Partnership Regulation). Consequently, the property consequences of a registered partnership means 'the set of rules concerning the property relationships of the partners, between themselves and in their relations with third parties, as a result of the legal relationship created by the registration of the partnership or its dissolution' (Article 3(1)(b)). Article 1(2) lists matters excluded from the scopes of the Twin Regulations. For example, pursuant to Article 1(2)(b) Twin Regulations, the existence, validity or recognition – respectively – of a marriage and of a registered partnership is excluded.[6]

2 Territorial Scope

#7 The Succession Regulation was adopted on the basis of Article 81(2) TFEU and not 81(3) as it was not perceived as a measure concerning family law. It is applicable in all MS except Denmark and Ireland. It was never applicable in the UK, even before the UK's withdrawal from the EU.

#8 As opposed to the Succession Regulation, the Twin Regulations do concern family law and therefore the possible basis for their adoption could have been Article 81(3) TFEU, which requires unanimity. As such unanimity was lacking, the Twin Regulations were adopted within separate procedure of **enhanced cooperation** on

5 P Quinzá Redondo, 'Matrimonial Property Regimes' in I Viarengo and F Villata (eds), *Planning the Future of Cross Border Families. A Path Through Coordination* (Hart 2020) 103; G Pallau Moreno, 'Property Consequences of Registered Partnerships' in I Viarengo and F Villata (eds) *Planning the Future of Cross Border Families. A Path Through Coordination* (Hart 2020) 109; MJ Cazorla Gonzalez and M Soto Moya, 'Main Concepts and Scope of Application of the Twin Regulations' in L Ruggeri, A Limanté and N Pogorelčnik Vogrinc, *The EU Regulations on Matrimonial Property Regimes and Property of Registered Partnerships* (Intersentia 2022) 41.

6 See A Rodríguez Benot, 'Article 1 Scope' in I Viarengo and P Franzina (eds), *The EU Regulations on the Property Regimes of International Couples. A Commentary* (Edward Elgar 2020) 17.

the basis of Article 328 TFEU, whose characterising feature is that a measure might be adopted only by some MS. As a result, the Twin Regulations were adopted by 18 participating MS these being Sweden, Belgium, Greece, Croatia, Slovenia, Spain, France, Portugal, Italy, Malta, Luxembourg, Germany, the Czech Republic, the Netherlands, Austria, Bulgaria, Finland and Cyprus.[7] The remaining MS may join the enhanced cooperation at a later stage, but so far none have decided to do so.

3 Temporal Scope

#9 The Succession Regulation became applicable on 17 August 2015 to the succession of persons deceased starting from this date (Article 83(1) and Article 84). It additionally contains special transitional provisions in Article 83, for instance concerning **a disposition of property upon death** (for example, a testament), which was made before 17 August 2015 by a person who died after that day.[8]

#10 Pursuant to Article 70, the Twin Regulations generally apply from 29 January 2019. Detailed transitional provisions are laid down in Article 69. The Twin Regulations apply to 'legal proceedings instituted, to authentic instruments formally drawn up or registered and to court settlements approved or concluded' starting from 29 January 2019 (Article 69(1)). If the proceedings in the MS of origin were instituted before 29 January 2019, decisions given after that date are also recognised and enforced in accordance with the Twin Regulations (Chapter IV) as long as the rules of jurisdiction applied comply with those set out in Chapter II of the Twin Regulations (Article 69(2)). Provisions on the **applicable law** (Chapter III) apply – respectively – only to spouses who have married or who specify the law applicable to the matrimonial property regime and to partners who register their partnership or who specify the law applicable to the property consequences of their registered partnership on or after 29 January 2019 (Article 69(3)).[9]

III Relation with International Agreements

#11 The Succession Regulation takes precedence over conventions (which concern succession matters) concluded exclusively between two or more Member States

7 E Kavoliūnaitė-Ragauskienė, 'The Twin Regulations: Development and Adoption' in L Ruggeri, A Limanté and N Pogorelčnik Vogrinc (eds), *The EU Regulations on Matrimonial Property Regimes and Property of Registered Partnerships* (Intersentia 2022) 25.

8 P Franzina, 'Article 83 Transitional Provisions' in A-L Calvo Caravaca, A Davi and H-P Mansel (eds), *The EU Succession Regulation. A Commentary* (CUP 2016) 852.

9 G Biagioni, 'Article 69 Transitional Provisions' in I Viarengo and P Franzina (eds), *The EU Regulations on the Property Regimes of International Couples. A Commentary* (Edward Elgar 2020) 483.

(Article 75(2)). Hence, the Succession Regulation takes precedence, for instance, over the bilateral agreement on judicial cooperation between Poland and Slovenia, which contains rules on succession matters. Almost identical provisions are included in the Twin Regulations (Article 62(2)). Because not all MS are participating in the enhanced cooperation (including Poland) and therefore are 'third states' for the purpose of the Twin Regulations, the very same bilateral agreement between Poland and Slovenia would not fall under Article 62(2) Twin Regulations, and therefore, the Twin Regulations (or rather Matrimonial Property Regulation) would not have precedence over this **bilateral agreement**.[10]

#12 The Succession Regulation 'shall not affect' the application of such international conventions to which one or more Member States are party at the time of the adoption of the Succession Regulation (Article 75(1)). The **Hague Convention on the Form of Wills**[11] is specifically mentioned. When read together, both paragraphs of Article 75 make it clear that the Succession Regulation 'shall not affect' the application of international convention to which at least one third state is a party to. In its judgment in the *OP* case[12] concerning the application of the Poland-Ukraine bilateral agreement on judicial cooperation, which contain rules on succession matters, the CJEU explained that 'where the EU legislature provides that the application of a regulation "shall not affect" existing international conventions, those conventions are to apply (. . .)'.

#13 Similar to Article 75(1) Succession Regulation, however slightly differently worded, provisions are included in the Twin Regulations (Article 62(1)). Based on Article 62 (1) Matrimonial Property Matters Regulation, the above-mentioned Poland-Slovenia bilateral agreement should be applied by Slovenian courts, instead of the Regulation. As the bilateral agreement seems not to cover registered partnership matters (as drafted in the 1960s), the Property Matters of Registered Partnership Regulation would apply.

#14 Both the Succession Regulation (Article 75(3)) and the Matrimonial Property Matters Regulation (Article 69(3)) regulate specifically the relation of these instruments – respectively – with respect to the Nordic Conventions.[13]

---

10 See A Wysocka-Bar, 'Enhanced Cooperation in Property Matters in the EU and Non-Participating Member States' (2019) 20 ERA Forum 187.

11 The Convention of 5 October 1961 on the Conflicts of Laws Relating to the Form of Testamentary Dispositions.

12 Case C-21/22 *OP* (12 October 2023) ECLI:EU:C:2023:766.

13 See M Jänterä-Jareborg, 'Inter-Nordic Exceptions in EU Regulations on Matters of Family and Inheritance Law. Legal "Irritants" or Necessary Concessions in the Citizens' Interest?' in A-L Verbeke and others (eds), *Confronting the Frontiers of Family and Succession Law: Liber Amicorum Walter Pintens* (Intersentia 2012) 733.

B International Jurisdiction

I Common Features

#15 All three regulations have some common features with respect to provisions related to jurisdiction. The most important feature is that the jurisdictional rules of these regulations are comprehensive and exhaustive, meaning that there is no place left (as opposed to, for example, the Brussels I-bis Regulation)[14] for domestic rules on jurisdiction.

#16 Where a court of a MS is seised of a matter over which it has no jurisdiction under a given regulation, it declares of its own motion that it has no jurisdiction (Article 15 Succession Regulation, Article 15 Twin Regulations).

#17 Safeguards aimed at assuring that the proceeding does not continue if a party was not properly **served** are in place in Article 16 Succession Regulation and Article 16 Twin Regulation. Depending on the case the **Service Regulation** or **Hague Service Convention** apply.[15]

#18 Article 17 Succession Regulation regulates **lis pendens**, concerning the situation where proceedings involving the same cause of action and between the same parties are brought in the courts of different MS. Traditionally, the **first in time rule** is in place, meaning that in the case of lis pendens, any court other than the court first seised shall of its own motion stay the proceedings. Once the jurisdiction of the court first seised is established, a court in another MS shall decline jurisdiction. The same mechanism is provided for in Article 17 Twin Regulations, however it is made clear, in their paragraph 2, that a court of a MS shall, upon request from another court of a MS seised of the dispute, inform without delay of the date when it was seised.

#19 **Related actions** are also regulated. In accordance with Article 18(3) Succession Regulation actions are deemed to be related if 'they are so closely connected that it is expedient to hear and determine them together to avoid the risk of irreconcilable decisions resulting from separate proceedings'. In case such actions are pending in the courts of different MS, any court other than the court first seised may stay its proceedings (Article 18(1) Succession Regulation). Where those actions are pending at first instance, any court other than the court first seised may also decline jurisdiction if the court first seised has jurisdiction and its law permits such consolidation. Such declining of jurisdiction requires, in accordance with Article 18(2) Succession Regulation, the application of one of the parties.

#20 Rules as to at which moment a court of a MS is **deemed to be seised** are to be found in Article 14 Succession Regulation and Article 14 Twin Regulations.

---

14 See P Franzina, Chapter 10, #24 et seq.

15 See W Kennett, Chapter 8.

#21 Just as in the Brussels I bis Regulation, the Succession Regulation and the Twin Regulations provide for specific jurisdiction with respect to **provisional, including protective, measures**. Application may be made to the courts of a MS for such measures as are available under the law of that MS, even if the courts of another MS have jurisdiction as to the substance of the matter (Article 19 Succession Regulation, Article 19 Twin Regulations).

#22 All three regulations contain a special rule on **forum necessitatis** (Article 11 Succession Regulation; Article 11 Twin Regulations). It applies in cases where no court of a Member State has jurisdiction pursuant to the other provisions of a given regulation and the proceedings cannot reasonably be brought or conducted or would be impossible in a third State with which the case is closely connected. In such a case, on an exceptional basis, the courts of a MS may exercise jurisdiction provided that the case has a sufficient connection with the MS of the court seised.

II Succession Regulation

1 General Rules on Jurisdiction

#23 Depending on where the deceased was **habitually resident at the time of death** a different jurisdictional rule of the Succession Regulation applies.[16] If the deceased was habitually resident in the EU MS bound by this regulation the general rule of Article 4 applies, and if the deceased was habitually resident in a third state (or EU MS, which does not apply this regulation) Article 10 applies.[17] In the former situation, in accordance with Article 4, the courts of the MS in which the deceased had his habitual residence at the time of death have jurisdiction. In the latter situation, in accordance with Article 10, the jurisdiction depends on the location of assets within a given MS. Pursuant to Article 10(1) Succession Regulation, the courts of a MS in which the assets of the estate are located have jurisdiction provided that an additional element is present. In accordance with Article 10(1)(a) the deceased must have held the nationality of that MS at the time of death. If the

16 M Kränzle, 'The Notion of Habitual Residence in Recitals 23 and 24' in S Bariatti, I Viarengo and FC Villata (eds), *EU Cross-Border Succession Law* (Edward Elgar 2022) 115.

17 Article 10 was already subject to the relatively rich case law of the CJEU (at least when compared with other provisions of the regulation). In case C-55/23 *Jurtukała* (17 July 2023) ECLI: ECLI:EU:C:2023:599 the CJEU had to explain that Article 10 Succession Regulation 'applies only where the habitual residence of the deceased at the time of death was located in a Member State not bound by that regulation or in a third State'. In case C-291/23 *Hantoch* (7 November 2024) ECLI: ECLI:EU:C:2024:938, the CJEU decided that in order to determine whether the subsidiary jurisdiction of the courts of the Member State in which the assets of the estate are located may be exercised, in order to rule on the succession 'as a whole' the assets must have been located in that MS at the time of the death of the deceased (and not at the time the court is seised).

deceased was not a national of that given MS, pursuant to Article 10(1)(a), the court of that MS has jurisdiction if the deceased had his previous habitual residence in that MS, provided that, at the time the court is seised, a period of not more than five years has elapsed since that habitual residence was changed.[18]

#24 Both Article 4 and Article 10(1) Succession Regulation underline that the jurisdiction is 'to rule on the succession as a whole'. Recital (37) explains what this expression means with respect to applicable law, however it can be helpful in understanding also rules on jurisdiction. Succession as a whole means 'all of the property forming part of the estate, irrespective of the nature of the assets and regardless of whether the assets are located in another Member State or in a third State'. Hence, jurisdiction derived by a court of a MS from Article 4 and Article 10(1) covers all the **assets** of the **estate** irrespective of their location, namely also any assets, including immovable property, located outside of the EU.

#25 If a court of a MS exercises jurisdiction in a succession case over assets located in a **third state**, there is always a risk that such a decision will not be recognised/ enforced in that third state. This risk was known to the EU legislator. Pursuant to Article 12(1) Succession Regulation, in a case where the estate consist of assets located in a third State, the court seised may decide not to rule on one or more of such assets if it may be expected that its decision in respect of those assets will not be recognised or declared not enforceable in that third State. This might happen, in accordance with Article 12(1), at the request of one of the parties.

2 Transfer of Jurisdiction in Succession Matters from One MS to Another MS

#26 As Recital (27) reminds, the rules of the Succession Regulation are 'devised so as to ensure that the authority dealing with the succession will, in most situations, be applying its own law'. This would be the case where both jurisdiction (in accordance with Article 4) and applicable law (in accordance with Article 21(1)) are based on the **habitual residence** of the deceased. In a case where the deceased has chosen the applicable law in accordance with Article 22(1), the court of a MS having jurisdiction over the case, depending on the circumstances, might be 'forced' to apply foreign law. Hence, the Succession Regulation 'provides for a series of mechanisms which would come into play where the deceased had chosen' the law applicable so that the coincidence between *forum* and *ius* might be restored (Recital (27)).

18 I Queirolo, 'Jurisdiction in Succession Matters: General Rules and Choice of Court' in S Bariatti, I Viarengo and FC Villata (eds), *EU Cross-Border Succession Law* (Edward Elgar 2022) 221.

#27 These ‘series of mechanisms’ are regulated in Articles 5–9 Succession Regulation. The prerequisite for the application of any of these mechanisms is that the deceased has chosen the law applicable to succession in accordance with Article 22, meaning the deceased has indicated in a disposition of property upon death their national law as being the law of one of the EU MS.[19]

#28 The first mechanism consists of the parties concerned agreeing on the jurisdiction of the court of the MS whose law was chosen by the deceased (Article 5(1)). Pursuant to Article 5(2) Succession Regulation, such an agreement must be expressed in writing, dated and signed by the parties concerned, while any communication by electronic means which provides a **durable record** is deemed equivalent to it being in writing. In the case of such an agreement being concluded, the court which would otherwise be competent declines jurisdiction in accordance with Article 6(a) Succession Regulation, whereas the court indicated in the choice-of-court agreement has jurisdiction in accordance with Article 7(b) Succession Regulation.

#29 Article 9 Succession Regulation envisages a situation where in the course of proceedings before a court of a MS exercising jurisdiction based on a **choice of court agreement**, it appears that not all the parties to those proceedings were party to that agreement. In such a case, in accordance with Article 9(1) Succession Regulation, the court continues to exercise jurisdiction if such parties enter an appearance without contesting the jurisdiction of the court. If on the other hand, this party contests the jurisdiction, pursuant to Article 9(2), the court declines jurisdiction.

#30 In the second mechanism the court of a MS may decline jurisdiction if it considers that the courts of the MS of the chosen law are better placed to rule on the succession. The court declines jurisdiction, in accordance with Article 6(a) at the request of one of the parties considering ‘the practical circumstances of the succession, such as the habitual residence of the parties and the location of the assets’. In such a case, pursuant to Article 7(a), the courts of this other MS have jurisdiction.

#31 The third mechanism operates when the parties to the proceedings have **expressly accepted the jurisdiction** of the court seised in accordance with Article 7(b). This mechanism assumes that the case was brought directly to the court of a MS of the chosen law.

---

19 See also C-422/20 *RK* (9 September 2021) ECLI:EU:C:2021:718 where the CJEU explained that the transfer is possible also ‘in the event that, in his or her will, drawn up before 17 August 2015, the deceased had not chosen the law applicable to the succession, and that the designation of that law can be inferred from Article 83(4) of that regulation alone’. Article 83(4) Succession Regulation provides that if a will was made prior to 17 August 2015 ‘in accordance with the law which the deceased could have chosen in accordance with this Regulation’, that law is deemed to have been chosen as applicable.

#32 Additionally, Article 8 Succession Regulation, provides a court which has opened succession proceedings of its own motion under Article 4 or Article 10 to close it if the parties have agreed to settle the succession **amicably out of court** in the MS of the chosen law.

3 Jurisdiction to Receive Declarations Relating to Succession

#33 Article 13 provides for a special, additional jurisdiction for accepting certain declarations,[20] this is 'a declaration concerning the acceptance or waiver of the succession, of a legacy or of a reserved share, or a declaration designed to limit the liability of the person concerned in respect of the liabilities under the succession'. The obvious purpose of this additional (to the general one) jurisdiction is, as Recital 32 explains, 'to simplify the lives of heirs and legatees'. Such a jurisdiction is vested in the courts of the MS of the individual's habitual residence, if that person wants to make such declaration. For this purpose Article 13 requires that the law applicable to the succession provides for the possibility of making such a declaration before a court and that under the law of the MS where such a declaration is to be received such declarations may be made before a court. Recital (32) adds that the possibility of making a declaration before a court should not preclude such declarations being made before other authorities in that MS which are competent to receive declarations under national law. Notaries constituting an example of such competent other authorities.[21]

20 Under this provision some doubts arose in practice. In case C-617/20 *TN and NN* (2 June 2022) ECLI: EU:C:2022:426 the CJEU (which mainly concern the form of a declaration) explained that 'according to the EU legislature, it is necessary that the declaration concerning the waiver of succession made before a court of the Member State of the habitual residence of the party waiving succession should be notified to the court having jurisdiction to rule on the succession. However, it must be noted that neither Article 13 nor Article 28 of that regulation provides for a mechanism for the communication of such declarations by the court of the Member State of the habitual residence of the party waiving succession to the court having jurisdiction to rule on the succession. On the other hand, Recital 32 presumes that persons who have made use of the right to make such declarations in the Member State of their habitual residence will assume the burden of communicating the existence of those declarations to the authorities responsible for the succession' (para 47). In case C-651/21 *M. Ya. M.* (30 March 2023) ECLI:EU:C:2023:277 the CJEU explained that an heir may make use of a declaration for which another heir applied for. In the currently pending case C-57/24 *Ławida* (27 March 2025) ECLI:EU:C:2025:217 will be faced with the question as to whether the jurisdiction based on Article 13 still exists in cases where 'in addition to a declaration of waiver of the succession being received, that declaration must additionally be approved by a court in order to be effective pursuant to the laws of the Member State of habitual residence of the person submitting it, for instance where the declaration is submitted after the expiry of the deadline'.

21 D Muritano, 'Acceptance and Waiver of the Succession' in S Bariatti, I Viarengoa and FC. Villata (eds), *EU Cross-Border Succession Law* (Edward Elgar 2022) 190.

III Twin Regulations

1 Jurisdiction in Cases Linked with Succession

#34 Pursuant to Article 4 Twin Regulations in the case a court of a MS is seised in matters of the succession of a spouse/registered partner pursuant to Succession Regulation, the courts of that MS have jurisdiction to rule on matters of the matrimonial property regime/on matters of the property consequences of the registered partnership arising in connection with that succession case. Article 13 Twin Regulations provides a rule where the estate of the deceased whose succession falls under the Succession Regulation comprises assets located in a third state. In such a case, the court seised to rule on the matrimonial property regime/on the property consequences of a registered partnership may decide not to rule on one or more of such assets if it may be expected that its decision in respect of those assets will not be recognised and, where applicable, declared enforceable in that third state. Just as in the succession case, this limiting of the proceedings requires the request of one of the parties. Pursuant to Article 13(2), the above does not affect the right of the parties to limit the scope of the proceedings under the law of the MS of the court seised.

2 Jurisdiction in Cases Linked with Divorce, Dissolution, Annulment of Marriage or Registered Partnership

#35 Article 5 Matrimonial Property Regimes Regulation relates to cases where a court of a MS is seised to rule on an application for **divorce**, **legal separation** or **marriage annulment** pursuant to the Brussels II ter Regulation. In such a case, in accordance with Article 5(1), the courts of that MS have also jurisdiction to rule on matters of the matrimonial property regime arising in connection with that application. In certain circumstances listed in Article 5(2) Matrimonial Property Regimes Regulation however additional **agreement between the spouses** is needed for the court seised on divorce, legal separation or marriage annulment to have jurisdiction also over matters of the matrimonial property regime. This is the case where the court seised assumed jurisdiction based on: Article 3(1)(a) fifth indent or sixth intent of the Brussels II ter Regulation; based on Article 5 of the Brussels II ter Regulation in cases of conversion of legal separation into divorce or based on Article 7 of the Brussels II ter Regulation in cases of residual jurisdiction.

#36 If the agreement required by Article 5(2) is concluded before the court is seised to rule on matters of matrimonial property regimes, the agreement must comply with requirements of Article 7(2) Matrimonial Property Regimes Regulation.

Namely, the agreement is to be expressed in writing[22] and dated and signed by the parties.

#37 The Property Consequences of Registered Partnership Regulation provides for a different solution in Article 5. Article 5 speaks about 'dissolution or **annulment**' of a registered partnership only. Pursuant to Article 5(1) a court of a MS seised to rule on the dissolution or annulment, the courts of that MS have jurisdiction to rule on the property consequences of the registered partnership arising in connection with that case, where the partners so agree. If such an agreement is concluded before the court is seised to rule on matters of the property consequences of the registered partnership, in accordance with Article 5(2), the agreement must comply with Article 7 Property Consequences of Registered Partnership Regulation. Namely, the agreement is to be expressed in writing[23] and dated and signed by the parties.

3 Jurisdiction in Other Cases

#38 Where no court of a MS has jurisdiction pursuant to Article 4 or 5 or in cases other than those provided for in those Articles, jurisdiction to rule on a matter of the spouses' matrimonial property regime is indicated by Article 6 Twin Regulations in the form of a so-called 'cascade' (or 'ladder').[24] The jurisdiction lies with the courts of the MS in whose territory the spouses are habitually resident at the time the court is seised. Failing that (meaning that spouses are not habitually resident in the same MS), the jurisdiction lies with the courts of the MS in whose territory the spouses were last habitually resident, insofar as one of them still resides there at the time the court is seised. Failing that the jurisdiction lies with the courts of the MS in whose territory the respondent is habitually resident at the time the court is seised. Failing that the jurisdiction lies with the courts of the MS of the spouses' common nationality at the time the court is seised. In Article 6 (e) Registered Partnership Property Regulation there is an additional level of the 'cascade'. Failing the possibility of applying the previous grounds of jurisdiction, the jurisdiction lies with the courts of the MS under whose laws the registered partnership was created.

22 Any communication by electronic means which provides a durable record of the agreement shall be deemed equivalent to writing.

23 Any communication by electronic means which provides a durable record of the agreement shall be deemed equivalent to writing.

24 P Franzina, 'Article 6 Jurisdiction in Other Cases' in I Viarengo and P Franzina (eds), *The EU Regulations on the Property Regimes of International Couples. A Commentary* (Edward Elgar 2020) 78.

#39 Pursuant to Article 7 Twin Regulations a **choice of court agreement** is admissible.[25] In cases covered by Article 6, the parties may agree that chosen court have exclusive jurisdiction to rule on matters of their property regime. The available options are the courts of the MS whose law is applicable pursuant to Article 22 Twin Regulations[26] or point (a) or (b) of Article 26(1) Matrimonial Property Regulation (and Article 26(1) Property Regimes of Registered Partnerships Regulation)[27] or the courts of the Member State of the conclusion of the marriage (in the case of Matrimonial Property Regulation). The choice of court agreement must be expressed in writing and dated and signed by the parties. Any communication by electronic means which provides a durable record of the agreement shall be deemed equivalent to writing. This solution is aimed at assuring the coincidence of *forum* and *ius*, meaning that the court applies its own **substantive law**.

#40 Article 8 Matrimonial Property Regulations provide for jurisdiction based on the **appearance** of the defendant (**submission**). Such submission is possible only before the courts of a MS whose law is applicable pursuant to Article 22 Twin Regulations or point (a) or (b) of Article 26(1) Matrimonial Property Regulation (and Article 26(1) Property Regimes of Registered Partnerships Regulation). This rule does not apply where the appearance was entered to contest the jurisdiction, or in cases covered by Article 4 or 5(1). Additionally, before assuming jurisdiction in this case, the court ensures that the defendant is informed of his right to contest the jurisdiction and of the consequences of entering or not entering an appearance. Also, this solution is aimed at assuring the coincidence of *forum* and *ius*.

#41 Article 9(1) Twin Regulations provide for situations where a court of the Member State that has jurisdiction holds that, under its private international law, the marriage in question is not recognised for the purposes of matrimonial property regime proceedings or does not provide for a registered partnership.[28] In such a case, by way of exception, the court may **decline jurisdiction**, without undue delay. Article 9(2) Twin Regulations indicates the courts which have jurisdiction in such case. This provision does not apply when the parties have obtained a divorce, legal separation or marriage annulment (or dissolution or annulment of a registered partnership) which is capable of being recognised in the MS of the forum.

25 P Franzina, 'Article 7 Choice of Court' in I Viarengo and P Franzina (eds), *The EU Regulations on the Property Regimes of International Couples. A Commentary* (Edward Elgar 2020) 85.

26 Twin Regulations contain quite detailed rules concerning party autonomy. Pursuant to Article 22 Twin Regulations (future or actual) spouses / partners are allowed to choose the law applicable to their property relations from among those listed (for instance, in accordance with Article 22(1)(b), spouses / partners may choose the national law of either the spouse / partner at the time the agreement is concluded).

27 Article 26 Twin Regulations designates the applicable law in case there is no choice of applicable law made by the spouses / partners.

28 Here the exact wording of the Twin Regulations differs one from another.

#42 Remaining rules on the jurisdiction of Twin Regulations (just as those commented upon above) are quite casuistic and therefore will only be mentioned in a very general way. In accordance with Article 10 Twin Regulations, in certain circumstances, where no court of a MS has jurisdiction or when jurisdiction was declined, the courts of a MS have jurisdiction in so far as the immoveable property of one or both spouses is located in the territory of that MS. In such a case the court has jurisdiction to rule only in respect of the immoveable property in question. Article 11 as already mentioned above provides for *forum neccessitatis*. In accordance with Article 12 Twin Regulations the court in which proceedings are pending, in general, has also jurisdiction to rule on a counterclaim if it falls within the scope of a given regulation.[29]

C Recognition and Enforcement of Judgments

I Common Features

#43 Rules on the recognition and enforcement of decisions of all three regulations are to a great extent identical. These provisions were based on the model of the Brussels I Regulation (before its recast of 2015), and therefore, enforcement requires **declaration of enforceability** (exequatur).[30]

#44 A decision given in a MS is recognised in another MS without any special procedure being required (Article 39(1) Succession Regulation; Article 36(1) Twin Regulations), including when the recognition concerns an incidental question (for instance, the recognition of a judgment indicating the heirs to the estate of the deceased within another proceeding which concerns a dispute over the ownership of one of the assets of the estate). A party wishing to have a foreign decision declared recognised once for all purposes may apply for such recognition in accordance with the procedure provided for enforcement (Article 39(2) Succession Regulation; Article 36(2) Twin Regulations).

29 See a detailed analysis in I Kunda and A Limanté, 'Jurisdictional Provisions in the Twin Regulations' in L Ruggeri, A Limanté and N Pogorelčnik Vogrinc (eds), *The EU Regulations on Matrimonial Property Regimes and Property of Registered Partnerships* (Intersentia 2022) 71.

30 See in this volume F Gascón Inchausti, Chapter 12, #16, #17 and W Hau, Chapter 13, #26, #27, #28. See also F Pesce and S Dominelli, 'Recognition and Enforcement of Foreign Decisions in Cross-Border Succession Matters' in S Bariatti, I Viarengo and FC Villata (eds), *EU Cross-Border Succession Law* (Edward Elgar 2022) 246.

#45 Decision[31] given in a MS[32] may be enforceable in another MS provided that it is enforceable in the MS of origin. A decision may be declared enforceable on the application of any interested party. The application should be supplemented by prescribed documents, including a **copy of the decision** and an **attestation** on a form provided for in the Implementing Regulation[33] (Article 46(3) and 47 Succession Regulation; Article 45(3) and Article 46 Twin Regulations).

#46 As for procedure this is partly described by the regulations themselves (in Articles 45–58 Succession Regulation; Article 44–57 Twin Regulations)[34] and in remaining aspects governed by the law of the MS of enforcement (Article 46(1) Succession; Article 45(1) Twin Regulations).[35] The application for a declaration of enforceability must be submitted to the court or other authority communicated by the MS (Article 45(1) Succession Regulation; Article 44(1) Twin Regulations). Also the internal territorial competence of the authorities of a MS is regulated (Article 45(2) and Article 44 Succession Regulation; Article 44(2) and Article 43 Twin Regulations). The decision is declared enforceable immediately upon completion of formalities without any review as to the grounds of refusal at that stage. At this stage of proceedings the other party (other than the applicant) is not entitled to make any submission (Article 48 Succession Regulation; Article 47 Twin Regulations). The declaration of enforceability is served on the other party (other than the applicant) together with the decision (Article 49(1) Succession Regulation; Article 48(2) Twin Regulations). The decision on the application is brought to the **notice** of the other party in accordance with the law of the MS of enforcement (Article 49(2) Succession Regulation; Article 48(1) Twin Regulations).

#47 The decision on enforceability may be appealed against (Article 50(1) Succession Regulation; Article 49(1) Twin Regulations). An appeal is to be lodged in the competent court (communicated by MS to the European Commission) within a time limit

---

31 In the context of Succession Regulation, in Case C-658/17 *WB* (23 May 2019) ECLI:EU:C:2019:444 the Court of Justice of the EU explained that a national certificate of succession, if produced by a notary public, who does not constitute a 'court' within the meaning of the Succession Regulation, is not a decision and therefore does not circulate in the EU based on the rules on recognition and enforcement of decisions but is an 'authentic instrument'.

32 MS means a MS which applies a given Regulation. For instance, for the purpose of recognition and enforcement of a decision on a succession matter, Ireland is not a MS within the meaning of the Succession Regulation.

33 Commission Implementing Regulation (EU) No. 1329/2014 of 9 December 2014 establishing the Forms referred to in Regulation (EU) No. 650/2012 of the European Parliament and of the Council on jurisdiction, applicable law, recognition and enforcement of decisions and acceptance and enforcement of authentic instruments in matters of succession and on the creation of a European Certificate of Succession [2014] OJ L359/30.

34 This procedure is based on the Brussels I Regulation model (before recast). See in this volume W Hau, Chapter 13, #26, #27, #28

35 ibid #41.

provided for in the regulations (30 days or 60 days depending on the circumstances of the case; Article 50(5) Succession Regulation; Article 49(5) Twin Regulations). The decision given on the appeal may be further appealed only in accordance with the procedure communicated by MS to the European Commission (Article 51 Successions Regulation). The court with which the appeal is lodged refuses or revokes a declaration of enforceability only on one of the grounds of refusal specified in Article 40 Succession Regulation. Grounds of refusal are the same for recognition and enforcement. All three regulations list four such grounds, which include public policy, the right to defence and irreconcilable judgments (Article 40 Succession Regulation; Article 37 Twin Regulations).[36] A decision may not be reviewed as to its substance (Article 41 Succession Regulation; Article 40 Twin Regulations).

II Specific Provisions in the Twin Regulations

#48 Article 38 Twin Regulations titled 'Fundamental rights' provides that previsions on refusal of recognition or enforcement must be applied in observance of the **fundamental rights** and principles recognised in the **Charter of Fundamental Rights**. The provisions indicates that this concerns in particular Article 21 of the Charter (the principle of non-discrimination). Recital (54) Twin Regulations explains that the courts of MS should not be able to apply the **public policy exception** in order to refuse to recognise/enforce a decision from another MS when doing so would be contrary to the Charter and in particular Article 21. Even though there is no equivalent of Article 38 Twin Regulations in the Succession Regulation, a very similar thought is expressed in its Recital (58).

#49 Additionally, Article 39(1) Twin Regulations, indicates that the jurisdiction of the court of the MS of origin may not be reviewed. Article 39(2) makes it clear that public policy as ground of refusal does not apply to the rules on jurisdiction. Even though the Succession Regulation lacks this provision, none of the grounds of refusal allows for a review of the jurisdiction of the court of origin in succession matters.

D Authentic Instruments and Court Settlements

#50 All three instruments contain rules on circulation of **authentic instruments** and **court settlements** between MS.[37] These rules are identical in all three regula-

36 ibid #16–23.

37 See J Fitchen, *The Private International Law of Authentic Instruments* (Hart 2020) 385–456; G Vallar, 'Authentic Instruments and Court Settlements' in S Bariatti, I Viarengo and FC Villata (eds), *EU Cross-Border Succession Law* (Edward Elgar 2022) 285; I Kunda and M Ticić, 'Authentic Instruments and Courts Settle-

tions. Article 3(1)(i) Succession Regulation defines an authentic instrument to be a document in a matter of succession which has been formally drawn up or registered as an authentic instrument in a MS. Two additional requirements are to be met. Firstly, the **authenticity**[38] of the authentic instrument must relate to the signature and the content. Secondly, that it has been established by a public authority or other authority empowered for that purpose by the MS of origin. An example of an authentic instrument might be a domestic certificate of succession produced by a notary public, who is not a 'court' within the meaning of the Succession Regulation.[39] Pursuant to 3(1)(h) Succession Regulation a court settlement means a settlement in a matter of succession which has been approved by a court or concluded before a court in the course of proceedings. Identical definitions of authentic instruments and court settlements are included in the Twin Regulation, except that they refer to – respectively – the matter of a matrimonial property regime and the matter of the property consequences of a registered partnership.

#51 Succession Regulation and Twin Regulations, as opposed to the Brussels I bis Regulation, differentiate between the **acceptance** of and the **enforceability** of authentic instruments. In the case of court settlements only enforcement is possible. 'Acceptance' means that an authentic instrument has the same evidentiary effects or the most comparable effects in another MS as it has in the MS of its origin.[40] The authentic instrument will not be accepted if giving such an effect would be manifestly contrary to public policy in the MS concerned (Article 59(1) Succession Regulation; Article 58(1) Twin Regulations). The evidentiary effects which the authentic instrument produces in the MS of origin are described in a form filled in on the application of the person wishing to employ an authentic instrument in another MS (Article 59(1) Succession Regulation; Article 58(1) Twin Regulations).

#52 A challenge relating to the authenticity[41] of an authentic instrument (for example the genuineness of the document) is made before the courts of the MS of origin. It

ments under the Twin Regulations' in L Ruggeri, A Limanté and N Pogorelčnik Vogrinc (eds), *The EU Regulations on Matrimonial Property Regimes and Property of Registered Partnerships* (Intersentia 2022) 157.

38 Recital (62) Succession Regulation explain that the 'authenticity' of an authentic instrument is an autonomous concept 'covering elements such as the genuineness of the instrument, the formal prerequisites of the instrument, the powers of the authority drawing up the instrument and the procedure under which the instrument is drawn up. It should also cover the factual elements recorded in the authentic instrument by the authority concerned, such as the fact that the parties indicated appeared before that authority on the date indicated and that they made the declarations indicated.' The same explanation is included in Recital (59) Twin Regulations.

39 For instance, domestic certificate of succession produced by a notary public in Poland. See case C-658/17 *WB* (23 May 2019) ECLI:EU:C:2019:444.

40 See P Beaumont, J Fitchen and J Holliday, *The Evidentiary Effects of Authentic Acts in the Member States of the European Union, in the Context of Successions. Study for the JURI Committee* (European Parliament 2016).

41 See Recital (62) Succession Regulation.

is also decided upon under the law of the MS of origin. The authentic instrument challenged does not produce any evidentiary effect in another MS as long as the challenge is pending before the competent court (Article 59(2) Succession, Article 58(2) Twin Regulations). A challenge relating to the legal acts or legal relationships recorded in an authentic instrument[42] is made before the courts having jurisdiction under a given regulation and is decided upon under the applicable law (for example, in succession cases under *lex successionis*). The authentic instrument challenged does not produce any evidentiary effect in a MS other than the MS of origin as regards the matter being challenged as long as the challenge is pending before the competent court.

#53 If the outcome of proceedings in a court of a Member State (for instance, a claim to recover payments from a debtor's heir)[43] depends on the determination of an **incidental question** relating to the legal acts or legal relationships recorded in an authentic instrument in matters of succession (for instance, the determination of who is the heir), that court shall have jurisdiction over that question.

#54 The rules on the enforcement of authentic instruments and court settlements are the same. An authentic instrument / court settlement which is enforceable in the MS of origin is declared enforceable in another MS on the application of any interested party in accordance with the procedure provided for in Articles 45 – 58 Succession Regulation (Articles 44 – 57 Twin Regulations). Hence, the procedure is the same as for the enforcement of court decisions. The appropriate form is produced by the authority which has established the authentic instrument. The court with which an appeal is lodged under Article 50 or Article 51 Succession Regulation (Article 49 or Article 50 Twin Regulations) refuses or revokes a declaration of enforceability only if the enforcement of the authentic instrument / court settlement is manifestly contrary to the **public policy** (ordre public) within the Member State of enforcement.

E European Certificate of Succession

#55 Chapter VI of the Succession Regulation creates and regulates the new instrument, which is the **European Certificate of Succession** ('ECS'). An ECS is issued

42 Recital (63) Succession Regulation explains that 'the legal acts or legal relationships recorded in an authentic instrument' should be interpreted as 'referring to the contents as to substance recorded in the authentic instrument.' The Recital also gives examples. The legal acts recorded in an authentic instrument can be a will or the agreement between the parties on the sharing-out or the distribution of the estate. The legal relationship recorded in the authentic instrument can be, for instance, the determination of the heirs under the law applicable to the succession.

43 An example taken from H-P Mansel, 'Acceptance of Authentic Instruments' in A-L Calvo Caravaca, A Davi and H-P Mansel (eds), *The EU Succession Regulation. A Commentary* (CUP 2016) 625.

in the MS having jurisdiction over the succession matters (Article 64 first sentence) to be employed in another MS (Article 62(1)). The ECS, as Article 63(1) Succession Regulation explains that it is for the use of heirs or legatees having direct rights in the succession or executors of wills or administrators of the estate and who need to invoke their status or to exercise their rights or their powers in another MS. An ECS may, in accordance with Article 63(2) Succession Regulation, be used to demonstrate, for example, the status and the rights of each heir or the attribution of a specific asset to the heir or the powers of the person mentioned in the ECS to execute the will. The use of an ECS is not mandatory (Article 62(2)), as it does not take the place of internal documents used for similar purposes in the MS.[44]

#56 An ECS is to be issued upon a detailed application by any person listed in Article 63(1), namely an heir, a legatee having direct rights in the succession, an executor or an administrator. Article 65(3) lists the detailed information and documents to be provided in the application. The applicant may use also a form provided for in the Implementing Regulation (Article 65(2)).[45] The ECS is issued by 'a court' (within the meaning of Article 3(2) Succession Regulation) or another authority which, under national law, has the competence to deal with matters of succession (Article 64).[46]

#57 Article 66 describes the procedure of the examination of the application for the ECS.[47] For instance, it explains the procedure of gathering evidence. The ECS is issued without delay when the elements to be certified have been established under the applicable law (Article 67(1)). The issuing authority will not issue an ECS in particular if the elements to be certified are being challenged or it would not be in conformity with a decision covering the same elements. In *Albausy*, the CJEU noted that any challenge raised within the procedure of issuing an ECS or another proceeding precludes the possibility of producing an ECS. It may be produced once the challenge is decided within a separate proceeding provided within national law or a challenge brought pursuant to Article 72 Succession Regulation.[48]

---

44 See CA Marcoz, 'The European Certificate of Succession: Creation, Purpose, Contents, and Effects' in S Bariatti, I Viarengo and FC Villata (eds), *EU Cross-Border Succession Law* (Edward Elgar 2022) 308.
45 The CJEU confirmed that the use of a standard form is optional in C-102/18 *Brisch* (17 January 2019) ECLI:EU:C:2019:34.
46 These courts and authorities are notified by Member States to the Commission. Information on these authorities is published by the European Commission on e-Justice Portal.
47 CA Marcoz, 'The European Certificate of Succession: Issuance Procedure' in S Bariatti, I Viarengo and FC Villata (eds), *EU Cross-Border Succession Law* (Edward Elgar 2022) 327.
48 Case C-187/23 *Albausy* (23 January 2025) ECLI:EU:C:2025:34, paras 44–60.

#58 Article 68 lists the detailed information to be contained in the ECS. The ECS is issued on Form V provided for in the Implementing Regulation.[49] Once issued, the ECS produces effects provided for in Article 69 of the Succession Regulation (Article 62(3)). These effects are produced 'without any special procedure being required' (Article 69(1)) and include a presumption that an ECS accurately demonstrate elements which have been established under the applicable law (Article 69(2)). A person indicated in the ECS as, for instance, an heir is presumed to have that status and to hold the rights stated in the ECS Article 69(2). Consequently, any person who, acting on the basis of the ECS, makes payments or passes on property to a person mentioned in the ECS as authorised is, in general, considered to have transacted with a person with authority to accept payment or property (Article 69(3)). Similarly, where a person mentioned in the ECS as authorised to dispose of succession property disposes of such property in favour of another person, that other person is considered to have transacted with a person of adequate authority (Article 69(4)). Additionally, the ECS in general constitutes a valid document for the recording of succession property in the relevant register of a MS (Article 69(5)).[50]

#59 Decisions taken by the issuing authority pursuant to Article 67 (namely, a decision to issue an ECS or a decision not to issue it) may be challenged by any person entitled to apply for the ECS. Decisions taken pursuant to Article 71 and Article 73 (1)(a) – namely, a decision concerning rectification, modification, withdrawal of the ECS and suspension of its effects – may be challenged by any person demonstrating a legitimate interest. The challenge is to be lodged before a judicial authority in the MS having jurisdiction in the succession case (Article 72(1)). The judicial authority, depending on the circumstances of the case, may rectify, modify or withdraw the ECS (or ensure that it is rectified, modified or withdrawn). If the issuance was refused, the competent judicial authority may issue the ECS (or ensure that the issuing authority re-assesses the case). Article 71 regulates rectification, modification or withdrawal of the ECS, whereas Article 73 regulates the suspension of the effects of the ECS (for instance, pending a challenge).[51]

---

49 Article 70 Succession Regulation explains the relation between the original ECS and its certified copies, which are subject to circulation. Such copies are valid for a fixed period of six months (Article 70(3)).

50 Compare C-354/21 *RJR* (9 March 2023) ECLI:EU:C:2023:184, where the Court of Justice of the EU found that an application for the registration of immovable property in the land register of a given Member State (in this case in Lithuania) may be rejected where the only document submitted in support of that application is an ECS, which does not mention this particular immovable property.

51 CA Marcoz, 'The European Certificate of Succession: Redress Procedure and Suspension of the Effects of the Certificate' in S Bariatti, I Viarengo and FC Villata (eds), *EU Cross-Border Succession Law* (Edward Elgar 2022) 345.

F Other Aspects of International Civil Procedure

#60 Article 56 of the Succession Regulation is devoted to **legal aid**. It concerns an applicant who has benefited from complete or partial legal aid or exemption from the costs or expenses in the MS of origin. If so, such an applicant, in any proceedings for a declaration of enforceability, is entitled to benefit from the most favourable legal aid or the most extensive exemption from the costs or expenses provided for by the law of the MS of enforcement. Identical provisions are included in Twin Property Regulations (Article 55).

#61 Article 74 Succession Regulation provides for exemption from **legalisation** and other similar formalities for documents issued in a MS in the context of the regulation. Identical provision is included in the Twin Regulations (Article 61).

#62 Article 57 Succession Regulation concerns **security**, **bond** or **deposit** 'however described'. It provides that a party who in one MS applies for recognition, enforceability or enforcement of a decision given in another MS may not be required to pay a security on the ground that he/she is a foreign national or that he/she is not domiciled or resident in the MS of enforcement. Identical provisions are included in the Twin Regulations (Article 56).

#63 Article 58 Succession Regulation concerns **charges**, **duties** or **fees**, which are calculated by reference to the value of the matter at issue. It provides that, in proceedings for the issue of a declaration of enforceability, no such payments may be levied in the MS of enforcement. Identical provisions are included in the Twin Regulations (Article 57).

References

Azcárraga Monzonís C, 'Succession' in I Viarengo and F Villata (eds), *Planning the Future of Cross Border Families. A Path Through Coordination* (Hart 2020) 93.

Beaumont P, Fitchen J and Holliday J, *The Evidentiary Effects of Authentic Acts in the Member States of the European Union, in the Context of Successions. Study for the JURI Committee* (European Parliament 2016).

Biagioni G, 'Article 69 Transitional Provisions' in Ilaria Viarengo and Pietro Franzina (eds), *The EU Regulations on the Property Regimes of International Couples. A Commentary* (Edward Elgar 2020) 483.

Cazorla Gonzalez MJ and Soto Moya M, 'Main Concepts and Scope of Application of the Twin Regulations' in L Ruggeri, A Limanté and N Pogorelčnik Vogrinc, *The EU Regulations on Matrimonial Property Regimes and Property of Registered Partnerships* (Intersentia 2022) 41.

Fitchen J, *The Private International Law of Authentic Instruments* (Hart 2020).

Franzina P, 'Article 83 Transitional Provisions' in A-L Calvo Caravaca, A Davi and H-P Mansel (eds) *The EU Succession Regulation. A Commentary* (CUP 2016) 852

—— 'Article 6 Jurisdiction in Other Cases' in I Viarengo and P Franzina (eds), *The EU Regulations on the Property Regimes of International Couples. A Commentary* (Edward Elgar 2020) 78.

—— 'Article 7 Choice of Court' in I Viarengo and P Franzina (eds), *The EU Regulations on the Property Regimes of International Couples. A Commentary* (Edward Elgar 2020) 85.

Jänterä-Jareborg M, 'Inter-Nordic Exceptions in EU Regulations on Matters of Family and Inheritance Law. Legal "Irritants" or Necessary Concessions in the Citizens' Interest?' in A-L Verbeke and others (eds), *Confronting the Frontiers of Family and Succession Law: Liber Amicorum Walter Pintens* (Intersentia 2012) 733.

Kavoliünaité-Ragauskiené E, 'The Twin Regulations: Development and Adoption' in Lucia Ruggeri, Agné Limanté and Neža Pogorelčnik Vogrinc (eds), *The EU Regulations on Matrimonial Property Regimes and Property of Registered Partnerships* (Intersentia 2022) 25.

Kränzle M, 'The Notion of Habitual Residence in Recitals 23 and 24' in S Bariatti, I Viarengo and Francesca C. Villata (eds), *EU Cross-Border Succession Law* (Edward Elgar 2022) 115.

Kunda I and Limanté A, 'Jurisdictional Provisions in the Twin Regulations' in L Ruggeri, A Limanté and N Pogorelčnik Vogrinc (eds), *The EU Regulations on Matrimonial Property Regimes and Property of Registered Partnerships* (Intersentia 2022) 71.#

Kunda I and Ticić M, 'Authentic Instruments and Courts Settlements under the Twin Regulations' in L Ruggeri, A Limanté and N Pogorelčnik Vogrinc (eds), *The EU Regulations on Matrimonial Property Regimes and Property of Registered Partnerships* (Intersentia 2022) 157.

Mansel H-P, 'Acceptance of Authentic Instruments' in A-L Calvo Caravaca, A Davi and H-P Mansel (eds), *The EU Succession Regulation. A Commentary* (CUP 2016) 625.

Marcoz CA, 'The European Certificate of Succession: Creation, Purpose, Contents, and Effects' in S Bariatti, I Viarengo and FC Villata (eds), *EU Cross-Border Succession Law* (Edward Elgar 2022) 308.

—— 'The European Certificate of Succession: Issuance Procedure' in S Bariatti, I Viarengo and FC Villata (eds), *EU Cross-Border Succession Law* (Edward Elgar 2022) 327.

—— 'The European Certificate of Succession: Redress Procedure and Suspension of the Effects of the Certificate' in S Bariatti, I Viarengo and FC Villata (eds), *EU Cross-Border Succession Law* (Edward Elgar 2022) 345.

Muritano D, 'Acceptance and Waiver of the Succession' in Stefania Bariatti, Ilaria Viarengoa and Francesca C. Villata (eds), *EU Cross-Border Succession Law* (Edward Elgar 2022) 190.

Pallau Moreno G, 'Property Consequences of Registered Partnerships' in Ilaria Viarengo and Francesca Villata (eds) *Planning the Future of Cross Border Families. A Path Through Coordination* (Hart 2020) 109.

Pesce F and Dominelli S, 'Recognition and Enforcement of Foreign Decisions in Cross-Border Succession Matters' in S Bariatti, I Viarengo and FC Villata (eds), *EU Cross-Border Succession* Law (Edward Elgar 2022) 246.

Queirolo I, 'Jurisdiction in Succession Matters: General Rules and Choice of Court' in Stefania Bariatti, Ilaria Viarengo and Francesca C. Villata (eds), *EU Cross-Border Succession Law* (Edward Elgar 2022) 221.

Quinzá Redondo P, 'Matrimonial Property Regimes' in I Viarengo and F Villata (eds), *Planning the Future of Cross Border Families. A Path Through Coordination* (Hart 2020) 103.

Rodríguez Benot A, 'Article 1 Scope' in Ilaria Viarengo and Pietro Franzina (eds), *The EU Regulations on the Property Regimes of International Couples. A Commentary* (Edward Elgar 2020) 17.

Vallar G, 'Authentic Instruments and *C*ourt *S*ettlements' in Stefania Bariatti, Ilaria Viarengo and Francesca C. Villata (eds), *EU Cross-Border Succession Law* (*Edward* Elgar 2022) 285

Wysocka-Bar A, 'Enhanced Cooperation in Property Matters in the EU and Non-Participating Member States' (2019) 20 ERA Forum 187.

Elena D'Alessandro*

Chapter 16
Debt Collection and Special Procedures: Small Claims and Orders for Payment

A Setting the Scene

#1 In the context of EU debt collection, the **European Small Claims Regulation**[1] and the **European Order for Payment Regulation**[2] play a central role. These second-generation of EU legislative instruments are designed to establish harmonised procedures across Member States, thereby facilitating the recovery of cross-border debts in civil and commercial disputes. By providing user-friendly forms and circumventing the intricacies of 26 distinct national procedural frameworks (with the exception of Denmark), these Regulations enhance efficiency in debt recovery. Creditors benefit from standardised forms, which obviates the need for legal representation, rendering the process more accessible, and the complexities associated with navigating different local legal systems. Furthermore, cross-border recognition and enforcement are facilitated, as the grounds for refusal under these regulations are fewer in number compared to those stipulated in the so called Brussels I Recast Regulation.[3]

#2 This **chapter** is devoted to the analysis of these Regulations and is divided into two parts: the first part addresses the European Small Claims Regulation (B), while the second part examines the European Order for Payment Regulation (C).

---

1 Regulation (EC) No 861/2007 of the European Parliament and of the Council of 11 July 2007 establishing a European small claims procedure [2007] OJ L199/1.

2 Regulation (EC) No 1896/2006 of the European Parliament and of the Council of 12 December 2006 creating a European order for payment procedure [2006] OJ L399/1.

3 Regulation (EU) No 1215/2012 of the European Parliament and of the Council of 12 December 2012 on jurisdiction and the recognition and enforcement of judgments in civil and commercial matters (recast) [2012] OJ L351/1.

***Corresponding author: Elena D'Alessandro**, University of Turin, e-mail: elena.dalessandro@unito.it

https://doi.org/10.1515/9783110781632-016

B European Small Claims Regulation

I Establishing the Context: Objectives of the European Small Claims Regulation

#3 The European Small Claims Regulation introduced a harmonised adversarial procedure for handling cross-border small claims. It has been applicable since 1 January 2009 across all Member States, with the exception of Denmark. The primary objective of the European small claims procedure is to address procedural inconsistencies and streamline litigation processes for small claims in cross-border disputes, ultimately **lowering** associated **costs.**[4] The decision, or the court settlement, concluding a European small claims procedure serves as a European enforcement title, thereby **facilitating cross-border small debt recovery** within the European judicial area.

#4 The European Small Claims Regulation was amended with improvements in 2015 through Regulation (EU) 2015/2421,[5] which has been applicable since July 14, 2017. Despite these improvements, the European Small Claims Regulation remains the least utilised of second-generation EU Regulations.[6]

#5 The Regulation doesn't comprehensively govern all aspects of small claims proceedings. When the provisions of the Regulation do not apply, the diverse national procedural laws of Member States come into play.

II Scope of Application

1 Value of the Claim

#6 The procedure outlined in the European Small Claims Regulation applies when the value of the claim does not exceed **€5,000** (originally, before the entry into

4 See X Kramer, 'Major Step in the Harmonization of Procedural Law in Europe: The European Small Claims Procedure Accomplishments, New Features and Some Fundamental Questions of European Harmonization' in T Jongbloed (ed), *The XIIIth World Congress of Procedural Law: The Belgian and Dutch Reports* (Intersentia 2008) 253, 283.

5 Regulation of the European Parliament and of the Council of 16 December 2015 amending Regulation (EC) No 861/2007 establishing a European small claims procedure and Regulation (EC) No 1896/2006 creating a European order for payment procedure [2015] OJ L341/1.

6 It is surpassed only by the European Account Preservation Order, as indicated in J von Hein and T Imm, 'Conclusions and Recommendations' in J von Hein and T Kruger (eds), *Informed Choices in Cross-Border Enforcement* (Intersentia 2021) 529, 557, Figure 2; M Buzzoni and C Santalò Goris, *Report on Practices in Comparative and Cross-Border Perspective. EFFORTS (Towards more EFfective enFORcemenT of claimS in civil and commercial matters within the EU)* (Project JUST-JCOO-AG-2019-881802) 55 <https://efforts.unimi.it/research-outputs/reports/> accessed 15 January 2025.

force of Regulation (EU) 2015/2421, the limit was €2,000) at the time the claim form is submitted to the competent court or tribunal. This valuation excludes interest, expenses, or disbursements. The Regulation encompasses disputes involving claims for the payment of a monetary sum or, for example, the delivery of a specific movable item, as long as its value remains within the €5,000 threshold.

#7 An **open issue** is whether a claimant, whose monetary claim exceeds €5,000, may initiate proceedings under the European Small Claims Regulation by limiting their claim to the Regulation's monetary ceiling while reserving the right to pursue the remaining amount in a separate proceeding. Certain Member States, such as Italy, explicitly prohibit such **fragmentation of claims**.[7]

2 Civil and Commercial Matters

#8 To apply the European Small Claims Regulation, it is also necessary that the case be of a civil and commercial matter nature. The concept of **civil and commercial matters**, as outlined in Article 2(2) of the European Small Claims Regulation, does not fully align with that set out in Article 1 of the Brussels I Recast Regulation. Specifically, the European Small Claims Regulation adopts a narrower scope of application. It explicitly excludes certain types of disputes from its coverage, such as those listed in Article 2(2)(h) ('violation of privacy and of rights relating to personality, including defamation'),[8] as well as those under subparagraphs (i) and (j).

3 Cross-Border Disputes

#9 Lastly, to apply the European Small Claims Regulation, it is furthermore required that the case be of a **cross-border** nature. A cross-border European small claim case is defined as one where, at the time the claim form is received, at least one party (either the applicant or the defendant) is domiciled in a Member State other than the State in which the court or tribunal is located. Domicile shall be determined in accordance with Articles 62 and 63 of the Brussels I Recast Regulation. Therefore, for natural persons, reference shall be made to the 'lex fori'. Conversely, a dispute in which both the applicant and the defendant are domiciled or habitually resident in the same Member State as the court or tribunal seized does not fall within the scope of the Regulation.[9]

---

7 The leading case in that respect is Cass civ 15 November 2007, no 23726, (2008) Rivista di diritto civile 335.

8 Eg, an infringement of the right to health protection would be regarded as a violation of personality rights and, as such, would fall outside the scope of application of the European Small Claims Regulation.

9 Case C-627/17 *ZSE Energia a.s.* v *R* (22 November 2018) ECLI:EU:C:2018:941.

III Filling the Application

#10 The claimant shall initiate the European small claims procedure by completing the standard claim **Form A,** which can be freely downloaded from the European e-Justice Portal.[10] Form A must be completed in the language of the court or tribunal in which the procedure is pending. Legal representation is not required.[11]

#11 In the claim form (Form A), the plaintiff must provide the following details:

a) Names and identification details of both parties;

b) Grounds of jurisdiction: The Brussels I Recast Regulation shall be applied to determine the international jurisdiction of the court seized, as confirmed in point 4 of Form A. Jurisdiction may be based on general[12] or special rules of jurisdiction or on a valid choice of court agreement.[13] Sometimes, the territorial jurisdiction of the competent court is also governed by these rules of the Brussels I Recast Regulation (eg, when Article 7 of the Brussels I Recast Regulation applies), which determine both the Member State having international jurisdiction and the specific court with territorial jurisdiction to hear the case. If this is not the case (eg, when Article 4 of the Brussels I Recast Regulation applies), the 'lex fori' will be applied to determine whether the seized court has venue;

c) Reasons why the dispute has a cross-border character pursuant to Article 3;

d) Whether it is a pecuniary claim or a claim for the restitution of property, specifying its presumed value;

e) Whether interest on the capital is sought and if a reimbursement of incurred legal expenses (lawyers' fees, translation costs, service costs) is requested;

f) Details of the claim (what happened, where, and when). In that respect, Article 12 of the European Small Claims Regulation specifies that the court or tribunal shall not require the parties to make any legal assessment of the claim;

g) The evidence presented in communication or the evidence to be obtained. However, new documents and requests for instructions are permitted at any stage of the proceedings.[14]

#12 Descriptions of supporting documents must be provided in the language of the proceedings. If they are not, the court may later request a translation, but only if it is deemed necessary for the judgment. If a party refuses a document on the grounds that it is not in the official language of the Member State or in a language which the addressee understands, the court or tribunal will inform the other party and invite it to provide a translation.

---

10 <https://e-justice.europa.eu/177/EN/small_claims_forms?init=true> accessed 19 February 2025.

11 Article 10.

12 Article 4 of the Brussels I Recast Regulation.

13 Article 25 of the Brussels I Recast Regulation.

14 Recital 12.

#13 When completing Form A, the claimant must also express his willingness, if any, to have a **hearing** scheduled, as the European small claims procedure is essentially written.

#14 With the implementation of the e-CODEX system under the e-Justice Regulation, which came into effect in May 2025,[15] Form A must now be submitted to the competent court exclusively through electronic means, utilising the e-CODEX system as the standard method for the transmission of documents. Prior to the implementation of e-CODEX, Form A was required to be submitted by traditional methods, such as post, or by alternative means of communication, including fax or email[16], as permitted by the Member State in which the procedure was initiated. The introduction of e-CODEX has thereby streamlined document transmission and significantly improved accessibility in cross-border small claims litigation.[17]

#15 **Before the adversarial process begins** and Form A is served on the defendant, the **court** or tribunal must **review** the claim to determine:

a) whether it falls within the scope of the European Small Claims Regulation. If the claim exceeds the scope of the Regulation, the court will inform the claimant in an appropriate manner, without using a specific form. The claimant will be notified that, unless the claim is withdrawn, the proceedings will continue under the 'lex fori'.[18] Since the European Small Claims Regulation does not specify a deadline for withdrawing the claim, national procedural law will govern this aspect. If no withdrawal is made, the proceedings must 'continue'. Consequently, the request in Form A should resemble a claim form filed in accordance with national procedural rules. However, if the claimant has filed the claim personally and legal representation is required under national procedural law, the court will set a deadline for rectifying this procedural defect;

b) whether it appears to be 'manifestly unfounded' or 'inadmissible'. If this is the case, Article 4(4) requires the court or tribunal to dismiss the claim without prior contradictory proceedings. The European Small Claims Regulation does not provide specific definitions for these terms ('manifestly unfounded' and 'inadmissible'), leaving them to the national procedural law of the Member State in which the proceedings are pending. An example of a manifestly

---

15 European Parliament and Council Regulation 2023/2844 of the European Parliament and of the Council of 13 December 2023 on the digitalisation of judicial cooperation and access to justice in cross-border civil, commercial and criminal matters, and amending certain acts in the field of judicial cooperation [2024] OJ L2023/2844.

16 Buzzoni and Santalò Goris (n 6) 56. For instance, Tribunal of Florence, 18 September 2023, admitted the filing of the defendant's defensive memory via certified email, on the grounds that in Italy it is equated to postal mail with return receipt.

17 See also A Nylund, Chapter 7.

18 Article 4(3).

unfounded claim could be a situation where the claimant demands payment and, at the same time, produces a receipt issued by the defendant;

c) whether Form A is correctly completed in all its sections and in the language of the Member State where the proceedings are taking place. If not, the court must request the claimant to complete or rectify Form A using Form B, specifying a deadline for these actions. While the deadline is mandatory, extensions may be granted, particularly in exceptional cases, to safeguard the claimant's right to action.[19]

IV Conduct of the Proceedings

#16 The European small claims proceedings are designed to be swift and straightforward. Upon receiving a properly completed Form A, the court or tribunal will fill out Part I of the standard answer **Form C**. A copy of the claim form, along with any supporting documents and the completed answer form, will be served on the defendant in accordance with Article 13 (which includes service through electronic means). These documents must be sent within 14 days of receiving the properly completed claim form.

#17 A **written response** must be submitted by the defendant within 30 days of receiving the claim and answer forms.[20] If the respondent chooses to actively defend the case, they may contest international jurisdiction, the applicability of the European Small Claims Regulation procedure, or the merits of the claim. The response may be submitted using the standard Form C or by filing a counterclaim. Within 14 days of receiving the respondent's response, the court or tribunal will provide the claimant with a copy of the response and any supporting documents.[21]

#18 In the event of a counterclaim, Form A must be used, which can be independently downloaded by the defendant from the European e-Justice Portal. Any counterclaim, along with relevant supporting documents, must be served on the claimant in accordance with Article 13. These documents should be dispatched within 14 days of receipt.

#19 However, if the counterclaim exceeds the threshold of EUR 5,000 set out in Article 2(1), both the claim and the counterclaim will not be dealt with under the Euro-

---

19 Article 14(2).

20 In France, Cour cass (1ère civ) 10 April 2019, no 17–13.307 emphasised that, in applying the European small claims procedure, French courts shall respect the parties' fundamental right to be heard. The Court overturned a lower court decision awarding compensation without allowing the defendant to respond.

21 In France, Cour cass (1ère civ) 27 November 2019, no 18–14.985 reversed a first instance European small claims decision declaring a claim inadmissible without giving the claimant an opportunity to provide observations.

pean small claims procedure. Instead, they will be dealt with in accordance with the relevant procedural law applicable in the Member State where the proceedings take place. In such a case, even if the original claim form was not submitted in accordance with the forms prescribed by the 'lex fori', its substantive and procedural effects remain valid. If the claimant submitted Form A in person and the local procedural law requires legal representation, the court or tribunal must set a time-limit for this procedural irregularity to be remedied.

V Oral Hearing

#20 The European small claims proceedings are **generally** conducted as a **written process** for cost-effectiveness reasons. An oral hearing may only be held if the court or tribunal considers it impossible to reach a judgment based solely on written evidence or if a party explicitly requests one. Such requests may arise from a party's preference for direct communication with the judge to present a personal perspective on the case, fostering greater comfort and confidence in the court's ability to facilitate a settlement between the parties.

#21 While the European Small Claims Regulation allows the court to refuse a request for an oral hearing if it considers it unnecessary to ensure a fair hearing,[22] it would be advisable for the court to grant such requests in the light of Article 6 of the European Convention on Human Rights. This is particularly important given that modern technological means, such as **videoconferencing**, can allow for a speedy and cost-effective hearing. This technological approach, which is quick, inexpensive and readily available to the court, should be considered the preferred method of conducting hearings. For example, a party who is summoned to attend an oral hearing in person and who claims that such attendance would entail disproportionate costs may request the use of remote communication technology. It should be noted, however, that an 'e-mail conference' may not in all cases satisfy the requirements of an oral hearing as provided for in the European Small Claims Regulation.[23]

#22 If, however, due to the particular circumstances of the case, the use of such technology is deemed inappropriate to ensure the fairness of the proceedings, a party required to participate in an oral hearing by means of remote communication technology retains the right to request an in-person hearing. In doing so, the party must provide substantiated reasons as to why the use of technology might undermine the fairness of the hearing.

22 Reasons for refusal will be provided in writing, and this refusal cannot be contested separately from a challenge to the judgment itself.

23 T Domej, 'Article 8 EuGFVO' in Stein-Jonas, *Kommentar zur Zivilprozessordnung* (23rd edn, Mohr Siebeck 2021) para 1.

VI Final Judgment

#23 The proceedings may end with a court settlement approved or concluded before the small claims court or tribunal.[24] Alternatively, where the defendant has presented a defence, the court may either uphold or dismiss the claimant's request. The court or tribunal is not obliged to use an EU-specific form, which means that the form of the judgment concluding the proceedings is left to national law.

#24 The judgment concluding the European small claims proceedings will also include a provision on costs. In accordance with Article 16 of the European Small Claims Regulation, the unsuccessful party is responsible for bearing the **costs** of the proceedings. However, the court or tribunal may refrain from awarding costs to the successful party if such costs were unnecessarily incurred or are deemed disproportionate to the nature of the small claim. This provision ensures that the costs remain reasonable and proportionate, in line with the simplified and accessible nature of the European small claims procedure. Court fees charged in a Member State for the European small claims procedure must not be disproportionate and should not exceed the court fees charged for national simplified court procedures in that Member State.

#25 A judgment in favour of the claimant is enforceable without the need for security, even if an appeal has been lodged.[25]

#26 The European Small Claims Regulation does not clarify when a European small claims **judgment** becomes **final**, leaving the matter to be determined by the procedural law of the legal system in which the proceedings took place.

#27 If the defendant receives Form A but fails to submit a defence or fails to do so in time, ie, within the time-limits set out in Article 5(3) or Article 6, the court or tribunal will render a **default judgment** on the claim in accordance with Article 7 (3). In this scenario, a 'default judgment' means that, following the defendant's failure to respond, the factual allegations supporting the claimant's case are deemed uncontested and no further evidence is required. Consequently, the court or tribunal will uphold the claim on its merits, provided that the facts submitted are sufficiently conclusive.

#28 Unless national procedural law requires additional mandatory checks (eg, public policy checks), the court or tribunal must also, as clarified by the CJEU in consumer-professional relations, examine 'ex officio' the existence of unfair terms under Directive 93/13/EEC before issuing a default judgment.[26]

---

24 Article 23a.

25 Article 15(1).

26 Case C-495/19 *Kancelaria Medius SA* v *RN* (4 June 2020) ECLI:EU:C:2020:431.

VII Appeals and Review in Exceptional Cases

#29 Appeals are subject to the procedural law of the Member State where the proceedings originated, which is a disadvantage of the European small claims procedure. This could potentially lead to inconsistencies between Member States, particularly regarding the length of the procedure and the costs involved. In Italy, for example, it is argued that Article 16 of the Regulation does not apply at the appeal stage, where only the 'lex fori' is considered relevant.[27]

#30 Even if a Member State chooses not to grant a right of appeal, a defendant who has not appeared in the European small claims proceedings should still be entitled to apply for a **review** under Article 18 **in exceptional circumstances**, to the court or tribunal of the Member State that delivered the judgment.

#31 Article 18 of the European Small Claims Regulation allows defendants in default to apply for a review of a default judgment, where:

a) they were not served with the claim form or duly summoned to a hearing in sufficient time and with sufficient information to enable them to prepare a defence; or
b) force majeure or extraordinary circumstances (eg, being in intensive care in hospital) prevented them from contesting the claim, provided that such circumstances were beyond their control and they did not fail to contest the judgment.

#32 An application for review must be made within 30 days of the date on which the defendant was served with the judgment and had an opportunity to respond. No extension is possible. For example:

(a) If the default judgment was given on 1 December 2024, but the defendant was not served with Form A and only became aware of it on 15 May 2025, the 30-day period would run from the latter date.
(b) If the defendant was served with Form A but, due to being in intensive care in hospital, did not have the opportunity to contest the claim, and therefore a default judgment was issued, the 30-day period will begin from the date when, having recovered their health, they are able to respond.

27 Consider, for example, the following Italian cases in which the amount of costs awarded on appeal pursuant to the *lex fori* exceeds the value of the claim: 1) In a case decided by the Court of Turin (decision of 5 October 2002) concerning a delayed flight with a claim value of €250 plus interest, the losing plaintiff was ordered to pay €792 in attorney's fees plus VAT on appeal. In addition, the plaintiff had to pay a court fee of twice the amount of the claim, ie, approximately €128; 2) In another case decided by the Tribunal of Ragusa (decision of 29 September 2002), concerning a cancelled flight, the court partially upheld the appeal. As a result, the passenger was ordered to reimburse the airline €502 (the value of the claim) and to pay the legal costs of both cases, totalling €2,174 plus VAT.

The 30-day time-limit for applying for a review runs at the latest from the date of the first enforcement measure that renders the defendant's assets unavailable[28] (eg, attachment or, in the case of Italy, 'pignoramento'), as it is assumed that the defendant was aware from that moment on that a European default judgment on a small claim had been delivered against him.

VIII Recognition, Enforceability and Enforcement

#33 A **judgment** delivered in a Member State under the European small claims procedure or a **court settlement approved** by or concluded before a court or tribunal in the course of such a procedure, shall be **automatically recognised and enforced** in any other Member State. The authentic copy of the judgment or of the court settlement must be accompanied by standard **form D**, which is available in all official EU languages on the European Judicial Portal,[29] with an optional translation in the language of the Member State of enforcement.

#34 To facilitate cross-border debt recovery, the party seeking enforcement benefits from exemptions such as the need for an authorised representative, a postal address, or a security, bond, or deposit in the Member State of enforcement, regardless of whether the party is a foreign national or not domiciled there.

#35 The use of the European small claims procedure has the advantage that the **grounds for non-enforcement** are more **limited** than those listed in Article 45 of the Brussels I Recast Regulation, being limited to irreconcilability and excluding substantive and procedural public policy. This even applies to cases involving a consumer debtor as provided for in Article 22, thus allowing efficient cross-border enforcement.

#36 The concept of 'irreconcilability' in the European Small Claims Procedure seems to be more in line with a 'European' approach than the analogous grounds for refusal in the Brussels I Recast Regulation. To put it clearly: In cases of irreconcilability under the European Small Claims Regulation, a strict chronological hierarchy is applied to determine which European (or national) small claims judgment takes precedence. In particular, the first judgment (or court settlement) given, whether by a national or a foreign court (ie, a court located in another Member State or in a third State), takes precedence. This approach promotes a more predictable and uniform framework for cross-border debt recovery, especially when the decision is in favour of the creditor. By prioritising chronological order over national origin, the European small claims procedure aims at creating a more creditor-friendly environment for cross-border enforcement. In contrast, Article

28 Article 18(2).
29 See n 10.

45 (c) of the Brussels I Recast Regulation[30] always gives priority to national judgments, regardless of the order in which they were delivered. This means that, even if a foreign condemnatory judgment was issued first, a later domestic judgment stating that the debt does not exist would take precedence.

C European Order for Payment Regulation

I Establishing the Context: Objectives of the European Order for Payment Proceedings

#37 The European Order for Payment Regulation, which became applicable in all Member States except Denmark on 12 December 2008, establishes a uniform, **optional order for payment procedure** for cross-border disputes. It is an **'ex parte' procedure**. Only the creditor participates, at least until the order for payment is issued, for the swift and effective recovery of uncontested claims, as late payment is a major cause of insolvency for small businesses and the procedural laws of the Member States did not provide uniform solutions in this respect.[31] For example, while Spain did not have a national injunction procedure when the order for payment regulation was conceived, France, Germany and Italy did.

#38 Creditors, regardless of their domicile in a Member State, have the choice between obtaining an order for payment through the single-stage and uniform European order for payment procedure, or, where available, through a procedure governed by national law.

#39 Article 1 and recitals 9 and 29 of the Regulation underline the objective of establishing a European order for payment procedure in order to simplify, speed up and reduce the costs of litigation in cross-border cases concerning uncontested pecuniary claims. In particular, the Regulation contains a set of harmonised – but not exhaustive – rules governing the application for, the examination of and the issuing of a European order for payment. Within this framework, Member States retain considerable discretion on a number of issues, such as the designation of the authorities competent to issue the order and to review it in exceptional circumstances. In particular, Article 26 provides that all procedural matters not specifically dealt with in the Regulation shall be governed by national law, including court fees.

30 See also F Gascon Inchausti, Chapter 12, and W Hau, Chapter 13.

31 Recital 6.

II Scope of Application

1 Civil and Commercial Matters

#40 The European Order for Payment Regulation applies to **civil and commercial matters**. Matters relating to revenue, customs or administrative matters and the liability of the State for acts and omissions in the exercise of State authority ('acta iure imperii') are excluded. Conversely, the European order for payment procedure cannot be used to enforce a claim arising out of a matter excluded under Article 2 of the Regulation.

#41 The matters excluded from the scope of the Regulation as set out in Article 2(2) are essentially the same as those listed in Article 1(2)(a)-(c) and (f) of the Brussels I Recast Regulation, bearing in mind that the legal status, legal capacity, capacity to act, as well as the legal representation of natural persons (Article 1(2)(a) of the Brussels I Recast Regulation) have been removed from the scope of application of the European Order for Payment Regulation because, in principle, they do not pertain to the recovery of pecuniary claims.[32]

2 Uncontested Claims

#42 To be eligible for European order for payment proceedings, a credit must be **uncontested**. This criterion clarifies why contractual claims fall within the scope of the Regulation, while non-contractual claims, which are more prone to disputes, are excluded.[33] The same exclusion applies to pre-contractual liability, which the CJEU[34] has classified as non-contractual for jurisdictional purposes under the Brussels Convention (now the Brussels I Recast Regulation) and as tort under the Rome II Regulation.

#43 German case-law[35] appears to include claims of unjust enrichment— where (unjust) payments are made to fulfil contractual obligations—within the scope of the European Order for Payment Regulation, arguing that these are not claims arising from non-contractual obligations.

---

32 B Ulrici, 'The European Order for Payment Procedure' in J von Hein and T Kruger (eds), *Informed Choices in Cross-Border Enforcement* (Intersentia 2021) 65.

33 Unless they have been the subject of an agreement between the parties or there has been an admission of debt, or they relate to liquidated debts arising from joint ownership of property.

34 Case C-334/00 *Fonderie Officine Meccaniche Tacconi SpA* v. *Heinrich Wagner Sinto Maschinenfabrik GmbH (HWS)* (17 September 2002) ECLI:EU:C:2002:499.

35 Amtsgericht Berlin-Wedding 10 February 2017, 70b C 6/17 (2017) BeckRS 108421; Amtsgericht Berlin-Wedding 13 April 2017, 70b C 5/17 (2017) BeckRS 108418.

3 Cross-Border Disputes

#44 To be eligible for European order for payment proceedings, the claim shall involve a credit arising from a **cross-border dispute**,[36] meaning that either the creditor or the debtor should be domiciled or habitually resident in a Member State other than the Member State where the court is seized. Domicile shall be determined in accordance with the corresponding notions of the Brussels I Recast Regulation.[37] The relevant moment for determining whether there is a cross-border case shall be the time when the application for a European order for payment is submitted.

III Filing the Application for a European Order for Payment

#45 The application for a European order for payment must be submitted to the **competent court** or authority.[38] Territorial jurisdiction is determined by national procedural law. While some Member States have adopted a decentralised system, aligning the jurisdiction for European orders for payment with that for national payment orders across their territory, others—such as Germany, Austria, and the Netherlands—have implemented a centralised system. In these countries, the relevant courts are the *Amtsgericht* Wedding in Berlin, the *Bezirksgericht für Handelssachen* in Vienna, and the District Court of The Hague.

#46 Croatia presents a unique case. Initially, it granted exclusive territorial jurisdiction for European order for payment proceedings to the Commercial Court in Zagreb. However, this approach was discontinued in 2019, when Croatia shifted to a decentralised system.

#47 To ensure the objectives of speed and uniformity in the procedure, the claimant shall use the standard **Form A**[39] and fill in the form in the language of the State where the court is located, without the need for legal representation.[40] The use of the standard Form A[41] is mandatory.[42] Recital 11 emphasises that the procedure should be based, as far as possible, on the use of standard forms for all communications between the court and the parties. This approach aims at streamlining the

36 Article 3.

37 Articles 62 and 63.

38 See Recital 16 and Article 5(3), which defines 'court' as any body of a Member State that has jurisdiction over European payment orders or other proceedings. In Hungary, European payment orders are issued by notaries.

39 Joined Cases C-453/18 and C-494/18 *Bondora AS* v *Carlos V. C. and XY* (19 December 2019) ECLI:EU:C:2019:1118, para 37 ('*Bondora*').

40 Article 24.

41 <https://e-justice.europa.eu/156/EN/european_payment_order_forms> accessed 17 February 2025.

42 Article 7(1).

administration of the procedure and encourages the use of automatic data processing. In addition, the use of standardised forms helps to reduce translation costs.

#48 The European Order for Payment Regulation specifies[43] the required information that must be included in the application, notably:

a) the names and addresses of the parties, and, where applicable, their representatives, and of the court to which the application is made;
b) the amount of the claim, including the principal and, where applicable, interest, contractual penalties and costs;
c) if interest on the claim is claimed, the interest rate and the period of time for which that interest is demanded unless statutory interest is automatically added to the principal under the law of the Member State of origin. As clarified by the CJEU, the claimant is not precluded from claiming interest for the period between the due date and the date of payment of the principal;[44]
d) the cause of the action, including a description of the circumstances on which the claim is based and, where appropriate, the interest claimed;
e) a description of evidence supporting the claim. In other words, the creditor is required to identify (but not necessarily to allege it in court) the evidence available to support the claim. Identifying the evidence may help the debtor to decide whether to lodge an opposition under Article 17. Due to differences between Member States, the Regulation does not provide guidance on the admissible means of evidence that may be referenced in Form A. As the creditor is not confined to a specific type of evidence, they may freely rely on various forms of evidence, such as witness testimony, documentary evidence, or other forms of proof permitted by the law of the forum.
f) the grounds for jurisdiction.

   To establish the grounds for international jurisdiction of the court seized, the provisions of the Brussels I Recast Regulation applies. This necessitates an evolving interpretation of the reference to the now-replaced Brussels I Regulation, as outlined in Article 6(1) of the European Order for Payment Regulation. Specifically, the jurisdiction of the court seized may be established not only by reference to the general[45] and special rules of jurisdiction[46] under the Brussels I Recast Regulation but also by any choice-of-court agreement entered into by the parties.[47]

43 Article 7(2).
44 Case C-215/11 *Iwona Szyrocka* v *SiGer Technologie GmbH* (13 December 2012) ECLI:EU:C:2012:794.
45 Article 4.
46 Article 7.
47 Pursuant to Article 25.

Article 6(2) of the European Order for Payment Regulation concerning claims arising out of contracts concluded by consumers for purposes outside their trade or profession is a specific jurisdiction rule for the European order for payment: if the creditor is a professional, the courts of the Member State where the debtor is domiciled have exclusive jurisdiction to issue an order for payment against consumer debtors. In other words, creditors cannot obtain a European order for payment against a consumer in a State other than that in which the consumer is domiciled. This provision provides consumer debtors with greater protection than Article 17 of the Brussels I Recast Regulation, since it does not impose any of the limitations or requirements set out therein, such as the professional's activities being in place or being directed towards the consumer's Member State.[48]

Where international jurisdiction is established by reference to the rules of Article 7 of the Brussels I Recast Regulation, these rules determine both, the legal system with jurisdiction, and the specific court with territorial jurisdiction (venue).

Furthermore, in situations where several national courts of first instance are competent to issue a European order for payment (eg, the justice of the peace or the tribunal in Italy, depending on the value thresholds), it is incumbent on the creditor to provide a reasoned justification for the choice of the specific national court. This justification must be based on the value of the claim and on the venue (for example, explaining why the Court of Turin was chosen rather than the Justice of the Peace in Rome). All relevant details must be clearly set out in section 11 of Form A, entitled 'Additional statements and further information (if necessary)', which includes a space specifically for this purpose;

g) the cross-border nature of the case within the meaning of Article 3.

#49 Form A includes several appendices. Specifically, **Appendix 2** of Form A provides the claimant (creditor) with the option to notify the court of their opposition to a transfer to national civil proceedings, as defined in Article 17, in the event of opposition by the debtor. Alternatively, the claimant may request that, in case of opposition by the debtor, the proceedings continue in accordance with the rules of the European Small Claims Regulation.

#50 If the debtor opposes and no such indication is given, the proceedings will continue under the national procedural law of the State where the order for payment was requested. This results in the loss of any benefits associated with the uniform European proceedings, such as familiarity with procedural rules and the absence of mandatory legal representation. However, failure to complete Appendix 2 at

48 Article 17(c).

the time of filing the judicial application does not prevent the claimant from informing the court of this subsequently, but, at least, before the order is issued.

#51 The claimant must declare that the information provided in Form A is true to the best of their knowledge and belief and must acknowledge that any deliberate false statement may result in appropriate penalties under the 'lex fori' of the Member State of origin. The specific consequences and deterrent effect of such a declaration vary depending on the provisions of the national procedural law applicable in this regard.

#52 Form A must be signed by the claimant or their representative. The Form allows for either a signature or a stamp (which is distinct from a physical or digital signature), and this occasionally results in completed Forms that are only stamped. Where the application is submitted electronically, it must be signed using a digital signature. However, an electronic signature is not required if, and to the extent that, an alternative electronic communications system is in place within the courts of the Member State of origin. Such a system must be accessible to a specific group of pre-registered and authenticated users and must enable the secure identification of those users.

#53 Pending the implementation of the **e-CODEX** system under the e-Justice Regulation,[49] the only way to submit Form A in Belgium, France, Italy, and Luxembourg was in hard copy. This could be done by either personally delivering the form or sending it via post to the office of the competent court or tribunal.[50] **Electronic submission** of the European payment order request was allowed **only in a few Member States**, including Croatia, Lithuania, and Germany. The lack of electronic filing may reduce the attractiveness of the European order for payment proceedings, particularly in countries where domestic payment orders can be requested electronically, such as in Italy. In such cases, domestic orders can then be utilised for cross-border recovery under the European Enforcement Order Regulation or the Brussels I Recast Regulation.

#54 However, the introduction of the e-CODEX system is expected to address this issue by establishing electronic communication as the standard method for submitting Form A to the court.[51] In line with advancements in technology and digitalisation, Article 8 of the European Order for Payment Regulation requires the court handling an application for a European order for payment to promptly re-

49 European Parliament and Council Regulation 2023/2844 of the European Parliament and of the Council of 13 December 2023 on the digitalisation of judicial cooperation and access to justice in cross-border civil, commercial and criminal matters, and amending certain acts in the field of judicial cooperation [2024] OJ L2023/2844.

50 M Buzzoni and C Santalò Goris (n 6) 47.

51 A Nylund, Chapter 7.

view the request. This review may be conducted using an **automated procedure**, as is currently the case in Germany.[52]

IV Safeguarding Consumer Debtors Ex Officio: A Complex Landscape

#55 The European Order for Payment Regulation does not require the creditor to present evidence of his claim, such as a copy of the contract establishing the credit. As a result, in cases where the debtor is a consumer and the creditor is a professional, the court handling the order for payment proceedings may not automatically detect an unfair term under the **EU Unfair Contract Terms Directive**[53] in consumer contracts, as required by the CJEU.[54] The situation becomes even more complex when automated procedures or a notary are responsible for issuing the European order for payment.[55]

#56 In order to fill this gap and to ensure an 'ex officio' examination of potentially unfair clauses in accordance with the EU Unfair Contract Terms Directive, the CJEU emphasised that a 'court' as defined in Article 5(b) of the European Order for Payment Regulation – a definition that includes not only state judges but also notaries and automated procedures – has the power to require the creditor to provide documentary evidence concerning the terms of the contract on which the claim is based. Consequently, national laws cannot consider documents intended for this review as inadmissible.[56]

#57 The 'reasoning' part of the European order for payment must state that the court has examined the possible existence of unfair terms.[57] If this requirement is not met, the issuance of a European order for payment does not prevent subsequent national courts from scrutinising unfair contractual clauses, if one or more contractual terms, whose potential unfairness has not been assessed in accordance with the EU Unfair Contract Terms Directive (on the basis of the reasoning of the European order for payment), are present.

---

52 See Section 1088 of the German Code of Civil Procedure (*Zivilprozessordnung*, ZPO).

53 Council Directive 93/13/EEC of 5 April 1993 on unfair terms in consumer contracts [1993] OJ L95/29.

54 Case C-618/10 *Banco Español de Crédito, SA* v *Joaquín Calderón Camino* (14 June 2012) ECLI:EU:C:2012:349.

55 According to Case C-49/14 *Finanmadrid EFC SA* v *Jesús Vicente Albán Zambrano and Others* (18 February 2016) ECLI:EU:C:2016:98, a court ruling on an order for payment must assess the unfairness of a contractual term, despite the creditor's urgency to terminate enforcement and quickly recover his credit.

56 *Bondora* (n 39).

57 Case C-421/14 *Banco Primus SA* v *Jesús Gutiérrez García* (26 January 2017) ECLI:EU:C:2017:60.

V Outcomes of the Proceedings

1 Rejection of the Application

#58 The court issuing the European order for payment may reject the creditor's request if it falls outside the scope of the Regulation (eg, non-cross-border claims), in cases of lack of jurisdiction or venue, or if the claim is manifestly unfounded under Article 8. As creditors are not required to present evidence to support their claims, cases of manifestly unfounded claims are uncommon. Such instances typically arise only in situations involving clearly time-barred debts.

#59 If Form A meets the mandatory requirements for only part of the claim, the court informs the claimant using Standard **Form C.**[58] Thereafter, the court presents the claimant with an alternative (as per Article 10 of the Regulation, which refers to a 'proposal'): either to accept that the court will issue an order for payment for a specified partial amount and to reply within a specified time-limit, or to refuse. Failure to reply or refusal will lead to the court rejecting the entire claim.

#60 If the claimant replies in the affirmative ('accepts the court's proposal' as per Article 10(2)), the court issues a **partial European order for payment** for the 'agreed' part of the claim, using the Form E. The consequences for the commencement of a judicial proceeding for the remaining part of the claim are governed by national law.

2 Issuing of a European Order for Payment

#61 If the requirements set out in Articles 2, 3, 4, 6 and 7 of the Regulation are met, the court will issue a European order for payment using **Form E,** normally within 30 days of the application being lodged. However, the European order for payment is **not immediately enforceable**. It only becomes enforceable if the debtor does not oppose[59] it or does not pay the amount owed to the creditor within 30 days of its notification. The declaration of enforceability shall be made on Form G. The European Order for Payment Regulation does not explicitly state whether the European order for payment acquires the status of ***'res judicata'*** in addition to its enforceability. However, Italian case-law[60] had clarified that the European order for payment does not have 'res judicata effects' as between the parties, their successors, heirs or representatives. Therefore, debtors may initiate subse-

58 Article 10.
59 Article 17.
60 Cass civ 26 May 2015, no. 10799.

quent legal proceedings to recover undue amounts and, more generally, to establish that the claimed debt did not exist.

#62 The European order for payment must be **served** on the debtor alongside a copy of the application form (Form A), excluding the information provided by the claimant in Appendices 1 and 2 to Form A. It must also be accompanied by a copy of Form F, which is used for filing objections. The procedures for serving the European order for payment on the debtor are governed by the national law of the Member State where service is to be carried-out. However, to ensure that the debtor is effectively informed of the European order for payment, irrespective of the provisions of national procedural law in the Member States, the Regulation[61] lays down specific rules for the service of the order. If these rules are not adhered to, resulting in a procedural error that affects the service of the European Order for Payment, the order will remain unenforceable[62] and the time-limit within which the defendant may file an opposition pursuant to Article 17, does not commence. As established by the CJEU, the European Order for Payment must be served in a **language** that the **debtor** can reasonably **understand.**[63]

3 Opposition

#63 Pursuant to Article 17 of the European Order for Payment Regulation, if a statement of opposition is filed within 30 days of receiving the notification of a Euro-

61 Articles 13, 14, 15.

62 Since the Regulation is silent as to the possible remedies available to the debtor if it only becomes apparent after a European order for payment has been declared enforceable that that order has not been served or has not been served in a manner which complies with the minimum standards laid down in Articles 13 to 15, those procedural issues are governed by national law: Case C-389/23, *Bulgarfrukt – Fruchthandels GmbH* v *Oranzherii Gimel II EOOD* (5 December 2024) ECLI:EU:C:2024:1001, para 41 ('*Bulgarfrukt*'). For example, Section 1092a of the German Code of Civil Procedure (*Zivilprozessordnung*, ZPO), titled 'Remedy in the event of failure to serve or to effect proper service of the European order for payment', establishes the debtor's right to seek annulment of a European order for payment where service was either not effected or did not comply with the requirements set out in Articles 13 to 15 of the European Order for Payment Regulation. To this end, the debtor must file an application for annulment within one month of becoming aware of the issuance of the order or the lack of service. If the court grants the application, the European order for payment shall be annulled.

63 Case C-21/17 *Catlin Europe SE* v. O.K. *Trans Praha spol. s r. o.* (6 September 2018) ECLI:EU:C:2018:675. The CJEU clarified that linguistic procedural irregularities affecting the service of the European order for payment and the associated Form A, (which was not accompanied by a translation into a language which the debtor is presumed to understand) preclude the defendant from filing a statement of opposition under Article 17. Consequently, the period in which the debtor may lodge a statement of opposition cannot start to run. Therefore, in such cases, it is Article 17 on opposition that must be applied, and not Article 20 of the European Order for Payment Regulation, which pertains to review in exceptional cases.

pean order for payment, proceedings continue in the 'competent courts' of the Member State where the order was issued, in accordance with its national procedural rules. The option of lodging a statement of opposition is designed to compensate for the fact that the system established by the European Order for Payment Regulation does not provide for the debtor's participation in the order for payment procedure, 'by enabling him or her to contest the claim after the European order for payment has been issued'.[64]

#64 The term 'competent courts' means, first and foremost, that they must have international jurisdiction to hear the claim under the Brussels I Recast Regulation. However, a statement of opposition which does not challenge the international jurisdiction of the court of the Member State of origin is not considered as entering an appearance under Article 25 of the Brussels I Recast Regulation.[65] The competent courts must also have territorial jurisdiction (venue).

#65 The statement of opposition may be submitted using standard **Form F,**[66] – ie, simply by expressing the intention to oppose, without the need to provide legal or factual reasons in support of one's request – but its use is not mandatory.[67]

#66 Defendants are free to use any appropriate claim form that allows them to contest the claim without formalities after the European order for payment has been issued.

#67 For the time being, pending the implementation of e-CODEX, Form F or other claim forms should preferably be submitted to the court in digital form in Member States where this is possible, or in paper form, where it is not yet possible.

#68 When submitting Form A, the creditor has to make a prognostic assessment of what is more advantageous: to continue the proceedings under the national procedural law of the court of the competent jurisdiction in the event of opposition by the debtor – which may be unfamiliar to the creditor and which may involve higher court fees than the European order for payment procedure as well as the obligation to provide legal representation – or to avoid these inconveniences by requesting the application of a uniform European procedure, namely the European small claims proceedings or, finally, to terminate the European order for payment procedure. In the latter two cases, the creditor must complete **Appendix 2.**

64 Eg, *Bulgarfrukt* (n 62) para 36; Case C-245/14 *Thomas Cook Belgium* v *Thurner Hotel GmbH* (22 October 2015) ECLI:EU:C:2015:715, para 28 ('*Thomas Cook*'); Case C–18/21 *Uniqa Versicherungen,* (15 September 2022) ECLI:EU:C:2022:682, para 24.

65 Case C-144/12 *Goldbet Sportwetten GmbH* v *Massimo Sperindeo* (13 June 2013) ECLI:EU:C:2013:393.

66 <https://e-justice.europa.eu/156/EN/european_payment_order_forms?init=true> accessed 17 February 2025.

67 See Recital 23.

#69 If the creditor does not seek to terminate the proceedings, they will be notified of any transfer to standard national civil proceedings upon the debtor filing a statement of opposition. The transfer is governed by:

a) the law of the Member State of origin ('lex fori'), which also encompasses court fees, or
b) by the **European Small Claims Regulation** for civil and commercial matters covered by the Regulation, provided that the creditor chooses this option by completing Appendix 2 to Form A.

#70 In relation to the possible outcomes of opposition proceedings, if the court determines that it lacks international jurisdiction under the Brussels I Recast Regulation, it is not obligated to independently review the European order for payment by analogy with Article 20 of the Regulation (review in exceptional cases).[68]

#71 When, on the other hand, the court has international jurisdiction over the case and national procedural law applies, the outcome of the opposition depends on the court's evaluation of the debtor's objections. Should the opposition be found unfounded and the debt confirmed, the effects of such a decision on the European order for payment may differ across jurisdictions. In Italy, for example, some court rulings on the merits uphold the validity of the European order for payment,[69] while others issue a condemnatory judgment which supersedes it.[70]

4 Review in Exceptional Cases

#72 Article 20 of the European Order for Payment Regulation provides that, after the expiry of the time limit laid down in Article 16(2), the debtor may still apply for a review of the European order for payment by the competent court of the Member State of origin, if the failure to comply with the 30-day time limit for lodging a statement of opposition is due to extraordinary or exceptional circumstances, in particular in the following cases:

a) when the order was served in accordance with one of the methods specified in Article 14, but the notification did not reach the debtor in time to allow them to raise their defences promptly (eg, when the European order for payment was served to persons living in the same household who, nevertheless, only delivered the order to the debtor after 25 days had passed from the date of notification);
b) when the debtor was unable to challenge the debt due to force majeure or other **extraordinary circumstances** beyond their control. These terms are

68 Case C- 94/14, *Flight Refund Ltd* v *Deutsche Lufthansa AG* (10 March 2016) ECLI:EU:C:2016:148.
69 Tribunal of Pavia, 29 February 2024, no 427.
70 Tribunal of Pisa, 26 February 2024, no 296; Tribunal of Naples, 8 February 2024, no 1584.

interpreted to include situations where the debtor was not served with the European order for payment because of unforeseeable events (eg, cases of mistaken identity (homonymy)), or where, despite being aware of the order's issuance in time, they were prevented from submitting a timely opposition due to unforeseen events (eg, an extended stay in intensive care or a coma in hospital). It is also necessary that there should be no fault on the part of the defendant and, third, that once the defendant becomes aware of the European order for payment, they must act promptly. The failure to meet any one of these conditions means that the defendant cannot claim to satisfy the requirements set out in that provision;[71] or

c) when the European Order for Payment was clearly issued in error or under other **exceptional circumstances.** In interpreting this expression, it should be borne in mind that a review in exceptional cases does not imply that the defendant is granted a second opportunity to oppose the claim. 'Exceptional circumstances' could include a situation where the European order for payment was based on false information provided in the application form.[72] However, they do not include cases in which a defendant, on whom a European order for payment has been duly served in accordance with the European Order for Payment Regulation, seeks to apply for a review of that order by arguing that the court of origin incorrectly asserted its international jurisdiction over the case, on the basis of allegedly false information provided by the claimant in application Form A.[73] Similarly, the incorrect calculation or transcription of the time limit for lodging the statement of opposition by the defendant's representative does not constitute 'exceptional circumstances'.[74]

#73 During the review procedure the merits of the claim should not be evaluated beyond the grounds resulting from the exceptional circumstances invoked by the defendant.[75]

VI Enforceability and Enforcement

#74 If no opposition is lodged with the court of origin, the European order for payment is promptly declared enforceable by means of **Form G**. Once enforceable in the Member State of origin, the European order for payment is automatically rec-

71 Case C-324/12 *Novontech-Zala kft.* v *Logicdata Electronic & Software Entwicklungs GmbH* (21 March 2013) ECLI:EU:C:2013:205, para 24 ('*Novontech-Zala*').

72 Recital 25.

73 *Thomas Cook* (n 64).

74 *Novontech-Zala* (n 71) para 20.

75 Recital 25.

ognisable and enforceable within the European judicial area, without requiring a declaration of enforceability, and with no possibility of opposing its recognition.[76]

#75 Even though, at present, national orders for payment are also automatically enforceable across the European judicial area under the Brussels I Recast Regulation, one factor that may lead a creditor to opt for European order for payment proceedings over a national procedure is the streamlined recognition and enforcement framework established by the European Order for Payment Regulation. Unlike Article 45 of the Brussels I Recast Regulation, the grounds for refusing recognition and enforcement under Article 22 are limited solely to irreconcilability, thereby excluding:

a) i) substantive and procedural public policy considerations, and
b) ii) challenges to jurisdictional competence, including cases where the debtor is a consumer.

#76 As is the case under the European Small Claims Regulation, in the event of irreconcilability, a strict chronological hierarchy is applied to determine whether a European order of payment or a national or a foreign judgment (ie, rendered by a court located in another Member State or in a third State), takes precedence.

References

Kramer X, 'Major Step in the Harmonization of Procedural Law in Europe: The European Small Claims Procedure Accomplishments, New Features and Some Fundamental Questions of European Harmonization' in T Jongbloed (ed), *The XIIIth World Congress of Procedural Law: The Belgian and Dutch Reports* (Intersentia 2008) 253.

Buzzoni M and Santalò Goris C, *Report on Practices in Comparative and Cross-Border Perspective. EFFORTS (Towards more EFfective enFORcemenT of claimS in civil and commercial matters within the EU)* (Project JUST-JCOO-AG-2019-881802) 55 <https://efforts.unimi.it/research-outputs/reports/> accessed 15 January 2025.

Domej T, 'Article 8 EuGFVO' in Stein-Jonas, *Kommentar zur Zivilprozessordnung* (23rd edn, Mohr Siebeck 2021).

Ulrici B, 'The European Order for Payment Procedure' in J von Hein and T Kruger (eds), *Informed Choices in Cross-Border Enforcement* (Intersentia 2021) 65.

von Hein J and Imm T, 'Conclusions and Recommendations' in Jan von Hein and Thalia Kruger (eds), *Informed Choices in Cross-Border Enforcement* (Intersentia 2021) 529.

76 Article 19.

Carlos Santaló Goris*

Chapter 17
Asset Preservation and Provisional Measures

A Provisional Measures in Cross-Border Civil Proceedings

#1 **Provisional measures** can be fundamental in ensuring the success of the future **enforcement** of a judgment which has not been rendered yet. Proceedings on the merits of a claim can take months, even years. When the courts render their judgments, there might not be assets left that would allow the recovery of the claim. Provisional measures serve to temporarily secure sufficient assets of the defendant to guarantee that, in case the court decides in the claimant's favour, that judgment can be effectively enforcement and the claim recovered.[1]

#2 In proceedings on claims with a cross-border dimension, provisional measures might result even more necessary than in purely domestic ones. Cross-border proceedings are often more complex, tend to last longer, and imply additional costs.[2] Furthermore, they often require the cross-border enforcement of the judgment resulting in those proceedings. For all these factors, claimants might feel more compelled to secure the recovery of their claim by relying on provisional measures. At the EU level, there are several civil procedural instruments that contain specific jurisdictional rules as well as rules on recognition and enforcement concerning provisional measures. The most representative of these instruments, is the Brussels I bis Regulation.[3] Besides these instruments, the EU legislator has

1 C Kessedjian, 'Note on Provisional and Protective Measures in Private International Law and Comparative Law' (Hague Conference on Private International Law, October 1998) 3.

2 J-F van Drooghenbroeck and C De Boe, 'Les mesures provisoires et conservatoires dans le règlement. Bruxelles I Bis' in E Guinchard (ed), *Le nouveau Règlement Bruxelles I bis. Règlement n°1215/2012 du 12 décembre 2012 concernant la compétence judiciaire, la reconnaissance et l'exécution des décisions en matière civile et commerciale* (Bruylant 2014) 167.

3 Regulation (EU) No 1215/2012 of the European Parliament and of the Council of 12 December 2012 on jurisdiction and the recognition and enforcement of judgments in civil and commercial matters (recast) [2012] OJ L351/1.

***Corresponding author: Carlos Santaló Goris**, Postdoctoral researcher at the University of Luxembourg, e-mail: carlos.santalo@uni.lu

https://doi.org/10.1515/9783110781632-017

also created a specific interim measure that allows the cross-border attachment of bank accounts: the **European Account Preservation Order** ('EAPO').[4]

#3 This chapter explores the main features of the provisional measures regime under the Brussels I bis Regulation as well as the EAPO procedure. It will provide a comprehensive roadmap of the two alternative paths offered by the EU legal order to provisional secure assets in cross-border civil and commercial claims.

B The Provisional Measures Regime Under the Brussels I bis Regulation

#4 The **Brussels I bis Regulation** contains special rules on jurisdiction, recognition, and enforcement for provisional measures. This special regime already existed under the 1968 Brussels Convention[5] and the Brussels I Regulation.[6] While the evolution of this regime from the 1968 Brussels Convention to the Brussels I bis Regulation might not reflect significant changes, it was the CJEU that has largely contributed to clarifying its boundaries and content. The CJEU case law is thus vital for a proper understanding of the provisional measures regime under the Brussels I bis Regulation.

I The Notion of 'Provisional, Including Protective, Measures'

#5 Under the Brussels I bis Regulation, the notion of '**provisional, including protective, measures**' is an autonomous concept of EU law. While the text of the Brussels I bis Regulation does not provide a definition of what is understood by provisional measures, the CJEU elaborated one when interpreting the 1968 Brussels Convention. In C-261/90, *Reichter*, the CJEU found that provisional measures are those measures which 'are intended to preserve a factual or legal situation so as to safeguard rights the recognition of which is sought elsewhere from the court having jurisdiction as to the substance of the matter'.[7] This definition remains rel-

4 Regulation (EU) No 655/2014 of the European Parliament and of the Council of 15 May 2014 establishing a European Account Preservation Order procedure to facilitate cross-border debt recovery in civil and commercial matters [2014] OJ L189/59 ('EAPO Regulation').
5 1968 Brussels Convention on jurisdiction and the enforcement of judgments in civil and commercial matters [1972] OJ L299/32.
6 Council Regulation (EC) No 44/2001 of 22 December 2000 on jurisdiction and the recognition and enforcement of judgments in civil and commercial matters [2001] OJ L12/1.
7 Case C-261/90 *Mario Reichert, Hans-Heinz Reichert and Ingeborg Kockler v Dresdner Bank AG* (26 March 1992) ECLI:EU:C:1992:149, para 34.

evant for the notion of 'provisional, including protective, measures' under the Brussels I bis Regulation.[8]

#6 The concept of provisional measures was revisited by the CJEU in C-391/95, *Van Uden*. In this case, the CJEU clarified that **interim payment** order under Dutch law (*kort geding*) could be qualified as a provisional measure under the 1968 Brussels Convention only if the 'payment to the defendant of the sum awarded is guaranteed if the plaintiff is unsuccessful as regards the substance of his claim' and if 'the measure sought relates only to specific assets of the defendant located or to be located within the confines of the territorial jurisdiction of the court to which application is made'.[9]

#7 The concept of 'provisional, including protective, measures' is only partially addressed in the Preamble of the Brussels I bis Regulation. Recital 14 clarifies that measures intended to gather evidence can also qualify as 'provisional, including protective, measures' as long as they have a protective character. Such protective character might exist, for instance, when the measure is intended to obtain documents at risk of disappearing at a later stage of the proceeding.[10] The Preambles also clarifies that hearing witnesses would not be considered a provisional measure.[11] It should be noted that in C-104/03, *St. Paul Diary*, the CJEU clarified that measures intended to gather **evidence** that would solely serve potential claimants to assess whether to file or not claim lack of the protective character necessary to be qualified as provisional measures in the sense of the Brussels I bis Regulation.[12]

II The Jurisdictional Regime for Provisional Measures

1 The Double-Track Jurisdictional System for Provisional Measures

#8 The Brussels I bis Regulation provides two jurisdictional possibilities for requesting provisional measures. One is requesting the provisional measures before the courts of the Member States with **jurisdiction to decide as to the substance of the matter**.[13] There is not a specific provision in the Brussels I bis Regulation in-

---

8 Case C-581/20 *Skarb Państwa Rzeczypospolitej Polskiej reprezentowany przez Generalnego Dyrektora Dróg Krajowych i Autostrad v TOTO SpA – Costruzioni Generali and Vianini Lavori SpA* (9 September 2021) ECLI:EU:C:2021:726, Opinion of Advocate General Rantos, para 32.

9 Case C-391/95 *Van Uden Maritime v Kommanditgesellschaft in Firma Deco-Line and Others* (17 November 1998) ECLI:EU:C:1998:543, para 47.

10 F Garcimartín Alférez, 'Provisional and Protective Measures in the Brussels I Regulation Recast' (2014/2015) 16 Yearbook of Private International Law 57, 80.

11 Recital 14 Brussels I bis Regulation.

12 Case C-104/03 *St. Paul Dairy Industries NV v Unibel Exser BVBA* (28 April 2005) ECLI:EU:C:2005:255, para 24.

13 T Garber, 'Art. 35 Brussels I bis' in U Magnus and P Mankowski (eds), *Brussels Ibis Regulation – Commentary* (2nd edn, Otto Schmidt 2023), para 21.

dicating that the courts of the Member State with jurisdiction as to the substance of the matter can grant provisional measures.[14] However, this is acknowledged in the definition of 'judgment' contained in Article 2 that states that only provisional measures granted by courts with jurisdiction as to the substance of the matter can profit from the simplified scheme of recognition and enforcement of the Brussels I bis Regulation.

#9 The second jurisdictional option to obtain provisional measures is the one provided by Article 35. This provision states that provisional measures can be granted by courts other than those with jurisdiction as to the substance of the matter. A literal interpretation of this provision would suggest that any court or any other Member State could grant provisional measures. That is not the case. The CJEU has clarified that there 'a **real connecting link** between the subject-matter of the measures sought and the territorial jurisdiction of the Contracting State of the court before which those measures are sought'.[15] How such real connecting link is established was something that the CJEU did not clarify and was object of discussions among scholars for a while after the judgment was rendered.[16] The Brussels I bis Regulation put a *de facto* end to this conundrum. Under the Brussels I bis Regulation, provisional measures granted by the courts of other Member States than those with jurisdiction as to the substance of the matter cannot be recognised and enforced in other Member States.[17] This means that provisional measures granted on the basis of Article 35 can be enforced only in the Member State they have been obtained. Since the Member State where provisional measures are granted is also the Member State of enforcement there is always a real connecting link between the provisional measure and the Member State the measure is requested.[18] The place of the enforcement serves as a connecting factor to establish that courts of a Member State have jurisdiction to grant provisional measures under Article 35.[19]

---

14 The Commission Proposal of the Brussels I bis Regulation intended to include the following provision: 'Where the courts of a Member State have jurisdiction as to the substance of a matter, those courts shall have jurisdiction to issue provisional, including protective measures as may be available under the law of that State' (Article 35 COM/2010/0748 final). However, it was decided to withdraw such provision.

15 Case C-391/95 *Van Uden Maritime v Kommanditgesellschaft in Firma Deco-Line and Others* (17 November 1998) ECLI:EU:C:1998:543, para 40.

16 van Drooghenbroeck and De Boe (n 2) 196–198.

17 See also below in text #16.

18 M-E Ancel and H Gaudemet-Tallon, *Compétence et exécution des jugements en Europe* (LGDJ 2018) 482.

19 However, some scholars consider that Article 35 does not establish an autonomous head of jurisdiction but rather contains a reference to the domestic jurisdictional rules of the Member States. In other words, if a provisional measure is requested through Article 35 of the Brussels I bis Regulation, the court examining the request would have to verify that it has jurisdiction to grant that provisional

2 Choice of Court Agreements and Article 35

#10 Article 25 of the Brussels I bis Regulation recognises parties the possibility of selecting the jurisdiction before which they might want to bring their disputes arising from their legal relationships through a choice of court agreement. It raises the question of whether the **choice of court agreement** prevents relying on Article 35 to ask for provisional measures other court than the one that has been selected by the parties.[20] That would depend on the terms in which the choice of court agreement is drafted.[21] If the choice of court agreement merely indicates that the dispute as to the substance of the matter is to be solved by a specific court, then, in principle, requesting provisional measures through Article 35 would not be excluded.[22] However, parties could expressly indicate that the selected jurisdiction is the only one competent to grant provisional measures.[23] If that were the case, then Article 35 would not be an option for the parties to request provisional measures before other courts.[24]

measure in light of its national law: AL Calvo Caravaca and J Carrascosa González, 'Medidas Cautelares y el Reglamento Bruselas I-Bis' (2015) 51 Rivista di diritto internazionale privato e processuale 55, 68–70; M Nioche, *La décision provisoire en droit international privé européen: Qualification et régime en matière civile et commerciale* (Bruylant 2012) para 407.

20 U Magnus, 'Art. 25 Brussels I bis' in U Magnus and P Mankowski (eds), *Brussels Ibis Regulation – Commentary* (2nd edn, Otto Schmidt 2023), para 152.

21 In C-581/20, *TOTO*, the CJEU has partially addressed this issue, stating that 'the parties may, by agreement, determine international jurisdiction in respect of provisional, including protective, measures and it can be presumed that a choice of forum clause drafted in general terms confers jurisdiction to adopt such measures on the chosen court' (Case C-581/20 *Skarb Państwa Rzeczypospolitej Polskiej reprezentowany przez Generalnego Dyrektora Dróg Krajowych i Autostrad v TOTO SpA – Costruzioni Generali and Vianini Lavori SpA* (6 October 2021) ECLI:EU:C:2021:808, para 50). However, the CJEU did not clarify to which extent the choice of court agreement excludes the courts of other Member States from granting provisional measures through Article 35. National courts have followed different interpretations of the impact that choice of court agreements have on the possibility of asking for provisional measures before other courts. For an overview of the national case law on this topic, see: Marlene Brosch and LM Kahl, 'Article 25' in M Requejo Isidro (ed), *Brussels I Bis. A Commentary on Regulation (EU) No 1215/2012* (Edward Elgar 2022) 344, paras 25.61–25.63.

22 R Gaier, 'Art. 32 Brüssel Ia-VO' in V Vorwerk and C Wolf (eds), *BeckOK ZPO* (CH Beck 2024), margin no. 80.1.

23 This was the interpretation made by the Regional Court of Dortmund (*Landgericht Dortmund*), which, upon examining the prorogation of jurisdiction clause in a contract, determined that its wording also covered interim measures. Therefore, no other court than the one selected by the parties could grant interim measures: LG Dortmund, Urteil vom 30.05.2018 – 8 O 10/18 Kart.

24 Magnus (n 20) para 152.

3 Article 35 and the Arbitration Exclusion

#11 **Arbitration** is one of the subject matters that are expressly excluded from the scope of application of the Brussels I bis Regulation.[25] The boundaries of the arbitration exclusion are not strictly clear and this explains the abundance of CJEU case law on this particular issue.[26] Under the 1968 Brussels Convention, the CJEU clarified is the possibility on relying on this instrument to obtain a provisional measure even if the dispute is being decided before an arbitration tribunal. In C-391/95, *Van Uden*, the CJEU determined that where the parties have validly excluded the jurisdiction of the courts in a dispute arising under a contract and have referred that dispute to arbitration, there are no courts of any State that have jurisdiction as to the substance of the case for the purposes of the Convention'.[27]

#12 However, at the same time, the CJEU acknowledged that it was possible to rely on Article 24 of the 1968 Brussels Convention (now Article 35 of the Brussels I bis Regulation) to obtain provisional measures in support of a claim brought before an arbitral tribunal.[28] The reason is that provision allows courts other than those with jurisdiction to decide as to the substance of the matter to render provisional measures.[29] What was relevant for the CJEU is that the nature of the rights to be protected by the provisional measure fall within the material scope of the 1968 Brussels Convention.[30] This means that the rights that the provisional measure intends to protect fall within the category of 'civil and commercial matter' and in none of the expressly excluded subject matters of its scope of application, such as arbitration. For instance, it would not be possible to ask for a provisional mea-

---

25 Article 1(2)(d) Brussels I bis Regulation.

26 For an overview of the CJEU case law on the arbitration exclusion on the Brussels I bis Regulation, see: P Rogerson and P Mankowski, 'Art. 1 Brussels I bis' in U Magnus and P Mankowski (eds), *Brussels Ibis Regulation – Commentary* (2nd edn, Otto Schmidt 2023) paras 41–59.

27 Case C-391/95 *Van Uden Maritime v Kommanditgesellschaft in Firma Deco-Line and Others* (17 November 1998) ECLI:EU:C:1998:543, para 24.

28 In this regard, it should be noted that numerous civil procedural systems recognise that courts can grant provisional measures in support of claims brought before arbitral tribunals. For instance, Article 722 of the Spanish Code of Civil Procedure (*Ley de Enjuiciamiento Civil*) expressly acknowledges this possibility. Another example is Article 9 of the UNCITRAL Model Law of Commercial Arbitration which states that 'It is not incompatible with an arbitration agreement for a party to request, before or during arbitral proceedings, from a court an interim measure of protection and for a court to grant such measure'.

29 Case C-391/95 *Van Uden Maritime v Kommanditgesellschaft in Firma Deco-Line and Others* (17 November 1998) ECLI:EU:C:1998:543, para 25.

30 ibid, para 28.

sure regarding an arbitrator's claim for the payment of his fee because that would materially fall within the arbitration exclusion as a subject matter.[31]

4 Parallel Requests of Provisional Measures and the *Lis Pendens* Rule

#13 The possibility of requesting provisional measures before the courts of the Member State with jurisdiction as to the substance of the matter and the courts of other Member State opens the question of whether a claimant could simultaneously apply for the same provisional measures concerning the same in two or more different Member States. Article 29, which enshrines the ***lis pendens* rule** which prevents the existence of two proceedings with the same parties, the same subject matter and the same cause of action pending before the courts of two different Member States.[32] Does the *lis pendens* rule apply to provisional measure proceedings? In C-581/20, *TOTO*, the CJEU replied that the *lis pendens* rule does not apply in case of provisional measures.[33] Hence, there are no impediments to requesting the same provisional measure involving the same case in two Member States.

#14 The existence of multiple provisional measure proceedings in several Member States can result in undermining the defendant's position with respect to the claimant.[34] This can occur in the hypothetical scenario that a claimant seeking to recover a claim asks for the provisional attachment of the debtors' bank accounts in Member States A and B. In each Member State, the total amount attached to the bank accounts covers the entire claim amount. However, the total amount of the funds attached in both Member States largely bypasses the amount of the claim. Such over-protection of the claim results from the lack of a coordination mechanism system between the different provisional measure proceedings.

#15 In the current ongoing discussions about the potential **reform the Brussels I bis Regulation**, it has been proposed to introduce a mechanism by which the court with jurisdiction as to the substance of the matter can withdraw provisional measures granted by the courts of other Member States.[35] This solution is inspired

---

31 G Cuniberti and S Migliorini, *The European Account Preservation Order Regulation: A Commentary* (Cambridge 2018) 27.

32 Case C-39/02 *Mærsk Olie & Gas A/S v Firma M. de Haan en W. de Boer* (14 October 2004) ECLI:EU:C:2004:615, para 34.

33 Case C-581/20 *Skarb Państwa Rzeczypospolitej Polskiej reprezentowany przez Generalnego Dyrektora Dróg Krajowych i Autostrad v TOTO SpA – Costruzioni Generali and Vianini Lavori SpA* (6 October 2021) ECLI:EU:C:2021:808, para 61.

34 T Garber, 'Art. 35 Brussels I bis' in U Magnus and P Mankowski (eds), *Brussels Ibis Regulation – Commentary* (2nd edn, Otto Schmidt 2023), para 89.

35 B Hess and others, 'The Reform of the Brussels Ibis Regulation – Academic Position Paper' (2024) Vienna Research Paper 39 <https://ssrn.com/abstract=4853421> accessed 30 December 2024.

in the mechanism to coordinate parallel requests for provisional measures under the **Brussels II-ter Regulation**.[36] By establishing that one single court with authority to withdraw provisional measures avoids defendants contesting provisional measures before the courts of several Member States.

III Recognition and Enforcement of Provisional Measures

#16 One of the innovations brought by the Brussels I bis Regulation with respect to the Brussels I Regulation is that it limited the cross-border enforcement of judgments on provisional measures.[37] Only provisional measures granted by courts with jurisdiction as the substance of the matter can benefit from the Brussels I bis Regulation simplified scheme of cross-border enforcement.

#17 Furthermore, the Brussels I bis Regulation also codified an already existing condition for the **cross-border enforcement** of provisional measures established by CJEU. In C-125/79, *Denilauer*, the CJEU determined that provisional measures which are granted ***inaudita altera parte*** can be recognised and enforced in other Member States through the 1968 Brussels Convention only if they are served on the defendant before seeking their enforcement in other Member State.[38] Since the defendant is informed about the provisional measure before its enforcement, this vanishes the surprise effect that the *inaudita altera parte* provisional measures intends to achieve. The Commission Proposal of the Brussels I bis Regulation allowed the circulation of *inaudita altera parte* provisional measures without their prior service on the defendant.[39] Nonetheless, the European legislator decided to codify the *Denilauler* doctrine instead.[40]

#18 One of the available grounds under the Brussels I bis Regulation to refuse the recognition and enforcement of a judgment granted in another Member State is if such judgment is **irreconcilable** with a judgment rendered in the Member State of enforcement.[41] This means that the both judgments 'entail legal consequences that are mutually exclusive'.[42] In C-80/00, *Italian Leather* the CJEU found that this

36 Article 15(3) Council Regulation (EU) 2019/1111 of 25 June 2019 on jurisdiction, the recognition and enforcement of decisions in matrimonial matters and the matters of parental responsibility, and on international child abduction (recast), ST/8214/2019/INIT [2019] OJ L178/1.

37 van Drooghenbroeck and De Boe (n 2) 199.

38 Case C-125/79 *Bernard Denilauler v SNC Couchet Frères* (21 May 1980) ECLI:EU:C:1980:130, para 17.

39 Article 2(a) COM/2010/0748 final.

40 I Pretelli, 'Chapter 5. Provisional and Protective Measures in the European Civil Procedure of the Brussels I System' in V Lazić and S Stuij (eds), *Brussels Ibis Regulation, Short Studies in Private International Law* (Springer 2017) 97, 114.

41 Article 45 Brussels I bis Regulation.

42 Case C-145/86 *Horst Ludwig Martin Hoffmann v Adelheid Krieg* (4 February 1988) ECLI:EU:C:1988:61, para 22.

ground to contest the recognition and enforcement of judgments also applies to judgments on provisional measures.[43] This solution is at odds with the CJEU found in C-581/20, *TOTO*, in which it determined that Article 29's *lis pendens* rule does not apply to provisional measure proceedings.[44] Both the the *lis pendens* rule and the ground on refusal of irreconcilable judgments respond to the same objective: avoiding the clash between irreconcilable judgments rendered in different Member States.[45] Paradoxically, the CJEU found that in case of provisional measures, one of these rules apply, but the other not.[46]

C The EAPO Regulation

#19 The EAPO Regulation introduced the first EU cross-border civil provisional measure that, as its name suggests, allows the provisional attachment of the debtors' bank accounts. It is an **alternative instrument**, meaning that creditors are not required to use an EAPO to provisionally secure a cross-border claim. The can opt instead for its national equivalent provisional freezing order relying on the jurisdictional regime for provisional measures of the Brussels I bis Regulation.[47] The EAPO is often referred to as a uniform instrument, though in reality, a hybrid procedure that combines certain uniform standards along with references to the domestic law of the Member States.[48] All procedural aspects that are not specifically addressed in the text of the EAPO Regulation depend on the national law of the Member States.[49] Furthermore, it is a proceedings that operates through pre-

43 Case C-80/00 *Italian Leather SpA v WECO Polstermöbel GmbH & Co* (6 June 2022) ECLI:EU:C:2002:342 para 41.

44 See above in text #15. After C-80/00, *Italian Leather*, some scholars defended that if the ground of refusal based on the irreconcilability of judgments applies to decisions between provisional measures, then the lis pendens rule should also apply between parallel proceedings on provisional measures. In this sense, see: X Kramer, 'Case C-80/00, Italian Leather SpA v. WECO Polstermöbel GmbH & Co., European Court of Justice, 6 June 2002' (2003) 40 Common Market Law Review 953, 961.

45 RG Fentiman, 'Art. 29 Brussels I bis' in U Magnus and P Mankowski (eds), *Brussels Ibis Regulation – Commentary* (2nd edn, Otto Schmidt 2023), paras 8–9.

46 Conversely, Advocate General Rantos advocated for the application of the *lis pendens* rule, among other reasons, because such solution would be coherent with what the CJEU stood in C-80/00, *Italian Leather*: Case C-581/20 *Skarb Państwa Rzeczypospolitej Polskiej reprezentowany przez Generalnego Dyrektora Dróg Krajowych i Autostrad v TOTO SpA – Costruzioni Generali and Vianini Lavori SpA* [(9 September 2021) ECLI:EU:C:2021:726, Opinion of Advocate General Rantos, paras 51–53.

47 Recital 6 EAPO Regulation; K Hilbig-Lugani, 'Art. 1 EuKoPf VO' in T Rauscher and W Krüger (eds), *Münchener Kommentar zur Zivilprozessordnung. Band 3* (6th edn, CH Beck 2022), marginal no. 4.

48 ML Villamarín López, 'Harmonisation of the Rules on Protective Measures? The European Account Preservation Order' in F Gascón Inchausti and B Hess (eds), *The Future of the European Law of Civil Procedure. Coordination or Harmonisation?* (Intersentia 2020) 111, 113.

49 Article 46(1) EAPO Regulation.

established **standards forms** that can be found in the EAPO Commission Implementing Regulation.[50]

I Scope of Application

1 Material Scope

#20 The EAPO Regulation can be only used in '**civil and commercial matters**'.[51] The notion of 'civil and commercial matters' is an autonomous concept of EU law, as the CJEU has repeatedly indicated concerning the identical expressly under the Brussels I bis Regulation.[52] While the CJEU has not elaborated a positive definition of what is meant by 'civil and commercial matters', it has adopted a broad interpretation of it.[53] In general, it covers all sort private parties contractual and non-contractual relations.[54]

#21 Besides the reference to 'civil and commercial matters', there are also specific subject matters that are excluded from the material scope of the EAPO Regulation. This does not apply 'to revenue, customs or administrative matters or to the liability of the State for acts and omissions in the exercise of State authority ('acta iure imperii')'.[55] It does neither apply to succession matters,[56] or claims regarding matrimonial or civil partnerships property regimes.[57] Debtors against whom an insolvency proceeding has been opened can be subject of an EAPO.[58] Another excluded matter are social security claims.[59] Like in the Brussels I bis Regulation, **arbitration** is also excluded.[60]

---

50 Commission Implementing Regulation (EU) 2016/1823 of 10 October 2016 establishing the forms referred to in Regulation (EU) No 655/2014 of the European Parliament and of the Council establishing a European Account Preservation Order procedure to facilitate cross-border debt recovery in civil and commercial matters, C/2016/6339 [2016] OJ L283/1.

51 Article 2(1) EAPO Regulation.

52 Case C-73/19 *Belgische Staat and Directeur-Generaal van de Algemene Directie Controle en Bemiddeling van de FOD Economie, K.M.O., Middenstand en Energie v Movic BV and Others* (16 July 2020) ECLI:EU:C:2020:568, para 33.

53 Case C-579/17 *BUAK Bauarbeiter-Urlaubs- u. Abfertigungskasse v Gradbeništvo Korana d.o.o.* (28 February 2019) ECLI:EU:C:2019:162, para 47.

54 Cuniberti and Migliorini (n 31) 65.

55 Article 2(1) EAPO Regulation.

56 Article 2(2)(b) EAPO Regulation.

57 Article 2(2)(a) EAPO Regulation.

58 Article 2(2)(c) EAPO Regulation.

59 Article 2(2)(d) EAPO Regulation.

60 Article 2(2)(e) EAPO Regulation. The contours of the arbitration exclusion are not clear, as discussions among scholars show. For an overview of the different approaches followed by courts and scholars concerning the arbitration exclusion, see: C Santaló Goris, 'The Boundaries of Arbitration Exclu-

#22 There are also certain types of **bank accounts** that cannot be attached by an EAPO, such as those that are immune to seizure under the law of the Member State of enforcement.[61] Bank accounts 'maintained in connection with the operation of any system as defined in point (a) of Article 2 of Directive 98/26/EC' can neither be attached.[62] Lastly, it is not possible to attach by accounts held by central banks when acting in their capacity of monetary authorities.[63]

2 Territorial Scope and Cross-Border Element

#23 The EAPO Regulation applies to all Member States except Denmark.[64] Only cases in which the court that issues the EAPO, the creditor's domicile, and the bank account to be attached are located in a Member State where the EAPO Regulation applies.[65] The debtor's domicile is irrelevant and could be even located in a third State.[66]

#24 The EAPO Regulation is only applicable in cases with a **cross-border dimension**.[67] The cross-border dimension of a claim exists when at least the creditor's domicile or the court that issues the EAPO is located in a different Member State than the bank account to be attached.[68] In case the EAPO were used to attach several bank accounts, the cross-border element needs to be established for each of the bank accounts.[69]

3 Stage of the EAPO Request

#25 Creditors can apply for an EAPO at three different **stages of the proceedings** as to the substance of the matters.[70] They can submit an EAPO application debtor

---

sion in the EAPO Regulation' (*EIPA Blog*, May 2023) <https://www.eipa.eu/publications/briefing/the-boundaries-of-arbitration-exclusion-eapo-regulation/> accessed on 30 December 2024.

61 Article 2(3) EAPO Regulation.

62 Article 2(3) EAPO Regulation.

63 Article 2(4) EAPO Regulation.

64 Recital 51 EAPO Regulation.

65 Article 4 EAPO Regulation.

66 M Walasik, 'Article 3' in E D'Alessandro and F Gascón Inchausti (eds), *The European Account Preservation Order. A Commentary on Regulation (EU) No 655/2014* (Edward Elgar 2022) 35, para 3.09.

67 Article 3 EAPO Regulation.

68 Article 3 EAPO Regulation.

69 D Wiedemann, 'Artikel 3 EU-Kpf VO' in T Rauscher (ed), *Europäisches Zivilprozess- und Kollisionsrecht* (5th edn, Otto Schmidt 2022), margin no. 6.

70 K Hilbig-Lugani, 'Art. 5 EuKoPf VO' in T Rauscher and W Krüger (eds), *Münchener Kommentar zur Zivilprozessordnung. Band 3* (6th edn, CH Beck 2022), margin no. 2.

the initiation of those proceedings (*ante demandam*), during those proceedings, or even once they have obtained an enforceable title. There are three kinds of titles that can be used to apply for an EAPO: judgments, court settlements, and authentic instruments.[71] While the text of the EAPO Regulation does not expressly mention that the titles have to be enforceable, the CJEU clarified this requirement in C-555/18, *K.H.K.*[72]

#26 When creditors apply for an EAPO before the initiation of the proceeding as to the substance of the matter, they are required to initiate that proceeding within a certain period of time. This is 'within 30 days of the date on which he (the creditor) lodged the application or within 14 days of the date of the issue of the Order, whichever date is the later'.[73] If creditors do not initiate the proceedings on the merits of the claim within the deadline, the courts can revoke the EAPO.

#27 The prerequisites to obtaining an EAPO and other procedural aspects vary depending on the stage at which the EAPO application is submitted. As is explained in the subsequent section, creditors without an enforceable title are subject to more stringent prerequisites than those with an enforceable title.[74]

II Preliminary Requirements

#28 In order to obtain an EAPO, creditors have to satisfy prerequisites. These prerequisites can be divided into two main categories: formal and material.

1 Material Prerequisites

#29 Any creditor who applies for an EAPO is required to prove a classic prerequisite to obtain national provisional measures: the ***periculum in mora***. The EAPO Regulation defines the *periculum in mora* as 'an urgent need for a protective measure in the form of a Preservation Order because there is a real risk that, without such a measure, the subsequent enforcement of the creditor's claim against the debtor will be impeded or made substantially more difficult'.[75] While the definition of

71 Article 5(b) EAPO Regulation.

72 Case C-555/18 *K.H.K. v B.A.C. and E.E.K.* (7 November 2019) ECLI:EU:C:2019:937, para 41. In C-291/21, *Starkinvest*, that a judgment on a penalty payment is not a valid title to apply for an EAPO. The reason was that the EAPO cannot be used to recover claims derived from penalty payments: Case C-291/21 *Starkinvest SRL* (20 April 2023) ECLI:EU:C:2023:299, paras 52 – 55.

73 Article 10(1) EAPO Regulation.

74 D Wiedemann, 'Artikel 5 EU-Kpf VO' in T Rauscher (ed), *Europäisches Zivilprozess- und Kollisionsrecht* (5th edn, Otto Schmidt 2022), margin no. 2.

75 Article 7(1) EAPO Regulation.

the *periculum in mora* is rather vague,[76] the Preamble offers some guidance on how the *periculum in mora* should be established Recital 14 indicates that the risk of frustration of the future enforcement of the claim has to be caused by debtors' actions adopted with the specific purpose of causing such frustration. Additionally, the Preamble provides examples of specific circumstances that might amount to the existence of the *periculum in mora* such as the existence of a 'previous dispute between the parties' or 'the debtor's credit history'. The Preamble also clarifies that the mere non-payment of the claim or the fact that debtors have several creditors amount to the existence of a *periculum in mora*.

#30 National case law shows domestic courts tend to rely on the Preamble when assessing the EAPO's *periculum in mora*.[77] As a result of this general reliance on the Preamble, in a certain degree uniformity has been attained across the EU in the way the *periculum in mora* is applied[78] In general, domestic courts seem reluctant to accept that the mere non-payment of a claim or the existence of an enforceable title is not enough to show the existence of the *periculum in mora*. They require

76 K Hilbig-Lugani, 'Art. 7 EuKoPf VO' in T Rauscher and W Krüger (eds), *Münchener Kommentar zur Zivilprozessordnung. Band 3* (6th edn, CH Beck 2022), margin no. 1.

77 References to the Preamble of the EAPO Regulation can be also found in national case law of other Member States concerning the EAPO's *periculum in mora*: Bulgaria: Gorna Oryahovitsa Regional Court, 11 February 2020, Order in Case No 2356/2019; Lovech District Court, 22 March 2022, Decision in Case No. 93/2022; Croatia: Visoki trgovački sud Republike Hrvatske, 05.05.2020, Pž-1847/2020–2 (unpublished); Estonia: Harju Maakohus, 31.07.2019, kohtuasja number: 2–18–19184, ECLI:EE:HMK:2019:2.18.19184.16326; Harju Maakohus, 05.09.2019, Tsiviilasja nr 2–19–13523. Germany: OLG Hamm, 14.01.2019, I-8 W 51/18, BeckRS 2019, 769 ECLI:DE:OLGHAM:2019:0114.8W51.18.00; LG Bremen Beschl. v. 7.1.2020 – 3 O 2166/19, BeckRS 2020, 4950,ECLI:DE:LGHB:2020:01.07.3O2166.19.00. Greece: Single Member District Court of Thessaloniki, Judgment no 12043/2018, TNP ISOKRATIS; Single Member District Court of Thessaloniki, Judgment no 12046/2018, TNP ISOKRATIS. Lithuania: Vilniaus apygardos teismas, 17.01.2019, byla 2S-65–653/2019. Poland: Sąd Rejonowy w Bydgoszczyz 23.03.2017, XII Co 1446/17; Sąd Apelacyjny w Katowicach z 22.05.2018, V AGz 317/18. Portugal: Tribunal da Relação de Guimarães, 29.06.2023, Acórdão no proceso no. 2854/17.2T8GMR-A.G2; Tribunal da Relação do Porto, 14.09.2023, Acórdão no proceso no. 69/23.0T8PRT-A.P1. Slovenia: Višje sodišče v Kopru, 08.01.2019, VSK00018612, ECLI:SI:VSKP:2019:I.IP.375.2018; Višje sodišče v Mariboru, 21.07.2021, VSM00048483, ECLI:SI:VSMB:2021:II.IP.356.2021. Slovakia: Krajský súd Žilina, 28.05.2018, 9Co/99/2018, ECLI:SK:KSZA:2018:5918200420.1; Okresný súd Banská Bystrica, 17.08.2018, 60Cb/106/2018, ECLI:SK:OSBB:2018:6118314375.1. Romania: Judecătoria Sectorul 1 București, 15.12.2021, 12326/2021, ECLI ECLI:RO:JDS1B:2021:010 (unpublished).

78 In March 2024, the Regional Court for Civil Matters of Vienna (*Landesgericht für Zivilrechtssachen Wien*) submitted a preliminary reference on the interpretation of the EAPO's periculum in mora, which reads as follows (C-198/24, *Green Limited*): 'Is Article 7(1) of Regulation (EU) No 655/2014 of the European Parliament and of the Council of 15 May 2014 establishing a European Account Preservation Order procedure to facilitate cross-border debt recovery in civil and commercial matters (OJ 2014 L 189, p. 59) to be interpreted as meaning that action taken by the debtor three years or more previously and/or obstacles to enforcement of the judgment in the Member State of the debtor are not to be taken into account?'.

creditors to prove that the debtor has adopted specific actions intended to frustrate the future enforcement of the claim.[79]

#31 Creditors with a non-enforceable title are also required to prove that there is a ***fumus boni iuris*** which means that they 'submit sufficient evidence to satisfy the court that he is likely to succeed on the substance of his claim against the debtor'.[80]

#32 Both the *periculum in mora* and *fumus boni iuris* have to be proven by the creditor. Concerning the means of **evidence** that can be used, the EAPO Regulation seems to favour the use of documentary evidence.[81] Nonetheless, it is also possible to 'use any other appropriate method of taking evidence available under its national law, such as an oral hearing of the creditor' as long as 'this does not delay the proceedings unduly'.[82]

#33 The provision of a **security** is the third of the prerequisites that creditors might have to satisfy.[83] In principle, creditors without an enforceable title are required to provide the security,[84] while creditors with one are exempt from it.[85] Nonetheless, there are exceptions for both cases. Attending to the circumstances of the case, courts can exempt creditors without an enforceable title from the security but also require creditors with an enforceable title to provide it.[86] For instance. if a creditor without an enforceable title lacks sufficient resources to provide the security, courts can take this into consideration to exempt the security.[87]

---

79 Against this general trend of interpreting the *periculum in mora* in light of the Preamble that national case law shows, Spanish courts appear to follow a more lenient approach. For instance, the Provincial Court of Cuenca (Audiencia Provincial de Cuenca) considered sufficient the existence of an enforceable title against the debtor to justify the *periculum in mora* (Audiencia Provincial de Cuenca, 13.06.2023, N° de Recurso: 72/2023, N° de Resolución: 54/2023, ECLI:ES:APCU:2023:56A). Such approach was also followed by the Provincial Court of Alicante (Audiencia Provincial de Alicante) (Audiencia Provincial de Alicante, 06.03.2023, N° de Recurso: 462/2022, N° de Resolución: 58/2023, ECLI:ES:APA:2023:198A).

80 Article 7(2) EAPO Regulation.

81 N Harbeck, 'Art. 7 EuKoPf VO' in J Kindl and C Meller-Hannich (eds), *Gesamtes Recht der Zwangsvollstreckung* (4th edn, Nomos 2021), margin no. 16. In Lithuania, the District Court of Utena (Utenos apylinkės teismas) rejected an EAPO application precisely because the creditor did not submit any evidence to sustain the facts invoked to justify the *periculum in mora*: Utenos apylinkės teismas, 22.01.2019, byla e2VP-216–477/2019.

82 Article 9(2) EAPO Regulation.

83 Article 12 EAPO Regulation.

84 Article 12(1) EAPO Regulation.

85 Article 12(2) EAPO Regulation.

86 Article 12(1)(2) EAPO Regulation.

87 Recital 18 EAPO Regulation.

#34 The form in which the security can be provided depends on the national law of Member States.[88] The Preamble though suggests different security forms that could be used such as a bank guarantee or a deposit in cash.[89]

#35 According to Article 12, courts are required to observe two criteria when calculating the amount of the security. First, the **amount** should be sufficient to dissuade creditors from abusing the EAPO procedure.[90] Secondly, the amount should serve to cover the potential **damages** that the EAPO might cause to the creditor.[91] For this, the court needs to take into consideration the applicable law to the creditor's liability.

#36 In this regard, Article 13 of the EAPO Regulation partially addresses the **creditors' liability**. On the one hand, it establishes some minimum uniform standards concerning the creditors' liability, such as fault based-liability standard.[92] On the other hand, it contains a conflict of law rule to determine which is the applicable law to the creditors' liability.[93] The Preamble indicates that the amount of the claim be used as a subsidiary 'guideline' to calculate the amount of the security 'in the absence of specific evidence as to the amount of the potential damage'.[94] In practice national courts seem often to rely on the amount of the claim as a term of reference to establish the amount of the security.[95] The amount of the security corresponds to a percentage of the amount of the claim.[96]

---

88 Article 12 EAPO Regulation.

89 In Portugal, a court accepted industrial factory machinery as a valid security to grant an EAPO: Tribunal da Relação de Guimarães, 20.05.2021, Acórdão no processo no. 3870/20.2T8GMR-A.G1.

90 D Wiedemann, 'Artikel 12 EU-Kpf VO' in T Rauscher (ed), *Europäisches Zivilprozess- und Kollisionsrecht* (5th edn, Otto Schmidt 2022), para 10.

91 N Harbeck, 'Art. 12 EuKoPf VO' in J Kindl and C Meller-Hannich (eds), *Gesamtes Recht der Zwangsvollstreckung* (4th edn, Nomos 2021), margin no. 9.

92 Article 13(1)(2) EAPO Regulation.

93 Article 13(4) EAPO Regulation.

94 Recital 18 EAPO Regulation.

95 This is something that some scholars already expected that it would occur: M Mann-Kommenda, 'Artikle 7 EuKoPf VO' in A Geroldinger and N Wallner-Friedl (eds), *IZVR Praxiskommentar Internationales Zivilverfahrensrech*t (LexisNexis 2021), para 13; P Peiteado Mariscal, 'Article 12' in E D'Alessandro and F Gascón Inchausti (eds), *The European Account Preservation Order. A Commentary on Regulation (EU) No 655/2014* (Edward Elgar 2022) 118, para 12.08.

96 For instance, in The Netherlands, the amount of the security often ranges between 10% and 30% of the amount of the claim: C van der Plas and D Beunk, 'Het Europees bankbeslag in de Nederlandse praktijk' [2018] Tijdschrift Financiering, Zekerheden en Insolventierechtpraktijk 30. In Austria, the High Regional Court of Innsbruck (*Oberlandesgericht Innsbruck*) used a 25 % of the amount of the claim: Oberlandesgericht Innsbruck, 07.05.2019, 10 R 25/19f, ECLI:AT:OLG0819:2019:01000R00025.19F.0507.000.

2 Formal Prerequisites

#37 Concerning the formal prerequisites, creditors are required to provide certain information concerning the case in the EAPO application. All this information is listed in Article 8. This includes information such as the name and contact details of the debtors;[97] or the identification of the bank accounts.[98] Bank accounts could be identified relying on the **IBAN**, the **BIC**, or the name and address of the bank.[99]

#38 The EAPO application has to be submitted relying on a pre-established standard form that can be found in the EAPO Commission Implementing Regulation.[100] The e-Justice portal allows to fill-in this standard form online.[101] Concerning the means of submission of the standard form to the competent court; to the present day this is a matter that depends on the national law of each Member State.[102] Nonetheless, **Regulation (EU) 2023/2844** on the digitalisation of judicial cooperation and access to justice in cross-border civil, commercial and criminal matters foresees that it will be possible to submit the EAPO application through the future European electronic access point, once this is established.[103] The European electronic access point is a portal which is accessible to natural and legal persons or their representatives, throughout the Union, and is connected to an interoperable access point in the context of the decentralised IT system.[104] The **European electronic access point** will be established in the e-Justice portal.[105]

III The EAPO's Information Mechanism

#39 It often occurs that creditors ignore the specific details of the debtor's bank accounts. They might just have mere suspicion that debtors have bank accounts.

97 Article 8(2)(c) EAPO Regulation.
98 Article 8(2)(d) EAPO Regulation.
99 Article 8(2)(d) EAPO Regulation.
100 Annex I Commission Implementing Regulation (EU) 2016/1823 of 10 October 2016 establishing the forms referred to in Regulation (EU) No 655/2014 of the European Parliament and of the Council establishing a European Account Preservation Order procedure to facilitate cross-border debt recovery in civil and commercial matters, C/2016/6339 [2016] OJ L283/1.
101 <https://e-justice.europa.eu/378/EN/european_account_preservation_order_forms?clang=en> accessed on 15 December 2024.
102 Article 8(4) EAPO Regulation.
103 Article 22 Regulation (EU) 2023/2844 of the European Parliament and of the Council of 13 December 2023 on the digitalisation of judicial cooperation and access to justice in cross-border civil, commercial and criminal matters, and amending certain acts in the field of judicial cooperation, PE/50/2023/REV/1 [2023] OJ L2023/2844, 27.12.2023 ('Regulation on digitalisation of judicial cooperation').
104 Article 2(4) Regulation on digitalisation of judicial cooperation.
105 Article 4(1) Regulation on digitalisation of judicial cooperation.

For such kind of situations, the EAPO Regulation provides a specific tool to discover the debtors' bank accounts. Along with the specific procedure of the Maintenance Regulation to trace the debtors' assets,[106] the **EAPO's information mechanism** is the other sole available procedure at the EU level to search for the debtors' bank accounts.

#40 The EAPO information mechanism is only available to creditors with a title,[107] though the title does not have to be enforceable.[108] These creditors have to submit the request for information within the same EAPO application.[109] They are required to indicate the reasons why they believe the debtor might have bank accounts in a specific Member State or States.[110] For creditors who have a non-enforceable title, there is an additional prerequisite. They need to probe that not obtaining the information about the bank accounts might frustrate the enforcement of the claim.[111] They also need to show that the amount of the claim is substantial attending to the circumstances of the case and that the non-recovery of the claim might 'lead to a substantial deterioration of the creditor's financial situation'.[112]

#41 Besides the referred specific requirements, access to the information mechanism is also conditioned to satisfying the general material prerequisites to obtain an EAPO, such as proving the *periculum in mora* or the provision of a security.[113]

#42 When all the conditions to access the information mechanism are duly fulfilled, the court will send the request to an **information authority** in the Member State where the bank accounts are suspected to exist. Information authorities are na-

---

106 Article 61(2)(c)(d) Council Regulation (EC) No 4/2009 of 18 December 2008 on jurisdiction, applicable law, recognition and enforcement of decisions and cooperation in matters relating to maintenance obligations [2009] OJ L7/1.

107 Article 14(1) EAPO Regulation.

108 Under the EAPO Commission Proposal, the information mechanism was available to all creditors, no matter if they had a title or not: Article 17 EAPO COM/2011/0445 final. During the *travaux préparatoires* of the EAPO Regulation, the French delegation defended restraining access to the EAPO's information mechanism to creditors with an enforceable title: Comments on Chapters I, II and III from the French delegation, 13260/11 JUSTCIV 205 CODEC 1280, 13140/12 ADD 13.

109 Article 8(2)(f) EAPO Regulation. K Hilbig-Lugani, 'Art. 14 EuKoPf VO' in T Rauscher and W Krüger (eds), *Münchener Kommentar zur Zivilprozessordnung. Band 3* (6th edn, CH Beck 2022), margin no. 2.

110 Article 14(2) EAPO Regulation. The Preamble offers two examples of grounds that serve to justify the search for the bank accounts in a Member State which are that 'the debtor works or exercises a professional activity in that Member State or has property there' (Recital 20).

111 Article 14(1) EAPO Regulation. While this prerequisite might resemble Article 7(1)'s *periculum in mora* that any creditor needs to satisfy to obtain an EAPO, they should not be confounded. They are two different prerequisites, one serves to obtain an EAPO and the other to access the EAPO's information mechanism: Cuniberti and Migliorini (n 31) 178.

112 Article 14(1) EAPO Regulation.

113 Article 14(3) EAPO Regulation.

tionally appointed bodies responsible for searching and providing information about the bank accounts.[114] For instance, in Germany, the role of information authority corresponds to the Federal Office of Justice (*Bundesamt für Justiz*).[115] The method to obtain information about the debtors' bank accounts is left to the discretion of the Member States as long as it is 'effective and efficient' and 'not disproportionately costly or time-consuming'.[116]

#43 There is no deadline for the information authorities to provide an answer to the court which requested to search for the bank accounts, though information authorities have to 'act expeditiously'.[117] Even if no bank accounts are found, information authorities will have to provide the requesting court with an answer.[118] Information authorities can require the payment of a fee for the costs they might incur while searching for the bank accounts.[119]

IV Jurisdiction to Grant the EAPO

#44 The rules to determine which is the court with jurisdiction to grant the EAPO vary depending on whether creditors have or do not have an enforceable title.[120] When creditors do not have an enforceable title, jurisdiction lies on the courts of the Member State with jurisdiction as to the substance of the matter.[121] This could be determined by observing the **rules on jurisdiction** contained in other EU instruments such as the Brussels I bis Regulation or the Maintenance Regulation, but also in light of national rules of jurisdiction[122] or international conventions with rules to determine jurisdiction.[123] It should be also noted that the EAPO Regulation does not require that the court which issues the EAPO coincides with the Member State where the proceedings as to the substance of the matter are effectively conducted.[124]

114 Article 4(13) EAPO Regulation.
115 Section 948(2) German Code of Civil Procedure (*Zivilprozessordnung*).
116 Article 14(5)(d) EAPO Regulation.
117 Article 14(5) EAPO Regulation.
118 Article 14(7) EAPO Regulation.
119 Article 44 EAPO Regulation.
120 Article 6 EAPO Regulation.
121 Article 6(1) EAPO Regulation.
122 For instance, in a case in Slovakia, the court relied on the Slovakian domestic rules on jurisdiction to determine whether it had to jurisdiction to grant the EAPO: Okresný súd Žilina, 13.08.2020, 50Cb/38/2020, ECLI:SK:OSZA:2020:5120208691.1, para 2.
123 P Franzina, 'Article 6' in E D'Alessandro and F Gascón Inchausti (eds), *The European Account Preservation Order. A Commentary on Regulation (EU) No 655/2014* (Edward Elgar 2022) 69, para 6.08.
124 For instance, in a case AP de Valencia (Sección 6ª), Auto núm. 192/2018 de 9 julio. JUR 2018\249114, ECLI:ES:APV:2018:2434A.

#45 If creditors do not have an enforceable title and the debtor is a consumer, then jurisdiction lies on the courts of the Member State where the consumer is domiciled.[125] This special jurisdictional fora for **consumers** applies to both passive and active consumers.[126] This means that it also applies when the trader with whom the consumer entered in the contractual relationship does not pursue or direct their professional or business activities in the Member State where the consumer is domiciled.[127]

#46 For those cases when creditors have already obtained an enforceable title, jurisdiction lies on the courts where the title used to obtain the EAPO has been obtained.[128]

#47 The EAPO Regulation expressly bars the possibility of requesting more than one EAPO 'against the same debtor aimed at securing the same claim'.[129] In case the claimant applies for an EAPO along with an equivalent domestic provisional attachment order, it has to inform the court which renders the EAPO about it.[130]

#48 The venue of the court that grants the EAPO is determined in light of the national civil procedural law of the Member States.[131] For example, in Finland, there is one single court that can issue EAPOs: the District Court of Helsinki.[132] An identical solution was adopted in Czechia, where the District Court of Prague 1 (*Obvodní soud pro Prahu 1*), has exclusive jurisdiction in this Member State to decide on EAPO applications.[133]

V Decision on the EAPO Application

#49 Once the court receives the EAPO application, it has to render the decision within a certain deadline. The deadline varies depending on whether the creditor applied for the EAPO with or without an enforceable title. For EAPO applications with an enforceable title, the deadline to render the decision is five working

125 Article 6(2) EAPO Regulation.
126 Franzina (n 123) para 6.19.
127 Article 17(1)(c) Brussels I bis Regulation.
128 Article 6(3)(4) EAPO Regulation.
129 Article 16(1) EAPO Regulation.
130 Article 16(2)(3) EAPO Regulation.
131 P Franzina, 'Article 6' in Elena D'Alessandro and Fernando Gascón Inchausti (eds), *The European Account Preservation Order. A Commentary on Regulation (EU) No 655/2014* (Edward Elgar 2022) 69, para 6.08.
132 Section 2 Act on the European Account Preservation Order Procedure (*Laki 17/2017 eurooppalaisesta tilivarojen turvaamismääräysmenettelystä*).
133 Section 37(13) Czech Act 6/2002 on Courts and Judges (*Zákon č. 6/2002 o soudech a soudcích*).

days.[134] When there is no enforceable title, then the deadline is ten working days.[135] If the application for the EAPO includes an information request, the decision on the EAPO is made immediately after the answer from the information authority is received[136]

#50 The court's **decision on the EAPO application** is adopted ***ex parte***.[137] The debtor is only informed once the EAPO has been effectively enforced. This prevents creditors from withdrawing the funds from their bank accounts before the EAPO is enforced.[138] The fact that the EAPO is granted *ex parte* and can circulate from one Member State to another without the debtor being informed is one of the main innovations brought by the EAPO Regulation to the field of judicial cooperation in civil matters within the EU.[139] As explained in the part of this chapter dedicated to the Brussels I bis Regulation, this instrument only allows the recognition and enforcement of *inaudita altera parte* provisional measures when the decision granting the provisional measure is served on the defendant before seeking its enforcement abroad.[140]

#51 If the court grants the EAPO, the decision will be adopted relying on a pre-established standard form which has two parts: A and B. Part A addresses banks, debtors, and creditors, while Part B is destined just for creditors and debtors.[141]

#52 If the court rejects the EAPO application, even partially (eg the EAPO is granted for a lesser amount than the creditor asked for), creditors have the possibility of lodging an appeal against this decision.[142] The EAPO Regulation establishes a 21 working days deadline to submit the request for the appeal.[143]

VI Enforcement and Implementation of the EAPO

#53 Once the EAPO is granted it has to be sent to the competent **enforcement authority** Member State where the banks accounts are found, in case it is not the Member State where the EAPO had been granted. The EAPO is automatically recognised and it can be enforced in other Member State without a declaration of

134 Article 18(2) EAPO Regulation.
135 Article 18(1) EAPO Regulation.
136 Article 18(5) EAPO Regulation.
137 Article 11 EAPO Regulation.
138 The so-called surprised effect of the *inaudita altera parte* provisional measures.
139 F Gascón Inchausti, 'Article 11' in E D'Alessandro and F Gascón Inchausti (eds), *The European Account Preservation Order. A Commentary on Regulation (EU) No 655/2014* (Edward Elgar 2022) 112, paras 11.05–11.06.
140 See above in text #24.
141 Article 19(1) EAPO Regulation.
142 Article 21 EAPO Regulation.
143 Article 21 EAPO Regulation.

enforceability granted in the Member State of enforcement.[144] In this regard, the EAPO Regulation aligns with other EU civil procedural instruments which have abolished the exequatur such as the Brussels I bis Regulation.[145]

#54 The enforcement procedure significantly relies on the national law of the Member State of enforcement.[146] The EAPO Regulation only provides some uniform standards concerning the enforcement. The most relevant one of these uniform aspects is the implementation of the EAPO by the bank. Once the bank is served with the EAPO by the enforcement authority, it has to implement it.[147] The implementation consists of the adoption of the necessary measures that will prevent the funds from being withdrawn from the accounts. Once the EAPO is implemented, the bank needs to issue a declaration relying on a pre-establishing standard form indicating that the amount of the funds that have been attached[148] The EAPO sets a rather short deadline to issue such declaration: three working days since the date the EAPO is implemented but in extraordinary circumstances, the declaration can be issued no later than the eighth working day.[149] Both the court which issued the EAPO and the creditor have to receive the **declaration on the attachment of the funds**.[150]

#55 The EAPO Regulation enables that certain amounts of funds may be exempted from attachment. This depends on the law of the Member State of enforcement.[151] Those exempted amounts can serve, for instance, 'to ensure the livelihood of the debtor and his family'.[152]

VII Service to the Debtor

#56 After the enforcement of the EAPO, debtors have to be informed about the attachment of their bank accounts. This is a fundamental step considering that EAPO is granted *inaudita altera parte*. Debtors can only contest the EAPO as long as they

144 Article 22 EAPO Regulation.
145 Eg Article 39 Brussels I bis Regulation.
146 Article 23(1) EAPO Regulation.
147 Article 24 EAPO Regulation.
148 Article 25 EAPO Regulation. The pre-established standard form can be found in Annex IV of the EAPO Commission Implementation Regulation.
149 Article 25(1) EAPO Regulation.
150 Article 25(2)(3) EAPO Regulation.
151 Relying on the law of the Member State of enforcement has been criticised by some authors who consider that such law does not take into consideration the vital needs of the debtor: Cuniberti and Migliorini (n 31) 272–273; ML Villamarín López, 'Article 31' in E D'Alessandro and F Gascón Inchausti (eds), *The European Account Preservation Order. A Commentary on Regulation (EU) No 655/2014* (Edward Elgar 2022) 286, para 31.01.
152 Recital 36 EAPO Regulation.

are duly informed about it. The EAPO Regulation contains certain rules concerning the documents that have to be served on the debtor, the language in which those documents have to be served, and the **means of service**. Debtors need to be served with the EAPO application as well as standard forms containing the decision EAPO application, both parts A and B.[153] All other documents submitted by the creditor in the EAPO application need to be served too.[154] They also have to be served the bank declaration indicating the funds that have been attached.[155]

#57 Concerning the language in which the documents have to be served, the decision issuing the EAPO and the EAPO application have to be translated into an official language of the Member State where the debtor is domiciled or a language that the debtor understands.[156] The court can require the translation of other documents accompanying the EAPO application if it considers this necessary.[157]

#58 The rules of service of the documents vary depending on the place where the debtor's domicile is located.[158] For instance, when the debtor's domicile is located in the Member State of origin, then the documents have to be served according to the national law of that Member State.[159] If debtors are domiciled in the Member State of enforcement, the service is done based on the national law of the Member State of enforcement.[160] It might occur that debtors are domiciled in a Member State which is not the issuing Member State nor the Member State of enforcement. In such a scenario, documents have to be sent to the competent authorities in the Member State where the debtor is domiciled, and the documents will be

153 Article 28(5)(a) EAPO Regulation.

154 Article 28(5)(b) EAPO Regulation.

155 Article 28(5)(c) EAPO Regulation.

156 Article 49(1) EAPO Regulation. The Preamble of the 2020 Service Regulation offers some examples of circumstances that can be used to determine that the recipient of a document can understand a language: 'when assessing the language skills of the addressee, the court or authority could take into account factual elements, for example documents written by the addressee in the language concerned, whether the addressee's profession involves particular language skills, whether the addressee is a citizen of the forum Member State or whether the addressee previously resided in that Member State for an extended period of time' (Recital 26 Regulation (EU) 2020/1784 of the European Parliament and of the Council of 25 November 2020 on the service in the Member States of judicial and extrajudicial documents in civil or commercial matters (service of documents) (recast) [2020] OJ L405/40). For instance, a Lithuanian found that a debtor domiciled in Germany could be served the documents in Lithuanian because he was a Lithuanian citizen and had lived in Lithuania. Because of that, the court considered that the debtor could understand Lithuanian: Klaipėdos apygardos teismas, 03.10.2019, byla e2S-1330–524/2019.

157 Article 49(1) EAPO Regulation.

158 K Hilbig-Lugani, 'Art. 28 EuKoPf VO' in T Rauscher and W Krüger (eds), *Münchener Kommentar zur Zivilprozessordnung. Band 3* (6th edn, CH Beck 2022), margin no. 2

159 Article 28(2) EAPO Regulation.

160 Article 28(3) EAPO Regulation.

served to the defendant according to the laws of that Member State.[161] The debtor's domicile can be located in a third State.[162] In those cases the service of the documents have to be done according to the applicable rules for the international service of documents of the Member State.[163]

VIII Debtor's remedies against the EAPO

#59 To compensate for the *ex parte* character of the EAPO, debtors are provided with a set of **remedies** to contest the EAPO or its enforcement. Debtors have the possibility of requesting the modification or revocation of the EAPO in the Member State of origin under a limited of grounds.[164] One of these grounds is that the prerequisites to grant an EAPO were not duly satisfied,[165] for instance, if the court did not jurisdiction to grant the EAPO,[166] or the *periculum in mora* had not been properly established.[167] Claimants could apply for the termination or limitation of the enforcement also under a limited number of grounds.[168] One of this grounds is the violation of public policy of the Member State of enforcement.[169] The EAPO Regulation sets some uniform standards concerning the proceeding to request the revocation of the EAPO or the termination of the enforcement, though those proceedings largely depend on the national procedural law of the Member States.[170] One of the procedural aspects addressed in the EAPO Regulation is the right to appeal against the decision on the request to revoke the EAPO or terminate its enforcement.[171] Both creditors and debtors are entitled to appeal those decisions. However, the way the appeal procedure is articulated depends largely on the national law of the Member State where the appeal procedure is lodged.

#60 Debtors also have the possibility of requesting to replace the funds attached by the EAPO with an **alternative security**.[172] They can do so in the Member State of

161 Article 28(3) EAPO Regulation.

162 See above in text #23.

163 Article 28(4) EAPO Regulation.

164 Article 33 EAPO Regulation.

165 Article 33(1)(a) EAPO Regulation.

166 Tribunal d'arrondissement de et à Luxembourg, 10 May 2024, No. Rôle: TAL-2024-02103, No. 2024TALREFO/00211.

167 The Netherlands: Rechtbank Gelderland, 21.01.2022,C/05/398652 / KGZA 22–7, ECLI:NL:RBGEL:2022:402. Poland: Sąd Okręgowy w Łodzi, 12.08.2021, Sygn. akt X Gz 108/21 (unpublished). Portugal: Tribunal da Relação de Guimarães, 20.05.2021, Acórdão no processo no. 3870/20.2T8GMR-A.G1.

168 Article 34 EAPO Regulation.

169 Article 34(2) EAPO Regulation.

170 Articles 36 and 37 EAPO Regulation.

171 Article 37 EAPO Regulation.

172 Article 38 EAPO Regulation.

origin or the Member State of enforcement.[173] Concerning the amount or value of the alternative security, this depends on the Member State where the security is provided.[174] If the alternative security is provided in the Member State of enforcement, the value of the alternative security has to be equal to the funds attached in that Member State.[175] Conversely, if the alternative security is provided in the Member State of origin, the value or amount of the alternative security has to equivalent to total amount of the funds attached by the EAPO.[176] The form in which the alternative security can be established depends on the national law of the Member State where the security is provided.[177]

References

Ancel M-E and Gaudemet-Tallon H, *Compétence et exécution des jugements en Europe* (LGDJ 2018) 482.

Brosch M and Leon Kahl LM, 'Article 25' in M Requejo Isidro (ed), *Brussels I Bis. A Commentary on Regulation (EU) No 1215/2012* (Edward Elgar 2022) 344.

Calvo Caravaca AL and Carrascosa González J, 'Medidas Cautelares y el Reglamento Bruselas I-Bis' (2015) 51 Rivista di diritto internazionale privato e processuale 55.

Cuniberti G and Migliorini S, *The European Account Preservation Order Regulation: A Commentary* (Cambridge 2018).

Drooghenbroeck van J-F and De Boe C, 'Les mesures provisoires et conservatoires dans le règlement. Bruxelles I Bis' in E Guinchard (ed), *Le nouveau Règlement Bruxelles I bis. Règlement n°1215/2012 du 12 décembre 2012 concernant la compétence judiciaire, la reconnaissance et l'exécution des décisions en matière civile et commerciale* (Bruylant 2014) 167.

Fentiman RG, 'Art. 29 Brussels I bis' in U Magnus and P Mankowski (eds), *Brussels Ibis Regulation – Commentary* (2nd edn 2023, Otto Schmidt).

Franzina P, 'Article 6' in E D'Alessandro and F Gascón Inchausti (eds*), The European Account Preservation Order. A Commentary on Regulation (EU) No 655/2014* (Edward Elgar 2022) 69.

Gaier R, 'Art. 32 Brüssel Ia-VO' in Volkert Vorwerk and Christian Wolf (eds), *BeckOK ZPO* (CH Beck 2024).

Garber T, 'Art. 35 Brussels I bis' in U Magnus and P Mankowski (eds), *Brussels Ibis Regulation – Commentary* (2nd edn, Otto Schmidt 2023).

Garcimartín Alférez F, 'Provisional and Protective Measures in the Brussels I Regulation Recast' (2014/2015) 16 Yearbook of Private International Law 57.

Gascón Inchausti F, 'Article 11' in E D'Alessandro and F Gascón Inchausti (eds), *The European Account Preservation Order. A Commentary on Regulation (EU) No 655/2014* (Edward Elgar 2022) 112.

173 Article 38(1) EAPO Regulation.

174 M Klöpfer, 'Art. 38 Verordnung (EU) Nr 655/2014' in R Geimer and RA Schütze (eds), *Internationaler Rechtsverkehr in Zivil- und Handelssachen* (CH Beck 2016), margin no. 2.

175 K Hilbig-Lugani, 'Art. 38 EuKoPf VO' in T Rauscher and W Krüger (eds), *Münchener Kommentar zur Zivilprozessordnung. Band 3* (6th edn, CH Beck 2022), margin no. 2.

176 D Wiedemann, 'Artikel 38 EU-Kpf VO' in T Rauscher (ed), *Europäisches Zivilprozess- und Kollisionsrecht* (5th edn, Otto Schmidt 2022), margin no. 3.

177 Article 38(1) EAPO Regulation. In this regard, Recital 35 of the Preamble provides three examples of the forms in which the security can be provided: 'a deposit in cash, a bank guarantee, and a mortgage'.

Harbeck N, 'Art. 7 EuKoPf VO' in J Kindl and C Meller-Hannich (eds), *Gesamtes Recht der Zwangsvollstreckung* (4th edn, Nomos 2021).

Hess B and others, 'The Reform of the Brussels Ibis Regulation – Academic Position Paper' (2024) Vienna Research Paper <https://ssrn.com/abstract=4853421> accessed 30 December 2024.

Hilbig-Lugani K, 'Art. 1 EuKoPf VO' in T Rauscher and W Krüger (eds), *Münchener Kommentar zur Zivilprozessordnung. Band 3* (6th edn, CH Beck 2022).

—— 'Art. 14 EuKoPf VO' in T Rauscher and W Krüger (eds), *Münchener Kommentar zur Zivilprozessordnung. Band 3* (6th edn, CH Beck 2022).

—— 'Art. 28 EuKoPf VO' in T Rauscher and W Krüger (eds), *Münchener Kommentar zur Zivilprozessordnung. Band 3* (6th edn, CH Beck 2022).

—— 'Art. 38 EuKoPf VO' in T Rauscher and W Krüger (eds), *Münchener Kommentar zur Zivilprozessordnung. Band 3* (6th edn, CH Beck 2022).

—— 'Art. 5 EuKoPf VO' in T Rauscher and W Krüger (eds), *Münchener Kommentar zur Zivilprozessordnung. Band 3* (6th edn, CH Beck 2022).

—— 'Artikel 7 EuKoPfVO' in T Rauscher and W Krüger (eds), *Münchener Kommentar zur Zivilprozessordnung. Band 3* (6th edn, CH Beck 2022).

Kessedjian C, 'Note on Provisional and Protective Measures in Private International Law and Comparative Law' (Hague Conference on Private International Law, October 1998).

Klöpfer M, 'Art. 38 Verordnung (EU) Nr 655/2014' in R Geimer and RA Schütze (eds), *Internationaler Rechtsverkehr in Zivil- und Handelssachen* (CH Beck 2016).

Kramer X, 'Case C-80/00, Italian Leather SpA v. WECO Polstermöbel GmbH & Co., European Court of Justice, 6 June 2002' (2003) 40 Common Market Law Review 953.

Magnus U, 'Art. 25 Brussels I bis' in U Magnus and P Mankowski (eds*), Brussels Ibis Regulation – Commentary* (2nd edn, Otto Schmidt 2023).

Mann-Kommenda M, 'Artikle 7 EuKoPf VO' in A Geroldinger and N Wallner-Friedl (eds), *IZVR Praxiskommentar Internationales Zivilverfahrensrech*t (LexisNexis 2021).

Nils Harbeck N, 'Art. 12 EuKoPf VO' in J Kindl and C Meller-Hannich (eds), *Gesamtes Recht der Zwangsvollstreckung* (4th edn, Nomos 2021).

Nioche M, *La décision provisoire en droit international privé européen: Qualification et régime en matière civile et commerciale* (Bruylant 2012), para 407.

Peiteado Mariscal P, 'Article 12' in E D'Alessandro and F Gascón Inchausti (eds), *The European Account Preservation Order. A Commentary on Regulation (EU) No 655/2014* (Edward Elgar 2022) 118.

Plas van der C and Beunk D, 'Het Europees bankbeslag in de Nederlandse praktijk' [2018] Tijdschrift Financiering, Zekerheden en Insolventierechtpraktijk 30.

Pretelli I, 'Chapter 5. Provisional and Protective Measures in the European Civil Procedure of the Brussels I System' in V Lazić and S Stuij (eds), *Brussels Ibis Regulation, Short Studies in Private International Law* (Springer 2017) 97.

Rogerson P and Mankowski P, 'Art. 1 Brussels I bis' in U Magnus and P Mankowski (eds), *Brussels Ibis Regulation – Commentary* (2nd edn, Otto Schmidt 2023).

Santaló Goris C, 'The Boundaries of Arbitration Exclusion in the EAPO Regulation' (EIPA Blog, May 2023) < https://www.eipa.eu/publications/briefing/the-boundaries-of-arbitration-exclusion-eapo-regulation/> accessed on 30 December 2024.

Villamarín López ML, 'Article 31' in E D'Alessandro and F Gascón Inchausti (eds), *The European Account Preservation Order. A Commentary on Regulation (EU) No 655/2014* (Edward Elgar 2022) 286.

—— 'Harmonisation of the Rules on Protective Measures? The European Account Preservation Order' in F Gascón Inchausti and B Hess (eds), *The Future of the European Law of Civil Procedure. Coordination or Harmonisation?* (Intersentia 2020) 111.

Walasik M, 'Article 3' in E D'Alessandro and F Gascón Inchausti (eds), *The European Account Preservation Order. A Commentary on Regulation (EU) No 655/2014* (Edward Elgar 2022) 35.

Wiedemann D, 'Artikel 12 EU-Kpf VO' in T Rauscher (ed), *Europäisches Zivilprozess- und Kollisionsrecht* (5th edn, Otto Schmidt 2022).
—— 'Artikel 3 EU-Kpf VO' in T Rauscher (ed), *Europäisches Zivilprozess- und Kollisionsrecht* (5th edn, Otto Schmidt 2022).
—— 'Artikel 38 EU-Kpf VO' in T Rauscher (ed), *Europäisches Zivilprozess- und Kollisionsrecht* (5th edn, Otto Schmidt 2022).
—— 'Artikel 5 EU-Kpf VO' in T Rauscher (ed), *Europäisches Zivilprozess- und Kollisionsrecht* (5th edn, Otto Schmidt 2022).

Vesna Lazić

Chapter 18
Insolvency Proceedings

A Introduction and Historical Background

#1 Private international law aspects of insolvency are unified at the EU level in the **Insolvency Regulation** of 2015 (EIR).[1] Its predecessor, Insolvency Regulation of 2000 (EIR 2000),[2] is the result of long-running negotiations within the European Economic Community and later within the European Community. The idea was that a unification of rules on cross-border insolvency would strengthen the legal protection of persons established in the Community.[3]

#2 Already at the first meeting of a Committee of Experts convened in 1960 it was decided to separate bankruptcy, compositions and analogous proceedings from the general convention on the recognition and the enforcement of judgments in civil and commercial matters. The work resulted in the 1995 Convention on Insolvency Proceedings and was accompanied by the Virgós-Schmit Report.[4] It never came into force, however, because ratification by all Member States was required and the UK ratification was missing. Nevertheless, the Convention was enacted as Regulation EIR 2000 when the Treaty of Amsterdam introduced the competence of the European Community to endorse legislation having a direct effect in the Member States without an implementation process. It became applicable on 31 May 2002 in all Member States except Demark. Compared to the text of the 1995 Convention, no substantial changes were made in EIR 2000. Consequently, the Virgós-Schmit Report remains an important source with regard to interpreting EIR and EIR 2000.

#3 According to a report on the application of EIR 2000 adopted by the Commission in 2012, although the Regulation generally was functioning well, it appeared desirable to improve the application of a number of its provisions 'in order to enhance the effective administration of cross-border insolvency proceedings' and conse-

1 Regulation (EU) 2015/848 of the European Parliament and of the Council of 20 May 2015 on insolvency proceedings [2015] OJ L141/19 (hereinafter: EIR).

2 Council Regulation (EC) No 1346/2000 of 29 May 2000 on insolvency proceedings [2020] OJ L160/1 (hereinafter: EIR 2000).

3 J Noël and J Lemontey, *Report on the Convention Relating to Bankruptcies, Compositions and Analogous Procedures* (Commission of the European Communities Working Document 16.775/XIV/70-F 1970); On the background of the Convention, see 6–9.

4 M Virgós and E Schmit, *Report on the Convention on Insolvency Proceedings* (EU Council of the EU Document 6500/96 1996) 7, para 3 (hereinafter: Virgós- Schmit Report).

Vesna Lazić, Utrecht University and Asser Institute, email: v.lazic@uu.nl

https://doi.org/10.1515/9783110781632-018

quently to recast in the interest of clarity'.[5] The EIR almost doubles the number of provisions, yet follows a structure similar to that of its predecessor. It contains provisions regarding the most important issues of international insolvency law, including: 1) jurisdiction for opening insolvency proceedings; 2) conflict of law rules for issues relating to insolvency proceedings (Article 7) and for specific matters that are not governed by *lex concursus* (Articles 8–18); 3) provisions on the recognition and enforcement of decisions issued in such proceedings; 4) the establishment and interconnecting of insolvency registers; and 5) the coordination of insolvency proceedings that relate to the same debtor or to several members of the same group of companies. As is clarified in Recital (66), matters covered by the Regulation, uniform rules on conflict of laws replace – within their scope of application – national rules of private international law.[6] In contrast to its predecessor, EIR introduces a number of important amendments: namely, it spans a wider range of pre-bankruptcy proceedings aimed at preventing liquidation; clarifies the concept of 'COMI'; describes the secondary proceedings in greater detail and aligns the co-operation between the main and secondary proceedings; improves the publicity with regard to legal actions relating to insolvency; and enhances the co-operation between courts and insolvency practitioners. Last but not least, EIR introduces detailed rules relating to the insolvency of proceedings with respect to groups of companies.

#4 Only insolvency proceedings that fall within the **substantive, personal, territorial, and temporal scope** of the Regulation's application need to comply with the requirements of the jurisdiction and may benefit from their extraterritorial effects in other Member States. Other proceedings remain subjected to the national laws of the Member States, both in terms of jurisdiction and regarding recognition of the effects of foreign insolvency proceedings.

#5 In this Chapter, how the scope of application is defined in EIR is addressed first, with the emphasis being on the substantive scope. Thereafter, the rule on international jurisdiction to open insolvency proceedings and the extent of such jurisdic-

5 Recital (1) EIR.

6 Whilst the EU legislative action initially was confined to the unification of private international law, it later expanded towards the approximation of certain aspects of insolvency law. The first step in that respect was Directive (EU) 2019/1023 of the European Parliament and of the Council of 20 June 2019 on preventive restructuring frameworks, on discharge of debt and disqualifications, and on measures to increase the efficiency of procedures concerning restructuring, insolvency and discharge of debt, and amending Directive (EU) 2017/1132. The Directive harmonises the restructuring procedures for the purpose of enhancing the coherence between national insolvency laws and reducing the inefficiencies of national laws which hamper the timely reorganisation of viable businesses in financial difficulties. In addition, the Proposal for a Directive on the European Parliament and of the Council harmonising certain aspects of insolvency laws COM/2022/702 can finally be mentioned amongst further developments in harmonising certain aspects of insolvency laws.

tion are discussed. Within this context, the focus is on delineating the scope of application between the EIR and the Brussels I-bis Regulation.[7]

B Material (Substantive) Scope of Application *(ratione materiae)*

#6 In contrast to its predecessor, the Regulation both expands the substantive scope and provides a more detailed definition. Article 1(1) describes the proceedings that fall within the scope of the Regulation, whereas Article 1(2) sets out the list of excluded matters.

I Proceedings Within the Scope of the Regulation: Article 1 Paragraph 1

#7 Article 1(1) is significantly wider compared to the corresponding provision under EIR 2000.[8] In order to fall within the scope of the Regulation, the procedure must, on the one hand, be one of those described in paragraph 1 and, on the other hand, it must be listed in Annex A. Thus, both requirements must cumulatively be met. In practice, however, it is the listing in Annex I that is decisive – if a type of proceedings is not listed in Annex A, it may not be considered to fall within the substantive scope,[9] regardless of whether it meets the standards of Article 1(1).[10]

#8 It is expected that only those proceedings that comply with these requirements will be listed in Annex A. The EIR applies to insolvency proceedings as long as the procedure appears in Annex A, regardless of whether a debtor is a legal or a natural person, a professional, or an individual. There will be no further examination by the court of another Member State as to whether the national procedure in Annex A actually meets the criteria.[11]

---

7 Regulation (EU) No 1215/2012 of the European Parliament and of the Council of 12 December 2012 on jurisdiction and the recognition and enforcement of judgments in civil and commercial matters [2012] OJ L351/1 (hereinafter: Brussels I-bis Regulation). See also, P Franzina, Chapter 10.

8 A Bornemann, M Brinkmann and M Dahl (eds), *European Insolvency Regulation: A Commentary* (CH Beck/Hart/Nomos 2020) 27.

9 Recital (9). Even though this was not expressed explicitly in EIR 2000, the same approach was followed, see eg Case C-461/11, *Ulf Kazimierz Radziejewski v Kronofogdemyndigheten i StockholmUlf* (8 November 2012) ECLI:EU:C:2012:704.

10 See also R Bork and K van Zwieten, *Commentary on the European Insolvency Regulation* (2nd edn, OUP 2022) 53, para 1.03.

11 Recital (9).

#9 Article 1(1) provides general characteristics and features that insolvency procedures must have as well as a detailed description of the type of proceedings that fall within the scope of the Regulation (under (a)-(c)), which consequently may be listed in Annex A. In other words, it determines the criteria that a particular procedure must meet in order to qualify as an Annex A procedure.

#10 Basic features of the procedures falling within the scope are described as 'public collective proceedings, including interim proceedings, which are based on laws relating to insolvency', the purpose of which is '**rescue, adjustment of debt, reorganisation** or **liquidation**'. This wording is followed by a description of the types of arrangements for liquidation and/or reorganisation that may be provided under national law.

1 'Public' nature of the proceedings

#11 The meaning of 'public' is clarified in Recitals (12) and (13). Recital (12) refers to the requirement for the opening of the procedure to be made public so that creditors can be made aware of the proceedings and therefore be in a position to file their claims as well as to challenge the jurisdiction of the opening court. Moreover, the fact that the EIR requires recognition of the effectiveness of an insolvency proceeding in other Member States justifies the requirement of publicity.[12] The provisions of Articles 24 et seq. relating to the establishment and interconnection of registers facilitate publicity. Therefore, Article 24 requires Member States to establish public registers in which relevant information about the insolvency proceedings, including their opening, must be published, with the exception of procedures relating to individuals not exercising an independent business or professional activity.[13]

#12 Only proceedings that are 'public' are eligible to be included in Annex A. Indeed, the Member States may maintain confidential procedures,[14] but they are outside the scope of the Regulation. Recital (13) is explicit in that respect. The commencement of insolvency proceedings must be registered so that third parties, especially creditors, may find out about the opening of proceedings through an accessible public register.[15]

12 See also, Bork and van Zwieten (n 10) 63, para. 1.16.

13 Article 24(4).

14 See INSOL Europe, *Study on a New Approach to Business Failure and Insolvency: Comparative Legal Analysis of the Member States Relevant Provisions and Practices* (12 May 2014) 21–23.

15 Bornemann, Brinkmann and Dahl (n 8) 28, para 14.

2 Collective proceedings

#13 The 'collective' nature of the proceedings is another condition for eligibility to be considered as an Annex A procedure. The definition is provided in Article 2(1) as follows: '"collective proceedings" means proceedings which include all or a significant part of a debtor's creditors, provided that, in the latter case, the proceedings do not affect the claims of creditors which are not involved in them'.

#14 Recital (14) provides further clarification regarding the definition of '**collective proceedings**'. The wording 'all or a significant part of the creditors' is meant to denote creditors to whom a debtor owes all or a substantial proportion of his outstanding debts. In the case of proceedings aimed at restructuring or reorganising a business, it is not required that all the creditors be involved. Since such proceedings may concern only a certain class of creditors, the definition requires that the claims of non-participating creditors remain unaffected. In addition, it clarifies that proceedings which include only the financial creditors of a debtor are also within the scope of the Regulation. Recital (14) offers no further explanation with respect to this part of the definition. This presumably implies that the claims of non-participating creditors may not be adjusted in terms of the amount or the date they become due.[16]

#15 Nevertheless, in contrast to reorganisation proceedings which may involve only a certain class of creditors, all creditors should be included in proceedings which lead to a definitive cessation of the debtor's activities or to the liquidation of the debtor's assets. Moreover, the fact that some insolvency proceedings involving natural persons exclude specific categories of claims – such as maintenance claims – from the possibility of a debt discharge should not mean that such proceedings are not collective.

#16 Even though Recital (14) does not mention secured creditors, it is suggested in the literature that proceedings which include all unsecured creditors and leave secured creditors unaffected should be considered as being compliant with the requirement of encompassing 'all' creditors.[17]

---

16 However, some point to the possibility of 'indirectly' affecting such claims 'if the restructuring arrangement enjoys a privileged status vis à vis claw-back rules', JJ Castelló Pastor and F Gómes Fonseca, 'Scope of Application of the Regulation (EU) 2015/848 on Insolvency Proceedings' in I Queirolo and S Dominelli (eds), *European and National Perspectives on the Application of the European Insolvency Regulation* (Aracne editrice 2017) 26, footnote 10. For a number of possible interpretations, see Bork and van Zwieten (n 10) 69–70, paras 1.19–1.20.

17 Bork and van Zwieten (n 10) 65, para 1.19. In a similar sense, Bornemann, Brinkmann and Dahl (n 8) 27, stating that even the proceedings which affect only a subgroup of creditors meet the requirement and consequently may be listed in Annex A, referring to Recital 14.

3 Proceedings 'based on law relating to insolvency'

#17 The EIR refers to **proceedings 'based on law relating to insolvency'** and in which, for the purpose of rescue, adjustment of debt, reorganisation or liquidation', a debtor is divested of the right to manage and dispose of the estate, or a debtor retains such right but under court control or supervision or there is a temporary stay of enforcement. Recital (10) clarifies that the Regulation extends its scope in particular to procedures that facilitate the restructuring of viable businesses and provide a second chance to entrepreneurs. Also included are proceedings for a discharge or an adjustment of debt in relation to consumers and self-employed individuals.

#18 Most importantly, EIR extends its application so as to cover not only the proceedings to liquidate or restructure an insolvent party but also procedures for restructuring at the stage of threatening insolvency. Article 1(1) refers to proceedings which in a particular Member State may be commenced if 'there is only a likelihood of insolvency', with the purpose of avoiding 'the debtor's insolvency or the cessation of its business activities'. Recital (10) also refers in particular to proceedings which facilitate the 'restructuring of a debtor at a stage where there is only a likelihood of insolvency'. Recital (17) confirms that the scope extends to proceedings in which the debtor is in non-financial difficulties, but they present a serious and real threat to the debtor's ability to meet the debts in future, and it further clarifies the situation with regard to threatening insolvency.[18]

#19 Article 1 refers to proceedings 'based on law relating to insolvency'. Such proceedings must be related to the purposes mentioned in the same provision: namely, rescue, adjustment of debt, reorganisation, or liquidation. Proceedings based on company law, but which are not intended for insolvency situations do not meet the standard and therefore do not qualify as Annex A proceedings. The same holds true for special procedures in which the debts of a natural person are written off, provided that this type of procedure never involves the payment of creditors.[19]

#20 As rightly put forward in the literature, laws which are those 'relating to insolvency' are to be determined by the national law of the Member States. A 'uniform interpretation' would be inappropriate in the absence of a unification of substantive insolvency law at the EU level and taking into account that national laws of the Member States are determinative within the Annex A system.[20]

18 See also, F Jault-Seseke, 'Article 1 Scope' in G Cuniberti and A Leandro, *The European Insolvency Regulation and Implementing Legislations* (Edward Elgar 2024) 28, para 1.009, pointing to the difference between an earlier reference in EIR 2000 to 'insolvency' which is in EIR 2025 replaced by 'insolvency law', which indeed includes situations of a threatening insolvency.

19 Recital (16).

20 G Van Calster, 'COMIng, and Here to Stay: The Review of the European Insolvency Regulation' (2016) 27 The Review of the European Insolvency Regulation 735, 740.

4 Interim proceedings

#21 According to Article 1(1), **interim proceedings** may also qualify as Annex A procedures. Recital (15) clarifies that EIR 'should also apply to proceedings that, under the law of some Member States, are opened and conducted for a certain period of time on an interim or provisional basis before a court issues an order confirming the continuation of the proceedings on a non-interim basis'. Although labelled as 'interim' such proceedings should meet all other requirements of this Regulation.'

#22 In addition, the definition of Article 2(5) clearly includes an '**insolvency practitioner**' appointed on an interim basis, and Article 2(7)(ii) specifies that the 'judgment opening insolvency proceedings' includes the decision of a court to appoint an insolvency practitioner. This reflects the CJEU reasoning in *Eurofood*[21] and seemingly exceeds its reach. Bork and Van Zwieten point out that the *Eurofood* decision was confined to the question of whether the appointment of the provisional liquidator qualified as a decision 'opening' the proceedings for the purposes of its recognition in other Member States.[22] However, the Regulation seems to give such opening judgments the effects for all purposes, including various obligations such as giving notice to foreign creditors.[23]

5 Types of procedures and their effects

#23 Article 1(1) refers to insolvency proceedings which are based on laws whose purpose is 'rescue, adjustment of debt, reorganisation or liquidation'. Furthermore, it defines in great detail the types of proceedings that fall within the scope of the Regulation in points (a)-(c). The types are determined by the effects that the opening of such proceedings will have on the debtor and the debtor's estate. The following three categories are envisaged: 1) proceedings that imply a full or partial dispossession of a debtor whereby the right of management and disposal of the estate is vested with an insolvency practitioner (Article. 1(1)(a)); 2) proceedings in which a debtor is not divested of the right to manage and dispose of the assets and no insolvency practitioner is appointed, but control or supervision by a court is required (Article. 1(1)(b)); and 3) a temporary stay of individual enforcements is granted either by law or by a court order (Article. 1(1)(c).

#24 Only the first type of proceedings entails the full or partial dispossession of a debtor and includes the appointment of an insolvency practitioner. Article 2(5)

---

21 Case C-341/04 *Eurofood IFSC* (2 May 2006) ECLI:EU:C:2006:281.

22 ibid para 58, referring to Article 16(1) of EIR 2000.

23 Bork and van Zwieten (n 10) 85, para 1.51.

provides a broad definition of 'insolvency practitioner' and refers to Annex B in which the persons and entities covered by the definition are listed.

#25 The two other types of proceedings do not entail **dispossession of a debtor**. Recital (10) further clarifies that EIR extends to proceedings for salvaging economically viable businesses and entrepreneurs, where **the debtor fully or partially retains the right of disposal and management** of the assets. Even though the proceedings do not necessarily entail dispossession of a debtor and appointing an insolvency practitioner, they are within the scope of the Regulation if they are carried out under the supervision or control of a court. Hereby the term 'control' in Article 1(1)(b) extends to court interventions upon application by a creditor or other interested parties.[24] According to the definition in Article 2(6)(i), the 'court' referred to in Article 1(1)(b) and (c) refers to a Member State's judicial body.

#26 Types of proceedings described in Article 1(1)(c) are those in which a debtor-in-possession has obtained a **temporary stay on the enforcement actions of individual creditors** in order to facilitate negotiations with them. According to Recital (11), the stay may be granted where such actions could adversely affect negotiations and chances for the business to be restructured. There are additional requirements for the eligibility of such a stay of enforcement to qualify as an Annex A procedure: 1) the stay, granted either by a court of by operation of law, must provide suitable measures to protect the general body of creditors, and 2) where no agreement is reached, the stay operates as a preliminary to one of the proceedings which are within the scope of the Regulation, ie, those referred to in Article 1(1)(a) or (b).

#27 The insolvency proceedings which fall within the scope of the EIR must be listed in Annex A. Recital (9) clarifies that the procedures not listed in Annex A are not covered by EIR.

II Excluded Proceedings: Article 1 Paragraph 2

#28 This Regulation shall not apply to proceedings referred to in paragraph 1 that concern: (a) insurance undertakings; (b) credit institutions; (c) investment firms and other firms, institutions, and undertakings to the extent that they are covered by Directive 2001/24/EC; or (d) collective investment undertakings.

#29 It is suggested in the literature that the definitions in the special directives should be used in the interest of the coherence between different EU legislation: Directive 2009/138/EC for insurance, Directive 2001/24/EC for credit institutions, Directive 2004/39/EC for investment firms and Directives 2009/65/EU and 2011/61/EC for collective investment undertakings.[25]

---

24 Recital (10).

25 Jault-Seseke (n 18) 54–55, paras 2.28–2.46.

C Personal (*ratione personae*) and Territorial Scope of Application

#30 The EIR refers to '**debtor**' but provides no definition. Yet Recital (9) refers to insolvency proceedings meeting the conditions under the Regulation 'irrespective of whether the debtor is a natural person or a legal person, a trader or an individual'.

#31 As far as the rules on jurisdiction are concerned, EIR applies only when the **'centre of main interest' (COMI)** is in a Member State. Recital (25) is explicit in this respect.[26] Before establishing its jurisdiction, a Member State court must examine whether the COMI is in a Member State. If it is so, the court must apply EIR regardless of whether or not there is an international element and may establish its jurisdiction on the basis of the Regulation's rules. The same holds true if the COMI is in another Member State: namely, the court may not open main proceedings on the basis of national law. Instead, it may only open the territorial proceedings as provided in Article 3 (2)-(4).

#32 As far as the rules on jurisdiction are concerned, no connection with another EU Member State is required for EIR to apply. Accordingly, it applies to the proceedings connected with a non-Member State as long as the COMI is in an EU Member State.[27] In *Schmid*, the CJEU held that the Regulation applies against a defendant domiciled in a third state. It reasoned that the applicability of Article 3(1) EIR 2000 could not, in principle, depend on the existence of an international link involving another Member State.[28] The CJEU held that the COMI has to be foreseeable for the defendant,[29] and rejected the argument on the uncertainty of recognition and enforcement of the decision in a third state.[30] Therefore, whenever a court in an EU Member State has been seised of a petition to open insolvency proceedings, it may apply EIR to establish its international jurisdiction with no need to engage in finding a link with a Member State unless its application is excluded under Article 1(2).[31] Indeed, other provisions of private international law, such as those relating to recognition and enforcement and to the applicable law, do require having a connection with a Member

---

26 See also P Mankowski, M Müller and J Schmidt, *EuInsVO 2015. Europäische Insolvenzverordnung 2015* (CH Beck 2016) Art. 1, n. 54f.

27 Case C-328/12 *Ralph Schmid v Lilly Hertel* (16 January 2014) ECLI:EU:C:2014:6, paras 24, 28f. For the commentary to the judgment, see G McCormack, *EU Insolvency Law. Cross Border Insolvency Law in Comparative Focus.* (Edward Elgar 2022) 96. See also Case C-649/13 *Comité d'entreprise de Nortel Networks and Others* (11 June 2015) ECLI:EU:C:2015:384, para. 52; Case C-295/13 *H v HK* (4 December 2014) ECLI:EU:C:2014:2410, para 34.

28 Case C-328/12 *Schmid* (16 January 2014) ECLI:EU:C:2014:6, para 29.

29 ibid para 35.

30 ibid paras 36–38.

31 Bornemann, Brinkmann and Dahl (n 8) 32, para 32.

State. With respect to the applicable law, a connection as defined in Articles 8–19 is needed.

#33 Where judgments are concerned, for **recognition** it is necessary that a decision on the opening of insolvency proceedings is made by a court in a Member State. Judgments brought by Member State courts having jurisdiction under Article 3, and concerning the **opening, the course, and the closure of insolvency proceedings** rendered by the courts of the Member States and their effects, must be recognised in all Member States automatically with no further formalities. Also, there may be no examination whether the court has properly established jurisdiction, ie, whether or not COMI is in that Member State (Arts. 19 and 32(1) EIR). The same holds true for **judgments in matters deriving directly from insolvency proceedings** and those closely linked with them, even though they are rendered by another court in the Member State in which insolvency proceedings were opened. They apply as well to judgments relating to preservation measures taken after the request for the opening of insolvency proceedings or in connection with them (Article 32(1)-(3) EIR). The judgments will be enforced according to Articles 39 to 44 and 47 to 57 of the Brussels I-bis Regulation. Public policy is the only reason for which recognition may be refused.

#34 According to Article 32(2), the recognition and enforcement of judgments over matters other than those referred to in paragraph 1 of this Article shall be governed by the Brussels I-bis Regulation, provided that the latter Regulation is applicable *ratione personae* and *ratione temporis*.

#35 Although EIR does not define expressly the territorial scope of its application,[32] Recital (88) clarifies that EIR applies in all EU Member States except Denmark. It refers to Articles 1 and 2 of Protocol on the position of Denmark annexed to the TEFU.

D Temporal Scope of Application (*ratione temporis*)

#36 The EIR applies to insolvency proceedings opened on or after 26 July 2017.[33] Proceedings opened before that date shall continue to be governed by EIR 2000.[34] The time of the opening of proceedings is defined in Article 2(8) as 'the time at which the judgment opening insolvency proceedings becomes effective, regardless of whether the judgment is final or not'.

32 R Bork and R Mangano, *European Cross-border Insolvency Law* (2nd edn, OUP 2022) 42, para 2.07.

33 Article 84(1) EIR.

34 Article 84(2) EIR.

E International Jurisdiction to Open Main Insolvency Proceedings (Article 3): COMI

#37 Article 3 contains the rules on international jurisdiction to open **main insolvency proceedings** as well as those to open **territorial and secondary proceedings**. There are two criteria regarding jurisdiction: firstly, the centre of main interest of the debtor (COMI) is the criterion attributing jurisdiction to open main insolvency proceedings; secondly, establishment of the debtor is the rule on jurisdiction for territorial and secondary proceedings. The effects of the opening of insolvency proceedings under Article 3 shall be recognised in all Member States. The effect of the opening of the proceedings under Article 3 para (2) shall be confined to the assets of the debtor situated in the territory of that Member State. Only the courts of the Member State in which the centre of the debtor's interest (COMI) is situated may open the main insolvency proceedings that comprise all of the debtor's assets wherever they are located.

#38 The effects of the opening of the main insolvency proceedings are recognised in all other Member States (Article 19(1)) except Denmark, without any examination of its 'correctness', namely, whether or not COMI was properly applied. This idea was already adhered to in *Eurofood*[35] as being in line with the principle of mutual trust between the Member States. It is now set out in Recital (65).

#39 Only secondary insolvency proceedings may subsequently be opened in another Member State where the debtor has their establishment after insolvency proceedings are opened in the Member State of the centre of main interests of the debtor.[36] Before the opening of the latter, territorial insolvency proceedings may be opened in another Member State under certain conditions defined in paragraph 4. As soon as the main insolvency proceedings are opened, the territorial proceedings may become secondary insolvency proceedings (Article 50 EIR).[37]

#40 The EIR 2000 did not contain a definition of COMI in its normative part, but it provided a clarification in Recital (13). EIR 2015 introduced the definition of COMI in Article 3. It is defined as the 'place where the debtor conducts the administration of interests on a regular basis, and which is ascertainable by third parties.' There is a presumption of COMI for companies and legal persons on the one hand and for individuals on the other. For legal persons, it is the registered office and for individuals it is the habitual residence, provided that the office or residence has not been moved to another Member State within a certain period of time

35 C-341/04 *Eurofood IFSC Ltd* (2 May 2006) ECLI:EU:C:2006:281

36 Article 3(2) EIR.

37 For more particulars on the two categories of insolvency proceedings, see, IF Fletcher, 'Scope and Jurisdiction' in G Moss, I Fletcher and S Isaacs (eds), *The EU Regulation on Insolvency Proceedings* (4th edn, Edward Elgar 2023) 57, paras 3.17 et seq.

prior to the request for insolvency proceedings. A 3-month period is provided for companies and legal persons and a 6-month period for individuals.[38] The presumption in both cases can be rebutted by proving otherwise: namely, if it is proven that the centre of main interest is elsewhere and not at the registered office or habitual residence.

#41 COMI must be interpreted autonomously, in a uniform way, with no reference to analogous concepts under national laws of the EU Member States.[39]

I The Extent of International Jurisdiction: Article 6

#42 EIR 2000 contained no provision corresponding to the current Article 6 EIR. The latter in paragraph 1 defines the **extent of jurisdiction** of the courts of the Member State that opened insolvency proceedings in accordance with Article 3. Article 6(1) refers to 'the courts' of a Member State, so that national rules apply to the allocation of internal jurisdiction. The jurisdiction of the courts in that Member State also encompasses 'any **action that derives directly from the insolvency proceedings and is closely linked with them**, such as avoidance actions'. Herewith Article 6(1) simply incorporates the two criteria developed in CJEU case law.[40] The provision of Article 25 of EIR 2000 (current Article 32 EIR) relating to the recognition and enforcement of judgments uses similar wording and embodies the same two criteria.

#43 The CJEU case law in that respect appears crucial in drawing the line between the scope of application of the EIR and the Brussels I-bis Regulation. However, the two criteria have not been interpreted and applied in a consistent manner by the CJEU. Uncertainties resulting from the CJEU interpretation will be discussed *infra* under II.

#44 In Article 6(2), the EIR introduces an option for the insolvency practitioner to submit true insolvency matters before the court of the domicile of the defendant, provided that it has jurisdiction in accordance with the Brussels I-bis Regulation. Where an action that derives directly from the insolvency proceedings and is closely linked with them is related to an action in civil and commercial matters against the same defendant, the insolvency practitioner may bring both actions before the courts of the Member State within whose territory the defendant is domiciled. Where the action is brought against several defendants, it can be brought before the courts of the Member State within whose territory any of them are domiciled, provided that those courts have jurisdiction pursuant to the

---

38 Herewith it is intended to combat 'mobile COMI' also referred to as 'bankruptcy tourism' or 'forum shopping, see Fletcher (n 37) 64, para 3.30.

39 C-396/09 *Interedil* (20 October 2011) ECLI:EU:C:2011:671.

40 Case C-133/78 *Henri Gourdain v Franz Nadler* (22 February 1979) ECLI:EU:C:1979:49 para 4.

Brussels I-bis Regulation. Such a joint filing will be available if the actions are so closely related that it is expedient to hear and determine them together to avoid the risk of irreconcilable judgments resulting from separate proceedings.[41]

The idea is that the insolvency practitioner should be able to pursue both actions in the courts of the defendant's domicile if that were to be considered more efficient. An example is a case where the insolvency practitioner wishes to combine an action for director's liability on the basis of insolvency law with an action based on company law or general tort law.[42] A debtor-in-possession may also rely on Article 6(2), provided that he/she is empowered to act on behalf of the estate under the *lex fori concursus*.[43]

#45 The option is available as long as the court or the courts have jurisdiction under the Brussels I-bis Regulation in accordance with Article 4. The criteria provided therein apply with respect to the scope of application as well as to the domicile as a ground of jurisdiction.[44] Accordingly, the definition under Article 63 of the Brussels I-bis Regulation applies if the defendant is a legal person. The conflict of law rule of Article 62 applies to determine the domicile of a natural person. In a case involving multiple defendants, the suit can be with a court in a Member State of the domicile of any of them. When opting for the possibility under Article 6(2) EIR, the insolvency practitioner may not rely on any jurisdiction ground of the Brussels I-bis Regulation other than that of the domicile of the defendant. Indeed, the option under Article 6(2) is not available if the action falls out of the substantive, personal, and temporal scope of application of the Brussels I-bis Regulation.

#46 This provision in paragraph 3 clarifies that 'actions are deemed to be related where they are so closely connected that it is expedient to hear and determine them together to avoid the risk of irreconcilable judgments resulting from separate proceedings'. It is argued in the literature that the reasons for connection and the assessment of it are not to be determined in a manner in which corresponding concepts are dealt with in the Brussels I-bis Regulation. The option under Article 6(2) is at the discretion of an insolvency practitioner. Hence, the assessment of the 'closeness' should not be reassessed or reversed by the court under the Brussels I-bis Regulation, since this is a matter falling under the exclusion of Article 1(2)(b).[45]

---

41 Insolvency Regulation, Article 6(3).

42 Recital 35 of the Insolvency Regulation.

43 Article 6(3).

44 In a similar sense when applied to the domicile as jurisdiction ground, see A Leandro, 'The Minefield at the Interface of the Brussels I-bis Regulation and the European Insolvency Regulation (Recast)' in P Mankowski (ed), *Research Handbook on The Brussels Ibis Regulation* (Edward Elgar 2020) 199.

45 ibid 200. *Contra*, see S Madaus, 'Article 6' in Bornemann, Brinkmann and Dahl (n 8) 82, para 27, arguing that the criteria of the analogous in Brussels I-bis should apply, since this provision in EIR is modelled along the lines of the Brussels I-bis Regulation.

II Interface Between the EIR and the Brussels I-bis Regulation

#47 Difficulties when delineating the scope of application between the two Regulations are likely to appear when: 1) determining the scope of application of the Brussels I-bis Regulation as a result of extending the scope of the EIR to a wider range of proceedings aiming at the rescue and reorganisation of businesses listed in Annex A, and 2) assessing the relevance of the extent of jurisdiction of the court opening insolvency when determining the scope of the 'insolvency exception' under Article 1(2)(b) of the Brussels I-bis Regulation. Determining the scope of application of the Regulation with regard to extending the scope of the EIR has mainly been discussed in the literature. In contrast, there is abundant CJEU case law on delineating the scope of application between the two Regulations, namely, when assessing the 'insolvency exception' under the Brussels I-bis Regulation and the extent of jurisdiction of the court opening insolvency proceedings under Article 3 EIR.

1 Types of proceedings within the EIR and 'insolvency exception' under the Brussels I-bis Regulation

#48 As already partly explained *supra* B.I.5., the definition of proceedings falling within the scope of the EIR adjusts the definition under EIR 2000. The possibility of including compositions and restructuring procedures in the scope of the EIR already existed under EIR 2000. This option is now spelled out in Article 1(1) EIR 2015 so as to give Member States the possibility of extending the application to a wide range of proceedings aiming at the restructuring or reorganisation of businesses in difficulties. The reference to 'the appointment of liquidator' is omitted from the current definition under Article 1(a) and the definition in Article 2(5) refers to the 'insolvency practitioner'.[46]

#49 Only the proceedings listed in Annex A are considered to meet the requirements of the definition in Article 1(1) and therefore to be within the EIR's scope of application. Recital 9 is clear in that respect: Proceedings that are not listed in Annex A do not fall within the scope of the EIR. It has been pointed out in the literature[47] that the amendment relating to annex procedures in the EIR may complicate the interpretation of the 'insolvency exception' under Article 1(2)(b) of the Brussels I-

46 See also Van Calster (n 20) 730.

47 Van Calster (n 20) 735; Leandro (n 44) 189; A Van Noe, 'The (not so Symbiotic?) Relationship Between Insolvency and the Brussels I Regime' in G van Calster and J Falconis (eds), *European Private International Law at 50* (Intersentia 2018) 66.

bis Regulation. In its rulings, the CJEU has held that the scope of application under the two Regulations must be interpreted in such a way as to avoid, on the one hand, any overlap between them[48] and, on the other hand, a gap or legal vacuum.[49] In the literature, it has been referred to as 'dovetailing' in reference to the relevant part of the Schlosser Report.[50]

#50 The point of concern is Recital (7) EIR, which seemingly abandons the 'dovetailing' concept. Clearly the wording 'the mere fact that a national procedure is not listed in Annex A to this Regulation should not imply that it is covered' automatically by the Brussels I-bis Regulation indicates that certain proceedings will not be within the scope of either of the two Regulations and will therefore be subjected to national law. Circumstances such as those in the CJEU judgment *Ulf Kazimierz Radziejewski*[51] present an obvious example of a procedure that falls outside the scope of both Regulations: namely, when a particular restructuring scheme or a debt relief procedure is not listed in Annex A but it is in the competence of an administrative authority that does not meet the definition of a 'court' under the Brussels I-bis Regulation. In certain circumstances, it will be more difficult to assess the true legal nature of the restructuring procedure, whether or not it is a 'civil and commercial' matter within the scope of the Brussels I-bis Regulation, the scheme of arrangement under English law being an example. Indeed, in the absence of clear criteria relating to Annex A proceedings,[52] it will be a new challenge when interpreting the 'insolvency exception'.

---

48 Case C-296/17 *Wiemer & Trachte GmbH v Zhan Oved Tadzher* (14 November 2018) ECLI:EU:C:2018:902, para 39; Case C-535/17 *NK v BNP Paribas Fortis NV* (6 February 2019) ECLI:EU:C:2019:96, para 24.

49 Case C-641/16 *Tünkers France and Tünkers Maschinenbau* (9 November 2017) ECLI:EU:C:2017:847, para 17. The necessity to avoid gaps and loopholes between the two legal instruments also follows from Recital 7 of the revised Insolvency Regulation. In a similar sense, Case C-133/78 *Henri Gourdain v Franz Nadler* (22 February 1979) ECLI:EU:C:1979:49, para 4; Case C-213/10 *F-Tex SIA v Lietuvos-Anglijos UAB 'Jadecloud-Vilma'* (19 April 2012) ECLI:EU:C:2012:215, paras 22 and 24; Case C-535/17 *NK v BNP Paribas Fortis NV* (6 February 2019) ECLI:EU:C:2019:96, para 30; Case C-641/16 *Tünkers France and Tünkers Maschinenbau* (9 November 2017) ECLI:EU:C:2017:847, para 17; Case C-157/13 *Nickel & Goeldner Spedition GmbH v 'Kintra' UAB* (4 September 2014) ECLI:EU:C:2014:2145, para 21.

50 Report by Schlosser on the convention on the Association of the Kingdom of Denmark, Ireland and the United Kingdom to the convention on jurisdiction and the enforcement of judgments in civil and commercial matters and to the Protocol on its interpretation by the Court of Justice [1979] OJ C 59/71, at p 90, no 53 stating that 'the two Conventions were intended to dovetail almost completely with each other'. For a more detailed analysis, see Van Calster (n 20) 741–743.

51 Case C-461/11 *Ulf Kazimierz Radziejewski v Kronofogdemyndigheten i Stockholm* (8 November 2012) ECLI:EU:C:2012:704.

52 Van Noe (n 47) 66. The literature refers to a possible extension of the Directive (EU) 2019/1023 of 20 June 2019 on preventive restructuring framework, on discharge of debt and disqualification, and on measures to increase the efficiency of procedures concerning restructuring, insolvency and discharge of debt, and amending Directive (EU) 2017/1132 (Directive on restructuring and insolvency) [2019] OJ L 172/18. B Hess, 'Introduction' in M Requejo Isidro (ed), *Brussels Ibis. A Commentary on Regulation (EU)No 1215/2012* (Edward Elgar 2022) 1, 7, para 0.17.

2 An 'action that derives directly from the insolvency proceedings and is closely linked with them' and 'insolvency exception' under the Brussels I-bis Regulation[53]

#51 This aspect of the relationship between the Regulations has proven to be most complex. The abundant CJEU case law illustrates that the national courts have encountered difficulties when deciding on the '**insolvency exception**' under Article 1(2)(b). CJEU case law has developed certain methods to be applied or rather steps to be taken when delineating the substantive scope between the two Regulations. The twofold criteria were established in the CJEU *Gourdain* judgment,[54] brought under the 1968 Brussels Convention, and were subsequently maintained in decisions brought under the Brussels I-bis Regulation. Whilst holding that jurisdiction under Article 3 encompasses not only insolvency proceedings but also actions related to such proceedings, the CJEU put forward the following dual criteria: 1) **an action which derives directly from insolvency proceedings** and 2) **an action which is closely connected** with them.

#52 The reference to an action deriving directly from or closely linked with insolvency proceedings is now spelled out in Article 6(1),[55] but regrettably no definition or more precise criteria for the determination of their meaning and reach has been provided.[56] Yet it expressly refers to avoidance actions as an example of such matters. However, the established formula has not been applied in a consistent manner in CJEU case law.

a) An action deriving directly from insolvency proceedings: Legal Basis of the Action

#53 In interpreting the first criterion, the CJEU maintains that the decisive factor for determining whether an action derives directly from insolvency proceedings is the legal basis of an action and not its procedural context. Thereby, it is conclu-

53 Certain remaining parts of this Chapter are to some extent based on the earlier research presented in V Lazić and P Mankowski, *Brussels I-bis Regulation. Interpretation and Implementation* (Edward Elgar 2023) 30–42 and the Note on CJEU C-394/22 *Oilchart International NV v O.W. Bunker (Netherlands) BV and ING Bank NV* (14 November 2024) ECLI:EU:C:2024:952, V Lazić, 'Comment on the CJEU C-394/22 Oilchart International NV v O.W. Bunker Netherlands) BV, ING Bank NV ECLI:EU:C:2024:952' (2025-2) Belgisch Tijdschrift voor Handelsrecht (BTHR) 308, also available on 2025-Note-rdc_tbh2025_2p308.pdf (last accessed 21 November 2025).

54 Case C-133/78 *Henri Gourdain v Franz Nadler* (22 February 1979) ECLI:EU:C:1979:49, para 4.

55 Although EIR 2000 did not contain a corresponding provision regarding the current Article 6(1), it did refer to judgments deriving directly from the insolvency proceedings and closely linked with them in Article 25 relating to recognition and enforcement. Also, in Recital (6), EIR 2000 refers to 'judgments which are delivered directly on the basis of the insolvency proceedings and are closely connected with such proceedings'.

56 For criticism on this point, see Mankowski, Müller and Schmidt (n 26) 160.

sive whether the right or the obligation which forms the basis of the action has its source in the ordinary rules of civil and commercial law or in derogating rules specific to insolvency proceedings.[57] Generally, a matter remains within the scope of the Brussels I-bis Regulation as long as the intervening insolvency proceeding does not substantially amend the nature of the claim so that the latter remains independent from the insolvency proceeding and is subjected to the rules of ordinary law. Later, in *PNK v BNP Paribas Fortis,*[58] seemingly another decisive factor was put forward. The CJEU examined whether the action could be pursued solely by an insolvency practitioner or could it instead also be filed by a creditor. If the latter is the case the CJEU ruled that such action then does not derive directly from the insolvency proceedings.

b) Actions closely linked with insolvency proceedings

#54 Regarding the second criterion, the CJEU has held that the closeness of the link between a court action and the insolvency proceedings is determinative for the applicability of the 'insolvency exclusion' under Article 1(2)(b) of the Brussels I-bis Regulation.[59] Thereby, 'contextual factors other than those relating to the legal basis of the action' may be taken into consideration.[60]

c) Inconsistency in the application of dual criteria

#55 The dual criteria have proven less cumbersome regarding the matters of insolvency law in a narrow sense, such as a decision on the opening of insolvency proceedings, the nomination of a trustee or a liquidator or the distribution of assets of a bankruptcy estate. They obviously fall within the substantive scope of EIR and accordingly within 'insolvency exclusion' under the Brussels I-bis Regulation.

---

57 Case C-157/13 *Nickel & Goeldner Spedition GmbH v 'Kintra' UAB* (4 September 2014) ECLI:EU:C:2014:2145, paras 27–28; Case C-535/17 *NK v BNP Paribas Fortis NV* (6 February 2019) ECLI:EU:C:2019:96 para 28; Case C-47/18 *Skarb Pánstwa Rzeczpospolitej Polskiej – Generalny Dyrektor Dróg Krajowych i Autostrad v Stephan Riel, en qualité d'administrateur judiciaire de Alpine Bau GmbH* (18 September 2019) ECLI:EU:C:2019:754, para 33; Case C-493/18 *Tiger and Others* (4 December 2019) ECLI:EU:C:2019:1046; C-394/22 *Oilchart International NV v O.W. Bunker (Netherlands) BV and ING Bank NV* (14 November 2024) ECLI:EU:C:2024:952.

58 Case C-535/17 *NK v BNP Paribas Fortis NV* (6 February 2019) ECLI:EU:C:2019:96, para 24.

59 Case C-649/16 *Peter Valach and Others v Waldviertler Sparkasse Bank AG and Others* (20 December 2017) ECLI:EU:C:2017:986, para 27 and the case law cited, and Case C-535/17 *NK v BNP Paribas Fortis NV* (6 February 2019) ECLI:EU:C:2019:96, para 30.

60 Case C-649/16 *Peter Valach and Others v Waldviertler Sparkasse Bank AG and Others* (20 December 2017) ECLI:EU:C:2017:986; Case C-641/16 *Tünkers France and Tünkers Maschinenbau* (9 November 2017) ECLI:EU:C:2017:847; Case C-292/08 *German Graphics Graphische Maschinen GMBH v Alice van der Schee* (10 September 2009) ECLI:EU:C:2009:544; Case C-394/22 *Oilchart International NV v O.W. Bunker (Netherlands) BV and ING Bank NV* (14 November 2024) ECLI:EU:C:2024:952, para 48.

Thus, the CJEU held to be matters within the EIR 'insolvency exception' the actions in respect of avoidance of fraudulent transactions,[61] an action against a manager of a company in insolvency proceedings to bear a part of the company's debt,[62] an action challenging a transfer of shares in a company made in the course of insolvency proceedings due to the lack of power of a liquidator to dispose of the assets in that Member State.[63]

#56 Other examples of 'the insolvency exclusion' are: if the outcome of the disputes depends on how proceeds from the sale of a debtor's assets are to be allocated between the main proceedings and the secondary proceedings,[64] an action for liability in tort against the member of a creditors' committee who rejected a restructuring plan in insolvency proceedings,[65] as well as an action for a declaration of the existence of claims for the purposes of the registration of these claims in a verification procedure.[66]

#57 On the other hand, actions requesting performance of the obligations under a contract concluded by the debtor prior to the opening of insolvency proceedings is not likely to derive directly from the insolvency proceedings. Thus, 'civil and commercial matters' within the scope of the Brussels I-bis Regulation is an action filed by an insolvency practitioner requesting payment for services provided by the debtor under a pre-insolvency contract,[67] as well as an action for unfair competition brought in the context of insolvency proceedings by the subsidiary of an insolvent company against the assignee of part of the business acquired in the course of the proceedings.

#58 However, in cases where the line of delineation is not obvious or easily drawn the CJEU case law does not offer clear guidelines. This is especially the case when a dispute concerning a transaction of a civil or commercial nature – such as a contract – arises in the context of insolvency proceedings. The conclusive factors

61 See eg Case C-339/07 *Christopher Seagon v Deko Marty Belgium NV* (12 February 2009) ECLI:EU:C:2009:83. See also Case C-296/17 *Wiemer & Trachte GmbH v Zhan Oved Tadzher* (14 November 2018) ECLI:EU:C:2018:902, holding that the court of the opening insolvency proceedings has exclusive jurisdiction over an action to set a transaction aside by virtue of the debtor's insolvency which has been brought against a defendant whose registered office or habitual residence is in another Member State.

62 Case C-133/78 *Henri Gourdain v Franz Nadler* (22 February 1979) ECLI:EU:C:1979:49.

63 Case C-111/08 *SCT Industri AB i likvidation v Alpenblume AB* (2 July 2009) ECLI:EU:C:2009:419, para 33.

64 Case C-157/13 *Nickel & Goeldner Spedition GmbH v 'Kintra' UAB* (4 September 2014) ECLI:EU:C:2014:2145, para 30; Case C-649/13 *Comité déntreprise de Nortel Networks SA and Others v Cosme Rogeau ans Cosme Rogeau v Alan Robert Bloom and Others* (11 June 2015) ECLI:EU:C:2015:384, para 28.

65 Case C-649/16 *Peter Valach and Others v Waldviertler Sparkasse Bank AG and Others* (20 December 2017) ECLI:EU:C:2017:986.

66 Case C-47/18 *Skarb Pánstwa Rzeczpospolitej Polskiej – Generalny Dyrektor Dróg Krajowych i Autostrad v Stephan Riel, en qualité d'administrateur judiciaire de Alpine Bau GmbH* (18 September 2019) ECLI:EU:C:2019:754.

67 Case C-157/13 *Nickel & Goeldner Spedition GmbH v 'Kintra' UAB* (4 September 2014) ECLI:EU:C:2014:2145.

suggested by the CJEU in both of the dual criteria have proved to be unsuitable and insufficient. This holds particularly true for the 'legal basis of the action'-test. A conclusion that a certain action may be pursued also when no insolvency proceedings are opened has been sufficient to characterise the action as a 'civil and commercial matter'. Thereby no characterisation is usually made for the purposes of the applicability of EIR. This resulted in a number of rulings in which certain **avoidance transactions** of the insolvency practitioner were characterised as a 'civil and commercial' matter within the scope of the BIbis.[68] This deviate from the CJEU earlier judgment in *Seagon,*[69] in which an action of the insolvency practitioner to avoid certain fraudulent transactions was held to be a matter deriving from insolvency law. Moreover, Article 6(1) now refers expressly to avoidance actions as examples of actions deriving directly from or closely connected with insolvency proceedings.

#59 In *Paribas Fortis NV,* the CJEU held that the '*Peeters/Gatzen*' action under Dutch law fell within the Brussels I-bis Regulation substantive scope of application. This type of claim is based on the Dutch Supreme Court's ruling in the *Peeters/Gatzen* case,[70] according to which the insolvency practitioner can bring an action for the benefit of the general body of creditors of the bankruptcy estate against a party that has acted unlawfully. The CJEU judgment is debatable in many respects, as was addressed extensively in the earlier publication.[71] It seems that another conclusive factor was introduced: the fact that the action allegedly is not in an exclusive competence of the insolvency practitioner but can be also pursued by a creditor. However, in the literature it has been put forward that an action against a third party exercised by a creditor on the basis of a wrongful act is usually not considered as a *Peeters/Gatzen* claim.[72]

---

68 Case C-535/17 *NK v BNP Paribas Fortis NV* (6 February 2019) ECLI:EU:C:2019:96; Case C-498/20 *ZK v BMA Braunschweigische Maschinenbaustalt AG* (10 March 2022) ECLI:EU:C:2022:173. For a criticism on both judgments, see Lazić and Mankowski (n 53) 41–42, paras 1.117–1.120. CJEU case law appears to be questionable also with respect to the application of the current Article 7 relating to the applicable law, certainly considering the ruling in C-198/18 *CeDe Group AB v KAN* (21 November 2019) ECLI:EU:C:2019:1001. See also, Case C-213/10 *F-Tex SIA v Lietuvos-Anglijos UAB 'Jadecloud-Vilma'* (19 April 2012) ECLI:EU:C:2012:215. The consequence of this CJEU ruling is less problematic, since the liquidator had assigned the claim. The assignee brought an action against a third party and was entitled to keep a major part of the proceeds obtained in an action pursuing the claim assigned. Only a certain percentage of the proceeds obtained was to be paid to the liquidator. Therefore, the major part was not to be returned to the estate but instead was to remain outside the insolvency proceedings in any case.

69 Case C-339/07 *Christopher Seagon v Deko Marty Belgium* (12 February 2009) *NV* ECLI:EU:C:2009:83.

70 ECLI:NL:HR:1983:AG:4521.

71 Lazić and Mankowski (n 53) 40–42, paras 1.116–1.120.

72 See eg, M Jonkers, 'European Court of Justice Resolves – Peeters/Gatzen Claim Falls within the Scope of Regulation (EU) 1215/2012 (Brussels I recast) instead of Regulation (EU) 2015/848 (Insolvency Regulation)' (*Stibbeblog*, 11 March 2019). For further points of criticism, see DFH Stein, noot onder HvJ 6 februari 2019, JBPR 2019/12, nr. 1; SM van den Braak, 'De Peeters/Gatzen-vordering in het internatio-

#60 Interestingly enough, as a consequence of the CJEU's subsequent judgment *ZK v BMA Braunschweigische Maschinenbaustalt AG,*[73] the jurisdiction over the '*Peeters/ Gatzen*' claim reverts to the Dutch court after all through the interpretation of the Brussels I-bis Regulation. The CJEU confirmed the Dutch court's characterisation of the claim as a matter of tort[74] within the meaning of Article 7(2). It held that the place where the harmful event occurred is 'the place of establishment of a company which is unable to satisfy its obligation towards its creditors because its "grand-mother" has breached its duty of care towards the creditors of that company'. Therefore, the place of harmful event will coincide with the *forum concursus* if the debtor's establishment is in the same Member State in which the debtor's centre of main interest is situated. This is likely to be so in many cases, meaning that courts in the Member State in which insolvency proceedings were opened will decide on both actions after all.[75] As was argued in the earlier publication,[76] it would be more in line with the provision of Article 6(1) to characterise the avoidance actions attributed exclusively to the insolvency practitioner as those falling within the reach of the EIR regardless of how they are termed in national laws.

#61 In its most recent ruling in *Oilchart*[77] CJEU held that **an action of a creditor** which was pursued individually in parallel proceedings before a 'foreign' court[78] did not meet the standards of the 'insolvency exception' under Article 1(2)(b) Brussels I-bis Regulation, since it was allegedly based on the ordinary rules of contract law. In doing so, the CJEU apparently deviated from its previous decision

---

naal privaatrecht: een overzicht naar aanleiding van Hof van Justitie EU 6 februari 2019, zaak C-535/17 (NK/Fortis)' (2019) 18 Tijsdchrift voor Insolventierecht 140, 142, nr 4.4. See also judgment of the Dutch Supreme Court (Hoge Raad) of 3 July 2020 ECLI:NL:HR:2020:1223 brought after the CJEU ruling and deciding on the jurisdiction on the basis of Article 7(2) in the same case.

73 Case C-498/20 *ZK v BMA Braunschweigische Maschinenbaustalt AG* (10 March 2022) ECLI:EU: C:2022:173. For a criticism on this judgment, see Lazić and Mankowski (n 53) 41–42, paras 1.119–1.120 and 133–134, paras 2.178–2. 181.

74 Since in an earlier decision in the Netherlands, the Supreme Court qualified this type of action as a 'tort', Judgment of 3 July 2020 ECLI:NL:HR: 2020:1223.

75 Although the ruling in *ZK v BMA Braunschweigische Maschinenbaustalt AG* mitigates to some extent the consequences of the *NK v BNP Paribas Fortis NV* judgment, the conclusion reached seems to be inconsistent with the CJEU ruling in Case C-337/17 *Feniks sp. z o.o. v Azteca Products & Services SL*, (4 October 2018) ECLI:EU:C:2018:805. In the latter, the CJEU characterised an *actio pauliana* as a matter of contract.

76 Lazić and Mankowski (n 53) 42, para 1.120.

77 C-394/22 *Oilchart International NV v O.W. Bunker (Netherlands) BV and ING Bank NV* (14 November 2024) ECLI:EU:C:2024:952.

78 Under the insolvency laws of the majority of legal systems, including those of the EU Member States, a claim of an ordinary unsecured creditor must be filed for verification in insolvency proceedings and may not be pursued in any other manner. For a comparative overview, see International Bar Association (IBA), 'IBA Toolkit on Insolvency and Arbitration' (IBA 2021), providing National Reports from a number of countries, as well as a Consolidated Report – both were prepared on the basis of the same Questionnaire.

in *H v H.K.*[79] It held that the fact that a claim may be pursued where no insolvency proceedings have been opened does not necessarily prevent such a claim from being characterised as a claim deriving directly from the insolvency proceedings. Hence, in the case at hand it is unclear how the CJEU applied its own test, now codified in Article 6(1) EIR. Also, the *Oilchart* judgment is not fully consistent with the earlier ruling in *Riel*,[80] in which the CJEU correctly ruled that a verification dispute falls within the 'insolvency exception' of Article 1(2)(b) of the Brussels I Regulation.

#62 When applying the 'close connectedness' test in *Oilchart,* the CJEU refrained again from accepting a 'correspondence' between the rules on jurisdiction and those on the applicable law – the position already taken in its earlier ruling in *German Graphic*.[81] The author of the present chapter has suggested in a number of other publications[82] that acceptance of the 'correspondence between the applicable law and jurisdiction' approach could resolve the existing inconsistencies created by the CJEU case law and thereby enhance the predictability and legal certainty. A connection with the insolvency proceeding is presumably the line of reasoning along which the provisions on the applicable law in EIR are drafted. As such, they are easily aligned with the criteria of jurisdiction in Article 6(1) – any action which derives directly from the insolvency proceedings and is closely linked with them.[83]

References

Bork R and Mangano R, *European Cross-border Insolvency Law* (2nd edn, OUP 2022).
Bork R and Zwieten van K, *Commentary on the European Insolvency Regulation* (2nd edn, OUP 2022).
Bornemann A, Brinkmann M and Dahl M (eds), *European Insolvency Regulation: A Commentary* (CH Beck/Hart/Nomos 2020).

79 Case C-295/13, *H v HK* (4 December 2014) ECLI:EU:C:2014:241.

80 The CJEU decision in Oilchart can hardly be reconcilable with its earlier ruling Case C-47/18 *Skarb Pánstwa Rzeczpospolitej Polskiej – Generalny Dyrektor Dróg Krajowych i Autostrad v Stephan Riel, en qualité d'administrateur judiciaire de Alpine Bau GmbH* (18 September 2019) ECLI:EU:C:2019:754, even though the CJEU refers to it in paras 32 and 37.

81 Case C-292/08 *German Graphics Graphische Maschinen GMBH v Alice van der Schee* (10 September 2009) ECLI:EU:C:2009:544

82 Lazić and Mankowski (n 53) 34 and 35, paras 1.098–1.100 and Vesna Lazić, CJEU C-394/22 *Oilchart International NV v O.W. Bunker Netherlands) BV and ING Bank* NV ECLI:EU:C:2024:952 [2025-2] Belgisch Tijdschrift voor Handelsrecht (BTHR) 308.

83 For a contrary view, see, Stephan Madaus and Bob Wessels, 'Identifying Annex Actions under Article 6(1) of the European Insolvency Regulation' in Conference on European Restructuring and Insolvency Law (CERIL), *CERIL Collection I, Improving European Restructuring and Insolvency Law, Statements and Reports 2017–2022* (Eleven International Publishing 2023) 162.

Braak van den SM, 'De Peeters/Gatzen-vordering in het internationaal privaatrecht: een overzicht naar aanleiding van Hof van Justitie EU 6 februari 2019, zaak C-535/17 (NK/Fortis)' (2019) 18 Tijsdchrift voor Insolventierecht 140.

Castelló Pastor JJ and Gómes Fonseca F, 'Scope of Application of the Regulation (EU) 2015/848 on Insolvency Proceedings' in I Queirolo and S Dominelli (eds), *European and National Perspectives on the Application of the European Insolvency Regulation* (Aracne editrice 2017) 26.

Conference on European Restructuring and Insolvency Law (CERIL), *CERIL Collection I, Improving European Restructuring and Insolvency Law, Statements and Reports 2017–2022* (Eleven International Publishing 2023) 162.

Fletcher I, 'Scope and Jurisdiction', in G Moss, I Fletcher and S Isaacs (eds), *The EU Regulation on Insolvency Proceedings* (4th edn, Edward Elgar 2023) 57.

Hess B, 'Introduction' in M Requejo Isidro (ed), *Brussels Ibis. A Commentary on Regulation (EU)No 1215/2012* (Edward Elgar 2022) 1.

INSOL Europe, *Study on a New Approach to Business Failure and Insolvency: Comparative Legal Analysis of the Member States Relevant Provisions and Practices* (12 May 2014).

International Bar Association (IBA), 'IBA Toolkit on Insolvency and Arbitration' (IBA 2021).

Jault-Seseke F, 'Article 1 Scope' in Gilles Cuniberti and Antonio Leandro, *The European Insolvency Regulation and Implementing Legislations* (Edward Elgar 2024) 28.

Jonkers M, 'European Court of Justice resolves – Peeters/Gatzen claim falls within the scope of Regulation (EU) 1215/2012 (Brussels I recast) instead of Regulation (EU) 2015/848 (Insolvency Regulation)' (*Stibbeblog*, 11 March 2019).

Lazić V and Mankowski P, *Brussels I-bis Regulation. Interpretation and Implementation* (Edward Elgar 2023).

Leandro A, 'The Minefield at the Interface of the Brussels I-bis Regulation and the European Insolvency Regulation (Recast)' in P Mankowski (ed), *Research Handbook on The Brussels Ibis Regulation* (Edward Elgar 2020) 199.

Madaus S and Wessels B, 'Identifying Annex Actions under Article 6(1) of the European Insolvency Regulation' in Conference on European Restructuring and Insolvency Law (CERIL), *CERIL Collection I, Improving European Restructuring and Insolvency Law, Statements and Reports 2017–2022* (Eleven International Publishing 2023) 162.

Mankowski P, Müller M and Schmidt J, *EuInsVO 2015. Europäische Insolvenzverordnung 2015* (CH Beck 2016).

Noël J and Lemontey J, *Report on the Convention Relating to Bankruptcies, Compositions and Analogous Procedures* (Commission of the European Communities Working Document 16.775/XIV/70-F 1970).

Stein DFH, noot onder HvJ 6 februari 2019, JBPR 2019/12, nr. 1.

Van Calster G, 'COMIng, and Here to Stay: The Review of the European Insolvency Regulation' (2016) 27 The Review of the European Insolvency Regulation 735.

Van Noe A, 'The (not so Symbiotic?) Relationship Between Insolvency and the Brussels I Regime' in G van Calster and J Falconis (eds), *European Private International Law at 50* (Intersentia 2018) 66.

Virgós M and Schmit E, *Report on the Convention on Insolvency Proceedings* (EU Council of the EU Document 6500/96 1996).

Georgia Antonopoulou

Chapter 19
Specialised Courts: The Unified Patent Court and International Commercial Courts

A Introduction

#1 Contrary to the increasing **specialisation** in the government and the society, national judiciaries have predominantly relied on generalist judges.[1] Yet, in recent years there is a growing trend towards court specialisation. Specialised courts are courts focusing on a specific sub-set of disputes such as family law, intellectual property law or commercial law disputes. Due to their narrow subject matter jurisdiction, specialised courts are often associated with more accurate and predictable outcomes, faster court proceedings, and therefore more efficient overall litigation.[2] It is for these reasons that court specialisation is also considered to enhance **access to justice**. Except for being a tool to improve court infrastructure and litigation, court specialisation is even considered a tool to address development needs, such as the need to improve the investment climate or the need to protect the environment.[3] However, due to their focus on a specific subset of disputes and litigants, judges at these courts might develop a 'tunnel vision' or become prone to 'capture' by interest groups.[4] Depending on their jurisdictional rules, specialised courts might also face difficulties in attracting a significant and income generating caseload.[5] The trend towards greater court specialisation has been therefore characterised as 'a major change in the judiciary'.[6]

1 DP Wood, 'Generalist Judges in a Specialised World' (1997) 50 SMU Law Review 1755; L Baum, *Specialising the Courts* (The University of Chicago Press 2010) 1–3.
2 Among others RC Dreyfuss, 'Specialised Adjudication' (1990) BYU Law Review 377; E Silvestri, 'The Pros and Cos of Judicial Specialisation' in X Kramer and others (eds), *New Pathways to Civil Justice in Europe* (Springer 2021) 245.
3 H Gramckow and B Walsh, 'Developing Specialised Court Services: International Experiences and Lessons Learned' (The World Bank, Justice and Development Working Paper Series 2013).
4 Baum (n 1) 2; L LoPucki, *Courting Failure: How Competition for Big Cases is Corrupting the Bankruptcy Courts* (University of Michigan Press 2005).
5 Among others S Bechtold, J Frankenreiter and D Klerman, 'Forum Selling Abroad' (2019) 92 South Calif L Rev 487; G Antonopoulou, 'Forum Marketing in International Commercial Courts?' (2024) 44 Oxford Journal of Legal Studies 860.
6 Baum (n 1).

Georgia Antonopoulou, Birmingham Law School, the University of Birmingham, UK,
e-mail: g.antonopoulou@bham.ac.uk

https://doi.org/10.1515/9783110781632-019

#2 This Chapter takes as its focus the **Unified Patent Court** (UPC) and **international commercial courts** (ICCs) being recently established specialised courts in Europe. The courts' specialised character is achieved through the focus on intellectual property law and international civil and commercial law disputes respectively, the appointment of judges with increased expertise, and tailormade court proceedings. The Chapter explores how the jurisdictional rules of the UPC and the ICCs interact with European rules on **international jurisdiction**; notably, the Brussels I-bis Regulation.[7] It is argued that despite differences, the UPC and the ICCs commonly raise a set of jurisdictional challenges that deserve closer examination. Due to their centralised structure and distinctive procedural features, both types of courts call into question their qualification as a 'court or tribunal' and blur the neat distinction between rules on the internal allocation of cases, territorial and international jurisdiction. This could bring about significant implications as regards the parties' procedural rights.

#3 The rest of this Chapter is structured as follows. Section B introduces the UPC and the ICCs, and outlines the courts' most distinctive procedural features as well as the reasons behind their establishment. Section C first examines the application of the Brussels I-bis Regulation to the UPC and the ICCs. It then explores the proposal for a European Commercial Court and considers how this court could draw insights from the UPC and ICCs. Based on this analysis, Section D draws the common jurisdictional challenges of specialised courts together and explains how the institutional and procedural design of these courts muddies traditional definitions of a 'court or tribunal' and blurs the distinctions between different types of court jurisdiction. The last section concludes that while specialised courts bear a promising potential for improving access to justice, their centralised nature and distinctive procedural features challenge **procedural fairness** and therefore call for a careful balancing between the need for greater specialisation and the parties' procedural rights.

B The UPC and ICCs

I The UPC

#4 On 1 June 2023, the **Agreement on a Unified Patent Court** (UPCA) entered into force and the UPC opened its doors.[8] The UPC is a court common to the UPCA

7 The Chapter is not examining the UPC's procedural rules available at <https://www.unified-patent-court.org/en/court/legal-documents> accessed 1 March 2025.

8 See UPC available at <https://www.unified-patent-court.org/en> accessed 1 March 2025.

Member States[9] and therefore part of their national judicial systems.[10] The UPC has exclusive jurisdiction over European patents with unitary effect and European patents granted under the provisions of the European Patent Convention.[11] Due to its focus on patent protection, the UPC deals with two main forms of actions; namely, infringement and revocation actions. It is comprised of a Court of First Instance with a central division in Paris, France and sections in Munich, Germany and Milan, Italy.[12] It also has various local and regional divisions in different UPCA Member States.[13] The Court of Appeal is seated in Luxemburg and decides on appeals against decisions of the Court of First Instance.[14] Panels have a multinational composition of both legally and technically qualified judges.[15] Except for its centralised structure and its distinct judicial composition, another outstanding feature of the UPC is its language regime. In broad strokes, according to the UPCA contracting Member States hosting a local or regional division shall designate their official language or one of their official languages as **the language of court proceedings**.[16] Alternatively, contracting Member States may designate one or more of the official languages of the European Patent Office as the language of proceedings.[17] Parties may also agree on the use of the language in which the patent was granted as the language of proceedings.[18] In principle, when a division has designated several languages as the languages of proceedings the choice lies with the claimant, but the defendant could object and request a change of language order.[19]

---

9 For a list of the UPC Member States, see <https://www.unified-patent-court.org/en/organisation/upc-member-states> accessed 1 March 2025.

10 Preamble to the UPCA.

11 Article 1 and 32 UPCA. However, Article 83(1) UPCA introduces a seven-year-long transition period during which the UPC and national courts have concurrent jurisdiction. For an analysis of the UPC's exclusive jurisdiction and the transition period, see P Torremans, 'Exclusive Jurisdiction and Competence' in D Matthews and PLC Torremans (eds), *European Patent Law: The Unified Patent Court and the European Patent Convention* (De Gruyter 2023) 197.

12 Article 7(2) UPCA.

13 For the locations of the divisions, see UPC, 'Locations' available at <https://www.unified-patent-court.org/en/court/locations> accessed 1 March 2025.

14 Article 9(5) UPCA.

15 Article 8 and 9 UPCA.

16 Article 49(1) UPCA.

17 Article 49(2) UPCA.

18 Article 49(3) UPCA.

19 See Article 49 UPCA and Rule 14 Rules of Procedure of the Unified Patent Court.

#5 The UPC marks the first time the European Union (EU) Member States have created a **common court** functioning in parallel to the EU's judicial system.[20] The idea for a European court specialising in patent disputes has been in the making for decades.[21] The UPC was created to safeguard the uniform application of European patent law and thereby contribute to the creation of the EU internal market. The UPC is expected to overcome the significant variations between national courts that impede innovation especially for small and medium-sized enterprises facing barriers in enforcing their patent rights.[22]

II ICCs in Europe

#6 The establishment of ICCs in Europe underlines a parallel commitment to court specialisation in the field of cross-border civil and commercial disputes. In 2011 and 2018, France established the International Chambers within the Paris Commercial Court and the Paris Court of Appeal respectively.[23] In 2017, Germany established a Chamber for International Commercial Disputes within the Frankfurt am Main Regional Court.[24] Similar chambers were also established in Hamburg, Stuttgart, and Mannheim.[25] In January 2019, the Netherlands created the Netherlands Commercial

20 H Ulrich, 'The Unified Patent Court' (2023) 42 Yearbook of European Law 135.

21 See Protocol on Litigation as annexed to the Agreement on Community Patents of 15 December 1989, OJEC 1989 L 401; Commission, Proposal for a Council Decision conferring jurisdiction on the Court of Justice in disputes relating to the Community patent, COM (2013) 827 of 23 December 2003; Commission, Proposal for a Council Decision establishing the Community Patent Court and concerning appeals before the Court of First Instance COM (2003) 828 of 23 December 2003; Council of the European Union, 'Draft Agreement on the European and Community Patents Court and Draft Statute—Revised Presidency Text' Doc 7928/09 of 23 March 2009.

22 Preamble to the UPCA.

23 Commercial Court Paris, (The International Chamber Official Website), available at <https://www.tribunal-de-commerce-de-paris.fr/> accessed 1 March 2025. See also A Biard, 'International Commercial Courts in France: Innovation without Revolution?' (2019) 12(1) Erasmus Law Review 24; E Jeuland, 'The International Chambers of Paris: A Gaul Village' in X Kramer and J Sorabji (eds), *International Business Courts: A European and Global Perspective* (Eleven International Publishing 2019) 65, 72.

24 Chamber for International Commercial Disputes at the Regional Court Frankfurt am Main Official Website, available at <https://ordentliche-gerichtsbarkeit.hessen.de/landgerichtsbezirk-frankfurt-am-main/landgericht-frankfurt-am-main/chamber-for-international-commercial-disputes> accessed 1 March 2025. See also B Hess and T Boerner, 'Chambers for International Commercial Disputes in Germany: The State of Affairs' (2019) 12(1) Erasmus Law Review 33

25 Commercial Court Stuttgart/ Mannheim Official Website, available at <https://www.commercial-court.de/commercial-court> accessed 1 March 2025. See also Justizstandort-Stärkungsgesetz of 7 October 2024, available at <https://www.recht.bund.de/bgbl/1/2024/302/VO.html> accessed 1 March 2025.

Court (NCC).[26] Lastly, in 2023 Cyprus added itself to the increasing number of EU Member States that have established an ICC.[27]

#7 ICCs are national courts focusing on cross-border commercial disputes that primarily base their jurisdiction on the parties' agreement.[28] The ICCs in Europe are staffed with national judges selected for their expertise in cross-border civil and commercial disputes and their English language skills. One of the courts' distinctive features is the use of English as the court language. Although different ICCs use English as the court language in varying degrees, the use of English is expected to align court proceedings with the practices of international commerce where English is the 'lingua franca' and thereby tailor proceedings to the particularities of business disputes.[29]

#8 Just as in the case of the UPC, access to justice as well as economic considerations explain the establishment of ICCs in Europe. Due to their focus on international civil and commercial disputes, ICCs are expected to enhance the efficiency of cross-border commercial court proceedings and improve access to justice.[30] While some ICCs charge higher than the ordinary courts fees, their establishment is considered especially important for small- and medium-sized enterprises that struggle with the increasing costs of arbitration or foreign commercial courts.

---

26 Netherlands Commercial Court Official Website, available at <https://www.rechtspraak.nl/English/NCC/Pages/default.aspx> accessed 1 March 2025. See also E Bauw, 'Commercial Litigation in Europe in Transformation: The Case of the Netherlands Commercial Court' (2019) 12(1) Erasmus Law Review 15; X Kramer and G Antonopoulou, 'Commercializing Litigation: The Case of the Netherlands Commercial Court' in A Henke and others (eds), *International Commercial Courts. A Paradigm for the Future of Adjudication?* (Edizioni Scientifiche Italiane 2023) 105.

27 G Antonopoulou and X Kramer, 'A New Court Open for International Business Soon: The Commercial Court in Cyprus' (*Conflict of Laws.Net*, 26 February 2023) <https://conflictoflaws.net/2023/a-new-court-open-for-international-business-soon-the-commercial-court-in-cyprus/> accessed 1 March 2025.

28 Protocol on Procedural Rules Applicable to the International Chamber of the Paris Commercial Court (21 February 2018) Art 1.3 (Protocol Paris International Chamber); 'Chamber for International Commercial Disputes' (*Ordentliche Gerichtsbarkeit Hessen*) available at <https://ordentliche-gerichtsbarkeit.hessen.de/landgerichtsbezirk-frankfurt-am-main/landgericht-frankfurt-am-main/kammer-fuer-internationale-handelssachen> accessed 1 March 2025; W van Burgerlijke Rechtsvordering (*Dutch Code of Civil Procedure*), Art 30r(1) (DCCP); Council for the Judiciary, *Rules of Procedure for the International Commercial Chambers of the Amsterdam District Court (NCC District Court) and the Amsterdam Court of Appeal (NCC Court of Appeal)* Art 1.3.1(c) (3rd edn, June 2023). However, note that according to Law 69(I)/2022 the Commercial Court in Cyprus also deals with domestic disputes.

29 X Kramer and J Sorabji, 'International Business Courts in Europe and Beyond: A Global Competition for Justice?' (2019) 12(1) Erasmus Law Review 1, 5.

30 X Kramer and J Sorabji, 'Introduction: The International Business of Courts' in X Kramer and J Sorabji (eds), *International Business Courts: A European and Global Perspective* (Eleven International Publishing 2019) 1, 3. See also M Yip and G Rühl, 'General Report: New International Commercial Courts' in M Yip and G Rühl (eds), *New International Commercial Courts: A Comparative Perspective* (Intersentia 2024) 1, 17–19.

ICCs are also considered to improve contract enforcement and thereby to enhance the attractiveness of their host jurisdictions to foreign investors.[31] Although most European ICCs date back to older initiatives aimed at improving civil justice in cross-border civil and commercial matters, the fact that most of these courts were created shortly after the United Kingdom's departure from the European Union hints at an underlying competition between national jurisdictions and civil courts in Europe.[32]

C The Interplay with European Civil Procedure Rules

I The UPC and the Brussels I-bis Regulation

#9 The UPCA regulates the internal allocation of cases between different divisions, but it does not regulate the jurisdiction of the UPC.[33] Article 31 UPCA indeed provides that the international jurisdiction of the court shall be established on the basis of the Brussels I-bis Regulation[34] or, where applicable, the Lugano Convention.[35] In addition, according to Article 89(1) UPCA, the agreement cannot enter into force before making the necessary amendments to the Brussels I-bis Regulation. Hence, **Regulation 542/2014** amended the Brussels I-bis Regulation to bring it in line with the UPCA and extend its application to the UPC.[36] It also addressed the issue of UPC's jurisdiction over defendants domiciled in third, non-European

---

31 See World Bank Group, *Doing Business 2020: Comparing Business Regulation in 190 Economies* (Word Bank 2020) 91, 96, 98, 109, 126; World Bank Group, *Business Enabling Environment* (Concept Note 2022).

32 Inter alia E Themeli, *The Great Race of Courts: Civil Justice System Competition in the European Union* (Eleven International Publishing 2018); P Bookman, 'The Adjudication Business' (2020) 45 Yale Journal of International Law 227, 270; G Van Calster, 'Brexit and the Competition of Dispute Resolution Fora in Europe' in S Brekoulakis and G Dimitropoulos (eds), *International Commercial Courts: The Future of Transnational Adjudication* (CUP 2022) 501.

33 See Article 71 Brussels I-bis Regulation which prohibits Member States from concluding new conventions dealing with jurisdiction or recognition or enforcement.

34 Regulation (EU) No. 1215/2012 of the European Parliament and of the Council of 12 December 2012 on Jurisdiction and the Recognition and Enforcement of Judgments in Civil and Commercial Matters (recast).

35 Convention on Jurisdiction and the Recognition and Enforcement of Judgments in Civil and Commercial Matters.

36 Regulation (EU) No 542/2014 of the European Parliament and of the Council of 15 May 2014 Amending Regulation (EU) No 1215/2012 as Regards the Rules to be Applied with Respect to the Unified Patent Court and the Benelux Court of Justice.

Union states.[37] By contrast, the Lugano Convention was not amended in light of the UPC's establishment.

#10 As the European Commission clarified in its proposal, while according to Recital 11 Brussels I-bis Regulation courts or tribunals common to several Member States are to be considered 'courts or tribunals' for the purposes of the regulation, the recital lacks binding character and can therefore not adequately safeguard the application of the Brussels I-bis Regulation to the UPC.[38] Hence, Regulation 542/2014 inserted Article 71a to the Brussels I-bis Regulation, according to which a court common to several Member States shall be deemed to be a court of a Member State when it exercises jurisdiction in matters falling within the scope of the regulation. It then lists the UPC as a 'common court'.[39]

#11 The provision is significant especially if we consider that the UPC consists of a central division as well as various regional and local divisions in UPCA Member States.[40] Due to the internal allocation of cases between different divisions of the UPC a defendant resident in a Member State might find themselves sued before a division in a Member State different from the Member State designated by the Brussels I-bis Regulation. For example, a defendant expecting to be sued at its domicile on the basis of Article 4(1) Brussels I-bis Regulation may be sued before the competent central, regional or local division depending on where regional or local divisions are set up.[41] As the Commission underlines, legal certainty and predictability for defendants requires that this change of territorial jurisdiction is clearly regulated in the Brussels I-bis Regulation.[42]

#12 While Article 71b(1) Brussels I-bis Regulation extends the regulation's provisions on international jurisdiction to the UPC, the Brussels I-bis Regulation does not in principle apply to **defendants domiciled in third states**. Extending the regulation to third country defendants was fiercely debated on the occasion of the revision of the Brussels I Regulation and eventually the proposal was dropped.[43] According to Article 6(1) Brussels I-bis Regulation, if the defendant is not domiciled

---

37 European Commission, 'Proposal for a Regulation of the European Parliament and of the Council Amending Regulation (EU) No. 1215/2012 on Jurisdiction and the Recognition and Enforcement of Judgments in Civil and Commercial Matters' COM (2013) 554 final, 2.

38 ibid 5.

39 Article 1 Regulation (EU) No 542/2014.

40 For an overview of the UPC Structure, see 'UPC Presentation' (Unified Patent Court) available at <https://www.unified-patent-court.org/en/court/presentation> accessed 1 March 2025.

41 European Commission (n 37) 3–4. See also PLC Torremans, 'Regulation 542/2014 on Jurisdiction' in D Matthews and P Torremans (eds), *European Patent Law: The Unified Patent Court and the European Patent Convention* (De Gruyter 2023) 187.

42 European Commission (n 37) 5.

43 M Poesen, 'Civil Litigation Against Third-Country Defendants in the EU: Effective Access to Justice as a Rationale for European Harmonization of the Law of International Jurisdiction' (2022) 59 Common Market Law Review 1597.

in a Member State, the jurisdiction of the courts of each Member State shall with a few exceptions be determined according to the national law of that Member State (*lex fori*). However, the exclusion of third state defendants from the jurisdictional scope of the Brussels I-bis Regulation leaves a gap as regards substantive patent law because many third country parties and their activities in the EU may give rise to disputes.[44] Furthermore, since the UPC is a court common to several Member States determining the applicable *lex fori* would be extremely challenging. Applying, for example, the national law of the state where the UPC division is located would turn an issue of the internal allocation of cases to an issue of international jurisdiction. It would also result in inconsistent approaches depending on the national law applicable and thereby give rise to unequal access to justice[45] and forum shopping between different divisions.[46] Hence, Article 71b(2) Brussels I-bis Regulation expands the regulation's scope and permits the UPC to establish jurisdiction based on the provisions of Chapter II Brussels I-bis Regulation regardless of the defendant's domicile.

#13 Despite these important considerations underlying Article 71b(1), its practical relevance is nevertheless limited. It is limited because Article 71b(1) applies only if the UPC cannot establish jurisdiction based on the other provisions of the Brussels I-bis Regulation. Given the subject matter of the disputes coming before the UPC, it is expected to more frequently establish jurisdiction on the basis of Article 24(4) second paragraph, Article 25(1), and Article 26(1) Brussels I-bis Regulation which similarly confer jurisdiction on Member State courts irrespective of the defendant's domicile.[47] Article 71b(2) becomes therefore mainly relevant when Article 7(2) Brussels I-bis Regulation applies.[48] Lastly, Article 71b(1) also ensures the UPC's jurisdiction to issue provisional, including protective, measures even when the courts of third States have jurisdiction as to the substance of the matter.[49]

#14 One of the most controversial provisions of Regulation 542/2014 is the new Article 71b(3) Brussels I-bis Regulation. Legal scholars have examined how the provision overly extends the jurisdiction of the UPC and have therefore characterised it as

44 PLC Torremans, *Intellectual Property and Private International Law* (OUP 2024) para 8.151.

45 European Commission (n 37) 6.

46 See also P Campolini, 'Unified Patent Court's International Jurisdiction and Related Issues Addressed by EU Regulation No. 542/2014: Much Ado About Nothing or New Playground for the CJEU?' in L Desaunettes-Barbero and others (eds), *The Unified Patent Court. Problems, Possible Improvements and Alternatives* (Ledizioni 2023) 323, 329.

47 See among others *Abbott Diabetes Care Inc. v Sibio Technology Limited and others*, UPC_CFI_131/2024 (Order 19 June 2024).

48 Campolini (n 46) 331.

49 Article 71b(2) second paragraph Brussels I-bis Regulation.

an '**exorbitant**'[50] and 'long-arm'[51] jurisdictional basis. According to Article 71b(3), where the UPC has jurisdiction over a third state defendant according to Article 71b(2) in a dispute relating to an infringement of a European patent giving rise to damage within the Union, it may also exercise jurisdiction in relation to damage arising outside the Union from such an infringement. The UPC's jurisdiction under Article 71b(3) may only be established, if property belonging to the defendant is located in any Member State party to the UPCA and the dispute has a sufficient connection with that Member State. Recital 7 clarifies that Article 71b(3) is a subsidiary rule of jurisdiction in the sense that it does not create an independent ground of jurisdiction and it applies only if the UPC already has jurisdiction over the defendant under Article 71b(2).[52] It notes that a sufficient connection exists if the claimant is domiciled in that Member State or the relevant evidence is available there. In addition, according to Recital 7, the property should be of significant value making enforcement possible.

#15 At first glance, the jurisdictional reach of Article 71b(3) seems limited. According to the settled case law of the Court of Justice of the European Union (CJEU) on Article 7(2) Brussels I-bis Regulation, the 'place where the harmful event occurred or may occur' covers both the place where the **harmful event** giving rise to the damage occurred as well as the place where the **damage** occurred, and the choice lies with the claimant.[53] The court has clarified that when suing where the event

---

50 PA de Miguel Asensio, 'Regulation (EU) No. 542/2014 and the International Jurisdiction of the Unified Patent Court' (2014) 45 International Review of Intellectual Property and Competition Law 868, 882.

51 P Véron, 'Extent of the Long-Arm Jurisdiction Conferred upon the Unified Patent Court by Art. 71 (b)(3) of the Brussels I Regulation as Amended by Regulation 542/2014 of May 15, 2014: Turkish Delight and a Bit of Swiss Chocolate for the Unified Patent Court' (2015) 27 European Intellectual Property Review 588; Torremans (n 41) 194; Torremans (n 44) para 8.159.

52 Campolini (n 46) 334; Torremans (n 44) para 8.159.

53 Case C-21/76 *Handelskwekerij Bier v Mines de Potasse d'Alsace* (30 November 1976) ECLI:EU:C:1976:166, paras 15-19 and 24-25; Case C-220/88 *Dumez France SA and Tracoba SARL v Hessische Landesbank and others* (11 June 1990) ECLI:EU:C:1990:8, para 10; Case C-68/93 *Shevill and Others v Presse Alliance* (7 March 1995) ECLI:EU:C:1995:61, para 20; Case C-364/93 *Marinari v Lloyd's Bank* (19 September 1995) ECLI:EU:C:1995:289, para 11; Case C-51/97 *Réunion européenne SA and Others v Spliethoff's Bevrachtingskantoor BV and the Master of the vessel Alblasgracht V002* (27 October 1998) ECLI:EU:C:1998:509, para 28; Case C-167/00 *Verein für Konsumenteninformation v Karl Heinz Henkel* (1 October 2002) ECLI:EU:C:2002:555, para 44; Case C-18/02 *Danmarks Rederiforening, acting on behalf of DFDS Torline A/S v LO Landsorganisationen i Sverige, acting on behalf of SEKO Sjöfolk Facket för Service och Kommunikation* (5 February 2004) ECLI:EU:C:2004:74, para 40; Case C-168/02 *Rudolf Kronhofer v Marianne Maier and Others* (10 June 2004) ECLI:EU:C:2004:364, para 16; Case C-189/08 *Zuid-Chemie BV v Philippo's Mineralenfabriek NV/SA* (16 July 2009) ECLI:EU:C:2009:475, para 24; Joined Cases C-509/09 and C-161/10 *eDate Advertising GmbH v X and Olivier Martinez and Robert Martinez v MGN Limited* (25 October 2011) ECLI:EU:C:2011:685, paras 40–41; Case C-523/10 *Wintersteiger AG v Products 4U Sondermaschinenbau GmbH* (19 April 2012) ECLI:EU:C:2012:220 paras 19–20; Case C-228/11 *Melzer v MF Global UK Ltd* (16 May 2013) ECLI:EU:C:2013:305, para 25; Case C-147/12 *ÖFAB, Östergötlands Fastigheter AB v Frank Koot and Evergreen Investments BV* (18 July 2013) ECLI:EU:C:2013:490, para 51; Case C-170/12 *Peter Pinckney v KDG Mediatech AG* (3 October 2013) ECLI:EU:

giving rise to the damage occurred a claimant can claim their 'worldwide' damage irrespective of where exactly it occurred. However, when suing at the place where the damage occurred the claimant can only claim the damage sustained there.[54] By limiting the amount of damages, the CJEU has limited the wide choice of fora Article 7(2) grants claimants.

#16 Therefore, on the basis of Article 7(2) Brussels I-bis Regulation, the UPC could have jurisdiction over a patent infringement which took place in an EU Member State which is also a contracting state to the UPCA even if this produces damage not only within the Union but also outside. However, in the context of patent infringement, distinguishing the place where the harmful event occurred from the place where the damage occurred can be challenging. Given that European patents continue to be governed by the national law of each state where they are granted, proceedings concerning the infringement of patents in different states are regarded as separate infringements.[55] It is therefore in these cases that 71b(3) Brussels I-bis Regulation becomes controversial. Given that the provision does not refer to property that is directly related to the infringement action, it could raise concerns of overly extending the UPC's jurisdiction.[56] If this is so, UPC judgements could be refused recognition and enforcement in third states.

#17 Lastly, Articles 71c and 71d extend the Brussels I-bis Regulation provisions on *lis pendens* and the recognition and enforcement of court judgements to the UPC and thereby fully integrate UPC court proceedings and judgements into the Brussels I-bis regime.

II ICCs and the Brussels I-bis Regulation

#18 Unlike their name suggests, the ICCs established thus far in Europe are not self-standing courts but chambers within existing national courts. For example, the **NCC** is a specialised chamber of the Amsterdam District Court.[57] On second in-

C:2013:635, para 26; Case C-45/13 *Andreas Kainz v Pantherwerke AG* (16 January 2014) ECLI:EU:C:2014:7, para 23; Case C-387/12 *Hi Hotel HCF SARL v Uwe Spoering* (3 April 2014) ECLI:EU:C:2014:215, para 27; Case C-360/12 *Coty Germany GmbH v First Note Perfumes NV* (5 June 2014) ECLI:EU:C:2014:1318, para 46; Case C-441/13 *Pez Hejduk v EnergieAgentur NRW GmbH* (22 January 2015) ECLI:EU:C:2015:28, para 18; Case C-375/13 *Harald Kolassa v Barclays Bank plc* (28 January 2015) ECLI:EU:C:2015:37, para 45.

54 Case C-68/93 *Shevill and Others v Presse Alliance* (7 March 1995) ECLI:EU:C:1995:61, paras 28–33.

55 See Case C-539/03 *Roche Nederland BV and Others v Frederick Primus and Milton Goldenberg (13 July 2006)* ECLI:EU:C:2006:458, para 27f.

56 The American Law Institute, *Intellectual Property: Principles Governing Jurisdiction, Choice of Law, and Judgments in Transnational Disputes* (2008); Asensio (n 50) 881–882.

57 Article 32a Dutch Code of Civil Procedure (*Wetboek van Burgerlijke Rechtsvordering*), available in English in Alex Burrough and others (eds), *Code of Civil Procedure, Selected Sections* (Amsterdam Court of Appeal 2025) (hereafter: DCCP); Article 1.1.1 Rules of Procedure for the International Commer-

stance, it is complemented by the **Netherlands Commercial Court of Appeal (NCCA)** which is a specialised chamber of the Amsterdam Court of Appeal.[58] The institutional set-up as chambers within courts was justified on the basis of time and budgetary constraints. Setting up ICCs as chambers within courts facilitated the rapid set up of these courts and enabled them to rely on existing administrative structures. While these practical and administrative considerations are fully justified, the institutional set-up of ICCs as chambers within courts coupled with their distinctive features could cast doubts on their qualification as 'courts or tribunals' and call into question the application of the Brussels I-bis Regulation.

#19 Being chambers of existing courts, ICCs' subject matter, territorial and international jurisdiction depends on the subject matter, **territorial and international jurisdiction** of the court which they form a part of. Thus, the NCC has jurisdiction over a dispute under the condition that the dispute falls under the jurisdiction of the Amsterdam District Court.[59] In a similar vein, the **Frankfurt Chamber for International Commercial Disputes** deals with disputes falling under the jurisdiction of a Chamber for Commercial Disputes.[60]

#20 In addition, ICCs lack compulsory jurisdiction and require the **parties' agreement** to litigate before them. Parties wishing to bring their dispute before the NCC should have expressly agreed in writing on the use of English as the court language and the application of the NCC Rules.[61] Similarly, parties wishing to litigate before the Frankfurt Chamber for International Commercial Disputes have to submit a relevant application. What explains the requirement for the parties' agreement to litigate before ICCs are the courts' distinctive features. For instance, by requiring parties to explicitly agree to litigate before it the NCC aims at ensuring the parties' will to litigate before a court which conducts proceedings in English and charges fees higher than the ordinary Dutch courts.[62] Thus, the requirement for an explicit and written agreement embodies some of the biggest challenges surrounding the creation of ICCs in Europe, namely the use of a foreign language in court and the more expensive court fees several ICCs, such as the NCC, introduce.

cial Chambers of the Amsterdam District Court (NCC District Court) and the Amsterdam Court of Appeal (NCC Court of Appeal) (Fourth Edition, December 2024) (hereafter: NCC Rules).

58 Article 1.1.1. NCC Rules.

59 Article 1.3.1.(c) NCC Rules; Explanatory notes to Article 1.3.1(c) NCC Rules.

60 Chamber for International Commercial Disputes at the Regional Court Frankfurt am Main Official Website (n 24).

61 Article 32a(1) DCCP; Article 1.3.1.(d) NCC Rules.

62 G Antonopoulou, 'Requirements upon Agreements in Favour of the NCC and the German Chambers: Clashing with the Brussels Ibis Regulation?' (2019) 12(1) Erasmus Law Review 56; G Antonopoulou, 'Procedure Before International Commercial and Ordinary Courts: A Comparative Perspective' in S Brekoulakis and G Dimitropoulos (eds), *International Commercial Courts: The Future of Transnational Adjudication* (CUP 2022) 421, 438–439.

#21 While these formal requirements safeguard the parties' will to bring their disputes before an ICC and thereby safeguard procedural justice, they are nevertheless stricter than the formal requirements Article 25(1) Brussels I-bis Regulation imposes on **choice of court agreements**. For example, contrary to the NCC Rules which exclude NCC agreements in general terms and conditions unless expressly accepted by the other party,[63] according to the settled case law of the CJEU where a jurisdiction clause is included in the general conditions printed on the back of a contract, the writing requirement is fulfilled if the contract signed by both parties expressly refers to those general conditions, if a party exercising reasonable care could check the express reference to the general terms and conditions and only if the latter have, in fact, been communicated to the party.[64] Article 25(1) paragraphs (b) and (c) also permit choice of court agreements in a form which is in accordance with established practices between the parties or with international trade and commerce usages. This discrepancy could result in clashes between ICCs' procedural rules and the Brussels I-bis Regulation.[65] However, whether the ICCs procedural rules and the Brussels I-bis Regulation actually clash depends on the characterisation of agreements in favour of ICCs.

#22 If such agreements are characterised as choice of court agreements, then they would clash with the Brussels I-bis Regulation and the latter would prevail. After all, the Brussels I-bis Regulation already protects weaker parties and ensures their agreement on the chosen court.[66] However, given that ICCs are chambers within courts, it would be more accurate to characterise agreements in their favour as **agreements on the internal allocation of cases** within a court, where parties merely agree on the jurisdiction of a chamber within a court.[67] If we follow this characterisation, then an agreement in favour of the NCC which abides by the formal requirements of Article 25(1) Brussels I-bis Regulation but not by the stricter formal requirements set by the NCC Rules would suffice to establish the jurisdiction of the Amsterdam District Court, but it would fail to establish the jurisdiction of the NCC as a chamber within this court.[68] Furthermore, irrespective of a clash with Article 25(1) Brussels I-bis Regulation, the divergence between the formal requirements on choice of court agreements under European rules on

63 Explanatory Notes to Article 1.3.1.(d) NCC Rules.

64 Case C-24/76 *Estasis Salotti di Colzani Aimo e Gianmario Colzani s.n.c. v Rüwa Polstereimaschinen GmbH* (14 December 1976) ECLI:EU:C:1976:177, paras. 9–12; Case C-64/17*Saey Home & Garden NV/SA v Lusavouga-Máquinas e Acessórios Industriais SA* (8 March 2018) ECLI:EU:C:2018:173, paras 27–29.

65 Antonopoulou, 'Requirements upon Agreements in Favour of the NCC and the German Chambers' (n 62); P Ortolani and B van Zelst, 'International Commercial Courts and EU Law: Easing the Tension' (2023) 14 JIDS 76, 79–82.

66 See Article 25(1), Sections 3, 4, and 5 Brussels I-bis Regulation.

67 In this respect, see Explanatory Memorandum 2017, 5–6.

68 Antonopoulou, 'Requirements upon Agreements in Favour of the NCC and the German Chambers' (n 62) 66.

one hand and the formal requirements on agreements in favour of the newly established ICCs on the other hand illustrates that the latter might overly complicate access to an ICC and undermine the courts' aim of attracting litigation.[69] Lastly, ICCs' structure as chambers within courts combined with the lack of compulsory jurisdiction might also call into question their qualification as a 'court or tribunal' under the Brussels I-bis Regulation and render the regulation's provisions on the recognition and enforcement of court judgements inapplicable to ICCs court judgements.[70]

#23 It becomes therefore apparent that, unlike Regulation 542/2014, which explicitly included the UPC under the definition of a **'court or tribunal'** of the Brussels I-bis Regulation, ICCs proper qualification remains debatable. To avoid these uncertainties Ortolani and van Zelst argue in favour of establishing ICCs as **self-standing courts** and vesting them with compulsory jurisdiction over certain matters, such as arbitration-related court proceedings.[71] While the aim of protecting parties from the use of a foreign language in court is a justifiable aim, they contend that the Brussels I-bis Regulation already safeguards the parties will to litigate before a court by regulating formal requirements on choice of court agreements and protecting weaker parties, including consumers.[72] Alternatively, they recommend establishing ICCs as chambers within courts but assigning to the court, not the parties, the task of referring cases to the ICCs by drawing into consideration the parties' size, the international nature of the dispute, or the language of the contractual documents. This recommendation clarifies the ICCs structure as chambers within courts. It also decouples issues of international jurisdiction from issues of the internal allocation of cases between different chambers and takes a case-by-case approach as regards the use of a foreign language in court proceedings.[73]

III The Proposal for a European Commercial Court

#24 Having examined the interplay between the European specialised courts and European rules on international jurisdiction, this part turns to the European Parliament's study on a **European Commercial Court**. If a European Commercial Court were to become reality, it would be the second common to Member States

---

69 ibid 68.

70 See Article 2(a) and Article 3 Brussels I-bis Regulation.

71 Ortolani and van Zelst (n 65) 88.

72 Article 25(1) and Article 17–19 Brussels I-bis Regulation.

73 For a similar approach as regards language at the UPC, see *Curio Bioscience Inc. v. 10x Genomics Inc.*, Order of the Court of Appeal of the Unified Patent Court issued on 17 April 2024 concerning language of proceedings (UPC_CoA_101/2024).

court after the UPC. While such a prospect appears distant at the time of writing, the proposal is a good illustration of the increasing pace of court specialisation in Europe. The UPC could yield significant lessons for the set up and design of a European Commercial Court.

#25 In September 2018, the **European Parliament published a study** on international commercial contracts in Europe. Leaving aside issues of applicable law, the study underlined that in Europe some commercial courts, such as the **London Commercial Court**, are more popular than others. While it noted that this is not a problem in itself, the study underscores that English courts might not be accessible to all parties, especially small- and medium-sized enterprises and microbusinesses,[74] due to the costly legal fees. Consequently, these parties have to fall back to national commercial courts which do not necessarily meet their expectations. In addition, after **'Brexit'** English court judgements will not benefit from the Brussels I-bis Regulation's favourable provisions on the recognition and enforcement of court judgements, and this will present one more reason for parties to seek litigation elsewhere in Europe.[75] However, the study remarked that, unlike France, the Netherlands, and Germany, which have established international commercial courts, most Member States lack commercial courts and cases are heard by general courts. Hence, it underlined the need to improve access to justice in commercial disputes resolution across Europe.[76]

#26 The study recommended various measures to improve commercial dispute resolution both at the level of Member State and at the level of the EU. At the EU level, it suggested the creation of a **European Commercial Court**[77] which would complement the Member State courts and offer parties an additional forum for the resolution of their disputes. In support of the proposal for a European Commercial Court, the study drew also into consideration the benefits of courts in other specialised fields of law including the UPC.[78]

#27 According to the study, a **European Commercial Court** would come with multiple advantages. Being composed of experienced commercial law judges from all Member States it would be a truly international court with increased legal expertise. Just as is the case with arbitral tribunals composed of arbitrators hailing from different jurisdictions, its multinational composition would also enhance its perception as a neutral and impartial court by parties.[79] Lastly, the study placed

---

74 G Rühl, *Building Competence in Commercial Law in the Member States* (Study for the Juri Committee, European Parliament 2018) para 4.3.

75 ibid para 1.3.

76 ibid para 1.2.

77 See also T Pfeiffer, 'Ein Europäisher Handelsgerichtshof und die Entwicklung des Europäishen Privatrechts' [2016] Zeitschrift für Europäisches Privatrecht 795.

78 Rühl (n 74) para 4.3.2.

79 ibid para 4.4.

the proposed court within the broader context of civil justice systems competition. It noted that unlike different international commercial courts scattered in different Member States, a uniform European Commercial Court would be better positioned to participate in the global competition for cases.[80] It recommended that the court should be qualified as a 'court or tribunal' and thereby the Brussels I-bis Regulation as well as the other EU instruments on judicial cooperation should be applicable to it.[81] The study also notes that the jurisdiction of the European Commercial Court should not be limited to parties domiciled in the Member States.[82] Lastly, the European Commercial Court would lack compulsory jurisdiction and its jurisdiction would depend on the parties' agreement.[83]

#28 While the proposal entails a limited discussion of the European Commercial Court's procedural features, nevertheless a few interesting similarities as well as differences with the UPC's jurisdictional rules are noticeable. Similar to the UPC, the European Commercial Court would be explicitly qualified as a 'court or tribunal' under the Brussels I-bis Regulation and would rely on the regulation to establish international jurisdiction. Just as in the case of the UPC, this would also require an extension of the regulation's provisions to parties domiciled in third states. However, unlike the UPC, the European Commercial Court is envisioned as a court lacking compulsory jurisdiction and only as an alternative to national courts. Explicitly qualifying the European Commercial Court as a 'court or tribunal' would lift any uncertainty around its nature despite the lack of compulsory jurisdiction. While the lack of compulsory jurisdiction preserves the caseload of Member State courts, it could however give rise to overlapping jurisdictions and it could add an additional layer of jurisdictional competition between national and supranational courts in Europe.

D The Jurisdictional Complexities of Specialised Courts

#29 The UPC is an international court established on the basis of an international agreement. By contrast, ICCs are national courts established on the basis of national laws. In addition, the UPC has exclusive jurisdiction over disputes relating to European and Unitary Patents, while the ICCs depend their jurisdiction on the parties' agreement.

80 ibid para 4.4.
81 ibid.
82 ibid para 4.4.2.
83 ibid.

#30 Despite these fundamental differences, both the UPC and ICCs raise common jurisdictional issues. The institutional set up and the distinctive features of the UPC and ICCs commonly invite us to reconsider traditional definitions of 'courts or tribunals'. The UPC's centralised structure with local and regional divisions in some but not all of the UPCA Member States calls into question its qualification as a 'court or tribunal' under the Brussels I-bis Regulation. As a result, Regulation 542/2014 was adopted to amend the Brussels I-bis Regulation and place under its scope courts common to several Member States. In a similar vein, the institutional set up of ICCs as chambers within courts and their voluntary jurisdiction calls into question their immediate qualification as a 'court or tribunal' and could create uncertainty.

#31 Moreover, the UPC's centralised structure with divisions set up in some but not all UPCA Member States and ICC's distinctive features, such as the use of English as the court language, also invite us to reconsider traditional distinctions between rules on the internal allocation of cases, territorial and international jurisdiction. In centralised courts, such as the UPC, rules on the internal allocation of cases between different divisions come closer to rules of territorial jurisdiction and therefore have important jurisdictional and procedural justice implications. Being sued in a UPC division set up in a Member State different from the Member State initially designated by the Brussels I-bis Regulation means that the defendant might find themselves sued in a court far from the otherwise competent court that they could not reasonably foresee. The defendant could also find themselves caught up in court proceedings conducted in a language they are not familiar with. These issues of court proximity and court language are inextricably linked to issues of **procedural justice**. One could similarly observe that an agreement in favour of the ICCs, even if only an agreement on the jurisdiction of a chamber within a court, has severe procedural implications. The ICCs' use of English as a court language or the adoption of higher court fees illustrate that litigating before an ICC comes with significant procedural and due process implications which exceed the ambit of rules on the internal allocation of cases. The analysis makes therefore apparent that specialised courts throw a spanner in the traditional distinction between rules on the internal allocation of cases, territorial and international jurisdiction. They also bring to the fore the close relationship between rules on jurisdiction on one hand and procedural justice on the other and thus challenge policy makers to reconcile administrative, jurisdictional as well as procedural justice issues.

E Conclusion

#32 By the end of January 2025, the UPC has received a total of 700 cases. These cases include 251 infringement actions, 259 counterclaims for revocation, 55 stand-alone revocations, and 69 applications for provisional measures. It is interesting to note that the German local divisions of Munich, Duesseldorf and Mannheim are the most popular among the local divisions having received the majority of infringement actions.[84] This might also explain why German is the most used court language with 47%, while English is the second most used language with 45%.[85] This trend is in line with previous trends according to which German courts were the most popular European courts in patent litigation.[86] Unlike the UPC and its booming case law, ICCs have had a slower uptake.[87] This is primarily owed to the fact that ICCs lack compulsory jurisdiction and their caseload relies on parties' choosing them in a choice of court agreement. However, as stakeholders underline it takes time for ICCs to raise awareness of their recent establishment and build a caseload.[88]

#33 Despite their varying degrees of popularity, the UPC and ICCs mark a turn in court administration in Europe and signal a broader trend towards court specialisation. As the background to the creation of specialised courts has shown, their establishment was frequently justified with small and medium-sized enterprises and their access to justice needs in mind. While these courts owe their establishment to access to justice considerations, it is at the same time such considerations that challenge their institutional design and procedural rules. The courts' centralised set up might undermine the predictability of the competent court to defendants and result in large geographic distances. Court language concerns have also resulted in complex rules which attempt to strike a balance between **court specialisation** and **procedural fairness**.

84 UPC, 'Case load of the Court since Start of Operation in June 2023 – Update End May 2024' available at <https://www.unified-patent-court.org/en/news/case-load-court-start-operation-june-2023-update-end-may-2024> last accessed 1 March 2025.

85 ibid.

86 Bechtold, Frankenreiter and Klerman (n 5).

87 For the caseload of the NCC, see <https://www.rechtspraak.nl/English/NCC/Pages/judgments.aspx>; for the Stuttgart Commercial Chambers, see <https://www.commercial-court.de/en/press-current-news/detail?tx_news_pi1%5Baction%5D=detail&tx_news_pi1%5Bcontroller%5D=News&tx_news_pi1%5Bnews%5D=12&cHash=8df82b39fa26cfdb80c940c8cab4c0d8> all accessed 1 March 2025.

88 'The Netherlands Commercial Court: Settling International Business Disputes in English' (*Iamsterdam*, 5 March 2024) <https://www.iamsterdam.com/en/business/the-netherlands-commercial-court-settling-business-disputes-in-english> accessed 1 March 2025.

References

'The Netherlands Commercial Court: Settling International Business Disputes in English' (*Iamsterdam*, 5 March 2024) <https://www.iamsterdam.com/en/business/the-netherlands-commercial-court-settling-business-disputes-in-english> accessed 1 March 2025.

Alex Burrough and others (eds), *Code of Civil Procedure, Selected Sections* (Amsterdam Court of Appeal 2025).

Antonopoulou G and Kramer X, 'A New Court Open for International Business Soon: The Commercial Court in Cyprus' (*Conflict of Laws.Net*, 26 February 2023) <https://conflictoflaws.net/2023/a-new-court-open-for-international-business-soon-the-commercial-court-in-cyprus/> accessed 1 March 2025.

Antonopoulou G, 'Requirements upon Agreements in Favour of the NCC and the German Chambers: Clashing with the Brussels Ibis Regulation?' (2019) 12(1) Erasmus Law Review 56.

—— 'Procedure Before International Commercial and Ordinary Courts: A Comparative Perspective' in S Brekoulakis and G Dimitropoulos (eds), *International Commercial Courts: The Future of Transnational Adjudication* (CUP 2022) 421.

—— 'Forum Marketing in International Commercial Courts?' (2024) 44 Oxford Journal of Legal Studies 860.

Asensio de Miguel PA, 'Regulation (EU) No. 542/2014 and the International Jurisdiction of the Unified Patent Court' (2014) 45 International Review of Intellectual Property and Competition Law 868.

Baum L, *Specializing the Courts* (The University of Chicago Press 2010).

Bauw E, 'Commercial Litigation in Europe in Transformation: The Case of the Netherlands Commercial Court' (2019) 12(1) Erasmus Law Review 15.

Bechtold S, Frankenreiter J and Klerman D, 'Forum Selling Abroad' (2019) 92 South Calif L Rev 487.

Biard A, 'International Commercial Courts in France: Innovation without Revolution?' (2019) 12(1) Erasmus Law Review 24.

Bookman P, 'The Adjudication Business' (2020) 45 Yale Journal of International Law 227.

Campolini P, 'Unified Patent Court's International Jurisdiction and Related Issues Addressed by EU Regulation No. 542/2014: Much Ado About Nothing or New Playground for the CJEU?' in L Desaunettes-Barbero and others (eds), *The Unified Patent Court. Problems, Possible Improvements and Alternatives* (Ledizioni 2023) 323.

Dreyfuss RC, 'Specialized Adjudication' (1990) BYU Law Review 377.

Gramckow H and Walsh B, 'Developing Specialized Court Services: International Experiences and Lessons Learned' (The World Bank, Justice and Development Working Paper Series 2013).

Jeuland E, 'The International Chambers of Paris: A Gaul Village' in X Kramer and J Sorabji (eds), *International Business Courts: A European and Global Perspective* (Eleven International Publishing 2019) 65.

Kramer X and Antonopoulou G, 'Commercializing Litigation: The Case of the Netherlands Commercial Court' in Albert Henke and others (eds), *International Commercial Courts. A Paradigm for the Future of Adjudication?* (Edizioni Scientifiche Italiane 2023) 105.

Kramer X and Sorabji J, 'International Business Courts in Europe and Beyond: A Global Competition for Justice?' (2019) 12(1) Erasmus Law Review 1, 5.

—— 'Introduction: The International Business of Courts' in X Kramer and J Sorabji (eds), *International Business Courts: A European and Global Perspective* (Eleven International Publishing 2019) 1.

LoPucki L, *Courting Failure: How Competition for Big Cases is Corrupting the Bankruptcy Courts* (University of Michigan Press 2005).

Ortolani P and Zelst van B, 'International Commercial Courts and EU Law: Easing the Tension' (2023) 14 JIDS 76.

Pfeiffer T, 'Ein Europäisher Handelsgerichtshof und die Entwicklung des Europäishen Privatrechts' [2016] Zeitschrift für Europäisches Privatrecht 795.

Poesen M, 'Civil Litigation Against Third-Country Defendants in the EU: Effective Access to Justice as a Rationale for European Harmonization of the Law of International Jurisdiction' (2022) 59 Common Market Law Review 1597.
Rühl G, *Building Competence in Commercial Law in the Member States* (Study for the Juri Committee, European Parliament 2018).
Silvestri E, 'The Pros and Cos of Judicial Specialization' in X Kramer and others (eds), *New Pathways to Civil Justice in Europe* (Springer 2021) 245.
The American Law Institute, *Intellectual Property: Principles Governing Jurisdiction, Choice of Law, and Judgments in Transnational Disputes* (2008).
Themeli E, *The Great Race of Courts: Civil Justice System Competition in the European Union* (Eleven International Publishing 2018).
Torremans PL, 'Exclusive Jurisdiction and Competence' in D Matthews and P Torremans (eds), *European Patent Law: The Unified Patent Court and the European Patent Convention* (De Gruyter 2023) 197.
—— 'Regulation 542/2014 on Jurisdiction' in D Matthews and P Torremans (eds), *European Patent Law: The Unified Patent Court and the European Patent Convention* (De Gruyter 2023) 187.
—— *Intellectual Property and Private International Law* (OUP 2024).
Ulrich h, 'The Unified Patent Court' (2023) 42 Yearbook of European Law 135.
Van Calster G, 'Brexit and the Competition of Dispute Resolution Fora in Europe' in S Brekoulakis and G Dimitropoulos (eds), *International Commercial Courts: The Future of Transnational Adjudication* (CUP 2022) 501.
Véron P, 'Extent of the Long-Arm Jurisdiction Conferred upon the Unified Patent Court by Art. 71(b)(3) of the Brussels I Regulation as Amended by Regulation 542/2014 of May 15, 2014: Turkish Delight and a Bit of Swiss Chocolate for the Unified Patent Court' (2015) 27 European Intellectual Property Review 588.
Wood DP, 'Generalist Judges in a Specialized World' (1997) 50 SMU Law Review 1755.
World Bank Group, *Doing Business 2020: Comparing Business Regulation in 190 Economies* (Word Bank 2020).
—— *Business Enabling Environment* (Concept Note 2022).
Yip M and Rühl G, 'General Report: New International Commercial Courts' in M Yip and G Rühl (eds), *New International Commercial Courts: A Comparative Perspective* (Intersentia 2024) 1.

Emma van Gelder*

Chapter 20 Alternative Pathways: ADR/ODR

A Introduction

#1 Out-of-court dispute resolution pathways form a vital part of contemporary civil justice systems throughout Europe. **Alternative Dispute Resolution (ADR)** refers to alternative forms of dispute resolution typically offered out of court, such as arbitration and mediation.[1] Since the 1990's, the European legislature has been actively encouraging the use of ADR as part of a broader effort to achieve access to justice, especially in the field of consumer protection.[2] Consumer redress has been and still is widely considered as the Achilles' heel of consumer protection as consumers often face difficulties in remedying their substantive rights.[3] Since consumers rarely seek judicial protection in view of the cost and formality of civil courts, the promotion of ADR as a less formal, swift and more affordable alternative to the court has been embraced by the EU legislature.[4]

#2 In 2013 the EU legislator adopted the first binding framework on consumer ADR: **the ADR Directive and the ODR Regulation.**[5] Consumer ADR forms a key component of a broader EU 'toolbox' consisting of legislative and non-legislative tools

1 E Bauw and others, *Rechtsstatelijke waarborging van buitengerechtelijke geschiloplossing* (Boom Juridisch 2018) 17.

2 European Commission, 'Green Paper on Alternative Dispute Resolution in Civil and Commercial Law' COM (2002) 196, 8; European Parliament and Council Directive 2008/52/EC of 21 May 2008 on certain aspects of mediation in civil and commercial matters [2008] OJ L136/3.

3 Parliamentary Assembly of the Council of Europe, Access to Justice and the Internet: Potential and Challenges, Resolution 2054, Report: Doc. 13918 of 10 November 2015; N Andrews, 'Fundamental Principles of Civil Procedure: Order Out of Chaos' in X Kramer and CH van Rhee (eds), *Civil Litigation in A Globalising World* (TMC Asser Press 2012) 19, 20.

4 A Fejös and C Willett, 'Consumer Access to Justice: The Role of the ADR Directive and the Member States' (2016) 24 ERPL 33, 34; H-W Micklitz and G Saumier, 'Enforcement and Effectiveness of Consumer Law' in H-W Micklitz and G Saumier (eds), *Enforcement and Effectiveness of Consumer Law* (Springer 2018) 3, 5; C Daniels, 'Alternative Dispute Resolution for European Consumers: A Question of Access to and Standards of Justice' in L Cadiet, B Hess and M Requejo Isidro (eds), *Privatizing Dispute Resolution* (Nomos 2019) 257.

5 Council Directive 2013/11/EU of 21 May 2013 on Alternative Dispute resolution for Consumer Disputes [2013] OJ L165/63; Council Regulation (EU) 524/2013 of 21 May 2013 on online dispute resolution for consumer disputes and amending Regulation 2006/2004 and Directive 2009/22/EC [2013] OJ L165/1.

***Corresponding author**: **Emma van Gelder,** Molengraaff Instituut, Utrecht University,
e-mail: e.m.vangelder@uu.nl

https://doi.org/10.1515/9783110781632-020

that aim to make consumer law enforcement more effective.[6] The EU legislature also addressed ADR through sector-specific legislation either encouraging or requiring access to ADR.[7] In addition to the aforementioned specific consumer ADR legislation, the EU legislator has adopted general ADR legislation for cross-border civil disputes including the **Mediation Directive**.[8]

#3 Where ADR procedures take disputes out of the court, **online dispute resolution** procedures (ODR) take procedures from a physical into a virtual space.[9] ODR refers to procedures that implement technology in their procedure to (assist in) resolving disputes.[10] There is no commonly accepted definition of ODR as the wide variety of ICT-enabled dispute resolution procedures as well as the degree in which technology is used make ODR difficult to define.[11] For instance, while some define ODR as procedures that are conducted online fully or substantially in part, others define it as any procedure in which some form of ICT is used.[12] This paper refers to ODR as out-of-court procedures that are conducted mostly online.[13]

#4 The field of ODR is quickly evolving across Europe as novel ODR providers are mushrooming and ADR bodies are increasingly relying on digital technologies, which development has been further fueled by the Covid-19 pandemic.[14] Also, the EU legislator has been keen in promoting the use of ODR.[15] Certainly, ODR has the potential to reduce barriers to **access to justice** even more than ADR by centralising the dispute online.[16]

6 European Commission, 'Report from the Commission to the European Parliament, the Council and the European Economic and Social Committee' COM (2019) 425 final.

7 For instance, adequate and effective ADR schemes are required to be put in place in the telecommunication and energy sectors.

8 E Storskrubb, 'Alternative Dispute Resolution in the EU: Regulatory Challenges' (2016) 24 ERPL 7, 21.

9 A Lodder and J Zeleznikow, 'Developing an Online Dispute Resolution Environment: Dialogue Tools and Negotiation Support Systems in a Three-Step Model' (2005) 10 Harvard Negotiation Law Review 287.

10 E Katsh and O Rabinovich-Einy, *Digital Justice. Technology and the Internet of Disputes* (OUP 2017) 10.

11 R Beretta, 'The Use of Technology in Dispute Resolution; A Framework for the Study of ODR' (2023) Vilnius University Open Series 19.

12 E van Gelder, *Consumer Online Dispute Resolution Pathways in Europe* (Eleven International Publishing 2022) 103.

13 The Chapter thus leaves judicial ODR (or 'court ODR'), referring to court processes that implement ODR techniques, outside its' scope; examples of Court ODR include the Civil Resolution Tribunal in British Columbia, the UK Pilot online Claim.

14 Van Gelder (n 12).

15 P Cortés and A Lodder, 'Consumer Dispute Resolution Goes Online' (2014) 21 Maastricht Journal of European and Comparative Law 16.

16 C Busch and S Reinhold, 'Standardisation of Online Dispute Resolution Services: Towards a More Technological Approach' (2015) 4(1–2) EuCML 50.

#5 ADR and ODR pathways are going through important developments in Europe, since the ADR Directive is under revision and the 2024 **Digital Services Act** (DSA) adds a whole new collection of ODR bodies to the existing field of pathways to consumer redress.[17] While these ongoing efforts in stimulating ADR and ODR can be applauded as they open up new redress pathways and modernise the existing ones, the diversity in legislative enactment risks a further fragmentation of the already difficult to navigate ADR and ODR field.

#6 This Chapter first introduces ADR and ODR (B) and then elaborates on the EU legislative policy (C). While this legislative policy concerns a broader ADR setting, this Chapter focuses on *consumer* ADR and Section C will thus mainly center around the functioning and revision of the ADR Directive. Sections D focuses on the Mediation Directive. Subsequently, the Chapter discusses the EU legislative efforts in promoting ODR (E). The Chapter then evaluates the overlap and connection between the different ADR and ODR routes (F) and concludes (G).

B The Rise of Alternative Dispute Resolution and Online Dispute Resolution

#7 ADR triumphed across Europe as a means to improve access to justice having significant potential to lower the court-related barriers by offering more affordable, more flexible and rapid procedures. ODR could lower these barriers even further by centralising procedures online. At the same time, critique began to be voiced against these rising forms of dispute resolution.

I The Rise of Alternative Dispute Resolution

#8 ADR emerged in the 1970's across Europe against the background of pertaining challenges to safeguard access to justice through the civil court including costs, organisational flaws and practical difficulties.[18] The Florence Access to Justice

---

17 Article 20 and 21 of Regulation (EU) 2022/2065 of the European Parliament and of the Council of 19 October 2022 on a Single Market For Digital Services and amending Directive 2000/31/EC (Digital Services Act) [2022] OJ L277/1; C Busch and V Mak, 'Putting the Digital Service Act into Context: Bridging the Gap between EU Consumer Law and Platform Regulation' (2021) 10 EuCML 109; C Busch, 'The P2B Regulation (EI) 2019/1150: Towards a "Procedural Turn" in EU Platform Regulation?' (2020) 9 EuCML 133; V Mak, 'Geschilbeslechting voor consumenten onder de Digital Services Act: Online Dispute Resolution 3.0' [2023–1] TvC 2.

18 M Piers, 'Europe's Role in Alternative Dispute Resolution: Off to a Good Start?' [2014–2] Journal of Dispute Resolution 269.

movement proposed several solutions for these obstacles amongst which was the extension of the scope of 'justice' to include remedies offered by ADR bodies.[19] It led to the acknowledgement that ADR is a proper means to achieve access to justice.[20]

#9 ADR bodies soon proliferated across Europe in different shapes and sizes offering procedures where parties have control over the process and outcome with the third-party acting as facilitator (eg **mediation** and **conciliation**) as well as procedures where a third-party is in charge of the process and outcome (eg **arbitration** and **binding advice**).[21] ADR was mainly promoted in the consumer redress field, characterised by the low-value claims and the difficulties to access courts.

II The Rise of Online Dispute Resolution

#10 The roots of ODR trace back to the mid-1990s in the United States with the appearance of online marketplaces and their quest for efficient means to resolve the growing amount of **e-commerce disputes** appearing on their platforms. Certainly, trust among their customers is key for the further growth of their business. Since available offline redress pathways often appeared too costly and complex to resolve these typical low-value and potential cross-border claims, the marketplaces explored the potential of technology in resolving disputes.[22] Also in the EU, consumers increasingly resort to such platforms for redress when encountering disputes with third-party sellers operating on the marketplaces owing to the emergence of online marketplaces in the EU internal market (eg Amazon Marketplace).[23]

#11 Next to ODR on **online intermediary platforms**, consumers can resort to ODR procedures offered by traditional ADR bodies using **ODR techniques** such as online complaint submission, case management systems and video hearings.[24] This growing uptake of technology by ADR bodies blurs the boundaries between *off-*

19 Other solutions regarded legal aid and collective representation; M Cappelletti, 'Alternative Dispute Resolution Process within the Framework of the World-Wide Access-to-Justice Movement' (1993) 56 The Modern Law Review 282.

20 M Galanter, 'Access to Justice in a World of Expanding Social Capability' (2009) 37 Fordham Urban Law Journal 115, 116; E Storskrubb and J Ziller, 'Access to Justice in European Comparative Law' in F Francioni (ed), *Access to Justice as a Human Right* (OUP 2007) 177, 178.

21 P Cortés, 'The New Landscape of Consumer Redress: The European Directive on Consumer Alternative Dispute Resolution and the Regulation on Online Dispute Resolution' in P Cortés (ed), *The New Regulatory Framework for Consumer Dispute Resolution* (OUP 2016) 17.

22 Van Gelder (n 12) 85.

23 A Carrel and N Ebner, 'Mind the Gap: Bringing Technology to the Mediation Table' [2019–2] Journal of Dispute Resolution 1, 25.

24 Van Gelder (n 12) 140.

line- and *online* dispute resolution.[25] In comparison with ADR, ODR, however, does have its unique features as technology enters the procedure as a **'fourth party'**[26] and can change the 'DNA' of the procedure presenting unique challenges to it.[27]

III ADR and ODR in relation to Access to Justice

#12 ADR and ODR are often hailed for their ability to enhance access to justice. Certainly, ODR can save time and costs related to travel, accommodation and scheduling appointments; online infrastructures are typically cheaper and faster than physical ones and the simplified guided interfaces can alleviate the need for costly and timely support.[28] How ADR and ODR influence access to justice, depends for a large share on the type of complaint underlying the case and the type of procedure used.

#13 Mediation and conciliation procedures are more focused on identifying parties' interests and reaching a solution based on them, rather than exploring their legal rights and promulgating a decision in compliance with the law. Critiques on ADR soon began to be voiced some even questioning whether ADR not rather was a 'deliberate escape' from justice.[29] Debates started as to whether ADR procedures – in particular conciliation and mediation – are actually designed to enforce substantive (consumer) rights and whether redress received through these procedures is actually similar to *justice*.[30] Furthermore, the typical private nature of ADR and ODR make it difficult to monitor the quality of the procedure and the outcomes, especially within consensual procedures which are typically less strictly regulated in comparison to adjudicative procedures.[31] As disputes increasingly move out of the court arena, the court cannot fulfill its public task to inter-

---

25 P Cortés, *Online Dispute Resolution for Consumers in the European Union* (Routledge 2011) 53.

26 This metaphor has been introduced by Katsh and Rifkin, emphasising the influential role of technology in procedures; see E Katsh and J Rifkin, *Online Dispute Resolution. Resolving Conflicts in Cyberspace* (Jossey-Bass 2001).

27 Van Gelder (n 12); E Vilalta, 'ODR and e-Commerce' in M Wahab, E Katsh and D Rainey (eds), *Online Dispute Resolution Theory and Practice* (Eleven International Publishing 2012) 125, 126.

28 O Rabinovich-Einy, 'Balancing the Scales: The Ford-Firestone Case, the Internet, and the Future Dispute Resolution Landscape' (2004) 6 Yale Journal of Law & Technology 1, 32.

29 PH Lindblom, 'ADR – The Opiate of the Legal System?' (2008) 16 ERPL 63, 67.

30 C Willet, 'Editorial: Special Edition on Access to Justice and Consumer ADR' (2016) 24 ERPL 1, 6; G Wagner, 'Private Law Enforcement Through ADR: Wonder Drug or Snake Oil?' (2014) 51 CMLR 165; Lindblom (n 29) 66.

31 G Wagner and H Eidenmüller, 'Digital Dispute Resolution' (2021) 28 <https://ssrn.com/abstract=3871612> accessed 10 April 2025.

pret the law or refer questions on interpretation in case of doubt. This may hinder a further development of the law.[32]

#14 Moreover, **quality concerns** continue to surround ADR and ODR. For instance, while ODR procedures have been hailed for their efficiency, the quality has been an issue sparking transparency concerns about what is happening behind the closed virtual doors of platforms.[33] As online marketplaces primarily act as private companies with the main objective to keep their customers satisfied and gain revenue, efficiency rather than quality standards is at the core of their ODR system design.[34] It also matters what type of technology is used and to what extent. For instance, while text-based online tools can keep the costs low and enhance the speed, consumers may not be able to adequately express themselves, the third party may misinterpret the text or be biased in favour of the party whose literacy skills are more solid.[35] For instance, consumers involved in more emotional disputes – in the health sector, for example – may wish to have an audio or video hearing where they can express their views, while consumers in other sectors – for instance, e-commerce – may prefer a faster and cheaper (automated) text-based procedure.

#15 While parties seeking redress through ADR and ODR retain the right to resort to court according to Art. 6 ECHR, individuals dealing with a low-value claims will likely not proceed to a costly and burdensome litigation procedure following an unsuccessful attempt to settle. ADR and ODR are *alternatives* to the court procedure and making them subject to a strict regulatory procedural framework may undermine their purpose to offer affordable, simple and quick alternatives to the elaborate and sophisticated civil court procedure.[36] In drawing up regulation for ADR and ODR it thus remains crucial that the quality remains at the core, especially in fields of law characterised by a power imbalance, while not losing touch of their flexibility assets.[37]

---

32 M Loos, 'Enforcing Consumer Rights through ADR at the Detriment of Consumer Law' (2016) 24 ERPL 61, 75.

33 E van Gelder and A van Duin, 'In de schaduw van het recht: over PayPal's Resolution Centre en kwaliteitsstandaarden voor cODR op online platforms' in P Wolters and others (eds), *Digitalisering en Conflictoplossing* (Wolters Kluwer 2021) 129.

34 V Mak, *Legal Pluralism in European Contract Law* (OUP 2020) 154.

35 Cortés (n 25) 150.

36 Lindblom (n 29) 66.

37 F Francioni, 'The Rights of Access to Justice under Customary International Law' in F Francioni (ed), *Access to Justice as a Human Right*, Collected Courses of the Academy of European Law (Oxford, 2007; online edn, Oxford Academic, 22 March 2012) 1; Daniels (n 4) 264.

C An Overview of the EU Legislative Policy on ADR and ODR

#16 There is a range of EU legislative initiatives that encourage or require the use of ADR within civil justice both within specific sectors – eg the consumer sector – and within broader areas encompassing civil and commercial disputes. This Section provides an overview of these initiatives, which overview attempts to follow a chronological approach in the rather patchy collection of initiatives. In line with the focus of the EU legislator in encouraging ADR, this overview also focuses on **consumer ADR**.

I EU Legislative Efforts on Encouraging the Use of ADR

#17 In a **1993 Green Paper** on consumer access to justice the European Commission expressed its ambition to develop ADR to lessen the imbalance between the costs of cross-border legal procedures and the value of the consumer dispute.[38] In the subsequent **1996 Action Plan**, it further promoted consumer ADR amidst the aforementioned proliferation of ADR across the Member States and notified the need to create minimum criteria to facilitate the creation and 'networking' of ADR at the internal market level.[39] In 1998 the EU legislature also identified mediation of transnational *family* disputes as a field that merited further examination and the EU legislature has made continued efforts ever since in promoting the use of cross-border mediation.[40]

#18 Among the first legislative ADR initiatives – following the Treaty of Amsterdam which allocated the EU the competence to legislate in the area of 'judicial cooperation in civil matters with cross-border implications'[41] – are two **non-binding Commission Recommendations of 1998 and 2001** aimed at creating and promoting quality ADR mechanisms across the EU, particularly in the field of consumer law. They respectively deal with ADR procedures that propose or impose a solution and with more consensual forms of ADR. Recommendation 1998 en-

38 European Commission, 'Green Paper on the Access of Consumers to Justice and the Settlement of Consumer Disputes in the Single Market' COM (93) 576.

39 European Commission, 'Action Plan on Consumer Access to Justice and the Settlement of Consumer Disputes in the Internal Market' COM (96) 13, 14.

40 This was part of the Action Plan of the European Commission and the European Council on how to best implement the provisions of the Treaty of Amsterdam.

41 This competence was introduced in Article 65 of the then EC Treaty and has been converted into Article 81 TFEU with the Treaty of Lisbon; G Wagner, 'Harmonisation of Civil Procedure: Policy Perspectives' in X Kramer and CH van Rhee (eds), *Civil Litigation in a Globalising World* (Asser Press 2012) 93, 94; Storskrubb (n 8) 9.

shrined the minimum quality standards of independence, transparency, adversarial proceedings, effectiveness, legality, and liberty, and Recommendation 2001 those of impartiality, transparency, effectiveness, and fairness.[42]

#19 In 2002, the European Commission issued a **Green Paper on ADR** which reached beyond the area of consumer law, applying to civil and commercial matters with the aim to familiarise a broad public with ADR.[43] It highlighted the growing interest in ADR across Europe and the political priority it had been given in many Member States.[44] A **2004 Code of Conduct on Mediation** stipulated quality principles mediators could adhere to including confidentiality, fairness and neutrality. Soon after, the Mediation Directive was adopted (See Section D).

#20 In 2011, the European Commission issued an **Impact Assessment** in which it identified that the fragmented reality of consumer ADR bodies in Europe negatively impacted the possibility for consumers to rely on ADR for cross-border disputes and thereby noted that improving cross-border ADR relied on improving national ADR.[45] In this regard, the IA highlighted the need for a binding EU framework harmonising ADR across Europe which eventually resulted in the adoption of the ADR Directive and ODR Regulation (see under III of this Section).

II EU Legislative Efforts on Promoting ODR

#21 The EU legislatures' efforts in improving access to justice also began to include references to ODR around the end of the 1990s. The **2000 e-Commerce Directive** supports ODR as it requires Member States to ensure that their legislation does not prevent the use of ADR, including appropriate electronic means.[46] In the 2010 'Digital Agenda for Europe', the European Commission acknowledged the potential of ODR by declaring its ambition to launch an EU-wide 'online redress tool' to

42 Commission Recommendation 98/257/EC on the Principles Applicable to the Bodies Responsible for Out-of-Court Settlement of Consumer Disputes [1998] OJ L155/31 and Commission Recommendation 2001/310/EC on the Principles for Out-of-Court Bodies involved in the Consensual Resolution of Consumer Disputes [2001] OJ L109/56.

43 European Commission, 'Green Paper on Alternative Dispute Resolution in Civil and Commercial Law' COM (2002) 196, 15.

44 ibid 5.

45 European Commission, 'Commission Staff Working Paper. Executive Summary of the Impact Assessment 2011' SEC (2011) 1409 final, 3, 4.

46 Directive 2000/31/EC of the European Parliament and of the Council of 8 June 2000 on certain legal aspects of information society services, in particular electronic commerce, in the Internal Market ('Directive on electronic commerce) [2000] OJ L178/1, Art. 17.

improve access to justice.[47] Furthermore, in the **ODR Regulation**, the EU legislature underscores the potential of ODR as a 'simple, efficient, fast and low-cost' redress option that can enhance consumers trust in e-commerce.[48] The EU legislature seems to take primarily a functional approach towards ODR, using it as a practical information and redirection tool.[49]

#22 The EU legislator also increasingly regulates ODR procedures offered by online marketplaces since they are fulfilling a growing role in consumer redress in the EU.[50] The **Platform-to-business Regulation** (P2B Regulation)[51] and the DSA lay down quality standards for internal procedures and also entitle platform users to challenge decisions stemming from such procedures to external ODR bodies.[52]

D The Consumer ADR Directive and ODR Regulation

I The Existing Framework

#23 The **ADR Directive** and **ODR Regulation** have been adopted on the basis of Articles 114 TFEU, the internal market basis, and 169(1)(a) TFEU.[53] The main purpose of the Directive is to tackle the shortcomings of the ADR landscapes existing across Europe to ease consumers' journey for redress and thereby achieve a high level of consumer protection.[54] The more specific objectives are to counter three shortcomings: the gaps in the geographical and sectoral coverage of ADR, the lack of awareness about ADR among consumers and traders and the uneven level of quality of ADR bodies.[55] Therefore, the Directive requires Member States to en-

---

47 European Commission, Communication from the Commission to the European Parliament, the Council, the European Economic and Social Committee and the Committee of the Regions a Digital Agenda for Europe, COM (2010) 245 final.

48 ODR Regulation, Recitals 6 and 8.

49 Beretta (n 11).

50 Mak (n 34) 138.

51 Regulation (EU) 2019/1150 of the European Parliament and of the Council of 20 June 2019 on promoting fairness and transparency for business users of online intermediation services [2019] OJ L186/57 (P2B Regulation).

52 P2B Regulation, Art. 12(1); DSA, Art. 18; Christoph Busch, 'Regulation of Digital Platforms as Infrastructures for Services of General Interest' WISO-Diskurs 09/2021 (Friedrich-Ebert-Stiftung) 19.

53 Cortés (n 21) 19.

54 European Commission, 'Impact Assessment accompanying the document Proposal for a Directive of the European Parliament and the Council on Alternative Dispute Resolution for consumer disputes (Directive on Consumer ADR) and Proposal for a Regulation of the European Parliament and of the Council on Online Dispute Resolution for consumer disputes (Regulation on consumer ODR)' SEC (2011) 1408 final, 21.

55 Van Gelder (n 12) 59.

sure full geographical and sectoral ADR coverage[56]; imposes information obligations on ADR entities and traders to notify consumers about ADR; and imposes a set of minimum quality criteria ADR entities must comply with including independence, impartiality, transparency, effectiveness and fairness.[57] It also includes the legality principle to safeguard that consumers are protected by mandatory national consumer law and the liberty principle safeguarding consumers' right to access court.[58]

#24 **The ADR Directive** follows a minimum harmonisation approach in order to provide what is needed for the different national ADR cultures and frameworks existing across the Member States.[59] It does not prescribe a specific type of ADR procedure, nor regulates whether participation in ADR is mandatory or voluntary nor regulates the (binding) nature of ADR.[60] The broad formulation of quality requirements may result in a (too) low common denominator and keep the low quality of ADR in existence.[61] For instance, the expertise principle requires staff to have a 'general knowledge in law' questioning whether this standard is sufficiently strict for such staff to be able to apply mandatory consumer law of the consumers' habitual residence.[62] While some Member States do apply a higher level of protection – e.g Germany requires its mediators to be fully qualified lawyers or certified mediators – most follow the minimum standards.[63] A lack of sufficient legal qualification may lead to erroneous outcomes.[64] Also, the legality principle exclusively applies to ADR procedures that impose a solution with the rational that consumers can still proceed to court following unsuccessful consensual procedures.[65] Consumers who already have spent time and effort to reach a settlement through a consensual procedure will likely just accept this outcome rather than going through a costly court procedure.

56 ADR Directive, Article 2.

57 ADR Directive, Articles 5–11.

58 ADR Directive, Article 10; J Zheng, *Online Resolution of E-Commerce Disputes. Perspectives from the EU, the UK and China* (Springer 2020) 229.

59 European Commission, 'Commission Staff Working Document Impact Assessment' SWD (2023) 335, 3.

60 ADR Directive, Article 2(2).

61 R Kirkham, 'Regulating ADR. Lessons from the UK' in P Cortés (ed), *The New Regulatory Framework for Consumer Dispute Resolution* (OUP 2016) 297, 302.

62 ADR Directive, Article 11; B Hess, 'Privatizing Dispute Resolution and its Limits' in L Cadiet, B Hess and M Requejo Isidro (eds), *Privatizing Dispute Resolution. Trends and Limits* (Nomos 2019) 17, 42; Wagner (n 30); A Biard, 'Impact of Directive 2013/11/EU on Consumer ADR Quality: Evidence from France and the UK' (2019) 42 Journal of Consumer Policy 109, 112.

63 BEUC, 'Alternative Dispute Resolution for Consumers: Time to Move up a Gear' (2022) 3.

64 M Faure, 'CADR and Settlement of Claims – A Few Economic Observations' in C Hodges and A Stadler (eds), *Resolving Mass Disputes. ADR and Settlement of Mass Claims* (Edward Elgar 2013) 38, 52.

65 M Knigge and C Pavillon, 'The Legality Requirement of the ADR Directive: Just Another Paper Tiger?' (2016) 5 EuCML 155, 157; Hess (n 62) 17, 32.

#25 The complementary **ODR Regulation** builds on the bedrock of ADR entities and establishes an **EU-wide ODR platform** enabling consumers to submit their online complaint against EU traders, to receive information and support, and to be forwarded to certified ADR entities.[66]

II The Revision of the ADR Framework

#26 Throughout the past decade, the **ADR Directive** has set up a horizontal legislative framework of accessible and quality consumer dispute resolution entities across the EU in almost all consumer sectors with monitoring authorities acting as guardians of the quality.[67] At the same time, the uptake of ADR remains limited due to three key issues that prevent the framework from flourishing: low levels of awareness among consumers and traders about ADR; limited trader participation and fragmentation of the ADR landscape encumbering a smooth navigation of the field.[68] In October 2023, the European Commission adopted a **proposal to amend the ADR Directive** in order to improve its uptake.[69] In March 2024, the European Parliament adopted its position and in September 2024 the Council adopted its proposal; both making amendments to the Commission proposal.[70]

#27 The European Commission proposes to extend the Directives' material and geographical scope in order to make the ADR Directive fit to answer to the digital

66 Van Gelder (n 12) 60.

67 European Commission, 'Report from the Commission to the European Parliament, the Council and the European Economic and Social Committee on the application of Directive 2013/11/EU of the European Parliament and of the Council on alternative disputes resolution for consumer disputes and Regulation (EU) No 524/2013 of the European Parliament and of the Council on online dispute resolution for consumer disputes' COM (2023) 648, 10.

68 European Commission, 'Report on the application of Directive 2013/11/EU of the European Parliament and of the Council on alternative dispute resolution for consumer disputes and Regulation (EU) No 524/2013 of the European Parliament and of the Council on online dispute resolution for consumer disputes' (COM) 2019 425 final, 9.

69 European Commission, 'Proposal for a Directive of the European Parliament and of the Council amending Directive 2013/11/EU on alternative dispute resolution for consumer disputes, as well as Directives (EU) 2015/2302, (EU) 2019/2161 and (EU) 2020/1828, Brussels 17 October 2023' COM(2023) 649 final; 'Proposal for a Regulation repealing Regulation (EU) No 524/2013 and amending Regulations (EU) 2017/2394 and (EU) 2018/1724 with regards the discontinuation of the European ODR Platform' COM (2023) 647 final.

70 European Parliament legislative resolution of 13 March 2024 on the proposal for a directive of the European Parliament and of the Council amending Directive 2013/11/EU on alternative dispute resolution for consumer disputes; Council of the European Union, Proposal for a directive of the European Parliament and of the Council amending Directive 2013/11/EU on alternative dispute resolution for consumer disputes 13398/24.

market and the increasing number of consumers purchasing outside the EU.[71] Regarding the **material scope**, it proposed to include all types of consumer disputes including pre-contractual obligations and disputes evolving from digital content and digital services as well as disputes against non-EU traders.[72] The EU Parliament follows this proposal.[73] The Council, however, reduces the scope to disputes stemming from a contract, thus deleting the commissions' proposal to extend the scope to non-contractual situations. The Council does note that contractual obligations can also include the stages preceding the conclusion of a contract, such as marketing and information provision, as well as those following the termination of a contract, such as use of digital content.[74] Regarding the **geographical scope**, the Commission proposed to extend the scope to voluntary ADR against traders established outside the EU that sell products to consumers in the EU. The Council, however, not goes along with this and determines to leave this to the discretion of the Member States.[75]

#28 Furthermore, the European Commission proposes the option of **collective ADR** by enabling ADR entities to bundle similar cases into one procedure, if consumers would not object. The European Parliament proposes that consumers must consent to such a collective ADR procedure, but the Council gives the discretion to the Member States on deciding the conditions for such a bundling of cases and thereby removes the obligation for consent.[76]

#29 The European Commission proposes to remove the information obligations on traders thereby stating that this is not effective for traders who do not want to participate in ADR anyway.[77] At the same time, such information could have an awareness function for consumers who have never heard of ADR. Simultaneously, the Commission aims to encourage traders to increase their participation by introducing a **duty to reply** requiring traders to respond to an ADR entity whether or not they intend to participate.[78] While the European Commission proposed a 20 day reply deadline, the Council extended this deadline to 40 working days in the case of complex disputes or in exceptional circumstances.[79] It adds that traders do not have to reply when their participation is mandatory and where ADR outcomes can be reached without traders' consent to participate.[80] Yet, participation in ADR is kept voluntary and thereby the revision fails to offer

71 European Commission (n 69).
72 ibid 1.
73 European Parliament (n 70) Amendment 5(5).
74 Council (n 70) 3.
75 ibid.
76 ibid 4.
77 European Commission (n 69).
78 While the Commission proposed 20 days, the Parliament amended it into 15 days.
79 Council (n 70) 4.
80 ibid.

a structural solution since they keep consumer redress dependent on the willingness of traders to participate. The European Parliament proposes mandatory ADR, but only for air carriers, provided that they are not prevented from accessing judicial systems.[81]

#30 In fact, whether or not to make ADR mandatory is an ongoing discussion both at the EU and the Member State level. For instance, in the Netherlands the prevailing doctrine used to be that mediation agreements were non-binding as was decided by the Dutch Supreme Court in 2006.[82] The Court of Justice of the European Union (CJEU) held in the 2009 *Alassini* case that mandatory mediation can be a justified restriction to the right to access court if certain conditions are fulfilled: the outcome is non-binding; there cannot be substantial delays in bringing legal proceedings; the time-barring period for claims is suspended for the duration of the settlement procedure; and the procedure is free or accessible.[83] Lastly, it holds that the effectiveness of procedures may be impossible or excessively difficult if the procedure can only be accessed by electronic means. In line with this EU case law, there seems to blow a new breeze in the Netherlands.[84] In her opinion of 26 January 2024, Advocate-General De Bock concludes that a mediation clause within a business agreement is legally binding thereby referring to the aforementioned CJEU case law.[85] On 12 July 2024, the Dutch Supreme Court decided that a mediation clause may be non-compulsory in nature, but may also oblige parties to attempt mediation before arbitration or legal proceedings.[86] It thereby stresses that a mediation clause cannot be applied if this would result in unacceptable interference with the parties' right to access to justice. It remains unclear why the EU legislator does not follow the trend towards making ADR mandatory providing that parties keep access to court, at least for traders operating in the most problematic sectors such as energy and telecom.

#31 Also the **ODR platform** failed to fully take off.[87] The annual evaluation reports on its functioning show similar results: while the number of submitted complaints

81 European Parliament (n 70) Amendment 23 Proposal for a Directive Article 1 – paragraph 1 – point – 1 (new).

82 HR 20 January 2006 ECLI:NL:HR:2006:AU3724; N Peters, 'The Enforcement of Mediation Agreements and Settlement Agreements Resulting from Mediation' [2019] CMJ 13, 15.

83 Joined Cases C-317/08, C-318/08, C-319/08 and C-320/08 *Rosalba Alassini and others vs Telecom Italia Spa* (18 March 2010) ECLI:EU:C:2010:146, para 64; M Villamarín López, 'Access to Civil Justice under European Case Law' (2017) 7 IJPL 130, 148.

84 E van Gelder and MS Thomas, 'Mediation Within the Modern Dutch Civil Justice System' in M Ahmed and D Sixsmith (eds), *The Place of Mediation Within the Modern Civil Justice System: Critical Perspectives* (Edward Elgar forthcoming).

85 Parket bij de Hoge Raad, 26 januari 2024, ECLI:NL:PHR:2024:103, 5.1.

86 Dutch Supreme Court, ECLI:NL:HR:2024:1078, 12 July 2024, Ro. 3.2.2

87 E van Gelder and S Voet, 'The EU ODR Platform – A Blessing in Disguise' (2022) 26 Nederlands-Vlaams Tijdschrift voor Mediation en conflictmanagement 31.

increases, around 85% of complaints automatically closes within the thirty-day deadline and only around 2% of complaints are ultimately submitted to an ADR entity.[88] The platform does have an incentive effect as many traders appear to contact consumers bilaterally after receiving a platform notification.[89] While the European Commission engaged in multiple efforts to improve the platforms' up-take by introducing a self-help tool for consumers and a direct communication channel enabling consumers to directly contact traders, the uptake remains low.[90]

#32 The European Parliament follows the Commission proposal to repeal the ODR platform due to its inefficiency and the disproportionate costs it raises for EU traders.[91] The European Parliament does recommend the Commission to develop and maintain a **'digital interactive tool'** providing information and redirection links to ADR. The Council follows the parliaments' proposal stressing that such a tool should aim to assist consumers to understand redress solutions and take appropriate action by also including direction links and a machine translation tool. The Council thereby adds that these commodities should be available no later than three months after the ADR Directives entry into force.[92] The discontinuation of the ODR platform seems a missed opportunity to further expand it into an online assisted negotiation tool providing a dispute resolution function in view of the growing number of consumers purchasing online and the related need for an accessible ODR platform.[93]

---

88 See for exact statistics: European Commission, Functioning of the European ODR platform. Statistical Reports of December 2018, December 2020 and December 2021.

89 European Commission, 'Report from the Commission to the European Parliament and the Council on the functioning of the European Online Dispute Resolution platform established under Regulation (EU) No 524/2013 on online dispute resolution for consumer disputes' COM (2017) 744, 6, 8; E van Gelder and A Biard, 'The Online Dispute Resolution Platform after one Year of Operation: A Work in Progress with Promising Potential' [2018–2] TvC 77.

90 European Commission, 'Functioning of the European ODR platform. Statistical report 2020' (December 2021) 2.

91 European Parliament, 'Discontinuation of the European ODR Platform. European Parliament legislative resolution of 13 March 2024 on the proposal for a regulation of the European Parliament and of the Council repealing Regulation (EU) No 524/2013 and amending Regulations (EU) 2017/2394 and (EU) 2018/1724 with regards to the discontinuation of the European ODR Platform (COM(2023)0647 – C9 – 0380/2023 – 2023/0375(COD)).

92 Council (n 70) 4.

93 In 2021 74% of internet users shopped online; Eurostat, 'E-commerce Statistics for Individuals' (2021) <https://ec.europa.eu/eurostat/statistics-explained/index.php?title=E-commerce_statistics_for_individuals> accessed 10 April 2025.

E The Mediation Directive

#33 The Mediation Directive aims to enhance access to justice by encouraging the use of mediation.

I The Purpose and Scope of the Mediation Directive

#34 The **Mediation Directive** has been adopted on the legal basis of Article 81 TFEU and has the broad purpose to improve access to justice through promoting the use of mediation as well as proposing common minimum rules and thereby contribute to the proper functioning of the EU internal market.[94] While the Directive applies to cross-border[95] civil and commercial matters, almost all Member States made use of the freedom to extend the application to domestic cases.

II The Functioning of the Mediation Directive

#35 While the **Mediation Directive** has undeniably achieved added value such as raising awareness among national legislators about the benefits of mediation and impacting the mediation legislation in several Member States, its overall uptake remains limited.[96] A 2016 European Commission evaluation identified difficulties: the existence of an adversarial tradition in many Member States and the lack of a mediation culture; limited awareness of mediation and the functioning of quality control mechanisms for mediators.[97] A 2017 European Parliament resolution illustrated the Directives' limited impact with mediation being used in only 1% of the cases in courts.[98] The resolution promulgates several recommendations to enhance the use of mediation including the call upon Member States to increase their efforts in promoting mediation; notifying the European Commission to as-

94 A Howard, *EU Cross-Border Commercial Mediation: Listening to Disputants: Changing the Frame, Framing The Changes* (Wolters Kluwer 2021) 11; E Storskrubb, *Civil Procedure and EU Law: A Policy Area Uncovered* (OUP 2008) 191.

95 The Directive does not prevent Member States from applying the provisions to internal mediation processes.

96 European Commission, 'Report from the Commission to the European Parliament, the Council and the European Economic and Social Committee on the application of Directive 2008/52/EC of the European Parliament and of the Council on certain aspects of mediation in civil and commercial matters' COM(2016) 542, 4.

97 ibid.

98 European Parliament, 'Rebooting' the Mediation Directive: Assessing the Limited Impact of its Implementation and Proposing Measures to Increase the Number of Mediations in the EU' (European Parliament 2017).

sess the need for EU-wide mediation quality standards and the need for Member States to establish a mediation register.[99]

F ODR Pathways Under the EU Digital Services Act

#36 In October 2022, the EU legislature adopted the DSA with the aim to contribute to the proper functioning of the internal market for intermediary services by stipulating harmonised rules for safe and trusted online environments.[100] The DSA adds a new ODR pathway for consumers objecting against content moderation decisions.[101] The DSA stipulates quality criteria for these ODR pathways.

I Procedural Safeguards for Internal ODR Procedures

#37 The DSA requires providers of online platforms to offer recipients of their service with an effective, easy accessible and user-friendly internal complaint handling scheme resolving complaints in a timely, diligent and non-arbitrary manner. The scheme must ensure reasoned decisions taken under supervision of appropriately qualified staff and the decisions cannot only be based on automated means.[102]

II Procedural Safeguards for External ODR Bodies

#38 In addition, the DSA entitles parties to select any certified ODR body to resolve disputes related to content moderation taken by the internal complaint systems.[103] It requires both parties to engage, in good faith, with this body thereby stipulating that the body cannot impose a binding settlement.[104] The DSA also lays down **quality criteria** requiring these bodies to be impartial, independent, easily accessible, cost-effective and to have a procedure that respects clear and fair rules of procedure that comply with the applicable law.[105]

#39 Scrutinising the procedural framework that is laid down by the DSA, it is observed that the DSA imposes stricter quality upon the external ODR bodies than on the

99 ibid.

100 Van Gelder (n 12) 282.

101 V Mak, 'Consumer ODR – Redefining Pathways to Dispute Settlement in a Post-Consumer Society' (*DSA Observatory Blog*, 22 January 2024).

102 DSA, Article 20.

103 DSA, Article 21(1); Busch (n 52) 19.

104 DSA, Article 21(2).

105 DSA, Article 21(3).

internal schemes while the majority of disputes is resolved in the internal phase. Also, the DSA does make engagement in the procedure mandatory for both parties.

G Recommendations and Conclusion: Towards an Interconnected Framework of ADR and ODR Pathways in the EU

#40 The EU legislator has built a framework consisting of various ADR pathways which, rather than isolated islands, potentially **overlap**. This Chapter argues the need for a more interconnected framework.

I Overlap of different ADR and ODR legislative instruments

#41 While the **Mediation Directive** and the **ADR Directive** share their purpose to enhance access to justice through ADR, the scope differs as the Mediation Directive covers cross-border civil and commercial disputes and the ADR Directive consumer disputes.[106] Mediation procedures resolving cross-border consumer disputes could thus fall within both scopes, but the ADR Directive stipulates that it is without prejudice to the Mediation Directive.[107]

#42 The **P2B Regulation** and the **DSA** both apply to online intermediary marketplaces, but in contrast to the P2B Regulation, the DSA applies to all platform users, which includes both consumers and traders, rather than only traders. The DSA notes that it is without prejudice to the P2B Regulation.[108] The instruments exist side by side for third-party sellers as they can file their complaint against platforms to both pathways, however, since the P2B Regulation has more specific procedural rules, this procedure likely will prevail.[109]

#43 Potential overlap also exists within the field of consumer redress. Whereas the **ADR Directive** and the **DSA** have different primary objectives and scopes, they intersect in areas related to consumer protection. The DSA holds that it is without prejudice to the ADR Directive and the ADR Directive notes it shall prevail when in conflict with another EU act.[110] The DSA, however, has important limitations,

106 U Gläßer, 'Linking ADR Discourses – Nine Lessons learned from Mediation Development for the Implementation of the EU Directive on Consumer ADR' in R Caponi and others (eds), *The Role of Consumer ADR in the Administration of Justice* (Sellier 2014) 115, 116.
107 ADR Directive, Recital 19.
108 DSA, Article 1(5)(g); Busch and Mak (n 17) 114.
109 Busch and Mak (n 17) 114.
110 ADR Directive, Article 3.

when it comes to available remedies eg with regard to unsafe products.[111] Consumers encountering other disputes than content moderation disputes, such as retail disputes (eg non-delivery or broken delivery), appear to fall beyond the protection that the DSA offers.[112] In the ADR revision, the European Commission acknowledges this potential intersect and attempts to draw a distinction between different types of disputes. Accordingly, it points out that the DSA's scope encompasses complaints on content moderation decisions and that even if such content concerns bad commercial practices of the third-party seller, the dispute will be settled according to the DSA.[113] The EP thereby adds that the DSA indeed lays down more detailed rules for such types of disputes.[114] The Commission further explains that the ADR Directive then will apply to more general disputes arising between consumers and third-party sellers such as those relating to repair, receiving money back and unfair terms.[115] For consumers, complaints they encounter on online marketplaces often will involve retail disputes (rather than content moderation) and thus for such disputes the DSA framework would be most relevant as an additional step to contact ADR entities operating under the ADR Directive appears cumbersome. Also, it must be seen if the theoretical distinction of disputes will also be so clear-cut in practice.

#44 Overlap may also arise in relation to different sets of quality standards applying to the same ODR scheme. Accordingly, the European Parliament encourages the adoption of a Regulation that is complementary to the ADR Directive and offers quality requirements for dispute resolution procedures by online marketplaces.[116] The DSA also stipulates quality requirements for online marketplaces and overburdening such platforms with requirements may have a countereffect.

II The Need for Interconnection

#45 There is a need for **interconnection** between the aforementioned routes to redress as synergy can contribute to enhanced consumer law enforcement. This connection must not only be sought between private ADR enforcement routes, but also between existing public and private consumer enforcement mechanisms. It goes beyond the scope of this Chapter to elaborate on such interconnection in detail, but this Section will highlight some insights.

111 Busch and Mak (n 17) 109.
112 Van Gelder (n 12).
113 European Commission (n 69) 4.
114 European Parliament (n 70) Recital 7.
115 European Commission (n 69) 3.
116 European Parliament (n 70) Amendment 6 Proposal for a Directive Recital 5 a (new).

#46 The need for interconnection is also acknowledged by the European Parliament highlighting the importance of connecting different enforcement actors to ensure overall consistency and coherence within the enforcement system. For instance, where the **Representative Actions Directive** (RAD) enables the bundling of similar consumer claims before court, the ADR Directive broadens this possibility for ADR with the rational that this makes outcomes consistent for consumers subject to the same illegal practices.[117] ODR offers numerous advantages to ease the bundling of claims as it can facilitate connection between consumers easing their communication and sharing of information to ultimately bundle their claims.[118] This Chapter recommends the continuance of the ODR platform to offer this function. Also, the platform can offer insights into what is occurring in the market supporting public regulators to intervene in rogue practices.[119]

#47 This Chapter has shown that the European legislature has been at the forefront of promoting ADR and ODR in its legislative ambition to improve access to justice since the 1990s. This policy has resulted in the emergence of numerous ADR and ODR pathways operating under the EU regulatory framework of which the ADR Directive represents a significant legislative milestone harmonising the field of ADR across the union. At the same time, this expansion of ADR/ODR pathways led to a fragmented field posing challenges for individuals to navigate the field. This **'patchwork'** may rather overwhelm than assist parties in their journey for redress. The revision of the ADR framework does signify the EU legislators' commitment to improving this fragmented landscape. Nonetheless, the task remains in place to prevent further fragmentation of the field and in this regard it is crucial to provide clarity within potential overlap and build further bridges between different enforcement mechanisms to ensure that the multiplicity of options does not counteract the objective of improved access to justice.

#48 It is paramount for maintaining parties' trust in the available mechanisms that their quality is assured. Therefore the EU's legislative approach towards promoting ADR and ODR must continue to prioritise the quality of the procedures while fostering the flexibility and efficiency that make ADR and ODR attractive alternatives to the formal court procedure. The integration of digital technologies in dispute resolution offers tremendous potential, but it must be carefully managed to ensure that it enhances rather than hinders the quest for justice. The procedural turn that the DSA makes in stipulating quality standards for ODR on platforms is a good step in this direction.

---

117 Directive (EU) 2020/1828 of the European Parliament and of the Council of 25 November 2020 on representative actions for the protection of the collective interests of consumers and repealing Directive 2009/22/EC [2020] OJ L409/2; European Parliament (n 70) Amendment 9.

118 M Azar-Baud and A Biard, 'The Dawn of Collective Redress 3.0 in France?' in A Uzelac and S Voet (eds), *Class Actions in Europe* (Springer 2021) 73, 78.

119 Van Gelder and Voet (n 87).

References

Andrews N, 'Fundamental Principles of Civil Procedure: Order Out of Chaos' in X Kramer and CH van Rhee (eds), *Civil Litigation in A Globalising World* (TMC Asser Press 2012) 19.

Azar-Baud M and Biard A, 'The Dawn of Collective Redress 3.0 in France?' in A Uzelac and S Voet (eds), *Class Actions in Europe* (Springer 2021) 73.

Bauw E and others, *Rechtsstatelijke waarborging van buitengerechtelijke geschiloplossing* (Boom Juridisch 2018).

Beretta R, 'The Use of Technology in Dispute Resolution; A Framework for the Study of ODR' (2023) Vilnius University Open Series 19.

BEUC, 'Alternative Dispute Resolution for Consumers: Time to Move up a Gear' (2022).

Biard A, 'Impact of Directive 2013/11/EU on Consumer ADR Quality: Evidence from France and the UK' (2019) 42 Journal of Consumer Policy 109.

Busch C and Mak V, 'Putting the Digital Service Act into Context: Bridging the Gap between EU Consumer Law and Platform Regulation' (2021) 10 EuCML 109.

Busch C and Reinhold S, 'Standardisation of Online Dispute Resolution Services: Towards a More Technological Approach' (2015) 4(1–2) EuCML 50.

Busch C, 'The P2B Regulation (EI) 2019/1150: Towards a "Procedural Turn" in EU Platform Regulation?' (2020) 9 EuCML 133.

Cappelletti M, 'Alternative Dispute Resolution Process within the Framework of the World-Wide Access-to-Justice Movement' (1993) 56 The Modern Law Review 282.

Carrel A and Ebner N, 'Mind the Gap: Bringing Technology to the Mediation Table' [2019–2] Journal of Dispute Resolution 1.

Christoph Busch, 'Regulation of Digital Platforms as Infrastructures for Services of General Interest' WISO-Diskurs 09/2021 (Friedrich-Ebert-Stiftung).

Cortés P and Lodder A, 'Consumer Dispute Resolution Goes Online' (2014) 21 Maastricht Journal of European and Comparative Law 16.

Cortés P, 'The New Landscape of Consumer Redress: The European Directive on Consumer Alternative Dispute Resolution and the Regulation on Online Dispute Resolution' in P Cortés (ed), *The New Regulatory Framework for Consumer Dispute Resolution* (OUP 2016) 17.

—— *Online Dispute Resolution for Consumers in the European Union* (Routledge 2011).

Daniels C, 'Alternative Dispute Resolution for European Consumers: A Question of Access to and Standards of Justice' in L Cadiet, B Hess and M Requejo Isidro (eds), *Privatizing Dispute Resolution* (Nomos 2019) 257.

European Commission, 'Green Paper on the Access of Consumers to Justice and the Settlement of Consumer Disputes in the Single Market' COM(93) 576.

—— 'Action Plan on Consumer Access to Justice and the Settlement of Consumer Disputes in the Internal Market' COM(96) 13.

—— 'Green Paper on Alternative Dispute Resolution in Civil and Commercial Law' COM(2002) 196, 15.

—— 'Commission Staff Working Paper. Executive Summary of the Impact Assessment 2011' SEC(2011) 1409 final.

—— 'Impact Assessment accompanying the document Proposal for a Directive of the European Parliament and the Council on Alternative Dispute Resolution for consumer disputes (Directive on Consumer ADR) and Proposal for a Regulation of the European Parliament and of the Council on Online Dispute Resolution for consumer disputes (Regulation on consumer ODR)' SEC(2011) 1408 final.

—— 'Report from the Commission to the European Parliament, the Council and the European Economic and Social Committee on the application of Directive 2008/52/EC of the European Parliament and of the Council on certain aspects of mediation in civil and commercial matters' COM(2016) 542.

—— 'Report from the Commission to the European Parliament and the Council on the functioning of the European Online Dispute Resolution platform established under Regulation (EU) No 524/2013 on online dispute resolution for consumer disputes' COM(2017) 744.
—— 'Functioning of the European ODR platform. Statistical Report' (December 2018).
—— 'Report from the Commission to the European Parliament, the Council and the European Economic and Social Committee' COM(2019) 425 final.
—— 'Report on the application of Directive 2013/11/EU of the European Parliament and of the Council on alternative dispute resolution for consumer disputes and Regulation (EU) No 524/2013 of the European Parliament and of the Council on online dispute resolution for consumer disputes' (COM) 2019 425 final.
—— 'Functioning of the European ODR platform. Statistical Report' (December 2020).
—— 'Functioning of the European ODR platform. Statistical report 2020' (December 2021).
—— 'Commission Staff Working Document Impact Assessment' SWD(2023) 335.
—— 'Proposal for a Directive of the European Parliament and of the Council amending Directive 2013/11/EU on alternative dispute resolution for consumer disputes, as well as Directives (EU) 2015/2302, (EU) 2019/2161 and (EU) 2020/1828, Brussels 17 October 2023' COM(2023) 649 final.
—— 'Proposal for a Regulation repealing Regulation (EU) No 524/2013 and amending Regulations (EU) 2017/2394 and (EU) 2018/1724 with regards the discontinuation of the European ODR Platform' COM(2023) 647 final.
—— 'Report from the Commission to the European Parliament, the Council and the European Economic and Social Committee on the application of Directive 2013/11/EU of the European Parliament and of the Council on alternative disputes resolution for consumer disputes and Regulation (EU) No 524/2013 of the European Parliament and of the Council on online dispute resolution for consumer disputes' COM(2023) 648.
European Parliament, 'Rebooting' the Mediation Directive: Assessing the Limited Impact of its Implementation and Proposing Measures to Increase the Number of Mediations in the EU' (European Parliament 2017).
Eurostat, 'E-commerce Statistics for Individuals' (2021) <https://ec.europa.eu/eurostat/statistics-explained/index.php?title=E-commerce_statistics_for_individuals> accessed 10 April 2025.
Faure M, 'CADR and Settlement of Claims – A Few Economic Observations' in C Hodges and A Stadler (eds), *Resolving Mass Disputes. ADR and Settlement of Mass Claims* (Edward Elgar 2013) 38.
Fejös A and Willett C, 'Consumer Access to Justice: The Role of the ADR Directive and the Member States' (2016) 24 ERPL 33, 34.
Francioni F, 'The Rights of Access to Justice under Customary International Law' in F Francioni (ed), *Access to Justice as a Human Right*, Collected Courses of the Academy of European Law (Oxford, 2007; online edn, Oxford Academic, 22 March 2012) 1.
Galanter M, 'Access to Justice in a World of Expanding Social Capability' (2009) 37 Fordham Urban Law Journal 115.
Gelder van E and Biard A, 'The Online Dispute Resolution Platform after one Year of Operation: A Work in Progress with Promising Potential' [2018–2] TvC 77.
Gelder van E and Duin van A, 'In de schaduw van het recht: over PayPal's Resolution Centre en kwaliteitsstandaarden voor cODR op online platforms' in P Wolters and others (eds), *Digitalisering en Conflictoplossing* (Wolters Kluwer 2021) 129.
Gelder van E and Thomas MS, 'Mediation Within the Modern Dutch Civil Justice System' in M Ahmed and D Sixsmith (eds), *The Place of Mediation Within the Modern Civil Justice System: Critical Perspectives* (Edward Elgar forthcoming).
Gelder van E and Voet S, 'The EU ODR Platform – A Blessing in Disguise' (2022) 26 Nederlands-Vlaams Tijdschrift voor Mediation en conflictmanagement 31.
Gelder van E, *Consumer Online Dispute Resolution Pathways in Europe* (Eleven International Publishing 2022).

Gläßer U, 'Linking ADR Discourses – Nine Lessons learned from Mediation Development for the Implementation of the EU Directive on Consumer ADR' in Caponi R and others (eds), *The Role of Consumer ADR in the Administration of Justice* (Sellier 2014) 115.
Hess B, 'Privatizing Dispute Resolution and its Limits' in L Cadiet, B Hess and M Requejo Isidro (eds), *Privatizing Dispute Resolution. Trends and Limits* (Nomos 2019) 17.
Howard A, *EU Cross-Border Commercial Mediation: Listening to Disputants: Changing the Frame, Framing the Changes* (Wolters Kluwer 2021).
Katsh E and Rabinovich-Einy O, *Digital Justice. Technology and the Internet of Disputes* (OUP 2017).
Katsh E and Rifkin J, *Online Dispute Resolution. Resolving Conflicts in Cyberspace* (Jossey-Bass 2001).
Kirkham R, 'Regulating ADR. Lessons from the UK' in P Cortés (ed), *The New Regulatory Framework for Consumer Dispute Resolution* (OUP 2016) 297.
Knigge M and Pavillon C, 'The Legality Requirement of the ADR Directive: Just Another Paper Tiger?' (2016) 5 EuCML 155.
Lindblom PH, 'ADR – The Opiate of the Legal System?' (2008) 16 ERPL 63.
Lodder A and Zeleznikow J, 'Developing an Online Dispute Resolution Environment: Dialogue Tools and Negotiation Support Systems in a Three-Step Model' (2005) 10 Harvard Negotiation Law Review 287.
Loos M, 'Enforcing Consumer Rights through ADR at the Detriment of Consumer Law' (2016) 24 ERPL 61.
Mak V, *Legal Pluralism in European Contract Law* (OUP 2020).
—— 'Geschilbeslechting voor consumenten onder de Digital Services Act: Online Dispute Resolution 3.0' [2023–1] TvC 2.
—— 'Consumer ODR – Redefining Pathways to Dispute Settlement in a Post-Consumer Society' (*DSA Observatory Blog*, 22 January 2024).
Micklitz H-W and Saumier G, 'Enforcement and Effectiveness of Consumer Law' in H-W Micklitz and G Saumier (eds), *Enforcement and Effectiveness of Consumer Law* (Springer 2018) 3.
Peters N, 'The Enforcement of Mediation Agreements and Settlement Agreements Resulting from Mediation' [2019] CMJ 13.
Piers M, 'Europe's Role in Alternative Dispute Resolution: Off to a Good Start?' [2014–2] Journal of Dispute Resolution 269.
Rabinovich-Einy O, 'Balancing the Scales: The Ford-Firestone Case, the Internet, and the Future Dispute Resolution Landscape' (2004) 6 Yale Journal of Law & Technology 1.
Storskrubb E and Ziller J, 'Access to Justice in European Comparative Law' in F Francioni (ed), *Access to Justice as a Human Right* (OUP 2007) 177.
Storskrubb E, *Civil Procedure and EU Law: A Policy Area Uncovered* (OUP 2008).
—— 'Alternative Dispute Resolution in the EU: Regulatory Challenges' (2016) 24 ERPL 7.
Vilalta E, 'ODR and e-Commerce' in M Wahab, E Katsh and D Rainey (eds), *Online Dispute Resolution Theory and Practice* (Eleven International Publishing 2012) 125.
Villamarín López M, 'Access to Civil Justice under European Case Law' (2017) 7 IJPL 130.
Wagner G and Eidenmüller H, 'Digital Dispute Resolution' (2021) <https://ssrn.com/abstract=3871612> accessed 10 April 2025.
Wagner G, 'Harmonisation of Civil Procedure: Policy Perspectives' in X Kramer and CH van Rhee (eds), *Civil Litigation in a Globalising World* (Asser Press 2012) 93.
—— 'Private Law Enforcement Through ADR: Wonder Drug or Snake Oil?' (2014) 51 CMLR 165.
Willet C, 'Editorial: Special Edition on Access to Justice and Consumer ADR' (2016) 24 ERPL 1.
Zheng J, *Online Resolution of E-Commerce Disputes. Perspectives from the EU, the UK and China* (Springer 2020).

Eva Lein*

Chapter 21 Collective Redress

A Introduction

#1 **Collective redress** is a procedural device used in litigation to determine the rights and remedies for large numbers of claimants whose cases involve common questions of law or fact. Historically, collective redress developed as equitable relief in cases with numerous litigants resulting in an **injunction** or declaratory judgment, before encompassing **compensatory relief**,[1] and it evolved from an **opt-in**-based regime towards an **opt-out** system, first in the US,[2] then slowly also across a few European jurisdictions.[3]

#2 The rationale behind Collective Redress is simple: both claimants and defendants can benefit from the fact that only one claim is brought where individual cases are analogous. Collective actions can comprise various types of claims from high-value litigation in areas such as **cartel claims** to low value cases such as systematic overcharging of fees or unfair terms in **consumer contracts**. Collective procedures save the defendant time and costs incurred by the defence against a multitude of lawsuits and provide legal certainty, once a single collective judgment is rendered or a mass settlement is concluded. The claimants involved in collective redress are able to share litigation costs, have a stronger collective bargaining power as to settlements and a strong case for third party litigation funding. In addition, actions for minor individual damage can be brought collectively in cases in which individual actions would not be practicable or economically sound, but where the overall damage for the collective of consumers is high and the behaviour of the defendant warrants a lawsuit. Courts can handle a single action instead of numerous cases,

1 Rule 23 FRCP enables class actions aiming at compensation of monetary damages, see also JG Harkins, 'Federal Rule 23 – The Early Years' (1997) 39 Ariz. L. Rev. 705.

2 Since 1966 unnamed parties to a class action In the US are bound by a judgment if their interests were adequately represented ('opt out').

3 Eg Portugal or the Netherlands. See also A Pato, *Jurisdiction and Cross-Border Collective Redress: A European Private International Law Perspective* (Hart 2019) 145ff; BIICL, Civic Consulting and RPA, 'State of Collective Redress in the EU in the Context of the Implementation of the Commission Recommendation' JUST/2016/JCOO/FW/CIVI/0099 (2017) <https://www.biicl.org/documents/1881_StudyontheStateofCollectiveRedress.pdf> accessed 1 April 2025 ('BIICL/CIVIC/RPA').

***Corresponding author: Eva Lein,** University of Lausanne and BIICL, e-mail: eva.lein@unil.ch

https://doi.org/10.1515/9783110781632-021

which allows for a more efficient use of court resources and prevents conflicting decisions.

#3 Effective **mass litigation** regimes require clear rules on standing, a participation mechanism with streamlined procedures, litigation funding options to enable the costly procedures, adequate rules on costs and on the distribution of compensation, as well as provision for low value claims or unclaimed sums.

B Collective Redress in Europe

#4 EU Member States have been traditionally reluctant to introduce collective redress.[4] This reservation stems from the experience with US **class actions**. In some instances, US class actions have led to complex procedures and to situations where the victims' individual interests were disregarded.[5] The existence of treble and **punitive damages** as well as contingency fees has been seen as an incentive for lawyers to 'boost' class actions.[6] From an EU Member States' perspective, the idea of a 'collective of claimants' also goes against the traditional 'individual suit approach' of civil procedure,[7] and opt-out mechanisms have long been criticised as incompatible with the constitutional right of a fair trial and the right to be heard which are a cornerstone of litigation in Europe.[8]

#5 Nonetheless, the practical need for a regime for mass claims, triggered in particular by the frequency of **investor claims**, led to an initially mostly sectoral legisla-

4 See European Commission, 'Towards a European Horizontal Framework for Collective Redress' COM/2013/0401 final; European Commission, 'Report from the Commission on the Implementation of the Commission Recommendation of 11 June 2013 on Common Principles for Injunctive and Compensatory Collective Redress Mechanisms in the Member States Concerning Violations of Rights Granted under Union Law (2013/396/EU)' COM (2018) 40 final; European Parliament, 'Collective Redress in the Member States of the European Union' PE 608.829 (2018); European Parliament, 'European Parliament legislative resolution of 26 March 2019 on the proposal for a directive of the European Parliament and of the Council on representative actions for the protection of the collective interests of consumers' (P8_TA(2019)0222) [2021] OJ C108/152; See also BIICL/Civic/RPA (n 3).

5 See eg <https://instituteforlegalreform.com/wp-content/uploads/2020/10/UnstableFoundation_Web.pdf> accessed 1 April 2025.

6 See recently on the discussion on contingency fees from the perspective of other jurisdictions: *R&B Investments Pty Ltd (Trustee) v Blue Sky (Reserved Question)* [2024] FCAFC 89 (AUS).

7 See also R Amaro and others, 'Collective Redress in the Member States of the European Union' (European Parliament 2018) 93, 96.

8 BIICL/Civic/RPA (n 3) 15ff.

tive activity across EU Member States.[9] Additionally, a recent reluctance in the US to accept foreign claimants in f-cubed class actions[10] revealed an acute need for alternative fora and collective redress options in Europe. Given the EU's internal market structure and the number of transactions taking place across borders, there is also a need for viable mechanisms permitting claimants based across various jurisdictions to bring joint cross-border collective actions. This evolution reanimated the debate on common minimum standards across EU Member States to avoid a lack of redress regimes, a problem of access to justice, and to keep forum shopping at bay.

I Commission Recommendation

#6 A first step towards collective redress in Europe was the **Commission Recommendation** (2013/396/EU).[11] Having the objective of ensuring the development of a European area of justice, a high level of consumer protection, an improved enforcement of EU law and **access to justice**, the instrument provided non-binding guidelines and political instructions to the Member States. As no political consensus for a binding uniform EU system could be found at the time, the Commission recommended and encouraged national legislation (injunctive and damages actions) based on certain common key principles.

#7 The Recommendation provided for strict requirements as to **standing**, requiring the designation of **representative entities** to bring actions on the basis of clearly defined conditions of eligibility.[12]

#8 The instrument was built upon the idea of an **opt-in** mechanism, but with some limited openness to **opt-out** procedures which were allowed when 'duly justified by reasons of sound administration of justice'.[13] This approach towards opt-out claims addressed the complexities of opt-in procedures which can be inefficient in practice due to high investigation costs, particularly in case of low value claims. In the latter cases, the constitutional concerns linked with opt-out regimes seem rather formalistic, as due to the low stakes for the individual claimants, the

9 See The Netherlands and Germany (*Kapitalanleger-Musterverfahrensgesetz*-KapMuG, now in its new version of 16 July 2024 (BGBl. 2024 I Nr. 240). The number of investor claims brought against Deutsche Telekom triggered the creation of the original version of the Act (16 August 2005 (BGBl. I 2437)).

10 *Morrison v National Australia Bank*, 561 U.S. 247 (2010).

11 Commission Recommendation of 11 June 2013 on common principles for injunctive and compensatory collective redress mechanisms in the Member States concerning violations of rights granted under Union Law [2013] OJ L201/60 ('Commission Recommendation').

12 ibid para 4.

13 Ibid para 21.

latter are not in a substantially better position if the regime follows the opt-in principle.[14]

#9 The Recommendation also expressly addressed the need to allow for **cross-border claims** (a 'single **collective action** in single forum should not be prevented by national rules on admissibility/standing of foreign claimants/entities' and 'Representative entities with standing . . . should be permitted to seize courts in other MS . . . '). However, the **Recommendation** itself did not provide for any further special rules or principles on cross-border redress, and EU private international law had not (and still has not) been aligned to the specifics of cross-border mass claims.[15]

#10 The **Recommendation** further explicitly prohibited **punitive damages** and **contingency fees** and was based on the loser pays principle for the distribution of costs, to clearly distinguish European collective redress and its underlying values from the features of US class actions.[16]

#11 Other key characteristics of the Recommendation included strict requirements as to **third party litigation funding**,[17] which was made dependent on various criteria: information on the origin of third-party funds; no undue influence of the funder on procedural decisions; no financing of claims against competitors; no charge of excessive interest; a prohibition to base remuneration or interest on the settlement amount or the compensation award; and a stay of proceedings in case of **conflict of interest** or in case of insufficient resources.[18]

II Developments in the Member States

#12 In the Member States, various types of procedures had already existed, or co-existed, although the picture was very diverse, and several different models of collective proceedings provided a 'broad spectrum of procedural diversity'.[19] The

14 E Hurter, 'Opting In or Opting Out in Class Action Proceedings: From Principles to Pragmatism?' De Jure (Pretoria) (2017) 50(1) 60; S Mezetović Međić, 'Collective Redress: Is There a Way for Both Opt-in and Opt-out?' (2022) 9 South East European Law Journal 62; J Stuyck, 'Class Actions in Europe? To Opt-In or to Opt-Out, that is the Question' (2017) 20 European Business Law Review 483.

15 See below C II. and D.

16 Recital 15 Commission Recommendation (n 11).

17 Recital 19ff and paras 14ff Commission Recommendation (n 11).

18 Paras 14ff Commission Recommendation (n 11).

19 Milieu Consulting, 'Study to Support the Preparation of A Report on the Application of Regulation (EU) No. 1215/2012 on Jurisdiction and the Recognition and Enforcement of Judgments in Civil and Commercial Matters (Brussels Ia Regulation) – Final Report' (Publications Office of the European Union 2023) 227ff ('Milieu Consulting Study'); M Stürner, 'Cross-border Issues' in A Stadler, E Jeuland and V Smith (eds), *Collective and Mass Litigation in Europe: Model Rules for Effective Dispute Resolution* (Edward Elgar 2020) 296.

mechanisms ranged from **representative actions** brought by entities such as **consumer associations** (see eg Lithuania, Poland, Belgium, Denmark, France, Malta, the Netherlands), **group litigation orders, group actions** (either led by lead claimants or ombudsmen (see eg, The Danish or Polish models) to **test-case proceedings** such as the German '***Musterfeststellungsklage***'.[20] The Netherlands have also been providing for a **settlement**-based procedure under the WCAM which was used with a certain frequency, including in cross-border cases.[21] Other methods of aggregating claims were based on traditional devices of multiparty practice, eg, the pooling of claims via **assignment**, more frequently used in areas such as cartel claims (eg in Germany, the Netherlands, Finland, Austria) and in some States backed up by litigation funding on a regular basis (eg in Austria).[22] In some jurisdictions (eg in Austria, Cyprus, Ireland, Estonia, the Czech Republic, Croatia, Slovakia, Latvia, Romania, Luxembourg), traditional procedural mechanisms such as **joinder** and **stay of proceedings** were the only available procedural tools to handle compensatory mass claims.[23]

#13 Following the Commission Recommendation of 2013, an accrued, mostly sectoral legislative activity across several Member States could be noted, albeit no EU-wide effort to introduce collective redress measures.[24] In the following years, reforms had been conducted which led to a broader acceptance of **opt-out** mechanisms, following the **Recommendation's** admittance of opt-out collective redress 'by law or court order, [but] only if duly justified by reasons of sound administration of justice' (see eg the Netherlands' WAMCA (opt-out), Portugal (opt-out), Belgium (both options), Denmark (both options), UK (both options), Slovenia (both options), Germany (opt-out settlement in **opt-in** test cases).[25] A shift from injunctive to compensatory redress and to cross-sectoral mechanisms could also be noted, for instance, in France (2014/2016),[26]

20 See above, KapMuG and Articles 606ff ZPO.

21 Collective Settlement of Mass Damage Act (WCAM), in force since 2005.

22 See BIICL/Civic/RPA (n 3) 120ff, 371ff.

23 ibid 9f.

24 See for details on the state of play after the Commission Recommendation: BIICL/Civic/RPA (n 3).

25 The UK is still mentioned here, as the reforms provided by the Consumer Rights Act 2015 led to an increased activity, with the UK leading in recent statistics on the number of collective claims brought per European jurisdiction.

26 Cf Loi 2014-344 relative à consommation du 17 mars 2014 (*Loi Hamon*) implemented in Articles L.623-1 to L.623-23 and R. 423-1 to R.423-23 Code de la consommation. Articles L.623-24 to L.623-26 of the Code de la consommation apply to competition law claims; Loi 2016-41 du 26 janvier 2016 and Article L.1143-1 ff Code de la santé publique; Loi 2016-1547 du 18 novembre 2016 de modernisation de la justice du XXIe siècle, see <https://www.le1gifrance.gouv.fr/loda/id/JORFTEXT000033418805> accessed 1 April 2025.

Belgium (2014),[27] UK (2015),[28] the Netherlands (2020),[29] Italy (2021),[30] and Germany (2018).[31]

#14 Although the process of introducing collective redress across Europe was rather slow and gradual, the number of cases brought has increased from 69 claims in 2019 to 133 claims filed in 2023,[32] with most actions brought in Portugal, the Netherlands and Germany, as well as in the UK, leading the statistics. Although no longer a Member State, it had reformed its legislation[33] following the Commission Recommendation of 2013. The year 2023 also saw the first time when opt-out class actions outnumbered opt-in class actions (68 versus 59) indicating an inclination in practice towards opt-out collective redress. Types of claims range from **product liability** and **consumer law** (32%) to **competition law** (19%), **shareholder claims** (13%), **Covid19**-related litigation (12%), **data protection** (11%) and **human rights** and **environmental disputes** (8%).[34] The increase also coincides with the transposition of the **Representative Actions Directive** (RAD).[35] The national implementation legislation is applicable to cases filed from 25 June 2023.[36]

---

27 Titre 2 du livre XVII du Code de droit économique (action en réparation collective au profit des consommateurs), see De H Wulf, 'Class Actions in Belgium' in BT Fitzpatrick and RS Thomas (eds), *The Cambridge Handbook of Class Actions: An International Survey* (CUP 2021) 194.

28 Consumer Rights Act (2015), Section 47B Competition Act 1998; See eg *Mastercard Incorporated and others (Appellants) v Walter Hugh Merricks CBE (Respondent)* UKSC/2019/0118.

29 Wet afwikkeling massaschade in collectieve actie, 1.1.2020. For cases see eg Rechtbank Amsterdam, 29 December 2021, ECLI:NL:RBAMS:2021:7647 (*TPC v Oracle and Salesforce*); Rechtbank Amsterdam, 25 October 2023, ECLI:NL:RBAMS:2023:6694 (*SOMI v TikTok*). All cases are registered in the WAMCA register, <https://www.rechtspraak.nl/Registers/centraal-register-voor-collectieve-vorderingen> accessed 1 April 2025.

30 Legge no. 31/2019, integrated in Article 840bisff *Codice di Procedura Civile* (CPC). Cf P Giudici and B Zuffi, 'The New Italian Regulation on Class Actions' in B Fitzpatrick and RS Thomas (eds), *The Cambridge Handbook of Class Actions: An International Survey* (CUP 2021) 217; A Giussani, 'La nuova azione di classe in Italia' (2020) 2 Revista Ítalo-Española de Derecho Procesal 7; P Massaro, 'The Italian Class Action Reform: A Redesigned Tool beyond Consumer Law' (2020) 4 European Review of Private Law 841; E Silvestri, 'Rebooting Italian Class Actions' in A Uzelac and S Voet (eds), *Class Actions in Europe* (Springer 2021) 201.

31 See the declaratory test case proceedings ('*Musterfeststellungsklage*') in Articles 606ff ZPO (now replaced by the redress action ('*Abhilfeklage*') introduced in transposition of the RAD); Cf A Halfmeier, 'Collective Litigation in German Civil Procedure' in BT Fitzpatrick and RS Thomas (eds), *The Cambridge Handbook of Class Actions: An International Survey* (CUP 2021) 233.

32 See CMS, 'Class Action Report 2024' <https://cms.law/en/int/publication/cms-european-class-action-report-2024> accessed 1 April 2025 ('CMS, 'Class Action Report 2024'').

33 Consumer Rights Act 2015, Section 47B Competition Act 1998.

34 See CMS, 'Class Action Report 2024' (n 32).

35 Directive (EU) 2020/1828 of the European Parliament and of the Council of 25 November 2020 on representative actions for the protection of the collective interests of consumers and repealing Directive 2009/22/EC [2020] OJ L409/1 ('RAD').

36 See Article 24(1)2 RAD.

C Representative Actions Directive (RAD)

#15 **Directive (EU) 2020/1828** of the European Parliament and of the Council of 25 November 2020 on representative actions for the protection of the collective interests of consumers and repealing Directive 2009/22/EC (RAD)[37] obliges the Member States to introduce representative actions or to adapt or supplement their existing collective proceedings in such a way that they fulfil the minimum standards for consumer protection laid down by the Directive. The RAD aims to protect the **collective interests of consumers** in the EU via representative actions brought by qualified entities and provides for the first uniform redress system across all EU Member States.[38] **Representative actions** are actions brought on behalf of groups of consumers seeking injunctive measures (ie to stop unlawful practices, as in the Injunctions Directive 2009/22/EC), or (newly introduced) redress measures such as compensation, or both. The RAD applies to representative actions brought against infringements of EU rules listed in its Annex I and protects the collective interests of consumers across many sectors, such as **data protection**, **financial services**, **travel and tourism**, **energy** and **telecommunications**. The RAD improves consumers' access to justice whilst creating appropriate safeguards to avoid **abusive litigation**. Examples are large-scale abusive practices (eg the use of **unfair contract terms** by banks) or massive travel/ flight cancellations without reimbursement as was the case during the Covid19 pandemic. Member States may apply the mechanism of representative actions in other or in all areas of law. However, it has been criticised that the Directive itself is limited to consumer collective redress and spares out other branches of law, such as environmental cases or business and human rights claims.[39]

#16 The RAD aims to ensure that EU consumers can effectively exercise the rights to which they are entitled under EU law. When EU regulations listed in the directive are disrespected, consumers are to be given the opportunity to file a representative action via a **'qualified entity'**, ie an organisation or public body representing consumer interests. Whilst the directive sets out minimum standards, it is not intended to regulate every aspect of a representative action. For example, it is largely up to the Member States to specify in detail the provisions regarding admissibility, evidence, or legal remedies. The scope of application of the directive can be gradually adapted if new EU provisions are added. According to Article 23

---

37 [2020] OJ L409/1.

38 B Gsell, 'The New European Directive on Representative Actions for the Protection of the Collective Interests of Consumers – A Huge, but Blurry Step Forward' (2021) 58 Common Market Law Review 1365; L Hornkohl, 'Up- and Downsides of the New EU Directive on Representative Actions for the Protection of the Collective Interests of Consumers – Comments on Key Aspects' (2021) 5 Journal of European Consumer and Market Law 189.

39 Milieu Consulting Study (n 19) 228.

RAD, the Commission will evaluate the Directive and its scope of application as well as its effectiveness in cross-border cases from mid-2028.[40]

I Legal Standing

#17 **qualified entities** have legal standing to bring **representative actions**. The authorisation of entities to bring such actions is subject to strict conditions relating to their independence and non-profit making character.[41] **Ad hoc entities** are only permitted if they fulfil the nationally set conditions for qualified entities and can only be designated to act in domestic representative actions.[42] Individual consumers are not authorised to bring a collective claim. They can either join the representative action brought by an organisation or bring an individual action. They are not exposed to an individual cost risk within the scope of a representative action.

II Cross-Border Actions

#18 Cross-border economic activity in the internal market and increasing digitalisation require that representative actions can be brought across borders so that **qualified entities** from abroad are also authorised to bring actions in a Member State. The European Commission maintains a **register** for this purpose, in which qualified entities authorised by an EU Member State are listed. These entities are deemed to be authorised to bring claims in the whole of the EU.[43] The RAD does otherwise not address the complexities of cases with an international element, and questions will arise regarding jurisdiction, the applicable law and the **recognition and enforcement** of judgments and **settlements**. Private International Law questions are subject to the **Brussels Ibis Regulation** and the **Rome I and II Regulations**, with several issues still unresolved.[44] None of the EU regulations on civil justice cooperation provides a collective litigation perspective and fre-

40 Cf Article 2, Annex I RAD. On the Directive in general, see A Biard, 'The Age of Consumer Law Enforcement in the European Union: High Hopes or Wishful Thinking?' (2024) 15 European Journal of Risk Regulation 625; A Vlahek, 'The Great Saga of Collective Redress in EU Competition Law: All Cry and No Wool?' (2024) 46 World Competition 53.

41 Article 4(3) RAD.

42 Article 4(6) and Recital 28 RAD.

43 Article 6(3) RAD.

44 P Leupold, 'Private International Law and Cross-Border Collective Redress – A Legal Analysis of Jurisdiction, Applicable Law, Pendency, Recognition and Enforcement under the Representative Actions Directive 1828/2020' (BEUC 2022) 11ff; F Rielaender, 'Aligning the Brussels Regime with the Representative Actions Directive' (2022) 71 International & Comparative Law Quarterly 107, 109.

quently, concentration of jurisdiction for all claims at one forum is difficult to achieve elsewhere than at the defendant's domicile. As the latter is usually in an economically strong position, in particular when sued in his home jurisdiction, this situation is not ideal for the claimants.[45] Moreover, European conflict of laws rules do not facilitate the application of one law to all claimants and no changes have been implemented so far in this respect but might be in the future.[46]

III Admissibility

#19 Rules concerning the similarity of individual claims or the minimum number of consumers participating in a representative action seeking redress are left to national legislators. However, national law must regulate these issues in such a way that national rules do not impair the efficiency of a representative action. In accordance with the principle of **non-discrimination**, the **admissibility** requirements for cross-border **representative actions** should not differ from the requirements for comparable domestic actions, nor should the decision to declare a representative action inadmissible affect the rights of the consumers concerned. Member States can prevent **abusive claims** either through specific provisions or through existing national law,[47] allowing a court or administrative authority to dismiss manifestly unfounded cases. Member States need to ensure that courts or administrative authorities can dismiss manifestly unfounded claims at the earliest possible stage of proceedings.[48]

IV Measures

#20 The directive provides for stronger sanctioning powers of **consumer associations**. They are enabled to assert not only injunctive relief but also **remedies** on behalf of consumers.[49] In addition to compensation, these remedies also include repair, replacement delivery, price reduction, contract termination or reimburse-

45 See below Section D.

46 On 31 January 2025 the European Commission published its report (COM(2025) 20 final) on the application of Regulation No 864/2007 on the law applicable to non-contractual obligations (Rome II), based on Article 30 of the Regulation. See the comments on collective redress at 3.4. See also Section D below.

47 Recital 39 RAD.

48 Article 7(7) RAD.

49 Articles 7(4), 8, 9 RAD.

ment of the price paid, as appropriate and as available under either EU or national law, depending on the circumstances of each case.[50] However, **punitive damages** are to be avoided, even though the latter were not completely and expressly excluded by the RAD, as was the case in the **Commission Recommendation** of 2013.[51]

V Mandate

#21 The implementing national legislation determines how and at what point within a reasonable period of time consumers must express their wish to participate in a **representative action** aiming at redress, and to be bound by it or not.[52] This can be done explicitly or implicitly at the discretion of the Member States.[53] The terms **'opt-in'** and **'opt-out'** which have stirred a heated debate over the years are avoided in the Directive and the Member States have some flexibility in setting up their national regimes. However, in the case of redress actions (ie compensatory collective redress), consumers domiciled outside the Member State in which the action is brought must expressly declare that they wish to participate (mandatory 'opt-in model').[54]

VI Litigation Funding

#22 The Directive provides a coordinated framework for **litigation funding**. It must be ensured that **conflicts of interest** are avoided in the case of third-party funded redress actions and that the economic interest of the third-party funder in the filing or outcome of a redress action does not outweigh the protection of the collective interests of consumers. Third-party funders must not unduly influence the proceedings to the detriment of consumers and must not fund proceedings against their competitors[55] in order to avoid conflicts of interest.[56] If there are

---

50 Articles 7(4) (a) and (b), 9(1), 3(10) RAD.

51 Recital 10 RAD.

52 Article 9(2) RAD.

53 Article 9(2): 'Member States shall lay down rules on how and at which stage of a representative action for redress measures the individual consumers concerned by that representative action explicitly or tacitly express their wish within an appropriate time limit after that representative action has been brought, to be represented or not by the qualified entity in that representative action and to be bound or not by the outcome of the representative action'.

54 Article 9(3) RAD.

55 Article 10(2)(b) RAD.

56 See BIICL and others, 'Mapping Third Party Litigation Funding in the European Union' JUST/2023/PR/JCOO/CIVI/0016 (2025) <https://commission.europa.eu/strategy-and-policy/policies/justice-and-funda

reasonable doubts as to compliance with these principles, a court may request the submission of a financial overview stating the sources of funding. It should also be noted that the **European Commission** is currently assessing the national frameworks for third party litigation funding, which is essential for the practical realisation of **collective actions**.[57]

#23 The Directive also recognises that procedural costs should not prevent qualified entities from bringing **representative actions**. The Member States should take the necessary measures to this end, eg impose a limit on the applicable court or administrative fees, grant legal aid if necessary, or provide public funds for bringing representative actions (structural support or other support measures). In the context of a representative action, no costs should be incurred by individual consumers, but in exceptional cases it should be possible to order individual consumers affected by a redress action to bear costs that they have caused intentionally or negligently – for example by delaying proceedings through unlawful acts. Member States may also provide that **qualified entities** may charge a moderate joining fee or a comparable fee for participating in the representative action.[58]

VII Limitation Period

#24 The filing of a **representative action** should lead to a suspension or interruption of the applicable **limitation periods** for consumers' individual claims, so that in the event of an unsuccessful action for redress, individual claims remain available or **consumers** can demand redress following an action for **injunctive relief**.[59]

mental-rights/civil-justice/civil-and-commercial-law/third-party-litigation-funding-tplf_en> accessed 1 April 2025 ('BIICL and others, 'Mapping Study''); C Cameron, J Kalajdzic and A Klement, 'Economic Enablers' in D Hensler, C Hodges and I Tzankova (eds), *Class Actions in Context: How Culture, Economics and Politics Shape Collective Litigation* (Edward Elgar 2016) 137; X Kramer and I Tillema, 'The Funding of Collective Redress by Entrepreneurial Parties: The EU and Dutch Context' 2020 (2) Revista Ítalo-Española de Derecho Procesal 165; I Tzankova and X Kramer, 'From Injunction and Settlement to Action: Collective Redress and Funding in the Netherlands' in A Uzelac and S Voet (eds), *Class Actions in Europe* (Springer 2021) 97; S Voet, 'Costs and Funding of Collective Redress Proceedings' in A Stadler, E Jeuland and V Smith (eds), *Collective and Mass Litigation in Europe: Model Rules for Effective Dispute Resolution* (Edward Elgar 2020) 264.

57 BIICL and others, 'Mapping Study' (n 56).

58 Article 20(3) RAD.

59 Article 16 RAD.

VIII Acceleration of Procedures

#25 The RAD also prescribes measures to speed up proceedings. **Representative actions** to obtain **injunctions** should be dealt with swiftly and, where appropriate, in summary proceedings in order to prevent harm or further harm.[60] **Redress** measures should benefit consumers without any need for a separate, follow-on action. However, Member States may set time limits within which a consumer may claim redress and determine the destination of any **compensation** not claimed within that time limit.[61]

IX Evidence

#26 Evidence is crucial to the merits of a representative action for both injunctive relief or redress. Due to frequent information asymmetries between traders and consumers, evidence might often not be accessible to qualified entities. The latter should have the right to make requests to the court or administrative authorities to order disclosure of evidence relevant to their claim, subject to applicable EU and national rules on **confidentiality** and **proportionality**. In turn, qualified entities may also be ordered to disclose relevant evidence on their side. Questions relating to the burden of proof are not covered by the RAD, but by the national procedural law of the EU Member State in question or the applicable law to the case. In many Member States' legal systems, the RAD evidence rules lead to a more comprehensive **disclosure** obligation than before.[62] A final decision by a court or administrative authority in a Member State on the existence of an infringement to the detriment of the **collective interests of consumers** can also be used as evidence in other redress actions against the same trader for the same practice. The national rules on the assessment of evidence apply.

X Settlements

#27 **Settlements** in a **redress** action may be proposed jointly by the parties to the court or an administrative authority. Alternatively, they may be initiated by the latter by requesting the parties to agree on a settlement within a reasonable pe-

60 Article 18 RAD.
61 Article 7(7) RAD.
62 However, a US-style disclosure obligation is not to be introduced, see Article 18 RAD ('in accordance with national procedural law') and Recital 68 RAD.

riod of time. Out-of-court settlements must be assessed by the court or authority.[63] If approved, settlements shall be binding upon the qualified entity, the defendant and the individual consumers concerned. Member States may provide that the individual consumer concerned by the representative action and the settlement has the choice of accepting or rejecting the settlement.[64]

XI Information

#28 In order to make **representative actions** practicable, **information** about ongoing and concluded representative actions should be provided in a way that is appropriate and proportionate to the circumstances of the case.[65] **Consumers** need to be informed in a timely manner and by appropriate means, in order to enable them to explicitly or tacitly express their wish to be represented in that representative action.[66] To diffuse information, the Directive refers to the website of the qualified entity or trader, to national electronic databases, social media, online marketplaces or high-circulation (also purely electronic) newspapers. Where possible and appropriate, the consumers concerned should be informed individually (by letter in electronic form or on paper). Both information about the qualified entities and information about ongoing and concluded representative actions should be provided.[67]

XII Transposition

#29 The RAD had to be transposed by 25 December 2022.[68] Despite delays in the transposition process, Member States have now implemented the directive, in many jurisdictions via the introduction of a new legal act (eg Germany,[69] Italy,[70] Ire-

63 Article 11(2) RAD.
64 Article 4(4) RAD.
65 Article 13 RAD.
66 Article 13(2), 9(2) RAD.
67 Article 14, Recital 63 RAD.
68 The adapted or newly introduced national provisions for representative actions apply to any actions filed on or after 25 June 2023. For the state of transposition and implementing legislation, see <https://eur-lex.europa.eu/legal-content/EN/NIM/?uri=CELEX:32020L1828> accessed 1 April 2025.
69 Gesetz zur Umsetzung der Richtlinie (EU) 2020/1828 über Verbandsklagen zum Schutz der Kollektivinteressen der Verbraucher und zur Aufhebung der Richtlinie 2009/22/EG (*Verbandsklagenrichtlinienumsetzungsgesetz* – VRUG) and *Verbraucherrechtedurchsetzungsgesetz* (VDuG), 8 October 2023 (BGBl. 2023 I Nr. 272, 2).
70 Decreto legislativo, 10 March 2023, n. 28 – Attuazione della direttiva (UE) 2020/1828 del Parlamento europeo e del Consiglio, del 25 novembre 2020, relativa alle azioni rappresentative a tutela degli inter-

land[71]), in others by integrating the new rules into existing legislation, with occasionally little need for additional measures due to existing modern **collective action** regimes aiming at compensatory redress (eg Sweden, France, Belgium, the Netherlands[72]). As the Directive only sets minimum standards, and many Member States maintained already existing collective redress measures,[73] the latter do not only provide representative actions, but continue to offer other cross-sectoral regimes for collective proceedings such as group actions (eg Italy) or collective settlements (eg the Netherlands), covering case scenarios beyond **consumer law**. In Italy, for instance, a collective action for violation of 'homogeneous individual rights' coexists with a representative action limited to consumer cases in accordance with the RAD.[74] In Germany, the newly transposed RAD partly replaced forms of collective redress that had been introduced following an acute need in the *Telekom*[75] and later the *Dieselgate*[76] mass claims. While the cross-sectoral ***Musterfeststellungsklage*** was replaced, the collective regime for investors under the German KapMuG[77] has been modernised and will continue to co-exist with the newly introduced ***Abhilfeklage*** which is based on the RAD.[78] In contrast,

essi collettivi dei consumatori e che abroga la direttiva 2009/22/CE. (23G00036) (GU Serie Generale n.70, 23.03.2023)

71 Representative Actions for the Protection of the Collective Interests of Consumers Act 2023, Iris Oifigiúl No 56, 14.7.2023, 839.

72 See eg, Loi modifiant les livres Ier, XV et XVII du Code de droit économique, et transposant la directive 2020/1828 du Parlement européen et du Conseil du 25 novembre 2020 relative aux actions représentatives visant à protéger les intérêts collectifs des consommateurs et abrogeant la directive 2009/22/CE (1), eli/loi/2024/04/21/2024005024/moniteur; O Kafi Cherrat, 'La transposition de la directive du 25 novembre 2020 sur les actions représentatives: la France à la croisée des chemins' (2023) 3 La Semaine Juridique 170; Wet van 2 november 2022 tot wijziging van Boek 3 van het Burgerlijk Wetboek en het Wetboek van Burgerlijke Rechtsvordering in verband met de omzetting van Richtlijn (EU) 2020/1828 van het Europees Parlement en de Raad van 25 november 2020 betreffende representatieve vorderingen ter bescherming van de collectieve belangen van consumenten en tot intrekking van Richtlijn 2009/22/EG (PbEU 2020, L 409) (Implementatiewet richtlijn representatieve vorderingen voor consumenten), 459, 1–8 (23 November 2022).

73 Recital 11 RAD.

74 See Legge no. 31/2019, integrated in Árticles 840bisff *Codice di Procedura Civile* (CPC); Decreto legislativo, 10 March 2023 (n 70), n 28.

75 A Halfmeier, 'Litigation Without End? The Deutsche Telekom Case and the German Approach to Private Enforcement of Securities Law' in D Hensler, C Hodges and I Tzankova (eds), *Class Actions in Context: How Culture, Economics and Politics Shape Collective Litigation* (Edward Elgar 2016) 279.

76 <https://www.bundesjustizamt.de/DE/Themen/Verbraucherrechte/VerbandsklageregisterMusterfeststellungsklagenregister/Verbandsklagenregister/Verbandsklagen/Klagen/202008/Verfahren/Verfahrensstand.html> accessed 1 April 2025.

77 *Kapitalanleger-Musterverfahrensgesetz*, 16 July 2024 (BGBl. 2024 I Nr. 240).

78 *Verbraucherrechtedurchsetzungsgesetz* (VDuG), 8 October 2023 (BGBl. 2023 I Nr. 272). See also H Schläfke and T Luhmann, 'Collective Redress in Germany and the Transposition of the Representative Actions Directive' [2023–2] Mass Claims 67.

several Member States introduced collective redress for the first time, and only in the form of a representative action.

#30 In order to achieve a greater collective legal protection, the material scope of application of the implementing legislation is often broad. In some countries, representative actions can not only be brought in the interests of a large number of consumers, but also to protect smaller companies (**SMEs**). In Germany, Belgium, and the Netherlands for example, these are included in the scope of the representative action.[79]

#31 It also varies across Member States how the question of an express or tacit **'mandate'** is addressed in the implementation process of the RAD. For instance, like Belgian law, the Dutch WAMCA follows an opt-out mechanism (or 'tacit mandate'). An exception to this approach is made for injured parties who have their habitual residence abroad, as prescribed by the RAD.[80] Member States also might not allow **opt-out** proceedings in collective actions for damages if the latter are aimed at compensating collective **physical** or **non-material damage** (eg in Belgium).

D Cross-Border Collective Actions

#32 The RAD expressly provides for the possibility of **cross-border representative actions**, which are defined as those in which a **qualified entity** brings a representative action in a Member State other than the one in which it was designated.[81] Qualified entities are designated by the Member State of origin, but the **European Commission** maintains a **register** of qualified entities which are authorised by an EU Member State and then deemed authorised to bring an action throughout the EU. The Directive does not exclude the possibility that individual Member States may also authorise third-country organisations to bring a representative action if **third-State** consumers are affected by EU legislation in the scope of application of the Directive.

#33 Recital 23 provides more detailed information on claims qualifying as **cross-border** or domestic actions. A **representative action** is regarded as a domestic action if a qualified entity brings it in the Member State in which it has been designated, even if it is brought against a trader domiciled in another Member State and **consumers** from several Member States are represented. Only a representative action brought abroad is considered a cross-border action in that respect. In cross-border cases, specific provisions on the **mandate** must also be observed. Ac-

79 See eg Article 1(2) VDuG.
80 Article 9(3) RAD.
81 Article 3(7) RAD.

cording to Article 9(3) RAD an express mandate is necessary for consumers based outside the forum State. However, cross-border representative actions as defined in the Directive still require that jurisdiction abroad is granted under European rules on cross-border civil procedure. According to Article 2(3), the RAD does not affect EU provisions on **jurisdiction** and on the **recognition and enforcement** of judgments in civil and commercial matters nor the provisions on the law applicable to contractual and non-contractual obligations.[82] These continue to apply in the same way as they would to two-person relationships and do not contain provisions on mass proceedings in which a large number of persons (possibly from several countries) intervene on the plaintiff's side.[83] In addition, cross-border cases can not only be brought as a representative action based on the RAD, but on the basis of other co-existing national collective redress regimes, and domestic actions against foreign defendants or involving foreign consumers are also cases with foreign elements.

#34 The **Brussels Ibis Regulation** to date only effectively facilitates **cross-border collective actions** involving consumers or organisations from several countries if it enables jurisdiction to be concentrated in one forum. In principle, this is only the case in the defendant's country of **domicile** (Article 4 Brussels Ibis Regulation) or in the country in which a tortious action was committed by the defendant (Article 7(2) Brussels Ibis Regulation[84]). However, the latter is often identical to the defendant's domicile, which is advantageous for the defendant as the claim will be brought in their home jurisdiction. The Brussels Ibis Regulation does not contain any jurisdiction rule that would allow for a **concentration of jurisdiction** at a different, more favourable place for the plaintiffs. Article 8(1) Brussels Ibis Regulation (which allows plaintiffs to sue several defendants in the Member State in which only one of them is domiciled if there is a close connection between the claims and a risk that irreconcilable judgments will be given in separate proceedings) does not apply by analogy to a majority of plaintiffs or affected parties in a collective action.[85] This leads to scenarios in which several actions are brought in

---

82 Regulation (EU) No 1215/2012 of the European Parliament and of the Council of 12 December 2012 on jurisdiction and the recognition and enforcement of judgments in civil and commercial matters (recast) [2012] OJ L351/1; Regulation (EC) No 593/2008 of the European Parliament and of the Council of 17 June 2008 on the law applicable to contractual obligations (Rome I) [2008] OJ L177/6; Regulation (EC) No 864/2007 of the European Parliament and of the Council of 11 July 2007 on the law applicable to non-contractual obligations (Rome II) [2007] OJ L199/40.

83 Rielaender (n 44); Amaro and others (n 7) 96.

84 At the place 'where the event giving rise to the damage' occurred, cf Case C-21/76 *Bier BV v Mines de potasse d'Alsace SA* (30 November 1976) ECLI:EU:C:1976:147.

85 Amsterdam Court of Appeal, *Converium* (12 November 2010) LJN BO3908.

different jurisdictions against the same defendant, as could be seen in the cases against *Volkswagen*.[86]

#35 As a matter of principle, following the *actor sequitur forum rei* maxim, the **Brussels Ibis Regulation** does not provide for jurisdiction at the place where the plaintiff is based, although the **domicile** of a majority of the affected parties had been discussed in the context of reform discussions for collective actions.[87] The place where damage was sustained for a majority of the parties[88] (eg in **product liability** cases) or where a contract was performed were also suggested.[89]

#36 So far, it has not been possible to bring an action involving foreign plaintiffs/consumers or organisations in the State with which the plaintiff side has the strongest territorial connection. In addition, the CJEU has also made it clear that in **assignment** cases, assignees cannot invoke consumer jurisdiction if they wish to assert claims involving foreign **consumers**.[90] The introduction of **representative actions** across the EU will at least partly solve access to justice problems in cross-border mass claims as defendants cannot escape collective proceedings altogether, based on a lack of collective action options in their country of **domicile**. Jurisdiction for a cross-border claim is, however, still granted at a forum favourable for the defendant and outside the scope of the RAD, there are still major differences between collective redress regimes available in the Member States. Tailored rules on jurisdiction for **cross-border mass claims** would provide a broader spectrum of fora for the claimants.

#37 With the revision of the **Brussels I Regulation**, **exequatur proceedings** were abolished so that judgments issued in one Member State are enforceable across borders without major formalities. However, Brussels Ibis provides for limited grounds for refusal of **recognition and enforcement**. In the area of collective redress, there has always been a risk, and debate, that foreign judgments based on an **opt-out** mechanism could potentially trigger an ***ordre public*** defence. Where plaintiffs are automatically included in a class, proper notice and procedural fairness require particular attention. Also, from the defendant's perspec-

---

86 <https://www.europarl.europa.eu/RegData/etudes/BRIE/2016/583793/EPRS_BRI(2016)583793_EN.pdf> accessed 1 April 2025.

87 Rielaender (n 44) 128; A Nuyts, 'The Consolidation of Collective Claims Under Brussels I' in A Nuyts and N Hatzimihail (eds), *Cross-Border Class Actions: The European Way* (Sellier 2014) 77; Amaro and others (n 7) 110; E Lein, 'Cross-Border Collective Redress and Jurisdiction under Brussels I: A Mismatch' in D Fairgrieve and E Lein, *Extraterritoriality and Collective Redress* (OUP 2012) paras 8.36f.

88 Rielaender (n 44) 113; Amaro and others (n 7) 97; Lein (n 87) paras 8.14f.

89 Rielaender (n 44) 119; ZS Tang, 'Consumer Collective Redress in European Private International Law' (2011) 7 Journal of Private International Law 101, 107.

90 Case C-498/16 *Maximilian Schrems v Facebook Ireland Limited* (25 January 2018) ECLI:EU:C:2018:37.

tive, the scope of the overall claim may not be accurately determined.[91] In France and Austria, for example, it was argued that opt-out proceedings contradict the principles enshrined in Article 6 ECHR, ia because the defendant cannot foresee the number and identities of the opposing parties.[92] However, recourse to the public policy exception can only be considered if recognition would lead to a manifest violation of rules regarded as essential in the requested State, or of a right recognised as fundamental.[93] Many Member States, such as Belgium and the Netherlands, have refuted public policy concerns even before the RAD[94] and have limited the *ordre public* control to extreme cases in which foreign proceedings can no longer be regarded as proper and constitutional (eg Germany).[95] Given that the RAD now expressly permits actions based on a tacit **mandate**, a refusal of recognition of a judgment in an opt-out collective action due to an *ordre public* violation seems increasingly unlikely.

#38 Under the **Brussels Ibis Regulation**, there is also a debate as to whether judicially confirmed collective **settlements** are to be considered judgments or fall under Article 59 Brussels Ibis Regulation. In the latter case, they would be enforceable in other Member States, subject to *ordre public*, but not subject to the other grounds for refusal in Article 45 Brussels Ibis Regulation. The question was mainly discussed in connection with WCAM settlements, for which it was predominantly assumed that they fall under Árticles 36 and 2(a) Brussels Ibis Regulation, because the court not only documents the settlement, but also examines its content to protect the claimants' interests.[96] If a settlement is part of a court-supervised procedure and is approved by the court, it should be considered a judgment and circulate as such, at least if the court has exercised a judicial function that goes beyond the mere confirmation of a private settlement.

91 Article 45(1)a Brussels Ibis. See also JT Nowak, 'Representative (Consumer) Collective Redress Decisions in the EU: Free Movement or Public Policy Obstacles?' in B Hess and K Lenaerts (eds), *The 50th Anniversary of the European Law of Civil Procedure* (Nomos 2020) 427.

92 French Senate, *Rapport d'information sur l'action de groupe*, 2009–2010, N° 499, 74–76; Österreichischer Bundesrat, *Begründete Stellungnahme von 27. Juni 2018*, 25/SB-BR/2018 <https://www.parlament.gv.at/PAKT/VHG/BR/SB-BR/SB-BR_00025/index.shtml> accessed 1 April 2025.

93 Case C-7/98 *Dieter Krombach v André Bamberski* (28 March 2000) ECLI:EU:C:2000:164, para 37.

94 In Belgium, it was clarified that the opt-out mechanism is often the most appropriate and efficient system for constituting a group and is compatible with Article 6 ECHR; see S Voet, 'Een Belgische vertegenwoordigende collectieve rechtsvordering: vier bouwstenen voor een Belgische class action' (2012) 18 *Rechtskundig Weekblad*, 682, 693: 'Opt-out is hardly an option. It probably is a necessity'. See also Gerechtshof Amsterdam (25 January 2007) NL:GHAMS:2007:AZ7033 paras 5.6–5.8.

95 BGHZ 48, 327, 331; OLG Frankfurt am Main, IPRax 2002, 523, 524.

96 A Stadler, 'Grenzüberschreitender kollektiver Rechtsschutz in Europa' (2009) 64 Juristenzeitung 131; A Halfmeier, 'Recognition of a WCAM Settlement in Germany' (2012) 1 Nederlands Internationaal Privaatrecht 176.

#39 As to the **applicable law**, in cases of cross-border actions seeking compensation for multiple parties domiciled or harmed in different jurisdictions, the court seised may have to apply several substantive laws to the different claimants of the group, dividing the action into batches according to the relevant applicable law. In a **product liability** case, for instance, Article 5 Rome II Regulation will most frequently lead to the applicable law at the habitual residence of the consumer, ie to a different law for **consumers** based in various Member States. This renders the assessment of a cross-border case complex and increases litigation costs and length of the proceedings. At the same time, subjecting multiparty claims to a different applicable law than individual claims, just because proceedings are collective, would affect **predictability** and **legal certainty**. The European Commission announced in their recent report on the application of the **Rome II Regulation**,[97] that this issue should be addressed and rediscussed in the review process of the latter.

References

Amaro R and others, 'Collective Redress in the Member States of the European Union' (European Parliament 2018).

Biard A, 'The Age of Consumer Law Enforcement in the European Union: High Hopes or Wishful Thinking?' (2024) 15 European Journal of Risk Regulation 625.

BIICL, Civic Consulting and RPA, 'State of Collective Redress in the EU in the Context of the Implementation of the Commission Recommendation' JUST/2016/JCOO/FW/CIVI/0099 (2017) < https://www.biicl.org/documents/1881_StudyontheStateofCollectiveRedress.pdf> accessed 1 April 2025.

BIICL and others, 'Mapping Third Party Litigation Funding in the European Union' JUST/2023/PR/JCOO/CIVI/0016 (2025) <https://commission.europa.eu/strategy-and-policy/policies/justice-and-fundamental-rights/civil-justice/civil-and-commercial-law/third-party-litigation-funding-tplf_en> accessed 1 April 2025.

Cameron C, Kalajdzic J and Klement A, 'Economic Enablers' in D Hensler, C Hodges and I Tzankova (eds), *Class Actions in Context: How Culture, Economics and Politics Shape Collective Litigation* (Edward Elgar 2016) 137.

De Wulf H, 'Class Actions in Belgium' in BT Fitzpatrick and RS Thomas (eds), *The Cambridge Handbook of Class Actions: An International Survey* (CUP 2021) 194

European Commission, 'Towards a European Horizontal Framework for Collective Redress' (COM) 2013 401 final.

——'Report from the Commission on the Implementation of the Commission Recommendation of 11 June 2013 on Common Principles for Injunctive and Compensatory Collective Redress Mechanisms in the Member States Concerning Violations of Rights Granted under Union Law (2013/396/EU)' (COM) 2018 40 final.

97 European Commission, 'Report from the Commission to the European Parliament, the Council and the European Economic and Social Committee on the Application of Regulation (EC) No 864/2007 on the Law Applicable to Non-contractual Obligations (Rome II Regulation)' COM (2025) 20 final.

——'Report from the Commission to the European Parliament, the Council and the European Economic and Social Committee on the Application of Regulation (EC) No 864/2007 on the Law Applicable to Non-contractual Obligations (Rome II Regulation)' COM (2025) 20 final.

European Parliament, 'Collective Redress in the Member States of the European Union' PE 608.829 (2018).

Giudici P and Zuffi B, 'The New Italian Regulation on Class Actions' in B Fitzpatrick and RS Thomas (eds), *The Cambridge Handbook of Class Actions: An International Survey* (CUP 2021) 217.

Giussani A, 'La nuova azione di classe in Italia' (2020) 2 Revista Ítalo-Española de Derecho Procesal 7.

Gsell B, 'The New European Directive on Representative Actions for the Protection of the Collective Interests of Consumers – A Huge, but Blurry Step Forward' (2021) 58 Common Market Law Review 1365.

Halfmeier A, 'Litigation Without End? The Deutsche Telekom Case and the German Approach to Private Enforcement of Securities Law' in D Hensler, C Hodges and I Tzankova (eds), *Class Actions in Context: How Culture, Economics and Politics Shape Collective Litigation* (Edward Elgar 2016) 279.

—— 'Collective Litigation in German Civil Procedure' in BT Fitzpatrick and RS Thomas (eds), *The Cambridge Handbook of Class Actions: An International Survey* (CUP 2021) 233.

Harkins JG, 'Federal Rule 23 – The Early Years' (1997) 39 Ariz. L. Rev. 705.

Hornkohl L, 'Up- and Downsides of the New EU Directive on Representative Actions for the Protection of the Collective Interests of Consumers – Comments on Key Aspects' (2021) 5 Journal of European Consumer and Market Law 189.

Hurter E, 'Opting In or Opting Out in Class Action Proceedings: From Principles to Pragmatism?' (2017) 50(1) De Jure (Pretoria) 60.

Kafi Cherrat O, 'La transposition de la directive du 25 novembre 2020 sur les actions représentatives: la France à la croisée des chemins' (2023) 3 La Semaine Juridique 170.

Kramer X and Tillema I, 'The Funding of Collective Redress by Entrepreneurial Parties: The EU and Dutch Context' (2020) 2 Revista Ítalo-Española de Derecho Procesal 165.

Lein E, 'Cross-Border Collective Redress and Jurisdiction under Brussels I: A Mismatch' in D Fairgrieve and E Lein, *Extraterritoriality and Collective Redress* (OUP 2012) 129.

Leupold P, 'Private International Law and Cross-Border Collective Redress – A Legal Analysis of Jurisdiction, Applicable Law, Pendency, Recognition and Enforcement under the Representative Actions Directive 1828/2020' (BEUC 2022).

Massaro P, 'The Italian Class Action Reform: A Redesigned Tool beyond Consumer Law' (2020) 4 European Review of Private Law 841.

Mezetović Međić S, 'Collective Redress: Is There a Way for Both Opt-in and Opt-out?' (2022) 9 South East European Law Journal 62.

Milieu Consulting, 'Study to Support the Preparation of A Report on the Application of Regulation (EU) No. 1215/2012 on Jurisdiction and the Recognition and Enforcement of Judgments in Civil and Commercial Matters (Brussels Ia Regulation) – Final Report' (Publications Office of the European Union 2023).

Nowak JT, 'Representative (Consumer) Collective Redress Decisions in the EU: Free Movement or Public Policy Obstacles?' in B Hess and K Lenaerts (eds), *The 50th Anniversary of the European Law of Civil Procedure* (Nomos 2020) 427.

Nuyts A, 'The Consolidation of Collective Claims Under Brussels I' in A Nuyts and N Hatzimihail (eds), *Cross-Border Class Actions: The European Way* (Sellier 2014) 77.

Pato A, *Jurisdiction and Cross-Border Collective Redress: A European Private International Law Perspective* (Hart 2019).

Rielaender F, 'Aligning the Brussels Regime with the Representative Actions Directive' (2022) 71 International & Comparative Law Quarterly 107.

Schläfke H and Luhmann T, 'Collective Redress in Germany and the Transposition of the Representative Actions Directive' [2023–2] Mass Claims 67.

Silvestri E, 'Rebooting Italian Class Actions' in A Uzelac and S Voet (eds), *Class Actions in Europe* (Springer 2021) 201.
Stadler A, 'Grenzüberschreitender kollektiver Rechtsschutz in Europa' (2009) 64 Juristenzeitung 131.
Stuyck J, 'Class Actions in Europe? To Opt-In or to Opt-Out, that is the Question' (2017) 20 European Business Law Review 483.
Stürner M, 'Cross-border Issues' in A Stadler, E Jeuland and V Smith (eds), *Collective and Mass Litigation in Europe: Model Rules for Effective Dispute Resolution* (Edward Elgar 2020) 296.
Tang ZS, 'Consumer Collective Redress in European Private International Law' (2011) 7 Journal of Private International Law 101.
Tzankova I and Kramer X, 'From Injunction and Settlement to Action: Collective Redress and Funding in the Netherlands' in A Uzelac and S Voet (eds), *Class Actions in Europe* (Springer 2021) 97.
Vlahek A, 'The Great Saga of Collective Redress in EU Competition Law: All Cry and No Wool?' (2024) 46 World Competition 53.
Voet S, 'Een Belgische vertegenwoordigende collectieve rechtsvordering: vier bouwstenen voor een Belgische class action' (2012) 18 Rechtskundig Weekblad 682.
—— 'Costs and Funding of Collective Redress Proceedings' in A Stadler, E Jeuland and V Smith (eds), *Collective and Mass Litigation in Europe: Model Rules for Effective Dispute Resolution* (Edward Elgar 2020) 264.

John Sorabji

Chapter 22
Legal Aid, Costs and Funding

A Introduction

#1 This chapter focuses on European approaches to litigation cost and public and private means of **litigation funding**, both of which are areas that have been rightly noted to be generally *'forgotten areas of civil procedure'*.[1] It does so through the lens of the right of access to justice guaranteed by both article 6 of the European Convention on Human Rights (ECHR) and article 47 of the Charter of Fundamental Rights of the European Union. Cost, funding and **access to justice** are intrinsically linked. Where litigation cost is, for example, too high, access to justice may be reduced as only those individuals or businesses with sufficient funds are likely to be able to litigate. As Bentham put it, high costs transform entry to the justice system into a lottery, and particularly one to which only those with a golden ticket, ie, wealth, are able to access.[2]

#2 Litigation cost levels equally have an impact on the nature and availability of litigation funding. They have, for instance, an impact on the level and availability of publicly funded legal aid both to individual disputes and to litigants generally. The higher the cost of litigation, the greater will be individual demands on legal aid, which in turn will either reduce its overall availability or require increasing amounts of taxpayer funding to be made available. High costs also have an impact on **private funding** methods. High costs may, for instance, lead to high insurance premiums and to lawyers and funders seeking high returns on any funding they provide to litigants. Increasingly higher returns for the provision of funding entail a commensurate reduction in any compensation secured by a funded party, thus undermining to an extent the vindication of their rights. From an alternative perspective, the availability of funding, even if for a high return to a funder, may be the only means by which a party may be able to secure rights-vindication.

#3 To explore the issues surrounding costs and funding, it is first necessary to identify the elements of each. Where litigation cost is concerned it is constituted of

1 C Hodges, S Vogenauer and M Tulibacka, 'The Oxford Study on Costs and Funding of Civil Litigation' in C Hodges, S Vogenauer and M Tulibacka (eds), *The Costs and Funding of Civil Litigation* (CH Beck/Hart 2010) 3, 5. This work provides the most detailed conspectus of approaches to costs across Europe.

2 J Bentham, *Letters on Scotch Reform* in *The Works of Jeremy Bentham* (ed. Bowring), vol 5 (William Tait 1843) 47.

John Sorabji, University College London, e-mail: j.sorabji@ucl.ac.uk

https://doi.org/10.1515/9783110781632-022

three things.[3] First, it concerns the cost to the state of funding the judiciary and the court administration. It thus encompasses, in respect of the former, the cost of securing judicial appointments, training, salaries and pensions. Where the latter is concerned, it covers the cost and maintenance of court buildings and infrastructure, including digital infrastructure, and administrative staff. To a certain extent these costs will be borne by the State through general taxation. However, they are also defrayed by court fees, ie, the fees states charge litigants to access the justice system. Such fees are traditionally kept at a low level, however, in some instances they have been set at levels that have undermined access to justice, while in other cases, such as those where low value claims are concerned court fees, even at a low level, may play a significant role in rendering them economically unviable.[4]

#4 The second, and most significant, aspect of litigation cost focuses on process **fees**. These fees are a function of two things. They are a product of a state's procedural code or rules and the fees that lawyers charge to provide litigants advice, assistance and **representation** consistently with that code or rules. The more complex or technical the code or rules, the more likely it will be that lawyers' fees will be high. Underpinning this point is the fact that to reduce litigation cost European states have consistently attempted to both reduce the general complexity of their civil justice systems through repeated reform efforts and most recently through attempts to digitise their justice systems, but have also introduced procedural case tracks of differing varieties that seek to match the nature and extent of procedure to the nature of the dispute.[5] Moreover, the more weight such a code or rules places on parties to carry out the conduct of litigation, e.g., to secure evidence, to make and attend pre-trial applications, and how they structure the litigation process, e.g., the greater the weight given to oral hearings with party presentation and testing of evidence, the higher lawyers' fees are likely to be. Conversely, where greater weight is placed on the court and the judiciary to manage the conduct of litigation, including the evidence-gathering and trial process, the lower those fees are likely to be. Albeit in such a case the cost to the state of the judiciary and court administration will be comparably higher. Process fees also necessarily include any costs of enforcement.[6]

3 AA Matić, *Just Words – The Effectiveness of Civil Justice in European Human Rights Jurisprudence* (CUP 2020) 174f; Hodges, Vogenauer and Tulibacka (n 1) 12.

4 In such cases, hence the need to develop effective small claims procedures and, where mass low value claims are concerned, effective representative or collective action mechanisms.

5 See, for instance, Civil Procedure Rules (England and Wales) Pts 26, 27, 28 and 29 (small, fast, intermediate and multi-tracks). Similarly, France has adopted a short, medium and long track, see E Jeuland, *Introduction to French Business Litigation* (Joly 2016) 128–130.

6 Depending on the structure of the system these may fall under process fees, as they would in England and Wales, or as part of the costs associated with court fees; see W Kennett, *Civil Enforcement in a Comparative Perspective: A Public Management Challenge* (Intersentia 2022).

#5 The final aspect of litigation cost concerns costs incurred by NGOs, charities and the State of providing free **legal advice** and assistance to individuals who are unable to access litigation funding. As this element of costs does not impact on litigants but on society in general it is often overlooked. It is, however, like the other two aspects of litigation costs linked to litigation funding and access to justice. To the extent that funding is unavailable, the cost burden in this respect will rise as individuals will, where they do seek to vindicate their rights through securing effective access to the courts, increasingly need to rely upon such advice and assistance.

#6 To meet these various aspects of litigation cost, three main mechanisms are available. Where possible parties to litigation will self-fund litigation, that is they will bear the cost of securing effective access to justice themselves. To do so they will draw on their income, savings or secure debt. Otherwise, there are two main funding sources: public and private. The primary source of public funding throughout Europe has been since the late 1940s the provision of state-funded civil **legal aid**; state funding provided to individuals to enable them to seek legal advice and assistance. To varying degrees European countries have also facilitated the use of a range of private funding mechanisms. These include both before-the-event and after-the event **legal expenses insurance**. It also includes insurance provided by or as a concomitant of Trade Union membership. They also include contingency fee funding provided by lawyers and **third party litigation funding** provided by specialist funding companies. Over the course of the last thirty years there has been a decided shift in emphasis both worldwide and across Europe where funding is concerned. That shift has been characterised by a reduction in the availability of public funding and its replacement by the market-based private funding mechanisms.

#7 To illustrate these issues, this chapter first considers the framework within which litigation cost and funding operates within Europe. It thus examines the right of access to justice, with specific reference to the **article 6 ECHR** right and the framework it provides for litigation cost and funding. It then turns to examine the extent to which cost affects the right of access, identifying steps taken to reduce cost across Europe. Finally, it considers European developments in the provision of litigation funding, particularly looking at recent developments in **third party funding**.

B Access to Justice, Costs and Funding

#8 Litigation cost, specifically high litigation cost, is well-known within Europe as posing a problem where access to justice is concerned. As Matić notes, in at least eight European jurisdictions the high incidence of costs has been identified by the

European Union Fundamental Rights Agency, as impeding effective access to justice.[7] While the concept of access to justice is one that has rightly been described as '*inherently ambiguous*',[8] in this context its meaning is clear: it refers to access to a fair trial before a court which concludes with an enforceable judgment being issued. The right of access to justice, in this sense, is an accepted right within European civil justice systems. It is not, however, explicit within the article 6 ECHR right to **fair trial** to which all Council of Europe member states are committed.[9] That being said, it is necessarily inherent in that right, as was made clear by the European Court of Human Rights (ECtHR) in *Golder v The UK*.[10] If it were not the right to a fair trial, and the substantive rights to which that is intended to give effect through judgment and enforcement, would be no more than words on paper. The right is not, however, absolute and may be subject to proportionate limitations where they pursue a legitimate aim and do not undermine the fundamental essence of the right itself.[11] That being noted the right of access cannot simply be a formal or theoretical one. It is a right that must be both practical and effective.[12] Within the framework provided by the right of access, the ECtHR has elaborated several a broad approach, which prohibits the placing of certain obstacles in the way of securing that right. This touches upon both litigation cost and funding.[13]

#9 Where cost is concerned, the ECtHR has held that court fees must not be such as to impede the right of access. That is to say that a litigant must not be subject to excessive court fees, as they would render the access right no more than theoretical.[14] Moreover, parties should not be subject to cost shifting rules that would improperly undermine the access right's practical efficacy.[15] In Europe the general approach to litigation costs is to employ cost shifting. In contrast to the United States of America, which typical does not do so on the basis that a no-cost shifting

7 Matić (n 3) 168.

8 *KA v London Borough of Croydon* [2017] EWHC 1723 (Admin) at [40].

9 It is also not fully explicit in article 47 of the EU Charter of Fundamental Rights. It is implicit in that right's provision that everyone is entitled to an effective remedy before a competent tribunal where their rights have been violated. It is, however, explicit in that article where the duty on EU member states to provide legal aid is concerned. See, *Unibet (Freedom to provide services)* [2007] ECR I-2271 at [36]-[37], for instance, on the right of access under article 47 and noting that it stemmed from the constitutional traditions of the EU member states.

10 *Golder v The UK* (1975) 1 EHRR 524 at [35]-[36].

11 *Ashingdane v The UK* (1985) 7 EHRR 528.

12 *Airey v Ireland* (1979) 2 EHRR 305; *Artico v Italy* [1980] ECHR 4; *Tolstoy Miloslavsky v The UK* (1995) 20 EHRR 442.

13 Matić (n 3) 195–205.

14 *Kreuz v Poland (No 1)* [2001] ECHR 398; *Stankov v Bulgaria* [2007] ECHR 582.

15 *Tolstoy Miloslavsky v The United Kingdom* [1995] ECHR 25, in the context of an application for security for costs.

rule promotes access to justice through lowering a party's potential cost liability,[16] in Europe states generally operate on the basis that the losing party should pay a proportion of the successful party's costs.[17] The rationale here is to ensure that meritorious claims and defences are not deterred due to the potential exposure to the costs of litigation that a party may incur. In other words, cost shifting is believed to encourage the pursuit of meritorious cases and thus increase access to justice. It is, however, important to ensure that where that is the case the potential costs to be paid by a losing party are not such as to impede the bringing of such claims; an issue developed further in Section C below.

#10 The nature and extent of litigation costs raises further questions than those concerning cost shifting. Excess costs, particularly lawyer's fees, may pose a problem for access to justice where they have a chilling effect on an individual's ability to obtain legal advice and representation or to bring proceedings in the first instance. As Hodges et al rightly note,

> *'the size and predictability of the costs of a dispute, and of a dispute resolution process, need to be evaluated to see whether the risks and benefits of using the process are favourable in pursuing a legal action . . . If the costs or risks are too high, and there is no better alternative pathway, the result will be a denial of access to justice, and potential wrongs will not be remedied or compensated.'*[18]

#11 Unpredictable costs may also impinge on the development of effective legal expenses insurance schemes, thus again having a chilling effect on an individual's ability to bring proceedings at all or effectively. It may do so as with an absence of such funding parties may not be able to obtain effective legal assistance.[19] Such issues raise further questions concerning European states' obligations to either control litigation costs or to provide legal aid. In respect of the former, a similar point arises as that applicable to court fees, ie, the extent to which the state ought to impose controls on parties' ability to incur litigation costs through or to control costs through capping them or rendering them subject to tariffs. Where the latter is concerned, the ECtHR has developed specific negative duties within the framework provided by the access to justice right, which have been placed on Council

16 See, for instance, M Rosenberg, 'Devising Procedures That Are Civil to Promote Justice That Is Civilized' (1970–1971) 69 Mich. L. Rev. 797, 802–803.

17 W van Boom, 'Litigation Costs and Third Party Funding' in W van Boom (ed), *Litigation, Costs, Funding and Behaviour* (Routledge 2017) 5, 6–7; ELI-UNIDROIT, *ELI-UNIDROIT Model European Rules of Procedure* (OUP 2021) 275. Also see, S Saarensola, 'The Risk of Legal Costs and its Effect on Access to Justice' in L Ervo and A Nylund, *The Future of Civil Litigation* (Springer 2014) 231, 235 on the adoption of the cost shifting rule in Finland, Norway, Sweden and Denmark.

18 Hodges, Vogenauer and Tulibacka (n 1) 4.

19 J Peysner, 'Costs in Personal Injury Cases: Searching for Predictable Costs' (2002) 2(2) Journal of Personal Injury Law 166.

of Europe member states. For instance, in *Airey v Ireland*, the ECtHR held that states had to make legal aid available to individuals where that was necessary, ie, essential, for them to secure practical and effective the access to justice right. It did not, however, provide that states had to provide legal aid. Where states could secure effective and practical access via other means, e.g., procedural simplification, the provision of pro bono legal advice and representation or, as now or in the future might well be the case, the provision of digitised court processes that are able to guide litigants through those processes, the provision of legal aid would not amount to a necessity.[20] In other cases, where the procedure is already straightforward, there may be no requirement whatsoever on a state to take any measures, as there will be no real obstacle to a litigant securing practical and effective access.[21]

#12 Any exposition of litigation cost and funding, and specifically the nature and prevalence of legal aid and other funding methods, has to be seen in the light of the approach taken by the ECtHR. Particularly, it needs to be considered by reference to the need to ensure that litigation costs, not least lawyer's fees, do not undermine parties' ability to gain practical and effective access to the courts. Moreover, funding mechanisms promoted and regulated by European states also need to be considered by reference to the fact that legal aid is no more and no less than the necessary backstop that a state must provide to secure practical and effective party access. That it does, places any consideration of funding mechanisms in the broader context that European states may promote other, and better, forms of litigation funding that legal aid. It is these issues that will now be explored.

C Access to Justice and Costs

#13 Two broad approaches to the allocation of litigation costs, within the general European approach to cost shifting, are evidenced within Europe.[22] As noted by the **ELI-UNIDROIT Model European Rules of Procedure**, the two approaches are exemplified by, on the one hand, France and England and Wales,[23] and on the

20 *Airey v Ireland* (1979) 2 EHRR 305 at [24]-[26].

21 For a detailed analysis of the development of this approach see Matić (n 3) 189–195.

22 ELI-UNIDROIT (n 17) 275.

23 E.g., Civil Procedure Rules (England and Wales), r.44.2:
'(1) *The court has discretion as to –*
(a) *whether costs are payable by one party to another;*
(b) *the amount of those costs; and*
(c) *when they are to be paid.*'
And, see CPR r.44.4 and r.44.5. Also see, Code of Civil Procedure (France) arts. 696 and 700.

other hand, Germany and Estonia.[24] The former adopt a discretionary approach to determining cost liability (as do the ELI-UNIDROIT Model Rules), leaving it to the court on a case-by-case basis to determine their incidence. The latter provide more or less detailed rules specifying their incidence. It ought to be clear that the former leaves costs at large during the course of the litigation, such that parties will not be aware of their potential cost liability until the end of the proceedings when the discretion is exercised and costs are determined. It is an approach that had been aptly described in England, consciously echoing Søren Kierkegaard, as an approach based on the idea that *'Litigation can only be understood backwards; but it can only be litigated forwards.'*[25] In the same vein, it could be said that costs can only be calculated at the conclusion of proceedings. By way of contrast, the rule-determined approach is one that provides greater advance certainty where cost liability is concerned.

#14 While it ought to be obvious that the discretionary approach renders litigation cost generally unpredictable, the more rule-determined approach also poses a potential problem where predictability is concerned. Simply determining where cost liability lies says nothing about the actual incidence of total party costs, ie, it does not in and of itself render the amount of party costs predictable, and hence it does not provide for any real predictability in the total costs that are to be subject to the cost shifting mechanism. As in discretionary cost regimes, in principle a rule-determined regime needs to control the extent to which parties incur costs if there is to be such predictability. As Van Boom notes across Europe different approaches to this aspect of cost shifting are adopted. In England and Wales, for instance, in principle the full amount of the successful party's costs can become payable by the losing party, whereas in Germany **cost shifting** operates according to a fixed tariff, i.e., the costs to be shifted are fixed and determined at the outset of the litigation whereas in England and Wales and England they are generally at large.[26] Where costs are at large, particularly where that is married with

24 E.g., German Code of Civil Procedure, s.92:

'(1) *Where each of the parties has prevailed for a part of its claim, but has not been able to enforce another part of its claim in the dispute, the costs are to be cancelled against each other, or they are to be shared proportionately. If the costs have been cancelled against each other, the parties shall bear the court costs at one half each.*

(2) *The court may impose the entire costs of the proceedings on one of the parties if:*

1. *The amount the other party claimed in excess was relatively small, or has resulted in only slightly higher costs, or*
2. *The amount of the claim brought by the other party depended on the judges determining it at their discretion, on the assessment by experts, or on the parties settling their reciprocal claims.'* And see art. 91(1).

25 *Sharp v Blank* [2017] EWHC 3390 (Ch) at [25].

26 van Boom (n 17) 6–7; B Hess and R Hübner, 'Germany' in C Hodges, S Vogenauer and M Tulibacka (eds), *The Costs and Funding of Civil Litigation* (CH Beck/Hart 2010) 349, 351–353.

a discretionary approach to the determination of the amount of costs that the losing party is to be liable for, a party's potential cost liability is unpredictable to a very significant degree, which poses a real risk to the delivery of effective and practical access to justice. Unpredictability can, for instance, adversely affect parties who are more risk averse than other parties, it can adversely affect those with fewer financial resources to fund litigation than those with sufficient or more than sufficient resources.

#15 Even in jurisdictions, such as Finland, where the court has discretion to reduce the amount of costs subject to its cost shifting rule in line with the need to protect access to justice, the exercise of that discretion in the absence of any principle or rules to secure a degree of predictability, is arguably problematic. The rationale for that, as pointed out by Saarensola is straightforward.[27] The absence of predictability and the fact that the court can interpret and apply its discretion in varying and different ways means that parties not only have no real way of predicting the potential cost liability that may arise under cost shifting but that they equally have no means of predicting whether and how the court could apply its discretion to reduce the amount of costs that are to be subject to cost shifting. The absence of predictability thus poses a real risk to access to justice. Where the amount of costs that are potentially to be shifted are subject to a tariff, which is determined and determinable before proceedings are commenced, the converse is true.

#16 The first issue that flows from the preceding points concerns the level of costs that are incurred in litigation across Europe, and how they are controlled. Jurisdictions, like England and Wales, where there is both a discretionary approach to cost shifting and discretion as to the amount of costs that a losing party may be liable to pay evidence high levels of litigation costs.[28] By way of contrast, Germany where a rule-determined approach to cost shifting and a tariff cost regime is in operation evidences a lower incidence of litigation costs.[29] This is not to say that these two factors are determinative of the level of costs. Two points needed to be noted here. First, these two factors are not wholly determinative of party costs. Such costs will also be a function of the nature of the procedural system and the balance struck between party and control responsibility for civil litigation, as noted above. Secondly, and as a necessary corollary of the first point, they will not be determinative of the global cost of proceedings. To determine that the other cost elements, e.g., **court costs**, etc, would need to be taken into account.

27 Saarensola (n 17) 244–245.
28 A Zuckerman, *Zuckerman on Civil Procedure* (Sweet & Maxwell 2021) 1413.
29 Hess and Hübner (n 26) 349.

#17 That caveat aside, to reduce the level of costs there has been a movement towards greater prospective control of litigation costs as a means to reduce the overall amount of costs that are subject to cost shifting. England and Wales, for instance, has introduced two different mechanisms of prospective costs control. In the first instance, it introduced a form of cost budgeting. This requires parties to prepare a schedule of their anticipated litigation costs at the outset of litigation. These costs are then subject to court scrutiny and approval at an appropriate level. That approved level then provides the basis on which the determination of the amount of costs that are subject to cost shifting at the conclusion of proceedings. In essence it provides an upper limit to such costs.[30] It has also introduced an approach, explicitly based on the German tariff costs regime, of fixed, predictable costs.[31] Similarly, albeit to a lesser extent, France also provides for fixed tariff costs for legal representation in certain proceedings.[32] Similarly, the approach taken in The Netherlands is one that sees the cost-shifting rule limited where lawyers' fees are concerned, so that only a proportion are subject to cost-shifting. Again, this is achieved via the imposition of a recoverability tariff.[33]

#18 The use of predictable cost regimes, and the level at which they set the amount of costs that successful parties can recover, is an important development where access to justice is concerned. They are an essential means by which the State strikes the balance between securing access to justice for meritorious claims and providing a cost-based disincentive for parties to pursue unmeritorious or frivolous litigation. Setting the tariff at too high a rate would act as a barrier to access to justice. Set at too low a rate, there would be a real risk that defendants would be troubled by frivolous litigation, and that the State would incur the cost of managing and determining such cases; a cost to the State that would impair its ability to allocate its resources to meritorious claims. This raises a question as to the basis on which European civil justice systems determine the level at which such costs should be determined. In respect of this different approaches can be discerned.

#19 Hodges et al noted that European systems rarely provided an explicit approach to the rules they adopt concerning costs.[34] England and Wales, it was noted, require costs to be consistent with the principle of proportionality.[35] It is also governed by the indemnity principle; that is to say, the losing party is only required to indemnify the successful party for those costs that the successful party is itself le-

30 CPR rr.3.12–3.18.

31 CPR Pt 45.

32 Law No. 71-1130 of 1971, art. 10 (France); Code of Civil Procedure (France), art. 699.

33 M Tuil, 'The Netherlands' in C Hodges, S Vogenauer and M Tulibacka (eds), *The Costs and Funding of Civil Litigation* (CH Beck/Hart 2010) 401, 415.

34 Hodges, Vogenauer and Tulibacka (n 1) 12.

35 Civil Procedure Rules (England and Wales) r.1.1(1).

gally obliged to pay to, e.g., its lawyers. It has also been said to be governed by the causation principle, i.e., that the losing party is required to compensate the successful party for the costs it wrongfully (tortiously) caused the successful party to incur by wrongfully bringing or defending the proceedings.[36] Rather than adopt a proportionality based approach, Germany operates its approach to its costs rules on the basis of necessity. Its predictable costs regime only permits costs necessarily incurred to be recovered, and they are recovered consistently with the tariff. Its primary principle governing costs is thus one of predictability and that serves the wider goal of promoting access to justice by enabling parties to determine whether and how they wish to litigate based on their prospects of success and not their financial resources. Implicitly, it thus promotes equal access to justice as it enables access to be determined not one their wealth or status. Germany's approach is also seen as serving a wider social objective, that of securing the efficient use of the State's resources by facilitating the prosecution and defence of meritorious claims, while deterring unmeritorious or frivolous claims.[37]

#20 Portugal also adopts a multi-factorial approach, as noted by Sousa Antunes and Hodges et al. As they explain, the Portuguese approach understands costs to be determined by reference to multiple principles: that they promote access to justice (a point implicit in the English and Welsh approach as proportionality is itself intended to secure access to justice[38]); to discourage frivolous claims; to ensure that the loser pays; that costs should only be paid where they have been caused by the losing party; and, proportionality.[39] The Netherlands takes a similarly detailed approach.[40] These are, as Tuil explains:[41] that litigation should not be free. It is a serious matter and parties should weigh up carefully whether to do so; that litigation cost should promote access to justice; that costs should be predictable; and that, the loser pays. That last principle is understood to be an incident of procedural fairness and not a question of tortious conduct.[42] In Norway, by contrast, the sole explicit principle governing cost shifting is that the successful party is entitled to full compensation for their costs, albeit the court retains a discretion to reduce the amount of costs subject that requirement. Hence, while it adopts

36 *Arkin v Borchard Lines Ltd (costs order)* [2005] EWCA Civ 655; [2005] 1 WLR 3055; although see the criticism of this in Zuckerman (n 28) 1432.
37 Hess and Hübner (n 26) 351.
38 Zuckerman (n 28) 31.
39 H Sousa Antunes, 'Portugal' in C Hodges, S Vogenauer and M Tulibacka (eds), *The Costs and Funding of Civil Litigation* (CH Beck/Hart 2010) 467, 469–470.
40 Tuil (n 33) 404.
41 ibid.
42 ibid.

the discretionary approach to cost-shifting, it does so explicitly further to a compensatory or indemnificatory approach.[43]

#21 The first point to take from these various approaches is that the approach to costs within Europe is either explicitly or implicitly intended to promote access to justice for meritorious claims and defences. It also rests on the idea that, as a matter of fairness, parties should not generally be out-of-pocket for bringing reasonable claims or defences, i.e., they should, to a degree, be indemnified, for seeking to vindicate their rights. The major departure between systems is how these objectives are achieved, e.g., whether they are to be achieved through the court's discretion or through the imposition of costs tariffs. That the jurisdiction – England and Wales – that has placed the greatest weight upon the court's discretion and abolished its own tariff cost regime in 1986 following a campaign by the Law Society (which represents the interests of the solicitor's branch of the legal profession in England and Wales, supportive of their abolition[44]), has moved back to a tariff-based cost regime, is indicative of predictability being a more effective means to secure the principles that underpin costs and cost-shifting. A tariff-based approach may not provide for a successful party to recover all their costs. It does, however, provide advance certainty as to all parties' potential **cost liability**. It thus provides a surer basis for parties to assess whether they ought to properly pursue their claim or defence. That such a regime means that even a successful party will be out-of-pocket for some of their litigation costs, i.e., those that the tariff renders irrecoverable from the loser party, also means that they take seriously the choice to litigate or not. Thus it properly promotes the appropriate use by individuals of the State's resources as they are provided to the civil justice system. In that respect, it also promotes the proportionate use of the justice system. In these ways it does not simply promote access to justice through controlling costs and rendering them predictable. It also enables the more effective promotion of litigation funding, and so further facilitates the promotion of access to justice.

D Access to Justice, Legal Aid and Other Forms of Funding

#22 Litigation cost, whether controlled, predictable or otherwise, can and does act as a barrier to access to justice. The extent to which it does so depends, however, upon the availability of litigation funding. European states generally take a mixed

43 Act relating to mediation and procedure in civil disputes (The Dispute Act) (Norway), chap. 20.
44 M Cook, *Cook on Costs* (LexisNexis 2012) 98.

approach to litigation funding, i.e., they promote the use of both publicly-funded, civil legal aid and various private forms of funding.

#23 All Council of Europe states provide some form of civil legal aid, although each state differs in respect of the basis on which they provide it and the exact manner in which it is provided. As CEPEJ note a broad distinction can be drawn between those states that provide legal aid (which for 38 Council of Europe states includes not only funding for legal advice and representation but also for civil mediation[45]) further to the aim of improving access to justice generally, whereas others target its availability based on need, i.e., it is only available for the impecunious. As it puts it, '*the second philosophy prevails in Europe, since the majority of the countries have income and assets evaluation as a prerequisite for granting legal aid*'.[46] States that provide legal aid on the former basis are, for instance, Cyprus, the Czech Republic and Romania. Those States that apply means-tests, which either consider an individual's assets and/or income, are, for instance, England and Wales, Hungary and Lithuania. One state, Denmark, only provides legal aid where legal expenses insurance is not available. Thus it places primary responsibility on individuals to put in place the means to fund litigation. Moreover, the majority of European State also apply a merits-assessment as a pre-condition to the grant of legal aid, i.e., the claim to be funded must demonstrate that it has a reasonable prospect of succeeding.[47] Examples of States that do not apply a merits test are, for instance, Cyprus, Greece, Portugal.[48]

#24 Public funding for legal aid has, however, been subject to significant reduction in several European states. In England and Wales, for instance, since the early 1980s it has been subject to sustained reduction, as successive governments have sought to shift the responsibility for litigation funding from the State to the private sector.[49] The last major reform, in 2012, saw civil legal aid's budget reduce by 40%.[50] This development is not an outlier. **CEPEJ** reports show that a long term trend can be seen where the provision of legal aid is concerned. From 2014 to 2016, 17 Council of Europe states, including England and Wales, The Netherlands and Portugal, reduced their legal aid budget, whereas 19 increased it.[51] From 2016 to 2018,

45 CEPEJ, *European Judicial Systems – CEPEJ Evaluation Report 2022* (Council of Europe 2022) 37 <https://rm.coe.int/cepej-report-2020-22-e-web/1680a86279> accessed 31 March 2025.

46 ibid.

47 For further detail see, CEPEJ (2022) 37f.

48 CEPEJ, *European Judicial Systems – CEPEJ Evaluation Report 2018*, (Council of Europe 2018) 75 <https://rm.coe.int/rapport-avec-couv-18-09-2018-en/16808def9c> accessed 31 March 2025.

49 J Peysner, *Access to Justice* (Palgrave Macmillan 2014).

50 Low Commission Report, 'Tackling the Advice Deficit. A Strategy for Access to Advice and Legal Support on Social Welfare Law in England and Wales' (Legal Action Group 2014), Annex 11 'National Public Sector funding', 1.

51 CEPEJ (2018) 86.

13 states decreased their budgets, while 25 increased theirs.[52] From 2018 to 2020 (the last period for which results are available), 22 states reduced their budgets, with 20 increasing theirs.[53] As CEPEJ noted in 2018, this picture was one that was underpinned by those States that had historically provided generous legal aid budgets retrenching and reducing them, whereas other States that had historically provided lower budgets increased them.[54]

#25 Public funding, if available, should not however be assumed to be the primary funding mechanism. As ought to be evident from the approach taken in Denmark, noted above, legal aid is very much a secondary form of funding, and one that – as the ECtHR has accepted – is a necessary backstop that need only be made available where other means to secure financial access to justice are unavailable. Historically, a similar approach has been taken in Germany where, for example, **self-funding** and the provision of legal expenses insurance have been the two primary means of litigation funding.[55] The approach in Germany is predicated upon one significant structural factor. For legal expenses insurance to develop effectively, it needs risk to be quantifiable to a reasonable extent.[56] Where litigation is concerned that requires predictability where cost is concerned. Where costs are predictable insurance companies can quantify risk effectively and set premiums accordingly. Where, as in England and Wales, litigation cost has historically been anything other than predictable due to the absence of prospective **costs controls** or fixed tariffs applicable to cost shifting, it is unsurprising that legal expenses insurance has been an under-developed funding mechanism. Equally, unsurprisingly, Denmark, which also relies primarily on legal expenses insurance also operates a tariff approach to lawyers' fees and thus, like Germany and increasingly England and Wales, makes provision for greater costs predictability.[57] One potential development consistent with the ECtHR's approach, which places how States make provision for access to justice, could – in principle – be the promotion across Europe of legal expenses insurance schemes as a substantial or the primary private funding mechanisms for litigation costs. Where that to happen it would require States to, however, promote greater predictability in costs, and hence cost shifting. Given the reduction in civil legal aid in many States, this may be the better policy choice than one that rests on, as at present, the promotion of

52 CEPEJ, *European Judicial Systems – CEPEJ Evaluation Report 2018* (Council of Europe 2020) 38 <https://rm.coe.int/evaluation-report-part-1-english/16809fc058> accessed 31 March 2025.

53 CEPEJ (2022) 38.

54 CEPEJ (2018) 86.

55 Hess and Hübner (n 26) 357. They also note that the expansion of legal expenses insurance did not result, as some critics suggested, result in an increasingly litigious society.

56 R Lewis, 'Litigation Costs and Before-the-event Insurance: The Key to Access to Justice?' (2011) 74 MLR 272; Hess and Hübner (n 26) 349.

57 Administration of Justice Act 2008 (Denmark), s. 316.

other forms of litigation funding, such as contingency fee agreements and third party litigation funding.

#26 In the absence of the wider development of litigation funding, the main policy debate in Europe has concerned the use of **contingency fee** and third party funding,[58] the former provided by lawyers who agree to act for no-fee if their client loses on the proviso that they will be reimbursed either by a share of the damages received by their client or by way of their ordinary fees plus an additional amount, whereas the latter sees funding provided to parties by businesses unconnected to the litigation in return for a share of the damages. Historically, both forms of funding were generally prohibited on various grounds, not least that what was viewed as speculation on litigation was understood to stir up litigation unnecessarily, and to pose a conflict of interest between lawyer and client where contingency fee funding was concerned. The latter argument, and particularly the point that such forms of funding were unethical, can for instance be seen to have lain behind the prohibition on contingency fees that historically existed, for instance, in England and Wales, Germany and in The Netherlands.[59]

#27 The recognition of these two types of private funding mechanism as valid forms of funding mechanism has rested on the claim that they promote access to justice, and where third party funding is concerned this is particularly the case where mass litigation pursued via collective proceedings is concerned.[60] It is noteworthy, however, that in England and Wales at least, the evidence suggests that arguments concerning access to justice may well be overstated. A recent empirical study suggests that third

58 On the historical development and issues concerning collective action funding via contingency fees, see for instance, M Tuil and L Visscher, *New Trends in Financing Civil Litigation in Europe* (Edward Elgar 2010); C Leskinen, 'Collective Actions: Rethinking Funding and National Cost Rules' (2011) 8 Comp. Law Review 87; X Kramer and I Tillema, 'The Funding of Collective Redress by Entrepreneurial Parties: The EU and Dutch Context' (2020) 2 Revista Ítalo-Española de Derecho Procesal 165. On concerns regarding third party funding see, A Cordina, 'Is It All That Fishy? A Critical Review of the Concerns Surrounding Third Party Litigation Funding in Europe' (2021) 14 ELR 270; J Saulnier, K Müllerwith and I Koronthalyova, 'Responsible Private Funding of Litigation' (European Parliamentary Research Service 2021); R Portenti, 'Three's a Crowd: The EU Should Safeguard Against Third-Party Funding' (2024) 15 Arb. L. Rev. 104.

59 Contingency fees were, for instance, historically unlawful and void for public policy reasons in England and Wales, but were rendered permissible via the Courts and Legal Services Act 1980. In Germany they were traditionally prohibited. They were rendered permissible by the German Constitutional Court in 2006 on the basis that they may promote access to justice in specific situations, see A Stadler, 'German Collective Actions – Is Litigation Funding in a Dead End?' in X Kramer and others (eds), *Frontiers in Civil Justice. Privatisation, Monetisation and Digitisation* (Edward Elgar 2022) 259; M Zander, 'Will the Revolution in the Funding of Civil Litigation in England eventually lead to Contingency Fees?' (2002) 52 DePaul Law Review 259; B van Velthoven and P van Wivck, 'Experimenting with Conditional Fees in the Netherlands' in W van Boom (ed), *Litigation, Costs, Funding and Behaviour* (Routledge 2017) 129.

60 Kramer and Tillema (n 58) 177.

party funding is focused on no more than 3 to 5% of cases that were eligible for funding. In other words it does not provide access to justice to any real extent other than in a tiny minority of disputes and that minority is focused upon collective actions.[61] Whether or not the access to justice rationale is overstated, it is generally recognised as the rationale justifying such funding being available. That that is so has been recognised by the European Parliament, notwithstanding its concerns that such funding may well be problematic. Recital C to its Resolution on Responsible Private Funding of Litigation (2023) specifically acknowledges that such funding can promote access to justice. That, however, is subject to the caveat that it is subject to effective regulation, which itself should be subject to minimum standards across the European Union.[62] These forms of funding are likely to continue to develop across Europe, with the policy debate concerning them focusing on, as it does currently, whether they should be subject to regulation and if so how best such regulation should be implemented. Different views can be taken on this point. The European Law Institute, for instance, recommended what could best be described as a light touch approach to the regulation of third party funding, focusing on the development of minimum standards.[63] The Voss Report to the European Commission, however, took a more conservative approach, one that focused more on regulation as a means to control the development of such funding and promote high standards in its providers.[64] Similarly, consideration of the future development of third party funding is also subject to specific consideration in England and Wales. Following the UK Supreme Court's interpretation of third party funding as a form of contingency fee agreement, its status and future development, particularly its regulation and whether it ought to be subject to specific rules where it is used in collective or representative proceedings, is subject to scrutiny by England and Wales' Civil Justice Council.[65]

61 R Mulheron, *A Review of Litigation Funding in England and Wales – A Legal Literature and Empirical Study* (Legal Services Board 2024).

62 European Parliament resolution of 13 September 2022 with recommendations to the Commission on Responsible private funding of litigation (2020/2130(INL)).

63 European Law Institute (ELI), *Principles Governing the Third Party Funding of Litigation* (2024) <https://www.europeanlawinstitute.eu/fileadmin/user_upload/p_eli/Publications/ELI_Principles_Governing_the_Third_Party_Funding_of_Litigation.pdf> accessed 31 March 2025.

64 A Vos, Report with recommendations to the Commission on Responsible private funding of litigation (2020/2130(INL)) <https://www.europarl.europa.eu/doceo/document/A-9-2022-0218_EN.pdf> accessed 31 March 2025. Future European Union developments are likely to be influenced by the European Commission study on third party funding, which was carried out by the British Institute of International and Comparative Law: *The Mapping Third Party Litigation Funding in the European Union* project. At the time of writing the study had not been published.

65 Civil Justice Council (England and Wales), Review of Litigation Funding. See Third Party Funding Working Party Terms of Reference <https://www.judiciary.uk/wp-content/uploads/2024/04/20240422-CJC-TPF-Review-TOR.pdf> accessed 31 March 2025) and the Review' Interim Report (<https://www.judiciary.uk/wp-content/uploads/2024/10/CJC-Review-of-Litigation-Funding-Interim-Report.pdf> accessed 31 March 2025). For a broader discussion on the interaction between third party funding and collective

#28 However these various reviews might develop, it might perhaps be anticipated that, where third party funding is concerned, it will – as in England and Wales – mainly focus on mass litigation and collective proceedings as they are the ones most likely to provide a basis on which funders can make a reasonable profit such as to make funding worthwhile from their perspective. Contingency fees are likely to also further develop, although in those jurisdictions where legal aid continues to increase in availability and those jurisdictions that have and can develop legal expenses insurance, those forms of funding may well become the primary means through which litigation cost is met. If the latter is the case, it might also be anticipated that the insurance sector will start to play an increasing role in policy arguments about how civil litigation should be carried out, i.e., it will become an increasingly powerful voice in respect of the reform of civil litigation, as it will seek to reduce litigation cost in general and render it more predictable. If that is the case, the possibility may arise that a form of litigation funding may become the means by which access to justice is promoted more generally than through the simple provision of funding.

E Conclusion

#29 Article 6 ECHR does not prescribe the approach which Council of Europe states must take to either litigation cost or funding. It sets a baseline. Some jurisdictions, such as England and Wales, skirt close to the baseline, as Smith noted where its approach to legal is concerned. He concluded that with the widescale reduction of legal aid following its introduction of the Legal Aid, Sentencing and Punishment of Offenders Act 2012, legal aid provision in that jurisdiction was at the *'lowest level of service that [would] comply with [its] minimum obligations under the European Convention on Human Rights at the least possible cost'*.[66] That being said legal aid is not the sole means by which England and Wales or other European jurisdictions secure compliance with the right to fair trial. The availability of legal expenses insurance in some jurisdictions, and the increasing availability of other private mechanisms, whether those are based on some form of contingency funding agreement or third party funding agreement provide the means by which individuals and businesses can secure effective access to justice. That re-

---

or representative actions see, for instance: X Kramer, 'The Quest for Funding Under the Dutch WAMCA: Third Party Funding and the Viability of a Procedural Fund' (2024) 38 Emory Int'l L. Rev. 767; X Kramer and others (eds), *Financing Collective Actions in the Netherlands – Towards a Litigation Fund?* (Eleven Publishing 2024).

66 R Smith, 'After the Act: What Future For Legal Aid?' Justice Tom Sargant Annual Lecture 2012 (16 October 2012) 2 <http://www.justice.org.uk/data/files/resources/332/After-the-Act-what-future-for-legal-aid.pdf> accessed 31 March 2025.

mains the case notwithstanding continuing concerns regarding both of these private funding mechanisms.

#30 The key though to securing an effective blend of public and private funding mechanisms, and particularly to promote legal aid and legal expenses insurance, is however litigation cost. Where that is concerned prospective costs control or management married is a necessity. Whether that is achieved through tariff costs, as is well-established in Germany and The Netherlands, for instance, or in the process of expansion, as in England and Wales, or through prospective court management of costs, European jurisdictions that provide greater degrees of predictability where costs, and particularly costs recoverable by successful parties from losing parties, is an essential feature. Jurisdictions, such as England and Wales, that have historically eschewed mechanisms to promote costs predictability are ones that have had the lowest levels of development of insurance-based funding mechanisms and the highest levels of legal aid costs. With the general decline in legal aid funding the promotion of such the various forms of private funding are likely to become increasingly relied upon across Europe, not least as European governments seek to maintain access to justice while minimising the cost of access to the State.

References

Bentham J, *Letters on Scotch Reform* in *The Works of Jeremy Bentham* (ed. Bowring), vol 5 (William Tait 1843).

Boom van W, 'Litigation Costs and Third Party Funding' in W van Boom (ed), *Litigation, Costs, Funding and Behaviour* (Routledge 2017) 5, 6–7; ELI-UNIDROIT, *ELI-UNIDROIT Model European Rules of Procedure* (OUP 2021) 275.

British Institute of International and Comparative Law, *The Mapping Third Party Litigation Funding in the European Union* (2025).

CEPEJ, *European Judicial Systems – CEPEJ Evaluation Report 2018* (Council of Europe 2018) 75 <https://rm.coe.int/rapport-avec-couv-18-09-2018-en/16808def9c> accessed 31 March 2025.

—— *European Judicial Systems – CEPEJ Evaluation Report 2018* (Council of Europe 2020) 38 <https://rm.coe.int/evaluation-report-part-1-english/16809fc058> accessed 31 March 2025.

—— *European Judicial Systems – CEPEJ Evaluation Report 2022* (Council of Europe 2022) <https://rm.coe.int/cepej-report-2020-22-e-web/1680a86279> accessed 31 March 2025.

Cook M, *Cook on Costs* (LexisNexis 2012) 98.

Cordina A, 'Is It All That Fishy? A Critical Review of the Concerns Surrounding Third Party Litigation Funding in Europe' (2021) 14 ELR 270.

European Law Institute (ELI), *Principles Governing the Third Party Funding of Litigation* (2024) <https://www.europeanlawinstitute.eu/fileadmin/user_upload/p_eli/Publications/ELI_Principles_Governing_the_Third_Party_Funding_of_Litigation.pdf> accessed 31 March 2025.

Hess B and Hübner R, 'Germany' in C Hodges, S Vogenauer and M Tulibacka (eds), *The Costs and Funding of Civil Litigation* (CH Beck/Hart 2010) 349.

Hodges C, Vogenauer S, Tulibacka M (eds), *The Costs and Funding of Civil Litigation* (CH Beck/Hart 2010).

Hodges C, Vogenauer S and Tulibacka M, 'The Oxford Study on Costs and Funding of Civil Litigation' in C Hodges, S Vogenauer and M Tulibacka (eds), *The Costs and Funding of Civil Litigation* (CH Beck/Hart 2010) 3.

Jeuland E, *Introduction to French Business Litigation* (Joly 2016).

Kennett W, *Civil Enforcement in a Comparative Perspective: A Public Management Challenge* (Intersentia 2022).

Kramer X and others (eds), *Financing Collective Actions in the Netherlands – Towards a Litigation Fund?* (Eleven Publishing 2024).

Kramer X and Tillema I, 'The Funding of Collective Redress by Entrepreneurial Parties: The EU and Dutch Context' (2020) 2 Revista Ítalo-Española de Derecho Procesal 165.

Kramer X, 'The Quest for Funding Under the Dutch WAMCA: Third Party Funding and the Viability of a Procedural Fund' (2024) 38 Emory Int'l L. Rev. 767.

Leskinen C, 'Collective Actions: Rethinking Funding and National Cost Rules' (2011) 8 Comp. Law Review 87.

Lewis R, 'Litigation Costs and Before-the-event Insurance: The Key to Access to Justice?' (2011) 74 MLR 272.

Low Commission Report, 'Tackling the Advice Deficit. A Strategy for Access to Advice and Legal Support on Social Welfare Law in England and Wales' (Legal Action Group 2014), Annex 11 'National Public Sector funding'.

Matić AA, *Just Words – The Effectiveness of Civil Justice in European Human Rights Jurisprudence* (CUP 2020)

Mulheron R, *A Review of Litigation Funding in England and Wales – A Legal Literature and Empirical Study* (Legal Services Board 2024).

Peysner J, 'Costs in Personal Injury Cases: Searching for Predictable Costs' (2002) 2(2) Journal of Personal Injury Law 166.

—— *Access to Justice* (Palgrave Macmillan 2014).

Portenti R, 'Three's a Crowd: The EU Should Safeguard Against Third-Party Funding' (2024) 15 Arb. L. Rev. 104.

Rosenberg M, 'Devising Procedures That Are Civil to Promote Justice That Is Civilized' (1970–1971) 69 Mich. L. Rev. 797.

Saarensola S, 'The Risk of Legal Costs and its Effect on Access to Justice' in L Ervo and A Nylund, *The Future of Civil Litigation* (Springer 2014) 231.

Saulnier J, Müllerwith K and Koronthalyova I, 'Responsible Private Funding of Litigation' (European Parliamentary Research Service 2021).

Smith R, 'After the Act: What Future For Legal Aid?' Justice Tom Sargant Annual Lecture 2012 (16 October 2012) <http://www.justice.org.uk/data/files/resources/332/After-the-Act-what-future-for-legal-aid.pdf> accessed 31 March 2025.

Sousa Antunes H, 'Portugal' in C Hodges, S Vogenauer and M Tulibacka (eds), *The Costs and Funding of Civil Litigation* (CH Beck/Hart 2010) 467.

Stadler A, 'German Collective Actions – Is Litigation Funding in a Dead End?' in X Kramer and others (eds), *Frontiers in Civil Justice. Privatisation, Monetisation and Digitisation* (Edward Elgar 2022) 259.

Tuil M and Visscher L, *New Trends in Financing Civil Litigation in Europe* (Edward Elgar 2010).

Tuil M, 'The Netherlands' in C Hodges, S Vogenauer and M Tulibacka (eds), *The Costs and Funding of Civil Litigation* (CH Beck/Hart 2010) 401.

Velthoven van B and Wivck van P, 'Experimenting with Conditional Fees in the Netherlands' in W van Boom (ed), *Litigation, Costs, Funding and Behaviour* (Routledge 2017) 129.

Zander M, 'Will the Revolution in the Funding of Civil Litigation in England eventually lead to Contingency Fees?' (2002) 52 DePaul Law Review 259.

Zuckerman A, *Zuckerman on Civil Procedure* (Sweet & Maxwell 2021) 1413.

Part III: **Outlooks on European Harmonisation and Beyond**

Emmanuel Jeuland*

Chapter 23
Harmonisation Through Soft Law, Common Standards, and Best Practices

A Introduction

#1 This chapter aims to give a look to soft law and other forms of informal **'Europeanisation'** of civil procedure. Examples are numerous and I could not pretend to be exhaustive. Since soft law is not mandatory by definition, there is no code or consolidation of its source. In consequence, I'll discuss the most important or illustrative ones and discuss how each of these does (or not) contribute, in part from a bottom-up approach, to EU civil justice. Since civil justice and civil procedure are linked to the cultural, political, economic and sociological context of each European country, soft law is a good tool for trying to get on the same wavelength and find common approaches without imposing them.

#2 I would argue that many aspects of this non-binding legislation seem to draw on both a **human rights approach** in terms of fair trial, principle of cooperation and adversarial procedures, and a **managerial approach** to civil justice in terms of indicators, efficiency and proportionality objectives, quality-based civil justice assessment. These two pillars are linked, because developing fair trial principles can be costly, so managerial principles are necessary (efficiency, quality, etc.). Many member states (eg Germany, France) were born through internal procedure (eg in France: helping to centralise litigations through appeals, prohibit duel during the Middle-Age and imposed a common language; in Germany, the ZPO the first code shortly after the formation of German State in 1877 contributes to structure this state); so that a European civil procedure may help to create a confederal state for transborder cases and at the same time create a common legal culture of civil justice.

#3 The term soft law refers to quasi-legal instruments (like recommendations or guidelines) which do not have any **legally binding force**, or whose binding force is somewhat weaker than the binding force of traditional law. Soft law can morph in hard law especially if a judge decides to do so. Article 288 of the Treaty on the Functioning of the European Union (TFEU) which describes the different EU legal acts that the Union may adopt to exercise its **competences** provides: 'Recommendations and opinions shall have no binding force'. It may be a

***Corresponding author: Emmanuel Jeuland,** University of Paris 1 – Panthéon-Sorbonne,
e-mail: emmanueljeuland@wanadoo.fr

https://doi.org/10.1515/9783110781632-023

faster way to prepare a change of law than pure preparation of a treaty or a directive. It may circulate easily through social media. The drawbacks of soft laws are that they may contradict, comes from many sources not hierarchical or public and blurs the aims.

#4 Common standards are a vaguer concept referring to common conduct in a field: the harmonisation may be made on common points. Best practices refer to practices which may be better than another at point of the time and may be influential in other countries. It is the idea that the **harmonisation** of EU law justice should be made with the best solutions and not with the least common denominators.

#5 Soft law is being used as a tool to bring civil justice closer together on a global scale, as demonstrated by the American Law Institute (ALI) and Unidroit principles of civil procedure[1] and even the latest OECD recommendation.[2] However, these documents remain very general. In Europe, a more integrative approach and even a degree of harmonisation may be envisaged through soft law.

#6 The chapter will focus on the ELI-Unidroit Model European Rules of Civil Procedure, the European Council's instruments and the soft law of various EU institutions and other bodies.

B ELI-Unidroit Model Rules

#7 Academic work is a form of soft law which may have an influence on civil procedure harmonisation.[3] In the field of civil procedure, a group of experts known as the **Storme Commission**, named after the Belgian professor who headed it, drew up a preliminary draft directive for the approximation of European civil procedures.[4] The European institutions did not follow up, notably because they did not consider themselves competent to deal with a matter which forms part of the

1 ALI/UNIDROIT, *Principles of Transnational Civil Procedure* (CUP 2004).

2 Recommendation on Access to Justice and People-Centred Justice Systems, OECD Council on 12 July 2023. Access to justice is globally recognised as a fundamental right underpinning quality democracies, inclusive growth and equality of opportunity. Under the United Nations (UN) 2030 Agenda for Sustainable Development (A/RES/70/1), all UN member countries committed to 'promot(ing) the rule of law at the national and international levels and ensur(ing) equal access to justice for all'.

3 A Nylund and M Strandberg (eds), *Civil Procedure and the Harmonisation of Law* (Intersentia 2019); R Stürner, 'The ELI/UNIDROIT Model European Rules of Civil Procedure' (2022) 86 Rabels Zeitschrift für ausländisches und internationales Privatrecht 421; B Hess and X Kramer (eds), *From Common Rules to Best Practices in European Civil Procedure* (Hart Publishing 2017); CA Kern, 'Harmonisation of the Rules on Judgments and Appeals in Europe: A Few Remarks from the Inside' in F Gascón Inchausti and B Hess (eds), *The Future of the European Law of Civil Procedure. Coordination or Harmonisation?* (Intersentia 2020) 223.

4 M Storme (ed), *Rapprochement du Droit Judiciaire de L'Union européenne/Approximation of Judiciary Law in the European Union* (Martinus Nijhoff Publishers 1994).

hard core of national sovereignty. Moreover, the timing was not right,[5] and the project was more concerned with common denominators than innovations.[6] A different approach was taken in developing the ELI-Unidroit European Rules of Civil Procedure.[7] Academics from many European countries (even outside the EU) came together to draw up common rules of procedure, without limiting themselves to one branch of law, such as consumer law, and without the influence of lobbying pressures. Some ten working groups (on notification, evidence, parties, appeals, res judicata, costs, etc) have met in the four corners of Europe, bringing about a veritable cultural cross-pollination. The procedural influences of different countries on one another are such (for example: the French Code of Civil Procedure of 1806 influenced several codes in the 19th century, including the German *Zivilprozessordnung* (ZPO) code of 1877; Franz Klein's Austrian code at the end of the 19th century created a kind of case management and influenced various codes, including the French *nouveau code de procédure civile* (NCPC) in 1976, followed by the English reform of 1999, which in turn, along with case management, influences many countries today, etc) that it seems possible to draw on the experience of other countries in the same way. It has become possible to propose solutions to even the most delicate issues (obtaining documents or disclosure, notification without a bailiff, class action, case management, etc). The **principle of cooperation,**[8] which implies taking into account the procedural relationships between the participants in the proceedings, appears to be the backbone of this purely procedural project. It could be backed up by a managerial approach based on the principle of coordination between the legal professions and the courts, rather than on the principle of efficiency alone.[9]

#8 The Model Rules of Civil Procedure were adopted on 15 July 2020 by the European Law Institute (ELI) and then by Unidroit in September 2020. They constitute a veritable code of civil procedure, comprising 245 articles. The project began in 2013, with the aim of producing a regional version of the ALI/Unidroit transnational

---

5 J Normand, 'Un droit judiciaire européen ?' in P de Vareilles-Sommières (ed), Le *droit privé européen* (Economica 1998) 124.

6 K Kerameus, 'Procedural Harmonisation in Europe' (1995) 43 Am. J. Comp. L. 401; K Kerameus, 'Procedural Unification: The Need and the Limitations' in I Richard Scott (ed), *International Perspectives on Civil Justice: Essays in Honour of Sir Jack I.H. Jacob, Q.C.* (Sweet & Maxwell 1990) 47; FK Juenger, 'Comments on European Procedural Harmonisation' (1997) 45 Am. J. Comp. L. 931.

7 European Law Institute and UNIDROIT, *ELI-Unidroit Model European Rules of Civil Procedure. From Transnational Principles to European Rules of Civil Procedure* (OUP 2021); E Jeuland, 'Les règles modèles ELI/Unidroit et la déconstruction des concepts de procédures civile' in X Lagarde and B Pireyre (eds) *Vers un renouvellement des catégories en procédure civile?* (IRJS 2022) 47.

8 See CH van Rhee, 'Principe de coopération – Cooperation Principle' in E Jeuland and S Lalani (eds), *Recherche lexicographique en procédure civile – Lexicographical Research in Civil Procedure* (IRJS 2017) 207.

9 E Jeuland (ed), *Court management, gestion du tribunal* (IRJS 2020).

principles of civil procedure adopted in 2004. The latter text contained just 35 principles. At the outset, it was influenced by American law, although by becoming a Unidroit project, it became **universalised**. The working language was mainly English, but in all sub-groups (nearly 10) a session on the French version helped to improve the English version.

#9 The overall result is coherent and fairly complete, even if there are no rules of jurisdiction (the European regulations Brussels 1bis and Brussels 2bis provide for this) or special rules of procedure in family or commercial matters. The **scope of application** is ordinary civil procedure (Article 1), which is very close to the scope of the Brussels 1 Regulation of 12 December 2012. The result is disruptive for all countries, as none of them has been taken as a model. All participants have had to negotiate or accept decisions taken against their will at one time or another.

#10 The **influences of these model rules** are manifold, starting with the procedural achievements of EU law (regulations and the directive on the cessation of practices contrary to consumer law) and the fundamental principles developed by the European Court of Human Rights (ECtHR). English law, reformed in 1999 and incorporating recent mechanisms, has been influential on certain points (case management, substitution of parties during proceedings, disclosure, redress). Dutch and Danish law have influenced the collective action mechanism. German law has influenced the scope of res judicata, the judge's office and the idea of main hearing. Italian law, like the law of other countries, has been taken into account with regard to the importance of facilitating settlements at all levels and for the substitutive action. **Continental countries** (including Austria) have collectively influenced the powers of the case manager judge to include pre-trial investigation. The French Code of Civil Procedure has served as a model for preliminary articles laying down guiding principles. The *astreinte* was enshrined under its name (even in the English version), as it is untranslatable. A rule on the standard of proof has been laid down, as exists in Germany and England (not in France). Croatian, Dutch and French academics insisted on the recognition of a principle of cooperation, while Scandinavian colleagues were in favor of a high degree of flexibility with regard to service. There is no need for **nationalism** in this field, even if certain national choices may correspond to a culture that should be defended. In fact, the balance between the powers of the judge and the rights of the parties is now part of **European culture**. There has, however, been a structural tension between members from **common law countries** or countries close to these (the Netherlands, Norway) with a rather flexible approach to procedure in the hands of a superior but neutral judge, and members from continental countries in favor of a more interventionist judge who is also more on an equal footing with the parties. A more specific tension existed between a member from a former Eastern bloc country who had experienced a system in which the judge was both omnipotent (the procedure being written and secret) and impotent (because the judge was not very independent and appointed by the State, and there was no activism on the part of the parties)[10] who expressed the need to give power back to the parties for reasons of efficiency, and those who defended the **powers of the judge** (English, German), also for reasons of efficiency (before 1999 in the UK, the judge had too few powers to speed up proceedings and make them less costly). The primacy of the principle of cooperation between the parties and the judge was at the heart of this debate.

#11 This model law could eventually serve as an instrument of standardisation in Europe and, more realistically, as an instrument of **harmonisation** for cross-border cases on a suppletive basis even beyond the European Union. The authors have tried not to make too many compromises, but rather to find the best solution each time, while seeking overall coherence. It is an instrument that can encourage each country to reflect on what is important in the procedure, what can be added or improved, and what is perhaps of secondary importance when it seems necessary. The principle of cooperation is mentioned first, which is not by chance, and comes just after the principle of proportionality, that of amicable resolution and the rights of the defence. Special mention is made of languages, as these are international rules.

#12 The **principle of cooperation** has a German-speaking origin, and some trace it back to Franz Klein, the Minister of Justice who imagined modern procedure, and particularly the case manager judge.[11] It expresses the idea of a balance of rights and powers between the judge and the parties in the search for facts and law.

#13 According to Rule 2 of the model rules, 'Parties, their lawyers and the court must co-operate to promote the fair, efficient and speedy resolution of the dispute'. The idea of **efficiency** and speed shows the economic and managerial angle of the project, as does the principle of proportionality.

#14 The **principle of cooperation** expresses the general spirit of the ELI/Unidroit model rules. It involves cooperation in matters of procedure, fact and law. Active parties are encouraged to act and to negotiate, and the judge can also be active, without making up for the lack of action by the parties, in preparing the case for trial, with investigative measures and by researching the applicable law. The parties must raise the law; in turn, the judge determines the law and may raise facts present in the file but not specifically invoked by a party. Rule 24 (3) provides that:

---

10 A Uzelac, 'Croatia: Omnipotent Judges as the Cause of Procedural Inefficiency and Impotence' in CH van Rhee and Y Fu (eds), *Civil Litigation in China and Europe: Essays on the Role of the Judge and the Parties* (Springer 2014) 197.

11 B Hahn, *Kooperationsmaxime im Zivilprozess?* (Carl Heymanns 1983) 1; see also R Wassermann, *Der soziale Zivilprozess* (Luchterhand 1978) 97f (the paragraph is entitled 'Der Zivilprozess als Arbeitsgemeinschaft', ie civil litigation as teamwork).

The court may consider such facts not specifically addressed by a party but that are necessarily implied by matters of fact put forward by the parties or which are contained within the case file. It may only do so if they are relevant to a party's claim or defence and the parties have been given a reasonable opportunity to respond.

#15 In matters of law, the judge has a general **obligation to determine the law**, but since he can only raise facts and the parties are obliged to raise legal arguments, the solution is more Belgian than German. According to Rule 26 (2) 'The court must determine the correct legal basis for its decision. This includes matters determined on the basis of foreign law. It may only do so having provided the parties a reasonable opportunity to present their arguments on the applicable law'. That said, the indicative 'determines' may correspond to the caselaw creation of the rule. This is why the solution has been accepted by the common law experts, and why the term is broad enough not to restrict the judge. It is true that Rule 26 (1) also states that 'While taking account of any applicable special provisions, the parties may present legal arguments supporting their claim or defence'. The parties are only obliged to present legal arguments if there is a special provision. However, Rule 53 (2) lays down a general provision for the parties whenever they act by unilateral means (the summons): 'The statement of claim should: (c) refer to the legal grounds that support the claim, including foreign law, in a way that is sufficient to permit the court to determine the claim's legal validity'.

#16 The **principle of proportionality** is sometimes associated with common law but is of German origin. According to the ELI/Unidroit rules, investigative measures must be proportionate (expert opinions are not suitable for all cases, the production of documents does not always have to be general), as must sanctions and legal costs. Under Rule 5 (1) 'The court must ensure that the dispute resolution process is proportionate'.

#17 The recognition of this principle in procedural matters is part of a global movement that began in the United Kingdom (inspired by the principle of proportionality existing in public law in Germany), spread to Canada,[12] the United States (Rule 26 Federal Rules of Civil Procedure) and Brazil (Rule 8 of the 2015 Code of Civil Procedure), before returning to Europe in the ECtHR's case law on excessive **formalism.**[13] The concern for amicable resolution is at the heart of the project, and for this reason constitutes a principle. Rule 9 (1) provides that 'Parties must co-operate in seeking to resolve their dispute consensually, both before and after proceedings begin'.

---

12 C Piché, 'La proportionnalité procédurale: une perspective comparative' (2009) 40 RDUS 551.

13 *Henrioud v France* App no 21444/11 (ECtHR, 5 November 2015); *Reichman v France* App no 50147/11 (ECtHR, 12 July 2016).

#18 The primary influence is undoubtedly that of the common law, but the concern for **amicable resolution** has spread to all countries, including the Netherlands and Italy. German, Austrian and even Croatian academics seem to have remained somewhat skeptical. It has to be said that in Germany, the quality of civil justice has hardly paved the way for the need for alternative justice. The cost of common law procedures, the concern for consensus in the Netherlands (particularly in class actions) or the congestion of the courts in Italy may explain the interest in amicable resolution.

#19 The principle of **adversarial proceedings** is one of the guiding principles, but it does not take the form of an abstract provision. Thus, Rule 11 states that 'The court must manage proceedings to ensure that parties have a fair opportunity to present their case and evidence, to respond to their respective claims and defences and to any court orders or matters raised by the court'. According to Rule 12 (2) 'The court must not base its decisions on issues that parties have not had an opportunity to address'. There is a kind of **pre-action protocol**. This is a prior **conciliation negotiation** which may involve an exchange of sufficient information (Rule 51). The model for this rule is English law, which favours prior negotiation, as it enables the parties to determine their chances of success if they do not reach an agreement.

#20 A number of rules concerning **evidence** corresponds to the most recent standards of civil procedure, whether in terms of access to evidence, **cross-examination** or **standards of proof**. In many countries a level of proof is set at which it is considered sufficiently probable that the facts have been established. The solution is still debated, as the standard is 51% in common law and around 77% in German law. The rule adopted lies somewhere between the two and is reminiscent of the 'intime conviction' rule in French criminal law. According to Rule 87, entitled 'Standard of proof', 'A disputed fact is proved if the judge is reasonably convinced of its truth'.

#21 Disloyalty in the search for evidence takes the form of the **illegality of the evidence** discussed, but an exception is made in favor of the **right to evidence** when it is the only means of establishing the facts (Rule 90). It seems that Croatia has been inspired by this rule in a recent reform.[14] There could be an impact in Scandinavian countries as well.[15] Indeed, Frederiksen and Stranberg conclude that:

---

14 CCP Amendments, Off. Gaz. (*Narodne novine*) 80/2022 of 11 July 2022. Quoted by A. Uzelac in Principles of Civil Procedure Under ELI-UNIDROIT Rules: Convergence Through a Uniform Approach to Procedural Obligations? Uniform Law review, to be released; the new Rule 90 Croatia Code of Civil Procedure amendment 11 July 2022 is about illegally obtained evidence; it's a literal translation of the model rules.

15 HH Fredriksen and M Strandberg, 'Impact of the ELI/UNIDROIT European Model Rules for Civil Procedure on National Law – the Case of Norway' (2023) 9 Oslo Law Review 152.

The ELI/UNIDROIT European Model Rules for Civil Procedure (ERCP) might come to influence Norwegian civil procedure as a source of inspiration for both academics and practitioners in debates over the best interpretation and application of the existing rules in the Code of Civil Procedure. The ERCP might also serve as a source of inspiration for the legislator in future attempts to improve the existing rules. As the ERCP are based on a pragmatic 'best practice' approach, they fit quite well with the Scandinavian way of legal thinking. This is also true for the style of the Model Rules – they are written in a relatively concise and open form that will be familiar to Scandinavian proceduralists.[16]

#22 The rules governing the **production of evidence** are broader than in continental law, but do not constitute a true American-style **discovery** system that can be used to go fishing for information. According to rule 100 (b), 'the court will, if the application is granted, direct the production of relevant, non-privileged, and sufficiently identified evidence held or controlled by another party or, if necessary, by a non- party, even if such production might be adverse to that person's interests'. Rule 102 specifies that precise categories of evidence may be identified by reference to their nature, content or date.

#23 Finally, **cross-examination** is now making its entry into civil procedure. According to Rule 115 (3):

A person giving evidence may be questioned first by the court or the party adducing their evidence. Where a witness has first been questioned by the court or by party other than the one adducing their evidence, that party must be given the opportunity to put supplemental questions directly to the witness.

Rule 118 allows cross-examination between the parties.

#24 **Service of a procedural document** is linked to the profession of bailiff in some countries. However, the model rules are not based on judicial professions, which vary widely from one European country to another. On the other hand, the 'service' group has been in contact with the **international association of bailiffs** to ensure that the rules are compatible with justice systems that include such a profession (notably the Netherlands, Belgium and France). There is considerable technical latitude in the way service is done under the rules, even at unknown addresses.

#25 A real filter is provided for **appeals**. Permission to appeal must be obtained from the Court of Appeal, which under Rule 166 takes into account several factors:

(a) whether the legal issue in dispute is of fundamental significance, or (b) the further development of the law, or the public interest in securing uniform adjudication require an appellate decision, or (c) fundamental procedural requirements have been violated.

A fortiori, there is filtering at the second level of appeal. Thus, an appeal may only be lodged against a contested judgment if such an appeal is necessary to

16 ibid.

sanction the violation of a fundamental right, to guarantee the uniformity of the law, to settle a legal question of principle, or to develop the law (Rule 172).

#26 A non-sectoral **group action** has been chosen; with the possibility of a **mass settlement** such as exists under Dutch law. The principle is **opt-in**, but there is an exception (opt-out) when the judge considers that the victims would not have acted, notably because the individual damage is too minimal (whereas the total damage is significant). This is the Scandinavian solution. It is not an action in representation, since the victims do not become parties and there is a qualified claimant (who may be an accredited organisation, an ad hoc organisation or a member of the group, Rule 208). The group action procedure gives rise (Rule 213) to an **admissibility** ruling enabling any person who believes he or she has suffered the same damage to determine whether he or she is part of the group. The rules also include a procedure for selecting the **qualified entity** best placed to act if several claimants come forward.[17]

#27 According to Norel Rosner (a member of the European institution which was an observer from the beginning), the model rules on service of **electronic service** have been a source of inspiration, as well as the access to evidence by **videoconference**.[18]

C Soft Law in European Civil Justice: Networks and Judicial Cooperation

#28 There are soft law texts in Europe on civil justice coming from networks. For example, the Resolution on Transparency and Access to Justice by the **European Network of Councils for the Judiciary** (ENCJ) states:

> An open and transparent justice system is one in which: Everyone, regardless of background or ability, has access to justice or to an alternative dispute resolution system, affordably and in accessible locations, so that all proceedings can be easily brought against any person, public or private, physical or moral.[19]

This brings together all the ingredients for a **transparent** justice system, including its relationship with the rule of law.

---

17 For further reading: A Stadler, E Jeuland and V Smith (eds), *Collective and Mass Litigation in Europe* (Edward Elgar 2020).

18 See ELI-Unidroit Dissemination Conference (Vienna, 5–6 February 2024).

19 European Network of Councils for the Judiciary (ENCJ), Resolution on Transparency and Access to Justice (Bucharest, May 2009) para 2a.

#29 The European Charter on the Statute for Judges[20] and the Magna Carta of Judges[21] stress the importance of **transparency** in the calculation of judges' remuneration, the budgets of each court and the allocation of cases to each judge (natural judge principle). According to the ECtHR, if systemic teleological interpretation is not sufficient to resolve a difficulty, recourse to external texts is possible, even if they are not binding.[22] Non-normative references to transparency and open justice from the Council of Europe could therefore take the form of an ECtHR ruling.

#30 The **European Commission for the Efficiency of Justice (CEPEJ)** was set up in 2002 to prepare for the entry of the former Eastern Bloc countries into the Council of Europe. It compares justice systems and offers indicators and assistance. The Council of Europe seems to have been at the origin of this movement (with the recommendations of the CEPEJ and the opinions issued by the Consultative Committees of European judges and prosecutors). Initially, it served to prepare the judiciaries of the so-called Eastern European countries to enter the canons of fair trial in terms of efficiency, quality, reasonable time, transparency and the fight against corruption. This would be the starting point for new judicial management in Europe.

D EU Soft Law: Governance, Evaluation, and Standardisation in Justice

#31 The **EU Justice Scoreboard** was set up in 2013 to help member countries improve the quality (by suggesting the development of new technology, ADR, communication) and efficiency of their justice systems. This Scoreboard is particularly influential in southern European countries. It is important to note, however, that the indicators proposed by the World Bank (for assessing a country's loan eligibility), the EU Justice Scoreboard (which, due to its comparison of judges' salaries, probably played a part in the temporary reduction in the salaries of Portuguese judges[23]) and the CEPEJ models are not neutral; they impose a certain conception

---

20 Consultative Council of European Judges (CCJE), European Charter on the Statute for Judges, 8–10 July 1998, DAJ/DOC(98)23 para 6.2.

21 Consultative Council of European Judges (CCJE), Magna Carta of Judges (Fundamental Principles), 17 November 2010, CCJE (2010)3 Final, para 14.

22 *Volkov v Ukraine* App no 21722/11 (ECtHR, 9 January 2013); *Denisov v Ukraine* App no 76639/11 (ECtHR, 25 September 2018) concerning the European Charter on the statute for judges and the Venice Commission.

23 See Case C-64/16 *Arrêt de la Cour, Associação Sindical dos Juízes Portugueses contre Tribunal de Contas* (27 February 2018) ECLI:EU:C:2018:117.

of justice and management. However, there is some debate among management specialists[24] and the objectives and indicators approach has been criticised.

#32 In some respects, the European Commission has taken up this standard approach, combining due process and **managerial methods**. European Regulation No 1382/2013 of 17 December 2013 replaced by Regulation 2021/693 of 28 April 2021 (for the period 2021–2027) concerns a large population of around 400 million people in an area that is not a territory in the sense of the attribute of a state. It provides for a program of action in judicial matters in Europe, and for funding. It is largely soft law, which in many respects can be likened to a form of standardisation. The regulation mixes managerial techniques – ie **standardisation** – with human rights (particularly victims' rights). European judicial law has thus given rise to a scoreboard, ie a document containing **indicators** for comparing different justice systems in Europe. The post-Stockholm program outlined in Regulation 1382/2013 and then in Regulation 2021/693 extends these guidelines, particularly with regard to practitioner training. The application of these principles involves the use of tools: the evaluation of European laws, the timetable, the training of legal professions, the exchange of best practices and the scoreboard. Public information is also taken into consideration through an e-justice portal. New technologies feature prominently in this text. The European Union's **Justice Scoreboard**[25] is an 'instrument designed to help the European Union and its Member States to increase the effectiveness of justice, by providing them with objective, reliable and comparable data on the operation of all national justice systems'. Justice is recognised as central to the construction of the European Union, as it contributes to making an 'economic environment attractive to business: the certainty of full respect for the rule of law has a direct influence on business confidence and investment in the economy'. The text adds: 'The Annual Growth Survey 2013 highlights the importance of improving the quality, independence and efficiency of national judicial systems'. The scoreboard is a cooperative mechanism, since it is the member states that provide the data, and it is not at all a question of 'establishing a ranking' or 'promoting a particular form of justice system'. The scoreboard comprises a number of **indicators**, largely based on CEPEJ indicators. Three quantitative indicators: 1) length of proceedings, 2) rate of change of stock, 3) number of cases pending. Four qualitative indicators 'that can contribute to improving the quality and efficiency of justice systems': 1) monitoring the evaluation of court activity, 2) information and communication technology systems used by courts, 3) alternative dispute resolution methods, 4) training of judges. An eighth indicator measures the perception of judges' independence by the public, in order to deter-

---

24 See eg C Grey and H Willmott, *Critical Management Studies: A Reader* (OUP 2005).

25 See Europa website on the Justice Scoreboard <https://commission.europa.eu/strategy-and-policy/policies/justice-and-fundamental-rights/upholding-rule-law/eu-justice-scoreboard_en> accessed 27 February 2025.

mine the 'degree of confidence in a judicial system'. The data comes from the member states concerned, as well as from the World Bank and the World Justice Project. The implementation of this scorecard shows that there are major disparities in the length of legal proceedings, the development of digital systems, and that 'business end-users of the justice system have a rather poor perception of its independence', which can 'discourage investment'. On the other hand, 'monitoring and evaluation help to speed up proceedings and increase the quality of justice', 'electronic systems for recording and managing cases improve the efficiency and quality of justice', and 'alternative dispute resolution methods lighten the workload of the courts'. Behind the apparent neutrality of these indicators lies a model of justice based on new technologies, evaluation and mediation. Of course, the scoreboard is not binding, but rather an incentive.

#33 Admittedly, the Stockholm program, Regulation 1382/2013, Regulation 2021/693 and the Justice Scoreboard can be seen as a **political discourse**, an action program and not law. In any case, this type of assessment goes beyond political propaganda. It is truly a complex thought process that is difficult to discuss, because it calls for adherence. How can we not want to see justice modernised, more swiftly, more efficiently and of better quality? The freedom and equality of those subject to the law legitimise an increasingly restrictive system (with new technologies, it is becoming even more rigid), not least because economies of scale are needed to make justice faster, cheaper and more efficient. How can we fail to be convinced by the need to set up an efficient, rapid and high-quality procedure? Isn't this the dream of every proceduralist?

#34 Moreover, there are **European judicial networks** comprising networks of judges (European judicial networks), jurisdictions (network of supreme courts) and even agencies (competition, financial, IT and freedom, etc.) and professional associations of lawyers (EJTN, CCBE, UEHJ). These networks are closely involved in all sorts of projects, they have their own resolutions and guidelines in vital areas of civil procedure and also influence EU legislation. A very concrete recent initiative is **EC-REACT**, which is a restricted platform for information exchange across the EU about representative actions.[26] Since civil justice is enshrined in national culture and economy, there is a need for exchange between lawyers of all member states. Soft law is a good tool to start finding out common approaches.

#35 It is worth noting in the same vein the existence of a platform (e-justice portal) and a technical network (**e-codex**). There are tools for simplifying judicial cooperation in civil matters in the administration of justice. This project was launched in June 2007, and is reflected in a European e-Justice strategy. **E-Justice** tools include: the European e-Justice portal, designed to facilitate access to justice for citizens and businesses throughout the Union; better use of **videoconferencing** in

26 See <https://representative-actions-collaboration.ec.europa.eu/en> accessed 27 February 2025.

legal proceedings; innovative **translation** tools, such as machine translation and dynamic online forms; and a European database of legal translators and interpreters.

#36 The European Parliament's research service produced a detailed report entitled '**Europeanisation** of civil procedure: Towards common minimum standards?' in June 2015. Rafael Manko, the author of this report, examined the potential for the introduction of common minimum standards. He looked at the existing **acquis** in the area of civil procedure. Then, the Legal Affairs Committee produced a 'Working document on establishing common minimum standards for civil procedure in the European Union – the legal basis' in December 2015.

#37 The **minimum standards** set out in the proposal[27] promotes the fair conduct of proceedings, the use of appropriate distance communication technology, such as videoconferencing or teleconference when the parties cannot physically be present, the use of proportionate provisional and protective measures, observing the rights of the defence, the right to an effective remedy and a fair trial, the principle of an adversarial process, in particular when deciding on the necessity of an oral hearing and on the means of obtaining evidence, the obligation for the courts to provide reasoned decisions within a reasonable time, an active management of cases by judges, the possibility for courts to grant legal aid to a party lacking appropriate means to finance the proceedings, the use of adequate service methods to ensure prompt and safe receipt of the served documents, the right to a lawyer of their choice for the parties to civil proceedings; providing citizens with transparent and easily available information regarding the commencement of various procedures, limitation or prescription periods, the competent courts to hear different disputes, and the necessary forms that need to be filled in for that purpose; the availability of interpretation during civil proceedings and a written translation of all essential documents essential to safeguard the fairness of the proceedings.

#38 The Radev report of 2019 pointed out that the EU has developed a complex regulatory framework related to the EU civil procedure. This framework includes sector-specific regulations, regulations covering specific elements of the procedure, and autonomous, optional EU procedures. This complexity lacks coherence and is heavily criticised by practitioners.[28] The adoption of an EU instrument on **minimum standards** of civil procedure is analyzed as one of the possible policy op-

27 European Parliament resolution of 4 July 2017 with recommendations to the Commission on common minimum standards of civil procedure in the European Union (2015/2084(INL)); see F Gascón Inchausti, 'The 2017 Directive Proposal on Common Minimum Standards of Civil Procedure in the European Union' in F Gascón Inchausti and B Hess (eds), *The Future of the European Law of Civil Procedure: Coordination or Harmonisation?* (Intersentia 2020) 241.

28 European Parliament: Directorate-General for Parliamentary Research Services, Evas T. and Ballegooij W., *Common Minimum Standards of Civil Procedure – European Added Value Assessment Accom-*

tions to optimise the current EU civil procedure system. The adoption of an EU legal instrument on minimum standards, applicable to all stages of the procedure, has the largest potential for cost-reduction. This policy option would generate the highest degree of certainty for the parties and contribute to the framework of mutual trust between judiciaries.[29]

#39 This report states:

> With the development of e-justice, the greater use of standard forms, as well as the increased emphasis on advice and information (for instance in the context of consumer protection) this element of pre-litigation activities may well be one to focus on. This is especially justified by the greater importance of ADR within the EU, and the resulting need to introduce potential litigants to the full choice of dispute resolution mechanisms available to them.[30]

E Conclusion

#40 Many soft law instruments are very general, such as the proposed 2017 Directive[31] and the recommendations of judicial networks in the EU or at Council of Europe level. Others are purely managerial (eg EU Justice Scoreboard). The most advanced tool is the ELI/Unidroit model rules on European civil procedure. They can influence national and European legislation. They seek to strike a balance between the power of the judge (in law, in facts and in the case management) and the rights and duties of the parties. They encompass both management principles such as efficiency, reasonable time and proportionality, and procedural principles such as the principle of cooperation and the right to be heard. They find a European path in terms of service, level of proof, disclosure, collective action.

#41 The future of Europe could lie in a common set of rules of civil procedure for cross-border cases. These soft law standards show that there is a balanced fair trial model in Europe, and a managerial and economic approach to civil justice as well. Let's hope the latter doesn't overwhelm the former.

panying the European Parliament's Legislative Own-initiative Report – (Rapporteur: Emil Radev) (Publications Office 2019) <https://data.europa.eu/doi/10.2861/136575> accessed 27 February 2025.

29 European Parliament: Committee on Legal Affairs, *Common Minimum Standards of Civil Procedure: European Added Value Assessment, Annex I, Research paper by Blomeyer & Sanz: Magdalena Tulibacka, Margarita Sanz, Roland Blomeyer* (June 2016) <https://www.europarl.europa.eu/cmsdata/105660/EPRS_CIVIL_PROCEDURE.pdf> accessed 27 February 2025.

30 ibid 35.

31 European Parliament resolution of 4 July 2017 with recommendations to the Commission on common minimum standards of civil procedure in the European Union (2015/2084(INL))

References

ALI/UNIDROIT, *Principles of Transnational Civil Procedure* (CUP 2004).

European Law Institute and UNIDROIT, *ELI-Unidroit Model European Rules of Civil Procedure. From Transnational Principles to European Rules of Civil Procedure* (OUP 2021).

European Parliament: Committee on Legal Affairs, *Common Minimum Standards of Civil Procedure: European Added Value Assessment, Annex I, Research paper by Blomeyer & Sanz: Magdalena Tulibacka, Margarita Sanz, Roland Blomeyer* (June 2016) <https://www.europarl.europa.eu/cmsdata/105660/EPRS_CIVIL_PROCEDURE.pdf> accessed 27 February 2025.

European Parliament: Directorate-General for Parliamentary Research Services, Evas T and Ballegooij W, *Common Minimum Standards of Civil Procedure – European Added Value Assessment* Accompanying the European Parliament's Legislative Own-initiative Report – (Rapporteur: Emil Radev) (Publications Office 2019) <https://data.europa.eu/doi/10.2861/136575> accessed 27 February 2025.

Fredriksen HH and Strandberg M, 'Impact of the ELI/UNIDROIT European Model Rules for Civil Procedure on National Law – the Case of Norway' (2023) 9 Oslo Law Review 152.

Gascón Inchausti F, 'The 2017 Directive Proposal on Common Minimum Standards of Civil Procedure in the European Union' in Fernando Gascón Inchausti and Burkhard Hess (eds), *The Future of the European Law of Civil Procedure: Coordination or Harmonisation?* (Intersentia 2020) 241.

Grey C and Willmott H, *Critical Management Studies: A Reader* (OUP 2005).

Hahn B, *Kooperationsmaxime im Zivilprozess?* (Carl Heymanns 1983).

Hess B and Kramer X (eds), *From Common Rules to Best Practices in European Civil Procedure* (Hart Publishing 2017).

Jeuland E (ed), *Court Management, gestion du tribunal* (IRJS 2020).

—— 'Les règles modèles ELI/Unidroit et la déconstruction des concepts de procédures civile' in X Lagarde and B Pireyre (eds), *Vers un renouvellement des catégories en procédure civile?* (IRJS 2022) 47.

Juenger FK, 'Comments on European Procedural Harmonisation' (1997) 45 Am. J. Comp. L. 931.

Kerameus K, 'Procedural Unification: The Need and the Limitations' in IR Scott (ed), *International Perspectives on Civil Justice: Essays in Honour of Sir Jack I.H. Jacob, Q.C.* (Sweet & Maxwell 1990) 47.

—— 'Procedural Harmonisation in Europe' (1995) 43 Am. J. Comp. L. 401.

Kern CA, 'Harmonisation of the Rules on Judgments and Appeals in Europe: A Few Remarks from the Inside' in F Gascón Inchausti and B Hess (eds), *The Future of the European Law of Civil Procedure: Coordination or Harmonisation?* (Intersentia 2020) 223.

Normand J, 'Un droit judiciaire européen ?' in P de Vareilles-Sommières (ed), *Le droit privé européen* (Economica 1998) 124.

Nylund A and Strandberg M (eds), *Civil Procedure and the Harmonisation of Law* (Intersentia 2019).

Piché C, 'La proportionnalité procédurale: une perspective comparative' (2009) 40 RDUS 551.

Rhee van CH, 'Principe de coopération – Cooperation Principle' in E Jeuland and S Lalani (eds), *Recherche lexicographique en procédure civile – Lexicographical Research in Civil Procedure* (IRJS 2017) 207.

Stadler A, Jeuland E and Smith V (eds), *Collective and Mass Litigation in Europe* (Edward Elgar 2020).

Storme M (ed), *Rapprochement du Droit Judiciaire de L'Union européenne/Approximation of Judiciary Law in the European Union* (Martinus Nijhoff Publishers 1994).

Stürner R, 'The ELI/UNIDROIT Model European Rules of Civil Procedure' (2022) 86 Rabels Zeitschrift für ausländisches und internationales Privatrecht 421.

Uzelac A, 'Croatia: Omnipotent Judges as the Cause of Procedural Inefficiency and Impotence' in CH van Rhee and Y Fu (eds), *Civil Litigation in China and Europe: Essays on the Role of the Judge and the Parties* (Springer 2014) 197.

Wassermann R, *Der soziale Zivilprozess* (Luchterhand 1978).

Monika Canco*, Ana Harvey*, and Iryna Izarova*

Chapter 24
European Civil Procedure and the EU Enlargement Process

A Background

#1 The European Union (EU) enlargement process has been a cornerstone of European integration, promoting stability, democracy, and the rule of law across the continent. Within the context of the EU enlargement – particularly with regard to the rule of law and the associated principles and values of judicial independence, access to justice, and judicial efficiency – European civil procedure has played a significant role from the outset. It is this role and impact of the European civil procedure (including the pertinent EU legislative instruments and the relevant case law of the European Court of Human Rights) on judicial and procedural reforms in EU candidate countries that this chapter will examine. Specifically, it will do so through analysing and evaluating the trajectories of three candidate countries – Albania, Serbia, and Ukraine – as they navigate the complex path toward EU membership. Whilst placed within a unique historical and political context, the three countries share common challenges and aspirations in aligning their legal and judicial systems with European standards.

#2 Comparatively, all three countries recognise the indispensable role of judicial reform and legal harmonisation in the EU accession process. Accordingly, they have undertaken significant overhauls of their judicial systems to enhance independence, combat corruption, and improve efficiency, reflecting the EU's stringent requirements regarding the rule of law and fundamental rights.

#3 However, as following sections shall demonstrate, their journeys have not been without obstacles. Albania grapples with internal political divisions that hinder consistent progress, while Serbia contends with the legacy of past conflicts, the uncertainty of present turbulent political developments, and the need for sustained institutional reforms. At the time of writing this chapter, Ukraine faces the dual challenge of ongoing external aggression and the imperative to transform its legal system amidst reconstruction efforts. Despite these challenges, the commitment of these nations to align with European standards underscores the transformative influence of the EU enlargement process.

*Corresponding author: Monika Canco, University of Tirana, e-mail: monika.canco@fdut.edu.al
*Corresponding author: Ana Harvey, University of Bedfordshire, e-mail: ana.harvey@beds.ac.uk
*Corresponding author: Iryna Izarova, Taras Shevchenko National University of Kyiv, e-mail: irina.izarova@knu.ua

https://doi.org/10.1515/9783110781632-024

#4 In analysing and evaluating the impact of European procedural law on each of the examined country's paths on the EU enlargement journey in turn, the chapter presents the reader with a brief background to the EU integration process of each country, followed by the analysis of procedural impact (including the discussion of the influence of the relevant instruments of EU civil procedural law on domestic reforms) and institutional impact (including the influence of the concepts developed by the ECtHR case law, ie judicial independence, quality and efficiency) on these countries' reformative processes. By examining their individual experiences within the broader context of EU enlargement, we gain insights into the complexities of legal integration and the pivotal role of judiciary reforms in shaping the future of these aspiring EU Member States.

B Albania

I Introduction

#5 During the early years of the 1990s, Albania's ruling politicians exalted the masses with the slogan 'Let's make Albania like all of Europe' (Alb.: 'Ta bëjmë Shqipërinë si e gjithë Europa').[1] The slogan remained a slogan as the ruling elite of those years turned out to be despotic and corrupt. After the abyss of years 1996–1997, Albania approved its current Constitution in 1998, which gave a new impetus to the political life of the country. As a result, in June 2003, the European Union (EU) identified Albania as a potential EU candidate and opened the process of negotiations for a **Stabilisation and Association Agreement (SAA)**.[2] This process concluded in 2006, and in 2009, Albania submitted its formal application for EU membership.

#6 In June 2014, Albania was granted **candidate status** by the EU. In April 2018, the Commission issued an unconditional recommendation to open accession negotiations with Albania in view of the deepening reforms in key areas such as the judiciary, fight against corruption and organised crime, intelligence services and public administration. In July 2022, the Commission started the screening process. Between 2024 and 2025, Albania opened accession negotiations on Cluster 1 (*Fundamentals*), Cluster 6 (*External Relations*), Cluster 2 (*Internal Mar-*

1 'Dhjetor '90, Ëndrra që na jep forcë për të punuar për Shqipërinë e gjeneratave të tjera' (8 December 2013) <https://www.kryeministria.al/newsroom/dhjetor-90-endrra-qe-na-jep-force-per-te-punuar-per-shqiperine-e-gjeneratave-te-tjera/> accessed 2 March 2025.

2 European Commission: Albania <https://neighbourhood-enlargement.ec.europa.eu/enlargement-policy/albania_en> and 2518th Council Meeting on External Relations (Luxembourg, 16 June 2003) doc no 10369/03 available at <https://www.consilium.europa.eu/ueDocs/cms_Data/docs/pressdata/en/gena/76201.pdf> accessed 2 March 2025.

ket), Cluster 3 (*Competitiveness and Inclusive Growth*) and Cluster 4 (*Green Agenda and Sustainable Connectivity*).

#7 However, this journey has not always been smooth. In addition to the diffidence that some Member States have towards Albania, Albania's membership path has been afflicted by an entrenched political class which spends a lot of energy on petty local conflicts and less on the proper implementation of reforms and progress at national level.

#8 An important upgrade in the Albanian journey towards the EU has been the adoption and implementation of judicial reform, significantly altering the Albanian legal and constitutional framework. The analysis below will highlight the impact of the EU on the Albanian legal framework, especially post-reform, with a focus on civil procedural law.

II Influence of European Procedural Law

1 Formal Adoption of EU or International Procedural Law Instruments During Negotiations

#9 Since the signing of the SAA with the EU, Albania has entered a process of approximation and implementation of the **EU *Acquis Communautaire***, including, *inter alia*, civil and civil procedural law. The SAA establishes that Albania shall ensure that the existing and future legislation shall be made compatible with *acquis* and properly implemented and enforced.[3] Skara argues that law approximation is mandatory for Albania, as SAA in Article 57 emphasises that account shall be taken in the progress of approximation of laws.[4] However, direct application of EU law is not mandatory. As explained below, the Albanian Constitutional Court concurs with the latter opinion. The general standing that EU secondary legislation is not (yet) obligatory to follow in Albania is often mentioned in the *travaux preparatoires* within the Albanian Parliament's **Commission on European Affairs (CEA)**.[5]

#10 Among numerous national bodies dealing with the process of EU integration, two crucial ones are the head of the executive – the Council of Ministers – that manages negotiations, and the Parliament that leads legislative approximation. The role of the Albanian Parliament in the EU integration process is regulated

3 Article 70(1) of SAA.

4 See also G Skara, *Europeanisation of Private Enforcement of Competition Law, the Case of Albania* (Springer 2022) 221.

5 See eg CEA, Meeting Minutes (28 March 2022) 8 <https://kuvendiwebfiles.blob.core.windows.net/webfiles/20220422121748Procesverbal%2C%20date%CC%88%2028.3.2022.pdf> accessed 2 March 2025.

by a 2015 law.[6] This law stipulates that Albania's integration into the EU is based on the principles of **rule of law**, protection of human rights and freedoms, legality, subsidiarity, proportionality, mutual cooperation, transparency, inclusiveness and market economy.[7] It provides several bodies implementing the above role, including CEA, directly responsible for the approximation of the Albanian legislation with the EU one. Draft laws aimed at aligning the Albanian legislation with acquis are reviewed in advance by the CEA before being assessed by other parliamentary committees.[8]

#11 Albanian civil procedural law is regulated by the Code of Civil Procedure (CCP).[9] It was adopted in 1996, prior to the actual Constitution and the signing of the SAA. Consequently, it has been subject to amendments, many of them due to the need for further approximation with EU law.

#12 A recent amendment of the CCP took place in 2021,[10] where significant changes were introduced following the justice reform, aimed at reducing the case backlog caused by judicial vacancies caused by the judges' vetting process. However, these challenges still persist, as acknowledged by the EU Commission's 2024 Progress Report on Albania, noting that the codes of procedure are hampered by formalities and do not provide adequate tools to address the high backlog. There are several moments where these amendments reflect the EU law influence. For instance, for the first time, Article 483/a of the CCP regulates **preliminary ruling.** The latest amendment of the CCP was made in 2022 by a decision[11] of the Constitutional Court of Albania. Required to rule on an article of the CCP contradicting Directive 2011/7/EU, the Court emphasised that EU secondary legislation is not part of the Albanian legal framework as long as Albania has not completed the procedures for EU integration.[12] However, the Court is eligible to **check the compatibility** of any normative act with ratified international agreements, including the SAA and European Convention on Human Rights (ECHR).[13] The Court referred to Articles 5, 116 and 122 of the Albanian Constitution, which provide that Albania applies the international law binding

6 Law No 15, dated 5 March 2015 'On the role of the Parliament in the integration process of the Republic of Albania in the European Union', amended (*Për rolin e Kuvendit në procesin e integrimit të Republikës së Shqipërisë në Bashkimin Europian, i ndryshuar).*

7 ibid Article 5.

8 ibid Article 17(1).

9 Law No 8116 dated 29 March 1996, Code of Civil Procedure of the Republic of Albania, amended (*Kodi i Procedurës Civile i Republikës së Shqipërisë, i ndryshuar*).

10 Law No 44/2021, dated 23 March 2021 On some additions and changes in the Law No 8116, dated 29 March 1996, Code of Civil Procedure of the Republic of Albania, amended (*Për disa shtesa dhe ndryshime në ligjin Nr 8116, datë 29.03.1996 Kodi i Procedurës Civile i Republikës së Shqipërisë, i ndryshuar*).

11 Decision No 30 dated 2 November 2022 of the Constitutional Court of the Republic of Albania.

12 ibid para 18.

13 ibid.

on it, ranking the ratified international agreements in the hierarchy of normative acts above its laws.[14] In this specific case, the Constitutional Court decided to amend Article 551(d) of the CCP on the grounds that it infringed the Constitution, not the SAA. However, this decision reflects the influence of international agreements and especially SAA in the Albanian legal framework.

#13 In addition, according to the SAA, Albania needs to approximate its legislation in **specific areas** of private law, including company law, intellectual property law and competition law. In particular, the 2022 EU Commission's Report on Albania highlighted that good progress was made with the adoption of the National Strategy for Intellectual Property 2022–2025 and the legislative alignment with the EU *acquis* in the areas of copyright and other related rights as well as industrial property rights.[15] The approximation of company and competition law, on the other hand, have faced more criticism. Company law in Albania has not aligned with EU *acquis* on the use of digital tools and the 2019 Directive on cross-border operations (mergers, divisions, conversions), as well as with rules on encouraging long-term shareholder engagement (Directive 2017/828),[16] and gender equality on boards of directors (Directive 2022/2381[17]).[18] Finally, regarding competition law, the 2023 Commission report stipulates that Albania's antitrust legislative framework is broadly in line with the EU *acquis* and the SAA, except for state aid rules which are only partially aligned.[19] However, antitrust law approximation may face problems in its implementation, as EU secondary law (Like Damages Directive[20] or

14 ibid para 73.

15 European Commission, 'Albania 2022 Report Accompanying the Document Communication from the Commission to the European Parliament, the Council, the European Economic and Social Committee and the Committee of the Regions 2022 Communication on EU Enlargement Policy' SWD (2022) 332 final 79.

16 Directive (EU) 2017/828 of the European Parliament and of the Council of 17 May 2017 amending Directive 2007/36/EC as regards the encouragement of long-term shareholder engagement [2017] OJ L132/1.

17 Directive (EU) 2022/2381 of the European Parliament and of the Council of 23 November 2022 on improving the gender balance among directors of listed companies and related measures [2022] OJ L315/44.

18 European Commission, 'Albania 2023 Report Accompanying the Document Communication from the Commission to the European Parliament, the Council, the European Economic and Social Committee and the Committee of the Regions 2023 Communication on EU Enlargement Policy' SWD (2023) 690 final, 85.

19 ibid 87.

20 Directive 2014/104/EU of the European Parliament and of the Council of 26 November 2014 on certain rules governing actions for damages under national law for infringements of the competition law provisions of the Member States and of the European Union [2014] OJ L349/1.

ECN+ Directive[21]) is transposed in competition authority's guidelines, not formal normative acts.[22]

#14 Albania adopted its actual private international law in 2011,[23] replacing a previous outdated and incomplete framework. It expressly provides that it is based on Rome I and Rome II Regulations,[24] governing contractual and non-contractual obligations. In drafting this law, orientation towards the **European *acquis*** was considered an obvious choice.[25] As a signing member of various international agreements with the EU and also as a future EU Member State, it is imperative for Albania to align private international law as closely as possible with the *acquis*. However, the recent EU Commission Progress Reports on Albania have highlighted issues regarding further alignment of legislation and better exchange of practices in judicial cooperation,[26] timely implementation of multilateral instruments and institutional capacity.[27]

#15 Albania has generally increased its efforts in approximating *acquis* with the civil and civil procedural domestic law. One key issue is the transposition of some EU instruments into national 'soft law' instead of formally normative acts- the case of competition law, mentioned above, is one example. Additionally, the effective implementation of the aligned framework is an additional challenge. Moreover, there is a standing that the transposition methodology needs to be 'tailored to the Albanian context', rather than directly transposed from the EU law. In any case, the approximation must also take into consideration the Albanian legal tradition as the countries of the region have been cautious in this regard.[28] However, it is worth mentioning that the SAA has been a

21 Directive (EU) 2019/1 of the European Parliament and of the Council of 11 December 2018 to empower the competition authorities of the Member States to be more effective enforcers and to ensure the proper functioning of the internal market [2019] OJ L11/3.

22 See also M Bogdani and M Canco, 'Private Enforcement of Competition Law: Albanian Challenges in Reflection of the EU Requirements' (2021) 1(8) SEE Law Journal Special Edition 54.

23 Law No 10 428/2011 On International private law *(Për të drejtën ndërkombëtare private)* dated 2 June 2011.

24 Council Regulation (EC) 593/2008 of 17 June 2008 on the law applicable to contractual obligations (Rome I) and Council Regulation (EC) 864/2007 of 11 July 2007 on the law applicable to non-contractual obligations (Rome II).

25 C Jessel-Holst, 'EU Harmonization of Private Law in South-East European Countries' in E Kurzinsky-Singer and R Kulms (eds), *Ukrainian Private Law and the European Area of Justice* (Mohr Siebeck 2019) 309, 314.

26 European Commission, 'Albania 2021 Report Accompanying the document Communication from the Commission to the European Parliament, the Council, the European Economic and Social Committee and the Committee of the Regions: 2021 Communication on EU Enlargement Policy' SWD (2021) 289 final, 50.

27 European Commission, 'Albania 2022 Report' (n 15) 47 and 'Albania 2023 Report' (n 18) 50.

28 A Bushati, *Europianizimi i të Drejtës Ndërkombëtare Private dhe Ndikimet në Legjislacionin Shqiptar të së Drejtës Ndërkombëtare Private* (DPhil thesis, University of Tirana 2016) 164.

cornerstone instrument, not only in the law approximation process, but also in the judicial practice, especially in higher courts.

2 The Discussion of the Procedural Law that Acted as a Catalyst for Changes at the National Level

#16 Featured with corruption, politicisation and arbitrariness, the judiciary in Albania has faced a historically low public trust. A dysfunctional judiciary system has affected the functioning of the state and society. Analysing the problems faced by the judiciary shows that the crisis of the judiciary is also a crisis of democracy.[29] A much-needed long-term strategy for **justice reform** was first mentioned in the EU Commission's 2010 Report on Albania. It pointed out that the main problems of the Albanian judiciary encompassed a lack of transparency, political interference, corruption, lack of coordinated control, lack of efficiency, and lack of management.[30] The EU representative of the time, Romana Vlahutin, considered the justice reform the most essential condition for the Albanian European integration process.[31]

#17 The justice reform in Albania was enacted in 2016, under the slogan 'If not now, when? If not us, who?' (Alb.: *'Në mos sot, kur? Në mos ne, kush?'*)[32] with the aim to promote and enhance the efficiency and integrity of the judicial system. Major constitutional amendments concerning the judiciary were followed by a **new legal framework** regulating six sectors: the judiciary (including amendments to the CCP), criminal justice, anti-corruption measures, legal education, legal services and financing.[33] These amendments were carried out by amending articles of the Constitution, adopting or amending more than forty laws and issuing tens of other normative acts, including decisions of the Council of Ministers.

---

29 A Anastasi, 'The Albanian Justice Reform in the Framework of the European Integration Process' (2021) 2 Euro-Balkan Law and Economics Review 1, 3.

30 European Commission, 'Analytical Report Accompanying the Communication from the Commission to the European Parliament and the Council Commission Opinion on Albania's Application for Membership of the European Union' SEC (2010) 1335, 94–95.

31 Top Channel Report, 'Vlahutin: Reforma në drejtësi, kushti kryesor për integrimin' (9 October 2015) <https://top-channel.tv/2015/10/09/vlahutin-reforma-ne-drejtesi-kushti-kryesor-per-integrimin/> accessed 2 March 2025; see also M Bregu and J Gjinko, 'The Impact of the European Union on the Endorsement of the Justice Reform in Albania' (2024) 13(3) Academic Journal of Interdisciplinary Studies 312.

32 The official website on the Judicial Reform in Albania <https://www.reformanedrejtesi.al/> accessed 2 March 2025.

33 ibid.

#18 Moreover, the newly created bodies like the High Judicial Council, High Prosecutorial Council, High Judicial Inspectorate, the Specialised Structure against Corruption and Organised Crime (SPAK) etc, are projected to strengthen the independence, integrity and impartiality of the judiciary and other bodies. The drafting and adoption of a new legal framework was challenging, but the most crucial test remains its **implementation**. The latter continues to be the focus of the EU Commission and other NGOs' reports. The EU Commission's 2023 report on Albania assessed the implementation of the reform in justice as 'overall good'.[34] However, despite the progress, corruption still remains an area of serious concern, as sectors most vulnerable to corruption require targeted risk assessments and dedicated actions.[35]

#19 One of the areas that was affected by justice reform in Albania was civil procedural law. The Albanian CCP underwent a major amendment in 2017.[36] The law does not mention the approximation level with the *acquis*. However, Albanian Parliament's 2015 Analytical Document on Albanian Judicial System preceding the amendment, provides that the CCP needs to **address EU secondary law**, especially regarding the **European order for payment procedure** (EU Regulation No 1896/2006[37]) and the **European small claims procedure** (EU Regulation No 861/2007[38]).[39] Analysing the 2017 amendments, authors confirm that some amendments, for instance, the provisions on small claims procedure, have mirrored EU standards[40] as anticipated by the 2015 Analytical Document. Aiming at increasing efficiency, time management and access to justice, more than one hundred changes or additions were made to the CCP in 2017. They address issues arising from: non-performing loans; the length of proceedings (for instance, determining the maximum duration of judicial processes at each level, the procedure of notices

---

34 European Commission '2023 Report Albania' (n 18) 4.

35 European Commission, 'Albania 2024 Report' Accompanying the document Communication from the Commission to the European Parliament, the Council, the European Economic and Social Committee and the Committee of Regions' SWD (2024) 699 final.

36 Law 38/2017 'On Some Additions and Amendments to Law 8116' dated 29 March 1996 'Code of Civil Procedure' of the Republic of Albania, amended (*Për disa shtesa dhe ndryshime të ligjit 8116 29.03.1996 'Kodi i Procedurës Civile' i Republikës së Shqipërisë, i ndryshuar*).

37 Regulation (EC) No 1896/2006 of the European Parliament and of the Council of 12 December 2006 creating a European order for payment procedure [2006] OJ L399/1.

38 Regulation (EC) No 861/2007 of the European Parliament and of the Council of 11 July 2007 establishing a European Small Claims Procedure [2007] OJ L199/1.

39 Special Parliamentary Commission on Judicial Reform, 'Analysis of Justice System in Albania' (2015) 88 <https://www.reformanedrejtesi.al/sites/default/files/dokumenti_shqip_0.pdf> accessed 2 March 2025.

40 See S Çinari, 'Zbatimi I Ndryshimeve Të Kodit Të Procedurës Civile Mbi Paditë Me Vlerë Të Vogël' in P Broka, S Çinari and L Ikonomi (eds), *Monitorimi i zbatimit të ndryshimeve të Kodit të Procedurës Civile për aksesin në drejtësi: Afati i arsyeshëm dhe paditë e vogla* (Fondacioni Shoqëria e Hapur për Shqipërinë 2020) 19, 21.

and the presentation of notices by electronic means, the simplified procedure for small claims); increasing the efficiency of courts' work (including amendments to the articles that regulate preparatory proceedings); expanding the competences of the High Court which receives more powers of a court of law, etc.

#20 The changes to civil procedural rules have had their impact in practice, even though they have not been fully exploited by the parties in civil processes yet. The 2020 Monitoring Report on Justice Reform confirmed that the number of claims for violation of the reasonable procedural time has increased year after year, since the entry into force of the changes in the CCP. However, this number remains low, compared to the number of cases where such a procedural tool could have potentially been utilised.[41] The number of small claims, on the other hand, did not change after the introduction of the 2017 changes, which is partly due to the lack of public awareness of the changes.[42] The positive impacts of these amendments appear to have been **only partially realised** as of 2023. The efficiency of the judicial system and access to justice continue to be affected by the long timescale of proceedings, increased workload and high backlog of cases, which remains particularly high in appeal and first instance courts.[43] The proper **implementation of civil procedure amendments** will also depend on increasing human resources and facilities in the judiciary, along with raising public awareness about procedural rights and building a stronger legal culture.

III Influence of European Institutions

1 The Impact of ECtHR Case Law on Procedural Aspects

#21 Albania has signed and ratified the European Convention on Human Rights (ECHR), which enjoys a special place in its hierarchy of legal instruments. Article 17(2) of the Albanian Constitution provides that '[The limitations to rights and freedoms] may not infringe the essence of the rights and freedoms and in no case may exceed the limitations provided for in the European Convention on Human Rights', granting to the ECHR a **superior status** compared to other international agreements or charters and elevating it to a constitutional level. By adhering to the **ECHR**, Albania has committed not only to guaranteeing human rights in the future, but also to adjusting its existing laws in the light of this Convention. For instance, in one of its latest decisions, the Albanian Constitutional Court decided on the amendment of Article 377 of the Albanian Civil

41 ibid 29.
42 ibid.
43 European Commission, '2023 Report Albania' (n 18) 4.

Code regulating testamentary rights, on the grounds that the limitation to the right to property did not pass the proportionality test as provided by the Constitution and the ECHR.[44]

#22 The **ECtHR** has dealt with an increasing volume of applications against Albania. Albania has (in)famously been found to infringe Article 6(1) ECHR on the right to a fair trial the most,[45] especially **procedural guarantees** like: access to a court, access to a lawyer, legal certainty and the right to be heard.[46] Other procedural issues identified by the ECtHR include the excessive length of proceedings in court and the lack of enforcement of decisions. As established by the Court, it is for the Contracting States to organise their legal systems in such a way that competent authorities can meet the requirements of Article 6 ECHR, including the obligation to take a decision within reasonable time.[47] Similarly, the Court has frequently emphasised the right to access the court.[48] These ECHR procedural guarantees are mirrored in Albanian domestic law. The 2017 amendment of the CCP aimed to strengthen these procedural guarantees[49] of the CCP explicitly regulate reasonable proceedings time.

#23 The **Albanian Constitutional Court** has been a **domestic promoter** of the ECtHR jurisprudence. Over the years, it has referenced ECHR standards and ECtHR jurisprudence in its rulings. While Kabashi argues that ECtHR jurisprudence has sometimes been applied inappropriately by the Albanian Constitutional Court,[50] or that sometimes the Court only mentions **ECtHR jurisprudence** without referring to specific case law,[51] its influence on decision-making and legal interpretation cannot be understated. Regarding the right to fair trial and other related procedural rights, the Constitutional Court has often referred to ECtHR jurisprudence concerning its interpretation of reasonable length of proceedings,[52] enforcement of court decisions,[53] reasoning of the decisions,[54] etc. Until 2016, the Albanian Constitutional Court could only review individual complaints regarding infringements of the right to a fair trial, mainly related to Article 6 ECHR. The 2016 constitutional amendments expanded the Constitutional Court's jurisdiction, providing that this

44 Decision No 69 dated 27 December 2023 of the Albanian Constitutional Court, paras 61 and 67.
45 See also V Kabashi, *The ECHR and the Western Balkans: Bringing the Convention Home* (EIZ Publishing 2023) 91.
46 ibid 105.
47 *Bici v Albania* App no 5250/07 (ECtHR, 3 March 2016) para 44; see also *Topallaj v Albania* App no 32913/03 (ECtHR, 21 July 2016).
48 *Ramadhi and others v Albania* App no 38222/02 (ECtHR, 2 June 2008) para 46.
49 Added by the 2017 amendments, mentioned above.
50 Kabashi (n 45) 82.
51 See eg Decision No 1 dated 21 January 2016 of the Constitutional Court of Albania, para 19.
52 See Decision No 35 dated 27 October 2010 of the Constitutional Court of Albania, para 9.
53 See Decision No 1 dated 19 January 2009 of the Constitutional Court of Albania, para 6.
54 See Decision No 6 dated 16 February 2015 of the Constitutional Court of Albania, para 19.

court can examine at a final stage the complaints of individuals against the acts of the public power or judicial acts impairing all fundamental rights and freedoms guaranteed by the ECHR.[55]

2 The Influence of Concepts: Judicial Independence, Quality, and Efficiency as Developed within the European AFSJ

#24 The EU, especially the EU Commission, have assisted the law approximation process in Albania by introducing some key concepts borrowed from **EU standards** that shaped the justice reform in Albania, including judicial independence, quality, and efficiency. **Judicial independence** in Albania has faced scrutiny, taking into consideration the deep-rooted issues of the judiciary. The justice reform set higher independence standards, starting with a self-governed High Judicial Council, which has an entirely new formula of constitution forming a balance between the powers[56] that replaced the previous politicised appointment of its members. An added guarantee has been the **'vetting process'** of judges and prosecutors, which aims to re-evaluate judges and prosecutors in Albania, based on asset, background and proficiency criteria.[57] Whereas the first criterion aims to combat corruption and increase judicial independence and impartiality, the last two criteria focus on increasing the quality of judicial practice. The 'vetting process', however, has led to **temporary challenges** in judicial efficiency, by creating vacancies in almost every level of the judiciary, paralysing the country's most important courts and tribunals for considerable periods of time.[58] To address this issue, the engagement of alternative dispute resolution could be a solution. However, the latter is underutilised in Albania. The new provisions on continual training of judges'[59] on the other hand, enhance the consistency and quality of judicial practice.

#25 The overall progress in promoting the independence of the judiciary in Albania was recognised by the Commission's 2023 and 2024 Progress Reports on Albania.[60] Regarding the **quality** of the Albanian jurisprudence, The 2023 Progress Report emphasised the need for a more comprehensive, in-line-with-EU-standards entry examination to the School of Magistrates, improved quality of its

55 Article 131(1)(f) of the Albanian Constitution.

56 J Bode and E Peppo, 'Issues of Implementation of the Fair Trial in the Albanian System: Analysis in the Framework of the Constitutional Court and ECHR's Jurisprudence on Albania's Cases' (2022) 11(6) Academic Journal of Interdisciplinary Studies 59.

57 Law No 84/2016 dated 30 August 2016 'On Transitional Re-evaluation of Judges and Prosecutors in the Republic of Albania', Article 4.

58 M Bakiasi, 'Albanian Judiciary under Construction' (2021) Institute for European Policy 3.

59 Law No 115/2016 dated 3 November 2016 'On Governing Bodies of the Justice System', Article 88.

60 European Commission, '2024 Report on Albania' (n 35).

academic staff, an enhanced methodology of continuous training, and further consolidation and unification of judicial practice. The more recent 2024 Progress Report established that the quality of justice needs to be improved and that further improvements to the judicial training system are still necessary.[61] Again, the the 2023 report underlined the lack of **efficiency** of the Albanian judiciary due to vacancies in the system, urging for a new integrated case management system through determined policy, planning and budgetary efforts. More specifically, the 2024 Report emphasised the need for improvement of judicial efficiency through ensuring the necessary budget for the Integrated Case Management System and rolling it out in a timely manner; and enacting the HJC roadmap to increase efficiency and reduce the backlog in the judicial system.[62]

3 EU projects directed at the improvement of the Albanian judiciary

#26 The EU has been a promoter of the judicial reform in Albania. During the adoption of the new legal framework as part of the judicial reform, the EU has assisted the **drafting and approximation** of laws. Following the judicial reform, the EU aims at further supporting its implementation, by contributing to the strengthening of rule of law, law enforcement and lower the corruption level in government agencies and judiciary.[63]

#27 One of the crucial EU Commission support programmes in the enlargement region is the **Instrument for Pre-accession Assistance (IPA),** consisting of financial and technical assistance.[64] The actual IPA III assistance program, covering the 2021–2027 timeframe, focusses on the progressive alignment with the EU rules, standards, policies and practices.[65] IPA assistance in Albania concentrates on several priority sectors, the first being democracy and governance.[66] Concerning the judiciary in Albania, IPA has been a key help during the 'vetting process' of judges and prosecutors (mentioned above) and in supporting specialised structures against corruption and organised crime.[67] Moreover, the EU

61 European Commission, '2023 Report on Albania' (n 18) 22 and '2024 Report on Albania' (n 35) 29.

62 European Commission, '2023 Report on Albania' (n 18) 24 and '2024 Report on Albania' (n 35) 5.

63 Delegation of the EU to Albania, 'Support to the Implementation of Justice Reform in Albania' (11 April 2024) <https://www.eeas.europa.eu/delegations/albania/support-implementation-justice-reform-albania_en> accessed 2 March 2025.

64 More information and an overview of the instrument for pre-accession assistance can be found at <https://neighbourhood-enlargement.ec.europa.eu/enlargement-policy/overview-instrument-pre-accession-assistance_en#:~:text=The%20general%20objective%20of%20the,Union%20rules%2C%20standards%2C%20policies%20and> accessed 2 March 2025.

65 ibid.

66 ibid.

67 European Commission, '2021 Report Albania' (n 26) 131.

Commission-led project named **International Monitoring Operation (IMO)** aims at overseeing the 'vetting' process in Albania, as provided in Article B of the Annex to the Constitution of Albania.[68] Another EU-funded project, EURALIUS, was designed to help with the consolidation of justice system in Albania from 2005 to 2021.[69] During these years, it provided continuous support before, during and in the first stages of implementation of the judicial reform.

#28 The **New Growth Plan for the Western Balkans** was introduced by the EU as a means to accelerate the speed of the enlargement process and the growth of the economies of the Western Balkans countries.[70] To support this process, a €6 billion financial instrument, the Reform and Growth Facility for the Western Balkans, was adopted for the period 2024–2027.[71] Even though it is not focused on the judiciary specifically, one of its four fundamental pillars concerns the acceleration of fundamental reforms.

#29 In addition, a project exclusively dedicated to the judiciary in Albania is the CEPEJ **Strengthening the Quality and Efficiency of Justice in Albania (SEJ IV)**, a co-funded project by the EU and the Council of Europe (CoE). The main activities of this project include usage of **cyberjustice** tools, court coaching projects, improvement of inspection guidelines and practices, efficiency and quality trainings for magistrates, support on introducing alternative dispute resolution tools, and workshops to improve judicial data analysis and statistics.[72] Regarding cyberjustice tools, an important project is the automatisation of proceedings by using information technology. For instance, an attempt to install of the court case management program (ICMIS) was first realised with funds from the World Bank and then with those of the European Union.[73]

#30 The EU and other connected international organisations have funded **trainings** or other career development programmes for Albanian judges and prosecutors, aiming at promoting the European standards in judicial practice. Some of these activities include: OSCE trainings on trafficking in human beings,[74] HELP

68 Delegation for the European Union in Albania, 'International Monitoring Operation' <https://www.eeas.europa.eu/delegations/albania/international-monitoring-operation_en?s=214> accessed 2 March 2025.

69 Euralius Publications <https://euralius.eu/index.php/en/library/euralius-publications> accessed 2 March 2025.

70 European Commission, 'New Growth Plan for the Western Balkans' available at <https://neighbourhood-enlargement.ec.europa.eu/enlargement-policy/growth-plan-western-balkans_en> accessed 2 March 2025.

71 ibid.

72 European Commission for the Efficiency of Justice (CEPEJ), 'Strengthening the Quality and Efficiency of Justice in Albania' (January 2023–December 2026) <https://www.coe.int/en/web/cepej/strengthening-the-quality-and-efficiency-of-justice-in-albania-sej-iv-> accessed 2 March 2025.

73 cf Special Parliamentary Commission on Judicial Reform (n 39) 307.

74 OSCE, 'Training of Trainers Guide for Judges and Prosecutors on Trafficking in Human Beings' (19 December 2023) <https://www.osce.org/presence-in-albania/560804> accessed 2 March 2025.

courses on the protection of human rights by CoE,[75] international labour standards trainings by ILO,[76] etc. Importantly, the European Judicial Training Network (EJTN), a network of EU judicial training institutions aimed at creating a common legal and judicial European culture, has collaborated with the Albanian School of Magistrates on trainings for judges. However, the Commission's report on Albania highlights the need for School of Magistrates to increase its participation in the network's activities and gaining of expertise.[77]

IV Summary

#31 The analysis above attempted to provide a comprehensive view of the alignment of civil procedural law in Albania with the EU *acquis* in the last three transitional decades, with a particular focus on the last one. This decade has been pivotal in the Albania's integration with the EU, marked by a significant judicial reform. This reform has helped 'Europeanise', *inter alia*, the domestic civil procedural law.

#32 European procedural law has influenced the Albanian one in several ways. In particular, the new concepts introduced during or after the judicial reform through legislative amendments, including preliminary ruling procedure, dealing with non-performing loans, special procedure for small claims, etc, have positively impacted the efficiency and quality in judicial practice. However, a major challenge that the Albanian judiciary is facing today is the incomplete implementation of this new legal framework.

#33 The European standards and legal framework are incorporated in the Albanian domestic system directly by cooperation with EU institutions, especially the Commission, but also indirectly, by the decisions of the ECtHR. The Strasbourg Court has influenced the enhancement of procedural guarantees provided in Article 6(1) ECHR, not only through its decisions against Albania, but also through the decisions of the Albanian Constitutional Court and High Court, which have been aligned with ECtHR jurisprudence.

75 See eg Council of Europe, 'Albanian Judges and Prosecutors to Expand Their Knowledge on Child-friendly Justice, through the HELP Online Course' (5 October 2021) <https://www.coe.int/en/web/help/-/albanian-candidate-judges-and-prosecutors-to-expand-their-knowledge-on-child-friendly-justice-through-the-help-online-course> OSCE, 'Training of Trainers Guide for Judges and Prosecutors on Trafficking in Human Beings' (19 December 2023) <https://www.osce.org/presence-in-albania/560804> accessed 2 March 2025.

76 United Nations Albania, 'The ILO Trains Albanian Judges and Magistrate Candidates on International Labour Standards' (16 June 2021) <https://albania.un.org/en/187487-ilo-trains-albanian-judges-and-magistrate-candidates-international-labour-standards> accessed 2 March 2025.

77 European Commission, '2023 Report Albania' (n 18) 23.

#34 The promotion of judicial independence, efficiency and quality has helped the establishment of new legal standards concerning the judicial practice. Most of these concepts have been integrated in the legal framework, and also included in trainings for judges and prosecutors, many of which funded by the EU institutions. While the 'vetting' process has contributed to a more independent and qualitative judicial practice, it has led to inefficiencies due to the increase of vacancies in the domestic courts.

C Serbia

I Background

#35 Historically speaking, the 'Europeanisation' of Serbian law (ie the mission aimed at shaping and reforming the Serbian legal system under the European influence)[78] is argued to have its roots in the **1349 Dušan Code** (Dušanov zakonik), at least in part.[79] The process continued in 19th century, in the context of the First and the Second uprising against the Ottomans,[80] resulting in the adoption of the **1844 Serbian Civil Code** – one of the very first of its kind in Europe – which was heavily influenced by the 1811 Austrian Civil Code.[81]

#36 In the more recent history, the process of harmonisation was renewed by the **Federal Republic of Yugoslavia**'s determination to speed up the process of integration with the EU following the break-up in Yugoslavia in the 1990s, by adopting a special Conclusion on the need to harmonise domestic law with EU law and thereby expressing its commitment to European goals. Guided by this objective, in 1996 the Federal Yugoslav Government recommended the harmonisation of internal rules and regulations with EU law, which started a new and long 'journey of Serbia towards Europe'.[82]

#37 Along the long journey taken down the EU route, Serbia has concluded a number of significant treaties and agreements, acknowledging, in particular, the necessity and importance of the harmonisation of its legislation with that of the

---

78 As put by Radovan Vukadinović: by 'looking up to European role models' ("ugledanjem na jevropejske uzore"), in R Vukadinović, 'Od ugledanja na jevropejske uzore do regionalne harmonizacije – druga strana medalje' in *Zbornik radova: Odnos prava u regionu i prava Evropske unije* (Pravni fakultet Univerziteta u Istočnom Sarajevu 2015) 37.

79 ibid.

80 M Pavlović, *Pravna evropeizacija Srbije, 1804–1914* (Kragujevac 2008) 32.

81 The 1844 Code was in force until 1946, with some provisions remaining in force even thereafter.

82 Vukadinović (n 78) 45.

EU. Crucial in this context is the **2008 Stabilisation and Association Agreement (SAA)**, which entered into force on 1 September 2013.[83]

#38 Serbia was granted the status of a **candidate** for EU membership on 1 March 2012, nine years following the Thessaloniki European Council Summit and two and a half years after its official application for the EU membership. This important step, preceded by a long Stabilisation and Association Process, signified the opening of a new chapter of Serbia's EU accession process.

#39 As observed by Vukadinović, in relation to the earlier 'imitation of European models', the new process of **harmonisation** differed in terms of goals, dynamics and subject matter.[84] In terms of goals, the new harmonisation process, based on the aforementioned Conclusion and the 2004 Resolution of the National Assembly on joining the European Union, is aimed at meeting the Copenhagen Criteria for admission to the EU, through the implementation of the SAA.

#40 For purposes of present discussion, it should be pointed out that the provisions of the SAA assigned a particularly crucial role to judiciary, with the objectives of strengthening of the **rule of law**, respect for its basic principles and judicial institutions set as priority from the very outset of the process.[85] With rule of law having been recognised as a key EU accession priority, the negotiating **Chapter 23** 'Judiciary and Fundamental Rights of the Union' became central to Serbia's accession process upon its opening on 18 July 2016, and, according to the official stance of the Serbian government, has remained 'a key focus throughout'.[86]

#41 In line with this, the basic principles of the **reform** of judiciary, including the **independence**, **impartiality**, expertise, responsibility and **efficiency** of the judiciary, were highlighted as the most important goal of the 'National Strategy for the Reform of the Judiciary' (NSRJ), adopted on 1 July 2013 by the National Assem-

---

83 Stabilisation and Association Agreement between the European Communities and their Member States of the one part, and the Republic of Serbia, of the other part [2013] OJ L278/14. This act has last been amended in 2023 by Decision No 1/2021 of the EU-Serbia Stabilisation and Association Council of 6 December 2021 amending the Stabilisation and Association Agreement between the European Communities and their Member States, of the one part, and the Republic of Serbia, of the other part, by replacing Protocol 3 thereto concerning the definition of the concept of 'originating products' and methods of administrative cooperation [2023/1320].

84 Vukadinović (n 78) 45.

85 D Bataveljić, 'Novi ustavni i zakonski okvir pravosuđa Republike Srbije posle reforme iz 2022. godine' (2023) Zbornik radova 'Usklađivanje pravnog sistema Srbije sa standardima EU' (Pravni fakultet Univerziteta u Kragujevcu) 105, 106.

86 EU For Justice: Support for Chapter 23, 'Booklet on Project Achievements: Judiciary and Fundamental Rights in the Context of Chapter 23 Accession Negotiations' (23 September 2020) 3.

bly of the Republic of Serbia.[87] The Government subsequently adopted its accompanying Action Plan for Implementation of the NSRJ.[88]

#42 The most recent revision of the NSRJ (in English known under the name '**Judicial Development Strategy**') was adopted for the period 2020–2025.[89] The document reemphasises 'the Republic of Serbia's commitment to the European **integration** process, as well as the direction of reforms and development set out in the recommendations issued by the European Commission in the Chapter 23 'Screening Report', and it:

> marks the completion of the reform process and creation of conditions for development continuity that is sustaining and enhancing the quality of the judiciary, as well as providing a clear and predictable framework for monitoring the achievements made thus far and the establishment of conditions for their sustainability.[90]

#43 It should be pointed out that the Ministry of Justice is the responsible institution overseeing the negotiation process for **Chapters 23 and 24**, and it is the key government body guiding, steering and monitoring the judicial reform process in Serbia. It is through the prism of these negotiating chapters that the discussion of the impact of European civil procedure on Serbia, as the candidate country, will take place.

#44 Accordingly, the following sections will explore in more detail the influence of EU civil procedural law instruments on Serbian legal system, including the relevant reforms at the national level that have taken place as a result (II), and, more broadly, the institutional impact, including the influence of the case law of the ECtHR and of the institutional concepts, such as **managerial accountability**, **judicial independence**, **quality** and **efficiency** as developed within the **European Area of Freedom, Security and Justice** (III).

---

87 National Judicial Reform Strategy for the 2013–2018 period, 'Official Gazette of the Republic of Serbia', no 57/13. The text of the National Strategy is available in the Serbian language at <https://vss.sud.rs/sites/default/files/document_category/Nacionalna-Strategija-reforme-pravosudja-za-period-2013-2018.pdf> accessed 2 March 2025.

88 The English text of the Action Plan for the Implementation of the National Strategy for the Reform of Judiciary for the period 2013–2018 is available at <https://www.mpravde.gov.rs/files/NSRJ_2013%20to%202018_Action%20Plan_English%20version.pdf> accessed 2 March 2025.

89 Government of the Republic of Serbia, 'Judicial Development Strategy for the Period 2020–2025' (July 2020). The text of the document is available in Serbian at <https://www.vrh.sud.rs/sr-lat/strategija-razvoja-pravosu%C4%91a-za-period-2020-2025-godine> accessed 2 March 2025.

90 ibid 6.

II Procedural Impact: The influence of EU Civil Procedure on Serbian legal system

#45 Since signing the SAA, Serbia has entered a process of approximation and implementation of the **EU *Acquis Communautaire***, including with respect to judiciary and **fundamental rights** as explicitly recognised in its Chapter 23 negotiation position.[91] In this context, there are several areas where the direct influence of the EU civil procedural instruments can be evidenced.

#46 The main piece of legislation regulating Serbian civil procedural law, the **Civil Procedural Law Act** (Zakon o parničnom postupku; hereinafter CPLA),[92] has been reformed several times since its adoption in 2011, with the latest amendments having been adopted in 2023. The reforms were officially driven by the need to harmonise the legislation in this area with the relevant EU acquis and especially to ensure '**procedural efficiency**'. However, the specific amendments that were ultimately adopted, following the backlash against the proposed draft,[93] seem to concern provisions of general nature, adopted in order

91 Government of the Republic of Serbia, 'Negotiating Position of the Republic of Serbia for Intergovernmental Conference on Accession of the Republic of Serbia to the European Union For Chapter 23 Judiciary and Fundamental Rights' (1 January 2016) available at <https://www.mei.gov.rs/upload/documents/pristupni_pregovori/pregovaracke_pozicije/ch_23_negotiation_position.pdf> accessed 2 March 2025.

92 Law on Civil Procedure, 'Official Gazette of the Republic of Serbia', no 72/11, 49/13 – Constitutional Court Decision, 74/13 – Constitutional Court Decision, 55/14, 87/18, 18/20 and 10/23.

93 It should be mentioned here that the draft CPLA, as published on 19 May 2021 by the Ministry of Justice, stirred significant criticism and, ultimately, led to protests by the general public and the members of the Serbian Bar Association. The main points of criticism included: the retroactive application of the provisions of the draft act; the proposed provision to consider a court submission withdrawn in event the court fee for the said submission is not paid within the deadline prescribed (draft Article 27); similarly, the proposed provision regarding the obligation of the plaintiff to deposit an advance payment for the costs of the appointment and work of a temporary legal representative, the failure of which would render the lawsuit withdrawn (draft Article 22); the curtailed right of a party to a special procedural remedy, the right to revision (second appeal on the points of law) before the Supreme Court in litigation proceedings (draft Article 106 concerning '*posebna revizija*') and the provision which foresaw the electronic submission for the legal profession as mandatory, instead of merely an option. None of these modifications – which were proposed in the name of ensuring procedural efficiency – were ultimately adopted. For a more detailed discussion of the 2021 CPLA draft, see: Vulić Law, 'Draft Law on Amendments to the Law on Civil Procedure: Challenges and Solutions' (17 June 2021) <https://vuliclaw.com/2021/06/17/draft-law-on-amendments-to-the-law-on-civil-procedure-challenges-and-solutions/> accessed 2 March 2025; V Rakić Vodinelić, 'Bio jednom Zakon o parničnom postupku . . .' (*Peščanik*, 25 May 2021) <https://pescanik.net/bio-jednom-zakon-o-parnicnom-postupku/> accessed 2 March 2025. For a detailed analysis of the legal remedy of revision (second appeal on the points of law) and the inspiration drawn from Slovenia and Croatia in drafting the provisions on general and special revision, see B Babović Vuksanović, 'Revision (Second Appeal on the Points of Law) in Serbian Litigation Proceedings' (2023) 4 Strani pravni život 707.

to facilitate the harmonisation of this instrument with legal acts regulating specific areas of civil procedure, discussed below.

#47 According to the National Programme for the Adoption of the **EU *Acquis Communautaire*** for the period 2024–2027, further reforms of the CPLA seem to be planned for the end of 2027.[94] The document specifically makes references to the following EU legislative acts which will be considered for purposes of reforming the CPLA going forward:[95] Directive 2020/1828 on representative actions for the protection of the collective interests of consumers;[96] Directive 2002/8/EC on access to justice in cross-border disputes;[97] the Succession Regulation 650/2012[98] and Regulation 2015/2421 amending the regulations on the European order for payment procedure and establishing a European Small Claims Procedure.[99] It is yet to be seen whether the controversial provisions proposed in 2021 will find their way into the new draft.

#48 Additionally, there are specific areas of civil and commercial matters where one may detect direct impact of legislative acts adopted in the context of European civil procedure. It is safe to say that most significant changes in this regard have been driven by the recognised need for procedural efficiency and the reduction in court caseload. One of the ways in which the legislator has attempted to improve this has been by encouraging the use of **alternative dispute resolution**. The notable example in this context has been the **Serbian Law on Mediation in Dispute Resolution** from 2014,[100] which replaced the much criticised 2005 Law on Mediation and is directly influenced by the Directive 2008/52/EC.[101] Notably, Article 4 prescribes the obligation to apply the 'principles and standards of mediation contained in the acts of the United Nations,

---

94 Nacionalni program za usvajanje pravnih tekovina Evropske unije (NPAA) 2024–2027 at < https://www.mei.gov.rs/upload/documents/nacionalna_dokumenta/npaa/npaa_2024-2027.pdf>.

95 ibid 10.

96 Directive (EU) 2020/1828 of the European Parliament and of the Council of 25 November 2020 on representative actions for the protection of the collective interests of consumers and repealing Directive 2009/22/EC [2020] OJ L409/1.

97 Council Directive 2003/8/EC of 27 January 2003 to improve access to justice in cross-border disputes by establishing minimum common rules relating to legal aid for such disputes [2003] OJ L26/41.

98 Regulation (EU) No 650/2012 of the European Parliament and of the Council of 4 July 2012 on jurisdiction, applicable law, recognition and enforcement of decisions and acceptance and enforcement of authentic instruments in matters of succession and on the creation of a European Certificate of Succession [2012] OJ L201/107.

99 Regulation (EU) 2015/2421 of the European Parliament and of the Council of 16 December 2015 amending Regulation (EC) No 861/2007 establishing a European Small Claims Procedure and Regulation (EC) No 1896/2006 creating a European order for payment procedure [2015] OJ L341/1.

100 Law on Mediation in Dispute Resolution (Zakon o posredovanju u rešavanju sporova) Official Gazette of the Republic of Serbia no 55/2014.

101 Directive 2008/52/EC of the European Parliament and of the Council of 21 May 2008 on certain aspects of mediation in civil and commercial matters [2008] OJ L136/3.

European Union and the Council of Europe' in matters not explicitly regulated by this Law. Furthermore, the Law prescribes that Articles 6–8 (concerning the 'cross-border proceedings') and 33(5) (prescribing the possibility for an EU citizen to act as a mediator in cross-border proceedings) will enter into force from the day Serbia becomes an EU member State.

#49 Likewise, it is important to note that the Law on Amendments and Supplements to the Law on Court Fees[102]) was enacted, encouraging parties to resolve their disputes by amicable means, through **mediation**, negotiated settlement, court settlement or any other amicable way, by postponing the collection of court fees and exempting parties from paying them if they achieve a settlement by the time of the first hearing. Serbia was also among the first signatories of the 2019 **Singapore Mediation Convention**,[103] showing initiative in promoting mediation.

#50 Despite these efforts, the number of instances in which mediation has been resorted to by the parties in civil and commercial matters has overall remained low: in 2019, only 40 commercial mediations were reported in the country, conducted by a total of 16 mediators (both court-connected and out-of-court cases). By contrast, commercial courts received 124,820 cases in the same year.[104] As a result, several projects, supported and/or funded by the EU, have been initiated with the view to promote mediation, especially in **commercial disputes**.[105]

#51 Another area in which there is clear evidence of the attempt to harmonise Serbian law with the EU community acquis includes **consumer law**. The new Law on Consumer Protection from 2021[106] seeks to change the shortcomings of the previous laws. In the official proposal of the adopted Law on Consumer Protection, it is stated that the main intention of its adoption is the harmonisation of consumer rights in the Republic of Serbia with EU consumer law – most specifically with EU Directive on Representative Actions for the Protection of the Col-

---

102 Official Gazette of RS, no 95/2018, entered into force on 1 January 2019.

103 United Nations Convention on International Settlement Agreements Resulting from Mediation (New York, 2018) adopted on 20 December 2018, opened for signature on 7 August 2019 (the 'Singapore Convention on Mediation').

104 EBRD in cooperation with IDLO, 'Comparative Study of the Legal and Institutional Frameworks and Best Practices on Commercial Mediation with Recommendations for the Republic of Serbia' (June 2021) 5 <https://www.drzavnauprava.gov.rs/files/ENG%20Study%20on%20Commercial%20Media tion%20in%20Serbia_Final.pdf> accessed 2 March 2025.

105 Some of these include: EBRD project 'Commercial Mediation in Serbia', funded by the UK Investment Climate and Governance Fund (hereinafter: EBRD project); IPA 2012 Judicial Efficiency Project; IPA 2015 'EU For Justice': Strengthening the Capacities of the Ministry of Justice in line with the Requirements of the EU Accession Negotiation Process (hereinafter: IPA 2015 'EU For Justice'); IPA 2016: EU for Supreme Court of Cassation.

106 Zakon o zaštiti potrošača, Official Gazette of RS 88/2021.

lective Interests of Consumers[107] – as well as the improvement of consumer protection, ie better and more efficient implementation of legal solutions. In the context of Serbian consumer law, it should be mentioned that one of the major novelties introduced by the legislation in 2014[108] (and kept in the 2021 revised legislation) included the introduction of the possibility to initiate **collective action** for the protection of consumers' interests, which is a procedural solution clearly inspired by the one adopted in the EU.

#52 Nevertheless, it should be pointed out that the Serbian regulatory framework only foresees such **collective protection** in the context of administrative proceedings.[109] Therefore, the decision as to whether there has been a violation of the collective interest is made by the competent ministry, which is at the same time authorised to adopt measures aimed at protecting the consumers' collective interests. Whether this legal framework is sufficient to enable effective and efficient consumer protection is questionable: bearing in mind the subject and the consequences of the decision (consumer's right to compensation), views have been expressed calling for such collective action to instead be regulated by the Serbian CPLA, as it had been between 2010 and 2013.[110]

#53 Finally, in the context of the discussion of consumer law, it should be pointed out that, while the right to out of court dispute resolution has been incorporated into the 2021 Law on Consumer Protection, one of the next initiatives within the harmonisation process is the establishment of the ODR platform, modelled upon the Regulation 524/2013 on consumer **ODR**.[111]

#54 Another area that should be mentioned in the context of the impact of European procedural law on Serbian procedural reforms is **access to justice**. Access to justice to all members of the society, especially the most vulnerable population, is one of the basic principles for the assessment of inclusivity and democracy of equal opportunity societies and it is considered an essential element of development, human rights, and the rule of law. In recognition of the significance of the **right to an effective remedy** before a tribunal and a fair trial, as guaranteed also by the EU Charter on Fundamental Rights, Serbia adopted the Law on Free Legal Aid,[112] which entered into force in October 2019. Nevertheless, despite the establishment of the free legal aid system five years

---

107 Directive (EU) 2020/1828 (n 96).

108 Zakon o zaštiti potrošača, Official Gazette of RS 62/2014.

109 For detailed discussion, see S Vukadinovic, 'Evropsko potrošačko pravo i njegov uticaj na razvoj potrošačkog prava Srbije' in J Ćeranić, V Đurić and A Višekruna (eds), *65 godina od Rimskih ugovora: Evropska unija i perspective evropskih integracija Srbije* (Institut za uporedno parvo 2022) 189.

110 ibid.

111 ibid 208. Regulation (EU) No 524/2013 of the European Parliament and of the Council of 21 May 2013 on online dispute resolution for consumer disputes and amending Regulation (EC) No 2006/2004 and Directive 2009/22/EC (Regulation on consumer ODR) [2013] OJ L165/1.

112 Zakon o besplatnoj pravnoj pomoći, Official gazette RS no 87/2018.

ago, there appears to remain a lack of awareness among citizens about their right to **free legal aid**, as well as several shortcomings in the implementation of the law.[113] According to the Commission's 2023 Report on Serbia, in the third year of implementation of the Law, local services in municipalities approved 95% of free legal aid requests; however, the report recognised the need to improve the existing capacity and cooperation between different service providers, including through training courses on application of good governance and antidiscrimination standards in decision-making.[114] Furthermore, while an analysis of the necessary amendments to the Law on free legal aid was finalised, the revision of procedural laws, the law on court fees and the tariff regulation has been delayed.[115]

#55 In order to raise the awareness of this Law and to promote the free legal aid mechanism in Serbia, the 'Free Legal Aid' project, implemented by the German International Cooperation Society (GIZ) and co-financed by the EU and the German Federal Ministry for Economic Development and Cooperation (BMZ) has been instituted.[116] The impact and the success of the implementation of the Free Legal Aid Law is yet to be evaluated: the most recent **Rule of Law Report** on Serbia from July 2025[117] does not mention this particular development.

#56 Finally, a few words should be said about **judicial cooperation** in civil matters, as something largely pertinent to the discussion on European civil procedure. This particular area of law is regulated by – what is today quite an outdated legal instrument from 1982 – adopted by the former Socialist Federal Republic of Yugoslavia (hereinafter: the 1982 PIL Code).[118] After the break-up of Yugoslavia, all the successor states, recognising a need for comprehensive reform, oriented themselves towards EU law, including in the area of **private international law**. As pointed out, this had 'an additional advantage [. . .] that the legal community can familiarise itself with an important part of the *acquis*

113 '"You Have the Right!" – Promoting the Free Legal Aid Campaign' (*WeBalkans.eu*, 22 June 2023) available at <https://webalkans.eu/en/news/you-have-the-right-promoting-the-free-legal-aid-campaign/> accessed 2 March 2025.

114 European Commission, 'Serbia 2023 Report: Accompanying the Document Communication from the Commission to the European Parliament, the Council, the European Economic and Social Committee and the Committee of the Regions: 2023 Communication on EU Enlargement Policy' SWD (2023) 695, 50.

115 ibid.

116 EU Za Tebe, 'Access to Justice for All -Free Legal Aid' (11 April 2024) <https://www.euzatebe.rs/en/news/access-to-justice-for-all-free-legal-aid> accessed 2 March 2025.

117 European Commission, '2025 Rule of Law Report: Country Chapter on the Rule of Law Situation in Serbia' SWD (2025) 931 final.

118 Zakon o rešavanju sukoba zakona sa propisima drugih zemalja – ZRSZ, Official gazette SFRY no 43/82 and 72/82-corr., Official Gazette FRY 46/96, Official Gazette RS 46/2006.

communautaire in advance of accession.'[119] Interestingly, Serbia, along with **Bosnia and Herzegovina,**[120] remain the only former Yugoslav states still applying the 1982 PIL Code.

#57 In her paper advocating for the reform of the 1982 PIL Code, Maja Stanivuković proposes two different routes to carry out such reforms (modelled upon **Slovenian** and **Croatian**, or **North Macedonian** and **Montenegrin** reforms respectively).[121] One of the listed reasons for these reforms is the need to harmonise Serbian private international law with the relevant EU instruments.[122] Furthermore, according to the same author, due to many changes that have taken place since its adoption, the application of the former Yugoslav Code as Serbian law has become increasingly difficult. Namely, the Code 'includes numerous terms and solutions that were based on the previously existing social, economic and political system and fails to respond to the altered needs of the Serbian citizens and companies'.[123] It should be pointed out that the PIL reform was attempted and was well underway in 2014: in January 2009, the Ministry of Justice established a Working Group for drafting of the new PIL Code for Serbia, which then completed its work and submitted a Draft consisting of 199 articles to the Ministry in June 2014.[124] Ultimately, however, the Draft PIL Code remained a draft, the reasons for which remain a mystery.

#58 In the same vein, it should be pointed out that, in the area of **recognition and enforcement of foreign judicial decisions** in civil and commercial matters, there has not been much discussion of the **2019 Hague Judgments Convention**[125] in Serbia, at least not beyond the academic circles.[126] Notably, Serbia is not a con-

119 Jessel-Holst (n 25) 315. Similarly, M Živković, 'Rad na novom Zakonu o međunarodnom privatnom pravu Republike Srbije – početne dileme i aktuelno stanje – Nacionalni izveštaj za Srbiju' in B Bordaš and M Stanivuković (eds), *Zbornik radova sa sedme Konferencije za međunarodno privatno pravo – Proširenje Evropskog pravosudnog prostora na države članice CEFTA* (2010 Novi Sad) 175, 185.

120 For critical discussion of the lack of harmonisation of private international law of Bosnia and Hercegovina with the EU acquis, see J Alihodžić and A Duraković, 'Zakon o međunarodnom privatnom pravu u Bosni i Hercegovini – Retrospektiva i perspektiva normativnog uređenja' (2023) 1 Zbornik radova Pravnog fakulteta u Tuzli 53.

121 M Stanivuković, '10 razloga zašto bi trebalo menjati Zakon o rešavanju sukoba zakona' (2020) 4 Branič 17, 26.

122 ibid 16–17.

123 ibid 27.

124 The text of the Draft Private International Law Act is available on the website of the Ministry of Justice <https://www.mpravde.gov.rs/obavestenje/6274/konacna-verzija-nacrta-zakona-o-medjunarodnom-privatnom-pravu-.php> accessed 2 March 2025.

125 HCCH, Convention of 2 July 2019 on the Recognition and Enforcement of Foreign Judgments in Civil or Commercial Matters ('HCCH 2019 Judgments Convention').

126 For a comprehensive analysis of the 2019 Hague Judgments Convention and its potential benefits and impact on Serbia, see S Đorđević, 'Kratak osvrt na Hašku konvenciju o priznanju i izvršenju stranih sudskih odluka u građanskim ili trgovačkim stvarima iz 2019' in S Soković (ed), *Usklađivanje prav-*

tracting state to any multilateral convention regulating the recognition and enforcement of foreign judgments in civil and commercial matters in the way that the Hague Judgments Convention does.[127] At the same time, however, Serbia has concluded numerous **bilateral agreements** containing provisions regulating these matters,[128] albeit not in the most satisfactory manner: in fact, it has been argued that acceding the Hague Judgments Convention would improve the recognition and enforcement of foreign judgments with those states with whom these bilateral agreements have already been concluded.[129] It remains to be seen whether any actual impact of European procedural instruments will be evidenced in the near future in this area of law.

III Institutional Impact

1 The Impact of the Case Law of the European Court of Human Rights on Some Procedural Aspects

#59 Serbia ratified the **ECHR** on 4 March 2004, whilst it was still part of the Union of Serbia and Montenegro.[130] By ratifying the Convention in 2004 and adopting a new Serbian Constitution in 2006 (replacing thereby the Constitution from 1990), the Serbian state 'signalled [their] objective to embrace a European vision of human rights protection'.[131]

#60 As per Article 16(2) of the 2006 Constitution,[132] ratified **international treaties** – including thus ECHR (to which, however, there is no explicit reference in the Constitution) – are an integral part of the Serbian legal system and shall be directly applicable. Moreover, Article 22 of the Constitution also provides that the citizens of Serbia 'shall have the right to address international institutions in order to protect their freedoms and rights guaranteed by the Constitution'.

nog sistema Srbije sa standardima EU (Kragujevac 2021) 407. See also D Marković-Bajalović 'Sporna pitanja izvršenja stranih sudskih odluka' in Slobodan Perović (ed), *Sudski postupak – pravda i pravičnost: međunarodna naučna konferencija: zbornik radova 35. susreta Kopaoničke škole prirodnog prava* (Kopaonik 2023) 477.

127 Đorđević (n 126) 418.

128 For instance, these include agreements with Bulgaria, Bosnia and Herzegovina, Montenegro, North Macedonia, Czech Republic, Slovakia, Hungary, Poland, Romania, Russian Federation, Cyprus, France and Greece.

129 Đorđević (n 126) 420.

130 Law on Ratification of the European Convention for the Protection of Human Rights and Fundamental Freedoms, Official Gazette of Serbia and Montenegro – International Agreements, no 9/2003, 5/2005, 7/2005.

131 Kabashi (n 45) 377.

132 The Constitution of the Republic of Serbia (Ustav Republike Srbije) Official Gazette RS no 98/06.

With respect to the obligation of the executive and legislative branches to ensure the compatibility of proposed legislation with ECHR standards, there is no specific procedure obliging lawmakers to ensure such compatibility. However, this is implied through the explicit obligation to ensure compatibility of legislation with the Constitution, which incorporates ECHR. This supra-legislative status of the Convention makes it possible for Serbian judges as well as for litigants to rely on the ECHR provisions and to enforce them directly at the domestic level.[133] While the **direct applicability of the Convention** and the ECtHR case law is undisputed, the issue that arises in practice is that of how often and how well the two are followed and implemented. This is a particularly acute issue, with Serbia being a country with the highest number of applications per capita before the ECtHR of all the Western Balkan countries.[134]

#61 By 2023, Serbia has been found in violation of **Article 6 ECHR** (often in conjunction with Article 13 ECHR) on more than 160 occasions in respect of many joined applications which reflects the repetitive nature of these violations.[135] According to the same source, the majority of these violations concerned the **length of proceedings** (the violation of the right to a fair hearing within reasonable time) and the failure to enforce final and binding judgments at domestic level. These areas, incidentally, appear to be the ones with most systemic faults and the ones where some legislative reforms have been detected.

#62 The most notable case concerning length of proceedings that initiated the dialogue and (ultimately) contributed to the legislative reforms in Serbia, was the ***V.A.M v Serbia*** case.[136] The case concerned the **excessive length of civil proceedings** brought by the applicant against her husband and the authorities' failure to enforce an interim access order. Despite Serbia's initial claims that its legal system provided for an effective legal remedy which the applicant had failed to exhaust, the Court reached a different conclusion due to the lack of any reference to the concrete remedy or case-law of the national courts proving its alleged effectiveness. As a result, the Court found a violation of Article 6 (the right to a fair hearing within a reasonable time) taken together with Article 13 of the Convention due to the lack of effective legal remedy at the domes-

133 D Popović, 'Uticaj Evropske konvencije za zaštitu ljudskih prava i osnovnih sloboda na sprsko zakonodavrstvo i sudsku praksu' (2011) 2 Pravni zapisi 356. The case-law of the national courts has also confirmed the direct applicability of international treaties and the generally accepted rules of international law; see Constitutional Court of Serbia, Decision No IU-149/2008, 28 May 2009.

134 Kabashi (n 45) 400.

135 ibid 406.

136 *V.A.M. v Serbia* App no 39177/05 (ECtHR, 13 March 2007); See also *Matijašević v Serbia* App no 23037/04 (ECtHR, 19 September 2006).

tic level. These findings were repeated in subsequent cases of *Ilić v Serbia*[137] and *Cvetković v Serbia.*[138]

#63 In response, Serbia introduced legislation in 2007 enabling litigants to seek the speeding up of the proceedings and/or just satisfaction through the constitutional complaint mechanism, modelled upon the Italian system (the so-called **Pinto law**).[139] This legal remedy was contained in Article 82(2) Constitutional Court Act as the means of protecting the right to a trial within reasonable time, which is both guaranteed by Article 6(1) ECHR and the Serbian Constitution.[140] According to the provision of the Constitutional Court Act, a **constitutional complaint** may be filed before the Constitutional Court even when the applicant has not exhausted the existing legal remedies in case where his right to a trial within reasonable time has been violated.[141]

#64 Initially, in *Vinčić and Others*, the Court declared the **constitutional appeal** to be a remedy that should, in principle, be considered effective in respect of applications lodged as of 7 August 2008.[142] Nevertheless, numerous problems arose with this remedy in terms of the amount of compensations awarded by Constitutional Court in these proceedings. In several instances, while actions taken by the Constitutional Court, ie finding a violation and awarding non-pecuniary damages 'constituted sufficient redress for the breach of the applicants' right to a hearing within a reasonable time',[143] the ECtHR held that the sums awarded to the applicants were not deemed sufficient and did not amount to appropriate redress,[144] rendering the **effectiveness of constitutional complaint** significantly poorer than was initially thought.[145]

#65 Serbia continued to operate without a specific law on **length of proceedings** until January 2016, when a new *lex specialis*, the 'Law on Protection of the Right to a Fair Trial Within Reasonable Time', entered into force.[146] The major novelty introduced by this legislation was sharing the burden among all domestic courts, which have now become responsible to deal with complaints regarding excessive length of proceedings. Under this legislation, interested parties were entitled to three types of legal actions: an objection to speed up the procedure which is submitted to the president of the court where the proceedings

137 *Ilić v Serbia* App no 30132/04 (ECtHR, 9 October 2007) para 105.
138 *Cvetković v Serbia* App no 17271/04 (ECtHR, 10 June 2008) para 59.
139 Popović (n 133) 347–348.
140 Article 32 Serbian Constitution.
141 Popović (n 133) 340, 346.
142 *Vinčić and Others v Serbia* App nos 4698/06 and 30 others (ECtHR, 1 December 2009) para 51.
143 *Borović and Others v Serbia*, App nos 58559/12 and 3 others (ECtHR, 11 April 2017) para 12.
144 ibid para 20; See Kabashi (n 45) 409–410.
145 For critical analysis of the issues with this particular mechanism, see Popović (n 133) 346–347.
146 Zakon o zaštiti prava na suđenje u razumnom roku, Official Gazette 40/2015.

are being conducted; an appeal following the result of such an objection; and a request for just satisfaction.[147]

#66 The legislation has since been amended once, in October 2023,[148] under the influence of the European Court of Human Rights subsequent case law. The reason for amending the Law was to incorporate provisions aimed at 'the execution of the European Court of Human Rights' judgment in the case *Kačapor and Others v Serbia*[149] concerning the **non-enforcement**, or **delayed enforcement**, of domestic judicial decisions given in the applicants' favour against socially/State-owned companies'.[150] The new 'Law on Amendments to the Law on the Protection of the Right to a Trial within a Reasonable Time' establishes the competence of the Constitutional Court to decide on the violation of the right to a trial within a reasonable time in bankruptcy and enforcement proceedings conducted for the purpose of settling claims in which the bankrupt, ie executive debtor, is a socially/State-owned enterprise. The Constitutional Court is authorised to decide whether there has been a violation of the right to a trial within a reasonable time, as well as the **right to compensation** for material and non-material damage, in a single procedure, based on a **constitutional appeal** that replaces the party's obligation to use different legal means.

#67 In addition, amendments to the law have introduced new grounds for appeal.[151] Finally, the Law stipulates that following the period of four months the judgment becomes final for the **voluntary enforcement** of the obligation. While this provides a form of certainty for parties regarding the settlement of obligations under these judgments, the provision in question does not stipulate any consequences in case of failure to fulfil such obligations, so the parties, in case voluntary enforcement fails would be forced to initiate appropriate enforcement proceedings.

#68 It remains to be seen whether the new legislative framework will assist Serbia in improving the average length of proceedings following the latest amend-

---

147 Kabashi (n 45) 411.

148 Zakon o zaštiti prava na suđenje u razumnom roku (n 146).

149 *R Kačapor and Others v Serbia* App nos 2269/06 and 5 others (ECtHR, 15 January 2008). The case concerned non-enforcement of numerous final judgments given in the applicants' favour against 'socially-owned' companies. The Court ordered Serbia to pay not only pecuniary damage but also what was owed to the applicants in accordance with the domestic judgments.

150 Council of Europe, 'Joint Programme Horizontal Facility, 'Public discussions on amendments to the Law on the Right to Trial Within Reasonable Time organised as part of Serbia's effort to execute the group of cases Kačapor and others' (5 August 2023) <https://pjp-eu.coe.int/en/web/horizontal-facility/-/public-discussions-on-amendments-to-the-law-on-the-right-to-trial-within-reasonable-time-organised-as-a-part-of-serbia-s-effort-to-execute-the-group-of-cases-kacapor-and-others> accessed 2 March 2025.

151 An appeal can now be filed if the court president, in a ruling granting the objection and recognizing a violation of the right to a trial within a reasonable time, fails to set a deadline for taking procedural actions that would expedite the proceedings.

ments. Despite the issues with the implementation of the ECHR and the less than favourable position of Serbia before the ECtHR, especially in cases triggered by Articles 6 and 13, the cases and reforms discussed in this section illustrate the clear impact that the Strasbourg case law has had, and continues to have, on the procedural developments in Serbia.

2 The Impact of Institutional Concepts: Judicial independence, Quality and Efficiency

#69 The present discussion concerning the impact of **institutional concepts**, such as judicial independence, quality and efficiency of the judiciary, is appropriate to be set against the background of the most recent **constitutional reforms** in Serbia. The amended Constitution was adopted in a referendum which was held on 16 January 2022, which was followed by an enaction of a set of judiciary laws in January 2023. This is the latest step in what has been a long process of substantial reforms of the Serbian justice system since the beginning of its EU integration journey.

#70 There have been several reasons for initiating constitutional reforms. Namely, from the very beginning of the implementation of the 2006 Constitution, a number of weaknesses were observed, primarily in the area of **judicial independence**.[152] The **Venice Commission**, through its numerous opinions, indicated the existence of a certain discrepancy between the constitutional framework of the Republic of Serbia and the desired standards that it strives for in the area of the rule of law.[153] Furthermore, as already pointed out previously, the SAA emphasises the importance of harmonisation with EU law in the field of judiciary: in this regard, the **Screening Report** on Chapter 23 indicated that Serbia should consider amending its Constitution in the area of judiciary, bearing in mind the recommendations the Venice Commission and European standards.[154]

#71 The constitutional revision included adopting several legislative acts aimed at achieving the following objectives: 1) changing the method of electing the holders of judicial positions; 2) reform of the way of work of the **judicial councils**,

152 Bataveljić (n 85) 107.

153 ibid 117. For general, critical discussion on the background to the issues concerning judicial independence in Serbia, see J Ćirić, 'Evropsko viđenje srpske reforme pravosuđa' in D Dimitrijević and B Miljuš (eds), *Harmonizacija zakonodavstva Republike Srbije sa pravom Evropske unije (II)* (Institut za međunarodnu politiku i privredu, Institut za uporedno pravo, Hans Zajdel Fondacija 2012) 117; A Kneževic Bojović and M Reljanović, 'Reforma pravosuđa' in A Rabrenović and J Ćeranić (eds), *Usklađivanje prava Republike Srbije sa pravnim tekovinama EU: Prioriteti, problemi, perspective* (Institut za uporedno pravo 2012) 89.

154 European Commission, 'Screening Report Serbia: Chapter 23 – Judiciary and Fundamental Rights' MD45/14 (15 May 2014) 22, 25.

whose jurisdiction has been greatly expanded; 3) strengthening the **constitutional guarantees** of the independence of the judiciary; 4) reducing the possibility of **politicisation** of the judiciary, and 5) strengthening the integrity and individual responsibility of **public prosecutors**.

#72 In its 2024 Report on the Rule of Law in Serbia, the Commission acknowledged the implementation of the constitutional reform to strengthen judicial independence as 'ongoing with further implementing laws to be amended'. In short, the Commission commended the establishment of a new appeal procedure to the Constitutional Court for **judicial appointments**, whilst cautioning against the delays in filling 'a considerable number of vacancies for judges and prosecutors'.[155] One of the main issues that have historically plagued the Serbian judiciary – the political pressure on it, resulting in a very low level of perceived judicial independence[156] – remains high in Commission's view.[157] Whether this will be somewhat remedied by the constitutional reforms is yet to be evaluated. Where quality of justice is concerned, the need for continued education and **judicial training** has been recognised as crucial and has received significant support by the EU. In terms of efficiency, according to the finding of the 2025 Report, Serbia still lacks a comprehensive court management system that interlinks cases across courts and prosecutor offices. While efficiency shows a positive trend for civil, commercial, and criminal cases, there are serious challenges in the handling of administrative cases and constitutional complaints.

#73 As noted above, the constitutional reforms had a specific objective to strengthen judicial independence. In an attempt to address the issues stemming from the excessive influence of the legislature and the executive on judiciary, the competence to appoint judges and prosecutors was finally transferred from the National Assembly to the **High Judicial Council** and the **High Prosecutorial Council**, which were established in May 2023. In terms of **separation of powers**, seeing how crucial it is to the matter of judicial independence, it should be pointed out that Article 4 of the amended Constitution now spells this out in more explicit terms. Namely, it underlines that the organisation of government rests on the division of power into legislative, executive and judicial, and specifically emphasises that the

---

155 European Commission, '2024 Rule of Law Report: Country Chapter on the Rule of Law Situation in Serbia' SWD (2024) 831 final.

156 According to Eurobarometer survey FL540 (conducted among the general public between 14 February and 27 February 2024) and Eurobarometer survey FL541 (conducted among companies between 14 February and 5 March 2024) in 2024, 36% of the general population and 34% of companies perceived the level of independence of courts and judges to be 'fairly or very good'. In 2025, the perceived judicial independence among the general public has decreased further (30%), according to the 2025 Rule of Law Report (n 117) 2.

157 European Commission, '2025 Rule of Law Report – Serbia' (n 117) 2.

relationship between the three main powers is now based on 'mutual **checks and balances**'.[158]

#74 In order to implement the constitutional changes, five laws were amended in February 2023: Law on the High Judicial Council, Law on the High Prosecutorial Council, Law on the Public Prosecutor's Office, Law on Judges and Law on the Organisation of Courts. These were overall positively assessed by the **Venice Commission**, whose opinions on draft laws (and revised drafts) have been particularly impactful.

#75 In its assessment of the constitutional reforms, the Commission did point out that an opportunity has been missed so far to carry out reforms of the **Constitutional Court**, in particular with regard to the introduction of a qualified majority with an anti-deadlock mechanism for the election of some of the judges by Parliament, as underlined by the Venice Commission.[159]

#76 A particularly strong institutional impact is visible in the context of the measures aimed at improving the quality of justice. The institution that has been responsible for initial and continuous judicial training, the **Judicial Academy**, was established in 2010, upon the Recommendations by the European Commission.[160] The Judicial Academy was founded as an institution that performs activities for the purpose of ensuring the exercise of rights established by the Law on the Judicial Academy, and of importance for the judicial system of the Republic of Serbia.[161] Its main goal is 'to meet the needs of technical expertise to respond to the challenges arising from the obligation to fully implement the European Convention on Human Rights, as well as from the EU accession negotiation process'.[162] In doing so, it is geared towards providing support and improve educational activities and new structures within the Judicial Academy and thereby contribute to the establishment of a consistent judicial system in the Republic of Serbia.

#77 The National Judicial Development Strategy for 2020–2025 acknowledged the necessity to further advance the Judicial Academy's training program by way of including new thematic areas arising from the processes, reforms and development steps connected to Serbia's accession to the EU, 'particularly those related to the **case law** of the European Court of Human Rights and the European

158 For further discussion, see Bataveljić (n 85) 108.

159 European Commission, '2024 Rule of Law Report – Serbia' (n 155) 3.

160 D Čvorović, 'Reform of Judiciary System in Serbia – Compliance with European Standards or Not?' in *Collection of Papers from the Conference 'Controversies of the Contemporary Law'* (East Sarajevo 2022) 466, 476.

161 The Judicial Academy of the Republic of Serbia (Pravosudna akademija Republike Srbije) Official webpage <https://www.pars.rs/en> accessed 2 March 2025.

162 ibid.

Court of Justice'.[163] The document further places a special emphasis on 'fulfilling the requirements contained in the interim benchmark to ensure that training needs are viewed as part of the judges' and prosecutors' performance appraisal.' In order to achieve this, '[I]t is necessary that the improvement of the training program be accompanied by appropriate infrastructure, administrative capacity of the Judicial Academy, and mechanisms to control the quality of training.'[164]

#78 In a similar manner, the 2023 Commission Report recommended that the Academy's capacity and internal expertise for delivering sufficient initial and continuous training should be further improved, in particular for training on EU law, and encouraged the Academy to benefit from its status as an observer in the **European Judicial Training Network** (EJTN).[165]

#79 Against this backdrop, it should finally be noted in this context that the Law on the Judicial Academy is one of the legislative acts that are currently awaiting an amendment: in doing so, the Serbian Government has already communicated their intentions to consult the European Commission and the Venice Commission on the draft Law,[166] which further demonstrates the impact of European institutions on judicial reforms in the area of rule of law and fundamental procedural rights.

IV Summary

#80 The brief analysis of the alignment of the Serbian law in the area of civil procedure and, more broadly, the rule of law, with the EU *acquis*, demonstrates the various ways in and the extent to which the European civil procedural and other instruments, as well as European institutions and concepts, have impacted the legal developments in Serbia over the last two decades.

#81 As evidenced in Part II, the reforms of Serbian civil procedural law have been strongly driven by the solutions adopted in European procedural law. This has been particularly evidenced by the reforms concerning alternative dispute resolution, small claims procedures, legal aid, and procedural mechanisms concerning consumer law, all of which have been carried out with the relevant corresponding EU legislative acts in mind.

#82 It can also be seen that the case law of the Strasbourg court has had, and continues to have, a particularly significant impact on legal developments in Serbia, as shown in Part III. This influence is particularly relevant in the context

163 Serbian Government, '2020–2025 Judicial Development Strategy' (n 89) 28.
164 ibid 28.
165 European Commission, '2023 Report Serbia' (n 114) 26.
166 European Commission, '2024 Rule of Law Report – Serbia' (n 155) 3.

of the right to a fair hearing within reasonable time and the right to a domestic remedy where important legislative (and jurisprudential) reforms have already taken place.

#83 Finally, in addition to the reforms of domestic laws being inspired by the specific EU legal instruments and the ECtHR case law, European standards and principles, with special emphasis on judicial independence, quality and efficiency of justice, have been (and are being) incorporated into the Serbian legal system by cooperation with the EU institutions (especially the Commission) and the Council of Europe. These institutional concepts have gradually been incorporated into Serbian legal framework and included in trainings for judges and prosecutors carried out by the Judicial Academy, supported by both the EU and the Council of Europe.

D Ukraine

I Introduction and Background Remarks

#84 Some historical remarks about **Ukraine's path to EU integration** will be necessary. They will help to understand the key points of the **Europeanisation** of procedural law and the background of the continuous judiciary reforms in Ukraine on the way to the EU Enlargement Process and the gradual implementation of European Civil Procedure. The Ukrainian legal system can only be studied within the European dimension of legal development,[167] considering the impact of the Council of Europe's recommendations and the ECtHR case law, and as part of a genuine European area of justice within the EU in the near future.[168] Despite strong traditions and a firm intention to further integrate into the European community, Ukrainian legislation and legal practice bear the burden of foreign elements imposed during periods of **occupation**,[169] as well

---

167 Ukraine is a UN co-founding state and, since the 9th century, has occupied a central territory in Europe with significant contributions to European legal traditions. These contributions include the foundational legal codes like 'Rus' Justice' or 'Rus' Truth' by Yaroslav the Wise, and the Lithuanian Statutes. This rich legal heritage has continued to evolve, shaping modern Ukrainian legal frameworks and its integration into European legal systems.

168 The intentions to integrate within the EU were announced by the Ukrainian government in the early 1990s, leading to a societal surge in support for further approximation with the EU community.

169 Historically, Ukrainian territories were divided among several empires and were forcibly included in the Soviet Union during the 20th century, an act widely considered as the occupation of Ukrainian lands after the declaration of Ukraine's independence in 1917–1918. See: I Bilas, *The Repressive and Punitive System in Ukraine, 1917–1953: Socio-Political and Historical-Legal Analysis*, vol 1–2, (Lybid, Viisko Ukrainy 1994); S Kulchytskyi, *Communism in Ukraine: The First Decade (1919–1928)* (Osnovy 1996); I Mazepa, *Bolshevism and the Occupation of Ukraine: Socio-Economic Reasons for the Im-*

as the consequences of the constant struggle for an independent path of development, distinct from former empires.

#85 Despite the longstanding desire **to join the EU** and the significant efforts made, Ukraine still has a considerable distance to cover. The idea of EU membership has been present in political discussions since the restoration of Ukrainian independence in 1991. Historically, Ukraine has deep European traditions, with its legislation and legal doctrine significantly influenced by European sources and the broader development of law in Europe.[170] Nevertheless, there is still room for necessary improvements in several key areas to achieve this goal.

#86 Ukraine is a founding member of the UN and has been a member of the Council of Europe since 1995, seeking EU membership for a considerable period of time. However, the period of **Soviet occupation** was characterised by the total disregard for national background and the specific regulations of the republic, the imposition of foreign elements and dubious concepts of protecting citizens' rights and their property.[171] Consequently, the independent legal profession was virtually destroyed,[172] judges were under control and significantly depen-

maturity of the Power of the Ukrainian Revolution (Lviv 1922); I Terlyuk, 'Political and Legal Nature of the Soviet Statehood in Ukraine as an Occupation' (2022) 5 Law of Ukraine 103; Y Tynchenko, *The First Ukrainian-Bolshevik War (December 1917 – March 1918)* (I Krypiakevych Institute of Ukrainian Studies 1996); D Yanevskyi, *Political Systems of Ukraine 1917–1920: Creation Attempts and Reasons for Defeat* (Dukh i litera 2003).

170 S Ivanovych Ishchuk, 'Civil Society in the Conditions of the European Integration Development of Ukraine: Theoretical and Legal Aspect' (DPhil thesis, King Danylo University 2021); Y Mykolaiovych Kostyuchenko, *Legal Regulation of Association Relations between Ukraine and the European Union* (Kyiv University 2019); M Kozjubra, 'The Tendencies of Development of the Sources of Law of Ukraine in the Context of the European Law-Integration Processes' (2004) 26 NaUKMA Research Papers: Law 3; I Oleksiivna Kresina (ed), *Strategic Priorities of Political and Legal Development of Ukraine in the Context of European Integration* (Norma Prava 2024); V Yevhenovych Marmazov and I Slavovych Pilyaev, *Ukraine in the Political and Legal Space of the Council of Europe: Experience and Problems* (Venturi 1999); V Andriiovych Zhuravel and others (eds), *Legal Science and Legislation of Ukraine: The European Vector of Development in the Conditions of Martial Law* (Pravo 2023).

171 'Legislation During the Days of Soviet Power in Ukraine (1920–1990)' (*Institute of Civil Society*, 18 July 2011) <https://www.csi.org.ua/publications/zakonotvorennya-za-doby-radyanskoyi-vl/> accessed 2 March 2025; I Leonovych Samsin and P Vitaliivna Kazakevich, *Organizational and Legal Cooperation of the Judicial Authorities of Ukraine with the Institutions of the Council of Europe* (Helvetica 2019); O Volodymyrivna Shkuratenko, 'International Recognition of Ukraine due to the Election of the Right to Membership in the UN (Historical Review)' (2001) 12 Law of Ukraine 142.

172 N Mezenivna Bakayanova, 'Functional and Organizational Foundations of the Legal Profession of Ukraine' (DPhil thesis, National University 'Odesa Juridical Academy' 2017); O Khotynska-Nor, 'Theoretical, Legal and Praxeological Principles of Judicial Reform in Ukraine' (DPhil thesis, Taras Shev-

dent on higher hierarchical courts,[173] including supervision procedures and direct interference in judicial proceedings of other state bodies representatives (see *Sovtransavto Holding v Ukraine*[174]).

#87 The signing of the **EU–Ukraine Association Agreement in 2014**[175] set forth the priority areas of cooperation and further plans for the harmonisation of Ukrainian legislation with EU laws. The Free and Comprehensive Trade Area was considered a basis for the further integration of Ukraine into the internal EU market. EU membership necessarily requires a level of judicial trust and efficiency of proceedings. Therefore, significant efforts were put into ensuring cooperation in the field of justice, which requires strengthening the judiciary, improving its efficiency, guaranteeing its independence and impartiality, and combating corruption. The major **reforms** of the judiciary and related institutions had various consequences, impacting multiple levels of judicial activities from new procedural regulations to the reshaping of the Supreme Court with new staff.[176]

#88 The current period is marked by active reforms under the **Ukraine Facility Plan**, aimed at advancing EU membership and supporting efforts.[177] The Ukraine Plan outlines reforms and investments, with qualitative and quantitative indicators, focusing on enhancing macro-economic and financial resilience and improving judicial accountability and integrity. To secure support, Ukraine must implement its recovery and reform plan while upholding the rule of law and human rights. Specific paths for implementing these reforms are discussed here.

---

chenko National University of Kyiv 2017); I Borysovych Usenko (ed), *Judicial Power in Ukraine: Historical Origins, Regularities, Peculiarities of Development* (Naukova dumka 2014).

173 B Oleksandrovych Potilchak, 'The Soviet Court and Justice Departments (Second Half of 1930-mid 1940-ies): Reception in the Modern Russian Historical-Legal Science' (2014) 28 Uzhhorod National University Herald, Series: Law 38.

174 *Sovtransavto Holding v Ukraine* App no 48553/99 (ECtHR, 25 July 2002).

175 'Association Agreement between the European Union and the European Atomic Energy Community and their member states, of the one part, and Ukraine, of the other part' [2014] OJ L161/3.

176 Decree of the President of Ukraine no 276/2015 of 20 May 2015 'On the Strategy for Reforming the Judiciary, Judiciary and Related Legal Institutions for 2015–2020' [2015] Official Gazette of Ukraine 41/1267; Decree of the President of Ukraine no 231/2021 of 11 June 2021 'On the Strategy for the Development of the Justice System and Constitutional Judiciary for 2021–2023' [2021] Official Gazette of Ukraine 48/2963; N Petrivna Demchik, 'Judicial Reform in the Conditions of European Integration Processes' (2023) 5 New Ukrainian Law 73; O Khotynska-Nor, *Theory and Practice of Judicial Reform in Ukraine* (Pravova yednist', Alerta 2016).

177 European Union, 'Plan for the Ukraine Facility' (*UA Ukraine Facility*, 2024) <https://www.ukrainefacility.me.gov.ua/en/> accessed 2 March 2025.

II Influence of European Procedural Law: The impact of CoE and ECtHR case law on procedural aspects of Ukrainian civil justice

#89 Perhaps the primary basis for major reforms of the Ukrainian judiciary ecosystem was Ukraine's accession to the **Council of Europe**. The ECHR was ratified in 1997, and the decisions of the ECtHR became an important and influential source of national case law.[178] This was an important step toward facilitating judicial cooperation and closer **approximation of the law** within the Council of Europe. The recommendations, resolutions, and guidelines slowly became impactful for Ukrainian legislative reforms.[179] Despite these efforts, Ukraine has been much criticised by the European Commission for Democracy through Law (Venice Commission) for legislative reforms, particularly those related to the judiciary and its institutions.[180]

#90 The most popular recommendations for improvements in civil procedure were only partly implemented into legislation and practice over the next few decades. For instance, **amicable and out of court settlements of disputes** before court proceedings have been instituted or in the course of proceedings were

---

178 Laws of Ukraine no 475/97-BP of 17 July 1997 'On the ratification of the Convention on the Protection of Human Rights and Fundamental Freedoms of 1950, the First Protocol and Protocols nos 2, 4, 7 and 11 to the Convention' [1997] Official Gazette of Ukraine 29/11.

179 L Leonidivna Bogachova, 'The Influence of the Council of Europe Law on the National Legal System of Ukraine' (2014) 28 State Building and Local Government 56; O Kaplina and A Tumanyants, 'ECtHR Decisions that Influenced the Criminal Procedure of Ukraine' (2021) 4 Access to Justice in Eastern Europe 102; V Komarov and T Tsuvina, 'The Impact of the ECHR and the Case Law of the ECtHR on Civil Procedure in Ukraine' (2021) 4 Access to Justice in Eastern Europe 79.

180 European Commission for Democracy Through Law (hereinafter: the Venice Commission), 'Ukraine – Information on the follow-up to the Urgent joint opinion on the draft law on amendments to certain legislative acts concerning the procedure for electing (appointing) members of the HCJ and the activities of disciplinary inspectors of the HCJ (Draft law no 5068) (CDL-AD(2021)018) and Joint Amicus curiae brief on certain questions related to the election and discipline of the members of the HCJ (CDL-AD(2022)023)' (13 June 2023); Venice Commission, 'Ukraine – Law on amendments to certain legislative acts of Ukraine to clarify provisions on the competitive selection of candidates for the position of judge of the Constitutional Court of Ukraine' (CDL-REF(2023)037) (20 September 2023); Venice Commission, 'Ukraine – Information on the follow-up to the Urgent follow-up opinion to the opinions on the Law 'On Amendments to certain legislative acts of Ukraine to clarify the provisions on the competitive selection of candidates for the position of judge of the Constitutional Court of Ukraine" (CDL-AD (2023)042) (20 December 2023); Venice Commission, 'Opinion no 999/2020 of 21 October 2021 Ukraine – Law on amendments to the Law 'On the judiciary and the status of judges' and selected laws regarding the resumption of operation of the high qualifications commission of judges' (CDL-REF(2021)079); Venice Commission, 'Opinion no 1129 / 2023 of 27 April 2023 Ukraine – Law on amending some legislative acts of Ukraine regarding improving procedure for selecting candidate Judges of the Constitutional Court of Ukraine on a competitive basis' (CDL-REF(2023)018).

introduced more or less widely only in 2017 with the implementation of the procedure of settlement with a judge[181] and in 2021 with the adoption of the **law on mediation** in Ukraine[182] (ie Recommendation No R (81) 7 on measures facilitating access to justice).[183] Simplified and more rapid forms of proceedings became available to the parties in Ukraine in a relatively recent past: the order for payment procedure was introduced in 2004, and the **simplified action procedure** only in 2017.[184] Only a small list of types of civil cases might be considered in simple manner where rules or sets of rules should be instituted in order to expedite the settlement of disputes according to the Recommendation No R (84) 5 on the principles of civil procedure designed to improve the functioning of justice.[185]

#91 However, **ECtHR case law** significantly impacts Ukrainian civil justice, and some positive, timely considerations were issues of attention and served as a catalyst for further reforms of procedural legislation. Despite Ukraine ranking third after Russia and Turkey in terms of the number of appeals to the European Court of Human Rights, the impact of the ECtHR's case law can be assessed as positive. The majority of complaints—95%—are related to the non-execution of court decisions.[186] Several landmark ECtHR decisions and statements have undoubtedly influenced the development of the Ukrainian legal and judicial system, such as the cases of *Yuriy Nikolayevich Ivanov v Ukraine*[187] and *Burmych and Others v Ukraine*.[188] In the former, the ECtHR obliged Ukraine to implement appropriate measures and ensure their compliance with the Convention regarding the execution of court decisions. In the latter, 12,143 cases filed between 2013

---

181 T Tsuvina and others, 'The Implementation of Consensual Tenet in Modern Civil Procedure: Comparative Analysis of Court-Connected Settlement Procedures Applied in Austria, Lithuania, and Ukraine' (2024) 7(1) Access to Justice in Eastern Europe 26.

182 CH van Rhee, 'Mandatory Mediation before Litigation in Civil and Commercial Matters: A European Perspective' (2021) 4(12) Access to Justice in Eastern Europe 7.

183 Recommendation no R (81) 7 of the Committee of Ministers to Member States on Measures Facilitating Access to Justice (adopted 14 May 1981) <https://rm.coe.int/168050e7e4> accessed 2 March 2025.

184 R Flejszar, I Izarova and V Vebraite, 'Access to Justice in Small Claims Procedure: Comparative Study of Civil Procedure in Lithuania, Poland and Ukraine' (2019) 9 International Journal of Procedural Law 97; Y Prytyka and S Kravtsov, 'Small Claims in Civil Procedure in Ukraine: Panacea or an Obstacle to Access Justice' (2023) (Spec) Revista Jurídica Portucalense 375.

185 Recommendation no R (84) 5 of the Committee of Ministers to Member States on the Principles of Civil Procedure Designed to Improve the Functioning of Justice (adopted 28 February 1984) <https://www.justice.gov.sk/dokumenty/2021/05/RECOMMENDATION-No.-R-84-5.pdf> accessed 2 March 2025.

186 Council of Europe, 'Report on a Mission to Ukraine for Bilateral Consultations with Ukrainian Authorities Concerning the Improvement of Enforcement Proceedings (for the Execution of Judgments of the European Court of Human Rights Yuriy Nikolayevich Ivanov v Ukraine and Burmych and others v Ukraine)' (August 2018) <https://rm.coe.int/report-on-a-mission-to-ukraine/16808f234c> accessed 2 March 2025.

187 *Yuriy Nikolayevich Ivanov v Ukraine* App no 40450/04 (ECtHR, 15 October 2009).

188 *Burmych and Others v Ukraine* App nos 46852/13, 47786/13, 54125/13 et al (ECtHR, 12 October 2017).

and 2017, concerning the **non-execution** of Ukrainian court decisions, were consolidated. These decisions laid the foundation for future reforms in the enforcement system in Ukraine.

#92 One of the most significant examples of the ECtHR's influence on the development of civil procedural law is the abolition of the **supervisory review protest institution**. This extraordinary appeal procedure allowed officials from various state bodies and courts to overturn court decisions after they had become final (cases such as *Sovtransavto Holding v Ukraine*[189] and *Tregubenko v Ukraine*[190]).

#93 Another classic example is the issue of **reasonable time** frames for case consideration. Numerous cases involved the appellate court repeatedly sending cases for new trials (*Sebova v Ukraine*,[191] *Pavlyulynets v Ukraine*,[192] *Moroz and Others v Ukraine*[193]), significant delays in case proceedings (in some cases over three years), and multiple retrials (some cases were sent back to the first instance court 4–5 times). Overall, it can be also considered that the differentiation of claim proceedings and the introduction of simplified proceedings aimed at the prompt resolution of uncomplicated cases was a response to these criticisms.

#94 The improvement of the procedure for reviewing decisions in connection with **newly discovered circumstances** (*Industrial Financial Consortium Investment Metallurgical Union v Ukraine*[194] and *Zheltyakov v Ukraine*[195]), and changes in the procedure for recognising a person as incapacitated or partially incapacitated (*Nataliya Mikhaylenko v Ukraine*[196] and others) are also noteworthy.

#95 The ECtHR case law regarding human rights violations and the **administration of justice in temporarily occupied territories**, as well as in wartime conditions, is of great importance. More than 5,000 complaints against Ukraine concern human rights violations in Crimea and the temporarily occupied territories of the Luhansk and Donetsk regions.[197] In the case *Tsezar and Others v Ukraine*,[198] the

189 *Sovtransavto Holding v Ukraine* App no 48553/99 (ECtHR, 25 July 2002).

190 *Tregubenko v Ukraine* App no 61333/00 (ECtHR, 2 November 2004).

191 *Sebova v Ukraine* App no 4430/04 (ECtHR, 30 July 2009).

192 *Pavlyulynets v Ukraine* App no 70767/01 (ECtHR, 6 September 2005).

193 *Moroz and Others v Ukraine* App no 36545/02 (ECtHR, 21 December 2006).

194 *Industrial Financial Consortium Investment Metallurgical Union v Ukraine* App no 10640/05 (ECtHR, 26 June 2018).

195 *Zheltyakov v Ukraine* App no 4994/04 (ECtHR, 9 June 2011).

196 *Nataliya Mikhaylenko v Ukraine* App no 49069/11 (ECtHR, 30 May 2013).

197 OHCHR, *Report on the Human Rights Situation in Ukraine, 1 August 2022 to 31 January 2023* (Office of the United Nations High Commissioner for Human Rights, 24 March 2023) <https://www.ohchr.org/en/documents/country-reports/report-human-rights-situation-ukraine-1-august-2022-31-january-2023> accessed 2 March 2025; *Ukraine v Russia (re Crimea)* App nos 20958/14 and 38334/18 (ECtHR, 25 June 2024).

198 *Tsezar and Others v Ukraine* App nos 73590/14, 73593/14, 73820/14, 4635/15, 5200/15, 5206/15, and 7289/15) (13 Feb 2018).

ECtHR emphasised that the applicants were not disproportionately restricted in their right to access a court located in government-controlled territory. Accordingly, the transfer of jurisdiction from non-controlled areas to corresponding courts in neighbouring regions under Ukrainian government control was positively assessed.

#96 It is also worth noting that the ECtHR enjoys considerable trust against the backdrop of a relatively low **level of trust** in the national judiciary.

#97 Both crises, the pandemic and the war have had a significant impact on the **digitalisation of the Ukrainian judiciary** and procedural instruments, making this example worth studying and following to some extent.[199] For instance, Ukraine maintains the largest **register of court decisions**, including interim orders, which are openly available to the public, participants, and lawyers.[200] This demonstrates the **transparency** and openness of the judiciary and serves as a basis for studies and further improvements. The introduction of digital services for judiciary purposes in the state-owned system **DIIA** significantly simplifies communication between participants and courts, providing a high level of data protection and reliability of service confirmation. The Ukrainian **e-justice** system is part of the broader concept of e-government, which has developed rapidly in recent years. The introduction of new modules for the e-justice system over the last few years reflects changes in the approaches to judicial service delivery for the citizens of Ukraine. The idea of facilitating easier access to justice for all is commendable. However, the Ukrainian e-justice system does not currently provide for the integration of the judicial system with a network of lawyers who can be easily found and contacted online, with the free legal aid network, or with online dispute resolution tools, including conciliators and mediators. Despite this, all the necessary prerequisites for intensifying such implementation have been created (see more later).

#98 Historically, the concept of private dispute resolution has deep roots in Ukrainian society, with **international commercial arbitration** being a prime example of such a flexible and adaptive mechanism.[201] Even amid the crises of the

---

199 I Izarova, 'Digitalization of Justice in Ukraine: Some Remarks on the Main Goal' in K Gajda-Roszczynialska (ed), *Impact of the COVID-19 Pandemic on Justice Systems: Reconstruction or Erosion of Justice Systems – Case Study and Suggested Solution* (V&R Unipress 2023) 235.

200 I Izarova and others, 'Advancing Sustainable Justice through AI-Based Case Law Analysis' (2024) 7(1) Access to Justice in Eastern Europe 127.

201 Law of Ukraine no 4002-XII of 24 February 1994 'On International Commercial Arbitration'; International Commercial Arbitration Court <https://icac.org.ua/en/> accessed 2 March 2025. See more in V Nekrošius and others, 'Legal, Social and Cultural Prerequisites for the Development of ADR Forms in Lithuania and Ukraine' (2020) 116 Teise 8.

pandemic and war, new and effective tools have been introduced to help parties defend their rights and resolve disputes efficiently. Among the recent changes is the implementation of combined procedures such as 'Arbitration-Mediation-Arbitration' and 'Mediation-Arbitration' since January 2023. The main reason for their introduction was the obstacles posed by crises and the martial law regime. Nevertheless, it is worth mentioning that this aligns with the general concept of out-of-court and amicable dispute resolution, which has been spreading in Ukraine recently.[202] The experience of the **International Commercial Arbitration Court** in Ukraine demonstrates how relatively simple steps taken to navigate crises can lead to the development of fundamental components of a modern judiciary for any rule of law democratic state.

III Influence of *European Institutions: Europeanisation of Ukrainian Procedural Law and Judiciary*: remarks on the latest steps and reflection on Facility Plan for Ukraine

#99 The first significant step towards the **Europeanisation** of Ukraine's procedural legislation occurred after the signing of the **Association Agreement** in 2014.[203] This development resulted from Ukraine's ongoing integration into the European Union and the shift in the social paradigm and the state's development trajectory. This milestone was marked by a **comprehensive reform of procedural law** and all related institutions, with provisions that advanced cooperation in the fields of justice, freedom, and security, including the strengthening of judicial cooperation in civil matters. The over 800-page draft law laid the foundation for Europeanisation of the judiciary, civil procedure, enforcement proceedings, laws on court fees, and other related areas.[204] This statute came into force with the commencement of the new Supreme Court as a cassation instance court on 15 December 2017.

#100 The primary goal of this reform in Ukraine was to align with **European standards of justice**, representing a new paradigm for a country formerly influ-

202 I Izarova and Y Prytyka, 'Evolution and Legal Framework of International Commercial Arbitration in Ukraine' in M Roth and M Geistlinger (eds), *Yearbook on International Arbitration and ADR*, vol VIII (Verlag Österreich 2024) 144.

203 See above n 175.

204 Strategy on development of justice <https://zakon.rada.gov.ua/laws/show/276/2015#Text> accessed 2 March 2025. It is worth noting that the law on the Nationwide Program for the Adaptation of Ukrainian Legislation to the Legislation of the European Union was adopted in 2004, but it did not lead to significant progress. Law of Ukraine no 1629-IV of 18 March 2004 'On the Nationwide Program of Adaptation of the Legislation of Ukraine to the Legislation of the European Union' <https://zakon.rada.gov.ua/laws/show/1629-15#Text> accessed 2 March 2025.

enced by Soviet legal traditions. In particular, Article 2 of the 2017 version of the Civil Procedure Code of Ukraine reflects this objective,[205] outlining the **goals and basic principles of Civil Procedure**, emphasising that the civil justice system's task is the fair, impartial, and timely consideration and resolution of civil cases. This aims to provide effective protection for violated, unrecognised, or disputed rights, freedoms, and interests of individuals and legal entities, as well as the interests of the state. The court and participants in the trial are mandated to prioritise the task of civil justice above any other considerations in the judicial process. For the first time in Ukrainian civil procedure the concept of preventing the abuse of the procedural rights was implemented.

#101 Contrary to the longstanding approach to civil procedure, which focused on the court's case consideration activities with particular emphasis on the neutrality of judges and a formal approach to the outcome, the reform introduced a more **active case management system** with more powerful judicial roles.[206] This new approach encourages judges **to facilitate amicable resolutions** and allows for greater flexibility in selecting the appropriate track for case consideration. The principle of proportionality and the idea of effective protection of civil rights, introduced in the 2017 civil procedure legislation, are among the most significant yet less implemented innovations.[207] These methods allow for improvements in case consideration and resolution, but they also present certain challenges.

#102 Like other Eastern European countries formerly part of the Soviet bloc, Ukraine never had a legislation on **small claims procedure**. In these legal systems, simplified procedures were not related to the amount at stake because the main purpose of civil proceedings was not merely to consider the case and resolve the dispute but to find the truth. In Ukraine, this reform marks the first attempt to differentiate civil proceedings and introduce a special simplified procedure for hearing cases whose value does not exceed a statutory amount. Notably, the 2004 Civil Procedure Code introduced the **payment order** procedure. This was a significant step in the development of Ukraine's judiciary, providing a timely and proportionate mechanism for debt collection and other

205 Law of Ukraine no 2147-VIII of 03.10.2017 'On Amendments to the Commercial Procedural Code of Ukraine, the Civil Procedural Code of Ukraine, the Code of Administrative Legal Proceedings of Ukraine, and other legislative acts' [2017] Official Gazette of Ukraine 96/2921; I Izarova, 'Civil Process Reform During Independence: New Goals and Principles' in Y Prytyka and I Izarova (eds), *Access to Justice in Conditions of Sustainable Development: to the 30th Anniversary of Ukraine's Independence* (Dakor 2021) 32.

206 I Izarova and E Silvestri, 'Case Management Principle in Civil Justice: A Comparative Study of the Legislation of Italy and Ukraine' (2018) 1 Bulletin of Taras Shevchenko National University of Kyiv 19.

207 O Terech, 'Implementation of the Principle of Proportionality in Civil Judiciary: Practice of the ECtHR' (2023) 2 Social Law 67; T Tsuvina, 'The Proportionality Principle in the Civil Court Procedure' (2018) 10 Law of Ukraine 50.

cases. The number of cases processed under this procedure has grown annually by approximately 20% of the total number of cases. It should be noted that the broadest grounds for application were ultimately removed from the CPC after the first year of its implementation, due to widespread violations of participants' rights and manipulations.

#103 However, the implementation of these provisions encountered a fundamental yet almost insurmountable obstacle—the human factor.[208] This issue pertains to the application of new tools by court employees and judges who, for three decades of independence, have been continuously subjected to turbulence, imminent reforms, and instability in various forms—from procedural legislation to political will and the level of **trust in the judiciary**. Despite substantial reshaping and renewal of the high court staff, around seven hundred courts of first and appeal instances retain the same judges who began their careers during the turbulent 1990s. During this period, the selection process for judges and the procedures for determining their qualifications were highly unsatisfactory. As a result, many of the interesting and useful concepts introduced into the new procedural legislation of Ukraine during the 2016–2017 reform remain largely unimplemented.

#104 The newly introduced proceedings for **small claims** consideration in Ukraine serve as a prime example of the legal community's misunderstanding of procedural instruments and their goals. The concept of simplifying the procedure by limiting the claim amount (as outlined in Article 274 of the Civil Procedure Code of Ukraine) was initially difficult for the legal community to grasp. This was due to a combination of complex grounds for its use and both objective and subjective reasons, such as the significance of the claim to the claimant. The early stages of implementation were fraught with difficulties and controversies, marked by numerous appeals against court decisions and restrictions on cassation. The culmination of the small claims saga in Ukraine was the Constitutional Court's decision, which upheld the institution of small cases as com-

---

208 See more in CH van Rhee and B Maan, 'Civil Procedure Reform: The Way Forward' (2020) 4 Access to Justice in Eastern Europe 179. Despite some useful and .. options in newly amended codes of procedural law, court staff quite ignored it in routine work, preferable to behave traditionally. The idea of so called 'judicial services' and general view to the judiciary as for service for citizens is very controversial among staff and conservative academics as well; See more: O Ivanchenko, 'System of Criteria for Evaluating the Effectiveness of Courts During the Provision of Court Services' (2017) 11 Entrepreneurship, Economy and Law 222 and Y Sedyk and I Storozhuk (eds), *Research of the Quality of the Work of Courts: Using the Methodology of Citizen Reporting Cards* (USAID project 'Ukraine: Rule of Law', Tviy Format 2010); USAID, *System for Evaluating the Quality of Court Work: Standards, Criteria, Indicators and Methods: Project* (USAID Project 'Fair Justice', Council of Judges of Ukraine, State Judicial Administration of Ukraine 2014); USAID, *Application of the Court Work Evaluation System: Methodical Guide* (USAID Project 'Fair Justice', Council of Judges of Ukraine, State Judicial Administration of Ukraine 2016).

pliant with the rule of law and the fundamental principles of judicial proceedings as defined by the Constitution of Ukraine. However, the court found the claim limit, approximately 6,000 euros, to be inconsistent with the Constitution, inappropriately reminding the European Small Claims Procedure.[209]

#105 The next stage of the Europeanisation of Ukraine's civil procedural law and judiciary could be the current period of Ukraine's integration into the EU. In 2022, four days after the large-scale war began, Ukraine submitted its application for **EU membership**. In June 2022, the European Commission delivered its Opinion, which the European Council endorsed, granting **candidate status** to Ukraine. In early 2024, the European Parliament and the Council reached a political agreement on the Ukraine Plan, initially proposed by the Commission.[210] Subsequently, the Commission endorsed Ukraine's comprehensive reform and investment strategy, known as the **Ukraine Plan**. The EU established the Ukraine Investment Framework to facilitate investments for the country's recovery and reconstruction.[211]

#106 The 2024–2027 **Ukraine Facility Plan** launch by the EU is a dedicated instrument which will allow the EU to provide Ukraine with financial support in its recovery, reconstruction and modernisation efforts and support Ukraine to make the reforms needed on its path to EU accession.[212] In April 2024, the European Commission endorsed the Ukraine Plan,[213] and Ukraine must implement its recovery and reform plan and also uphold the rule of law and human rights.

#107 In the **EU 2023 report**, it was rightly mentioned that, despite the ongoing Russian aggression, Ukraine has maintained its judiciary's functionality and made

---

209 Prytyka and Kravtsov (n 184); see also 'The Constitutional Court of Ukraine Delivered a Decision in the Case on Guaranteeing the Right to Judicial Protection in Minor Disputes' (*Constitutional Court of Ukraine*, 22 November 2023) <https://ccu.gov.ua/en/novina/constitutional-court-ukraine-delivered-decision-case-guaranteeing-right-judicial-protection> accessed 2 March 2025.

210 Communication from the Commission to the European Parliament, the European Council and the Council: Commission Opinion on Ukraine's application for membership of the European Union COM (2022) 407 final (17 June 2022); European Commission, 'Commission welcomes political agreement on the up to €50 billion Ukraine Facility' (6 February 2024) <https://ec.europa.eu/commission/presscorner/detail/en/ip_24_658> accessed 2 March 2025.

211 European Commission, 'Questions and Answers – A new Ukraine Facility' (20 June 2023) <https://ec.europa.eu/commission/presscorner/detail/en/qanda_23_3353> accessed 20 March 2025.

212 European Union, 'Plan for the Ukraine Facility' (*UA Ukraine Facility*, 2024) <https://www.ukrainefacility.me.gov.ua/en/> accessed 2 March 2025.

213 'Commission endorses Ukraine Plan, paving the way for regular payments under the Ukraine Facility' (European Commission, 15 April 2024) <https://neighbourhood-enlargement.ec.europa.eu/news/commission-endorses-ukraine-plan-paving-way-regular-payments-under-ukraine-facility-2024-04-15_en> accessed March 2025.

significant progress in implementing the 2021 judicial governance reforms and most courts maintained to deliver justice.[214]

#108 Among key points of the reforms are judiciary and **enforcement**, **bankruptcy** and further **digitalisation**. Chapter 3 of the Plan provides a comprehensive analysis of the current state of Ukraine's judiciary and prosecution systems and outlines the main directions for reforms from 2024 to 2027. These reforms, encompassed within Component I of the Ukraine Facility, aim to restore **public and business trust** in the judicial system, enhance judicial efficiency, and align Ukrainian law with European standards.

#109 The reforms under Component I of the Ukraine Facility also include significant changes in **bankruptcy and insolvency regulations**, as well as the enforcement of court decisions. This begins with the adoption of legislation aimed at improving the bankruptcy regime and introducing systems for preventing insolvency and early warning tools for both legal and natural persons, aligning with the EU acquis, particularly Directive (EU) 2019/1023 on preventive restructuring frameworks. The reforms also involve the introduction of simplified bankruptcy procedures for micro, small, and medium-sized enterprises (MSMEs).

#110 It is worth noting that **bankruptcy** in Ukraine has been subjected to quite active reforms. In 1992, a relevant law on bankruptcy was adopted, focusing on a pro-creditor position.[215] This condition met the needs of the challenging period of building an independent state. However, this approach was later shifted to a pro-debtor position, emphasising the restoration of the debtor's solvency. The Bankruptcy Code of Ukraine was adopted in 2019, marking a significant update to the institution and its alignment with European and global standards. In 2023, the next step towards improving the bankruptcy procedure was taken. Specifically, applications from participants in bankruptcy proceedings are now considered within the framework of the bankruptcy case according to simplified or general claim proceedings rules. Furthermore, the implementation of Directive (EU) 2019/1023[216] is expected in the future, which the Ministry of Justice is currently working on.

---

214 European Commission, 'Ukraine 2023 Report: Accompanying the document Communication from the Commission to the European Parliament, the Council, the European Economic and Social Committee and the Committee of the Regions: 2023 Communication on EU Enlargement Policy' (SWD) 2023 699 final.

215 A Biryukov, 'Ukrainian Bankruptcy Law in the Context of Regional and International Developments' (2007) 13 Annual Survey of International & Comparative Law 13; A Engels, O Biryukov and R Chumak, *Bankruptcy in Ukraine: GAP-Analysis (II) Jul 2019 – Aug 2020, Draft Version 25_2020/09/06* (EU-funded Project PRAVO-Justice, 2020) <https://www.pravojustice.eu/storage/app/uploads/public/5f8/550/206/5f85502060694705727020.pdf> accessed 2 March 2025.

216 Directive (EU) 2019/1023 of the European Parliament and of the Council of 20 June 2019 on preventive restructuring frameworks, on discharge of debt and disqualifications, and on measures to in-

#111 Additionally, a roadmap under Component I of the Ukraine Facility will be developed to reform the **enforcement of court decisions** and enhance the functioning of both state and private bailiffs. A law on the enforcement of court decisions concerning property and non-property obligations is expected to be implemented, along with the launch of a data collection system on the enforcement of court decisions. Furthermore, an updated IT system for enforcement proceedings will be operational, facilitating asset tracking, bank account blocking, and debt collection.

#112 It must be acknowledged that the system of **enforcing court decisions** in Ukraine is one of the weakest areas of judiciary. This issue reflects more complex problems than just non-execution, inefficiency of bailiffs, and the significant duration of proceedings. The inability to implement court decisions is often caused by the content of the decision itself and the peculiarities of its adoption, such as the limited application of protective and provisional measures during the court proceedings, and the lack of effective tools for judges and bailiffs to ensure execution, including the freezing of funds in accounts and access to property registers. Additionally, state debts and the absence of funds in the state budget to fulfil such court decisions are also conditions for non-execution. A mix of objective and subjective reasons has caused extremely large-scale enforcement issues since 2017 when the ECtHR consolidated more than 12,000 applications against Ukraine regarding the non-execution of court decisions between 2013 and 2017.[217]

#113 In response to these challenges, in 2016, Ukraine launched the development of a **mixed system of enforcement of court decisions**, which provides for the activities of public and private enforcement officers. As noted in the report, over the years of their existence, private enforcement officers have proven their effectiveness, in particular, in 2019, debts totalling almost UAH 798.6 billion (approximately UAH 17.75 billion) were subject to enforcement. However, only about 2.6% was recovered in favour of the plaintiffs, in particular, due to the efforts of 213 private enforcement officers.[218] Further development and denationalisation

crease the efficiency of procedures concerning restructuring, insolvency and discharge of debt, and amending Directive (EU) 2017/1132 (Directive on restructuring and insolvency) [2019] OJ L172/18.

217 *Burmych and Others v Ukraine* App nos 46852/13, 47786/13, 54125/13 et al (ECtHR, 12 October 2017). Currently we expect more outcomes from the Council of Europe project 'Strengthening Ukrainian Law Enforcement Agencies During War and Post-War Period' (Council of Europe: Implementation of Human Rights, Justice and Legal Co-Operation Standards, 2023) more at <https://www.coe.int/en/web/implementation/ukraine-strengthening-ukrainian-law-enforcement-agencies-during-war-and-post-war-period> accessed 2 March 2025.

218 Association of Private Performers of Ukraine, *5 Steps to Effective Execution of Court Decisions: Conceptual Principles of the Draft Law 'On Executive Proceedings'* (APVU 2020) <https://apvu.com.ua/europacket> accessed 2 March 2025.

of performance is considered desirable in the community and reflecting European values.

#114 Reforming and improving the system of enforcing court decisions in Ukraine should start with a conceptual review of the provisions regarding the consideration and **resolution of debt payment cases by the courts**. The existing procedures for the European Enforcement Order and European Order for Payment contain provisions that can be applied much more broadly than the provisions on court orders and notarial writs of execution under Ukrainian law, which can be used for debt collection. Accordingly, easier access and simplified procedures for collecting small debts should be considered as effective measures on the way of integration.

#115 The enhancement of the automated arrest of debtors' funds is another critical measure according to Component I of the Ukraine Facility. It is noteworthy to remind that during the adoption of the draft law on amendments to the procedural codes in 2017, the article providing for the arrest of funds in the debtor's accounts sparked discussions and unfounded objections from members of parliament, leading to its removal from the draft law. At the same time, understanding the necessity of introducing effective mechanisms for the automatic arrest of funds in the debtor's account, the Ministry of Justice developed subordinate regulatory acts, including the adoption of relevant orders and amendments in 2019 and 2021.[219] Subsequently, it would be logical to expand the list of grounds and improve the procedure for such automation and align the legislation with Regulation (EU) No 655/2014.[220]

#116 The reforms under Component I of the Ukraine Facility also include the **digitalisation** of the judicial system. There are plans for a significant reengineering of business processes, supported by digital transformation, to improve the efficiency, quality, and accessibility of judicial management. These reforms collectively aim to rebuild trust in the judicial system and enhance its overall functionality. This involves expanding access to justice during wartime, improving the transparency, efficiency, and effectiveness of court operations, and reducing operational costs. Additionally, the reforms aim to facilitate evidence-based policy-making within the judicial system.

219 Order of the Ministry Justice of Ukraine No 1203/5 of 16 April 2019 'On the approval of the Procedure for automated seizure of funds/electronic money of debtors on accounts/electronic wallets opened by providers of payment services for account maintenance, issuers of electronic money' [2019] Official Gazette of Ukraine 34/1237; Order of the Ministry of Justice of Ukraine No 4464/5 of 13 December 2021 'On the approval of the Amendments to the Procedure for Automated Seizure of Debtors' Funds in Bank Accounts' [2021] Official Gazette of Ukraine 98/6477.

220 Regulation (EU) No 655/2014 of the European Parliament and of the Council of 15 May 2014 establishing a European Account Preservation Order procedure to facilitate cross-border debt recovery in civil and commercial matters [2014] OJ L189/59.

#117 It is noteworthy, that in recent years, Ukraine has made significant strides in digitalisation, driven by challenges such as the pandemic and war, which highlighted the strengths and weaknesses of digital systems. One notable achievement is the **'DIIA' service**, launched in 2020, which mediates the relationship between government agencies and citizens by providing access to identification documents and a range of public services. As of 2024, DIIA was used by 20 million people, majority of Ukrainian population. Among digital services currently introduced are court penalties and court cases; enforcement procedures notifications were already available in the app.[221]

#118 First steps of **digitalisation of judicial services** in Ukraine started more than decades ago with the Automated Court Document Management System, operating since 2011, which ensured the distribution of cases and provided information on case statuses. In 2017, the Unified Judicial Information and Telecommunication System (UJITS), which supports electronic record keeping, centralised document storage, and real-time video conferencing, was introduced. UJITS aims to enhance transparency, efficiency, and access to justice. It was announced a prominent perspective, which are slowly implemented during last years. Additionally, the unique Unified State Register of Judgments allows for the analysis and processing of over a million anonymised judgments.[222]

#119 **Enforcement proceedings**, traditionally a weak point in Ukrainian justice, have also seen digital advancements. The automated enforcement system facilitates the collection and processing of enforcement proceedings, and the Unified Register of Debtors helps prevent the alienation of property by debtors. According to the Component I of the Ukraine Facility, there will be an expansion of the functionalities of the automated enforcement system and the integration of the **Unified Debtors Register** with other registers to prevent debtors from disposing of their property. Nevertheless, despite announced implementation of the enforcement register with the UJITS, there is no any significant achievement yet, as well as openly available information on enforcement outcomes.

#120 The **digitalisation** of judiciary in Ukraine faces obstacles. Despite efforts, the large size of the state and the number of employees in the justice sector have slowed implementation, in terms of necessary computer equipment available in courts, trainings of the staff etc despite over decades of progress with permanent digitalisation of judicial services. The most important disadvantage is the lack of machine-readable formats for documents, accompanied by the lack of

221 DIIA: Government services online <https://diia.gov.ua> accessed 2 March 2025.

222 'Functioning of the Unified Judicial Information and Communication System' (State Judicial Administration of Ukraine, 2024) <https://dsa.court.gov.ua/dsa/inshe/func_ecits> accessed 2 March 2025; Unified State Register of Court Decisions <https://reyestr.court.gov.ua>.

interaction between various providers of legal services and courts, such as attorneys, mediators, and the enforcement register.[223] This makes the e-justice system of Ukraine quite disorganised and ineffective for objective and transparent monitoring of the judiciary and access to justice. During wartime, the **e-justice system**'s weaknesses became apparent, with access to key services temporarily suspended. This underscores the need for robust digital infrastructure to ensure continuity.

#121 While Ukraine has made notable progress in judicial digitalisation, significant work remains to fully integrate and optimise systems. The focus should be on ensuring broad accessibility and **effective implementation** to achieve the goals of **e-justice**, as well as on integration with the EU portal of e-justice. Finally, it is vital to achieve the necessary level of interaction with **e-Codex** and enable Ukrainian public services in the area of justice to be exposed to a cross-border dimension with other EU member states by adopting the Regulation (EU) 2022/850 on a computerised system for the cross-border electronic exchange of data in the area of judicial cooperation in civil and criminal matters (e-CODEX system).[224]

#122 Real challenge for Ukrainian judiciary will be **the integration with a genuine European area of justice,** where it supposes to exercise rights fully for all. The **judicial cooperation** in civil matters in particular between various Ukrainian and EU countries; authorities aimed at mutual recognition and enforcement of foreign judgments, access to justice and harmonisation of national legislation depend on joint efforts of academics and practitioners from both sides put together for facilitating reforms and further movement to announced goals.

#123 The **EU 'Pravo-Justice' Project** supports Ukraine's justice sector reforms across four main areas: prosecutorial reform and accountability for international crimes, judicial reform, enforcement of court decisions and protection of property rights, and support for EU integration in the justice sector. This involves enhancing efficiency, ensuring accountability, providing expert support, strengthening institutional capacity, and promoting dialogue for EU accession.[225]

#124 The **USAID-funded 'Fair Justice'** project has been operating in Ukraine since October 2011. It was developed to continue the initiatives of the USAID 'Ukraine: Rule of Law' (UROL) project, which ran from 2006 to 2011. In collaboration with the Ukrainian government and civil society, the 'Fair Justice' project supports the enhancement of key legislation to complete judicial reforms, improve judicial

223 Izarova and others (n 200) 127.

224 Regulation (EU) 2022/850 of the European Parliament and of the Council of 30 May 2022 on a computerised system for the cross-border electronic exchange of data in the area of judicial cooperation in civil and criminal matters (e-CODEX system), and amending Regulation (EU) 2018/1726 [2022] OJ L150/1.

225 EU Project PRAVO-Justice <https://www.pravojustice.eu/en> accessed 2 March 2025.

practices and procedures, and establish a more efficient, accountable, and transparent judiciary.

#125 The **USAID 'Justice for All'** program builds on the successes of previous USAID programs "Fair Justice" and 'New Justice'. It coordinates closely with Ukrainian partners, USAID and US Government projects, and other international donor initiatives in Ukraine. Running from 1 October 2021 to 30 September 2026, the program aims to promote justice for everyone seeking to protect their rights. It addresses legal issues and needs of Ukrainians by improving the justice system, enhancing justice services, and engaging society. The program supports Ukraine in advancing people-centred justice in close cooperation with Ukrainian and international partners.[226]

#126 Overall, these projects highlight USAID's long-term commitment to **advancing justice** and the rule of law in Ukraine through comprehensive reforms, institutional improvements, and stakeholder engagement. They also shed light on the origins of many proposed legislative initiatives and other reforms in Ukraine in recent years.

IV Summary

#127 Ukraine is actively reforming its legal and judicial systems to align with European procedural law as part of its EU integration efforts. Influenced by its historical background and legacy, Ukraine's legal framework is slowly but steadily transitioning to incorporate recommendations from the Council of Europe and the ECtHR case law into general legal practice and legislative policy. The ECtHR has significantly impacted Ukrainian civil justice through landmark cases addressing systemic issues like non-execution of court decisions and unreasonable delays in legal proceedings. These cases prompted complex reforms. Digitalisation efforts have improved transparency and access to justice, exemplified by the extensive public access to court decisions and the development of electronic justice services.

#128 The 2014 EU–Ukraine Association Agreement marked a pivotal step, leading to comprehensive reforms of procedural law to meet European standards. The 2017 overhaul introduced active case management, enhanced judicial roles, and principles like proportionality and effective protection of civil rights. Despite these advances, challenges remain due to entrenched practices within the legal community and some level of resistance to change.

226 'The USAID 'Justice for All' Program' (High Qualification Commission of Judges of Ukraine 2021) < https://www.vkksu.gov.ua/en/page/usaid-justice-all-program-0> accessed 2 March 2025.

#129 The Ukraine Facility Plan as a significant initiative focuses on judiciary reforms, enforcement of court decisions, bankruptcy law alignment with EU directives, and extensive digitalisation of the judicial system. These reforms aim to restore public trust, enhance efficiency, and ensure legal compatibility with the EU. The plan includes improving the enforcement of court decisions, integrating digital systems like the Unified Judicial Information and Telecommunication System, and aligning with EU regulations such as e-CODEX.

#130 International support from EU projects like 'Pravo-Justice' and USAID-funded programs is instrumental in facilitating these reforms through expertise, capacity building, and promoting dialogue for EU accession. However, Ukraine still faces obstacles such as ineffective enforcement mechanisms, incomplete digital integration, and the need for cultural shifts in judicial practices. Ongoing efforts are directed at overcoming these challenges to fully integrate Ukraine into the European legal and judicial landscape.

#131 The experiences of other candidate states could provide more insights to achieve positive effects, but further collaboration and knowledge exchange are necessary to address Ukraine's unique challenges.

E Conclusions

#132 The pursuit of the EU membership has profoundly influenced the legal and judicial reforms undertaken by Albania, Serbia, and Ukraine. While each country operates within its unique historical and political context, their shared objective of aligning with EU standards has led to notable similarities in their reform efforts. At the same time, differences in their approaches reflect distinct national challenges and priorities.

#133 At the time of writing, Serbia has been experiencing waves of student-led civil protests against corruption, which have significantly disrupted the functioning of the judiciary and which is expected to have a detrimental impact on the accession negotiation process. Notably, the lack of genuine support of the EU key institutions (with the exception of several MEPs) for the civil protests – at the heart of which are the requirements for the respect for the rule of law, including independent judiciary – have the potential of further alienating the EU from the Serbian citizens and deepen the anti-EU sentiment. This is all the more so given the brutality of the force by Serbian authorities applied to those protesting peacefully. Therefore, while the most recent judicial reforms may appear as a step towards EU accession theoretically, when translated into the specific Serbian socio-political context – especially in light of the currently turbulent political situation in the country – and defective culture of judicial independence, its path to EU remains wobbly and uncertain.

#134 The beginning of the **journeys towards the EU membership** for all three countries started in the early 1990s. Albania has since aspired to align itself with EU, but political instability and corruption initially hindered progress toward **European integration**. The adoption of a new Constitution in 1998 marked a turning point, leading to Albania's application for EU membership in 2009. After achieving candidate status in 2014, the screening process started in 2022. Judicial reform's success was central to Albania's efforts to meet EU criteria, including in reshaping its civil procedural law. While Serbia's efforts toward European integration are rooted in its historical legal traditions influenced by European models that predate the EU, it was following the disintegration of Yugoslavia in the 1990s, that Serbia officially established its commitment to EU integrations. Key milestones include the signing of the SAA in 2008 and attaining the candidate status in 2012. Judicial reform has been a focal point in Serbia's accession negotiations, aiming to enhance judicial independence and efficiency and strengthen the rule of law. Similarly, Ukraine has sought closer ties with Europe since gaining independence in 1991, culminating in the EU–Ukraine Association Agreement in 2014. The agreement prioritises harmonising Ukrainian laws with EU legislation and strengthening the judiciary. Ukraine faces the challenge of overcoming historical influences and resources that undermined judicial independence. Current reforms, particularly under the Ukraine Facility Plan, aim to modernise its legal and judicial institutions in line with EU expectations.

#135 As the previous discussion hopefully demonstrates, there is a striking resemblance among the three countries in terms of their emphasis on strengthening the **rule of law** and ensuring **judicial independence**, as well as the measures undertaken in this regard. Recognising that an autonomous and efficient judiciary is fundamental to EU integration, Albania, Serbia, and Ukraine have prioritised reforms aimed at achieving these objectives. This shared focus is directly linked to the requirements outlined in Chapters 23 and 24 of the EU accession negotiations.

#136 One of the areas significantly affected by justice reforms in Albania and Ukraine is **civil procedural law**. The Albanian Code of Civil Procedure (CCP) underwent a major amendment in 2017, introducing substantial changes aimed at enhancing judicial efficiency and aligning with EU standards. Similarly, Ukraine overhauled its Civil Procedure Code in the same year, introducing principles such as proportionality, case management, and simplified proceedings to improve judicial efficiency. However, while Albania's amendments brought its procedural laws closer to EU secondary legislation, Ukraine's new rules, though modernising its civil procedure, diverged in certain aspects from EU secondary law. This divergence reflects Ukraine's unique legal challenges and the necessity to tailor reforms to its specific context. The multiple Civil Procedural Law Act (CPLA) reforms in Serbia have been a point of significant contention, resulting in overall less radical changes than projected, however, at the same time strongly focusing on the measures aimed at improving judicial efficiency, similarly to its counterparts. It is yet to be seen how many of the objectives set by the Serbian government are in fact going to be met in the next wave of reforms of the CPLA and related instruments.

#137 In terms of procedural reforms, there are two additional points of convergence – and challenges – among all three countries that should be noted. These include the promotion of ADR and the objective of developing effective collective protection mechanisms in the area of consumer law.

#138 With the view to alleviate court burdens and enhance access to justice, all three countries have enacted the relevant legislation to encourage **ADR**. In Albania, despite the introduction of provisions encouraging mediation and continuous training of judges, ADR remains underdeveloped and underutilised. Serbia faces a similar situation; although mediation has been reformed to align with EU law, its practical application remains limited. Serbia has attempted to incentivise mediation through legislative measures, such as postponing or exempting court fees for the parties who resolve disputes amicably before the first court hearing. Ukraine has also adopted similar measures to encourage amicable settlements, yet the uptake of mediation in civil and commercial matters remains low. These shared challenges highlight a common obstacle in fully integrating ADR into legal practice. Cultural factors, lack of awareness, and insufficient infrastructure contribute to the underutilisation of mediation, despite legislative efforts. The situation suggests that merely aligning laws with EU legislation is insufficient without accompanying measures to promote and facilitate the use of ADR among legal professionals and the public.

#139 Furthermore, developing effective collective protection mechanisms is essential for safeguarding consumer rights and ensuring access to justice in alignment with European Union (EU) standards. In Serbia, **collective protection of consumer rights** is primarily conducted through administrative proceedings, with the competent ministry responsible for determining violations of collective interests. This approach has raised concerns regarding its effectiveness, particularly in securing compensation for affected consumers. As a result, there have been calls to reintroduce collective actions, reinstating provisions that existed between 2010 and 2013 to enhance judicial recourse for consumers. Albania similarly lacks comprehensive legal frameworks for collective actions, limiting consumers' ability to enforce their rights collectively. The absence of such mechanisms hinders effective consumer protection and falls short of EU expectations for member and candidate countries in providing accessible justice for collective grievances. Ukraine faces comparable challenges, with no extensive mechanisms for collective actions in civil and commercial matters. To address these gaps, innovative approaches are being considered within its administrative justice system – typical and model administrative cases. Although not traditional collective actions, these initiatives aim to enhance efficiency and consistency in handling numerous similar cases.

#140 All three countries have undertaken significant reforms to improve **access to justice**, including the introduction and development of free legal aid. However, challenges remain, such as limited public awareness of these services, inconsistent implementation, and capacity constraints among service providers. Addressing these gaps is essential for ensuring equal access to justice, a core EU value.

#141 The judiciary reforms and EU integration processes in these countries underscore the importance of sustained **international support and collaboration**. By aligning their legal frameworks and adopting common practices, candidate countries can collectively advance toward EU membership while contributing to the broader goal of establishing a unified European area of justice. These efforts highlight the need for a holistic approach that combines legislative reforms, institutional strengthening, training programs, and regional collaboration to create lasting and effective changes.

#142 **Judicial training** emerges as pivotal issues shared by Albania, Serbia, and Ukraine in their paths toward EU integration. Enhancing the skills and knowledge of judges, prosecutors, and court staff is critical to aligning judicial practices with EU standards. In all three countries, judicial training institutions have been supported by EU projects, yet the need for further capacity-building, particularly in areas such as European procedural law and ADR, remains evident. Strengthening these programs can improve judicial efficiency, foster a stronger rule of law, and advance the broader goals of EU integration.

#143 As Ukraine continues to navigate its challenging path toward EU membership, it will benefit greatly from studying the experiences of other candidate countries and leveraging opportunities for joint initiatives. Similarly, Albania and Serbia can draw from Ukraine's recent advances in judicial digitalisation and its reforms under the Ukraine Facility Plan. Together, these countries can set a powerful precedent for achieving judicial and procedural harmonisation, ultimately fostering a stronger and **more inclusive European Union**.

References

'"You Have the Right!" – Promoting the Free Legal Aid Campaign' (*WeBalkans.eu*, 22 June 2023) available at <https://webalkans.eu/en/news/you-have-the-right-promoting-the-free-legal-aid-campaign/> accessed 2 March 2025.

'Dhjetor '90, Ëndrra që na jep forcë për të punuar për Shqipërinë e gjeneratave të tjera' (8 December 2013) <https://www.kryeministria.al/newsroom/dhjetor-90-endrra-qe-na-jep-force-per-te-punuar-per-shqiperine-e-gjeneratave-te-tjera/> accessed 2 March 2025.

'Legislation During the Days of Soviet Power in Ukraine (1920–1990)' (*Institute of Civil Society*, 18 July 2011) < https://www.csi.org.ua/publications/zakonotvorennya-za-doby-radyanskoyi-vl/> accessed 2 March 2025.

'The Constitutional Court of Ukraine Delivered a Decision in the Case on Guaranteeing the Right to Judicial Protection in Minor Disputes' (*Constitutional Court of Ukraine*, 22 November 2023) <https://ccu.gov.ua/en/novina/constitutional-court-ukraine-delivered-decision-case-guaranteeing-right-judicial-protection> accessed 2 March 2025.

Alihodžić J and Duraković A, 'Zakon o međunarodnom privatnom pravu u Bosni i Hercegovini – Retrospektiva i perspektiva normativnog uređenja' (2023) 1 Zbornik radova Pravnog fakulteta u Tuzli 53.

Andriiovych Zhuravel V and others (eds), *Legal Science and Legislation of Ukraine: The European Vector of Development in the Conditions of Martial Law* (Pravo 2023).

Babović Vuksanović B, 'Revision (Second Appeal on the Points of Law) in Serbian Litigation Proceedings' (2023) 4 Strani pravni život 707.

Bataveljić D, 'Novi ustavni i zakonski okvir pravosuđa Republike Srbije posle reforme iz 2022. godine' (2023) Zbornik radova 'Usklađivanje pravnog sistema Srbije sa standardima EU' (Pravni fakultet Univerziteta u Kragujevcu) 105.

Bilas I, *The Repressive and Punitive System in Ukraine, 1917–1953: Socio-Political and Historical-Legal Analysis*, vol 1–2, (Lybid, Viisko Ukrainy 1994).

Biryukov A, 'Ukrainian Bankruptcy Law in the Context of Regional and International Developments' (2007) 13 Annual Survey of International & Comparative Law 13.

Bode J and Peppo E, 'Issues of Implementation of the Fair Trial in the Albanian System: Analysis in the Framework of the Constitutional Court and ECHR's Jurisprudence on Albania's Cases' (2022) 11(6) Academic Journal of Interdisciplinary Studies 59.

Bogdani M and Canco M, 'Private Enforcement of Competition Law: Albanian Challenges in Reflection of the EU Requirements' (2021) 1(8) SEE Law Journal Special Edition 54.

Borysovych Usenko I (ed), *Judicial Power in Ukraine: Historical Origins, Regularities, Peculiarities of Development* (Naukova dumka 2014).

Bregu M and Gjinko J, 'The Impact of the European Union on the Endorsement of the Justice Reform in Albania' (2024) 13(3) Academic Journal of Interdisciplinary Studies 312.

Bushati A, *Europianizimi i të Drejtës Ndërkombëtare Private dhe Ndikimet në Legjislacionin Shqiptar të së Drejtës Ndërkombëtare Private* (DPhil thesis, University of Tirana 2016).

Çinari S, 'Zbatimi I Ndryshimeve Të Kodit Të Procedurës Civile Mbi Paditë Me Vlerë Të Vogël' in P Broka, S Çinari and L Ikonomi (eds), *Monitorimi i zbatimit të ndryshimeve të Kodit të Procedurës Civile për aksesin në drejtësi: Afati i arsyeshëm dhe paditë e vogla* (Fondacioni Shoqëria e Hapur për Shqipërinë 2020) 19.

Ćirić J, 'Evropsko viđenje srpske reforme pravosuđa' in D Dimitrijević and B Miljuš (eds), *Harmonizacija zakonodavstva Republike Srbije sa pravom Evropske unije (II)* (Institut za međunarodnu politiku i privredu, Institut za uporedno pravo, Hans Zajdel Fondacija 2012) 117.

Council of Europe, 'Report on a Mission to Ukraine for Bilateral Consultations with Ukrainian Authorities Concerning the Improvement of Enforcement Proceedings (for the Execution of Judgments of the European Court of Human Rights Yuriy Nikolayevich Ivanov v Ukraine and Burmych and others v Ukraine)' (August 2018) <https://rm.coe.int/report-on-a-mission-to-ukraine/16808f234c> accessed 2 March 2025.

Čvorović D, 'Reform of Judiciary System in Serbia – Compliance with European Standards or Not?' in *Collection of Papers from the Conference 'Controversies of the Contemporary Law'* (East Sarajevo 2022) 466.

Đorđević S, 'Kratak osvrt na Hašku konvenciju o priznanju i izvršenju stranih sudskih odluka u građanskim ili trgovačkim stvarima iz 2019' in S Soković (ed), *Usklađivanje pravnog sistema Srbije sa standardima EU* (Kragujevac 2021) 407.

EBRD in cooperation with IDLO, 'Comparative Study of the Legal and Institutional Frameworks and Best Practices on Commercial Mediation with Recommendations for the Republic of Serbia' (June 2021).

Engels A, Biryukov O and Chumak R, *Bankruptcy in Ukraine: GAP-Analysis (II) Jul 2019 – Aug 2020, Draft Version 25_2020/09/06* (EU-funded Project PRAVO-Justice, 2020) <https://www.pravojustice.eu/storage/app/uploads/public/5f8/550/206/5f8550206069470572 7020.pdf> accessed 2 March 2025.

EU For Justice: Support for Chapter 23, 'Booklet on Project Achievements: Judiciary and Fundamental Rights in the Context of Chapter 23 Accession Negotiations' (23 September 2020).

EU Za Tebe, 'Access to Justice for All -Free Legal Aid' (11 April 2024) <https://www.euzatebe.rs/en/news/access-to-justice-for-all-free-legal-aid> accessed 2 March 2025.

Flejszar R, Izarova I and Vebraite V, 'Access to Justice in Small Claims Procedure: Comparative Study of Civil Procedure in Lithuania, Poland and Ukraine' (2019) 9 International Journal of Procedural Law 97.

Government of the Republic of Serbia, 'Negotiating Position of the Republic of Serbia for Intergovernmental Conference on Accession of the Republic of Serbia to the European Union For Chapter 23 Judiciary and Fundamental Rights' (1 January 2016) available at <https://www.mei.gov.rs/upload/documents/pristupni_pregovori/pregovaracke_pozicije/ch_23_negotiation_position.pdf> accessed 2 March 2025.

—— 'Judicial Development Strategy for the Period 2020–2025' (July 2020).

Ivanchenko O, 'System of Criteria for Evaluating the Effectiveness of Courts During the Provision of Court Services' (2017) 11 Entrepreneurship, Economy and Law 222.

Ivanovych Ishchuk S, 'Civil Society in the Conditions of the European Integration Development of Ukraine: Theoretical and Legal Aspect' (DPhil thesis, King Danylo University 2021).

Izarova I and others, 'Advancing Sustainable Justice through AI-Based Case Law Analysis' (2024) 7(1) Access to Justice in Eastern Europe 127.

Izarova I and Prytyka Y, 'Evolution and Legal Framework of International Commercial Arbitration in Ukraine' in M Roth and M Geistlinger (eds), *Yearbook on International Arbitration and ADR*, vol VIII (Verlag Österreich 2024) 144.

Izarova I and Silvestri E, 'Case Management Principle in Civil Justice: A Comparative Study of the Legislation of Italy and Ukraine' (2018) 1 Bulletin of Taras Shevchenko National University of Kyiv 19.

Izarova I, 'Civil Process Reform During Independence: New Goals and Principles' in Y Prytyka and I Izarova (eds), *Access to Justice in Conditions of Sustainable Development: to the 30th Anniversary of Ukraine's Independence* (Dakor 2021) 32.

—— 'Digitalization of Justice in Ukraine: Some Remarks on the Main Goal' in K Gajda-Roszczynialska (ed), *Impact of the COVID-19 Pandemic on Justice Systems: Reconstruction or Erosion of Justice Systems – Case Study and Suggested Solution* (V&R Unipress 2023) 235.

Jessel-Holst C, 'EU Harmonization of Private Law in South-East European Countries' in E Kurzinsky-Singer and R Kulms (eds), *Ukrainian Private Law and the European Area of Justice* (Mohr Siebeck 2019) 309.

Kabashi V, *The ECHR and the Western Balkans: Bringing the* Convention *Home* (EIZ Publishing 2023).

Kaplina O and Tumanyants A, 'ECtHR Decisions that Influenced the Criminal Procedure of Ukraine' (2021) 4 Access to Justice in Eastern Europe 102.

Khotynska-Nor O, *Theory and Practice of Judicial Reform in Ukraine* (Pravova yednist', Alerta 2016).

—— 'Theoretical, Legal and Praxeological Principles of Judicial Reform in Ukraine' (DPhil thesis, Taras Shevchenko National University of Kyiv 2017).

Kneževic Bojović A and Reljanović M, 'Reforma pravosuđa' in A Rabrenović and J Ćeranić (eds), *Usklađivanje prava Republike Srbije sa pravnim tekovinama EU: Prioriteti, problemi, perspective* (Institut za uporedno pravo 2012) 89.

Komarov V and Tsuvina T, 'The Impact of the ECHR and the Case Law of the ECtHR on Civil Procedure in Ukraine' (2021) 4 Access to Justice in Eastern Europe 79.

Kozjubra M, 'The Tendencies of Development of the Sources of Law of Ukraine in the Context of the European Law-Integration Processes' (2004) 26 NaUKMA Research Papers: Law 3.

Kulchytskyi S, *Communism in Ukraine: The First Decade (1919–1928)* (Osnovy 1996).

Leonidivna Bogachova L, 'The Influence of the Council of Europe Law on the National Legal System of Ukraine' (2014) 28 State Building and Local Government 56.

Leonovych Samsin I and Vitaliivna Kazakevich P, *Organizational and Legal Cooperation of the Judicial Authorities of Ukraine with the Institutions of the Council of Europe* (Helvetica 2019).

Marković-Bajalović D, 'Sporna pitanja izvršenja stranih sudskih odluka' in Slobodan Perović (ed), *Sudski postupak – pravda i pravičnost: međunarodna naučna konferencija: zbornik radova 35. susreta Kopaoničke škole prirodnog prava* (Kopaonik 2023) 477.

Mazepa I, *Bolshevism and the Occupation of Ukraine: Socio-Economic Reasons for the Immaturity of the Power of the Ukrainian Revolution* (Lviv 1922).

Mezenivna Bakayanova N, 'Functional and Organizational Foundations of the Legal Profession of Ukraine' (DPhil thesis, National University 'Odesa Juridical Academy' 2017).

Mykolaiovych Kostyuchenko Y, *Legal Regulation of Association Relations between Ukraine and the European Union* (Kyiv University 2019).

Nekrošius V and others, 'Legal, Social and Cultural Prerequisites for the Development of ADR Forms in Lithuania and Ukraine' (2020) 116 Teise 8.

OHCHR, *Report on the Human Rights Situation in Ukraine, 1 August 2022 to 31 January 2023* (Office of the United Nations High Commissioner for Human Rights, 24 March 2023) <https://www.ohchr.org/en/documents/country-reports/report-human-rights-situation-ukraine-1-august-2022-31-january-2023> accessed 2 March 2025.

Oleksandrovych Potilchak B, 'The Soviet Court and Justice Departments (Second Half of 1930-mid 1940-ies): Reception in the Modern Russian Historical-Legal Science' (2014) 28 Uzhhorod National University Herald, Series: Law 38.

Oleksiivna Kresina I (ed), *Strategic Priorities of Political and Legal Development of Ukraine in the Context of European Integration* (Norma Prava 2024).

OSCE, 'Training of Trainers Guide for Judges and Prosecutors on Trafficking in Human Beings' (19 December 2023) <https://www.osce.org/presence-in-albania/560804> accessed 2 March 2025.

Pavlović M, *Pravna evropeizacija Srbije, 1804–1914* (Kragujevac 2008).

Petrivna Demchik N, 'Judicial Reform in the Conditions of European Integration Processes' (2023) 5 New Ukrainian Law 73

Popović D, 'Uticaj Evropske konvencije za zaštitu ljudskih prava i osnovnih sloboda na sprsko zakonodavrstvo i sudsku praksu' (2011) 2 Pravni zapisi 356.

Prytyka Y and Kravtsov S, 'Small Claims in Civil Procedure in Ukraine: Panacea or an Obstacle to Access Justice' (2023) (Spec) Revista Jurídica Portucalense 375.

Rakić Vodinelić V, 'Bio jednom Zakon o parničnom postupku . . . ' (*Peščanik*, 25 May 2021) < https://pescanik.net/bio-jednom-zakon-o-parnicnom-postupku/> accessed 2 March 2025.

Rhee van CH and Maan B, 'Civil Procedure Reform: The Way Forward' (2020) 4 Access to Justice in Eastern Europe 179.

Rhee van CH, 'Mandatory Mediation before Litigation in Civil and Commercial Matters: A European Perspective' (2021) 4(12) Access to Justice in Eastern Europe 7.

Sedyk Y and Storozhuk I (eds), *Research of the Quality of the Work of Courts: Using the Methodology of Citizen Reporting Cards* (USAID project 'Ukraine: Rule of Law', Tviy Format 2010).

Skara G, *Europeanisation of Private Enforcement of Competition Law, the Case of Albania* (Springer 2022).

Special Parliamentary Commission on Judicial Reform, 'Analysis of Justice System in Albania' (2015) < https://www.reformanedrejtesi.al/sites/default/files/dokumenti_shqip_0.pdf> accessed 2 March 2025.

Stanivuković M, '10 razloga zašto bi trebalo menjati Zakon o rešavanju sukoba zakona' (2020) 4 Branič 17.

Terech O, 'Implementation of the Principle of Proportionality in Civil Judiciary: Practice of the ECtHR' (2023) 2 Social Law 67.

Terlyuk I, 'Political and Legal Nature of the Soviet Statehood in Ukraine as an Occupation' (2022) 5 Law of Ukraine 103.

Top Channel Report, 'Vlahutin: Reforma në drejtësi, kushti kryesor për integrimin' (9 October 2015) <https://top-channel.tv/2015/10/09/vlahutin-reforma-ne-drejtesi-kushti-kryesor-per-integrimin/> accessed 2 March 2025.

Tsuvina T and others, 'The Implementation of Consensual Tenet in Modern Civil Procedure: Comparative Analysis of Court-Connected Settlement Procedures Applied in Austria, Lithuania, and Ukraine' (2024) 7(1) Access to Justice in Eastern Europe 26.

Tsuvina T, 'The Proportionality Principle in the Civil Court Procedure' (2018) 10 Law of Ukraine 50.

Tynchenko Y, *The First Ukrainian-Bolshevik War (December 1917 – March 1918)* (I Krypiakevych Institute of Ukrainian Studies 1996).

USAID, *Application of the Court Work Evaluation System: Methodical Guide* (USAID Project 'Fair Justice', Council of Judges of Ukraine, State Judicial Administration of Ukraine 2016).

—— *System for Evaluating the Quality of Court Work: Standards, Criteria, Indicators and Methods: Project* (USAID Project 'Fair Justice', Council of Judges of Ukraine, State Judicial Administration of Ukraine 2014).

Volodymyrivna Shkuratenko O, 'International Recognition of Ukraine due to the Election of the Right to Membership in the UN (Historical Review)' (2001) 12 Law of Ukraine 142.

Vukadinović R, 'Od ugledanja na jevropejske uzore do regionalne harmonizacije – druga strana medalje' in *Zbornik radova: Odnos prava u regionu i prava Evropske unije* (Pravni fakultet Univerziteta u Istočnom Sarajevu 2015) 37.

Vukadinovic S, 'Evropsko potrošačko pravo i njegov uticaj na razvoj potrošačkog prava Srbije' in J Ćeranić, V Đurić and A Višekruna (eds), *65 godina od Rimskih ugovora: Evropska unija i perspective evropskih integracija Srbije* (Institut za uporedno parvo 2022) 189.

Vulić Law, 'Draft Law on Amendments to the Law on Civil Procedure: Challenges and Solutions' (17 June 2021) <https://vuliclaw.com/2021/06/17/draft-law-on-amendments-to-the-law-on-civil-procedure-challenges-and-solutions/> accessed 2 March 2025.

Yanevskyi D, *Political Systems of Ukraine 1917–1920: Creation Attempts and Reasons for Defeat* (Dukh i litera 2003).

Yevhenovych Marmazov V and Slavovych Pilyaev I, *Ukraine in the Political and Legal Space of the Council of Europe: Experience and Problems* (Venturi 1999).

Živković M, 'Rad na novom Zakonu o međunarodnom privatnom pravu Republike Srbije – početne dileme i aktuelno stanje – Nacionalni izveštaj za Srbiju' in B Bordaš and M Stanivuković (eds), *Zbornik radova sa sedme Konferencije za međunarodno privatno pravo – Proširenje Evropskog pravosudnog prostora na države članice CEFTA* (2010 Novi Sad) 185.

—— 'Rad na novom Zakonu o međunarodnom privatnom pravu Republike Srbije – početne dileme i aktuelno stanje – Nacionalni izveštaj za Srbiju' in B Bordaš and M Stanivuković (eds), *Zbornik radova sa sedme Konferencije za međunarodno privatno pravo – Proširenje Evropskog pravosudnog prostora na države članice CEFTA* (2010 Novi Sad) 175.

Magdalena Tulibacka,* Peter C.H. Chan*, Mohamed Paleker*, and Eduardo Silva de Freitas*

Chapter 25 European Civil Procedure From a Non-European Perspective

A Introduction

#1 Significant developments have taken place in civil procedure over the past decade with the goal of enhancing access to justice. The developments are not limited to Europe, as procedural innovations and reforms are observed and engaged with in other regions. This chapter examines civil justice from a non-European perspective, focusing on selected jurisdictions: the United States, Brazil, China, and South Africa. Key areas of focus differ between these jurisdictions, but they largely include case management, digitalisation of justice, public interest litigation, litigation funding, alternative dispute resolution, and the role of specialised courts. Whenever this is possible, the chapter's authors explore how these jurisdictions engage with European procedural traditions, innovations, and reforms—whether through influence, divergence, or mutual learning in shaping their own procedural frameworks.

B United States

I Introduction

#2 The U.S. civil justice system is well known for robust access to justice, for entrepreneurial lawyers funding individual and class litigation, and for aggregate

*Corresponding author: Magdalena Tulibacka, Emory University School of Law, e-mail: magdalena.tulibacka@emory.edu
*Corresponding author: Peter C.H. Chan, City University of Hong Kong, e-mail: pchchan@cityu.edu.hk
*Corresponding author: Mohamed Paleker, Department of Private Law, University of Cape Town, e-mail: mohamed.paleker@uct.ac.za
*Corresponding author: Eduardo Silva de Freitas, Erasmus University Rotterdam, within the NWO-funded Vici project 'Affordable Access to Justice: Towards Sustainable Cost and Funding Mechanisms for Civil Litigation in Europe' (No. VI.C.191.082); A junior researcher in Private International Law at the T.M.C. Asser Institute, and a Brazil-qualified attorney, e-mail: e.silva.de.freitas@asser.nl

https://doi.org/10.1515/9783110781632-025

justice through class actions and multidistrict litigation.[1] The **U.S. civil procedure** has some unique **features** such as the elaborate, concentrated trial, the presence of juries, and substantial compensation awards, including punitive damages. These features endure despite quite significant reforms of civil procedure, both at the federal and state levels. American litigation is a public, open process founded on ideals of transparency and equality before the law.[2] It is meant to resolve disputes, but also to regulate relations between the people and between the government and the people.[3] In writings of American scholars, one observes the continued emphasis on fundamental goals of litigation such as accuracy, efficiency, fairness, political legitimacy, provision of information to society,[4] and fostering discussions about important social and cultural issues. Some of the recent reforms of civil procedure aimed at achieving efficiency have caused concern in policy and academic circles.[5]

#3 This short overview introduces some of the key aspects of the American civil procedure, with special emphasis on areas where we observed recent changes and reforms.

II The Fundamentals of Civil Procedure

#4 The federal system of the U.S. is reflected in its court structure and in the applicable rules of civil procedure. Two distinct court systems, the federal and state courts, op-

1 The 'American way of law', also referred to as 'adversarial legalism' has been examined by RA Kagan, *Adversarial Legalism: The American Way of Law* (Harvard University Press 2001); see also SB Burbank, S Farhang and HM Kritzer, 'Private Enforcement of Statutory and Administrative Law in the United States (And Other Common Law Countries)' in P Gottwald and B Hess (eds), *Procedural Justice* (Gieseking 2014) 197, 216; and more recently S Issacharoff and I Samuel, 'The Institutional Dimension of Consumer Protection' in F Cafaggi and H-W Micklitz (eds), *New Frontiers of Consumer Protection. The Interplay Between Private and Public Enforcement* (Intersentia 2009) 9.

2 The concept of openness and publicity as guaranteeing justice is not unique to the United States. It was recognised, for instance, by Jeremy Bentham who said that 'publicity is the very soul of justice' (J Bentham, 'Draught of a New Plan for the Organisation of the Judicial Establishment in France: With Critical Observations on the Draught Proposed by the National Assembly Committee, in the Form of Perpetual Commentary' in J Bowring (ed), *The Works of Jeremy Bentham* (Tait 1843) vol IV, 316, as quoted by TCW Farrow, 'Civil Justice, Privatization and Democracy' (2010) <https://ssrn.com/abstract=1795407> accessed 26 February 2025; see also RD Freer, 'Exodus from and Transformation of American Civil Litigation' (2016) 65 Emory Law Journal 1491.

3 MH Redish, 'Electronic Discovery and the Litigation Matrix' (2001) 51 Duke Law Journal 561.

4 See the six 'foundational goals' of litigation by MH Redish (n 3). Also, AD Lahav, 'The Political Justification for Group Litigation' (2013) 81 Fordham Law Review 3193, 3199.

5 Freer (n 2); Lahav (n 4) 3199.

erate according to two distinct, yet related, systems of civil procedure rules.[6] The **federal courts** are structured in three levels: district courts (trial courts), circuit courts (first level of appeal), and the U.S. Supreme Court. While the latter is the court of last appeal, its jurisdiction, granted by the U.S. Constitution, is subject to exceptions and regulations made by the U.S. Congress.[7] There are also specialist federal courts for specific areas, in particular bankruptcy, tax and international trade.[8] The federal courts operate under the provisions of the Federal Rules of Civil Procedure (FRCP).[9] **State courts** have a similar structure to federal courts, also with specialist courts for some areas, for example, family law. They operate under state rules of civil procedure. Most U.S. states shaped those to reflect the FRCP.[10]

#5 The powers of these different courts to consider cases are bound in the intricate and ever-evolving rules on **jurisdiction**. These rules are provided by the U.S Constitution, by federal and state legislation, and by extensive case law (concerning personal jurisdiction, subject matter jurisdiction, original and appellate jurisdiction).[11] The recent case law of the Supreme Court concerning personal jurisdiction,[12] as noted by scholars,[13] to some extent, limits access to courts.[14]

#6 The structure of civil proceedings, once the case is brought and jurisdiction and venue confirmed, reflects their party-driven, **adversarial** spirit. The trial is the cornerstone of the process. However, recent changes brought in greater powers of the court to front-load procedural work of the parties and their attorneys, and to encourage settlement, thus avoiding trial.[15] The sentiments that brought the re-

6 PK Bookman and CF Shanahan, 'A Tale of Two Civil Procedures' (2022) 122 Columbia Law Review 1183.

7 U.S. Constitution, Article III, Section 2, Clause 2. See also RD Doerfler and S Moyn, 'Democratizing the Supreme Court' (2021) 109 California Law Review 1703.

8 RL Revesz, 'Specialised Courts and the Administrative Lawmaking System' (1990) 138 University of Pennsylvania Law Review 1111.

9 Rules of Civil Procedure for the United States District Courts, 1938. The amended version, as of 1 December 2024, is available at <https://www.uscourts.gov/file/78323/download> accessed 26 February 2025.

10 For the links to all relevant state laws see <https://www.law.cornell.edu/wex/table_civil_procedure> accessed 26 February 2025.

11 RD Freer, *Civil Procedure* (4th edn, Wolters Kluwer 2017) 39–149 and 193–279.

12 For some reflections on the applicability of those limitations to class actions – see eg C Sarchio, J Tam and L Wilson, '9th Circ. Jurisdiction Ruling Guides on Class Action Strategy' (*LAW 360*, 12 November 2021) and AN Steinman, 'Beyond Bristol-Myers: Personal Jurisdiction Over Class Action' (2022) 97 New York University Law Review 1215.

13 Freer (n 2) 1515; also, AR Miller, 'McIntyre in Context: A Very Personal Perspective' (2012) 63 South Carolina Law Review 465.

14 *J. McIntyre Mach. Ltd. v Nicastro,* 131 S. Ct. 2780, 2788 (2011); *Daimler AG v Bauman* 134 S. Ct. 746, 760 (2014).

15 M Galanter, 'The Vanishing Trial: An Examination of Trials and Related Matters in Federal and State Courts' (2004) 1 Journal of Empirical Legal Studies 459, 500f; Freer (n 2) 1513–1516.

forms of civil procedure in England and Wales in 1999 – the need for **efficiency**[16] – have been heard in the U.S. as well.[17] Many reforms were not the result of legislation but rather **judicial activism**. For example, the relatively straightforward '**notice pleadings**' approach allowing the plaintiff to effectively bring in the complaint by giving the defendant 'fair notice of what [his] claim is and the grounds upon which it rests'[18] was changed dramatically – the result of the U.S. Supreme Court decisions in *Iqbal* and *Twombly*.[19] Following these two judgements, plaintiffs are required to 'plead factual content that allows the court to draw the reasonable inference that the defendant is liable for misconduct alleged'.[20] The courts are expected to use their 'judicial experience and common sense' to establish whether the claim meets the 'plausibility' requirement.[21]

#7 Civil **discovery process**,[22] for so many years the cornerstone of the U.S. litigation but also an expensive and time-consuming exercise,[23] was already amended several times and recently limited.[24] Further reforms may be forthcoming.

III Aggregate Litigation

#8 The fundamentals of **class actions** are established by Rule 23 of the FRCP and by state laws that largely follow FRCP.[25] The prominence of class actions, their illustrious history in the past 50 years, their successes and their dramatic failures were all extensively documented in the popular press, films, books, and scholarly writings. While there were at least three significant attempts at **reforming class actions**, some motivated by the need to help the plaintiffs, some by the need to

16 Coleman wrote that 'efficiency norm' guides policy makers, law makers, and judges in the United States to introduce changes on many levels of civil litigation. See BD Coleman, 'The "Efficiency Norm"' (2015) 56 Boston College Law Review 1777.

17 As noted by Freer (n 2) 1513.

18 *Conley v Gibson*, 335 U.S. 41, 47 (1957). Rule 8(a)(2) FRCP.

19 *Ashcroft v Iqbal*, 556 U.S. 662 (2009); *Bell Atl. Corp. v Twombly*, 550 U.S. 544 (2007).

20 *Ashcroft v Iqbal*, 556 U.S. 662 (2009), 678.

21 *Fowler v UPMC Shadyside*, 578 F. 3d 203, 211 (3d Cir. 2009).

22 Rule 26 FRCP.

23 According to some reports, discovery costs now amount to between 50 per cent and 90 per cent of the overall costs of litigation; see *The Third Branch: The Newsletter of the Federal Courts, The Third Branch: The Newsletter of the Federal Courts*, vol 31, no 10 (October 1999).

24 See, eg, Private Securities Litigation Reform Act, Pub. L. No. 104–67, 109 Stat. 737 (1995).

25 For an example of how complex the interactions of state and federal rules of civil procedure and jurisdiction can be, see the U.S. Supreme Court judgement in *Shady Glove Orthopaedic Associates, P.S. v Allstate Insurance Company*, 595 U.S. 393 (2010).

help the defendants, some also motivated by the need to refocus the U.S. civil justice system,[26] class actions retain their prominence in the United States.

#9 Another form of aggregation of claims that is also important in the U.S. system is **multidistrict litigation**. It allows multiple lawsuits 'involving one or more common questions of fact [. . .] pending in different districts' to be 'transferred to any district for coordinated or consolidated pretrial proceedings' if the judicial panel on multidistrict litigation determines 'that transfers for such proceedings will be for the convenience of parties and witnesses and will promote the just and efficient conduct of such actions'.[27]

IV Public Interest Litigation

#10 **Public interest litigation** blossomed between 1965 and 1980. Following President Johnson's War on Poverty, the newly established Office of Economic Opportunity's (OEO) Legal Services Program, as well as the Legal Services Corporation, supported many notable public interest lawsuits, further supported by the growing number of private bodies, charities and other entities (funded through membership dues and donations).[28] Since then, as the LSC's resources have been limited, public interest litigation has been supported by many organisations. Public interest also remains an attractive career path for young lawyers.

#11 Another source of funding for public interest litigation is funds from **cy-pres awards**. Cy-pres (next best) damages are often agreed in class action settlements. Courts usually approve settlement awards, including cy-pres arrangements, as this allows the money that cannot be paid to any individual class members to be paid to an organisation whose aims align with the subject of the litigation.[29]

---

26 For a brilliant reflection on these reforms, see LS Mullenix, 'The Politics of Class Action Reform: Reflections on the American Experience' (1 January 2023) Public Law and Legal Theory Research Paper Series 595/2023.

27 Codified by 28 U.S. Code para 1407: 'When civil actions involving one or more common questions of fact are pending in different districts, such actions may be transferred to any district for coordinated or consolidated pretrial proceedings. Such transfers shall be made by the judicial panel on multidistrict litigation authorised by this section upon its determination that transfers for such proceedings will be for the convenience of parties and witnesses and will promote the just and efficient conduct of such actions . . .'.

28 C Albiston and L Nielsen, 'Funding the Cause: How Public Interest Law Organisations Fund Their Activities and Why It Matters for Social Change' (2014) 39 Law and Social Inquiry 62.

29 See the recent decision in *Hawes v Macy's Inc.*, No. 1:17-CV-754, 2023 WL 8811499 (S.D. Ohio, 20 December 2023)—the entire settlement was rejected by the court because the cy-pres arrangements were not 'appropriate'.

V Funding of Litigation

#12 The American system is known for its **costs rule**, where each party bears the costs of their own attorneys' fees irrespective of the result of the case.[30] There are plenty of exemptions from this general rule, including in civil rights, constitutional torts, consumer protection cases, employment law cases, intellectual property suits, or public interest litigation, where statutes introduced **attorney fee shifting**, either **two-way shifting** or **one-way shifting** in favour of the plaintiff.[31] **Contingency fees** remain the key mechanism for funding civil litigation. Under the American Bar Association's Model Rules of Professional Conduct,[32] contingency fee agreements must be signed, in writing, by the client and must state the method through which the fee will be determined. At the positive conclusion of the case, lawyers are paid the agreed **percentage of the winnings**, usually between 20 per cent and 40 per cent.

#13 **Third-party funding**, which arrived in the U.S. later than in Australia or the United Kingdom, is now a booming market.[33] Funding is provided directly to litigants, especially in large business disputes, or as portfolio funding arrangements to law firms that engage in consumer or other class actions. Third-party funding is not yet regulated at the federal level, but there are some state-level initiatives where fees or interest rates that funders charge may be capped or where transparency is required (often by courts, not statute).[34] It is likely that these state initiatives, as well as regulation of third-party funding in Australia, Canada, or soon to be proposed by the European Union, may influence further U.S. states to introduce their own rules on the matter.

#14 **Legal aid** is severely limited in the U.S., and there is no constitutional right to legal aid in civil cases.[35]

---

30 For some fundamentals see for instance: DA Root, 'Attorney Fee-Shifting in America: Comparing, Contrasting, and Combining the "American Rule" and "English Rule"' (2005) 15 Indiana International and Comparative Law Review 583.

31 M Carroll, 'Fee-Shifting Statutes and Compensation for Risk' (2020) 95 Indiana Law Journal 1021.

32 Available at <https://www.americanbar.org/groups/professional_responsibility/publications/model_rules_of_professional_conduct/?login> accessed 26 February 2025.

33 J Lewis, 'Third-Party Litigation Funding: A Boon or Bane to the Progress of Civil Justice?' (2020) 33 The Georgetown Journal of Legal Ethics 687. See also the report produced for the U.S. Government Accountability Office, *Third-Party Litigation Financing: Market Characteristics, Data and Trends*, GAO-23-105210 (20 December 2022) <https://www.gao.gov/products/gao-23-105210> accessed 26 February 2025.

34 Scholars have not yet examined these reform attempts comprehensively. For an analysis of reform proposals in Arizona, Georgia, and other states, see <https://landline.media/legislation-in-six-states-would-enact-third-party-litigation-reform/#:~:text=In%20the%20past%20year%2C%20multiple,a%20similar%20rule%20in%202023> accessed 26 February 2025.

35 On the implications of this, see MYK Woo, C Cox and S Rosen, 'Access to Civil Justice' (2022) 70(Supplement_1) The American Journal of Comparative Law 89.

VI Alternative Dispute Resolution

#15 **Alternative dispute resolution (ADR)** is widely used in a wide variety of cases, increasingly also online (ODR).[36] ADR was also expressly authorised by 28 U.S.-C. para 651. U.S. district courts must authorise the use of ADR in all civil actions. The courts are also expected to establish their own ADR programs to encourage and promote the use of ADR, and to improve the effectiveness of programs already operating.[37]

#16 One form of ADR – **arbitration** – has recently gained significant popularity in consumer, employment, civil rights and other cases. **Consumers** and employees in particular were finding that contractual arrangements they were involved in contained clauses that entailed waiver of the right to bring or take part in litigation and waiver of the right to bring or be part of a class action. These clauses were enforced by courts, including the U.S. Supreme Court, interpreting the Federal Arbitration Act of 1925 as part of the 'liberal policy favoring arbitration' and the 'fundamental principle that arbitration is a matter of contract'.[38] Recently, as a result of significant discontent with **mandatory arbitration, especially in consumer cases**, plaintiff law firms started bringing very large numbers of individual arbitration proceedings. Businesses were left with very significant costs of these proceedings.[39]

C Brazil

I Introduction

#17 The following overview of selected topics in **comparative civil procedure** between Brazil and the EU highlights aspects in three areas of growing relevance in both jurisdictions: digitalisation of justice, consumer collective actions, and private enforcement of competition law. Initially, this section will explain the basic structure of the Brazilian judiciary in order to contextualise civil jurisdic-

36 EE Greenberg and N Ebner, 'How Much Justice Can You Afford?' (2020) St. John's Legal Studies Research Paper No. 20-0016 <https://ssrn.com/abstract=3864194> accessed 26 February 2026.
37 28 U.S.C. para 651 (c).
38 *AT&T Mobility LLC v Concepcion*, 563 U.S. 333, 339 (2011) (first quoting *Moses H. Cone Mem'l Hosp. v Mercy Constr. Corp.*, 460 U.S. 1, 24 (1983); then quoting *Rent-A-Ctr., W., Inc. v Jackson*, 561 U.S. 63, 67 (2010)).
39 JM Glover, 'Recent Developments in Mandatory Arbitration Warfare: Winners and Losers (So Far) in Mass Arbitration' (2023) 100 Washington University Law Review 1617; LS Mullenix, 'Class Action Waivers in Arbitration Agreements: The Twenty-First Century Arbitration Battleground and Implications for the EU Countries' (2024) 38 Emory International Law Review 785.

tion within it. Secondly, there will be a comparison between key issues dealt with by the EU's Digitalisation of Justice Regulation and developments in Brazilian civil justice in such area, specially those triggered by the COVID-19 pandemic. Thirdly, in the area of consumer collective actions, a comparative overview was undertaken contrasting the approach that Brazil's Consumer Protection Code and the EU's Representative Actions Directive give to this matter. Finally, there is an outline, from a procedural perspective, of the inspiration drawn from the EU's Antitrust Damages Directive for the recent reform of Brazil's system of private enforcement of competition law.

II Civil Jurisdiction in the Brazilian Legal System

#18 In order to understand the functionality of civil justice in Brazil, one must first be able to identify the divisions of the Brazilian judiciary. Hence, a brief incursion into the structure of the Brazilian judiciary is necessary. The **Brazilian judiciary** is divided in five branches, operating in distinctive levels within the federal state structure. Four of these five branches belong to the Union's judicial power (*Poder Judiciário da União*): the electoral judiciary, the labor judiciary, the military judiciary, and the federal judiciary (ordinary and small claims courts). Despite the latter's name, all these four branches are organised at the federal level. The fifth branch are the state judiciaries. Every Brazilian state has its own judiciary, also composed of ordinary and small claims courts.[40] The Maritime Court[41] and the Union's Audit Court[42] belong, respectively, to the executive and legislative powers, and therefore are not branches of the judiciary as such. The same goes for the Brazilian sports judiciary which, despite its name and constitutional status,[43] is organised by private entities.

#19 Apart from the Union's military judiciary, each of these branches has its own **High Court system**. The **electoral judiciary** has 27 electoral High Courts (TREs), one for each Brazilian state.[44] The labor judiciary has 24 labor High Courts (TRTs). Most are responsible for cases from a single state, while some handle cases from multiple states. São Paulo is the only state with two labor High Courts.[45] The federal

40 cf 'Functional Structure' (*Superior Tribunal de Justiça*) <https://international.stj.jus.br/en/Brazilian-Judicial-Branch/Functional-Structure> accessed 3 February 2025.

41 BRASIL. Lei nº 2.180, de 5 de fevereiro de 1954. Dispõe sôbre o Tribunal Marítimo.

42 BRASIL. Constituição (1988).

43 BRASIL. Constituição (1988).

44 BRASIL. Constituição (1988).

45 cf 'Tribunais Regionais do Trabalho' (*Tribunal Superior do Trabalho*) <https://www.tst.jus.br/web/acesso-a-informacao/trts> accessed 4 February 2025.

judiciary has 6 federal High Courts (TRFs), one corresponding to each federal circuit. Each Brazilian state judiciary has its own High Court (TJs).[46]

#20 Finally, three out of these five branches have their own **Court of Appeal**: the labor Court of Appeal (TST), the electoral Court of Appeal (TSE), and the military Court of Appeal (STM). The *Superior Tribunal de Justiça* (STJ) is a Court of Appeal for non-constitutional issues, responsible for ruling on appeals from the federal and state High Courts.[47] All the courts mentioned so far, from all instances, are under the jurisdiction of the Supreme Court (STF).[48] The Figure 25.1 below displays the judiciary organisation just described:

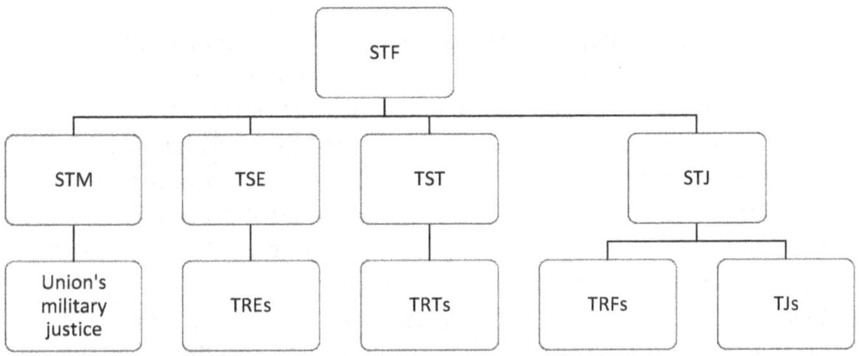

Figure 25.1: Brazilian judiciary organisation.

#21 Neither the electoral judiciary nor the military judiciary have **civil jurisdiction**. Conversely, the labor judiciary has a relatively broad civil jurisdiction. For a labor court to establish jurisdiction, it suffices that the underlying dispute *arises* from the employment relationship, irrespectively of whether it concerns the labor contract as such or its associated obligations.[49] In its turn, the federal judiciary has civil jurisdiction whenever the Union, a federal agency, or a federal state-owned enterprise is either a claimant or a defendant in the proceedings.[50] It is with the state judiciaries, however, that the (residual) competence for the vast majority of civil cases lie, and where quintessentially civil proceedings such as divorces, probate, ejectment, and boundary disputes are handled.

46 BRASIL. Constituição (1988).

47 BRASIL. Constituição (1988).

48 BRASIL. Constituição (1988).

49 BRASIL. Supremo Tribunal Federal. Recurso Extraordinário nº 238.737-4. Relator: Sepúlveda Pertence. Brasília, DF, 17 de novembro de 1998.

50 BRASIL. Constituição (1988).

#22 This incursion was necessary because some of the topics dealt with below concern developments taking place with regards to a specific branch of the judiciary rather than a specific field of law. However, because most of the branches, as just explained, have at least some civil jurisdiction, such developments have a direct impact on civil cases too. The best example of that is digitalisation of justice, to which I now turn.

III Digitalisation of Justice: Developments in Brazil and Europe, and the Role of the COVID-19 Pandemic

#23 **COVID-19** played a decisive role in speeding up the **digitalisation** of Brazil's justice system, though it is fair to say that it was already quite advanced when the pandemic began. Upon the enactment of the justice reform brought about by Constitutional Amendment n. 45 in 2004, several projects aiming at the informatisation of the judiciary were incentivised by the Ministry of Justice, such as the 'Paperless Justice' project.[51] This same Constitutional Amendment also created the National Council of Justice (CNJ), which later came to be a very important rules-setter for electronic proceedings, especially during the pandemic.

#24 However, the first relevant driver of digitalisation of justice in Brazil came with the enactment of Law no 11.419/2006 (**Electronic Procedure Act**), which aims primarily at enhancing the legal value of electronic judicial proceedings and official judicial documents in electronic means. This Act also allowed, but did not demand, all branches of the judiciary to start taking practical steps towards having fully digitalised proceedings.[52]

#25 From that point onwards, the digitalisation of the Brazilian justice system progressed quite unevenly and, to this day, Brazil lacks a uniform system for **electronic proceedings** – although digitalisation as such is mandatory since the aftermath of the COVID-19 pandemic.[53] Article 194 of the 2015 Brazilian Code of Civil Procedure ensures **interoperability** by requiring such systems to be platform-independent and accessible while guaranteeing the integration of systems, services, data, and information. Although the labor and electoral branches of the judiciary use the ***Processo Judicial Eletrônico*** (PJe) system in their entire court structure, many state and federal judiciaries operate their own systems for electronic proceedings. The same goes for the STJ and the STF.

---

51 PR Pegoraro Junior, *O processo eletrônico e a evolução disruptiva do direito processual civil* (PhD thesis, Pontifícia Universidade Católica do Rio Grande do Sul 2018) 93–106.

52 BRASIL. Lei nº 11.419, de 19 de dezembro de 2006. Dispõe sobre a informatização do processo judicial.

53 BRASIL. Conselho Nacional de Justiça. Ato Normativo nº 0006956-27.2021.2.00.0000. Relator: Luiz Fux. Brasília, DF, 21 de setembro de 2021.

#26 With the onset of COVID-19 and a partnership between the CNJ and the United Nations Development Program named **Program Justice 4.0**, many resolutions by the CNJ set rules for electronic proceedings in Brazil. In comparison, the EU addressed similar topics through **Regulation (EU) 2023/2844** on the digitalisation of judicial cooperation (Digitalisation of Justice Regulation).[54] A relevant difference, however, is that while the latter deals with cooperation between different EU Member States, the CNJ resolutions deal with both internal and cooperation-related matters within the Brazilian judiciary and between judiciaries of different Brazilian states or different federal circuits.

#27 However, before turning to such topics, two pandemic-related developments are worthy of note. Firstly, during this time, the CNJ published a resolution which allowed all paper-based proceedings to be turned into digital.[55] Secondly, another **CNJ resolution** created the **'100% digital justice'** program, which, on an optional basis, digitalises the entire judicial process, including phases that are traditionally held in person, such as hearings.[56]

#28 Regarding communication between judicial authorities in Brazil, CNJ resolution 455/2022 established the **'judiciary service portal'** (*Portal de Serviços do Poder Judiciário* – PSPJ) as the form of electronic communication between all bodies of the Brazilian judiciary.[57] The PJSP is also accessible to all citizens, be they or not a party to ongoing proceedings. The services available depend on the user's profile. For similar purposes, the Digitalisation of Justice Regulation establishes an electronic form of communication between judicial authorities of EU Member States (Article 3) and the European electronic access point (Article 4).[58] The latter is a **platform** for judicial services within the EU.

#29 The Brazilian approach to **hearings** through videoconferencing is enshrined in CNJ resolution 481/2022, which places great emphasis on initiative by the parties,

---

54 Discussing the Digitalisation of Justice Regulation only scratches the surface of the topic's relevance in the EU. For a deeper exploration, see E Storskrubb, 'E-Justice, Innovation and the EU' in B Hess and X Kramer (eds), *From Common Rules to Best Practices in European Civil Procedure* (Nomos 2017) 271.

55 BRASIL. Conselho Nacional de Justiça. Resolução nº 314, de 20 de abril de 2020. Prorroga, no âmbito do Poder Judiciário, em parte, o regime instituído pela Resolução n. 313, de 19 de março de 2020, que estabelece regime de Plantão Extraordinário para uniformizar o funcionamento dos serviços judiciários, com o objetivo de prevenir o contágio pelo Novo coronavírus (Covid-19), e garantir o acesso à justiça neste período emergencial.

56 BRASIL. Conselho Nacional de Justiça. Resolução nº 345, de 09 de outubro de 2020. Dispõe sobre o "Juízo 100% Digital".

57 BRASIL. Conselho Nacional de Justiça. Resolução nº 455, de 27 de abril de 2022. Institui o Portal de Serviços do Poder Judiciário (PSPJ), na Plataforma Digital do Poder Judiciário (PDPJ-Br), para usuários externos.

58 Regulation (EU) 2023/2844 of 13 December 2023 on the digitalisation of judicial cooperation and access to justice in cross-border civil, commercial and criminal matters, and amending certain acts in the field of judicial cooperation [2023] OJ L/27.12.2023.

allowing the judge to determine *ex officio* a hearing through videoconferencing only in specific occasions (Article 3º, §1º).[59] In the EU, Article 5 Digitalisation of Justice Regulation established the conditions under which hearings in cross-border civil proceedings may take place electronically. This provision clarifies that the possibility of a hearing through videoconferencing is contingent upon its permissibility under national law and that the opinion of the parties must be taken into account (Article 5(1)(a)).[60]

#30 Finally, both Brazil's Electronic Procedure Act (Articles 1º, §2º, III, a) and 4º, §1º)[61] and the EU's Digitalisation of Justice Regulation (Articles 7 and 8)[62] attach legal value to **electronic signatures** and provide for the equal legal effects of electronic court documents.

IV Consumer Collective Redress: The EU's Representative Actions Directive and Brazil's Consumer Protection Code

#31 Brazil has a relatively long experience with **consumer collective redress** and a distinct set of actors involved. The Law on Public Civil Action (Law no 7.347/85), which is still the most important piece of legislation on the Brazilian legal framework for collective actions, was already in force when the **Brazilian Consumer Protection Code (CDC)** came into force in 1990. The latter, in is turn, contains specific rules on collective actions concerning consumer rights, which I shall now compare to those dealing with similar matters in Directive (EU) 2020/1828 on representative actions for the protection of the collective interests of consumers (Representative Actions Directive – RAD). Consumer collective actions may take place before both state and federal courts, the latter contingent upon the assignment of civil jurisdiction to federal courts as explained above.

#32 In terms of scope, Article 81 CDC defines the three occasions in which a violation of consumer **law** allows for the **filing of collective actions**: (a) when it concerns 'diffuse rights and interests', meaning those which affect an undetermined population (ie, an ecologically balanced environment); (b) when it concerns 'collective rights and interests', meaning those which affect an ascertainable group of people in an indivisible manner (ie, right to adequate provision of collective transportation services); (c) when it concerns 'homogeneous individual rights', mean-

59 BRASIL. Conselho Nacional de Justiça. Resolução nº 481, de 22 de novembro de 2022. Revoga as Resoluções vigentes à época da pandemia do Coronavírus e altera as Resoluções CNJ n. 227/2016, 343/2020,345/2020, 354/2020 e 465/2022.

60 Regulation (EU) 2023/2844 (n 58).

61 BRASIL. Lei nº 11.419, de 19 de dezembro de 2006. Dispõe sobre a informatização do processo judicial.

62 Regulation (EU) 2023/2844 (n 58).

ing those which affect a specific target population and have a common origin (ie, illegal charging of cancellation fees).[63] On this matter, the RAD has a slightly more vague **scope**. Article 3(3) RAD defines 'collective interests of consumers' as 'the general interest of consumers and, in particular for the purposes of redress measures, the interests of a group of consumers'. Such **collective interests** would be violated due to 'infringements by traders of the provisions of Union law' (Article 2(1) RAD). However, the RAD is silent as to any standard for assessing the degree upon which such infringement would amount to a violation of the 'collective interests of consumers', which is left for the procedural autonomy of the Member States.[64] From a procedural point of view, the RAD clarifies that, for injunctive measures, the claimant entities should not be required to prove 'loss or damage on the part of the individual consumers' (Article 8(3)(a) RAD). For redress measures, it is sufficient that the claimant entity is able to describe the group of consumers affected (Article 9(5) RAD).[65]

#33 With regards to **standing**, the RAD and the CDC have a similar range of actors that are entitled to bring collective actions. Under the RAD consumer organisations (Article 4(2)) and public bodies (Article 4(7)) may be designated by Member States as '**qualified entities**' for the purposes of bringing both domestic and cross-border collective actions.[66] The CDC is very similar to the RAD in this aspect, as Article 82 CDC lists a range of public bodies that can bring collective actions on matters of consumer law alongside consumer associations.[67] That said, two key differences should be highlighted. The first difference is that, when it comes to consumer associations, the standing requirements contained in the CDC (Article 82, IV)[68] are somewhat more lax compared to the RAD (Article 4(3)).[69] Furthermore, in collective actions concerning homogeneous individual rights, such requirements may even by waived by the judge depending on the seriousness of the case concerned (Article 82, §1° CDC).[70] The second difference is that,

63 BRASIL. Lei nº 8.078, de 11 de setembro de 1990. Dispõe sobre a proteção do consumidor e dá outras providências.

64 B Gsell, 'The New European Directive on Representative Actions for the Protection of the Collective Interests of Consumers – A Huge, But Blurry Step Forward' (2021) 58 Common Market Law Review 1365.

65 Directive (EU) 2020/1828 of 25 November 2020 on representative actions for the protection of the collective interests of consumers and repealing Directive 2009/22/EC [2020] OJ L409/1.

66 Directive (EU) 2020/1828 (n 65).

67 BRASIL. Lei nº 8.078, de 11 de setembro de 1990. Dispõe sobre a proteção do consumidor e dá outras providências.

68 BRASIL. Lei nº 8.078, de 11 de setembro de 1990. Dispõe sobre a proteção do consumidor e dá outras providências.

69 Directive (EU) 2020/1828 (n 65).

70 BRASIL. Lei nº 8.078, de 11 de setembro de 1990. Dispõe sobre a proteção do consumidor e dá outras providências.

in practice, Public Prosecutors take on a rather prominent role in consumer collective redress – both the Federal Public Prosecutors (MPF) and the State Public Prosecutors (MPs) – and also public interest litigation more generally.[71]

#34 On the topic of **litigation costs**, the CDC has taken a more friendly approach towards claimant associations when compared to the RAD. Under Article 87 CDC, claimant associations are exempt from any litigation costs of whichever nature and are immune to **adverse costs orders**, meaning they are also not liable for attorney's fees.[72] Conversely, the RAD explicitly adopts the **loser pays principle** in Article 12, including for when claims are dismissed to the detriment of the claimant association. Article 20(2) RAD, however, states that Member States must take steps to prevent that litigation costs form a barrier to access to justice in the context of collective actions for the protection of consumers.[73]

V Private Enforcement of Competition Law: The EU Model as a Direct Inspiration for Brazil

#35 In Brazil, both individual and collective actions for antitrust damages are governed by Article 47 of the **Brazilian Competition Law (LDC)**. This provision establishes **injunctive and compensatory relief** in both **stand-alone** and **follow-on claims**. Unlike in the United States, where federal courts have exclusive jurisdiction over the federal antitrust laws, both individual and collective actions for breaches of competition law may take place in Brazilian state courts. The assignment of (civil) jurisdiction between state and federal courts for antitrust damages actions largely follows the division explained above. However, if either the MPF files the collective action[74] and/or the Brazilian Competition Authority (CADE) decides to intervene in the proceedings,[75] only federal courts have jurisdiction.

#36 With the enactment of Law 14.470/2022, key changes were introduced to the framework for collective redress in **antitrust** cases under the LDC. Two of these changes concern procedural law and were inspired by Directive 2014/104/EU on

71 For a critical perspective on this topic, see K Denari Gomes de Mattos, '"We the prosecutors": Challenges to Social Participation in Brazilian Public Law Litigation' (2021) 19 International Journal of Constitutional Law 1084.

72 BRASIL. Lei nº 8.078, de 11 de setembro de 1990. Dispõe sobre a proteção do consumidor e dá outras providências.

73 Directive (EU) 2020/1828 (n 65).

74 BRASIL. Superior Tribunal de Justiça. Conflito de Competência nº 40.534. Relator: Teori Zavascki. Brasília, DF, 17 de maio de 2004.

75 BRASIL. Superior Tribunal de Justiça. Conflito de Competência nº 34.977. Relator: Laurita Vaz. Brasília, DF, 7 de abril de 2003.

actions for damages for infringements of competition law (Antitrust Damages Directive).[76]

#37 The LDC now explicitly assigns the **burden of proof** for passing-on defences to the defendant (Article 47, § 4º). This defence is commonly used by cartel members, who claim that the plaintiff did not incur any actual losses because the financial impact of the antitrust violation was transferred to the next level in the supply chain. Under the revised LDC, it is the responsibility of alleged cartel members, rather than the claimants, to substantiate any **passing-on allegations**.[77] This change was inspired by Article 13 Antitrust Damages Directive,[78] under which the burden of proof for passing-on allegations also lies with the defendant, though under such provision there is also a possibility to request disclosure of evidence that the claimant may possess.[79]

#38 Moreover, the LDC now authorises courts to grant **provisional relief** (*tutela de evidência*) once CADE's plenary court has issued a final ruling on an antitrust violation (Article 47-A). Introduced as part of Brazil's 2015 procedural reform, *tutela de evidência* differs from traditional civil law preliminary injunctions, as it does not require proof of urgency (*periculum in mora*). Rather than preserving the *status quo*, its purpose is to ensure that claimants can exercise their rights without unnecessary delays.[80]

#39 Under the new law, CADE's decisions can serve as grounds for granting advance provisional relief at any stage of the legal proceedings. In practical terms, once CADE's plenary has issued a final decision confirming an infringement, a judge handling collective actions can order the termination of the unlawful practices without requiring a prior hearing for the defendant.[81] This new regime was inspired by Article 9 Antitrust Damages Directive,[82] which provides for the **irrefutability**, in actions for damages before national courts, of the establishment of infringements of antitrust law by competition authorities.[83]

---

76 C Ragazzo and I Veloso, *Ações de reparação de danos concorrenciais no brasil: obstáculos e sugestões* (2023) <https://direitorio.fgv.br/sites/default/files/arquivos/2023_07_19%20Vers%C3%A3o%20Final%20relat%C3%B3rio%20FDD_site.pdf> accessed 16 February 2025.

77 L Macedo and E Silva de Freitas, 'A Silent Revolution? The Revamped Brazilian Private Enforcement System and Third-Party Funding' (*Lexology*, 10 March 2023) <https://www.lexology.com/library/detail.aspx?g=f13fa643-dfc6-48cf-9bc9-fee60343e23e> accessed 24 February 2025.

78 Ragazzo and Veloso (n 76).

79 Directive 2014/104/EU of 26 November 2014 on certain rules governing actions for damages under national law for infringements of the competition law provisions of the Member States and of the European Union [2014] OJ L349/1.

80 Macedo and Silva de Freitas (n 77).

81 Macedo and Silva de Freitas (n 77).

82 Ragazzo and Veloso (n 76).

83 Directive 2014/104/EU (n 79).

D South Africa

I Context

#40 South Africa has a **mixed legal system**. Its civil procedure is an amalgam of Roman-Dutch law and English Law. Like many other countries, South Africa's adversarial civil justice system is often criticised for being expensive, slow, complex, and overly adversarial, making it inaccessible to most people.[84] The country is characterised by extreme societal inequality, which disempowers the majority from accessing the courts despite a strong constitutional emphasis on the rule of law.[85]

#41 To address systemic difficulties, efforts have been made to tackle various civil justice challenges and enhance **access to justice**. Many initiatives have been shaped by comparative law from Europe and other parts of Africa. However, care has been taken to infuse the law with homegrown values often influenced by the **Bill of Rights in the South African Constitution**.[86]

II Funding of Litigation

1 The Split Bar System and the Winner-Takes-All Costs Structure: A Problem?

#42 Lawyers are either attorneys (**solicitors**) or advocates (**barristers**). Attorneys handle cases in lower courts, prepare legal documents, manage property transfers, handle deceased estates, and more.[87] Advocates specialise in litigation in superior courts.[88]

---

84 S Ngcobo, 'Enhancing Access to Justice: The Search for Better Justice', Opening Remarks Access to Justice Conference: Towards Delivering Accessible and Quality Justice for All (7–10 July 2011) 15 <https://constitutionallyspeaking.co.za/wp-content/uploads/2011/07/Speech-of-the-Chief-Justice-2011.pdf> accessed 27 June 2024.

85 In 2023, South Africa had the highest income inequality, with a Gini score of 63, while Namibia followed second. The Gini coefficient measures the difference between the income (or consumption) distribution among individuals or households within a country and a perfectly equal distribution. See <https://www.statista.com/statistics/264627/ranking-of-the-20-countries-with-the-biggest-inequality-in-income-distribution/> accessed 4 July 2024.

86 Constitution of the Republic of South Africa, 1996.

87 See Code of Conduct of All Legal Practitioners, Candidate Legal Practitioners and Juristic Entities GN 198 in *Government Gazette* 42364 of 29 March 2019, rule 23.2'. See also *Rösemann v General Council of the Bar of SA* 2004 (1) SA 568 (SCA) para 26.

88 The superior courts include the High Courts in the nine provinces, the Supreme Court of Appeal in Bloemfontein, and the Constitutional Court in Braamfontein, Johannesburg. Attorneys can appear in all superior courts but often use advocates instead. See Rights of Appearance in Courts Act 62 of 1995.

There was some discussion to remove the split, but the the Legal Practice Act of 2014 maintained the divided **legal profession**.[89]

#43 Due to the split legal profession, litigants are generally required to hire an attorney before hiring an advocate so that the attorney can instruct the advocate.[90] Both attorneys and advocates have different **fee** criteria. Attorneys charge an average of ZAR 800 to ZAR 2,500 per hour[91] based on experience and case complexity, while advocates charge ZAR 3,500 to ZAR 5,000[92] per hour, depending on the counsel's seniority.[93] Some may charge more. There are plans to regulate fees better to make professional services more affordable.[94]

#44 In South Africa, the '**winner-takes-all**' system allows the winning party to recover legal costs from the losing party,[95] but usually not 100 per cent of the **legal costs**. Full cost recovery occurs in less than 1 per cent of cases and only if abusive litigation practices are proven.[96] Costs are awarded on a party-party or attorney-client basis,[97] with the default being party-party costs.[98] Attorney-client costs are granted if a prior agreement allows for this[99] or if a litigant acts vexa-

89 Parliamentary Monitoring Group (PMG), 'Legal Practice Bill [B20-2012]: Deliberations on Amendments Proposed by Negotiating Mandates' (*PMG*, 26 February 2014) <https://pmg.org.za/committee-meeting/17001/> accessed 4 July 2024.

90 Code of Conduct (n 87) rule 27. However, section 34(2)(b) of the Legal Practice Act allows for a third type of practitioner, namely an advocate who operates a trust account and can take instructions from the public. This is a new concept and there aren't many practitioners like this.

91 'How Much Do Lawyers and Attorneys Charge?' (*ChatLegal*) <https://www.chatlegal.co.za/cost/how-much-do-lawyers-and-attorneys-charge/> accessed 27 June 2024.

92 'How Much is a Lawyer Consultation Fee in South Africa' (*LegalAdvice*, 7 March 2024) <https://legaladvice.org.za/how-much-is-a-lawyer-consultation-fee-in-south-africa/> accessed 27 June 2024.

93 To be elevated to Senior Counsel, one must meet certain criteria: see GN 4495 in *Government Gazette* 50290 of 13 March 2024. Some Senior Counsels are estimated to charge up to R60 000 per day, and junior advocates charge R20 000 per day; see South African Law Reform Commission, 'Report Project 142: Investigation into Legal Fees – Including Access to Justice and other Interventions' (South African Law Reform Commission 2021) 118 (hereinafter referred to as 'Report').

94 Report (n 93) 189ff.

95 T Bekker, 'The Apportionment of Legal Costs in South Africa: A Comparative Analysis' [2022] Tydskrif vir die Suid-Afrikaanse Reg 457, 458–476.

96 See, eg, *KT v AT* 2020 (2) SA 516 (WCC).

97 M Dendy, 'Vol 10: Costs' in *The Law of South Africa* (3rd edn, LexisNexis 2017) para 276 (hereinafter referred to as '*LAWSA*').

98 AC Cilliers, C Loots and HC Nel (eds), *Herbstein & Van Winsen: The Civil Practice of the High Courts and the Supreme Court of Appeal of South Africa* (5th edn, Juta 2009) 971 (hereinafter referred to as *Herbstein & Van Winsen*). There are exceptions: for example, Promotion of Equality and Unfair Discrimination Act 4 of 2000, section 21(2)(a).

99 Often, a contract will include a provision stating that the successful party can recover costs on an attorney-client basis if litigation ensues. See *LAWSA* (n 97) para 277.

tiously. However, it is important to note that it does not allow full **cost recovery** for the innocent party.[100]

#45 Party-party and attorney-client costs are determined by a **pre-determined tariff** table in the Rules of the Magistrates' Courts and the Uniform Rules of the High Court.[101] Party-party costs are generally lower than attorney-client costs. The tariff tables do not differentiate between attorney-client and party-party costs, but party-party costs cover 'reasonable and necessary' litigation costs, while attorney-client costs cover **'reasonable' costs**, making the latter higher.[102] All bills undergo a process called 'taxation' before a Taxing Master to prevent overcharging.[103]

#46 The Rules Board for Courts of Law regularly updates **tariff tables**,[104] assigning specific amounts to activities performed by legal practitioners based on the nature and value of the claim.[105] Tariffs are higher in superior courts relative to the complexity of litigation and higher monetary sums involved.[106]

#47 Since party-party and attorney-client costs do not fully cover expenses, the client must pay the difference between what is recovered according to the tariffs and the amount stipulated in the **fee agreement** between the client and the practitioner, which is usually based on an hourly rate.

#48 In a winner-takes-all system, the **losing party** faces significant costs, paying the winner's legal fees as well as their own. South African law is largely uncodified, and litigation outcomes can be uncertain, discouraging many from entering into

---

100 *Herbstein & Van Winsen* (n 98) 974f. See also *In re Alluvial Creek Ltd* 1929 CPD 532; *Mahomed & Son v Mahomed* 1959 (2) SA 688 (T); *Levinsohn's Meat Products (Edms) Bpk v Addisionele Landdros, Keimoes* 1981 (2) SA 562 (NC) at 570A–B; *Delfante v Delta Electrical Industries Ltd* 1992 (2) SA 221 (C) at 233A–F.

101 Uniform Rules Regulating the Conduct of the Proceedings of the Several Provincial and Local Divisions of the High Court of South Africa GN R48 in *Government Gazette* 999 of 12 January 1965, as amended (hereinafter referred to as the 'URC'); Rules Regulating the Conduct of the Proceedings of the Magistrates' Courts of South Africa GN R740 in *Government Gazette* 33487 of 23 August 2010 (hereinafter referred to as the 'MCR').

102 *Herbstein & Van Winsen* (n 98) 952f.

103 The Taxing Master is a court official who reviews the Bill of Costs in the presence of the attorneys.

104 See Rules Board for Courts of Law Act 107 of 1985, section 6.

105 Different amounts are assigned for litigation work in District Magistrates' Courts and Regional Courts. The superior courts also have their own tariffs.

106 The District Magistrates' Courts have a jurisdictional limit of ZAR 200,000, while the Regional Magistrates' Courts have a limit ranging from ZAR 200,000 to ZAR 400,000. While the High Courts have concurrent jurisdiction over these matters, in practice, cases are usually filed in the High Court only when the value of the claim exceeds the monetary jurisdiction of the Magistrates' Courts. However, parties can consent per section 45 of the Magistrates' Courts Act 32 of 1944 to bring the claim to the Magistrates' Court in cases where value of the claim exceeds the Magistrates Courts' monetary jurisdiction.

legal battles lightly. On the other hand, the **winner-takes-all** system discourages **frivolous litigation.**[107]

#49 To address access to justice, in *Biowatch Trust v Registrar Genetic* Resources, the Constitutional Court introduced a new approach to costs in **constitutional matters**. If the State loses, it must pay the winning party's costs. If the State wins, each party must pay their own costs.[108] Other courts in non-constitutional matters have sometimes ordered parties to pay their own costs.[109] However, courts have generally hesitated to deviate from the winner-take-all approach.[110] There may be a need to reevaluate the winner-takes-all system and identify civil disputes and instances where it may not be applicable.

2 Legal Aid

#50 Access to legal services for individuals with limited financial resources is primarily through legal aid. According to the **Legal Aid South Africa Act** 39 of 2014,[111] the objectives of Legal Aid South Africa include providing legal representation and advice to individuals at state expense and offering education and information about legal rights and responsibilities.[112] The Legal Aid Board may use a **means test**[113] and other criteria to determine **eligibility** for financial assistance and decide on funding for certain types of litigation.[114] Some civil matters may not receive funding, such as cases involving financial inquiries, administration orders, estate administration, voluntary surrender or sequestration of an estate, liquidation of a legal entity, and others.[115] Legal aid can be granted in permitted civil cases based on the likelihood of success and tangible positive results.[116]

107 See N Bedford 'The Winner Takes It All: Legal Costs as Mechanism of Control of Public Law' (2018) 30 Bond Law Review 119.

108 *Biowatch Trust v Registrar, Genetic Resources* 2009 (6) SA 232 (CC) para 43.

109 For example, see *Sekeleni v Sekeleni* (1986) 3 All SA 136 (TKS); *Mnyama v Gxalaba* [1990] 3 All SA 1042 (C). Under common law, such a deviation is possible because the ordering of costs is ultimately an issue in the court's discretion.

110 *Herbstein & Van Winsen* (n 98) 955; AC Cilliers, *Law of Costs* (Issue 49 LexisNexis 2024) §2.05.

111 Act 39 of 2014 was preceded by Act 22 of 1969.

112 Legal Aid South Africa Act (n 111) section 3.

113 Legal Aid Act section 23. To qualify for legal aid at State expense, an individual person must earn less than R8700 per month after tax, and less than R9500 per month after tax for households <https://legal-aid.co.za/how-it-works> accessed on 5 July 2024.

114 Legal Aid Act (n 111) section 23.

115 Legal Aid South African Regulations GN 745 in *Government Gazette* 41005 of 26 July 2017, Regulation 11(2).

116 Legal Aid Regulations (n 115) Regulation 9.

Demonstrating a reasonable prospect of success can be challenging in an uncodified legal system.

#51 In certain situations, like **domestic violence** cases, the client's age is important for determining their eligibility for legal aid.[117] It's also relevant if the opposing party has legal representation. In **child maintenance** cases, the duration of missed payments and the likelihood of court administration failure or abuse of process are important factors when deciding whether a litigant should qualify for legal aid.[118] If no extenuating circumstances exist, the litigant is encouraged to represent themselves. This is problematic in a legal system known to be inefficient and complicated, compounded by low levels of literacy among some litigants.[119] These limitations are, however, necessary due to **budget constraints**, which have worsened over time.[120] Legal Aid South Africa has historically spent more on criminal litigation than civil litigation[121] because the Constitution guarantees legal representation to anyone facing criminal charges if substantial injustice would otherwise result. In contrast, the same guarantee does not apply in civil cases.[122]

#52 The means test for legal aid disproportionately affects **middle-income citizens**. It sets a low threshold, creating a significant 'missing middle' problem.[123] The middle class is neither wealthy enough for legal representation nor poor enough for aid, creating an unfair situation in a country with a wide wealth gap between the rich and the less well off.[124]

#53 The legal aid legislation fails to recognise and address the needs of **vulnerable groups** such as youth, older people, persons with disabilities, women, and those who do not conform to gender stereotypes. Treating gender-based violence and abuse as similar to other civil cases is unacceptable, given the prevalence of gender-based violence in the country.[125]

---

117 ibid Regulation 13.

118 ibid Regulation 13.

119 South Africa's adult literacy rate is only 85.8 per cent, see Stats SA, *General Household Survey* (2019), key statistics available at <https://www.statssa.gov.za/?page_id=737&id=4> accessed 29 June 2024.

120 Over the past three years, Legal Aid SA's budget has been reduced by 15 per cent. See Legal Aid South Africa, *Integrated Annual Report 2022–2023* (Legal Aid SA 2023) 15.

121 Report (n 93) 167.

122 Constitution of the Republic of South Africa, 1996, sections 35(2)(c) and 35(3)(g). See J Brickhill, 'The Right to A Fair Civil Trial: The Duties of Lawyers and Law Students to Act Pro Bono' (2005) 21 South African Journal on Human Rights 293, 295. And see *Legal Aid South Africa v Magidiwana* 2015 (6) SA 494 (CC).

123 Report (n 93) 158ff.

124 L Greenbaum, 'Access to Justice for All: A Reality of Unfulfilled Expectations?' (2020) 53 De Jure 248, 253. See also *Report* 51.

125 Report (n 93) 131.

3 Contingency Fees

#54 Following developments in Europe and many other regions, South Africa introduced **contingency fees** in 1997. Under Roman-Dutch law, such agreements were considered against public policy, falling into the same category as betting and wagering agreements. The **Contingency Fees Act 66 of 1997** regulates contingency fees, which are not allowed in criminal and family cases but are commonly used in civil cases like personal injury, medical malpractice, and non-litigious matters.[126] The Act was intended to ensure that people who cannot afford legal representation have access to courts and justice.

#55 According to the Act, there must be a written and signed **agreement** between the attorney and the client. If the case is unsuccessful, the attorney works for free, and the client only pays for disbursements such as sheriffs' fees and travel costs. In the event of a successful case, the attorney can receive either a higher fee or 25 per cent of the claim, whichever is lower. The attorney could also charge their standard ('normal') fee[127] or 25 per cent of the claim, whichever is lower. If the attorney's fee is higher, it cannot exceed the standard fee by more than 100 per cent.[128]

4 Public Interest Litigation

#56 Since the advent of the constitutional dispensation in 1994, **public interest litigation** has been pivotal in transforming the legal system. Section 38 of the Constitution, which recognises public interest litigation, has broadened the principles of ***locus standi***, allowing individuals or organisations to litigate **constitutional matters** to safeguard the public interest.[129] Constitutional issues are not limited to advancing human rights. More broadly, they can also include preventing corruption and promoting open and transparent government.

---

126 Contingency Fees Act 66 of 1997, s 1.

127 But most attorneys would not.

128 Contingency Fees Act, s 2(2). See also *Masango v Road Accident Fund* 2016 (6) SA 508 (GJ); *Mathimba v Nonxuba* (2019 (1) SA 550 (ECG).

129 Section 38 provides: 'Anyone listed in this section has the right to approach a competent court, alleging that a right in the Bill of Rights has been infringed or threatened, and the court may grant appropriate relief, including a declaration of rights. The persons who may approach a court are -

a. anyone acting in their own interest;
b. anyone acting on behalf of another person who cannot act in their own name;
c. anyone acting as a member of, or in the interest of, a group or class of persons;
d. anyone acting in the public interest; and
e. an association acting in the interest of its members.'

#57 Public interest litigation has been used to challenge health policies,[130] contest COVID-19 restrictions,[131] protect the rights of marginalised communities,[132] safeguard the environment, and secure basic services.[133] While some argue that it serves a counter-revolutionary agenda and has been instrumental in protecting **'white' privilege'**,[134] it has undoubtedly contributed to the advancement of law in South Africa.

#58 Public interest litigation faces the challenge of **screening bias**, which can result in many cases not receiving support. Organisations carefully select suitable litigants for test cases that advance their aims, such as promoting the rights of vulnerable groups. Without an ideal test case, they are unlikely to support a cause, as a loss could set back their strategic agenda for years.[135]

5 Class Actions

#59 These are relatively new phenomena in South Africa. **Class action** lawsuits did not exist before the constitutional dispensation. However, the courts have held that class action lawsuits are implicitly recognised by section 38(c) of the Constitution.[136] Using their inherent jurisdiction under the common law, as confirmed in section 172 of the Constitution, the courts have fashioned a certification procedure for recognising class actions.[137] The procedure also allows litigants to **'opt-in'** or **'opt-out'** of class action litigation.[138]

#60 Class actions are a powerful mechanism for vindicating and protecting the rights of vulnerable members of society who may lack the financial resources or the

---

130 For example, see *Minister of Health and v Treatment Action Campaign* 2002 (5) SA 721 (CC).

131 For example, see *Esau v Minister of Co-Operative Governance and Traditional Affairs* 2021 (3) SA 593 (SCA); *One South Africa Movement v President of the Republic of South Africa* (2020) JOL 47527 (GP).

132 See, for example, *Satchwell v President of Republic of South Africa* 2002 (6) SA 1; *Gory v Kolver NO* 2007 (4) SA 97 (CC); *Minister of Home Affairs v Fourie* 2006 (1) SA 524 (CC).

133 See, for example, *Mvumvu v Minister of Transport* 2011 (2) SA 473 (CC); *Highveldridge Residents Concerned Party v Highveldridge Transitional Local Council* 2002 (6) SA 66 (T); *Joseph v City of Johannesburg* 2010 (4) SA 55 (CC); *Malan v City of Cape Town* 2014 6 SA 315 (CC); *Occupiers of 51 Olivia Road, Berea Township and 197 Main Street Johannesburg v City of Johannesburg* 2008 (3) SA 208 (CC). *National Coalition for Gay and Lesbian Equality v Minister of Home Affairs* 2000 (2) SA 1 (CC).

134 J Brickhill (ed), *Public Interest Litigation in South Africa* (Juta 2018) 30, 39.

135 S Budlender, G Marcus and N Ferreira, *Public Interest Litigation and Social Change in South Africa: Strategies, Tactics and Lessons* (The Atlantic Philanthropies 2014) 115.

136 *Trustees Children's Resource Centre Trust v Pioneer Food (Pty) Ltd* 2013 (2) SA 213 (SCA); S Woolman and M Bishop, *Constitutional Law of South Africa*, Original Service (2nd edn, Juta 2013) 32–155.

137 ibid. See also *Mukaddam v Pioneer Foods (Pty) Ltd* 2013 (5) SA 89 (CC); *Nkala v Harmony Gold Mining Company Limited* 2016 (5) SA 240 (GJ).

138 T Broodryk, 'The South African Class Action Mechanism: Comparing the Opt-in Regime to the Opt-out Regime' (2019) 22 PER / PELJ 1.

acumen to pursue cases on their own. Furthermore, class actions allow litigants to aggregate smaller cases that may not be financially viable on their own.[139]

#61 **Class** action lawsuits have been utilised to prevent illegal competition, hold mines accountable for harmful practices, ensure credit providers are consumer-centric, and guarantee better judicial oversight when commercial entities sue vulnerable members of society.[140]

III Special Procedures

#62 South African civil procedure textbooks typically do not include a section on 'special procedures' as may be found in other jurisdictions. The procedural system does not generally differentiate between subject matter jurisdiction to create special procedures, although some do exist on closer inspection.

1 Small Claims

#63 The **Small Claims Courts Act**[141] and Rules[142] govern the 413 Small Claims Courts in the country. These courts can hear most contract and tort cases if the claim does not exceed ZAR 20,000.[143] Despite needing to increase their monetary jurisdiction to keep up with inflation, their widespread presence significantly improves access to justice.

#64 The Act and the Rules have simplified the court procedure by disallowing **legal representation.**[144] The new Small Claims Rules of 2022 have significantly improved the process by streamlining court documents and enhancing administrative processes. Unlike other courts, which operate **adversarially**, small claims courts operate **inquisitorially**, with relaxed rules of evidence and decisions that may not be appealed,[145] making them more accessible to the public.

#65 While the Rules were amended by the Rules Board, the Act urgently requires **amendment** by Parliament. The Act needs to be revised to address the enforcement of court judgments, which must be enforced by the local magistrate's court,

139 See *Permanent Secretary, Department of Welfare, Eastern Cape v Ngxuza* 2001 (4) SA 1184 (SCA) para 5.

140 See *Mukaddam v Pioneer Foods (Pty) Ltd* (2013 (5) SA 89 (CC); *Nkala v Harmony Gold Mining Company Limited and Others* 2016 (5) SA 240 (GJ); *Stellenbosch University Law Clinic v Lifestyle Direct Group International (Pty) Ltd and Others* 2022 (2) SA 237 (WCC).

141 Small Claims Courts Act 61 of 1984.

142 NO R 2573 in *Government Gazette* No. 47254 of 7 October 2022.

143 GN 296 in *Government Gazette* 42282 of 5 March 2019.

144 Small Claims Courts Act section 14.

145 ibid section 45.

causing delays.[146] The jurisdiction rules are too rigid and should be relaxed to make the courts more accessible. Furthermore, the concurrent jurisdiction of Magistrates' Courts with Small Claims Courts is problematic because it allows wealthy litigant plaintiffs to initiate lawsuits in the Magistrates' Courts. Creating a small claims track in the Magistrates' Courts – similar to the position in England and Wales – could help divert less complex matters to the Small Claims Courts.[147] In the past, the Small Claims Courts dealt with consumer matters, but the **Consumer Protection Act** of 2008 removed their jurisdiction, requiring all consumer protection matters to be referred to the Consumer Protection Commission and Tribunal.[148] This would have been a positive change had it not been for the fact that the Commission and Tribunal do not function optimally and if the Commission could make binding decisions because currently, it does not.[149]

2 Provisional Sentence

#66 **Provisional sentence** is a summary Roman-Dutch procedure allowing a creditor with clear evidence of a claim to swiftly obtain a judgment without going through the conventional trial process.[150]

#67 The defendant is served with a provisional sentence summons, requiring them to appear in court on a specified date to admit or deny liability. If provisional sentence is granted, it serves as an interim (provisional) judgment that gives the defendant time to enter the main case. The **provisional judgment** becomes final if the defendant does not take appropriate action within the given time.[151]

#68 During the provisional stage, the plaintiff can demand **immediate payment**, but the defendant can ask for **security** for the value of the claim and costs.[152] Regardless of whether payment is claimed, the plaintiff must wait two calendar months before the judgment becomes final.[153] During this period, the defendant could pay the debt and the claim and, in so doing, enter the main case again and continue the action.[154] However, if the defendant paid the debt but the plaintiff

---

146 ibid section 41.
147 See M Paleker, *The Re-Engineering of South African Small Claims Courts* (PhD thesis, University of Cape Town 2018) 27.
148 T Naude and S Eiselen (eds), *Commentary on the Consumer Protection Act 2008*, Revision Service 8 (Juta 2022) 69–1.
149 See R Sharrock, *Business Transactions Law* (9th edn, Juta 2016) ch 25.
150 DE van Loggerenberg, *Erasmus Superior Court Practice* (Revision Service 22, 2023) D1 Rule 8–2.
151 URC 8(11); MCR 14A(11).
152 ibid URC 8(9); MCR 14A(9).
153 ibid URC 8(11); MCR 14A(11).
154 ibid URC 8(10); MCR 14A(10).

failed to put up security as requested, the usual action procedure ensues with the exchange of pleadings, the pretrial stage and eventually trial.[155]

#69 In ***Twee Jonge Gezellen (Pty) Ltd v Land and Agricultural Development Bank of South Africa***,[156] the Constitutional Court found the provisional sentence procedure limited the defendant's right to a **fair trial**. The court ordered the development of the common law to allow courts the discretion to refuse provisional sentence in specific circumstances. This was to address situations where the defendant could not demonstrate a balance of success without oral evidence and was unable to settle the judgment debt. The court held that the common law must be developed so that courts will have the discretion to refuse provisional sentence only if the defendant can demonstrate: (a) an inability to satisfy the judgment debt, (b) an equal likelihood of success in the main case based on the available documents; and (c) a reasonable prospect that oral evidence may change the likelihood of success in their favour.[157]

#70 Interestingly, *Twee Jonge Gezellen* did not strike down the entire procedure for being cumbersome but upheld the essence of the procedure subject to modification. In so doing, the court rendered the procedure less ineffectual, resulting in the procedure being hardly utilised. It is much simpler to issue a simple summons for liquid claims, file the necessary preliminary pleadings and apply for summary judgment than going through the cumbersome provisional sentence procedure.[158]

3 Uniform Rule of the High Court 43 / Magistrates' Courts Rule 58 procedure

#71 In **matrimonial proceedings** at the High Court and Regional Magistrates' Courts, a financially constrained spouse can request interim maintenance for themselves and their children. This process also enables spouses to seek court orders for the care and contact of minor children, as well as for one spouse to contribute to the legal costs of the divorce litigation. However, it is important to note that the procedure is only available if there is a pending divorce action.[159]

#72 Initially, the fees for these applications were restricted to prevent **excessive legal costs**. However, in 2013, the Rules Board lifted this restriction following

155 ibid URC 8(11); MCR 14A(11).

156 *Twee Jonge Gezellen (Pty) Ltd v Land and Agricultural Development Bank of South Africa t/a The Land Bank* 2011 (3) SA 1 (CC).

157 ibid paras 66–69.

158 M Dendy and C Loots, *Herbstein and Van Winsen: The Civil Practice of the Superior Courts of South Africa* (Revision Service 1, 2021) vol 1, 9–30. But see van F Dyk, 'Provisional Sentence Proceedings – Tailored for Liquid Documentary Debts' (January/February 2024) De Rebus 18.

159 URC 43(1)(b).

complaints from practitioners. Since then, some lawyers have exploited the process, increasing **divorce costs** and more acrimonious proceedings.[160]

#73 The procedure only allows for two sets of affidavits in which the parties must set out the facts but no evidence supporting the facts.[161] But, courts have expressed concern about the **length of papers** submitted in some cases. In *KT v AT*, the court admonished counsel for filing an application of 368 pages peppered with salacious information.[162] The court ruled that the plaintiff's attorneys should cover 100 per cent of the legal costs of both the applicant and the respondent out of their pocket.[163] Nevertheless, this procedure is a mainstay of South African divorce litigation and is frequently used to assist impoverished spouses.

4 Tailoring the General Application Procedure

#74 There is a clear distinction between actions and applications in South African procedure. The **application procedure** provide special remedies. To understand the point, it is useful to consider a few examples.

#75 The ***mandament van spolie*** is a Roman-Dutch legal remedy that restores possession to someone unlawfully deprived of their property rights. For example, a tenant who finds the landlord has changed the locks due to a dispute can seek this remedy. According to common law, the person seeking this remedy must immediately assert their right to possession. If proven, the court must restore possession without delving into the merits of the case.[164]

#76 The application process is well-suited to enforce the *mandament*. The notice of motion initiates the *mandament* by outlining the relief sought. The founding affidavit captures the applicant's testimony without the need for **oral evidence** or a trial. The *mandament* can be brought urgently before the court with or without notice (ie ***ex parte***) to the respondent. Overall, procedural law complements substantive law to provide a swift and **cost-effective** remedy to protect the rights of the dispossessed.

#77 Another example: The **presumption of death** typically involves someone applying to declare another person dead due to their unexplained disappearance for a significant period. One can initiate the procedure by submitting an *ex parte* applica-

160 See, for example, *KT v AT* 2020 (2) SA 516 (WCC).

161 Usually, affidavits set out facts and evidence. However, the Rule 43 and Rule 58 applications are *sui generis* and according to the rules the affidavits must be drafted similar to a plea in an action. This means that one must set out the facts. See P Van Blerk, *Precedents for Applications in Civil Proceedings* (Juta 2022) 181.

162 *KT v AT* 2020 (2) SA 516 (WCC) para 29.

163 ibid para 33f.

164 S Peté and others, *Civil Procedure: A Practical Guide* (4th edn, OUP 2024) 543f.

tion. At the first hearing, if the applicant satisfies the evidential burden, the court grants an **interim order** (*rule nisi*). This interim order is published in newspapers and on social media, requiring any person with an interest in the matter to appear in court on the return date to explain why a final order should not be granted.

#78 In administrative law and access to information matters, the application procedure is adapted to the requirements of the relevant substantive remedy.[165] South African procedural law contains numerous instances where the application procedure is adapted to create a **special procedure**.[166]

IV Alternative Dispute Resolution

#79 Following developments in Europe and other parts of the globe, including Africa, Uniform Rule of Court 41A and Chapter 2 of the Magistrates' Courts Rules were enacted to introduce **ADR** as part of the litigation rules.[167] Previously, courts only informally recognised the value of referring matters to ADR, especially in family law cases.[168]

#80 **Mediation** is voluntary and applicable to actions and applications. The plaintiff must include a form with the summons or notice of motion to indicate whether they want to mediate or give reasons for refusing mediation.[169] The defendant can also use a similar form to show their desire to mediate and reasons for refusing mediation.[170] The form is not filed with the court but exchanged between the parties.[171]

#81 Even if the parties choose not to mediate, they can do so at any stage of litigation.[172] However, court permission is needed once the trial or hearing has com-

165 Rules of Court for Application to Court in terms of the Promotion of Access to Information Act 2 of 2000 GNR 1284 *in Government* Gazette 42740 of 4 October 2019; Promotion of Administrative Justice Act, 2000 – Adminstrative Review Rules, 2019 GNR 1284 *in Government* Gazette 42740 of 4 October 2019.

166 See, for example, T Broodryk, *Eckard's Principles of Civil Procedure in the Magistrates' Courts* (6th edn, Juta 2019) 47f.

167 Rule 41A came into operation on 9 March 2020. Chapter 2 as amended came into operation on 5 May 2023. For a discussion see EC Muller and CL Nel, 'A Critical Analysis of the Inefficacy of CAM in SA' (2021) 46 Journal for Juridical Science 26.

168 See for example, *Port Elizabeth Municipality v Various Occupiers* 2005 (1) SA 217 (CC) para 39; *MB v NB* 2010 (3) SA 220 (GSJ) para 50.

169 URC41A(2)(a); MCR72(1).

170 URC41A(2)(b); MCR 72(2).

171 URC41A(2)9(d); MCR 72(4).

172 URC41A(3)(a); MCR73(1).

menced.[173] Since mediation is **voluntary**, a judge cannot force the parties to mediate but can encourage it as part of their judicial case management functions.[174]

#82 When parties agree to mediate, they must file a **joint minute** with the court registrar,[175] which suspends the court rules and allows 30 days for mediation. An optional 30-day extension can be requested in writing.[176]

#83 The parties must enter into a **mediation agreement** that includes choosing a mediator, determining the costs, and deciding on the venue for the meetings.[177] Most courts are unsuitable for hosting mediation sessions as they do not have the facilities; thus the parties must arrange a venue.

#84 All information shared during mediation is **confidential** except for **discoverable documentary evidence.**[178]

#85 In **multiparty litigation**, some parties may opt for mediation.[179] However, the effectiveness of mediation depends on the specifics of the case and the possibility of reaching a partial settlement without affecting non-mediating parties. Any **settlement** reached through mediation is binding only on the parties involved in the mediation.

#86 **Mediation settlements** can be made an order of court or enforced as contracts under common law, and courts generally cannot interfere with the settlement terms due to the principle of freedom of contract.[180]

#87 The usual litigation rules will be reinstated if mediation is unsuccessful or the period expires.[181]

V Judicial Case Management

#88 **Judicial case management** was introduced in 2019 in the High Courts and in 2022 in the Magistrates' Courts to address congested trial schedules and delays in finalising cases.[182] **European developments** have highly influenced South African judicial case management as a mechanism to introduce some judicial oversight in an **adversarial** litigation system to prevent protracted litigation.

---

173 URC41A(3)(a) proviso; MCR 73(1) proviso.
174 URC41A(3)b); MCR 73(2).
175 URC41A(4)(a); MCR 73(3)(a).
176 URC41A(4)(c)-(d); MCR74.
177 URC 41A(4)(b); MCR73(3)(b).
178 URC41A(6).; MCR76.
179 URC41A(5)(a); MCR75.
180 URC41A(8)(e); MCR77(7). See also *Ubisi v Road Accident Fund* 2024 JDR 2383 (SCA).
181 URC41A(8)(a); MCR 77(3).
182 URC 37A(2)(a). See *Report* (n 93).

#89 The judicial case management rules do not lessen the **responsibility of parties** and their legal representatives for case preparation, compliance with court rules, and ethical conduct to expedite proceedings.[183]

#90 In matters designated for case management, the court registrar or clerk can send **compliance letters** to parties who miss filing deadlines and refer non-compliant matters to a case management judge or magistrate.[184]

#91 For a case to proceed to trial, it must be **certified as trial-ready** by a case management judge or magistrate.[185] This certification depends on whether all non-trial issues have been addressed, remaining trial issues are defined, discovery requirements are met, and potential trial delays have been minimised.[186] If any of these requirements are unmet, the presiding officer will provide directions to make the case trial-ready.[187]

#92 Before a case management conference, the parties must have a **pre-trial meeting**. During this meeting, they need to discuss reaching a settlement, narrowing the issues, setting a timeline for procedures, deciding on expert testimony, and using electronic means for proceedings. They should strive to reduce the number of witnesses (including expert witnesses) and consider examining witnesses via videoconferencing.[188]

#93 During the **case management conference**, parties must submit a joint minute outlining the meeting outcomes. The judge or magistrate should explore settlement options, feasibility of voluntary mediation, limit trial witnesses, avoid unnecessary evidence, and document trial issues.[189]

#94 At the **end of the case management conference**, the judge or magistrate can:

(a) Certify the case as trial-ready.
(b) Refuse certification.
(c) Impose terms on the parties for trial readiness and set a date for the next conference.
(d) Remove the matter from case management and re-enroll it after resolving any non-compliance.
(e) Give directions for the expedited hearing of opposed interlocutory applications.
(f) Order separation of issues in appropriate cases.
(g) Record decisions and direct the plaintiff to file a record if necessary.

---

183 URC 37A(2)(c), see also DE van Loggerenberg, *Erasmus: Superior Court Practice* (Revision service 22, 2023) D1, Rule 37A-1).
184 URC 37A(4); MCR 25(4).
185 URC 37A(5)(a); MCR 25(5)(a).
186 URC 37A(5)(b); MCR 25(5)(b).
187 URC 37A(5)(c); MCR 25(5)(c).
188 URC37A(7),(10); MCR25(7),(10).
189 URC37A (11); MCR25(11).

(h) Make orders regarding costs, including against legal representatives or others who unreasonably frustrate the case management process.[190]

VI Online Civil Justice Initiatives

#95 The Office of the Chief Justice is leading an initiative to implement e-filing, digital case management, and evidence systems for the High Courts.[191] This allows lawyers to file documents electronically and simplifies court scheduling and administrative tasks.[192] The **Court Online system** allows for automatic sending of electronic documents to the assigned court official. It also facilitates the exchange and sharing of legal documents among involved parties and enables judges to adjudicate disputes electronically.[193] Currently, the system is only available for civil court proceedings.[194]

#96 The Court Online system can be accessed on any laptop or tablet with internet access and an HTML5-compliant web browser. No specialised **software** is needed.[195] However, South Africa's **electricity crisis** has caused difficulties with the online system, though the situation has improved considerably with the adoption of renewable energy.

#97 Courts increasingly use electronic methods for hearings, and **video-conferencing** technology is often used to examine witnesses.[196] The Rules Board is developing **e-justice** rules to accommodate technology, and court rules already allow for **electronic signatures** and document service between parties.[197] Many law firms use cloud-based solutions for communications and document exchange. Extensive technology use is expected to address infrastructure issues,[198] reduce costs, and alleviate case backlogs.[199] **Artificial intelligence** is also anticipated to play a role in

---

190 URC37A(12); MCR25(12).

191 M Sedutla, 'Court Digitisation – The Future Is Here' (*De Rebus*, 1 April 2021) <https://www.derebus.org.za/court-digitisation-the-future-is-here/> accessed 5 July 2024.

192 B Batchelor, 'Online Litigation – Preparing For the New Normal' (*De Rebus*, 1 August 2023) <https://www.derebus.org.za/online-litigation-preparing-for-the-new-normal/> accessed 5 July 2024.

193 C Ncube and others, *Artificial Intelligence and the Law in Africa* (LexisNexis 2023) 250.

194 'Court Online' (*The South African Judiciary*, 2024) <https://www.judiciary.org.za/index.php/63-caselines?start=3> accessed 5 July 2024.

195 ibid.

196 Batchelor (note 192).

197 Rules Board for Courts of Law, 'E-rules: Draft Amended Uniform Rules' (2021) <https://www.justice.gov.za/rules_board/invite/20210309-E-Rules-AnnexureA.pdf> accessed on 5 July 2024; See also Report (n 93) 45.

198 Report (n 93) 84.

199 Batchelor (n 192).

court administration and dispute resolution in the future.[200] However, South Africa still has a long way to go, and perhaps with some public-private partnerships, the use of technology in courts can be significantly enhanced.

E China

I Efficiency of Case Management

1 Historical Context of Case Management in Europe

#98 The litigation explosion that began in the mid-19th century and the problem of insufficient judicial resources plagued most European countries.[201] Under the pressure of increasing case numbers, both efficiency and the quality of justice were compromised.[202] These issues prompted **judicial reforms across Europe**, aimed at enhancing the effectiveness of litigation. In the field of civil litigation, the reforms focused on strengthening judges' management of civil procedure and promoting the resolution of civil cases within a reasonable timeframe.[203] The Austrian Code of Civil Procedure, which came into effect in 1898, marked a new era in the development of civil procedural law in Europe—the era of case management.[204] Subsequently, many European countries undertook civil justice reforms centered on strengthening the authority of the courts.[205]

#99 '**Case management**' in European jurisdictions share the following characteristics: First, the characteristics of the case itself determine its procedural approach.[206] There is unprecedented emphasis and value placed on procedural flexibility.[207] Legislators no longer design a strict set of procedural norms to be

200 Ncube (n 193).

201 L Grinin, 'The European Revolutions and Revolutionary Waves of the 19th Century: Their Causes and Consequences' in JA Goldstone, L Grinin and A Korotayev (eds), *Handbook of Revolutions in the 21st Century: The New Waves of Revolutions, and the Causes and Effects of Disruptive Political Change* (Springer 2022) 281, 285.

202 ibid 292.

203 M Cappelletti, 'Social and Political Aspects of Civil Procedure—Reforms and Trends in Western and Eastern Europe' (1970) 69 Michigan Law Review 847.

204 CH van Rhee, 'The Development of Civil Procedural Law in Twentieth-Century Europe: From Party Autonomy to Judicial Case Management and Efficiency' in CH van Rhee (ed), *Judicial Case Management and Efficiency in Civil Litigation* (Intersentia 2008) 11, 12f.

205 CH van Rhee, 'Civil Litigation in Twentieth Century Europe' (2007) 75 Tijdschrift voor Rechtsgeschiedenis / Revue d'histoire du droit / The Legal History Review 308.

206 A Cabral, 'New Trends and Perspectives on Case Management' (2018) 8 International Journal of Procedural Law 10.

207 Van Rhee (n 204) 12f.

applied to different types of cases; instead, they design different procedures based on the characteristics of different case types.[208] Thus, the development of case management has promoted the differentiation and refinement of procedures, including procedures for family trials, small claims, and intellectual property cases.[209] Second, case management seeks to enhance litigation efficiency.[210] During the preparatory phase of the proceedings, judges assist parties in organising issues, determining the scope and order of evidence submission, and speeding up the process. Judges also ensure that procedural deadlines are met. Third, case management promotes the use of mediation or other forms of ADR. In some cases, the judge would initiate this process.[211] Case management is not an end in itself, but a means to achieve an end. The control of judges over procedural matters is not unlimited, but is guided by the legislative purpose of enhancing the efficiency of dispute resolution.[212]

2 Adoption and Adaptation in China

#100 In response to these European advancements, China has embarked on its own **judicial reforms**, mirroring some of the European approaches while adapting them to local conditions. In China, the number of civil disputes has been increasing with economic and social development, and as public legal awareness has risen, the **number of civil cases in courts** has also increased.[213] In 2023, courts at all levels across the nation accepted 45.574 million cases and concluded 45.268 million cases, representing year-over-year increases of 15.6 per cent and 13.4 per cent, respectively.[214] However, the **number of judges** in local courts at all levels has not increased correspondingly, and the 'many cases, few judges' issue is a common problem faced by courts nationwide.[215] The case management system in Europe, which emphasises efficiency and transparency, has had a cer-

208 S Gensler, 'Judicial Case Management: Caught in the Crossfire' (2010) 60 Duke Law Journal 669.
209 M Payne, 'The Politics of Case Management and Social Work' (2000) 9 International Journal of Social Welfare 85.
210 Van Rhee (n 204) 13.
211 WH Rechberger, *Civil Procedure in Austria* (Walters Kluwer 2011) 17.
212 IN Tzankova, 'Case Management: The Stepchild of Mass Claim Dispute Resolution' (2014) 19 Uniform Law Review 329, 330.
213 CF Minzner, 'China's Turn Against Law' (2011) 59 American Journal of Comparative Law 937.
214 '2023年全国法院收结案均超4500万件' ('In 2023, National Courts Handled More Than 45 Million Cases') (最高人民法院, 8 March 2024) <https://www.court.gov.cn/zixun/xiangqing/427022.html> accessed 20 June 2024.
215 程金华, '中国法院"案多人少"的实证评估与应对策略' ('Empirical Assessment and Response Strategies for the "Many Cases, Few People" Issue in Chinese Courts') [2022–6] 中国法学 ('Chinese Legal Science') 238.

tain influence over China's civil litigation system, mainly reflected in the following aspects.

#101 First, **case diversion** and **preliminary screening**: Some European countries have adopted a case diversion system that, through preliminary case screening and classification management, effectively speeds up case handling.[216] This method has influenced the Chinese court system to place greater emphasis on preliminary management and diversion of cases, introducing similar preliminary review systems to improve litigation efficiency. The Supreme People's Court proposed the idea of 'dividing complex and simple cases, separating light and serious cases, and differentiating fast and slow tracks', ('繁简分流、轻重分离、快慢分道') and on 28 December 2019, it was authorised by the Standing Committee of the National People's Congress to pilot the simplification of civil litigation procedures in certain regional courts.[217] As a significant outcome of the reform pilot, on 19 October 2021, the Supreme People's Court submitted the '**Civil Procedure Law of the People's Republic of China (Amendment Draft)**' to the Standing Committee of the National People's Congress.[218] The amendment made the following changes to improve the application scope and methods of the small claims procedure:[219] firstly, it lowered the threshold for applying the small claims procedure, changing the applicable amount from thirty per cent to fifty per cent of the average annual wage of employed persons in each province, autonomous region, and municipality directly under the Central Government of the previous year.[220] Secondly, it stipulated that for cases not exceeding a certain limit, parties could voluntarily agree to apply the small claims litigation procedure.[221] Thirdly, it simplified the trial methods for small claims cases, shortening the deadlines for document delivery, evidence submission, and trial, and simplifying the procedures for filing, responding, summoning, servicing of documents, and court hearings.[222] The Amendment Draft aims to develop a multi-level and

---

216 DH Choe, 'Discretion at the Pre-Trial Stage: A Comparative Study' (2014) 20 Eur J on Crim Policy and Res 101.

217 '破解"案多人少" 民事诉讼繁简分流改革' ('Solving the "Many Cases, Few People" Issue through the Streamlining Reform of Civil Litigation') (人民网, 13 May 2020) <http://henan.people.com.cn/n2/2020/0513/c351638-34013968.html> accessed 20 June 2024.

218 '关于《中华人民共和国民事诉讼法 (修正草案)》的说明' ('Explanation on the "Civil Procedure Law of the People's Republic of China (Draft Amendment)"') (中国人大网, 27 December 2021) <http://www.npc.gov.cn/npc/c2/c30834/202112/t20211227_315637.html> accessed 20 June 2024.

219 '降低门槛简化审理,民诉法拟修改完善小额诉讼程序' ('Reducing Thresholds and Simplifying Trials, Civil Procedure Law Plans to Amend and Improve Small Claims Procedure') (新华网, 19 October 2021) <http://www.news.cn/legal/2021-10/19/c_1127972768.htm> accessed 20 June 2024.

220 Civil Procedure Law of the People's Republic of China (Draft Amendment), Article 165(1).

221 Civil Procedure Law of the People's Republic of China (Draft Amendment), Article 165(2).

222 Civil Procedure Law of the People's Republic of China (Draft Amendment), Article 162.

refined civil litigation procedural system, thereby improving the dispute resolution capabilities of the people's courts and increasing litigation efficiency.[223]

#102 Secondly, **procedural simplification**: Some of Europe's summary procedures and fast-track decision-making mechanisms have reduced the burden on courts and accelerated case handling.[224] Building on these experiences, Chinese courts have tried to increase litigation **efficiency** by simplifying certain procedures and introducing fast-track procedures, thus speeding up case handling and reducing backlogs. For example, the Amendment Draft lifted the limitation that only collegial panels could conduct trials of first-instance ordinary procedures and second-instance procedures. The Amendment Draft provided that if the basic facts are simple and clear and the rights and obligations are clear, first-instance civil cases under ordinary procedures adjudicated by primary people's courts could be handled by a single judge. Intermediate people's courts and specialised courts handling second-instance civil cases that applied summary procedures for case closure or appeals against civil rulings could also adopt a single-judge bench if the facts are clear and the rights and obligations are clear.[225] Additionally, regarding the delivery of judicial documents, the Amendment Draft retained the possibility of delivering judgments, rulings, and mediation documents electronically.[226] Lastly, another simplification is also reflected in the service process. The current Civil Procedure Law stipulates a sixty-day public notice service period. The Amendment Draft shortened it to thirty days.[227] These new provisions in the Amendment Draft are expected to significantly enhance the efficiency of the operation of China's civil justice system, prevent an 'equal effort' approach for all cases, and enhance overall judicial quality and efficiency.[228]

---

223 任重, '"案多人少"的成因与出路——对本轮民事诉讼法修正之省思' ('The Causes and Solutions of "Many Cases, Few People" – Reflections on the Current Round of Civil Procedure Law Amendments') (2022) 40 法学评论 ('Law Review') 138.

224 E Guinchard and M-P Granger (eds), *The New EU Judiciary: An Analysis of Current Judicial Reforms* (Kluwer Law International 2016).

225 Civil Procedure Law of the People's Republic of China (Draft Amendment), Article 40.

226 Civil Procedure Law of the People's Republic of China (Draft Amendment), Article 90.

227 Civil Procedure Law of the People's Republic of China (Draft Amendment), Article 95.

228 谢冰斌, '论我国民事"独任制+普通程序"组织模式的完善' ('On the Improvement of the "Sole Responsibility + Ordinary Procedure" Organisational Model in China's Civil Justice System') (2021) 29(2) 成都理工大学学报 (社会科学版) ('Journal of Chengdu University of Technology (Social Sciences)') 43.

II E-Justice

1 Development of E-Justice in the EU

#103 With the development of e-commerce, the European Union has continuously improved its **consumer protection** policies in terms of procedural rules.[229] To further safeguard consumer interests, enhance **online dispute resolution (ODR)** mechanisms, boost consumer confidence in e-commerce, and achieve the goals of a digital integrated market in Europe, the European Parliament and the Council of the European Union enacted Regulation No 524/2013 on May 21, 2013, on online resolution of consumer disputes and amending Regulation (EC) No 2006/2004 and Directive 2009/22/EC, as well as Directive 2013/11/EU on alternative dispute resolution for consumers, which also amends Regulation (EC) No 2006/2004 and Directive 2009/22/EC.[230] Following the enactment of these regulations, member states began to utilise the online dispute resolution platform (ODR platform) established under the EU internal market environment.[231] These platforms employ Information and Communication Technology (ICT) to resolve e-commerce disputes.[232]

#104 The **EU ODR platform** provides a one-stop website for out-of-court dispute resolution for consumers and businesses. The platform organically links all eligible ADR entities of member states.[233] When a dispute arises, consumers can access the ODR platform via a link publicly provided by the business to submit their application.[234] Once the business and consumer mutually select an ADR entity, the platform submits the dispute to the agreed-upon ADR entity to handle the dispute. This includes proposing solutions for resolving the dispute and providing a communication platform to assist in discussing resolution options.[235]

---

229 J Devenney and M Kenny (eds), *European Consumer Protection: Theory and Practice* (CUP 2012).

230 P Cortés and AR Lodder, 'Consumer Dispute Resolution Goes Online: Reflections on the Evolution of European Law for Out-of-Court Redress' (2014) 21 Maastricht Journal of European and Comparative Law 14.

231 D Clifford and YS Van Der Sype, 'Online Dispute Resolution: Settling Data Protection Disputes in a Digital World of Customers' (2016) 32 Computer Law & Security Review 272.

232 A Plevri, 'Alternative Dispute Resolution (ADR) & Online Dispute Resolution (ODR) for EU Consumers: The European and Cypriot Framework' in T-E Synodinou and others (eds), *EU Internet Law in the Digital Era: Regulation and Enforcement* (Springer 2020) 367.

233 M Bakhramova, 'Theoretical and Legal Regulation of ODR in the European Union Countries' (2022) 2 European Journal of Innovation in Nonformal Education 299.

234 U Jeretina, 'Consumer Online Dispute Resolution (ODR)—A Mechanism for Innovative E-Governance in EU' (2018) 16 Cent Eur Pub Admin Rev 45.

235 J Page and L Bonnyman, 'ADR and ODR—Achieving Better Dispute Resolution for Consumers in the EU' (2016) 17 ERA Forum 2.

2 China's Integration of E-Justice

#105 In recent years, as the ODR mechanism has matured, the European model of **e-justice**, particularly its robust implementation of ODR platforms, has encouraged China to integrate similar technologies. This is evident in the growing adoption of **online courts** and dispute resolution mechanisms that allow for the handling of cases digitally. On the other hand, China's extensive deployment of internet courts in major cities offers a unique model for Europe in terms of scale and integration with the national judicial system. The Chinese experience in handling a vast number of cases online could provide valuable insights into operational efficiencies and the digital management of judicial processes.

a) Development of Internet Courts

#106 Inspired by Europe's digital strides, China has not only adopted but also expanded the concept of E-Justice to suit its vast and varied legal landscape. In 2018, the Supreme People's Court issued the 'Provisions on Several Issues Concerning the Handling of Cases by Internet Courts', to provide a legal foundation for the development of **Internet Courts in China**.[236] As grassroots people's courts with centralised jurisdiction over Internet-related cases, Internet Courts primarily operate under a novel mechanism whereby pretrial procedures are handled online and court hearings are conducted online.[237] They have jurisdiction over 11 types of Internet-related cases within their municipal areas, including disputes over online financial loans, online shopping contracts, online service contracts, online torts, and online intellectual property rights, covering the most common dispute types in the e-commerce sector.[238] In 2017 and 2018, Internet Courts were successively established in Hangzhou, Beijing, and Guangzhou.[239] By the end of October 2023, the Beijing Internet Court had accepted 197,000 cases and concluded 186,000 cases.[240] The Beijing Internet Court has developed a 'multi-functional, full-process, integrated' **electronic litigation platform**, completely transitioning the litigation model from off-

236 '关于互联网法院审理案件若干问题的规定' ('Provisions on Several Issues Concerning the Handling of Cases by Internet Courts') (最高人民法院公报, 6 September 2018) <http://gongbao.court.gov.cn/Details/7e594961f195254a863d6cc90be5cd.html> accessed 20 June 2024.

237 张芳芳和骆嘉仕, '我国互联网法院管辖制度研究' ('Research on the Jurisdiction System of Internet Courts in China') (2024) 41(1) 政法学刊 ('Journal of Political Science and Law') 120–128.

238 ibid.

239 '首个互联网法院——展现互联网司法治理的"中国智慧"' ('The First Internet Court—Demonstrating the "Chinese Wisdom" in Internet Judicial Governance') (中国法院网, 2 January 2019) <https://www.chinacourt.org/article/detail/2019/01/id/3640671.shtml> accessed 20 June 2024.

240 '以高质量互联网司法护航中国式现代化——北京互联网法院成立五年工作综述' ('Safeguarding Chinese-style Modernization with High-Quality Internet Justice: A Five-Year Review of the Beijing Internet Court') 中国法院网 (29 October 2023) <https://www.chinacourt.org/article/detail/2023/10/id/7600832.shtml> accessed 20 June 2024.

line to online. The online case filing submission rate reached 100 per cent, the online litigation fee payment rate was 92.24 per cent, and the online trial rate was 99.89 per cent, showing a clear transition to a fully online mode of procedure.[241] Significant improvements have been made in case handling, platform construction, litigation rules, technology application, and network governance.

b) Development of Online Mediation

#107 In 2016, the Supreme People's Court issued the 'Opinions on Further Deepening the Reform of the Diversified Dispute Resolution Mechanism of the People's Courts', which proposed building a fully functional, diverse, and well-regulated platform for integrating litigation and mediation and improving dispute resolution channels.[242] Specific measures included 'innovating online dispute resolution methods', clearly stipulating the establishment of an integrated information platform for **online mediation**, online case filing, online judicial confirmation, online trial, electronic payment procedures, and electronic service of documents.[243]

#108 In February 2017, the Supreme People's Court initiated a pilot project for an **online mediation** platform.[244] In February 2018, the People's Court Mediation Platform developed by the Supreme People's Court officially launched and began trial operation across all courts nationwide.[245] In February 2021, the Supreme People's Court announced at a press conference that, by the end of 2020, all 3502 courts had integrated with the mediation platform, achieving a 100per cent implementation rate. The platform hosts 32,937 mediation organisations and 165,333 mediators, having mediated over 13.6 million cases with an average mediation duration of 23.33 days. In 2020, the platform added approximately 5.1988 million successfully mediated cases, with a success rate of 65.04 per cent.[246] Fuelled by the efforts of the Supreme People's Court, local courts and authorities also estab-

241 '北京互联网法院:5年审结18.2万件案件 著作权权属侵权纠纷超七成' ('Beijing Internet Court: 182,000 Cases Concluded in 5 Years, Over 70% Are Copyright Ownership and Infringement Disputes') (人民网,9 September 2023) <http://society.people.com.cn/n1/2023/0909/c1008-40073886.html> accessed 20 June 2024.

242 '关于人民法院进一步深化多元化纠纷解决机制改革的意见' ('Opinions on Further Deepening the Reform of Diversified Dispute Resolution Mechanisms in People's Courts') (中国法院网,28 June 2016) <https://www.chinacourt.org/law/detail/2016/06/id/148740.shtml> accessed 20 June 2024.

243 ibid.

244 '最高法启动在线调解平台建设试点工作' ('The Supreme Court Initiates Pilot Project for Building an Online Mediation Platform') (中国法院网 28 February 2017) <https://www.chinacourt.org/article/detail/2017/02/id/2546606.shtml> accessed 20 June 2024.

245 '人民法院调解平台正式上线' ('The People's Court Mediation Platform Officially Launched') (最高人民法院,28 February 2018) <https://www.court.gov.cn/zixun/xiangqing/82582.html> accessed 20 June 2024.

246 '每分钟66件,看人民法院调解平台如何为民解纷' ('66 Cases per Minute: How the People's Court Mediation Platform Resolves Disputes for the Public') (最高人民法院新闻. 20 February 2021) <https://www.court.gov.cn/zixun/xiangqing/287441.html> accessed 20 June 2024.

lished online mediation platforms. In January 2019, the **'Tianfu Citizen Cloud'** legal services section in Chengdu officially launched the 'Hehe Zhijie' service, providing parties with economical, convenient, and efficient dispute resolution channels.[247] In December 2019, the Huangdao District People's Court in Qingdao launched the **People's Court Mediation Platform** to provide user-friendly online mediation tools for parties.[248]

#109 The **Chinese online court mediation platform** allows mediation data to flow freely online among parties, overcomes geographical limitations and provides parties with flexible and convenient online services such as legal consultation, judicial confirmation and fast track dispute resolution tools.[249]

III Collective Litigation

1 European Framework for Collective Litigation

#110 In the field of collective litigation, countries like Sweden and the Netherlands have significantly enhanced their case-processing capabilities through the establishment of **group litigation** systems.[250] In the realm of consumer protection, the European Union's system for collective consumer litigation has played a vital role in 'levelling the playing field'.[251] It deprives defendants of unlawful gains and serves as a deterrent to unlawful business operators, thereby preventing future unlawful or irresponsible business practices.[252]

#111 Overall, the main functions of **EU consumer collective litigation** include: (1) Compensating consumers whose legal rights have been infringed. Generally, small claims are difficult to resolve through other procedures, but they can be

---

247 '成都中院全国首创"和合智解"e调解平台探索"o2o"零距离司法服务新机制' ('Chengdu Intermediate People's Court Pioneers the "Hehe Zhijie" E-Mediation Platform to Explore New "O2O" Proximity-Free Judicial Service Mechanisms') (成都法院网 15 April 2019) <http://cdfy.scssfw.gov.cn/article/detail/2019/05/id/3890054.shtml> accessed 20 June 2024.

248 '19起案件5天结案!黄岛法院率先成功运行互联网远程调解' ('19 Cases Concluded in 5 Days! Huangdao Court First to Successfully Operate Internet Remote Mediation') (青报网, 27 December 2019) <https://www.shiminjia.com/news/detail/MDAwMDAwMDAwMKSMzuy8rZeM> accessed 20 June 2024.

249 吕宗澄和夏培元, '新时代法院在线调解平台建设现状及优化策略研究' ('Research on the Current Status and Optimization Strategies of Online Mediation Platform Construction by Courts in the New Era') (2022) 23(4) 南华大学学报 (社会科学版) ('Journal of Nanhua University (Social Science Edition)') 76.

250 P van der Grinten, 'A Dutch Perspective on Civil Litigation and Its Harmonisation' in XE Kramer and CH van Rhee (eds), *Civil Litigation in a Globalizing World* (OUP 2012) 286.

251 F Cafaggi, 'Collective Enforcement of Consumer Law: A Framework for Comparative Assessment' (2008) 16 European Review of Private Law 3.

252 I Benöhr, 'Collective Redress in the Field of European Consumer Law' (2014) 41 Legal Issues of Economic Integration 18.

relatively easily addressed through consumer collective litigation.[253] This is because the damages to individual consumers are low, litigation costs are high, and the legal system is complex.[254] Consumer collective litigation consolidates multiple small claims, thereby enabling the recovery of compensation efficiently that would otherwise be difficult to obtain.[255] (2) Depriving operators of undue profits and preventing their continuation of illegal activities. The establishment of the consumer collective litigation system aligns with the equitable legal principle that no one should profit from their illegal actions.[256] Moreover, the establishment of this system also serves as a warning to operators, making them realise that they cannot profit at the expense of consumer interests.[257] (3) Saving judicial resources and avoiding conflicting judgments. By consolidating the claims of hundreds and thousands of individuals into one lawsuit, it saves limited judicial resources.[258] At the same time, it also prevents conflicting judicial decisions, which could affect the credibility of the judiciary.[259]

2 China's Emerging Practices in Collective Litigation

#112 As Europe has refined its collective litigation frameworks, China has cautiously begun to explore these mechanisms, ensuring they align with societal values and legal traditions. In **China, the collective litigation system** is still in its initial stages, but its development and reform show a clear trend of legal adaptation to societal needs. Strictly speaking, the term 'collective litigation' does not exist under Chinese law; the professional terms are **'joint litigation'** or **'representative litigation'**.[260] In practice, China's representative litigation mainly focuses on labour

253 B Haar, 'Regulation Through Litigation—Collective Redress in Need of a New Balance Between Individual Rights and Regulatory Objectives in Europe' (2018) 19 Theoretical Inquiries in Law 203.
254 ibid.
255 ibid.
256 R Van den Bergh and L Visscher, 'The Preventive Function of Collective Actions for Damages in Consumer Law' (2007) 1 Erasmus Law Review 5.
257 ibid.
258 KW Dam, 'Class Actions: Efficiency, Compensation, Deterrence, and Conflict of Interest' (1975) 4 The Journal of Legal Studies 47.
259 ibid.
260 张明继, '论我国群体诉讼解决机制的完善路径' ('On the Improvement Path of Group Litigation Resolution Mechanism in China') [2020–1] 黑龙江省政法管理干部学院学报 ('Journal of Heilongjiang Administrative Cadre College of Politics and Law') 92.

disputes[261] and securities disputes.[262] In these cases, courts tend to use representative collective filing and the consolidation of individual cases to improve judicial efficiency and fairness.[263] Notably, in 2020, the Supreme People's Court issued the **'Provisions on Several Issues Concerning Representative Litigation in Securities Disputes'**, to provide a structured legal framework for collective litigation in the securities industry.[264]

#113 However, the conditions for accepting collective lawsuits are strict, and courts often have wide discretion in deciding whether to accept such cases.[265] Moreover, **China's litigation culture** traditionally favours mediation and settlement over litigation, which influences public attitudes towards collective litigation.[266] Despite facing many challenges, the potential of collective litigation in China cannot be underestimated. In the future, as the legal system is improved and public legal awareness is raised, collective litigation is expected to play a more significant role in China. The implementation of representative litigation in **securities disputes** has already provided valuable lessons for collective litigation in other areas.[267] This not only helps to simplify litigation procedures and enhance efficiency but, most importantly, better protects the rights and interests of consumers and retail investors.

IV Litigation Funding

#114 Litigation costs in China has soared in the past decade or so, giving rise to access to justice concerns.[268] These costs not only include the litigation fees charged by

261 葛进, '群体性劳动争议解决机制研究' ('Research on the Mechanism for Resolving Collective Labour Disputes') (2014) 13(6) 安徽警官职业学院学报 ('Journal of Anhui Police College') 26.
262 毛立琦, '论中国式证券集体诉讼的功能定位' ('On the Functional Positioning of Chinese-Style Securities Class Actions') (2022) 59(1) 南京大学学报 (哲学·人文科学·社会科学) ('Journal of Nanjing University (Philosophy, Humanities and Social Sciences)') 146.
263 ibid.
264 '最高人民法院关于证券纠纷代表人诉讼若干问题的规定' ('Supreme People's Court Provisions on Several Issues Concerning Representative Litigation in Securities Disputes') (最高人民法院, 31 July 2020) <https://www.court.gov.cn/fabu/xiangqing/245501.html> accessed 20 June 2024.
265 冷静, '康美启示:证券集团诉讼首案的制度突破与未尽议题' ('Kangmei Inspiration: Institutional Breakthroughs and Unresolved Issues in the First Case of Securities Group Litigation') [2022–1] 中国法律评论 ('China Law Review') 78.
266 王国龙, '法院诉源治理的司法理念及功能定位' ('Judicial Philosophy and Functional Positioning of Court Litigation Source Management') [2022–6] 政法论丛 ('Tribune of Political Science and Law') 133.
267 王雪羽, '证券特别代表人诉讼的制度创新与规则完善' ('Institutional Innovation and Rule Improvement in Securities Special Representative Litigation') (2024) 42(3) 法律科学 (西北政法大学学报) ('Legal Science (Journal of Northwest University of Political Science and Law)') 183–200.
268 王福华, '民诉法修改背景下的诉讼费用改革' ('Reform of Litigation Costs in the Context of the Amendment of the Civil Procedure Law') (2022) 40(2) 法学评论 ('Law Review') 126.

the courts but also the expensive legal service fees and other expenses necessary for litigation.[269] In recent years, as the types and number of cases have increased, **litigation costs** have also increased, leading parties to either abandon litigation altogether due to their inability to bear the costs or, even if they can afford it, hastily settle their lawsuits due to the fear of losing the case.[270]

1 Overview of Litigation Funding in Europe

#115 Over the past two decades, **third-party litigation funding** has emerged and developed rapidly in common law countries and has gradually gained traction in civil law countries like Germany, Austria, and Switzerland.[271] Third-party litigation funding involves a third party external to the litigation covering the litigation costs, from which they profit if the outcome is favourable. If the party loses, the funder has no right to any returns.[272]

#116 Litigation funding has multiple attributes. First, it is a method of enhancing access to justice.[273] **Legal aid** supported by state finances has a narrow reach and is insufficient to meet the litigation needs of average litigants.[274] Thus, litigation funding, through market resource allocation, can help channel resources to litigants in need of funding.[275] Secondly, it is a way of **transferring litigation risk**; many businesses capable of bearing litigation costs are unwilling to take on the associated risks.[276] Introducing third-party litigation funding allows companies to transfer these risks to funders, potentially transforming their legal departments from cost centres into profit centres.[277] Thirdly, it is also a form of **venture investment**. Third-party litigation funding essentially combines venture capital from the financial sector with the legal services industry.[278] Since the funds are non-recourse, funders conduct independent and rigorous assessments

---

269 ibid.

270 周庆和张永利, '我国民事诉讼和解权的法律问题研究' ('Legal Issues of Settlement Rights in Civil Litigation in China') (2018) 39(4) 湖北文理学院学报 ('Journal of Hubei University of Arts and Science') 39.

271 See M de Morpurgo, 'A Comparative Legal and Economic Approach to Third-Party Litigation Funding' (2011) 19 Cardozo Journal of International and Comparative Law 343, 364.

272 M Steinitz, 'Whose Claim is This Anyway? Third-Party Litigation Funding' (2010) 95 Minnesota Law Review 1268.

273 De Morpurgo (n 271).

274 J Charn, 'Legal Services for All: Is the Profession Ready' (2008) 42 Loyola of Los Angeles Law Review 1021.

275 Steinitz (n 272) 1269.

276 KN Hylton, 'Toward a Regulatory Framework for Third-Party Funding of Litigation' (2013) 63 DePaul Law Review 527.

277 ibid.

278 M Steinitz, 'The Litigation Finance Contract' (2012) 54 William & Mary Law Review 455.

of the cases they support.[279] High-value claims, as lower-risk assets, are unaffected by capital market fluctuations and can offer more favourable returns to investors.[280]

2 China's Approach to Litigation Costs and Funding

#117 As **capital markets** become increasingly globalised and litigation becomes the primary method of dispute resolution, the commercialisation of third-party litigation funding offers a way to share litigation costs and disperse litigation risk, which could serve as a model for China to alleviate some of the difficulties associated with rising litigation costs.[281] With the development of litigation financing globally, China has seen the emergence of **litigation financing practices** in recent years. Since 2015, companies specialising in litigation financing have appeared, innovatively introducing the concept of '**legal finance**' by integrating financial elements with legal services.[282] In 2016, China's first litigation financing fund was established—Duomeng Litigation Financing Fund—specialising in investing in disputes between businesses and providing litigation funding to individuals within companies, such as executives.[283] In 2017, China's first legal **public welfare project** for litigation financing was established, which, through legal aid and litigation funding, supports cases matches appropriate lawyers with the funded individuals.[284] Once the case is won and executed, the funded party returns the litigation costs to the fund pool to support other cases. Currently, aside from litigation fee waivers, legal aid, and lawyer risk representation, China lacks specific and explicit mechanisms for sharing litigation costs and dispersing the risk of losing a case.[285] More needs to be done in this area going forward.

---

279 ibid.

280 ibid.

281 李欢, '第三方诉讼融资: 域外实践与我国的引入' ('Third-Party Litigation Financing: Foreign Practices and Its Introduction in China') [2018–9] 市场周刊 ('Market Weekly') 140.

282 程雪梅, '第三方诉讼融资: 效力、发展及对我国的启示' ('Third-Party Litigation Financing: Efficacy, Development, and Implications for China') [2014–4] 学术界 ('Academic Community') 211.

283 '中国首只诉讼融资基金在武汉成立' ('China's First Litigation Financing Fund Established in Wuhan') (荆楚网, 12 March 2016) <http://www.cnhubei.com/xw/jj/201603/t3566300.shtml> accessed 20 June 2024.

284 This project is called the 'Bangying Public Interest Litigation Financing Platform', and the website for the project is <https://www.bangying.tech/new-home/#/login> accessed 20 June 2024.

285 张光磊, '第三方诉讼融资: 通往司法救济的商业化路径' ('Third-Party Litigation Financing: The Commercial Path to Judicial Relief') [2016–3] 中国政法大学学报 ('Journal of China University of Political Science and Law') 24.

V Specialised Courts

1 Development of Specialised Courts in Europe and China

The establishment of **specialised courts** highlights a shared objective between China and Europe to refine judicial expertise and enhance **procedural efficiency** for complex cases. For instance, both have made breakthroughs in the specialisation of their intellectual property adjudication systems in recent years. In February 2013, 24 EU member states signed the Agreement on a Unified Patent Court, initiating the establishment of the **European Unified Patent Court**.[286] In August 2014, the Standing Committee of the National People's Congress in China passed a decision to establish intellectual property courts in Beijing, Shanghai, and Guangzhou.[287]

2 Benefits of Specialisation

a) Unified Judicial Standards

#118 **Specialised intellectual property courts** play a crucial role in unifying judicial standards.[288] In the EU, patent trials are conducted by national courts separately, affecting the uniformity of judicial protection standards. For example, regarding the validity of patents, the American company DSS once filed a lawsuit against the European Central Bank concerning European Patent No. 04555750 (which involves technology to prevent the illegal copying of documents). Courts in Germany, the Netherlands, and Spain upheld the patent's validity, while courts in the UK, Austria, and France declared it invalid.[289] EU member states have different patent infringement compensation systems, inevitably leading to variations in compensation amounts and encouraging forum shopping by parties.[290] Similarly, in China, due to the vast number of courts handling intellectual property cases across a wide geographic area, there are regional disparities which are ex-

286 J Tumbridge, 'Unified Patent Court: Harmonising Patent Law Throughout Europe' (2014) 15 Business Law International 55.

287 '全国人民代表大会常务委员会关于在北京、上海、广州设立知识产权法院的决定' ('Decision of the Standing Committee of the National People's Congress on Establishing Intellectual Property Courts in Beijing, Shanghai, and Guangzhou') (中国人大网,31 August 2014) <http://www.npc.gov.cn/zgrdw/npc/xinwen/2014-09/01/content_1877042.htm> accessed 20 June 2024.

288 P Drahos, 'The Universality of Intellectual Property Rights: Origins and Development' in *Intellectual Property and Human Rights* (World Intellectual Property Organisation 1999) 13.

289 JM Smits and WA Bull, 'European Harmonisation of Intellectual Property Law: Towards a Competitive Model and a Critique of the Proposed Unified Patent Court' in A Ohly and J Pila (eds), *The Europeanization of Intellectual Property Law: Towards a European Legal Methodology* (OUP 2013) 39, 41.

290 B Jacobsmeyer, 'Forum Shopping in Patent Cases: Lessons for the Unified Patent Court' (2018) 25 Michigan Technology Law Review 131.

acerbated by local protectionism. The low predictability of intellectual property protection leads to a lower willingness of right holders to seek formal channels to enforce their rights.[291] Specialised intellectual property courts can help address this issue.

b) Avoiding Repetitive Litigation

#119 Specialised intellectual property courts, by **centralising jurisdiction**, can prevent repetitive litigation and reduce the cost burden for right holders.[292] The **fragmentation of patent trials** in Europe has caused the skyrocketing of litigation costs.[293] According to some analyses, the costs of applying for and maintaining patents in six major European countries (Germany, the UK, France, Italy, the Netherlands, and Switzerland) are six times higher than that in the US.[294] The **costs of litigation** are also exceptionally high. In the UK, the cost of a patent litigation can be as high as between £1 million to £6 million.[295] Under the Agreement on a Unified Patent Court, right-holders need only participate in one trial and have their rights enforced in multiple countries. This has significantly reduced enforcement costs as well.[296] In China, based on the basic principle of civil litigation jurisdiction over the defendant, parties typically need to initiate lawsuits in the location of the infringement act or where the defendant is located.[297] As such, repetitive litigations across multiple regions have emerged.[298] The centralisation and cross-regional jurisdiction of specialised intellectual property courts are conducive in reducing the occurrence of multiple litigations for similar infringement acts.[299]

---

291 PP Soo, 'Enforcing a Unitary Patent in Europe: What the US Federal Courts and Community Design Courts Teach Us' (2012) 35 Loyola of Los Angeles International and Comparative Law Review 57.

292 余希, '专门审判机构设立研究' ('Research on the Establishment of Specialised Judicial Organs') [2022–4] 法律适用 ('Application of Law') 147.

293 L Dijkman and C Van Paddenburgh, 'The Unified Patent Court as Part of a New European Patent Landscape: Wholesale Harmonization or Experiment in Legal Pluralism?' (2018) 26 European Review of Private Law 97.

294 刘强, '中欧知识产权专门法院比较研究' ('Comparative Study of Intellectual Property Specialised Courts in China and Europe') (2015) 39(6) 湘潭大学学报 (哲学社会科学版) ('Journal of Xiangtan University (Philosophy and Social Sciences)') 89.

295 'UK Patent Litigation Is a Complex Area and Can Be Daunting' (*Marks & Clerk*, 18 October 2017) <https://www.marks-clerk.com/insights/articles/uk-patent-litigation-is-a-complex-area-and-can-be-daunting/> accessed 20 June 2024.

296 Tumbridge (n 286).

297 杨雪婷, '我国民事重复诉讼研究综述' ('Overview of Research on Civil Re-litigation in China') [2021–14] 西部学刊 ('Western Academic Journal') 100.

298 ibid.

299 N Lee and L Zhang, 'Specialised IP Courts in China—Judicial Governance of Intellectual Property Rights' (2017) 48 IIC-International Review of Intellectual Property and Competition Law 900.

F Conclusion

#120 The comparative endeavour conducted in this Chapter reveals several intricacies of the European influence on foreign procedural systems. Specifically, it reveals that the **challenges** in promoting access to justice are contemporary to legal systems on a global scale. In this context, the solutions to achieving a fairer and more equitable justice system require analytical efforts that acknowledge how mutually shared experiences, such as the COVID-19 pandemic, are addressed by multiple perspectives and approaches. **Cross-fertilisation** of procedural concepts and solutions is always beneficial to improving the procedural systems of the jurisdictions involved. Europe has taken a lead in the **harmonisation** of civil procedure and would continue to be an important case study for the rest of the world.

References

'Court Online' (*The South African Judiciary*, 2024) <https://www.judiciary.org.za/index.php/63-caselines?start=3> accessed 5 July 2024.

'How Much Do Lawyers and Attorneys Charge?' (*ChatLegal*) <https://www.chatlegal.co.za/cost/how-much-do-lawyers-and-attorneys-charge/> accessed 27 June 2024.

'How Much is a Lawyer Consultation Fee in South Africa' (*LegalAdvice*, 7 March 2024) <https://legaladvice.org.za/how-much-is-a-lawyer-consultation-fee-in-south-africa/> accessed 27 June 2024.

Albiston C and Nielsen L, 'Funding the Cause: How Public Interest Law Organisations Fund Their Activities and Why It Matters for Social Change' (2014) 39 Law and Social Inquiry 62.

Bakhramova M, 'Theoretical and Legal Regulation of ODR in the European Union Countries' (2022) 2 European Journal of Innovation in Nonformal Education 299.

Batchelor B, 'Online Litigation – Preparing For the New Normal' (*De Rebus*, 1 August 2023) <https://www.derebus.org.za/online-litigation-preparing-for-the-new-normal/> accessed 5 July 2024.

Bedford N, 'The Winner Takes It All: Legal Costs as Mechanism of Control of Public Law' (2018) 30 Bond Law Review 119.

Bekker T, 'The Apportionment of Legal Costs in South Africa: A Comparative Analysis' [2022] Tydskrif vir die SuidAfrikaanse Reg 457.

Benöhr I, 'Collective Redress in the Field of European Consumer Law' (2014) 41 Legal Issues of Economic Integration 18.

Bentham J, 'Draught of a New Plan for the Organization of the Judicial Establishment in France: With Critical Observations on the Draught Proposed by the National Assembly Committee, in the Form of Perpetual Commentary' in J Bowring (ed), *The Works of Jeremy Bentham* (Tait 1843) vol IV, 316.

Bookman PK and Shanahan CF, 'A Tale of Two Civil Procedures' (2022) 122 Columbia Law Review 1183.

Brickhill J (ed), *Public Interest Litigation in South Africa* (Juta 2018).

Brickhill J, 'The Right to A Fair Civil Trial: The Duties of Lawyers and Law Students to Act Pro Bono' (2005) 21 South African Journal on Human Rights 293.

Broodryk T, 'The South African Class Action Mechanism: Comparing the Opt-in Regime to the Opt-out Regime' (2019) 22 PER / PELJ 1.

—— *Eckard's Principles of Civil Procedure in the Magistrates' Courts* (6th edn, Juta 2019).

Budlender S, Marcus G and Ferreira N, *Public Interest Litigation and Social Change in South Africa: Strategies, Tactics and Lessons* (The Atlantic Philanthropies 2014).

Burbank SB, Farhang S and Kritzer HM, 'Private Enforcement of Statutory and Administrative Law in the United States (And Other Common Law Countries)' in P Gottwald and B Hess (eds), *Procedural Justice* (Gieseking 2014) 197.

C Ragazzo and I Veloso, *Ações de reparação de danos concorrenciais no brasil: obstáculos e sugestões* (2023) <https://direitorio.fgv.br/sites/default/files/arquivos/2023_07_19%20Vers%C3%A3o%20Final%20relat%C3%B3rio%20FDD_site.pdf> accessed 16 February 2025.

Cabral A, 'New Trends and Perspectives on Case Management' (2018) 8 International Journal of Procedural Law 10.

Cafaggi F, 'Collective Enforcement of Consumer Law: A Framework for Comparative Assessment' (2008) 16 European Review of Private Law 3.

Cappelletti M, 'Social and Political Aspects of Civil Procedure—Reforms and Trends in Western and Eastern Europe' (1970) 69 Michigan Law Review 847.

Carroll M, 'Fee-Shifting Statutes and Compensation for Risk' (2020) 95 Indiana Law Journal 1021.

Charn J, 'Legal Services for All: Is the Profession Ready' (2008) 42 Loyola of Los Angeles Law Review 1021.

Choe DH, 'Discretion at the Pre-Trial Stage: A Comparative Study' (2014) 20 European Journal on Criminal Policy and Research 101.

Cilliers AC, Loots C and Nel HC (eds), *Herbstein & Van Winsen: The Civil Practice of the High Courts and the Supreme Court of Appeal of South Africa* (5th edn, Juta 2009).

Clifford D and Van Der Sype YS, 'Online Dispute Resolution: Settling Data Protection Disputes in a Digital World of Customers' (2016) 32 Computer Law & Security Review 272.

Coleman BD, 'The "Efficiency Norm"' (2015) 56 Boston College Law Review 1777.

Cortés P and Lodder AR, 'Consumer Dispute Resolution Goes Online: Reflections on the Evolution of European Law for Out-of-Court Redress' (2014) 21 Maastricht Journal of European and Comparative Law 14

Dam KW, 'Class Actions: Efficiency, Compensation, Deterrence, and Conflict of Interest' (1975) 4 The Journal of Legal Studies 47.

Dendy M and C Loots, *Herbstein and Van Winsen: The Civil Practice of the Superior Courts of South Africa* (Revision Service 1, 2021) vol 1, 9.

Dendy M, 'Vol 10: Costs' in *The Law of South Africa* (3rd edn, LexisNexis 2017).

Devenney J and Kenny M (eds), *European Consumer Protection: Theory and Practice* (CUP 2012).

Dijkman L and Van Paddenburgh C, 'The Unified Patent Court as Part of a New European Patent Landscape: Wholesale Harmonization or Experiment in Legal Pluralism?' (2018) 26 European Review of Private Law 97.

Doerfler RD and Moyn S, 'Democratizing the Supreme Court' (2021) 109 California Law Review 1703.

Drahos P, 'The Universality of Intellectual Property Rights: Origins and Development' in *Intellectual Property and Human Rights* (World Intellectual Property Organization 1999) 13.

Dyk F, 'Provisional Sentence Proceedings – Tailored for Liquid Documentary Debts' (January/February 2024) De Rebus 18.

Farrow TCW, 'Civil Justice, Privatization and Democracy' (2010) <https://ssrn.com/abstract=1795407> accessed 26 February 2025.

Freer RD, 'Exodus from and Transformation of American Civil Litigation' (2016) 65 Emory Law Journal 1491.

—— *Civil Procedure* (4th edn, Wolters Kluwer 2017).

Galanter M, 'The Vanishing Trial: An Examination of Trials and Related Matters in Federal and State Courts' (2004) 1 Journal of Empirical Legal Studies 459.

Gensler S, 'Judicial Case Management: Caught in the Crossfire' (2010) 60 Duke Law Journal 669.

Glover JM, 'Recent Developments in Mandatory Arbitration Warfare: Winners and Losers (So Far) in Mass Arbitration' (2023) 100 Washington University Law Review 1617.

Greenbaum L, 'Access to Justice for All: A Reality of Unfulfilled Expectations?' (2020) 53 De Jure 248.
Greenberg EE and N Ebner, 'How Much Justice Can You Afford?' (2020) St. John's Legal Studies Research Paper No. 20-0016 <https://ssrn.com/abstract=3864194> accessed 26 February 2026.
Grinin, 'The European Revolutions and Revolutionary Waves of the 19th Century: Their Causes and Consequences' in JA Goldstone, L Grinin and A Korotayev (eds), *Handbook of Revolutions in the 21st Century: The New Waves of Revolutions, and the Causes and Effects of Disruptive Political Change* (Springer 2022) 281.
Grinten van der P, 'A Dutch Perspective on Civil Litigation and Its Harmonisation' in XE Kramer and CH van Rhee (eds), *Civil Litigation in a Globalizing World* (OUP 2012).
Gsell B, 'The New European Directive on Representative Actions for the Protection of the Collective Interests of Consumers—A Huge, But Blurry Step Forward' (2021) 58 Common Market Law Review 1365.
Guinchard E and Granger M-P (eds), *The New EU Judiciary: An Analysis of Current Judicial Reforms* (Kluwer Law International 2016).
Haar B, 'Regulation Through Litigation—Collective Redress in Need of a New Balance Between Individual Rights and Regulatory Objectives in Europe' (2018) 19 Theoretical Inquiries in Law 203.
Hylton KN, 'Toward a Regulatory Framework for Third-Party Funding of Litigation' (2013) 63 DePaul Law Review 527.
Issacharoff S and Samuel I, 'The Institutional Dimension of Consumer Protection' in F Cafaggi and H-W Micklitz (eds), *New Frontiers of Consumer Protection. The Interplay Between Private and Public Enforcement* (Intersentia 2009) 9.
Jacobsmeyer B, 'Forum Shopping in Patent Cases: Lessons for the Unified Patent Court' (2018) 25 Michigan Technology Law Review 131.
Kagan RA, *Adversarial Legalism: The American Way of Law* (Harvard University Press 2001).
Lahav AD, 'The Political Justification for Group Litigation' (2013) 81 Fordham Law Review 3193.
Lee N and Zhang L, 'Specialized IP Courts in China—Judicial Governance of Intellectual Property Rights' (2017) 48 IIC-International Review of Intellectual Property and Competition Law 900.
Legal Aid South Africa, *Integrated Annual Report 2022–2023* (Legal Aid SA 2023).
Lewis J, 'Third-Party Litigation Funding: A Boon or Bane to the Progress of Civil Justice?' (2020) 33 Georgetown Journal of Legal Ethics 687.
Loggerenberg van DE, *Erasmus Superior Court Practice* (Revision Service 22, 2023).
Macedo L and Silva de Freitas E, 'A Silent Revolution? The Revamped Brazilian Private Enforcement System and Third-Party Funding' (*Lexology*, 10 March 2023) <https://www.lexology.com/library/detail.aspx?g=f13fa643-dfc6-48cf-9bc9-fee60343e23e> accessed 24 February 2025.
Miller AR, 'McIntyre in Context: A Very Personal Perspective' (2012) 63 South Carolina Law Review 465.
Minzner CF, 'China's Turn Against Law' (2011) 59 American Journal of Comparative Law 937.
Morpurgo de M, 'A Comparative Legal and Economic Approach to Third-Party Litigation Funding' (2011) 19 Cardozo Journal of International and Comparative Law 343.
Mullenix LS, 'The Politics of Class Action Reform: Reflections on the American Experience' (1 January 2023) Public Law and Legal Theory Research Paper Series 595/2023.
—— 'Class Action Waivers in Arbitration Agreements: The Twenty-First Century Arbitration Battleground and Implications for the EU Countries' (2024) 38 Emory International Law Review 785.
Muller EC and CL Nel, 'A Critical Analysis of the Inefficacy of CAM in SA' (2021) 46 Journal for Juridical Science 26.
Naude T and Eiselen S (eds), *Commentary on the Consumer Protection Act 2008*, Revision Service 8 (Juta 2022) 69–1.
Ncube C and others, *Artificial Intelligence and the Law in Africa* (LexisNexis 2023).
Ngcobo S, 'Enhancing Access to Justice: The Search for Better Justice', Opening Remarks Access to Justice Conference: Towards Delivering Accessible and Quality Justice for All (7–10 July 2011) 15 <

https://constitutionallyspeaking.co.za/wp-content/uploads/2011/07/Speech-of-the-Chief-Justice-2011.pdf> accessed 27 June 2024.

Page J and Bonnyman L, 'ADR and ODR—Achieving Better Dispute Resolution for Consumers in the EU' (2016) 17 ERA Forum 2.

Paleker M, *The Re-Engineering of South African Small Claims Courts* (PhD thesis, University of Cape Town 2018).

Parliamentary Monitoring Group (PMG), 'Legal Practice Bill [B20–2012]: Deliberations on Amendments Proposed by Negotiating Mandates' (*PMG*, 26 February 2014) <https://pmg.org.za/committee-meeting/17001/> accessed 4 July 2024.

Payne M, 'The Politics of Case Management and Social Work' (2000) 9 International Journal of Social Welfare 85.

Pegoraro Junior PR, *O processo eletrônico e a evolução disruptiva do direito processual civil* (PhD thesis, Pontifícia Universidade Católica do Rio Grande do Sul 2018).

Peté S and others, *Civil Procedure: A Practical Guide* (4th edn, OUP 2024).

Plevri A, 'Alternative Dispute Resolution (ADR) & Online Dispute Resolution (ODR) for EU Consumers: The European and Cypriot Framework' in T-E Synodinou and others (eds), *EU Internet Law in the Digital Era: Regulation and Enforcement* (Springer 2020) 367.

Rechberger WH, *Civil Procedure in Austria* (Walters Kluwer 2011).

Redish MH, 'Electronic Discovery and the Litigation Matrix' (2001) 51 Duke Law Journal 561.

Revesz RL, 'Specialized Courts and the Administrative Lawmaking System' (1990) 138 University of Pennsylvania Law Review 1111.

Rhee van CH, 'Civil Litigation in Twentieth Century Europe' (2007) 75 Tijdschrift voor Rechtsgeschiedenis / Revue d'histoire du droit / The Legal History Review 308.

—— 'The Development of Civil Procedural Law in Twentieth-Century Europe: From Party Autonomy to Judicial Case Management and Efficiency' in CH van Rhee (ed), *Judicial Case Management and Efficiency in Civil Litigation* (Intersentia 2008) 11.

Root DA, 'Attorney Fee-Shifting in America: Comparing, Contrasting, and Combining the "American Rule" and "English Rule"' (2005) 15 Indiana International and Comparative Law Review 583.

Sarchio C, Tam J and Wilson L, '9th Circ. Jurisdiction Ruling Guides on Class Action Strategy' (*Law 360*, 12 November 2021).

Sedutla M, 'Court Digitisation – The Future Is Here' (*De Rebus*, 1 April 2021) <https://www.derebus.org.za/court-digitisation-the-future-is-here/> accessed 5 July 2024.

Sharrock R, *Business Transactions Law* (9th edn, Juta 2016).

Smits JM and Bull WA, 'European Harmonisation of Intellectual Property Law: Towards a Competitive Model and a Critique of the Proposed Unified Patent Court' in A Ohly and J Pila (eds), *The Europeanization of Intellectual Property Law: Towards a European Legal Methodology* (OUP 2013) 39.

Soo PP, 'Enforcing a Unitary Patent in Europe: What the US Federal Courts and Community Design Courts Teach Us' (2012) 35 Loyola of Los Angeles International and Comparative Law Review 57.

South African Law Reform Commission, 'Report Project 142: Investigation into Legal Fees – Including Access to Justice and other Interventions' (South African Law Reform Commission 2021).

Stats SA, *General Household Survey* (2019) <https://www.statssa.gov.za/?page_id=737&id=4> accessed 29 June 2024.

Steinitz M, 'The Litigation Finance Contract' (2012) 54 William & Mary Law Review 455.

—— 'Whose Claim is This Anyway? Third-Party Litigation Funding' (2010) 95 Minnesota Law Review 1268.

Steinman AN, 'Beyond Bristol-Myers: Personal Jurisdiction Over Class Action' (2022) 97 New York University Law Review 1215.

Storskrubb E, 'E-Justice, Innovation and the EU' in B Hess and X Kramer (eds), *From Common Rules to Best Practices in European Civil Procedure* (Nomos 2017) 271.

The Third Branch: The Newsletter of the Federal Courts, The Third Branch: The Newsletter of the Federal Courts, vol 31, no 10 (October 1999).

Tumbridge J, 'Unified Patent Court: Harmonising Patent Law Throughout Europe' (2014) 15 Business Law International 55.

Tzankova IN, 'Case Management: The Stepchild of Mass Claim Dispute Resolution' (2014) 19 Uniform Law Review 329.

U.S. Government Accountability Office, *Third-Party Litigation Financing: Market Characteristics, Data and Trends*, GAO-23-105210 (20 December 2022) <https://www.gao.gov/products/gao-23-105210> accessed 26 February 2025.

UK Patent Litigation Is a Complex Area and Can Be Daunting' (*Marks & Clerk*, 18 October 2017) <https://www.marks-clerk.com/insights/articles/uk-patent-litigation-is-a-complex-area-and-can-be-daunting/> accessed 20 June 2024.

Van den Bergh R and Visscher L, 'The Preventive Function of Collective Actions for Damages in Consumer Law' (2007) 1 Erasmus Law Review 5.

Woo MYK, Cox C and Rosen S, 'Access to Civil Justice' (2022) 70(Supplement_1) The American Journal of Comparative Law 89.

Woolman S and Bishop M, *Constitutional Law of South Africa*, Original Service (2nd edn, Juta 2013).

Entries in Asian Languages

'19起案件5天结案!黄岛法院率先成功运行互联网远程调解' ('19 Cases Concluded in 5 Days! Huangdao Court First to Successfully Operate Internet Remote Mediation') (青报网, 27 December 2019) <https://www.shiminjia.com/news/detail/MDAwMDAwMDAwMKSMzuy8rZeM> accessed 20 June 2024.

'2023年全国法院收结案均超4500万件' ('In 2023, National Courts Handled More Than 45 Million Cases') (最高人民法院, 8 March 2024) <https://www.court.gov.cn/zixun/xiangqing/427022.html> accessed 20 June 2024.

'中国首只诉讼融资基金在武汉成立.' ('China's First Litigation Financing Fund Established in Wuhan') (荆楚网, 12 March 2016) <http://www.cnhubei.com/xw/jj/201603/t3566300.shtml> accessed 20 June 2024.

'人民法院调解平台正式上线' ('The People's Court Mediation Platform Officially Launched') (最高人民法院,28 February 2018) <https://www.court.gov.cn/zixun/xiangqing/82582.html> accessed 20 June 2024.

'以高质量互联网司法护航中国式现代化——北京互联网法院成立五年工作综述' ('Safeguarding Chinese-style Modernization with High-Quality Internet Justice: A Five-Year Review of the Beijing Internet Court') 中国法院网 (29 October 2023) <https://www.chinacourt.org/article/detail/2023/10/id/7600832.shtml> accessed 20 June 2024.

'全国人民代表大会常务委员会关于在北京、上海、广州设立知识产权法院的决定' ('Decision of the Standing Committee of the National People's Congress on Establishing Intellectual Property Courts in Beijing, Shanghai, and Guangzhou') (中国人大网,31 August 2014) <http://www.npc.gov.cn/zgrdw/npc/xinwen/2014-09/01/content_1877042.htm> accessed 20 June 2024.

'关于《中华人民共和国民事诉讼法 (修正草案) 》的说明' ('Explanation on the "Civil Procedure Law of the People's Republic of China (Draft Amendment)"') (中国人大网, 27 December 2021) <http://www.npc.gov.cn/npc/c2/c30834/202112/t20211227_315637.html> accessed 20 June 2024.

'关于人民法院进一步深化多元化纠纷解决机制改革的意见' ('Opinions on Further Deepening the Reform of Diversified Dispute Resolution Mechanisms in People's Courts') (中国法院网,28 June 2016) <https://www.chinacourt.org/law/detail/2016/06/id/148740.shtml> accessed 20 June 2024.

'北京互联网法院:5年审结18.2万件案件 著作权权属侵权纠纷超七成' ('Beijing Internet Court: 182,000 Cases Concluded in 5 Years, Over 70% Are Copyright Ownership and Infringement Disputes') (人民网,9 September 2023) <http://society.people.com.cn/n1/2023/0909/c1008-40073886.html> accessed 20 June 2024.

'成都中院全国首创"和合智解"e调解平台探索"o2o"零距离司法服务新机制' ('Chengdu Intermediate People's Court Pioneers the "Hehe Zhijie" E-Mediation Platform to Explore New "O2O" Proximity-Free Judicial Service Mechanisms') (成都法院网 15 April 2019) <http://cdfy.scssfw.gov.cn/article/detail/2019/05/id/3890054.shtml> accessed 20 June 2024.

'最高人民法院关于证券纠纷代表人诉讼若干问题的规定' ('Supreme People's Court Provisions on Several Issues Concerning Representative Litigation in Securities Disputes') (最高人民法院,31 July 2020) <https://www.court.gov.cn/fabu/xiangqing/245501.html> accessed 20 June 2024.

'最高法启动在线调解平台建设试点工作' ('The Supreme Court Initiates Pilot Project for Building an Online Mediation Platform') (中国法院网 28 February 2017) <https://www.chinacourt.org/article/detail/2017/02/id/2546606.shtml> accessed 20 June 2024.

'每分钟66件,看人民法院调解平台如何为民解纷' ('66 Cases per Minute: How the People's Court Mediation Platform Resolves Disputes for the Public') (最高人民法院新闻. 20 February 2021) <https://www.court.gov.cn/zixun/xiangqing/287441.html> accessed 20 June 2024.

'破解"案多人少" 民事诉讼繁简分流改革' ('Solving the "Many Cases, Few People" Issue through the Streamlining Reform of Civil Litigation') (人民网, 13 May 2020) <http://henan.people.com.cn/n2/2020/0513/c351638-34013968.html> accessed 20 June 2024.

'降低门槛简化审理,民诉法拟修改完善小额诉讼程序' ('Reducing Thresholds and Simplifying Trials, Civil Procedure Law Plans to Amend and Improve Small Claims Procedure') (新华网, 19 October 2021) <http://www.news.cn/legal/2021-10/19/c_1127972768.htm> accessed 20 June 2024.

'首个互联网法院——展现互联网司法治理的"中国智慧"' ('The First Internet Court—Demonstrating the "Chinese Wisdom" in Internet Judicial Governance') (中国法院网, 2 January 2019) <https://www.chinacourt.org/article/detail/2019/01/id/3640671.shtml> accessed 20 June 2024.

任重, '"案多人少"的成因与出路——对本轮民事诉讼法修正之省思' ('The Causes and Solutions of "Many Cases, Few People" – Reflections on the Current Round of Civil Procedure Law Amendments') (2022) 40 法学评论 ('Law Review') 138

余希, '专门审判机构设立研究' ('Research on the Establishment of Specialized Judicial Organs') [2022–4] 法律适用 ('Application of Law') 147.

关于互联网法院审理案件若干问题的规定' ('Provisions on Several Issues Concerning the Handling of Cases by Internet Courts') (最高人民法院公报, 6 September 2018) <http://gongbao.court.gov.cn/Details/7e594961f195254a863d6cc90be5cd.html> accessed 20 June 2024.

冷静, '康美启示:证券集团诉讼首案的制度突破与未尽议题' ('Kangmei Inspiration: Institutional Breakthroughs and Unresolved Issues in the First Case of Securities Group Litigation') [2022–1] 中国法律评论 ('China Law Review') 78.

刘强, '中欧知识产权专门法院比较研究' ('Comparative Study of Intellectual Property Specialized Courts in China and Europe') (2015) 39(6) 湘潭大学学报 (哲学社会科学版) ('Journal of Xiangtan University (Philosophy and Social Sciences)') 89.

吕宗澄和夏培元, '新时代法院在线调解平台建设现状及优化策略研究' ('Research on the Current Status and Optimization Strategies of Online Mediation Platform Construction by Courts in the New Era') (2022) 23(4) 南华大学学报 (社会科学版) ('Journal of Nanhua University (Social Science Edition)') 76.

周庆和张永利, '我国民事诉讼和解权的法律问题研究' ('Legal Issues of Settlement Rights in Civil Litigation in China') (2018) 39(4) 湖北文理学院学报 ('Journal of Hubei University of Arts and Science') 39.

张光磊, ‘第三方诉讼融资: 通往司法救济的商业化路径’ (‘Third-Party Litigation Financing: The Commercial Path to Judicial Relief’) [2016–3] 中国政法大学学报 (‘Journal of China University of Political Science and Law’) 24.
张明继, ‘论我国群体诉讼解决机制的完善路径’ (‘On the Improvement Path of Group Litigation Resolution Mechanism in China’) [2020–1] 黑龙江省政法管理干部学院学报 (‘Journal of Heilongjiang Administrative Cadre College of Politics and Law’) 92.
张芳芳和骆嘉仕, ‘我国互联网法院管辖制度研究’ (‘Research on the Jurisdiction System of Internet Courts in China’) (2024) 41(1) 政法学刊 (‘Journal of Political Science and Law’) 120–128.
李欢, ‘第三方诉讼融资: 域外实践与我国的引入’ (‘Third-Party Litigation Financing: Foreign Practices and Its Introduction in China’) [2018–9] 市场周刊 (‘Market Weekly’) 140.
杨雪婷, ‘我国民事重复诉讼研究综述’ (‘Overview of Research on Civil Re-litigation in China’) [2021–14] 西部学刊 (‘Western Academic Journal’) 100.
毛立琦, ‘论中国式证券集体诉讼的功能定位’ (‘On the Functional Positioning of Chinese-Style Securities Class Actions’) (2022) 59(1) 南京大学学报 (哲学·人文科学·社会科学) (‘Journal of Nanjing University (Philosophy, Humanities and Social Sciences)’) 146.
王国龙, ‘法院诉源治理的司法理念及功能定位’ (‘Judicial Philosophy and Functional Positioning of Court Litigation Source Management’) [2022–6] 政法论丛 (‘Tribune of Political Science and Law’) 133.
王福华, ‘民诉法修改背景下的诉讼费用改革’ (‘Reform of Litigation Costs in the Context of the Amendment of the Civil Procedure Law’) (2022) 40(2) 法学评论 (‘Law Review’) 126.
王雪羽, ‘证券特别代表人诉讼的制度创新与规则完善’ (‘Institutional Innovation and Rule Improvement in Securities Special Representative Litigation’) (2024) 42(3) 法律科学 (西北政法大学学报) (‘Legal Science (Journal of Northwest University of Political Science and Law)’) 183–200.
程金华, ‘中国法院“案多人少”的实证评估与应对策略’ (‘Empirical Assessment and Response Strategies for the “Many Cases, Few People” Issue in Chinese Courts’) [2022–6] 中国法学 (‘Chinese Legal Science’) 238.
程雪梅, ‘第三方诉讼融资: 效力、发展及对我国的启示’ (‘Third-Party Litigation Financing: Efficacy, Development, and Implications for China’) [2014–4] 学术界 (‘Academic Community’) 211.
葛进, ‘群体性劳动争议解决机制研究’ (‘Research on the Mechanism for Resolving Collective Labour Disputes’) (2014) 13(6) 安徽警官职业学院学报 (‘Journal of Anhui Police College’) 26.
谢冰斌, ‘论我国民事“独任制+普通程序”组织模式的完善’ (‘On the Improvement of the “Sole Responsibility + Ordinary Procedure” Organizational Model in China’s Civil Justice System’) (2021) 29(2) 成都理工大学学报 (社会科学版) (‘Journal of Chengdu University of Technology (Social Sciences)’) 43.

Alan Uzelac*

Chapter 26
Wider Challenges: The EU, Europe, and the World

A Mutual (Dis)trust – An Illusory Area of Justice?

I Not All (National) Courts Are Made Equal!

#1 European civil procedure is part of the broader framework of European integration. Its fundamental ideological foundation, most clearly defined in the **1999 Tampere** milestones, is rooted in the creation of an area of freedom, security, and justice. The cornerstone of a genuine European area of justice is the principle of **mutual trust** and respect.[1] While the mutual trust may be the 'most elusive principle' of EU law, it is certainly related to inter-institutional trust which *inter alia* assumes that, for the protection of their civil rights and obligations, EU citizens can equally rely on the courts of their home jurisdiction, as well as on the courts of any other Member State. An alleged adherence to the shared values, and the effective protection of EU law form the basis for the broad mutual recognition of judgments. In short, an ideal common area of justice would be one in which every European citizen enjoys equal protection of their rights, regardless of the EU Member State in which the court handling their legal matter is situated.

#2 The requirement of **mutual trust** applies both to individual decisions and to the legal and judicial systems of the Member States as a whole.[2] While the principle of mutual trust holds constitutional status in the EU, it is by no means absolute. The President of the CJEU argued that it should not be mistaken for **blind trust**.[3] However, he also emphasised that exceptions—limitations to mutual trust—must remain rare and should not weaken the overall force of the principle, which should be restored as soon as possible.[4] Ultimately, trust in judicial institutions

1 See more on the development of the doctrine of mutual trust in Chapter 4 by M Weller.

2 E Brouwer, 'Mutual Trust and Judicial Control in the Area of Freedom, Security, and Justice: An Anatomy of Trust' in E Brouwer and D Gerard (eds), *Mapping Mutual Trust: Understanding and Framing the Role of Mutual Trust in EU Law* (EUI Working Papers MWP 2016/13) 59, 61.

3 K Lenaerts, 'La vie après l'avis: Exploring the Principle of Mutual (Yet Not Blind) Trust' (2017) 54 Common Market Law Review 805.

4 ibid 805.

*Corresponding author: Alan Uzelac, University of Zagreb, e-mail: auzelac@pravo.hr

https://doi.org/10.1515/9783110781632-026

that apply EU law—both EU courts and national courts—must exist; or, at the very least, it must be presumed to exist.

#3 In the present time, trust can be evaluated and quantified, which may reveal a more fundamental challenge to the **ideological foundations of mutual trust**. The doctrine of mutual trust—namely, the presumption that the judicial systems of Member States are capable of fairly and independently upholding the **rule of law**—has been questioned, particularly in light of several infringement procedures initiated by the European Commission against Poland. Similarly, Hungary's EU funding was suspended 'to protect the Union budget from breaches of the principles of the rule of law in Hungary'.[5] The public and political nature of these procedures suggests that, empirically, not all civil justice systems in Europe are equally trusted by all EU Member States.

#4 If the judicial systems in the EU are not unequivocally trusted among Member States, questions also arise about their internal trustworthiness. Do European citizens trust their courts and judges, including their ability to uphold the fundamental values of a state governed by the principles of the rule of law? Can these institutions be relied upon when they apply civil procedural law or EU law? The instruments created by the EU to foster **harmonisation** of civil and criminal justice systems suggest that the level of **trust** enjoyed by courts and judges within the Member States is hardly satisfactory. Indeed, only a slim majority—53% in 2023—of EU citizens view their national courts and judges positively.[6] The 2023 **EU Justice Scoreboard** indicates that this unimpressive level of trust has persisted for at least a decade.[7]

#5 From this information, it may be inferred that when **trust in (civil) justice** is concerned, the glass is half empty. But is it also half full? Some comfort may be found in the fact that, in many other areas of the world, courts and judges enjoy even less trust. For instance, in **Latin America**, **trust levels** are significantly lower, ranging between 23% and 37%.[8] However, this level of trust is still far from the public trust traditionally enjoyed by the judicial branch of government in the **US**, where 'a great deal' or 'a fair amount' of trust used to be expressed by up to 80% of US citizens.[9]

5 European Commission, 'Questions and Answers on Hungary: Rule of Law and EU Funding' (December 2023) <https://ec.europa.eu/commission/presscorner/detail/en/qanda_23_6466> accessed 15 February 2025.

6 Flash Eurobarometer 519, 'Perceived Independence of the National Justice Systems in the EU among the General Public – January 2023 Report' (June 2023) <https://europa.eu/eurobarometer/surveys/detail/2667> accessed 15 February 2025.

7 The *2023 EU Justice Scoreboard*, COM (2023)309, 41, Figure 49.

8 Latinobarometro, Informe 2021, 'Confianza en el poder judicial 1995–2020', <http://www.latinobarometro.org> accessed 15 February 2025 70.

9 Gallup, data from 2000–2010. In recent years, after highly controversial appointments of Supreme Court judges in the first Trump's mandate and the shift of its case law, this level was of trust is how-

#6 Since EU civil procedure is applied by national courts, it is more important to note that **public (dis)trust** in courts is not evenly distributed among European states. Quite the opposite, this trust is greatly divergent from state to state. When asked 'how would you rate your justice system', European citizens gave ratings that ranged from almost complete trust to almost complete distrust. For instance, a positive assessment of the national justice system was given by 89% of Finns, but only by 17% of Croatians.[10]

#7 The official **mutual trust narrative**, which assumes that equivalent and effective enforcement of EU law can be equally granted by all national courts, is further jeopardised by clear regional and geographic lines in the distribution of public (dis)trust. On one side, the highest level of **public trust** is visible in the **North and West** of the EU. Scandinavian countries are at the top (Finland, Denmark, Sweden), followed by the traditionally solid judiciaries of Germany and Austria, and by the Benelux states. Ireland is also among the 'trusted' group (as was England while it belonged to the EU). France is the last member of the group in which the public has more trust than distrust in the national judiciary—it is approximately at the average European levels of **'slim trust'**.

#8 However, the other half of EU member states, consisting of countries from the **European South and East**, clearly displays a group where distrust predominates. This group is divided into two parts: Mediterranean countries (Italy, Greece, Spain, Portugal) and former Socialist countries (Romania, Bulgaria, Poland, Hungary, Czechia, Slovakia, Slovenia, Croatia, etc). Quite consistently, in these countries, **negative public assessments** of the courts outweigh the positive ones.

#9 In about a decade since public trust in courts has been surveyed, there have been only a few major changes and exceptions to the above delineation of 'trusted' and 'distrusted' groups of national judiciaries. Reforms in Portugal have significantly raised the level of trust in its judiciary. Some **Baltic states (Estonia, Lithuania)** have also raised their profile and now even belong to the countries above the EU trust average, with Estonia leading by a solid 10 percent increase.[11]

#10 A few successful reform stories may give rise to cautious optimism, but the fact remains that **divergences in public perception** of courts and judges, as well as

ever dramatically reduced, see <https://news.gallup.com/poll/402737/trust-federal-government-branches-continues-falter.aspx> accessed 15 February 2025.

10 Flash Eurobarometer 489, 'Perceived Independence of the National Justice Systems in the EU among the General Public' (July 2021) <http://data.europa.eu/euodp/en/data/dataset/S2272_489_ENG> accessed 15 February 2025, Croatia, 2021 (4% 'very good' and 13% 'fairly good'). This should be contrasted to 35% of those who assessed the situation in judiciary as 'fairly bad' and 43% as 'very bad'.

11 See 2023 EU Justice Scoreboard (n 7). Of course, the Scoreboard as 'the first attempt of the European Commision to venture into the field of evidence-based justice policies' is not a perfect instrument, but in the area of measuring attitudes of citizens and businesses towards judiciary, it provides a solid starting point. On its limits and use in another area, see A Dori, 'In Data We Trust? Quantifying the Costs of Adjudication in the EU Justice Scoreboard' [2021–4] ELR 281.

the **differences in the level of trust** they enjoy both at home and among knowledgeable outside observers, remain enormous. Some countries, which are supposed to belong to the EU because they share fundamental judicial values and observe the same rule of law principles, obviously struggle with the practical implementation of these values and principles. For any further integrative processes—which include the further development of European civil procedure—overcoming this challenge will be a great hurdle. How can we aim to develop joint judicial practices in the common area of justice if we cannot trust our own courts? Pretending that all courts in the Member States are equal, and equally competent and capable of providing the same level of effective protection of European law is hardly convincing if there is no basic public trust in their capability to render effective judicial protection domestically. So far, the Union has not proved that it can foster significant progress in this area, and in the future, this may lead to further problems.

II Same but Different: Dissimilar Understanding of Common Procedural *Acquis*

#11 As an emerging area of law, European civil procedure has evolved from simple forms of judicial cooperation in civil and commercial matters—such as mutual recognition of judgments and assistance in service of documents and taking of evidence—to more complex and demanding ones. The development of **optional autonomous European procedures** gives national courts the opportunity to apply uniform procedural regimes in a select number of matters, both **contentious and non-contentious.** This includes processing small claims, issuing payment orders, enforcing various enforceable instruments, and even some forms of provisional and protective relief through tentatively uniform and harmonised common European procedures. Future procedural arrangements, which aim to further develop collective redress, promote alternative dispute resolution (ADR), and introduce third-party funding, are even more ambitious.

#12 The prolific production of European procedural instruments is, however, not accompanied by an enthusiastic embrace among those for whom they were intended to benefit. **Uniform European procedures**, such as **European payment orders** or **European small claims**, have generally achieved underwhelming effects. EU-backed studies aimed at analysing and comparing European procedures designed to foster and improve the **cross-border enforcement of civil claims** show a rather disappointing use of optional European instruments. These studies identify 'horizontal deficiencies' and 'major weaknesses of the system', as well as 'a number of defects and divergences in Member States' legislations which impair the effectiveness' of EU acquis in the field of civil procedure.[12]

#13 For some ambitiously drafted EU instruments, like the **European Account Preservation Order (EAPO)**, the balance sheet of the first five years of application is practically empty. A recent book that provided a systematic insight into case law answers the question 'Is the EAPO fulfilling its purpose?' with a confirmation that it is 'seldom being used', which may be taken as an understatement, as there were a few or none successful instances of EAPO issuance, even in countries with fairly efficient domestic systems of enforcement on monetary funds.[13] Among legal practitioners, the negative perception of such EU instruments is more the rule than the exception, to the extent that the very announcement of the EAPO Regulation was accompanied by views that it would 'join the **club of largely unused EU civil justice instruments**'.[14]

#14 Among the reasons for the underuse of **EU procedural *acquis***, an important one is the deceptive impression that EU procedural regulations create uniform procedural regimes. As expressed by a learned observer, there is a 'counterintuitive' plurality of regimes for the implementation of EU acts that are, in theory, directly applicable and uniformly interpreted by the CJEU.[15] While the 'law in books'—the text of EU instruments in the civil procedure field—is easy to locate, the 'law in action,' which includes national operative rules and implementation practices, is not simple to trace. Without proper guides and commentaries (and even more, personal knowledge from a few individuals responsible for the rare cross-border cases submitted to national courts), it is difficult to navigate the system. Europeans entangled in cross-border civil cases often find it easier to use well-established **local procedures** and **local lawyers** rather than experiment with the 'rare birds' of 'uniform' EU procedures, which are differently understood and applied from country to country. Instead of a uniform interface, there is a **dissonant interplay of EU instruments with national rules (and customs)**, signifying a major weakness of the current sys-

---

12 See FC Villata and B Hess (eds), 'Towards more EFfective enFORcemenT of claimS in civil and commercial matters within the EU – "EFFORTS": Final Study' (Project JUST-JCOO-AG2019-881802) 1 <https://efforts.unimi.it> accessed 15 February 2025 ('EFFORTS Final Study'). See similar results of other studies at <https://www.ipr.uni-heidelberg.de/forschung/studien_en.html> and <https://ec.europa.eu/newsroom/just/document.cfm?action=display&doc_id=18575> all accessed 15 February 2025.

13 See N Mouttotos, 'Is the EAPO Fulfilling its Purpose' in N Kyriakides, HA Huhtamäki and N Mouttotos (eds), *European Account Preservation Order: A Multi-Jurisdictional Guide with Commentary* (Bruylant 2024) 27.

14 See Clifford Chance, 'European Account Preservation Orders: Must Try Harder' (Briefing Note, September 2014) <https://www.cliffordchance.com/content/dam/cliffordchance/briefings/2014/09/european-account-preservation-orders-must-try-harder-10-september-2014.pdf> accessed 15 February 2025.

15 G Cuniberti, 'Preface' in N Kyriakides, HA Huhtamäki and N Mouttotos (eds), *European Account Preservation Order: A Multi-Jurisdictional Guide with Commentary* (Bruylant 2024) 9.

tem. This makes it difficult for practitioners, and even more so for consumers and businesses, to be cognizant of the mere existence and practical functioning of the available procedures and mechanisms.[16]

III Crippling Nomotechnical Effects of EU Consensus Policies

#15 A constantly present challenge to EU civil procedure arises from the nature of **European legislation**. The principles of **nomotechnics** ('the science of good lawmaking') require clarity, consistency, precision, and ease of use. Historically, procedural legislation in Europe was drafted in codes that were transparent, precise, and comprehensive. Their design was universal and intended to last for at least a few decades, considering that legal practitioners needed a stable and generally applicable framework to use daily, irrespective of the nature of the legal matter assigned to a particular procedure. Judged from that perspective, the EU procedural acquis is far from being a model of well-structured and accessible legal infrastructure. The words 'fragmented', 'inconsistent', 'cumbersome', and 'user-unfriendly' regularly appear in the honest descriptions of European procedural instruments.

#16 The unappealing character of the EU procedural *acquis* is not the result of accidental mistakes. It is the inevitable outcome of the **EU legislative process and policies**, which makes it difficult, if not impossible, to repair. Seeking **consensus** among the key players—the European Commission, Parliament, and Council—has two disabling effects. First, it impairs comprehensive and general legislative projects. Even disregarding the **limited competences of the Union**, EU law progresses only in baby steps, by incremental progress achieved through acts targeted to reach minor improvements in limited fields and largely insignificant 'recasts' of previous normative documents.

#17 Secondly, the **strive towards unanimity** results in an inconsistent patchwork of rules and exceptions, tailored to satisfy the interests of individual states or other specific interests. This leads to the dilution of the scope of adopted instruments (typically: optional procedures reduced to a cross-border environment), exceptions and exclusions for individual Member States (Denmark is not the only such example), and even departures from fundamental principles and definitions as a trade-off for the formal blessing of individual states.[17] In the field of procedural law, which is governed by key principles of equality and fairness, this is deeply discouraging. Whether

---

16 M Buzzoni, 'The Certification of Judgments under the EFFORTS Regulations' in EFFORTS Final Study (n 12) 7, 11.

17 For instance, due to an exception in Article 3(a) of Brussels Ibis Regulation, Hungarian public notaries are considered a 'court' under EU law in summary payment order proceedings. However, despite having an almost identical role and status, Croatian public notaries were for the same purpose declared **not** to be a 'court' under the Brussels Ibis Regulation by the CJEU in the *Pula Parking* and *Zulfi-*

or not national civil justice systems are rooted in antiquated and outdated procedural codes and models, for insiders they will continue to be preferable due to their relative familiarity and simplicity. A clear framework, no matter how archaic, is always perceived to be better than progress wrapped in a set of **fragmented**, inconsistent, and opaque rules. In such a way, paradoxically, the harmonising EU efforts in the field of civil procedure may stimulate parochial sentiments and inspire centripetal and anti-European forces within the national civil justice systems.

IV Procedural Autonomy 2.0: From Procedural Cohesion to Procedural Autarchy?

#18 The lacking efficiency of optional EU civil procedures ultimately means that national systems of civil procedure remain the key guarantee of the effectiveness of legal protection, both in respect to local and EU substantive law. But will local courts and their procedures continue to be the glue that connects national justice systems to EU law? The precondition for this is to embrace **procedural autonomy** as the vehicle for enforcing EU law and to take the **principles of equivalence and effectiveness** seriously. So far, the CJEU has ensured that these principles are enforced, but its authority has depended on the willingness of national courts to exercise their power to submit **preliminary references**. Historically, the number of such references has varied significantly from jurisdiction to jurisdiction. Even in areas of European 'success stories', such as **consumer protection** law, the number of cases per jurisdiction has been relatively modest.[18]

#19 According to research from the **Max Planck Institute Luxembourg** in 2016, the number of CJEU judgments in **consumer protection cases** fluctuated from two to eighteen per annum, with eleven Member States having no cases in the period between 2006–2016.[19] In the following period, there were increasingly significant judgments. Over the past five years, the **CJEU** issued over 400 judgments dealing with consumer protection.[20] However, the proliferation of judgments may also indicate the **uncertainty of EU law** in this field and the lacking interface of EU law

karpašić cases (Case C-551/15 *Pula Parking* (9 March 2017) ECLI:EU:C:2017:193 and Case C-484/15 *Zulfikarpašić* (9 March 2017) ECLI:EU:C:2017:199).

18 See also Chapter 21 by E Lein on the development of collective consumer protection rights in the EU.

19 See European Commission: Directorate-General for Justice and Consumers, 'An Evaluation Study of National Procedural Laws and Practices in Terms of Their Impact on the Free Circulation of Judgments and on the Equivalence and Effectiveness of the Procedural Protection of Consumers under EU Lonsumer Law – Strand 2 – Procedural Protection of Consumers', Study JUST/2014/RCON/PR/CIVI/0082 (Publications Office 2017).

20 The search in the CJEU database for 2020–2025 period reveals 418 judgments tagged with subject matter 'consumer protection' <https://curia.europa.eu/> accessed 15 February 2025.

with national procedural mechanisms. The selective availability of recourse to the highest EU court has been used by various courts and economic players to protract proceedings and deflect and/or discourage litigation of consumer cases. At the same time, some of the highest national courts are still struggling with consumer protection cases that were the product of the **2008 economic crisis**, with no intent to refer the disputed issues to the CJEU.[21]

#20 The complexity of national procedural instruments and the differences in **national legal cultures** significantly limit the unification of approaches to enforcing core EU policies in the area of civil procedure. The emerging centripetal trends do not create a conducive environment for the voluntary submission of national courts to institutions that challenge core procedural principles of national law. Civil courts in many EU countries are traditionally reluctant to act ex officio, often adhering to **formalism** and perceiving enforcement procedures as merely formal and technical processes.

#21 This *status quo* remained unchallenged until the CJEU intervened, reshaping expectations through its case law. The **CJEU** now requires that courts exert **ex officio control** over the fairness of consumer contract clauses as part of mandatory EU law. If necessary, such control should also extend to enforcement proceedings initiated based on abstract instruments like bills of exchange or uncontested payment orders. While this tectonic shift is undoubtedly well-intended and progressive, it has not been enthusiastically embraced by all European national courts. Their reaction could potentially be a retreat into autarchy. While this has not yet occurred on a large scale, it does not mean that such a development is not on the horizon.

#22 While the CJEU's case law on **consumer protection** is still a good example of a relatively well-functioning system that collaborates with the national judiciary, efforts to introduce effective alternative means of consumer protection have met with much higher levels of resistance.[22] After ten years since their adoption, the EU instruments aimed at introducing **effective, low-cost, and fair alternative procedures** for resolving disputes between consumers and traders have failed to

---

21 For instance, the Supreme Court of Croatia has been split for quite some time regarding the interpretation of the consequences of consumer loan conversion, which was based on the national legislation, enabling conversion of loans denominated in Swiss Francs to Euro-denominated loans. Later, the original consumer contracts were found to contain unfair consumer terms. The validity of the converted contracts, although closely connected to EU law, was never referred to the CJEU by the Supreme Court. When a reference was finally made by a first-instance court, the results were underwhelming. See Case C-567/20 *Zagrebačka banka* (5 May 2022) ECLI:EU:C:2022:352).

22 On alternative dispute resolution in consumer cases see more in Chapter 20 by E Van Gelder.

achieve almost any of their objectives.[23] This is particularly evident with the **ODR** Regulation, which is being repealed, and the ODR platform, which is on the way to being permanently closed. Over a whole decade, the EU has been unable to change the landscape of consumer dispute resolution, which remains divided between a few countries with effective out-of-court consumer dispute resolution mechanisms and the majority that have not been able to make any significant progress in this sector.

#23 More importantly, the fundamental ideals of the EU framework, such as **transparency, affordability,** and **effectiveness**, did not materialise in most EU countries. The **ADR entities** generally failed to provide meaningful **activity reports**, the behaviour of the traders was not affected, and the entire procedure was perceived in many jurisdictions as a waste of the consumer's time and money. Consequently, the ambitiously designed European system clashed with the **national procedural autarchy**, resulting in the ADR instruments joining the club of 'largely unused EU instruments.'

#24 The current proposals to amend the **ADR Directive** to 'improve' and 'simplify' ADR may, from a certain angle, be viewed as an admission of failure, especially as they fundamentally abandon some of the most innovative elements of the directive related to information obligations. Moving away from all elements of traders' obligation to participate in **CADR (Consumer Alternative Dispute Resolution)** proceedings and comply with the recommendations and evaluations of the dispute resolution bodies will hardly promote the use of alternative dispute resolution. Reducing **C2B** (Consumer to Business) dispute resolution to voluntary mediation will likely have the same effect as mediation in **C2C** (Consumer to Consumer) and **B2B** (Business to Business) disputes: no more than a fraction of disputes will be successfully resolved in this manner.[24]

#25 The fate of **ADR instruments** has apparently not altered the trajectory of EU policies. History often shows that those involved have difficulty learning from past mistakes. The same test of the **(in)efficiency of ADR procedures** will likely occur in the context of new, ambitious EU instruments like the **Digital Services Act** (DSA).[25] Under the DSA, for dispute settlement between users of online platforms, out-of-court dispute settlement bodies are provided to supplement the internal

---

23 See Directive (2013/11/EU) on alternative dispute resolution for consumer disputes (the 'ADR Directive') [2013] OJ L165/63 and Regulation (EU) No 524/2013 on online dispute resolution for consumer disputes (the 'ODR Regulation') [2013] OJ L165/1.

24 As a 2014 study of the European Parliament showed, only about one percent of court cases are submitted to mediation. G De Pal and others, 'Rebooting' the Mediation Directive: Assessing the Limited Impact of its Implementation and Proposing Measures to Increase the Number of Mediations in the EU' (European Parliament 2014).

25 Regulation (EU) 2022/2065 of the European Parliament and of the Council of 19 October 2022 on a Single Market for Digital Services [2022] OJ L277/1.

complaint-handling systems of platforms and offer later judicial redress. The ambition is to enable engagement in an optional ADR procedure by certified dispute resolution bodies that are 'independent' and 'have the means and expertise to carry out . . . fair, swift, and cost-effective' proceedings under fees that are 'reasonable, accessible, attractive, inexpensive for consumers, and proportionate, and assessed on a case-by-case basis'. However, just as with previous ADR instruments, almost everything regarding the process is fully optional and non-binding: Member States are not required to establish ADR bodies, engaging in proceedings before them may be refused by both providers and users, there is no pressure to reach a settlement, and any result of the process is further subject to contestation in judicial proceedings.[26] For the ADR bodies tasked with resolving disputes regarding digital services, there is even no obligation to offer native digital handling of these inherently digital disputes.

#26 The generous drafting of the **out-of-court dispute settlement** schemes, which operate like an 'empire of freedom', will most likely result in the same outcome across most EU jurisdictions—they will be irrelevant or even practically non-existent, satisfying only the interests of a narrow group of private ADR providers who will successfully capitalise on the remaining EU verbal support for **'certified' ADR schemes**. There is already evidence supporting this conclusion. Since the end of August 2023, the 'VLOPs' and 'VLOSEs' (ie, the very large providers of digital services) have an obligation to submit their transparency reports, which include data about the functioning of internal and external dispute settlement mechanisms.[27] The first empirical test is already present and it conforms to our expectations. For instance, the latest Facebook report on out-of-court dispute settlement submissions reported that 'as of 30 September 2024, we did not receive any disputes from certified out-of-court settlement bodies pursuant to Article 21 DSA'.[28] The gravity of this fact is underscored by information about complaints received through Facebook's internal complaint-handling systems, which reports on millions of complaints and enforced decisions in the same period.[29]

#27 Thus, in this area, as well as in many other areas of genuine EU consumer protection jurisdiction, the EU-backed dispute settlement mechanisms are being overshadowed and absorbed by another form of **'procedural autonomy'**— the autonomy

---

26 See in particular para 59 of the Preamble and Art 21 DSA.

27 Compare <https://digital-strategy.ec.europa.eu/en/policies/dsa-brings-transparency> accessed 15 February 2025.

28 Meta, 'Regulation (EU) 2022/2065 Digital Services Act Transparency Report for Facebook' (25 October 2024) 25 <https://transparency.meta.com/reports/regulatory-transparency-reports/> accessed 15 February 2025.

29 ibid 16–17 (Table 15.1.d.(1)): only in one category (organic content removal complaints) there were 3,5 million complaints and 870 thousand affirmative decisions (restored content after removal complaint).

(or, rather, autarchy) of **private providers**, in particular those very large ones – the VLOPs and VLOSEs.

B *Sicut Rota Sine Axis*: Disintegration Trends After Brexit

I How to Stay Calm and Go on Without Perfidious Albion?

#28 Among the wider challenges to the successful development of European civil procedure, several arise from the broader geopolitical landscape. The foundational premise of the EU, as expressed in Article 1 of the Treaty on European Union (TEU), is that it aims to create an **'ever closer Union'**. For a long time, it was also an 'ever growing Union' with a continuous policy of enlargement. As the Nobel Committee noted when the EU won the Nobel Peace Prize in 2012, the global achievements of the EU were seen in its promotion of peace and reconciliation between former enemies, the expansion of democracy and human rights, and the creation of a stable and cooperative economic and political environment that reduced the likelihood of conflict.[30] A decade later, many of these achievements have been questioned: peace and stability have faded, tensions and polarisations have grown, and the previously stable and cooperative economic and political environment is receding. For the development of European civil procedure, the first case of the **shrinking** of the 'ever closer Union' is especially significant. The 'leave' vote for **Brexit** in 2016 and the UK's departure from the EU in 2020 meant much more than simply reducing the number of EU Member States by one.

#29 This significant event not only altered the geopolitical landscape but also impacted the legal framework within the EU. During the 1973–2020 period of its membership in the European Union, the UK's contributions to the EU were substantial. Despite often being seen as a 'reluctant European', the UK played a pivotal role in shaping EU policies, governance, and global influence. With its historic influence on the development of **constitutionalism, democracy, human rights, and judicial independence** worldwide, the **UK** was instrumental in drafting EU instruments that harmonised civil procedures across the member states. The UK was a key architect of the **Brussels I Regulation**, which aims to simplify the rules of jurisdiction and the recognition and enforcement of judgments across EU countries. Additionally, the UK played crucial roles in the drafting of regulations such as the European Enforcement Order (**EEO**), the European Payment Order (**EPO**), and the European Small Claims Procedure (**ESCP**).

30 See <https://www.nobelprize.org/prizes/peace/2012/press-release/> accessed 15 February 2025.

#30 The UK's experience in handling **insolvency** cases, characterised by its corporate rescue culture and expertise in restructuring and bankruptcy law, helped establish a more efficient insolvency system across the EU. This influence extended beyond merely procedural aspects, influencing substantive legal frameworks and fostering a more integrated legal environment.

#31 Moreover, the UK's historical experience in reaching compromises and drafting legislation for an empire full of divergence, amplified by the native use of English, which is the most used language in the EU, facilitated its significant role in legal drafting and policy-making.[31] But these are not the only reasons why **post-Brexit development** of the EU civil procedure will be challenging.

#32 The legal interplay between the UK and the EU was a story of mutual influence between **common law** and **civil law** traditions. Legal and institutional reforms in the UK, which took place as a result of EU membership and its willingness to adopt decisions of the **CJEU** and the **ECtHR**, demonstrated that harmonisation between the two most influential global legal traditions is not impossible. Conversely, the EU benefited from the pragmatism and diplomatic skills of UK representatives and incorporated progressive elements inspired by common law best practices in shaping the EU procedural *acquis*. With the UK's departure, the divide between common law and civil law traditions may begin to widen once again. As Ireland, and to a certain extent Malta and Cyprus, remain the only common law jurisdictions within the EU, there is a likelihood that the traditionally conservative civil law approach will dominate future projects in the area of civil justice, leaving less room for innovation and change. Without the UK's influence, procedural harmonisation efforts may become more rigid, potentially slowing the evolution of EU civil procedure.

#33 The potentially devastating impact of Brexit on the future development of EU civil procedural law is further underscored by the fact that the most influential contemporary reforms of civil procedure in the West originate in England. The **Woolf Reforms**, which led to the 1999 changes in the Civil Procedure Rules in England, marked a series of reform actions that are widely regarded as a rare example of coherent and successful modernisation efforts in civil procedure. These reforms have served as a model for procedural reform worldwide, demonstrating how procedural efficiency, access to justice, and judicial case management can be improved through well-structured changes. Within the EU, both the

31 The contribution of UK reaches beyond drafting binding EU legal instruments. The most important project of drafting model legislation for civil procedure in Europe would be impossible without the skilful and diplomatic leadership of Diana Wallis as the past president of the European Law Institute. See more on ERCP in European Law Institute and Unidroit, *ELI-Unidroit Model European Rules of Civil Procedure. From Transnational Principles to European Rules of Civil Procedure* (OUP 2021). On the role of ELI-UNIDROIT project in the context of soft law harmonisation of procedural law in Europe see Chapter 23 by E Jeuland.

Woolf and **Jackson reforms** were closely observed by several Member States, influencing procedural reform efforts. Some of their principles—such as judicial case management, cost proportionality, and active court involvement in planning of proceedings—have been partially echoed in EU civil procedure, but there remains significant room for further improvement. However, after Brexit, promoting procedural reforms modelled on UK examples will become increasingly difficult.

#34 In many civil law countries, traditionalist forces that adhere to the old reactive style of civil procedure—where judicial intervention is minimal, and proceedings are predominantly party-driven—continue to resist the introduction of more dynamic, multi-dimensional procedures based on the overriding objective, procedural cooperation, and proportionality. Without the UK's influence within EU legislative processes, these forces are more likely to hinder future reforms, weaken EU legislative initiatives, and potentially undermine past achievements in modernising civil procedure.[32] The absence of the UK's pragmatic approach to **procedural efficiency** may ultimately slow or even stall the evolution of EU civil procedural law, reinforcing rigid, formalistic procedural traditions rather than fostering flexibility and innovation.

II Beyond EU enlargement: how much of the East can be digested without digestive disorders?

#35 Exiting the EU is not the only wider geopolitical challenge. Entering the EU can also create tensions and affect further developments. From 2004 to 2013, the last three waves of **EU enlargement** brought thirteen (13) new EU Member States, which is almost half of the present EU membership. A large number of the new Member States belong to the group of post-Socialist states. They come from three different regions: Central Europe (Czechia, Hungary, Poland, Slovakia), Baltic States (Estonia, Latvia and Lithuania) and Western Balkans/Southeastern Europe (Slovenia, Croatia, Bulgaria, Romania). The current list of **candidates** and potential candidates includes ten (10) further countries. These include more Western Balkan nations (Albania, Bosnia and Herzegovina, Montenegro, Serbia, and Kosovo) but also extend further into Eastern Europe (Moldova, Ukraine) and even into Western Asia (Georgia, Turkey).

---

32 The development of CDR (dispute resolution in consumer disputes) in the EU was under strong influence of English approach, marked by a functional landscape of public and private dispute resolution bodies (ombudsmen and other DR entities). Key elements of the underlying approach like transparency, regulatory objectives and systemic pressure on traders (all best described in the works of Christopher Hodges) are after Brexit being gradually dismantled.

#36 The prospects for a quick further expansion of the EU are, at present, more unlikely than likely. However, rapidly changing geopolitical realities may accelerate this process, as the EU has expressed a renewed commitment to enlargement in light of **Russia's invasion of Ukraine**. Officially, the precondition for enlargement is a rigorous accession process that requires alignment with EU standards, including those on the rule of law and human rights. In practice, however, past accessions have demonstrated the significance of political considerations. While some EU standards relate to civil justice systems (such as an independent and accountable judiciary, fair and efficient judicial proceedings, effective access to justice, and a functional legal aid system), they remain fluid in many aspects and subject to interpretation. Therefore, as clearly shown in the case of accession of **Bulgaria** and **Romania**, EU enlargement could proceed irrespective of whether sufficient reforms in justice sector have been made.[33]

#37 The past two decades have proven that the idea of a quick transition from old regimes to modern democracies is illusory. Particularly in the field of the rule of law and justice, tectonic changes are difficult to achieve. Statistics from the ECtHR show that among the top ten countries in terms of pending applications concerning human rights violations, five are EU members. Of these, three (Romania, Poland, and Slovenia) belong to **post-Socialist countries**, while two (Greece and Italy) are from Southern Europe.[34] The challenges the EU has faced with attacks on **judicial independence** in Hungary and Poland[35] demonstrate that accession reforms have not fundamentally changed some features of these legal systems. The persistence of the **Socialist legal tradition**, which appears capable of surviving even without the ideological foundation of communism, has been raised by various authors and remains a subject of interest among procedural scholars and legal theorists who developed the concept of 'legal survivals'.[36]

---

33 On the experiences with the 'two laggards of the Eastern Enlargement' see more in F Trauner, 'Post-accession Compliance with EU Law in Bulgaria and Romania: A Comparative Perspective' in F Schimmelfennig and F Trauner (eds), 'Post-accession Compliance in the EU's New Member States' (2009) European Integration online Papers (EIoP), Special Issue 2, Vol. 13, Art. 21, <http://eiop.or.at/eiop/texte/2009-021a.htm.> accessed 15 February 2025.

34 See <https://www.echr.coe.int/documents/d/echr/stats-pending-month-2025-bil> accessed 15 February 2025.

35 See UA Kos, 'Signalling in European Rule of Law Cases: Hungary and Poland as Case Studies' (2023) 23 Human Rights Law Review <https://doi.org/10.1093/hrlr/ngad035> accessed 15 February 2025; J Freeberg, 'Don't Judge Me: Declining Judicial Independence in Hungary and Poland' (2022) WWU Honors College Senior Projects 601 <https://cedar.wwu.edu/wwu_honors/601> accessed 15 February 2025.

36 See for instance R Mańko, 'Survival of the Socialist Legal Tradition? A Polish Perspective' (2013) 4(2) Comparative Law Review 1–28; A Uzelac, 'Survival of the Third Legal Tradition?' in J Walker and Oscar C (eds), *Common Law, Civil Law and the Future of Categories* (Lexis Nexis 2010) 377.

#38 The further aspects of the EU enlargement process, together with its many open issues, is elaborated in detail in the next chapter.[37] However, in the context of the wider challenges to European civil procedure, it is worth noting that the changing composition of the Union may have far-reaching consequences for its further development. If we assume that the EU will, in ten years, be composed of 37 Member States, 20 of them—or 54%—would be **post-Socialist countries**. These states would encompass approximately 165 million people, representing about 30% of the EU population. How would this affect the development of civil procedure, both at the EU and national levels? Various scenarios are possible.

#39 On one side, this change could further accelerate a move towards **procedural autarchy**. At present, over two-thirds of all applications before the **ECtHR** relate to human rights violations in just four countries—Turkey (35.4%), Russia (13.3%), Ukraine (12.5%), and Romania (6.4%).[38] Many of these cases stem from dysfunctions within their justice systems. The experience of current **post-Socialist EU Member States** has shown that while justice sector reforms were partially effective during the accession period, they were often slowed down, stalled, or even reversed after full membership was achieved.[39] A shift in EU composition could exacerbate difficulties in reaching consensus on procedural reforms. The divide between national dispute resolution systems and EU procedural instruments could widen further, and in the worst-case scenario, we will experience a process of **de-Europeanisation** of national civil courts. EU civil procedure could become illusory and obsolete.

#40 On the opposite side, the multiplication of **dysfunctional justice systems** could serve as a strong motivation for further **harmonisation** and **unification**. However, this scenario is not very likely, as it would require a shared awareness of the problems rather than a top-down modernisation effort led by 'advanced' EU jurisdictions. Additionally, even if political consensus were achievable, the independent judicial structures of an enlarged EU would have the means to resist and neutralise such efforts. The involvement of large jurisdictions with serious rule of law challenges, such as **Ukraine** or **Turkey**, would introduce further obstacles, making meaningful procedural reform even more difficult to implement.

---

37 Chapter 24 by M Canco, A Harvey and I Izarova.

38 Compare figures in ECtHR chart (n 34).

39 For instance, in Croatia, efforts to implement the recommendations of European observers were half-hearted and met with reluctance from judicial insiders. Once Croatia's accession to the EU became certain, the reforms necessary for the modernisation of the judiciary were either interrupted or reversed. Examples of reversed judicial reforms include dismantling the private bailiff system, which had been introduced based on agreements with EU experts, abandoning efforts to introduce objective criteria for the selection of judges, and degrading the State School for Judicial Officials and the Judicial Academy to the level of optional courses or evening schools. A Uzelac, 'Judiciary in Croatia 2020. Current Situation, Causes of Crisis and Possible Reform Measures' 5 <https://www.alanuzelac.from.hr/pubs/C04_Judiciary_in_Croatia_preprint.pdf> accessed 15 February 2025.

#41 Therefore, the only viable path to a sustainable EU approach to civil procedure in an enlarged Europe seems to be gradual progress and a slow process of supporting reforms that begin with improvements to national civil procedure. Experience in the **Western Balkans** has shown that the presence of European experts or even an EU protectorate, accompanied by a supervised overhaul of procedural legislation, does not guarantee lasting **harmonisation of procedural law.**[40] Change must come from within: the harmonisation of national law and practice with EU procedural standards should be the result of conscious and voluntary adoption rather than external imposition. In this context, model instruments such as the **ELI-UNIDROIT European Rules of Civil Procedure** may ultimately prove more important and influential than EU directives and regulations, as they offer a framework that jurisdictions can integrate at their own pace, fostering a more organic and sustainable alignment with European procedural norms and standards.

III From the EU to a United States of Europe: Where Does the American Path Lead?

#42 Continuing the project of an **'ever closer Union'** that can substantially guarantee **mutual trust** in the justice sector calls for further **harmonisation** of procedural law, which does not only affect 'law in books' but brings a common set of convictions, affecting behaviour of all involved. Achieving harmonisation that is substantial and effective, rather than formal and illusory, requires a positive environment, inspiring role models, and, above all, a shared determination to move forward together on a common path. In the past, encouraging examples that diversity can be overcome were regularly coming from the United States. ***E pluribus unum***, strength through diversity, is the ideal that Europe was also striving to achieve.

#43 In the area of justice and legal reforms, Europe has often followed the **American** path – and *vice versa*. Many contemporary achievements in European civil procedure either originated from or were inspired by American models. These include promotion of **alternative dispute resolution** (ADR), a high level of **consumer protection** through various legal mechanisms, the development of **collective redress**, strong **judicial independence**, and broad availability of **legal aid**. American procedural models, despite their special features that were difficult to be adopted elsewhere (often referred to in the literature as aspects of **American ex-**

---

40 Examples of such developments are most visible in Kosovo and Bosnia and Herzegovina. Despite significant progress, old practices have re-emerged whenever external monitoring has been reduced.

ceptionalism[41]), were for a long time perceived as modern and progressive, serving as an inspiration for future-oriented procedural reforms in Europe.

#44 For some time, it seemed that this mutual respect was reciprocal. At least some American law professors, such as John Langbein and James Maxeiner, studied and praised certain elements of the **European tradition in civil procedure**, describing them as 'civilised' and 'advantageous'.[42] Leading American scholars of civil procedure, such as Geoffrey Hazard, contributed to important projects aimed at the **international harmonisation of procedural law**.[43] It seemed that there was a 'modern trend towards **convergence** between the United States and the rest of the world'.[44]

#45 From a European perspective, the United States of America has also provided an appealing example of a federal state in which a diverse mosaic of state and federal courts manages to operate harmoniously, creating the impression of a coherent and functional system. The binding force of this system has traditionally been a highly respected judicial institution—the Supreme Court of the United States (**SCOTUS**). Highly regarded both domestically and internationally for its independence and progressive impact on legal development, SCOTUS was once praised as the 'least dangerous branch' of government.[45] It was an institution that could serve as a valuable reference point for Europe's highest tribunals.

#46 In the preface to the ALI-UNIDROIT Principles, the reporters—a diverse team from the United States, Europe, and Brazil—concluded their introduction with an insightful remark on the future trajectory of civil procedure. Their perspective on the bifurcation of this path was as follows:

> *In this era of globalisation, the world is marching in two paths. One path is of separation and isolationism, with war and turmoil: in such a world, this project is useless and unwelcome. The other path is increasing exchange of products and ideas among the peoples of the world; this path underscores the need for a transnational civil procedure.*[46]

---

41 See OG Chase, 'American "Exceptionalism" and Comparative Procedure' (2002) 50 Am J Comp L 277, 288–292; R Marcus, 'Putting American Procedural Exceptionalism into a Globalized Context' (2005) 53 Am J Comp L 709.

42 See JH Langbein, 'The German Advantage in Civil Procedure' (1985) 52 U Chi L Rev 823; EC Stiefel and JR Maxeiner, 'Civil Justice Reform in the United States—Opportunity for Learning from "Civilized" European Procedure Instead of Continued Isolation?' (1994) 42 Am J Comp L 147, 157.

43 See American Law Institute and UNIDROIT, *Principles of Transnational Civil Procedure* (CUP 2006).

44 S Dodson, 'Global Civil Procedure Trends in the Twenty-First Century' (2011) 34 Boston College Int and Comp L Rev 1.

45 A Hamilton, in *The Federalist* No. 78 (28 May 1788).

46 See ALI-UNIDROIT Principles (n 43) (signed by G Hazard, R Stürner, M Taruffo and A Gidi).

#47 Evaluating the current state of this 'fork in the road,' it appears that the world is moving toward the first path—the path of **separation** and **isolationism**. This may present the ultimate wider challenge to European unity—and with it, to the very **idea of a common European area of justice.** By the mid-2020s, both the American and European political and socio-legal landscapes have changed significantly. What has also shifted—especially during the second term of President Trump—is the perception that the EU and the US remain strategic allies. The promotion of the **'MAGA' doctrine** and the concrete political moves of Trump's administration increasingly position much of the world as either latent or actual adversaries of the United States. In this adversarial environment, the potential for using American procedural models as a template for the development of EUstitia,[47] based on convergence with U.S. legal and procedural frameworks, is severely compromised.

#48 But this is not the only reason why following the American path is becoming increasingly unlikely. It is also becoming more difficult to define what the 'American path' in civil justice and civil procedure reforms actually entails. The main U.S.-inspired achievements in European justice are, in the meantime, becoming less and less recognisable in their country of origin. While Europe was once guided by the high level of **consumer protection** in the United States, the 2011 SCOTUS decision in *AT&T Mobility LLC v. Concepcion*[48] marked a turning point. By allowing traders to bypass state courts and class actions through arbitration clauses in consumer contracts, the ruling significantly weakened consumer protections in the U.S., leaving American consumers virtually unprotected in many cases.[49] Europe has often looked to the United States as a model when promoting human rights, the rule of law, and a high level of **judicial independence**. However, in the present time, the U.S. is experiencing an unprecedented level of challenges to human rights and judicial independence.[50] The **American Supreme Court**, once praised and highly respected, is now facing a crisis of legitimacy,

---

47 On the notion of EUstitia as both pragmatic and aspirational concept of the Euroepan governance project see more in H Hartnell, 'EUstitia: Institutionalizing Justice in the European Union' (2002) 23 NW J Int'l Law & Bus 65, 67.

48 *AT&T Mobility LLC v Concepcion*, 131 S. Ct. 1740, 1753 (2011).

49 See J Resnik, 'Diffusing Disputes: The Public in the Private of Arbitration, the Private in Courts, and the Erasure of Rights' (2015) 124 Yale Law J <https://ssrn.com/abstract=2601132> accessed 15 February 2025.

50 The threats made by an American president who opposes judicial decisions and declares that 'maybe we have to look at the judges,' while qualifying court rulings prohibiting government actions as 'a very serious violation,' have not been seen since President Jackson's refusal to enforce a Supreme Court decision in the Cherokee case in 1832. See <https://www.npr.org/2025/02/12/nx-s1-5294666/trump-white-house-constitutional-crisis-judges> accessed 15 February 2025.

with historically low public approval ratings. For the first time, its trust levels have fallen below the average levels of **public trust** in courts across the EU.[51]

#49 There is an even more dangerous turn in the 'American path'. The United States has historically supported the European integration process, viewing it as a means to promote stability, economic prosperity, and transatlantic security. Free trade with an integrated Europe was seen as beneficial, and the process of EU enlargement was actively supported. However, much of this has significantly changed, bringing new challenges to integration efforts in Europe. The failure of the **Transatlantic Trade and Investment Partnership (TTIP)** and the imposition of tariffs on EU goods exported to the U.S. have not only made economic cooperation more difficult but also prevented the creation of mutually trusted judicial institutions for dispute settlement. The current U.S. administration has aggressively undermined the work of **international tribunals.**[52] It praised Brexit, openly supporting **disintegrative forces** within the EU. The effect of this shift in policy remains to be seen. At present, the EU is 'bracing for a new era',[53] and it is certain that the effort to strengthen Europe as 'a genuine area of justice' will face multiple challenges. All we can do is hope that, despite the stern warning of the ALI-UNIDROIT team, the project of further developing European civil procedure will not become 'useless and unwelcome'.

C Conclusion: Progress Should Not Be Taken for Granted, It Should Be Earned

#50 The project of creating **'a genuine European area of justice'** is a grand and ambitious task. Such an area is unimaginable without a coherent and meaningful **Europeanisation of civil procedure**. It is only natural that a project of this magnitude requires time, sustained efforts, and a fair amount of luck in navigating internal and external geopolitical and social developments.

#51 In July 2000, the French Justice Minister stated: 'If it has taken forty years to create an Internal Market, and thirty years to create a single currency, we will be doing well if we achieve a single judicial space within twenty years.'[54] Twenty-five years later, this statement seems overly optimistic. However, the challenge

51 For the evolution of public reception of the SCOTUS see S Dodson, 'The Supreme Court and Public Opinion' (2024) 111(1) Iowa Law Review 1.

52 See <https://www.whitehouse.gov/presidential-actions/2025/02/imposing-sanctions-on-the-international-criminal-court/> accessed 15 February 2025.

53 See Jeanna Smialek, 'Europe Braces for a New Trump Era, Uncertain About What It Means' *New York Times* (21 January 2025) <https://www.nytimes.com/2025/01/21/world/europe/trump-eu-policy.html> accessed 15 February 2025.

54 Guigou, cited in Hartnell (n 47) at 65.

lies not only in the timeline but also in the assessment itself: while the criteria for establishing an Internal Market or a single currency are clear and measurable, defining what exactly constitutes a **'single judicial space'** remains uncertain and open to interpretation.

#52 This 'brave new horizon for the rule of law in the European Union'[55] is not a fixed destination, but rather a continually evolving goal, where new perspectives are constantly being explored. For some—to extend the metaphor—it is a place where dreamers are chasing rainbows.

#53 In this chapter, wider challenges on the path toward developing a **common European approach to civil procedure** have been identified. While these challenges are significant, they are not insurmountable. However, successfully addressing them requires persistent efforts. These efforts cannot be limited to the proliferation of new rules or the recasting of old ones in European civil procedure.

#54 The institutionalists' claim that it is sufficient to create common rules and expect them to 'generate a self-sustaining dynamic' and lead to a 'gradual deepening of integration'[56] has proved to be flawed. Europe needs a clear and comprehensive concept of civil procedure that goes beyond the current **'minimal standards of civil procedure'** and results in simpler, more coherent, and more user-friendly rules. It must work harder to develop a **common procedural culture** of efficient and accessible **judicial and extrajudicial institutions**, drawing on **best practices**—whether from within or outside the EU.

#55 Last but not least, Europe needs a renewed confidence in the idea that **European civil justice** should continue to develop as a ***ius commune***—a **common area of justice** that ensures the highest and most equal level of protection of human and other rights for everyone under the jurisdiction of any EU Member State.

References

American Law Institute and UNIDROIT, *Principles of Transnational Civil Procedure* (CUP 2006).

Brouwer E, 'Mutual Trust and Judicial Control in the Area of Freedom, Security, and Justice: An Anatomy of Trust' in E Brouwer and D Gerard (eds), *Mapping Mutual Trust: Understanding and Framing the Role of Mutual Trust in EU Law* (EUI Working Papers MWP 2016/13) 59.

Buzzoni M, 'The Certification of Judgments under the EFFORTS Regulations' in FC Villata and B Hess (eds), Towards more EFfective enFORcemenT of claimS in civil and commercial matters within the EU – "EFFORTS": Final Study' (Project JUST-JCOO-AG2019-881802) 7 <https://efforts.unimi.it> accessed 15 February 2025.

Chase OG, 'American "Exceptionalism" and Comparative Procedure' (2002) 50 Am J Comp L 277.

55 ibid at 66.

56 Alec Stone Sweet and Wayne Sandholtz, 'Integration, Supranational Governance, and the Institutionalisation of the European Polity' in Alec Stone Sweet, Wayne Sandholtz and Neil Fligstein (eds), *The Institutionalisation of Europe* (Oxford 2001) 1, 5.

Clifford Chance, 'European Account Preservation Orders: Must Try Harder' (Briefing Note, September 2014) <https://www.cliffordchance.com/content/dam/cliffordchance/briefings/2014/09/european-account-preservation-orders-must-try-harder-10-september-2014.pdf> accessed 15 February 2025.

Cuniberti G, 'Preface' in N Kyriakides, HA Huhtamäki and N Mouttotos (eds), *European Account Preservation Order: A Multi-Jurisdictional Guide with Commentary* (Bruylant 2024) 9.

De Pal G and others, '"Rebooting" the Mediation Directive: Assessing the Limited Impact of its Implementation and Proposing Measures to Increase the Number of Mediations in the EU' (European Parliament 2014).

Dodson S, 'Global Civil Procedure Trends in the Twenty-First Century' (2011) 34 Boston College Int and Comp L Rev 1.

—— 'The Supreme Court and Public Opinion' (2024) 111(1) Iowa L Rev 1.

Dori A, 'In Data We Trust? Quantifying the Costs of Adjudication in the EU Justice Scoreboard' [2021–4] ELR 281.

European Commission, 'Questions and Answers on Hungary: Rule of Law and EU Funding' (December 2023) <https://ec.europa.eu/commission/presscorner/detail/en/qanda_23_6466> accessed 15 February 2025.

European Commission: Directorate-General for Justice and Consumers, 'An Evaluation Study of National Procedural Laws and Practices in Terms of Their Impact on the Free Circulation of Judgments and on the Equivalence and Effectiveness of the Procedural Protection of Consumers under EU Consumer Law – Strand 2 – Procedural Protection of Consumers', Study JUST/2014/RCON/PR/CIVI/0082 (Publications Office 2017).

European Law Institute and Unidroit, *ELI-Unidroit Model European Rules of Civil Procedure. From Transnational Principles to European Rules of Civil Procedure* (OUP 2021).

Flash Eurobarometer 489, 'Perceived Independence of the National Justice Systems in the EU among the General Public' (July 2021) <http://data.europa.eu/euodp/en/data/dataset/S2272_489_ENG> accessed 15 February 2025.

Flash Eurobarometer 519, 'Perceived Independence of the National Justice Systems in the EU among the General Public – January 2023 Report' (June 2023) <https://europa.eu/eurobarometer/surveys/detail/2667> accessed 15 February 2025.

Freeberg J, 'Don't Judge Me: Declining Judicial Independence in Hungary and Poland' (2022) WWU Honors College Senior Projects 601 <https://cedar.wwu.edu/wwu_honors/601> accessed 15 February 2025.

Gallup, 'Trust in Federal Government Branches Continues to Falter' (2022) <https://news.gallup.com/poll/402737/trust-federal-government-branches-continues-falter.aspx> accessed 15 February 2025.

Hartnell H, 'EUstitia: Institutionalizing Justice in the European Union' (2002) 23 NW J Int'l Law & Bus 65.

Kos UA, 'Signalling in European Rule of Law Cases: Hungary and Poland as Case Studies' (2023) 23 Human Rights Law Review <https://doi.org/10.1093/hrlr/ngad035> accessed 15 February 2025.

Langbein JH, 'The German Advantage in Civil Procedure' (1985) 52 U Chi L Rev 823.

Latinobarometro, *Informe 2021: Confianza en el poder judicial 1995–2020* <http://www.latinobarometro.org> accessed 15 February 2025

Lenaerts K, 'La vie après l'avis: Exploring the Principle of Mutual (yet not Blind) Trust' (2017) 54 *Common Market Law Review* 805

Mańko R, 'Survival of the Socialist Legal Tradition? A Polish Perspective' (2013) 4(2) Comparative Law Review 1.

Marcus R, 'Putting American Procedural Exceptionalism into a Globalized Context' (2005) 53 Am J Comp L 709.

Meta, 'Regulation (EU) 2022/2065 Digital Services Act Transparency Report for Facebook' (25 October 2024) 25 <https://transparency.meta.com/reports/regulatory-transparency-reports/> accessed 15 February 2025.

Mouttotos N, 'Is the EAPO Fulfilling its Purpose' in N Kyriakides, HA Huhtamäki and N Mouttotos (eds), *European Account Preservation Order: A Multi-Jurisdictional Guide with Commentary* (Bruylant 2024) 27.

Resnik J, 'Diffusing Disputes: The Public in the Private of Arbitration, the Private in Courts, and the Erasure of Rights' (2015) 124 Yale Law J <https://ssrn.com/abstract=2601132> accessed 15 February 2025.

Smialek J, 'Europe Braces for a New Trump Era, Uncertain About What It Means' *New York Times* (21 January 2025) <https://www.nytimes.com/2025/01/21/world/europe/trump-eu-policy.html> accessed 15 February 2025.

Stiefel EC and Maxeiner JR, 'Civil Justice Reform in the United States—Opportunity for Learning from "Civilized" European Procedure Instead of Continued Isolation?' (1994) 42 Am J Comp L 147.

Stone Sweet A and Sandholtz W, 'Integration, Supranational Governance, and the Institutionalization of the European Polity' in A Stone Sweet, W Sandholtz and N Fligstein (eds), *The Institutionalization of Europe* (OUP 2001) 1.

Trauner F, 'Post-accession Compliance with EU Law in Bulgaria and Romania: A Comparative Perspective' in F Schimmelfennig and F Trauner (eds), 'Post-accession Compliance in the EU's New Member States' (2009) European Integration online Papers (EIoP), Special Issue 2, Vol. 13, Art. 21 <http://eiop.or.at/eiop/texte/2009-021a.htm> accessed 15 February 2025.

Uzelac A, 'Survival of the Third Legal Tradition?' in J Walker and O Chase (eds), *Common Law, Civil Law and the Future of Categories* (Lexis Nexis 2010) 377.

—— 2020. Current Situation, Causes of Crisis and Possible Reform Measures' <https://www.alanuzelac.from.hr/pubs/C04_Judiciary_in_Croatia_preprint.pdf> accessed 15 February 2025.

Villata FC and Hess B (eds), 'Towards more EFfective enFORcemenT of claimS in civil and commercial matters within the EU – "EFFORTS": Final Study' (Project JUST-JCOO-AG2019-881802) <https://efforts.unimi.it> accessed 15 February 2025.

Index

https://doi.org/10.1515/9783110781632-027

Fictitious service 138, 140, 145